Reading STREET

Grade 2, Unit 2

Working Together

D1402978

PEARSON

Scott Foresman

scottforesman.com

Editorial Offices: Glenview, Illinois • Parsippany, New Jersey • New York, New York
Sales Offices: Needham, Massachusetts • Duluth, Georgia • Glenview, Illinois
Coppell, Texas • Ontario, California • Mesa, Arizona

Cover Scott Gustafson

About the Cover Artist
When Scott Gustafson was in grade school, he spent most of his spare time drawing pictures. Now he gets to make pictures for a living. Before he starts a painting, he photographs his family, pets, or friends posing as characters that will appear in the illustration. He then uses the photos to inspire the finished picture.

ISBN: 0-328-10855-3

1 2 3 4 5 6 7 8 9 10 V064 14 13 12 11 10 09 08 07 06 05

Reading STREET

Welcome!

Let us be your guide.

Ready to go? Our expert authorship team makes it easy to navigate a research-based approach to reading instruction.

Program Authors

Peter Afflerbach, Ph.D.
Professor, Department of Curriculum and Instruction University of Maryland at College Park
Assessment, Comprehension, Engagement, Motivation

Camille L. Z. Blachowicz, Ph.D.
Professor of Education National-Louis University
Comprehension, Fluency, Vocabulary

Candy Dawson Boyd, Ph.D.
Professor, School of Education, Saint Mary's College of California
Children's Literature, Professional Development

Wendy Cheyney, Ed.D.
Professor of Special Education and Literacy Florida International University
Phonological and Phonemic Awareness, Early Literacy

Connie Juel, Ph.D.
Professor of Education School of Education, Stanford University
Phonics, Oral Vocabulary, Anchored Vocabulary, Literacy Development, Intervention

Edward J. Kame'enui, Ph.D.
Professor of Special Education; Director, Institute for the Development of Educational Achievement and Center on Teaching and Learning, University of Oregon
Assessment, Elements of Reading First, Intervention, Progress Monitoring, Vocabulary

Donald J. Leu, Ph.D.
John and Maria Neag Endowed Chair in Literacy and Technology University of Connecticut
Comprehension, Technology, New Literacies

"By teaching a child to read, we change the world."
Donald J. Leu, Ph.D.

Jeanne R. Paratore, Ed.D.
Associate Professor of
Education, Department
of Literacy and Language
Development, Boston
University
*Intervention, Grouping,
Professional Development*

P. David Pearson, Ph.D.
Professor and Dean
Graduate School of
Education, University of
California, Berkeley
*Comprehension, Assessment,
Reading Informational Text,
Concept Integration*

Sam L. Sebesta, Ed.D.
Professor Emeritus, College
of Education, University of
Washington, Seattle
*Children's Literature, Reader
Response, Motivation*

Deborah Simmons, Ph.D.
Professor, College of
Education and Human
Development
Texas A&M University
*Literacy Development,
Phonics, Elements of
Reading First, Intervention*

Sharon Vaughn, Ph.D.
H. E. Hartfelder/Southland
Corporation Regents
Professor, University
of Texas
*Literacy Development,
Elements of Reading First,
Intervention, Professional
Development*

Susan Watts-Taffe, Ed.D.
Independent Literacy
Researcher
Cincinnati, Ohio
*Professional Development,
Vocabulary, Comprehension*

Karen Kring Wixson, Ph.D.
Professor of Education
University of Michigan
*Alignment of Curriculum
and Assessment,
Concept Integration*

Research contributions for *Reading Street* are set in italics.

Consultants and Reviewers

Let us lead the way.

Reading Street provides proven teaching methods that are classroom-tested and validated by research.

Have a great trip!

Consulting Authors

Jim Cummins, Ph.D.
Professor
Department of Curriculum, Teaching and Learning, University of Toronto
Toronto, Canada
English Language Learners

Lily Wong Fillmore, Ph.D.
Professor Emerita
Graduate School of Education
University of California, Berkeley
English Language Learners

Barbara Kay Foots, M.Ed.
Science Education Consultant
Houston, Texas
Science Integration

Georgia Earnest García, Ph.D.
Professor
Language and Literacy Division, University of Illinois at Urbana-Champaign
English Language Learners

George González, Ph.D.
Professor (Retired)
School of Education, University of Texas Pan-American, Edinburg
English Language Learners, Bilingual Education

Valerie Ooka Pang, Ph.D.
Professor
School of Teacher Education
San Diego State University
Social Studies Integration

Sally M. Reis, Ph.D.
Professor and Department Head
Educational Psychology
University of Connecticut
Gifted and Talented

Consultants

V. Karen Hatfield, Ed.D.
Harrodsburg, Kentucky
Assessment

Lynn F. Howard, M.Ed.
Huntersville, North Carolina
Assessment

Student Edition Reviewers

Lahna Anhalt
Reading Coordinator
DeForest Area School District
DeForest, Wisconsin

Teresa M. Beard
Cary Elementary School
Cary, North Carolina

Ebony Cross
Glassmanor Elementary School
Oxon Hill, Maryland

Melisa G. Figurelli
Fourth and Fifth Grade Teacher
Hans Herr Elementary School
Lampeter, Pennsylvania

Jennifer Flynn
Second Grade Teacher
Weatherstone Elementary School
Cary, North Carolina

Linda Halbert
Centennial Elementary School
Springfield, Oregon

Angela Hartman
Hutto Elementary School, Hutto, Texas

Judy Holiday
Program Coordinator for Special Education
Woodmen Center, Academy SD #20
Colorado Springs, Colorado

Victoria Holman
Third Grade Teacher
Mount Pleasant Elementary School
San Jose, California

Harriett Horton
Barnwell Elementary School
Alpharetta, Georgia

Mary Beth Huber
Elementary Curriculum Specialist
Calcasieu Parish School System
Lake Charles, Louisiana

Jeff James
Fay Wright Elementary School
Salem, Oregon

Debbie Jessen
Learning Strategist
Clifford J. Lawrence Jr. High School
Las Vegas, Nevada

Sherry Johnston
Literacy Coach
Bruce Elementary School
Milwaukee, Wisconsin

Carol Kelly
Hudson School, Union City, New Jersey

Linda Lindley
Fort Hall Elementary School
Pocatello, Idaho

Karen McCarthy
Goddard School, Brockton, Massachusetts

Patsy Mogush
Educational Coordinator
Central Kindergarten Center
Eden Prairie, Minnesota

Stacie Moncrief
Ventura Park Elementary School
Portland, Oregon

Nancy Novickis
Support Services
Douglass Valley Elementary School
United States Air Force Academy, Colorado

Betty Parsons
Past President
Santa Clara Reading Council
San Jose, California

Greta Peay
Clark County School District
North Las Vegas, Nevada

Leslie Potter
Blackwood Elementary School
Blackwood, New Jersey

Cyndy Reynolds
Williams Elementary School
Georgetown, Texas

Sharyle Shaffer
Fourth Grade Teacher
Summit Elementary School, Smithfield, Utah

Barbara Smith
Goddard School, Brockton, Massachusetts

Jane Stewart
Lakeshore Elementary School
Monroe, Louisiana

Nancey Volenstine
Chinle Elementary School, Chinle, Arizona

Teacher's Edition Reviewers

Alyssa E. Agoston
First Grade Teacher
Elms Elementary School, Jackson, New Jersey

Laura Beltchenko
Wauconda CUSD #118
Wauconda, Illinois

Lisa Bostick
NSU Elementary Lab School
Natchitoches, Louisiana

Debra O. Brown
First Grade Teacher
McFadden School, Murfreesboro, Tennessee

Cheri S. DeLaune
Paulina Elementary School
Paulina, Louisiana

Dr. Susan B. Dold
Elementary English/Language Arts Staff
Development Coordinator
Memphis City Schools, Memphis, Tennessee

Amy Francis
Montview Elementary School
Aurora, Colorado

Dawn Julian
First Grade Teacher
Elms Elementary School, Jackson, New Jersey

Suzette Kelly
Woodmen-Roberts Elementary School
Colorado Springs, Colorado

Suzanne Lank
Primary Teacher
Maury Elementary School
Alexandria, Virginia

Sharon Loos
Foothills Elementary School
Colorado Springs, Colorado

R. Franklin Mace
Title I Teacher
Bridgeview Elementary Center
South Charleston, West Virginia

Carol Masur
Second Grade Teacher
Elms Elementary School, Jackson, New Jersey

Jennifer D. Montgomery
Houston, Texas

Diana B. Nicholson
Cynthia Mann Elementary School
Boise, Idaho

Richard Potts
Memphis, Tennessee

Antonia Rogers
Richardson Independent School District
Richardson, Texas

Audrey Sander
Brooklyn, New York

Dr. Johnny Warrick
Gaston County Schools
Gastonia, North Carolina

Diane Weatherstone
Second Grade Teacher
Elms Elementary School, Jackson, New Jersey

Becky Worlds
Charlotte, North Carolina

Literature

Who will you meet on *Reading Street*?

Spine-tingling adventures, fascinating facts, hilarious characters!
Reading Street takes students as far as the imagination will go.

Expository Text Ahead

With a greater emphasis on informational text, *Reading Street* prepares your students for the kinds of selections they'll encounter on state assessments.

Grades 1–3
50% Fiction
50% Nonfiction

Grades 4–6
40% Fiction
60% Nonfiction

Life in an Ocean

ENCYCLOPEDIA Brown and the Case of the Slippery Salamander

JIM THORPE'S BRIGHT PATH

THE GREAT KAPOK TREE
A TALE OF THE AMAZON RAIN FOREST
by Lynne Cherry

Penguin Chick

Connect to Content Areas

Reading Street supports your **science** and **social studies** instruction, too. Look for content-area connections every week!

STREET GUIDE
Did you know?

All phonics elements, story vocabulary, and high-frequency words are pretaught prior to each selection. This helps students read successfully every week and every day.

Priority Skills

This way to AYP!

Reading Street *is built on solid research. You can feel confident you're teaching the* **right skill** *at the* **right time** *with the* **right emphasis.**

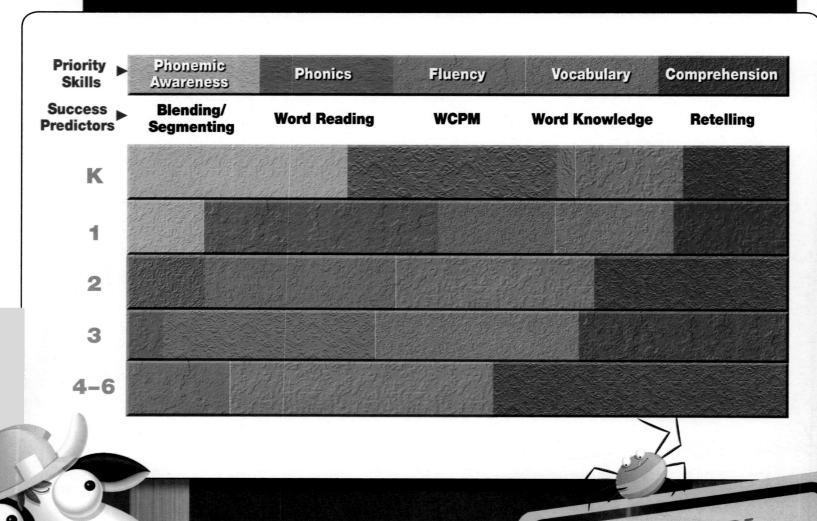

PRIORITIZING SKILL INSTRUCTION

Priority Skills ▶	Phonemic Awareness	Phonics	Fluency	Vocabulary	Comprehension
Success Predictors ▶	Blending/ Segmenting	Word Reading	WCPM	Word Knowledge	Retelling
K					
1					
2					
3					
4–6					

STREET GUIDE
Did you know?
Research tells us there are predictors for reading success. *Reading Street* identifies the **Success Predictors** for each Priority Skill to help you monitor progress and guide instruction.

Focus on Priorities

Not every skill at every grade is equally important! *Reading Street* prioritizes the five core areas of reading instruction for every grade.

Success Predictors for the Road Ahead

How do you get where you need to go? *Reading Street* identifies **Success Predictors** for each Priority Skill.

Progress Monitoring to Guide You

The **Monitor Progress** boxes throughout *Reading Street* tell you where students are, so you can focus instruction—and go!

Differentiated Instruction

Reading Street supports all your students with **Group-Time Lessons and Routines** to smooth out any bumps in the road.

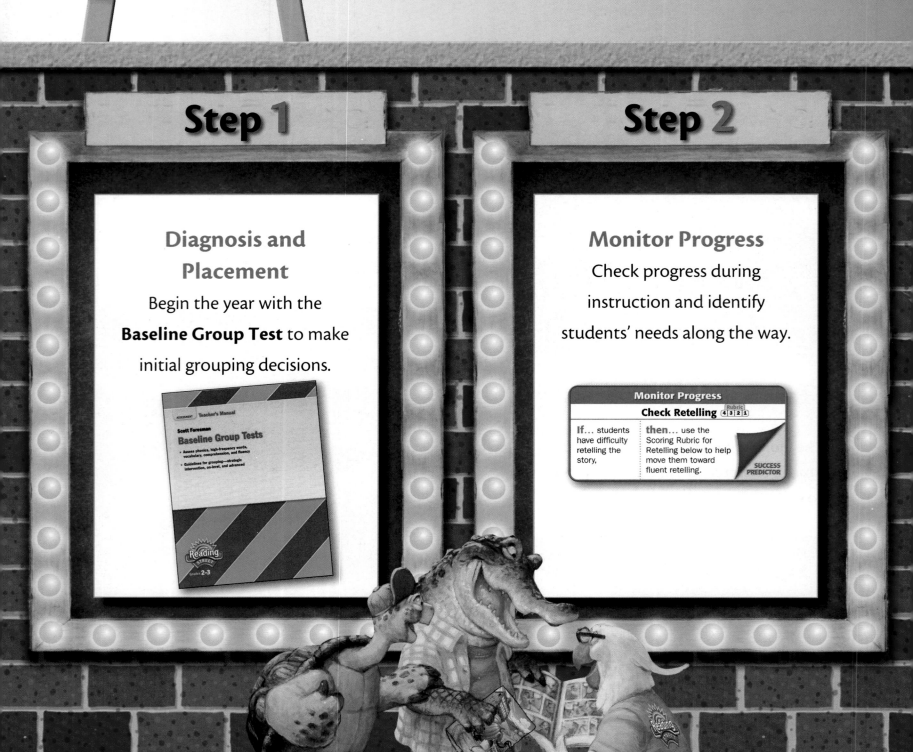

Assessment

You'll never get lost on the way.

A **four-step assessment plan** *provides a clear pathway that ensures all your students reach the final destination . . . reading!*

Step 1

Diagnosis and Placement

Begin the year with the **Baseline Group Test** to make initial grouping decisions.

Step 2

Monitor Progress

Check progress during instruction and identify students' needs along the way.

Monitor Progress

Check Retelling Rubric 4 3 2 1

If... students have difficulty retelling the story,

then... use the Scoring Rubric for Retelling below to help move them toward fluent retelling.

SUCCESS PREDICTOR

Step 3

Assess and Regroup
Use the **Unit Benchmark Test**
to measure performance
and to regroup.

Step 4

Summative Assessment
See how far students have
come with the **End-of-Year
Benchmark Test.**

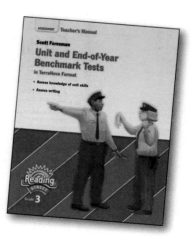

STREET GUIDE
Did you know?
Success Tracker™ is your online data
management system. It assesses students,
records results, prescribes practice, and
disaggregates and aggregates data.

Differentiated Instruction

Bring every child with you.

Need an alternate route? On Reading Street, instruction is systematic, explicit, and highly focused for all ability levels.

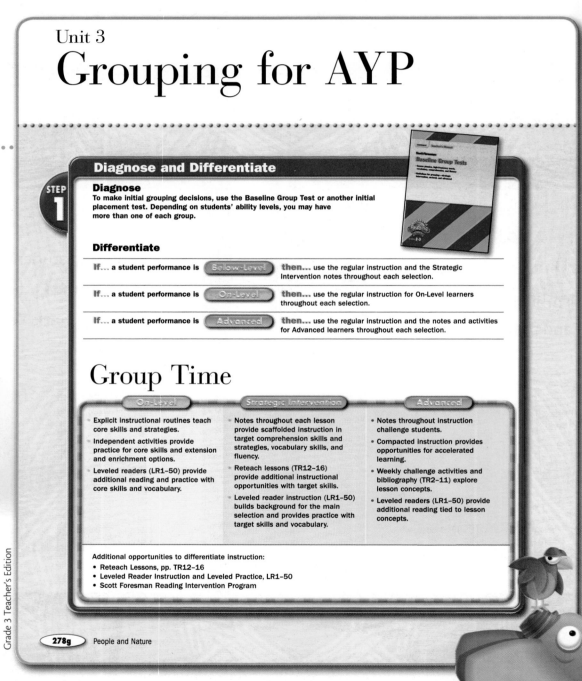

Unit 3
Grouping for AYP

Diagnose and Differentiate

STEP 1

Diagnose
To make initial grouping decisions, use the Baseline Group Test or another initial placement test. Depending on students' ability levels, you may have more than one of each group.

Differentiate

If... a student performance is **Below-Level** then... use the regular instruction and the Strategic Intervention notes throughout each selection.

If... a student performance is **On-Level** then... use the regular instruction for On-Level learners throughout each selection.

If... a student performance is **Advanced** then... use the regular instruction and the notes and activities for Advanced learners throughout each selection.

Group Time

On-Level	**Strategic Intervention**	**Advanced**
• Explicit instructional routines teach core skills and strategies. • Independent activities provide practice for core skills and extension and enrichment options. • Leveled readers (LR1–50) provide additional reading and practice with core skills and vocabulary.	• Notes throughout each lesson provide scaffolded instruction in target comprehension skills and strategies, vocabulary skills, and fluency. • Reteach lessons (TR12–16) provide additional instructional opportunities with target skills. • Leveled reader instruction (LR1–50) builds background for the main selection and provides practice with target skills and vocabulary.	• Notes throughout instruction challenge students. • Compacted instruction provides opportunities for accelerated learning. • Weekly challenge activities and bibliography (TR2–11) explore lesson concepts. • Leveled readers (LR1–50) provide additional reading tied to lesson concepts.

Additional opportunities to differentiate instruction:
• Reteach Lessons, pp. TR12–16
• Leveled Reader Instruction and Leveled Practice, LR1–50
• Scott Foresman Reading Intervention Program

Grade 3 Teacher's Edition

278g People and Nature

Which Students Need More Support?

Each unit gives you a clear road map to differentiate instruction for **On-Level, Strategic Intervention,** and **Advanced** readers.

Group Time

On-Level	Strategic Intervention	Advanced
If you began a web on p. 282a, students can use the information they contributed to set a purpose for reading. Students should also take notes in the web as they read.	Students can use the question on p. 285 of the Student Edition to set a purpose for reading. Students should read for causes and effects.	Students may set their own purposes for reading based on the preview of the selection. Students should use the illustrations to help set a purpose.

Strategies at Point of Use

Group Time throughout each lesson provides scaffolded instruction for all your readers.

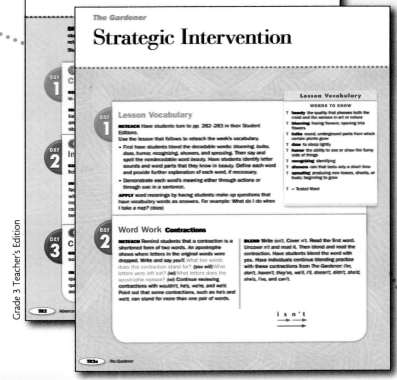

The Gardener
Advanced Challenge Activities

The Gardener
Strategic Intervention

More Reading for Group Time

Weekly **Leveled Readers** and **Leveled Practice** help every student practice and apply comprehension skills and vocabulary in appropriate texts.

More Lessons for Group Time

Built-in lessons for **Strategic Intervention** and **Advanced** learners supplement your core instruction every day.

STREET GUIDE
Did you know?
You can access more than 1,000 Leveled Readers online. Download, e-mail, and print from our **Leveled Reader Database**—anytime! **sfsuccessnet.com**

xv

Eliminate road blocks.

How do you empower your ELL students? Reading Street paves the way with highly focused ELL instruction, practice, and resources.

Grade 3 Teacher's Edition

ELL

Access Content Use ELL Poster 11 to preteach vocabulary. Choose from the following to meet language proficiency levels.

Beginning Point out the *-ing* ending on *blooming, sprouting,* and *recognizing.* Tell students that this ending goes on action words (verbs). Invite students to use each word in a sentence.

Intermediate After reading, students can use a Venn diagram to sort words that go with gardening, words that do not, and words that may go with both.

Advanced Teach the lesson on pp. 282–283. Students can report on the names of these gardening-related words in their home languages.

Resources for home-language words may include parents, bilingual staff members, bilingual dictionaries, or online translation sources.

ELL Strategies in the Lesson

ELL strategies support your instruction to meet all proficiency levels.

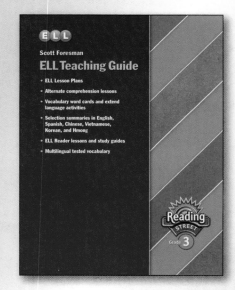

ELL Zone This Exit!

The **ELL Teaching Guide** provides an alternate lesson each week plus multilingual selection summaries, word cards, language activities, and more.

ELL Teaching Posters

Preteach vocabulary, build background, and access content with the weekly **ELL Poster**.

More ELL Tools

The **ELL and Transition Handbook** is your all-in-one guide for best practices, research, strategies, assessment tools, and activities.

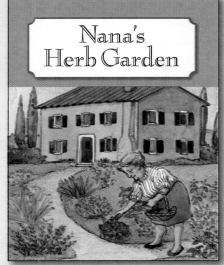

More Reading Practice

Reading Street provides an **ELL Reader** every week to build vocabulary, provide text support, and enrich language skills.

A **Teaching Guide** supports you every step of the way!

STREET GUIDE
Did you know?

Ten Important Sentences helps the ELL reader access content and develop comprehension skills for every selection.

Let the journey begin!

KINDERGARTEN

19 Big Books
(including alphabet book)

18 Read Aloud
Trade Books

36 Kindergarten
Readers

Talk with Me Chart
Sing with Me Chart
Phonics Songs and Rhymes Chart
(3 charts per week)

6 Teacher's Editions (1 per Unit)

GRADE 1

Student Edition (Unit 1)

Student Edition (Unit 2)

Student Edition (Unit 3)

Student Edition (Unit 4)

Student Edition (Unit 5)

5 Teacher's Editions (1 per Unit)

GRADE 2

Student Edition
(Units 1–3)

Student Edition
(Units 4–6)

6 Teacher's Editions
(1 per Unit)

GRADE 3

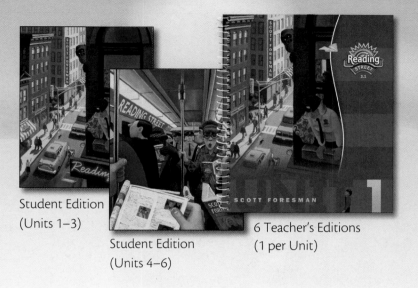

Student Edition
(Units 1–3)

Student Edition
(Units 4–6)

6 Teacher's Editions
(1 per Unit)

GRADE 4

Student Edition

6 Teacher's Editions (1 per unit)

GRADE 5

Student Edition

6 Teacher's Editions (1 per Unit)

GRADE 6

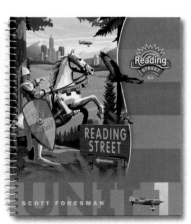

Student Edition

6 Teacher's Editions (1 per Unit)

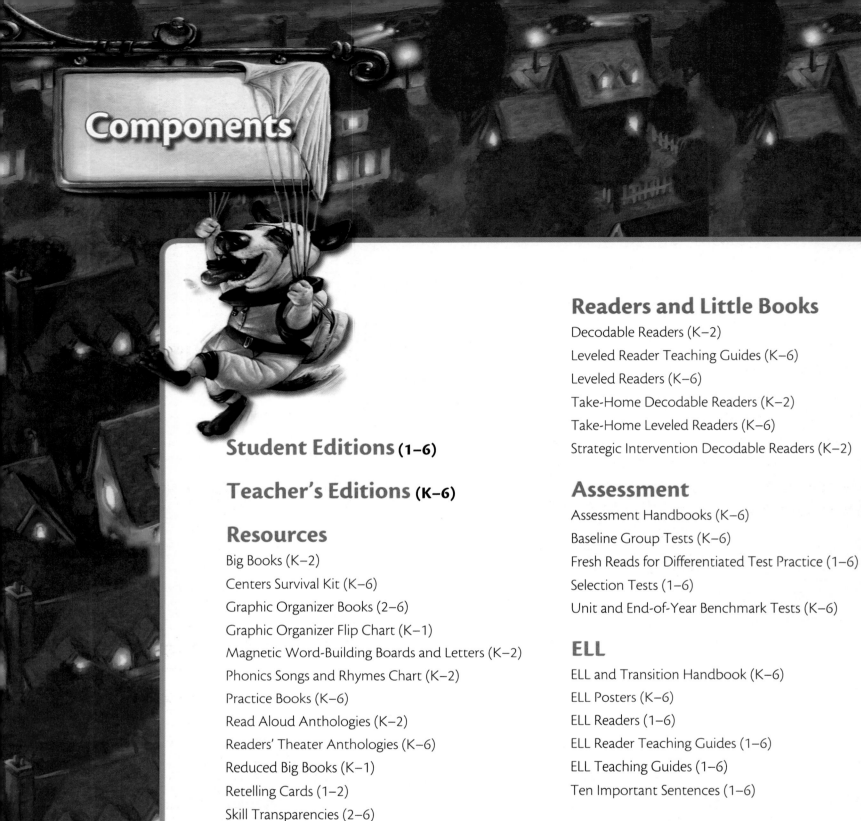

Components

Student Editions (1–6)

Teacher's Editions (K–6)

Resources

Big Books (K–2)

Centers Survival Kit (K–6)

Graphic Organizer Books (2–6)

Graphic Organizer Flip Chart (K–1)

Magnetic Word-Building Boards and Letters (K–2)

Phonics Songs and Rhymes Chart (K–2)

Practice Books (K–6)

Read Aloud Anthologies (K–2)

Readers' Theater Anthologies (K–6)

Reduced Big Books (K–1)

Retelling Cards (1–2)

Skill Transparencies (2–6)

Sound Spelling Cards (1–2)

Vocabulary Transparencies (1)

Tested Vocabulary Cards (K–6)

Trade Book Library and Teaching Guide (1–6)

Readers and Little Books

Decodable Readers (K–2)

Leveled Reader Teaching Guides (K–6)

Leveled Readers (K–6)

Take-Home Decodable Readers (K–2)

Take-Home Leveled Readers (K–6)

Strategic Intervention Decodable Readers (K–2)

Assessment

Assessment Handbooks (K–6)

Baseline Group Tests (K–6)

Fresh Reads for Differentiated Test Practice (1–6)

Selection Tests (1–6)

Unit and End-of-Year Benchmark Tests (K–6)

ELL

ELL and Transition Handbook (K–6)

ELL Posters (K–6)

ELL Readers (1–6)

ELL Reader Teaching Guides (1–6)

ELL Teaching Guides (1–6)

Ten Important Sentences (1–6)

Intervention

Intervention Assessment (1–6)

Intervention Assessment Benchmark Books (1–6)

Intervention Decodable Readers (3)

Intervention Leveled Readers (1–6)

Intervention Teaching Guides (1–5)

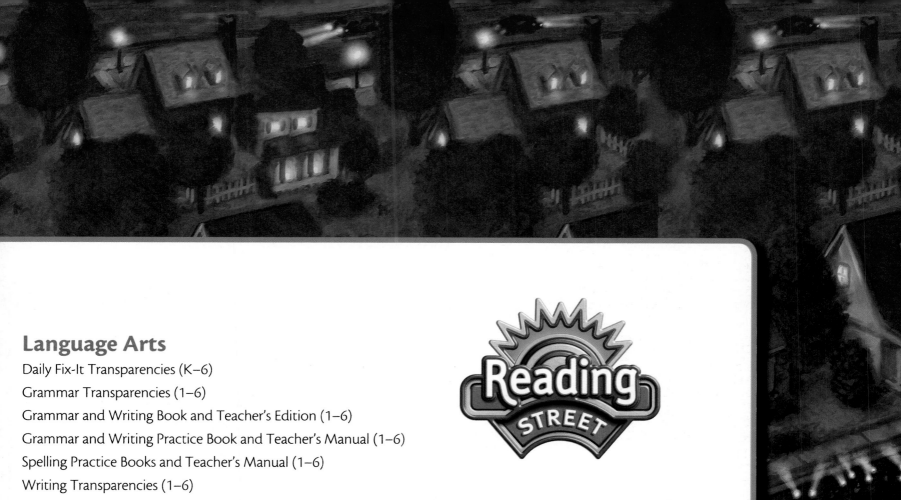

Language Arts

Daily Fix-It Transparencies (K–6)

Grammar Transparencies (1–6)

Grammar and Writing Book and Teacher's Edition (1–6)

Grammar and Writing Practice Book and Teacher's Manual (1–6)

Spelling Practice Books and Teacher's Manual (1–6)

Writing Transparencies (1–6)

Writing Rubrics and Anchor Papers (1–6)

Professional Development (K–6)

Technology

AudioText CDs (K–6)

Background-Building Audio CDs (K–6)

ExamView® CD-ROM (2–6)

Fluency Coach Voice Recognition Software (2–6)

Online Activities (K–6)

Online Decodable Readers (K–2)

Online Lesson Planner (K–6)

Online Leveled Readers (K–6)

Online New Literacies Activities (1–6)

Online Student Editions (1–6)

Online Teacher's Editions (K–6)

Phonics Activities (K–2)

Phonics Songs and Rhymes Audio CD (K–2)

Success Tracker™ Data Management (K–6)

W-H-E-E... enjoy the ride!

Grade 2
Priority Skills

Priority skills are the critical elements of reading—phonemic awareness, phonics, fluency, vocabulary, and text comprehension—as they are developed across and within grades to assure that instructional emphasis is placed on the right skills at the right time and to maintain a systematic sequence of skill instruction.

Key
- ● = Taught/Unit priority
- ◐ = Reviewed and practiced
- ○ = Integrated practice

	UNIT 1		UNIT 2	
	Weeks		**Weeks**	
	1–2	**3–5**	**1–2**	**3–5**
Phonemic Awareness	Appears in Strategic Intervention lessons (pp. DI•14–DI•64)			
Phonics				
Know letter-sound relationships	●	●	●	●
Blend sounds of letters to decode				
Consonants	●	◐	○	◐
Consonant blends and digraphs	●	●	◐	◐
Short Vowels	●	◐	◐	◐
Long Vowels	●	◐	◐	◐
r-Controlled Vowels			●	●
Vowel Digraphs				●
Diphthongs				
Other vowel patterns	●	◐	◐	○
Phonograms/word families	●	●	○	○
Decode words with common word parts				
Base words and inflected endings		●	◐	●
Contractions			●	◐
Compounds				
Suffixes and prefixes				
Blend syllables to decode multisyllabic words	◐	◐	●	●
Fluency				
Read aloud with accuracy, comprehension, and appropriate rate	●	●	●	○
Read aloud with expression		●	●	●
Attend to punctuation and use appropriate phrasing		●	●	●
Practice fluency in a variety of ways, including choral reading, paired reading, and repeated oral reading	●	●	●	●
Work toward appropriate fluency goals	50–60 WCPM	50–60 WCPM	58–68 WCPM	58–68 WCPM
Vocabulary				
Read high-frequency words and lesson vocabulary automatically	●	●	●	●
Develop vocabulary through direct instruction, concrete experiences, reading, and listening to text read aloud	●	●	●	●
Use word structure to figure out word meaning				
Use context clues to determine word meaning of unfamiliar words, multiple-meaning words, homonyms, homographs				●
Use grade-appropriate references sources to learn word meanings			●	○
Use new words in a variety of contexts	○	○	○	○
Use graphic organizers to group, study, and retain vocabulary	●	●	●	●
Classify and categorize words				
Understand antonyms and synonyms		●		
Examine word usage and effectiveness	●	●	●	●

UNIT 3		UNIT 4		UNIT 5		UNIT 6	
Weeks		**Weeks**		**Weeks**		**Weeks**	
1–2	3–5	1–2	3–5	1–2	3–5	1–2	3–5

UNIT 3 1–2	UNIT 3 3–5	UNIT 4 1–2	UNIT 4 3–5	UNIT 5 1–2	UNIT 5 3–5	UNIT 6 1–2	UNIT 6 3–5
66–76 WCPM	66–76 WCPM	74–84 WCPM	74–84 WCPM	82–92 WCPM	82–92 WCPM	90–100 WCPM	90–100 WCPM

Grade 2
Priority Skills

Key
- ● = Taught/Unit priority
- ◐ = Reviewed and practiced
- ○ = Integrated practice

Text Comprehension	UNIT 1 Weeks 1–2	UNIT 1 Weeks 3–5	UNIT 2 Weeks 1–2	UNIT 2 Weeks 3–5
Strategies				
Preview the text	○	○	○	○
Set and monitor purpose for reading	○	○	○	○
Activate and use prior knowledge			●	○
Make and confirm predictions	●	○	●	○
Monitor comprehension and use fix-up strategies		●	○	○
Use graphic organizers to focus on text structure, to represent relationships in text, or to summarize text	○	○	○	○
Answer questions	○	○	○	○
Generate questions				
Recognize text structure: story and informational	●	●	○	●
Summarize text by retelling stories or identifying main ideas	○	○	○	●
Visualize; use mental imagery				●
Make connections: text to self, text to text, text to world	○	○	○	○
Use parts of a book to locate information		●	●	○
Skills				
Author's purpose	◐	○	○	●
Cause and effect				
Compare and contrast		◐	○	○
Draw conclusions				●
Fact and opinion				
Graphic sources (charts, diagrams, graphs, maps, tables)			●	○
Main idea and supporting details	●	●	○	○
Realism/fantasy		●	●	◐
Sequence of events			●	●
Literary Elements				
Character (Recognize characters' traits, actions, feelings, and motives)	●	●	◐	○
Plot and plot structure				
Setting	●	●	◐	○
Theme				

UNIT 3		UNIT 4		UNIT 5		UNIT 6	
Weeks		Weeks		Weeks		Weeks	
1–2	3–5	1–2	3–5	1–2	3–5	1–2	3–5
○	○	○	○	○	○	○	○
○	○	○	○	○	○	○	○
○	○	○	○	○	●	○	●
○	●	○	○	○	○	○	○
○	●	○	○	○	●	●	○
○	○	○	●	●	○	○	●
○	○	○	○	○	○	○	○
		●	●	○	●	○	○
●	○	●	○	●	○	○	○
○	○	○	●	○	○	○	●
●	○	○	○	○	○	●	○
○	○	○	○	○	○	○	○
●	○	○	○	○	○	○	○
●	○	○	○	◑	●	○	○
	●	○	○	○	○	○	●
○	○	●	●	○	○	●	○
●	◑	○	◑	○	○	○	●
		●	●	○	○	●	◑
●	●	●	●	●	●	●	●
○	○	○	◑	●	○	◑	○
○	○	○	○	○	●	○	○
◑	○	○	○	●	◑	○	○
○	○	◑	○	○	○	○	●
	●	○	●	◑	●	○	●
○	○	◑	○	○	○	○	●
	●	○	●	◑	●	○	○

You Are Here

Table of Contents

Unit 2
Working Together

Unit 3
Creative Ideas

Unit 4
Our Changing World

Unit 5
Responsibility

Working Together

How can we work together?

Unit 2
Skills Overview

166–187

Tara and Tiree
Fearless Friends/
Rescue Dogs

NARRATIVE
NONFICTION

194–215

Ronald Morgan
Goes to Bat/Spaceball

REALISTIC
FICTION

Oral Language	*What can we do in a dangerous situation?*	*What makes a team?*
Word Work — Phonics	T ↻ *r*-Controlled *ar, or, ore* T REVIEW Consonant Digraphs	T ↻ Contractions T REVIEW *r*-Controlled *ar, or, ore*
Spelling	T Words with *r*-Controlled *ar, or, ore*	T Words with Contractions
High-Frequency Words	T *family, once, pull, listen, heard, break*	T *laugh, great, you're, either, certainly, second, worst*
Reading — Comprehension	T ↻ **Skill** Sequence ↻ **Strategy** Predict REVIEW **Skill** Characters	T ↻ **Skill** Realism and Fantasy ↻ **Strategy** Prior Knowledge REVIEW **Skill** Sequence
Vocabulary	Position and Direction Words	Descriptive Words: Verbs
Fluency	Accuracy and Appropriate Pace	Read with Expression/Intonation
Language Arts — Writing	**Weekly Writing** How-to Report **Unit Process Writing**	**Weekly Writing** How-to Report **Unit Process Writing**
Grammar	T Nouns	T Proper Nouns
Speaking, Listening, Viewing	Narrate in Sequence	Types of Media
Research/Study Skills	Glossary: Guide Words	Newspaper/Periodicals
Integrate Science and Social Studies Standards	Time for SOCIAL STUDIES Heroes, Community Service	Time for SOCIAL STUDIES Cultural Heritage, Production of Goods, Personal Responsibility

↻ Target Skill   T Tested Skill

Big Idea — How can we work together?

WEEK 3	WEEK 4	WEEK 5
222–249 **Turtle's Race with Beaver/** **The Secret Life of Ponds** FOLKTALE	256–279 **The Bremen Town Musicians/** **Animals Helping Animals** FAIRY TALE	286–309 **A Turkey for Thanksgiving/** **Thanksgiving USA** ANIMAL FANTASY
When does sharing make sense?	*When should we work together?* *When should we work alone?*	*How can we contribute to a celebration?*
T *r*-controlled *er, ir, ur* **T** REVIEW Contractions	**T** Plurals REVIEW *r*-Controlled *er, ir, ur*	**T** Long *a: a, ai, ay* **T** REVIEW Plurals
T Words with *r*-controlled *er, ir, ur*	**T** Words with Plurals –*s, es, ies*	**T** Words with Long *a: a, ai, ay*
T *enough, toward, above, ago, word, whole*	**T** *people, sign, shall, bought, probably, pleasant, scared*	**T** *door, behind, brought, minute, promise, sorry, everybody*
T **Skill** Sequence **Strategy** Summarize REVIEW **Skill** Realism and Fantasy	**T** **Skill** Author's Purpose **Strategy** Story Structure REVIEW **Skill** Realism and Fantasy	**T** **Skill** Draw Conclusions **Strategy** Visualize REVIEW **Skill** Author's Purpose
Time and Order Words for Sequence	Homophones	Similes
Express Characterization	Appropriate Phrasing	Read Silently with Fluency
Weekly Writing How-to Report **Unit Process Writing**	**Weekly Writing** How-to Report **Unit Process Writing**	**Weekly Writing** How-to Report **Unit Process Writing**
T Singular and Plural Nouns	Plural Nouns That Change Spelling	Possessive Nouns
Follow and Give Directions	Compare and Contrast Characters	Make Introductions
Alphabetical Order: Second Letter	Advertisement/Poster	Read a Web Page
Time for **Science** Physical Environment, Habitat, Ecosystems	Time for **Science** Interdependence, Living Things, Environment	Time for **SOCIAL STUDIES** National Celebrations, Patriotism

Unit 2
Monitor Progress

Predictors of Reading Success	WEEK 1	WEEK 2	WEEK 3	WEEK 4
Word Reading / **Phonics**	⚙️ 🎯 *r*-Controlled *ar, or, ore*	⚙️ 🎯 Contractions	⚙️ 🎯 *r*-Controlled *er, ir, ur*	⚙️ 🎯 Plurals
WCPM / **Fluency**	Read with Accuracy and Appropriate Pace/Rate 58–68 WCPM	Read with Expression/ Intonation Attend to Punctuation 58–68 WCPM	Express Characterization 58–68 WCPM	Read with Appropriate Phrasing 58–68 WCPM
High-Frequency Words / **High Frequency Words/ Vocabulary**	⚙️ break ⚙️ family ⚙️ heard ⚙️ listen ⚙️ once ⚙️ pull	⚙️ certainly ⚙️ either ⚙️ great ⚙️ laugh ⚙️ second ⚙️ worst ⚙️ you're	⚙️ above ⚙️ ago ⚙️ enough ⚙️ toward ⚙️ whole ⚙️ word	⚙️ bought ⚙️ people ⚙️ pleasant ⚙️ probably ⚙️ scared ⚙️ shall ⚙️ sign
Oral Vocabulary / **Vocabulary/ Concept Development** (assessed informally)	avalanche blustery courageous fast-paced hazard instinct rescue skittish	actuate aloft compete contribute deserve mope recreation tinker	coax conflict inhabit ramp resolve serape startle vacation	faithful miserable misgivings occasion partnership solution struggle survival
Retelling / **Text Comprehension**	⚙️ 🎯 **Skill** Sequence 🎯 **Strategy** Predict	⚙️ 🎯 **Skill** Realism and Fantasy 🎯 **Strategy** Prior Knowledge	⚙️ 🎯 **Skill** Sequence 🎯 **Strategy** Summarize	⚙️ 🎯 **Skill** Author's Purpose 🎯 **Strategy** Story Structure

🎯 Target Skill   ⚙️ SuccessTracker/Unit 2 Benchmark Tested Skills

Make Data–Driven Decisions

Data Management
- Assess
- Diagnose
- Prescribe
- Disaggregate

Classroom Management
- Monitor Progress
- Group
- Differentiate Instruction
- Inform Parents

Reading STREET

Success Tracker

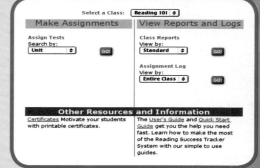

ONLINE CLASSROOM

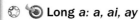

WEEK 5

Long *a: a, ai, ay*

Read Silently with Fluency

58–68 WCPM

- behind
- brought
- door
- everybody
- minute
- promise
- sorry

---

banquet
decorate
dine
flare
glimmer
holiday
participate
whispery

Skill Draw Conclusions

Strategy Visualize

Manage Data

- Assign the Unit 2 Benchmark Test for students to take online.

- SuccessTracker records results and generates reports by school, grade, classroom, or student.

- Use reports to disaggregate and aggregate Unit 2 skills and standards data to monitor progress.

- Based on class lists created to support the categories important for AYP (gender, ethnicity, migrant education, English proficiency, disabilities, economic status), reports let you track adequate yearly progress every six weeks.

Group

- Use results from Unit 2 Benchmark Tests taken online through SuccessTracker to regroup students.

- Reports in SuccessTracker suggest appropriate groups for students based on test results.

On-Level

Strategic Intervention

Advanced

Individualize Instruction

- Tests are correlated to Unit 2 tested skills and standards so that prescriptions for individual teaching and learning plans can be created.

- Individualized prescriptions target instruction and accelerate student progress toward learning outcome goals.

- Prescriptions include resources to reteach Unit 2 skills and standards.

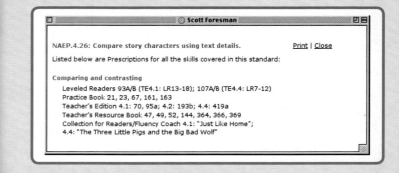

NAEP.4.26: Compare story characters using text details.   Print | Close

Listed below are Prescriptions for all the skills covered in this standard:

Comparing and contrasting
  Leveled Readers 93A/B (TE4.1: LR13-18); 107A/B (TE4.4: LR7-12)
  Practice Book 21, 23, 67, 161, 163
  Teacher's Edition 4.1: 70, 95a; 4.2: 193b; 4.4: 419a
  Teacher's Resource Book 47, 49, 52, 144, 364, 366, 369
  Collection for Readers/Fluency Coach 4.1: "Just Like Home";
  4.4: "The Three Little Pigs and the Big Bad Wolf"

Grouping for AYP

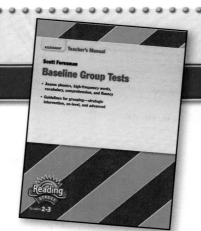

Diagnose and Differentiate

STEP 1

Diagnose
To make initial grouping decisions, use the Baseline Group Test or another initial placement test. Depending on children's ability levels, you may have more than one of each group.

Differentiate

If... a child's performance is	**Below-Level**	**then...** use the regular instruction and the daily Strategic Intervention, pp. DI·14–DI·62.
If... a child's performance is	**On-Level**	**then...** use the regular instruction for On-Level learners throughout each week.
If... a child's performance is	**Advanced**	**then...** use the regular instruction and the daily instruction for Advanced learners, pp. DI·9–DI·63.

Group Time

On-Level
- Explicit instructional routines teach core skills and strategies.
- Ample practice for core skills.
- Independent activities provide practice for core skills.
- Leveled readers (LR1–50) and decodable readers provide additional reading and practice with core skills and vocabulary.

Strategic Intervention
- Daily Strategic Intervention provides more intensive instruction, more scaffolding, more practice with critical skills, and more opportunities to respond.
- Decodable readers practice word reading skills.
- Reteach lessons (DI·64–DI·68) provide additional instructional opportunities with target skills.
- Leveled readers (LR1–50) build background for the selections and practice target skills and vocabulary.

Advanced
- Daily Advanced lessons provide compacted instruction for accelerated learning, options for independent investigative work, and challenging reading content.
- Leveled readers (LR1–50) provide additional reading tied to lesson concepts.

Additional opportunities to differentiate instruction:
- Reteach Lessons, pp. DI·64–DI·68
- Leveled Reader Instruction and Leveled Practice, LR1–50
- Scott Foresman Reading Intervention Program

4–Step Plan for Assessment

1	**Diagnose and Differentiate**
2	**Monitor Progress**
3	**Assess and Regroup**
4	**Summative Assessment**

Monitor Progress

STEP 2

- **Monitor Progress boxes** to check word reading, high-frequency words, retelling, and fluency
- **Weekly Assessments** on Day 5 for phonics, high-frequency words, comprehension, fluency, and retelling
- **Guiding comprehension questions** and skill and strategy instruction during reading
- **Practice Book** pages at point of use
- **Weekly Selection Tests** or **Fresh Reads for Differentiated Test Practice**

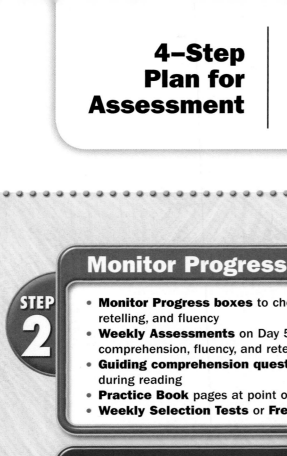

Assess and Regroup

STEP 3

- **Day 5 Assessments** Record results of weekly Day 5 assessments for phonics, high-frequency words, and fluency (pp. 313j–k) to track children's progress.
- **Unit 2 Benchmark Test** Administer this test to check mastery of unit skills.
- Use weekly assessment information, Unit Benchmark Test performance, and the Unit 2 Assess and Regroup (p. 313l) to make regrouping decisions. See the timeline below.

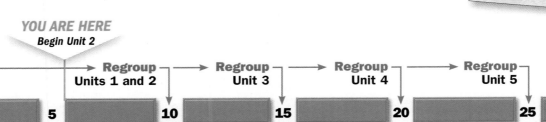

YOU ARE HERE
Begin Unit 2

SCOTT FORESMAN ASSESSMENT

Group Baseline Group Test		Regroup Units 1 and 2	Regroup Unit 3	Regroup Unit 4	Regroup Unit 5	END OF YEAR
Week 1	5	10	15	20	25	30

OUTSIDE ASSESSMENT

Initial placement → Outside assessment for regrouping → Outside assessment for regrouping

Outside assessments (e.g., DIBELS) may recommend regrouping at other times during the year.

Summative Assessment

STEP 4

- **Benchmark Assessment** Use to measure a child's mastery of each unit's skills.
- **End-of-Year Benchmark Assessment** Use to measure a child's mastery of program skills covered in all six units.

Unit 2
Theme Launch

Discuss the Big Idea

Read and discuss the theme question. Explain

- there are many ways to show that you are a good friend (sharing, taking care of others, making sure others are safe)

- there are many ways to be a good team member (do your part, be a good sport, support others, take turns)

- there are many ways to cooperate to make things work (take turns, share, work together, take charge, listen, help others)

Have children use the pictures along the side of the page to preview the selections in this unit. Read the titles and captions together. Ask children how each selection might be about how we can work together.

Read Aloud

Read the big book *From Me to You.*

- What event changes the way Rat acts every day?

- How does Rat feel when he helps his friends?

- How do Rat and his friends work together to make Bat feel better?

- How can friends show one another that they care about each other?

- How does knowing that someone cares about you make you feel?

For more read alouds related to the theme, see the Read Aloud Anthology.

UNIT 2

Working Together

How can we work together?

Read It ONLINE
sfsuccessnet.com

160

CONNECTING CULTURES

You can use the following selection to help children learn about their own and other cultures and explore common elements of culture.

Ronald Morgan Goes to Bat Children can talk about different sports that children play around the word and discuss how teams are alike, no matter how the game is played. Discuss how team cooperation and team spirit help a team play well.

connect to SOCIAL STUDIES

Tara and Tiree, Fearless Friends
Faithful pets work together to save a life.
Narrative Nonfiction

connect to SOCIAL STUDIES

Ronald Morgan Goes to Bat
Ronald provides his team with spirit.
Realistic Fiction

connect to SCIENCE

Turtle's Race with Beaver
Beaver learns the importance of cooperation.
Folk Tale

connect to SCIENCE

The Bremen Town Musicians
Animals work together to stop the robbers.
Fairy Tale

connect to SOCIAL STUDIES

A Turkey for Thanksgiving
The animals work together to make a happy Thanksgiving.
Animal Fantasy

Unit Inquiry Project
Organize a Club

Children can work together in groups of 5–6 to organize a school club to solve a problem in the school or community.

PROJECT TIMETABLE

WEEK	ACTIVITY/SKILL CONNECTION
1	**BRAINSTORM AND INTERVIEW** Children think of needs their school or community has. They can interview community leaders or family members for ideas. Have children form groups and choose one need to address.
2	**ORGANIZE A CLUB** Children organize a club to address the need of the school or community.
3	**ELECT OFFICERS** Decide on officers to elect and hold an election.
4	**PLAN ACTIVITIES** Hold club meetings to discuss problems. Begin planning how to address identified needs.
5	**PRESENT** Children present their plan to the class.

Presentation options and assessment rubric can be found on p. 313. **Rubric 4 3 2 1**

Concept Development
to Foster Reading Comprehension

Working Together

How can we work together?

WEEK 1	WEEK 2	WEEK 3	WEEK 4	WEEK 5

EXPAND THE CONCEPT

Lesson Focus • What can we do in a dangerous situation?	**Lesson Focus** • What makes a team?	**Lesson Focus** • When does sharing make sense?	**Lesson Focus** • When should we work together? When should we work alone?	**Lesson Focus** • How can we contribute to a celebration?

DEVELOP LANGUAGE

READ THE LITERATURE

• *Tara and Tiree, Fearless Friends* • "Rescue Dogs"	• *Ronald Morgan Goes to Bat* • "Spaceball"	• *Turtle's Race with Beaver* • "The Secret Life of Ponds"	• *The Bremen Town Musicians* • "Animals Helping Animals"	• *A Turkey for Thanksgiving* • "Thanksgiving USA"

TEACH CONTENT

Time for SOCIAL STUDIES	Time for SOCIAL STUDIES	TIME FOR Science	TIME FOR Science	Time for SOCIAL STUDIES
• Heroes • Community Services	• Cultural Heritage • Production of Goods • Self Direction • Personal Responsibility • Cooperation • Teamwork	• Physical Environment • Survival • Habitat • Ecosystems	• Interdependence • Survival • Living Things • Environment	• National Celebrations • Patriotism • Traditions

Tara and Tiree
Fearless Friends

Preview Your Week

What can we do in a dangerous situation?

Tara and Tiree
Fearless Friends
by Andrew Clements
illustrated by Scott Gustafson

What makes Tara and Tiree fearless friends?

166

Student Edition pages 166–183

Audio CD

Genre Narrative Nonfiction
Phonics r-Controlled *ar, or, ore*
Comprehension Skill Sequence
Comprehension Strategy Predict

Paired Selection

Reading Across Texts
Training Rescue Dogs

Genre
Expository Nonfiction

Text Features
Photographs
Headlines

Time for **SOCIAL STUDIES**

Social Studies in Reading

Rescue Dogs

by Rena Moran

Do you know that dogs can be trained to save lives? These dogs are called rescue dogs. When people are in danger, rescue dogs are ready to help them.

Who do they help?

Rescue dogs find lost hikers and campers. They find people who are trapped after an earthquake or an avalanche. When people get lost in a snowstorm, rescue dogs search for them. Some dogs can even save people from drowning.

What kinds of dogs make good rescue dogs?

Good rescue dogs must be strong and smart. They also must listen to the people who train and handle them. Saint Bernards have been working as rescue dogs for many years. They help rescue people who get lost in snowstorms or get trapped under deep snow.

Bloodhounds, Labrador retrievers, and German shepherds are good at following the trails of lost people. German shepherds also are good at finding people who are trapped under snow. Newfoundlands do a great job with water rescues.

184

Student Edition pages 184–187

Audio CD

Read It ONLINE
sfsuccessnet.com

- Student Edition
- Leveled Readers
- Decodable Reader

Leveled Readers

🎯 **Skill** Sequence

🎯 **Strategy** Predict

Lesson Vocabulary

Below-Level

On-Level

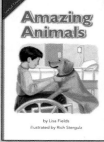

Advanced

 **ELL Reader**

- Concept Vocabulary
- Text Support
- Language Enrichment

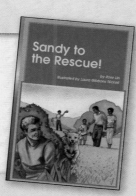

Decodable Reader

Apply Phonics

· *A Trip to the Farm*

Time for **SOCIAL STUDIES**

Integrate Social Studies Standards

- Heroes
- Community Services

✓ **Read**

Tara and Tiree, Fearless Friends pp. 166–183

"Rescue Dogs" pp. 184–187

✓ **Read**

Leveled Readers

Below-Level   **On-Level**   **Advanced**

- Support Concepts
- Develop Concepts
- Extend Concepts
- Social Studies Extension Activity

✓ **Read**

ELL Reader

✓ **Build Concept Vocabulary**
Working Together,
pp. 162r, 162–163

✓ **Teach Social Studies Concepts**
Service Dogs, pp. 180–181
Natural Hazards, pp. 172–173

✓ **Explore Social Studies Center**
Acting in an Emergency,
p. 162k

Planner

My Lesson Planner
ONLINE
sfsuccessnet.com

THIS WEEK
CHILDREN WILL LEARN
Phonics *r*-Controlled *ar, or, ore*
Comprehension Skill Sequence
Comprehension Strategy Predict

DAY 1

DAY 2

Oral Language *10–15 minutes*

- Build Concepts
- Share Literature

Oral Language 162l–162m
QUESTION OF THE WEEK *What can we do in a dangerous situation?*
Share Literature
Sing with Me Big Book, 6

Oral Language 164a–164b
QUESTION OF THE DAY *What are some ways that dogs can help people?*
Share Literature
Read Aloud Anthology "Snoop, the Search Dog"

Word Work *25–30 minutes*

- Phonics
- Spelling
- High-Frequency Words

Word Work 162n–162p
Phonics
Introduce *r*-Controlled *ar, or, ore* **T**

Spelling Pretest

Word Work 164c–164d, 164–165a
Phonics
r-Controlled *ar, or, ore* **T**

Spelling Dictation
High-Frequency Words T
Introduce *family, once, pull, listen, heard, break*

Reading *60–75 minutes*

- Vocabulary
- Comprehension
- Fluency

- Cross-Curricular Connections

- Independent Reading

Reading 162q–163b
Vocabulary
Decodable Word Meaning
Read Decodable Reader 6
Comprehension Check
Fluency
Paired Reading
Build Background
Let's Talk About Working Together
Comprehension
Sequence **T**

SOCIAL STUDIES Concept Chart

Leveled Readers, LR1–9
Self-Selected Reading, TR22–23

Decodable Reader 6
A Trip to the Farm
Written by Andrew Crum
Illustrated by Dana Combs

Reading 164e–164f, 166a–181a
Vocabulary
Introduce *slipped, collar, brave*
Comprehension
Sequence **T**
Predict

Read *Tara and Tiree: Fearless Friends*, 166–181

REVIEW **Comprehension Skill**
Character and Setting

SOCIAL STUDIES Service Dogs
SCIENCE Natural Hazards
SOCIAL STUDIES Concept Chart

Leveled Readers, LR1–9
Self-Selected Reading, TR22–23

Tara and Tiree

Language Arts *20–30 minutes*

- Writing
- Grammar
- Speaking, Listening, Viewing
- Research/Study Skills

Language Arts 163c–163d
Shared Writing
Directions
DAILY WRITING
Write about things people do that are courageous and explain why.
Grammar
Introduce Nouns **T**

Language Arts 181b–181c
Interactive Writing
Notes
DAILY WRITING
Write about an animal you know or heard of who helped someone.
Grammar
Practice Nouns **T**

Monitor Progress

Daily SUCCESS PREDICTORS for
Adequate Yearly Progress

Day 1 Check 162o
Check Word Reading
Spiral **REVIEW** Phonics

Phonics

Day 2 Check 165a
Check High-Frequency Words
Spiral **REVIEW** High-Frequency Words

Fluency

162d | Vocabulary | **Check Oral Vocabulary** See p. DI·2.

Student Edition 166–181

▶ ▶

Leveled Readers

▶ ▶

Student Edition 184–187

DAY 3

Oral Language 182a–182b

QUESTION OF THE DAY *When would people need to use a dog like Snoop?*

Share Literature
Read Aloud Anthology "Snoop, the Search Dog"

Word Work 182c–182d

Phonics
REVIEW Consonant Digraphs

Spelling Practice

High-Frequency Words T
Practice *family, once, pull, listen, heard, break*

Reading 166–181, 182e–183

Vocabulary
Position and Direction Words

Comprehension
Read *Tara and Tiree: Fearless Friends,* 166–183

Think and Share

Fluency
Choral Reading

SOCIAL STUDIES Concept Chart

Leveled Readers, LR1–9
Self-Selected Reading, TR22–23

Language Arts 183a–183b

Independent Writing
Respond to Literature

DAILY WRITING
Write a journal entry about a dangerous situation you've heard or read about.

Grammar
Write with Nouns T

DAY 4

Oral Language 184a–184b

QUESTION OF THE DAY *What kind of work do dogs do?*

Share Literature
Read Aloud Anthology "Porpoise Savers"

Word Work 184c–184d

Phonics
REVIEW Sentence Reading

Spelling Partner Review

High-Frequency Words T
Practice *family, once, pull, listen, heard, break*

Reading 184–187a

Vocabulary
Position and Direction Words

Comprehension
Read *Rescue Dogs,* 184–187
Social Studies in Reading
Reading Across Texts

Fluency
Choral Reading

SOCIAL STUDIES Heroes, Community Services
SOCIAL STUDIES CENTER Think and Act

Leveled Readers, LR1–9
Self-Selected Reading, TR22–23

Language Arts 187b–187d

Writing Across the Curriculum
List

DAILY WRITING
Write about when you helped someone.

Grammar
Review Nouns T

Speaking and Listening
Narrate in Sequence

DAY 5

Oral Language 188a–188b

QUESTION OF THE DAY *How can we help during dangerous events?*

Share Literature
Read Aloud Anthology "Porpoise Savers"

Word Work 188c–188f

Phonics
REVIEW Review *r*-Controlled Vowels *ar, or, ore*

Spelling Test

High-Frequency Words T
Review *family, once, pull, listen, heard, break*

Reading 188b, 188e–188g

Vocabulary
Position and Direction Words

Monitor Progress
Read the Sentences
Read the Story

SOCIAL STUDIES Concept Chart

Leveled Readers, LR1–9
Self-Selected Reading, TR22–23

Language Arts 188–189a

Grammar and Writing
Use Nouns

Connect to Unit Writing
How-to Report

DAILY WRITING
Write about when you helped someone.

Research/Study Skills
Glossary: Guide Words

KEY

↻ = Target Skill

T = Tested Skill

THIS WEEK'S RESOURCES

Practice Book pp. 51–60

Spelling Practice Book pp. 21–24

Grammar and Writing Practice Book pp. 21–24

Selection Test pp. 21–24

Fresh Reads for Differentiated Test Practice pp. 31–36

Phonics Songs and Rhymes Chart 6

Day 3 Check 182g
Check Retelling

Comprehension

Day 4 Check 187a
Check Fluency WCPM
Spiral REVIEW Phonics, High-Frequency Words

Fluency

Day 5 Check 188e
r-Controlled *ar, or, ore*
High-Frequency Words
Fluency
Comprehension

SUCCESS PREDICTOR

Resources for Differentiated Instruction

LEVELED READERS

▶ **Comprehension**

🔁 **Skill** Sequence

🔁 **Strategy** Predict

▶ **Lesson Vocabulary**

High-Frequency Words

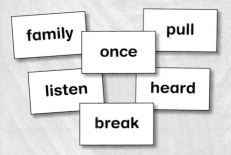

family
pull
once
listen
heard
break

▶ **Social Studies Standards**

• Heroes

• Community Services

Leveled Reader Database

ONLINE

sfsuccessnet.com

Use the Online Database of over 600 books to

• Download and print additional copies of this week's leveled readers

• Locate more titles at various levels to practice this week's skill—sequence

• Search for more titles focused on this week's topic and content

---

On-Level

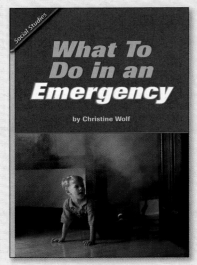

Social Studies

What To Do in an Emergency
by Christine Wolf

On-Level Reader

Sequence
Sequence refers to the order of events in both fiction and nonfiction. Sequence can also refer to the steps in a process.

Read the steps on how to be safe in case of a fire. They are listed out of order. Put them in order by writing them on the correct line below.

> • Break windows to get out if you must.
> • Don't stop to take anything with you.
> • First get down low. The air is easier to breathe.
> • Next, check your clothes. If they are on fire, stop drop and roll.
> • After you are out of danger, you can call 9-1-1.

1. *First get down low...*

2. *Next, check your clothes...*

3. *Don't stop to take anything...*

4. *Break windows to get out...*

5. *Call 9-1-1!*

On-Level Practice TE p. LR5

Vocabulary

Words to Know
break family heard listen once pull

Draw a line to match the word to its meaning.

1. break   a. people that are related to each other

2. family   b. to sense sounds through your ear

3. heard   c. a single time

4. listen   d. to hurt or damage

5. once   e. to pay attention to sounds

6. pull   f. to move by dragging or tugging

7-8. Write the meaning of the word *heard*.

answer reflects their understanding

9-10. Wite the meaning of the word *listen*.

answer reflects their understanding

On-Level Practice TE p. LR6

Strategic Intervention

Social Studies

Dogs to the Rescue
by Jessica Quilty **POLICE**

Below-Level Reader

Sequence
Sequence refers to the order of events in both fiction and nonfiction. Sequence can also refer to the steps in a process.

Read the story. Then, read what happened next. Put the sentences in order by writing the correct number between 1–5 next to each one.

> Rachel went on a walk in the forest. She tripped and fell on a rock. Her ankle hurt so she could not walk back to her car. She used her mobile phone to call for help. A rescue worker named Miguel was sent to the forest to help Rachel.

5 1. Miguel looks at Rachel's leg to see if it is broken.

4 2. Next, Rachel smiles when she sees Miguel and Max.

2 3. After Max picks up Rachel's smell, he follows a path into the woods.

3 4. Then, Max stopped and held up his head. Max and Miguel hear Rachel cry for help.

1 5. First, Miguel and his rescue dog Max found Rachel's car.

Below-Level Practice TE p. LR2

Vocabulary
Unscramble each word below. Look at the words in the Word Box to help you. Write the word on the line. Say the word aloud. Count the number of syllables.

Words to Know
break family heard listen once pull

1. ymifal   **family**   How many syllables? **3**

2. draeh   **heard**   How many syllables? **1**

3. enltis   **listen**   How many syllables? **2**

4. lpul   **pull**   How many syllables? **1**

5. ceon   **once**   How many syllables? **1**

6. akbre   **break**   How many syllables? **1**

7-8. Write the meaning of the word *heard*.

answer reflects their understanding

9-10. Write the meaning of the word *listen*.

answer reflects their understanding

Below-Level Practice TE p. LR3

Advanced

Amazing Animals

by Lisa Fields
illustrated by Rich Stergulz

Advanced Reader

Sequence

Sequence refers to the order of events in both fictional and nonfiction. Sequence can also refer to the steps in a process.

Re-read pages 4 and 5 of *Amazing Animals*. Then number each of the sentences below to put them into the correct order.

 5 1. Guide dogs like Max have special permission to enter the grocery stores to help their owners.

 3 2. Peg trusts Max to know when it is safe to cross the street.

 2 3. Peg holds on to Max's harness as he leads her safely down the steps and onto the sidewalk.

 1 4. Max is Peg's guide dog.

 4 5. Max lets Peg know when there is a hazard and leads her around the danger.

Advanced Practice TE p. LR8

Vocabulary

Complete each sentence below using the correct vocabulary word.

Words to Know
courageous depends groom
hazard rescue tasks therapy

1. Rescue dogs have to be very **courageous**.
2. Before riding on a therapy horse, the person learns how to **groom** the horse.
3. A **therapy** dog visits children and adults in nursing homes and hospitals.
4. Therapy monkeys help their owners with many **tasks**, such as turning lights on and off.
5. Some dogs are trained to **rescue** people who are lost in the snow or the woods.
6. A guide dog helps lead its owner around a **hazard**.
7. An owner **depends** on his or her service animal in many different ways.

Advanced Practice TE p. LR9

ELL

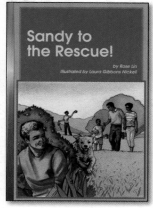

Sandy to the Rescue!

by Rose Lin
illustrated by Laura Gibbons Nickell

ELL Reader

ELL Poster 6

Teacher's Edition Notes

ELL notes throughout this lesson support instruction and reference additional resources at point of use.

**Teaching Guide
pp. 36–42, 222–223**

- Multilingual summaries of the main selection
- Comprehension lesson
- Vocabulary strategies and word cards
- ELL Reader 6 lesson

ELL and Transition Handbook

Ten Important Sentences

- Key ideas from every selection in the Student Edition
- Activities to build sentence power

More Reading

Reader's Theater Anthology

- Fluency practice
- Five scripts to build fluency
- Poetry for oral interpretation

Leveled Trade Books

- Extend reading tied to the unit concept
- Lessons in Trade Book Library Teaching Guide

School + Home

Homework

- Family Times Newsletter
- ELL Multilingual Selection Summaries

Take-Home Books

- Decodable Readers
- Leveled Readers

Family Times

Weekly Plan for Group Time
Differentiated Instruction

See Group Time pp. 162p, 166a, 182e, 184d, 188d.

DAILY PLAN

WHOLE GROUP

- Morning Warm-Up
- Share Literature
- Phonics
- Spelling
- Vocabulary

1 2 3 4 5

DAILY GROUP TIME

- **Reading Support**
- **Skill Support**
- **Fluency Practice**

WHOLE GROUP

- Fluency
- Writing
- Grammar
- Wrap Up Your Day

Look for the **(i)**

Independent Activities

See Group Time pp. 162p, 166a, 182e, 184d, 188d.

✓ **Fluency Reading**
Choral Reading

✓ **Journal Writing**
See the Planner for daily writing prompts, pp. 162d–162e.

✓ **Homework**
Practice Book, pp. 51–60
Spelling Practice Book, pp. 21–24
Grammar and Writing Practice Book, pp. 21–24

✓ **Literacy Centers**
pp. 162j–162k
- Listening
- Reading/Library
- Word Work
- Writing
- Social Studies
- Technology

DAY 1

On-Level

Page 162q
- Read Decodable Reader 6
- Reread for Fluency

Strategic Intervention

Page DI•14
- Read Decodable Reader 6
- Blend Words with r-Controlled ar, or, ore
- Reread for Fluency

Advanced

Page DI•15
- Read Advanced Selection 6
- Extend Word Reading
- Introduce Concept Inquiry

DAY 2

On-Level

Pages 166–181
- Read *Tara and Tiree Fearless Friends*
- Reread for Fluency

Strategic Intervention

Page DI•16
- Read SI Decodable Reader 6
- Read or Listen to *Tara and Tiree Fearless Friends*
- Blend Words with r-Controlled ar, or, ore

Advanced

Page DI•17
- Read *Tara and Tiree Fearless Friends*
- Continue Concept Inquiry

DAY 3

On-Level

Pages 166–183
- Reread *Tara and Tiree Fearless Friends*

Strategic Intervention

Page DI•18
- Reread *Tara and Tiree Fearless Friends*
- Read Words and Sentences
- Review Sequence and Predict
- Reread for Fluency

Advanced

Page DI•19
- Self-Selected Reading
- Continue Concept Inquiry

On-Level

Pages 184–187
- Read "Rescue Dogs"

Strategic Intervention

Page DI•20
- Read or Listen to "Rescue Dogs"
- Reread for Fluency
- Build Concepts

Advanced

Page DI•21
- Read "Rescue Dogs"
- Expand Vocabulary
- Continue Concept Inquiry

DAY 4

On-Level

Pages 188e–188g
- Sentence Reading, Set B

> **Set B**
> 1. Barb said, "Once I went to see Martin."
> 2. I will have a birthday party with my family.
> 3. You must listen and do each chore in the army.
> 4. He heard me tell corny jokes to Mr. Marshall.
> 5. Did you see the farmer pull the short, fat pig in?
> 6. Do not break the vase with the border because I

Strategic Intervention

Page DI•22
- Practice Word Reading
- Sentence Reading, Set A

> **Set A**
> 1. My family went to a large farm.
> 2. I heard a dog bark from the north.
> 3. Once we saw corn by the barn.
> 4. Pull the cord before you go.
> 5. Listen to Carl give the order.
> 6. Art did not break his arm.

Advanced

Page DI•23
- Sentence Reading, Set C
- Share Concept Inquiry
- Monitor Fluency and Comprehension

> **Set C**
> 1. Once they made the formula, they sold a portion.
> 2. It is an ordinary day, because I did not take a break from my boring work.
> 3. Listen and do not ignore me, or you will make things much harder.
> 4. The superstar will come and perform the songs for my family.
> 5. I heard him inform you that the artwork will go on sale in a day or two.
> 6. The gardener will pull up weeds by the ballpark.

DAY 5

Grouping Place English language learners in the groups that correspond to their reading abilities in English.

ELL

Use the appropriate Leveled Reader or other text at children's instructional level.

TIP Send home the appropriate Multilingual Summary of the main selection on Day 1.

MORE READING FOR Group Time

Below-Level   On-Level   Advanced

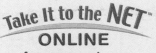

Take It to the NET ONLINE
sfsuccessnet.com

P. David Pearson
For ideas and activities to build comprehension, see the article "Comprehension Instruction in the Primary Grades" by Scott Foresman author P. D. Pearson and N. Duke.

TEACHING TIP **Help children develop a sense of how long it takes to do a task.** Give constant feedback on time as children work independently or take tests. Say: "You have been working 5 minutes. That is half the time you have."

TEACHER TALK

An **r-Controlled vowel** is a vowel followed by the letter *r*. The *r* influences the sound of the vowel, which is neither long nor short.

Looking Ahead

Be sure to schedule time for children to work on the unit inquiry project "Organize a Club." This week children should list needs of the school or community, choose one need, and form a group to address it.

Literacy Centers

Listening

Let's Read
Along

MATERIALS `SINGLES`
CD player, headphones, print copies of recorded pieces

LISTEN TO LITERATURE As children listen to the following recordings, have them follow along or read along in the print version.

AudioText
Tara and Tiree, Fearless Friends
"Rescue Dogs"

Sing with Me Background Building Audio "To the Rescue"

Phonics Songs and Rhymes Audio
"Safe from Harm"

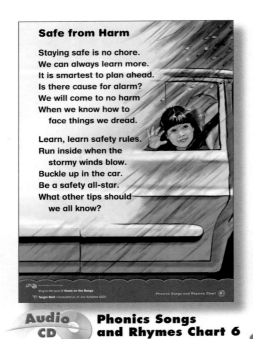

Reading/Library

Read It
Again!

MATERIALS `GROUPS`
collection of books for self-selected reading, reading logs

REREAD BOOKS Have children select previously read books from the appropriate book box and record titles of books they read in their logs. Use these previously read books:

- Decodable Readers
- Leveled Readers
- ELL Readers
- Stories written by classmates
- Book from the library

TEN IMPORTANT SENTENCES Have children read the Ten Important Sentences for *Tara and Tiree, Fearless Friends* and locate the sentences in the Student Edition.

BOOK CLUB Use p. 183 of the Student Edition to set up an "Author Study" of Andrew Clements and have children their share favorites.

Word Work

Car
Puzzle

MATERIALS `PAIRS`
puzzle pieces

r*-CONTROLLED *ar, or, ore Have children put together a puzzle whose pieces use *r*-controlled words with *ar, or,* and *ore.*

1. Cut a car shape out of cardboard and cut it into puzzle pieces. On each piece, write an *r*-controlled word with *ar, or,* or *ore*. Cut extra puzzle pieces that are not part of the car and write a word that is not *r*-controlled on each.
2. Put all of the pieces in one pile.
3. Children read the words and put together the puzzle using only *r*-controlled words.

 This interactive CD provides additional practice.

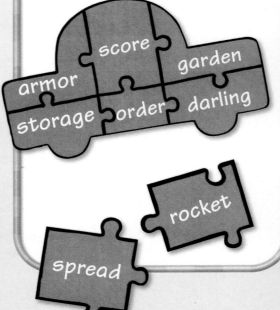

Scott Foresman Reading Street Centers Survival Kit

Use the *Tara and Tiree* materials from the Reading Street
Centers Survival Kit to organize this week's centers.

Writing

Social Studies

Technology

Out of Danger

MATERIALS   **SINGLES**
paper, pencils, crayons

WRITE A NARRATIVE Recall that Tara and Tiree help Jim when he is in danger.

1. Ask children to think of people who have been helped out of dangerous situations.
2. Have them write about one of the situations.
3. Then have them draw a picture to accompany their writing.

LEVELED WRITING Encourage children to write at their own ability level. Some may only label their picture. Others will be able to write a simple sentence with some attention to mechanics and spelling. Your best writers will write two or more sentences with greater detail and more attention to mechanics and spelling.

I went to the beach last summer. I saw a lifeguard rescue a man. He pulled him out of the water. He did CPR to help him breathe.

Emergency 911

MATERIALS   **PAIRS**
Emergency 911 chart

THINK AND ACT Talk to children about what to do in an emergency and review the Emergency 911 chart.

1. Have partners practice emergency calls.
2. Have one child be the caller and the other answer the 911 call.
3. Children should provide correct information and then switch roles.

Emergency 911

When you call 911:

- Give your name.
- Give your address and telephone number.
- Explain the emergency.
- Stay on the phone.

Helping Jobs

MATERIALS   **SINGLES** **PAIRS**
computer, CD-ROM
encyclopedia, pencils,
markers, poster board

RESEARCH HELPING JOBS Review helping jobs such as police officers, teachers, and firefighters.

1. Have children turn on the computer and access a CD-ROM encyclopedia.
2. Ask them to research a helping job of their choice.
3. Then have children design posters that illustrate and explain the job.

Encyclopedia

Police officers arrest people who break the law. They help people who have car wrecks. They help lost children get home. They keep us safe.

ALL CENTERS

Day 1
AT A GLANCE

Materials

- *Sing with Me Big Book*
- Letter Tiles
- Decodable Reader 6
- Student Edition 162–163
- Graphic Organizer 25
- Writing Transparency 6
- Grammar Transparency 6

Take It to the NET™ ONLINE

Professional Development
To learn more about modeling, go to sfsuccessnet.com and read "Modeling Mental Processes . . ." by G. Duffy and others.

Morning Warm~Up!

Fires, tornadoes, and getting lost are hazards.
People can often get hurt.
What can we do in a dangerous situation?

QUESTION OF THE WEEK Tell children they will talk, sing, read, and write about what we can do in a dangerous situation. Write and read the message and discuss the question.

CONNECT CONCEPTS Ask questions to connect to Unit 1 selections.

- It would be fun to explore a desert, as discussed in *A Walk in the Desert*. What hazards might you find in the desert?
- *Exploring Space* is about the people who learn about space by going there. What is a problem astronauts might have? How could they be helped if they were in danger?

REVIEW HIGH-FREQUENCY WORDS

- Circle the high-frequency word *often* in the message.
- Have children say and spell the word as they write it in the air.

ELL

Build Background Use the Day 1 instruction on ELL Poster 6 to assess knowledge and develop concepts.

ELL Poster 6

Share Literature

BUILD ORAL VOCABULARY Display p. 6 of the *Sing with Me Big Book.* Tell children that the class is going to sing a song about helping someone who is in trouble. Read the title. Ask children to listen for the Amazing Words **courageous**, **hazard**, and **rescue** as you sing. Then sing the song again and encourage children to sing along with you. Have children demonstrate their understanding of *courageous, hazard,* and *rescue* by asking:

* How is a fireman courageous?

* What is a type of safety hazard?

* When is someone in need of being rescued?

To the Rescue!
When you see a friend who's in trouble
And facing a hazard or two,
Then run to get help on the double.
Your friend will be counting on you.

Call 9-1-1,
Or find an adult who knows what to do.
You'll be helping
To make a courageous rescue.

Sing with Me Big Book

**Sing with Me/
Background Building Audio**

OBJECTIVE

● Build oral vocabulary.

Amazing Words to build oral vocabulary

	MONITOR PROGRESS
courageous **hazard** **rescue**	**If...** children lack oral vocabulary experiences about the concept Working Together, **then...** use the Oral Vocabulary Routine on pp. DI·1–DI·3 to develop the Amazing Words.

Access Content Help children understand the meaning of the English phrase *counting on you* in "To the Rescue!" by telling them it means "depending or relying on you."

r-Controlled *ar, or, ore*

TEACH/MODEL

Blending Strategy

ROUTINE

1 **Connect** Write *had* and *spot.* What do you know about these words? (The *a* in *had* and the *o* in *hot* are short vowel sounds.) Today we'll learn about the sounds of *a* and *o* when followed by *r.*

2 **Use Sound-Spelling Card** Display Card 3. This is *artist. Artist* has the sounds /är/ at the beginning. /är/ is the *r*-controlled sound of *a.* Say it with me: /är/.

3 **Model** Write *hard.* When the letter *a* is followed by *r,* the *a* has an *r*-controlled sound. Listen as I blend this word. Blend the sounds continuously across the word. Let's blend this word together: /härd/, *hard.* Have children compare vowel sounds in *had* and *hard.*

Repeat steps 2 and 3. Use Card 25 *orchestra* for *or, ore*/ôr/, and model blending with *sport* and *more.*

Write *darling.* You can blend longer words with /är/ and /ôr/ by dividing them into smaller parts. We usually divide words between two consonants. Read one syllable at a time and then blend them together. Model blending *darling.* Let's blend together: *dar/ling, darling.*

4 **Group Practice** Blend these words together. Continue with *born, part, score, garden, morning, armor, target.*

5 **Review** What do you know about reading these words? The letters *ar* stand for /är/; the letters *or* and *ore* stand for /ôr/.

ar

Sound-Spelling Card 3

or, ore

Sound-Spelling Card 25

BLEND WORDS

INDIVIDUALS BLEND *ar, or,* AND *ore* WORDS Have children blend *party, store, short, artist, carpet, correct, forget.* Ask what they know about each word before reading it. For feedback, see step five of the Blending Strategy Routine.

BUILD WORDS

INDIVIDUALS MAKE *ar*, *or*, AND *ore* WORDS Write *hard* and have the class blend it. Have children spell *hard* with letter tiles. Monitor work and provide feedback.

- Change the *d* in *hard* to *m*. What is the new word?

- Change the *h* in *harm* to *f*. What is the new word?

- Change the *a* in *farm* to *o*. What is the new word?

- Change the *m* in *form* to *e*, and change the *f* to *m*. What is the new word?

- Change the *m* in *more* to *ch*. What is the new word?

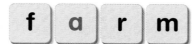

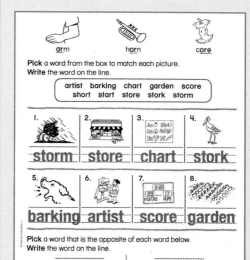

Vocabulary TIP

You may wish to explain the meanings of these words.

armor a covering worn to protect the body

batch a group or bunch

market an open space where people buy and sell things

▲ **Practice Book 2.1** p. 53, *r*-Controlled *ar, or, ore*

Monitor Progress | **Check Word Reading *r*-Controlled *ar, or, ore***

Write the following words and have individuals read them.

shark	market	charm	armor	start
porch	corner	thorn	store	morning
shore	chop	art	pocket	batch

If... children cannot blend words with *ar*, *or*, and *ore* at this point,

then... continue to monitor their progress using other instructional opportunities during the week so that they can be successful with the Day 5 Assessment. See the Skills Trace on p. 162n.

Spiral REVIEW

- Rows 1 and 2 review consonant blends and digraphs.
- Row 3 contrasts short *a* and *o* with *r*-controlled *ar* and *ore*.

▶ **Day 1 Check Word Reading** : **Day 2 Check** High-Frequency Words : **Day 3 Check** Retelling : **Day 4 Check** Fluency : **Day 5 Assess** Progress

- Segment sounds and word parts to spell words.
- Spell words with *r*-controlled *ar, or* and *ore*.

Spelling Words

r-Controlled *ar, or, ore*

1.	part*	7.	smart*
2.	hard*	8.	farm
3.	born	9.	porch
4.	horse*	10.	corn
5.	before	11.	chore
6.	more*	12.	score

Challenge Words

13.	cardinal	15.	morning
14.	therefore		

* Words from the Selection

Words with *ar, or, ore*

Generalization The vowel sound /är/ is spelled ar: p**ar**t. The vowel sound /ôr/ can be spelled or and ore: b**or**n, m**ore**.

Sort the list words by *ar, or,* and *ore*.

ar
1. part
2. hard
3. smart
4. farm

ore
5. before
6. more
7. chore
8. score

or
9. born
10. corn
11. porch
12. horse

Challenge Words
ar
13. cardinal

or
14. morning

ore
15. therefore

Spelling Words
1. part
2. hard
3. born
4. horse
5. before
6. more
7. smart
8. farm
9. porch
10. corn
11. chore
12. score
Challenge Words
13. cardinal
14. therefore
15. morning

 **Home Activity** Your child is learning to spell words with ar, or, and ore. To practice at home, have your child look at the word, pronounce it, spell it aloud, and then write it.

▲ **Spelling Practice Book** p. 21

ELL

Support Spelling Before giving the spelling pretest, clarify the meaning of each spelling word with examples, such as saying a *horse* is an animal people can ride and that on a *farm* we find lots of animals like horses.

Spelling

PRETEST *r*-Controlled *ar, or,* and *ore*

MODEL WRITING FOR SOUNDS Each spelling word has an /är/ or /ôr/ vowel sound. Before administering the spelling pretest, model how to segment *ar, or,* and *ore* words to spell them.

- What sounds do you hear in *harp?* (/h/ /är/ /p/)
- What is the letter for /h/? Write *h.* Continue with *ar* /är/ and *p* /p/.
- What letters stand for the /är/ sound? *(ar)*
- What sounds do you hear in *cord* and *store?* (/c/ /ôr/ /d/) (/s/ /t/ /ôr/)
- What is the letter for /k/ in *cord?* Write *c.* Continue with the *or* /ôr/ and *d* /d/.
- What is the letter for /s/ in *store?* Write *s.* Continue with the *t* /t/ and *ore* /ôr/.
- What letters stand for the /ôr/ sound? (*or* and *ore*)

PRETEST Dictate the spelling words. Segment the words for children if necessary. Have children check their pretests and correct misspelled words.

HOMEWORK Spelling Practice Book, p. 21

Group Time

K-9 Paul, Police Dog

"Did you hear about today's special assembly?" Joe asked Nate. "There's going to be a police dog." Nate was excited by this news. He loved dogs, and having a police dog visit school was much more fun than a math test.

Nate and Joe sat together for the assembly. They listened as the principal introduced Officer Reynolds and his four-footed partner, K-9 Paul, a big German Shepherd.

Decodable Reader 6
A Trip to the Farm
Written by Andrea Erwin
Illustrated by Steve Cowden

DAY 1

On-Level	Strategic Intervention	Advanced
Read Decodable Reader 6. • Use pp. 162q.	**Read** Decodable Reader 6. • Use the **Routine** on p. DI·14.	**Read** Advanced Selection 6. • Use the **Routine** on p. DI·15.

ELL Place English language learners in the groups that correspond to their reading abilities in English.

ⓘ Independent Activities

Fluency Reading Pair children to reread Leveled Readers or the ELL Reader from the previous week or other text at children's independent level.

Journal Writing Write about things people do that are courageous and explain why. Share writing.

Independent Reading See p. 162j for Reading/Library activities and suggestions.

Literacy Centers To practice *r*-controlled *ar, ore, ore* you may use Word Work, p. 162j.

Practice Book 2.1 *r*-Controlled *ar, or, ore,* p. 53 Sequence, p. 54

Break into small groups after Spelling and before Build Background.

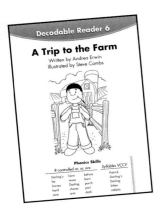

Apply Phonics

⟳ PRACTICE
r-Controlled *ar, or,* and *ore*

HIGH-FREQUENCY WORDS Review *before, gone, there,* and *work.*

READ DECODABLE READER 6

- Pages 42–43 Read aloud quietly with the group.
- Pages 44–45 Have the group read aloud without you.
- Pages 46–48 Select individuals to read aloud.

CHECK COMPREHENSION AND DECODING Ask children the following questions about *A Trip to the Farm:*

- Who are the characters in the story? (Rick, Jon, Mom)
- Where does the story take place? (Jon Darling's farm)
- What does Rick do on the farm? (He helps with the chores.)

Then have children locate *r*-controlled *ar, or,* and *ore* words in the story. Review *ar, or,* and *ore* spelling patterns. Sort words according to their spelling patterns.

ar: are, arm, barn, dark, Darling, Darling's, far, farm, hard, part

or: horses, porch

ore: before, chore, more, sore

HOMEWORK Take-Home Decodable Reader 6

REREAD FOR FLUENCY

Paired Reading

ROUTINE

1 **Reader 1 Begins** Children read the entire story, switching readers at the end of each page.

2 **Reader 2 Begins** Have partners reread; now the other partner begins.

3 **Reread** For optimal fluency, children should reread three or four times.

4 **Provide Feedback** Listen to children read and provide corrective feedback regarding their oral reading and their use of the blending strategy.

OBJECTIVES

- Apply knowledge of letter-sounds and word parts to decode unknown words when reading.
- Use context with letter-sounds and word parts to confirm the identification of unknown words.
- Practice fluency in paired reading.

Monitor Progress

Decoding

If... children have difficulty decoding a word,	then... prompt them to blend the word.
	• What is the new word?
	• Is the new word a word you know?
	• Does it make sense in the story?

Access Content

Beginning Lead children on a picture walk through *A Trip to the Farm,* identifying *farm* and *horses* in the pictures and print.

Intermediate Preview *A Trip to the Farm,* explaining *ar, or,* and *ore* words such as *barn, porch,* and *chore.*

Advanced Explain that *chore* is another word for *job.* Have children discuss what kinds of chores they do at home. Guide children using the sentence frame: *One chore I do at home is _____.*

Strategic Intervention

Have children choose one of the situations from the chart and illustrate what people should do in that situation.

Advanced

Have children search the library for information about people and animals that have been involved in rescue situations.

Activate Prior Knowledge
Invite children who share a home language to identify things in the pictures in that language and in English.

Build Background

LET'S TALK ABOUT Working Together

GENERATE DISCUSSION Read the title and ask questions to generate language. Encourage children to respond in complete sentences.

- What are these animals and people doing?
- Why do these animals and people need to work together?

BUILD ORAL VOCABULARY Lead the class in a discussion that focuses on concepts and today's Amazing Words, *courageous, hazard, rescue.*

Look at all the courageous people and animals in the pictures. They are helping one another escape hazards. Some of the pictures show people helping to rescue animals, and others show people helping other people. Which picture shows animals helping a person? This week we will read about how two dogs, Tara and Tiree, help their owner, Jim.

VOCABULARY

CONCEPT CHART Remind children of the question of the week.

- What can we do in a dangerous situation?

Display Graphic Organizer 25. Label the columns "Dangerous Situation" and "What We Should Do." Using the pictures on the student page as a starting point, help children identify dangerous situations and appropriate responses that fit each category. Encourage children to think of other dangerous situations, especially those that involve people. Display the chart for use throughout the week.

- Why would someone throw a life preserver to another person? (if they're having trouble swimming)
- What is a phone number you know to call in an emergency? (911)

Build Background

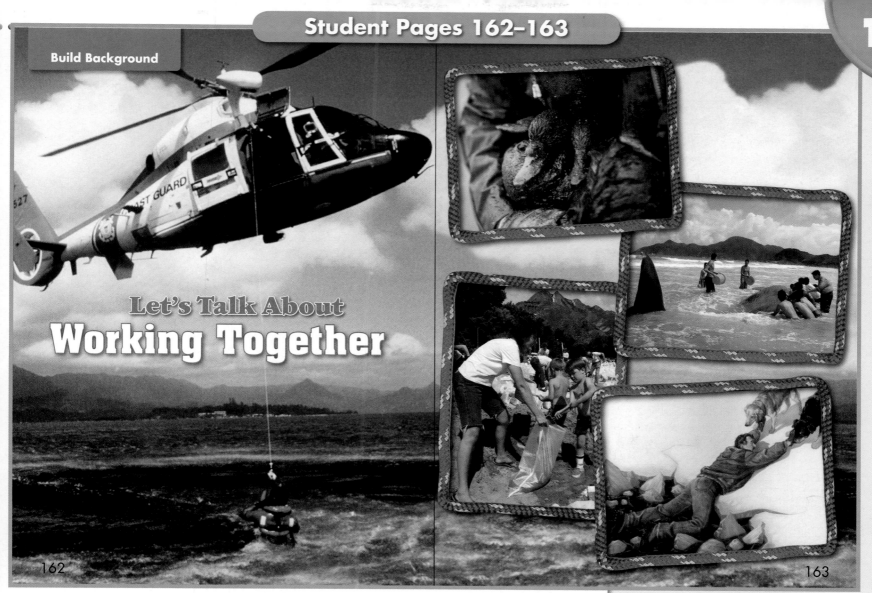

Let's Talk About
Working Together

162

163

Dangerous Situation	What We Should Do
An animal is stuck in a pipe.	Call animal workers.
A person needs help swimming.	Throw the person a life preserver.
A man falls into a lake.	Pull him out.
A person gets lost.	Use search dogs and people to find the lost person.
There is a fire.	Get out of the building; call 911.
There is a tornado.	Seek shelter.

▲ **Graphic Organizer 25**

Take It to the NET™
ONLINE

For a Web site that tells more about helpful animals, do an Internet search using the keywords *service animals*.

Access Content To prepare children for reading *Tara and Tiree, Fearless Friends*, send home the story summary in English and/or the home language. See the ELL Teaching Guide, pp. 40–42.

OBJECTIVE

◎ Identify sequence.

Skills Trace	
◎ **Sequence**	
Introduce/Teach	TE: 2.2 163a–b, 164e, 219a–b, 220e; 2.5 180r, 180–181
Practice	PB: 2.1 54–55, 67, 74–75, 107; 2.2 64–65, 77
Reteach/Review	TE: 2.2 204–205, DI·64, DI·66; 2.3 330–331; 2.5 216–217, DI·65
Assess/Test	TE: 2.2 21–24, 29–32; 2.5 85–88; Benchmark Test, Unit 2

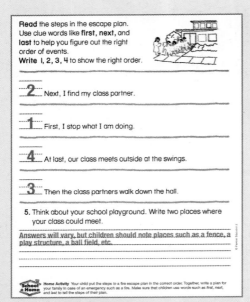

Read the steps in the escape plan. Use clue words like **first**, **next**, and **last** to help you figure out the right order of events.
Write 1, 2, 3, 4 to show the right order.

___2___ Next, I find my class partner.

___1___ First, I stop what I am doing.

___4___ At last, our class meets outside at the swings.

___3___ Then the class partners walk down the hall.

5. Think about your school playground. Write two places where your class could meet.

Answers will vary, but children should note places such as a fence, a play structure, a ball field, etc.

Home Activity Your child put the steps to a fire escape plan in the correct order. Together, write a plan for your family in case of an emergency such as a fire. Make sure that children use words such as first, next, and last to tell the steps of their plan.

▲ **Practice Book 2.1** p. 54, Sequence

Access Content For a Picture It! lesson on sequence, see the ELL Teaching Guide, pp. 36–37 .

Listening Comprehension

◎ TEACH/MODEL Sequence

DEFINE SEQUENCE

- Sequence is the order in which things happen.
- As you read, think about what happens first, next, and last.
- Good readers pay attention to the order of the events in a story.

READ ALOUD Read "The Rescue" and model how to identify the sequence.

MODEL As I read, I think about what happens first, next, and last. The first thing that happened was that the girl, father, and dog were playing with a soccer ball. The word *then* tells me what happened next. The ball went over the cliff, and the dog followed it. The word *next* tells me that that is what happened next.

PRACTICE

CLUES TO SEQUENCE Ask children to order the events in the selection. (The dog disappears over the cliff. Maya sees the dog on a ledge. Maya's dad steps down on the ledge. Maya and her dad help the dog back onto the lawn.)

IDENTIFY SEQUENCE Have children recall the sequence of events in *Henry and Mudge and the Starry Night.*

- What is the first thing that happens in this story? (Henry talks to Mudge about what they will see when they go camping.)
- What happens next? (Henry and his family hike while Mudge smells things.) Then what happens? (They set up camp.)
- What happens last in the story? (Henry and his family look at the stars while Mudge chews on a log.)

CONNECT TO READING Tell children that when they read any story, they should think about the order of the events so they can keep track of what happens.

The Rescue

Sometimes being courageous happens when you least expect it. At least, that's what happened to me.

Read ALOUD

I'm afraid of heights. I can't climb a tree. Going up a ladder makes my feet tingle and I start sweating. Nothing has cured me from my fear, either. I'm just a scaredy-cat when it comes to high places.

Last July my family was on vacation at the beach. The place where we stayed had these enormous cliffs that overlooked the ocean. There was a huge lawn in front of the cliff, and my dad and I were playing soccer on the grassy field. My dog, Sandy, chased the ball. Pretty soon Dad and I were playing keep-away from the dog.

Then, all of the sudden, the ball went sailing over the cliff. Dad and I watched in horror as Sandy chased it. One minute Sandy was there, and the next minute, she had disappeared!

We raced to the side of the cliff. I looked down, and there she was, standing on a ledge. She was shaking, and I knew why. Two more inches, and she might fall! I was so worried about her, I didn't even notice how high up we were.

Dad carefully stepped down on the ledge with Sandy. Then he picked her up and held her up to me. I reached down and pulled the dog back up on the grass to safety.

Dad then jumped back onto the lawn. That was when I realized what I had done. I looked back down and saw the soccer ball far below on the beach.
A sliver of fear ran down my back.

"Maya, are you still afraid of high places?" my dad asked me.

"Yes," I said.

Sandy was wagging her tail, as if thanking me the only way she knew how.

I felt really good. I was still a scaredy-cat when it came to high places, but at least I knew that courage wins over fear when it has to.

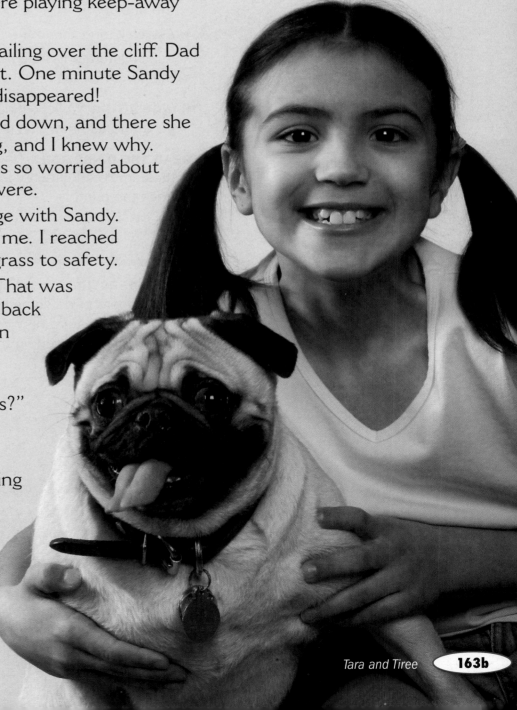

Tara and Tiree 163b

Shared Writing

WRITE Directions

GENERATE IDEAS Tell children that a new student needs directions to get from their classroom to the lunchroom. What would they tell the student?

WRITE DIRECTIONS Explain that the class will write directions that can help a new student find his or her way from the classroom to the lunchroom. Put the directions in order.

COMPREHENSION SKILL Have children think of the sequence—order of events—for their directions.

- Display Writing Transparency 6 and read the title.
- Ask children to read the first step.
- Ask children to list the remaining steps in the correct order.

HANDWRITING While writing, model the letter forms as shown on pp. TR18–21.

READ THE DIRECTIONS Have children read the completed directions aloud as you track the print.

> ### How to Get There
>
> 1. Go out our classroom door. .
>   **Possible answers:**
> 2. __Turn right__ .
> 3. __Walk to the end of the hall__ .
> 4. __Turn left__ .
> 5. __Go down the stairs__ .
>
> Unit 2 Tara and Tiree   Writing Model **6**

▲ **Writing Transparency 6**

INDEPENDENT WRITING

WRITE DIRECTIONS Have children write their own directions about how to get somewhere or do something. Encourage them to use words from the Word Wall and the Amazing Words board. Let children illustrate their writing. You may place children's work in their portfolios.

OBJECTIVE

- Write directions.

DAILY FIX-IT

1. that dog is smart
   T̲hat dog is smart.̲

2. it's exciteing to see it
   work hard.
   I̲t's exciting̲ to see it work hard.

This week's practice sentences appear on Daily Fix-It Transparency 6.

Strategic Intervention

Children who are not able to write independently may copy one or more of the sentences containing directions and add an illustration.

Advanced

Have children write directions explaining how to play their favorite game—for example, how to play baseball.

Support Writing Let beginning English speakers dictate their sentences that give directions to a more proficient English speaker.

Grammar

TEACH/MODEL NOUNS

IDENTIFY NOUNS Display Grammar Transparency 6. Read the definition aloud.

- A *park* is a place and *snow* is a thing. Names for people, places, animals, and things are called nouns.

Continue modeling with items 2–4.

PRACTICE

SUGGEST NOUNS Have children name other nouns. Write the nouns.

- Name a place we have read about.
- What kind of animals do you remember from our stories?
- Name some of the things from the stories you have read.

Nouns

A noun names a person, place, animal, or thing.

man	lake	dog	ice
↑ person	↑ place	↑ animal	↑ thing

Circle the nouns. Write them in the chart.

1. The park was covered in snow.
2. The ducks and geese had no food.
3. Two children lived across the street.
4. The girl and the boy brought bread to the birds.

Person	Place	Animal	Thing
children	park	ducks	snow
girl	street	geese	food
boy		birds	bread

Unit 2 Tara and Tiree   Grammar **6**

▲ **Grammar Transparency 6**

Wrap Up Your Day!

 r*-CONTROLLED *ar, or, ore Write *bark* and ask children what sound the *ar* in *bark* has. (/är/) Repeat with *born* and *sore*.

 SPELLING *r*-CONTROLLED *ar, or, ore* Have children name and write the letters for each sound in *bark*. Name a different beginning consonant and have children write the word, such as *m (mark)*. Continue with *born* and *sore*.

 SEQUENCE To help children recognize the importance of sequence, ask: Could the story "The Rescue" have occurred in a different order—for example, could Dad have stepped down on the ledge at the beginning of the story? Why not?

LET'S TALK ABOUT IT Recall that Maya helped her Dad save her dog from falling off of a ledge. What can we do for someone who is in a dangerous situation? (Call 911 or get an adult to help)

 HOMEWORK Send home this week's Family Times newsletter.

PREVIEW Day 2

Tell children that tomorrow the class will read about dogs and a person in a dangerous situation.

Day 2
AT A GLANCE

Materials

- *Sing with Me Big Book*
- Read Aloud Anthology
- Phonics Songs and Rhymes Chart 6
- Background Building Audio CD
- Graphic Organizer 25
- Decodable Reader 6
- Tested Word Cards
- Vocabulary Transparency 6
- Student Edition 164–181

Morning Warm~Up!

Today we will read about Jim and his smart dogs. We will read about how the dogs try hard to help Jim before it's too late. What are some ways for dogs to help people?

QUESTION OF THE DAY Encourage children to sing "To the Rescue!" from the *Sing with Me Big Book* as you gather. Write and read the message and discuss the question.

REVIEW *r*-CONTROLLED *ar, or, ore*

- Read the message.
- Have children raise their hands when they hear a word with *r*-controlled *ar, or,* or *ore*. (*smart, hard, before, for*)

Build Background Use the Day 2 instruction on ELL Poster 6 to preview high-frequency words.

ELL Poster 6

Share Literature

BUILD CONCEPTS

REVIEW NONFICTION Have children read the title. Identify the author. Review that books about real people and animals doing real things are nonfiction.

BUILD ORAL VOCABULARY Ask children what they know about dogs that have jobs. Point out that a dog that herds cows or sheep is a working dog. Dogs that help people who are in danger are also working dogs. Explain that a dog that searches for lost people might be put to work after an **avalanche** occurs, which is when snow or rock rushes down a mountainside. Suggest that as you read, children listen to find out other times dogs might be needed to help people.

Read Aloud Anthology
Snoop, the Search Dog

- What are some dangerous events that call for a search dog's help? (Possible answers: following an **avalanche,** earthquake, mudslide, tornado)

- How do search dogs find people? (They use their sense of smell.)

MONITOR LISTENING COMPREHENSION

- What happens after a search dog finds someone? (Possible response: The team of people working with the dog rescue the person by moving him or her to a safe place.)

- How do you think people who are lost or hurt feel when a search dog finds them? (Possible response: relieved, happy, grateful)

OBJECTIVES

- Discuss characteristics of nonfiction.
- Set purpose for listening.
- Build oral vocabulary.

Amazing Words to build oral vocabulary

	MONITOR PROGRESS
courageous **hazard** **rescue** **avalanche**	**If...** children lack oral vocabulary experiences about the concept Working Together, **then...** use the Oral Vocabulary Routine on pp. DI·1–DI·3 to develop the Amazing Words.

Build Concepts Search dogs are the main topic in "Snoop, the Search Dog." Point out to children that the dogs are part of a team. They work with a *handler*. The handler is in charge of the dog. This person teaches the dog what it needs to do, gives it commands, and then rewards it for hard work. Have children demonstrate their understanding by giving commands a handler might give a dog. *(Go find! Come, Good dog!)*

r-Controlled *ar, or, ore*

- Review *r*-Controlled *ar, or,* and *ore* words.
- Sort *r*-Controlled *ar, or,* and *ore* words.
- Preview words before reading them.
- Spell *r*-Controlled *ar, or,* and *ore* words.

Strategic Intervention

Use **Statgeic Intervention Decodable Reader 6** for more practice with *r*-Controlled *ar, or, ore.*

Support Phonics Invite children to act out the two safety tips in "Safe from Harm" as you replay the Phonics Songs and Rhymes Audio CD.

TEACH/MODEL

Fluent Word Reading

ROUTINE

1 **Connect** Write *barn.* You can read this word because you know how to read words with *r*-Controlled vowels. What sounds do the letters *ar* stand for in this word? (/är/) What's the word? *(barn)* Do the same with *sore.*

2 **Model** When you come to new word, look at the letters from left to right and think about the vowel sounds. Say the sounds in the word to yourself and then read the word. **Model** reading *drugstore, hardly, shortstop.* When you come to a new word, what are you going to do?

3 **Group Practice** Write *farmer, cartoon, charming, therefore, seashore, stormy.* Read these words. Look at the letters, think about the vowel sounds, say the sounds to yourself, and then read the word aloud together. Allow 2–3 seconds previewing time.

WORD READING

PHONICS SONGS AND RHYMES CHART 6 Frame each of the following words on Phonics Songs and Rhymes Chart 6. Call on individuals to read them. Guide children in previewing.

stormy	car	star
chore	more	far
alarm	harm	smartest

Sing "Safe from Harm" to the tune of "Home on the Range," or play the CD. Have children follow along on the chart as they sing. Then have individuals take turns locating *ar, or,* and *ore* words on the chart.

 **Phonics Songs and Rhymes Audio**

Safe from Harm

Staying safe is no chore.
We can always learn more.
It is smartest to plan ahead.
Is there cause for alarm?
We will come to no harm
When we know how to
   face things we dread.

Learn, learn safety rules.
Run inside when the
   stormy winds blow.
Buckle up in the car.
Be a safety all-star.
What other tips should
   we all know?

Phonics Songs and Rhymes Chart 6

SORT WORDS

INDIVIDUALS SORT *ar, or,* AND *ore* WORDS Write *ar, or,* and *ore* as headings. Have individuals write *ar, or,* and *ore* words from the Phonics Chart under the appropriate headings and circle the letters that stand for the /är/ and /ôr/ sounds. Have all children complete the activity on paper. Ask individuals to read the completed lists. Provide feedback as necessary.

ar	*or*	*ore*
darken	storm	before
start	fork	store
bark	scorch	adore
arch		

Spelling

PRACTICE *r*-Controlled *ar, or, ore*

WRITE DICTATION SENTENCES Have children write these sentences. Repeat words slowly, allowing children to hear each sound. Children may use the Word Wall to help with spelling high-frequency words. Word Wall

That horse was born on a farm.

We picked more corn by the porch.

Do this chore before you go out.

HOMEWORK Spelling Practice Book, p. 22

Spelling Words

r-Controlled *ar, or, ore*

1. part*
2. hard*
3. born
4. horse
5. before
6. more*
7. smart*
8. farm
9. porch
10. corn
11. chore
12. score

Challenge Words

13. cardinal
14. therefore
15. morning

* Words from the Selection

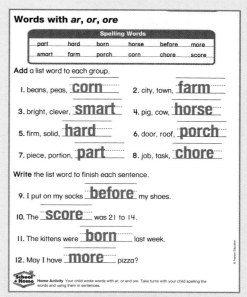

Words with *ar, or, ore*

Spelling Words					
part	hard	born	horse	before	more
smart	farm	porch	corn	chore	score

Add a list word to each group.

1. beans, peas, **corn**   2. city, town, **farm**

3. bright, clever, **smart**   4. pig, cow, **horse**

5. firm, solid, **hard**   6. door, roof, **porch**

7. piece, portion, **part**   8. job, task, **chore**

Write the list word to finish each sentence.

9. I put on my socks **before** my shoes.

10. The **score** was 21 to 14.

11. The kittens were **born** last week.

12. May I have **more** pizza?

Home Activity Your child wrote words with ar, or and ore. Take turns with your child spelling the words and using them in sentences.

▲ **Spelling Practice Book** p. 22

Comprehension

◎ SKILL Sequence

RECOGNIZE SEQUENCE Review that the sequence of a story is the order in which things happen. Have children tell the sequence of several previously read stories.

CONNECT TO READING

- As you read, ask yourself what happens first, next, and last.
- Notice clue words such as *first* and *then* and picture clues that tell about the order of events.

◎ STRATEGY Predict

INTRODUCE THE STRATEGY Tell children that it is sometimes fun to guess what is going to happen next in a story. Trying to guess what might happen, and then finding out what really happens, makes reading more fun.

Think Aloud **MODEL** When I read a story, I think about the words and pictures and I try to figure out what will happen next. When I'm right, I know that I understand the story. Sometimes I'm surprised by what happens.

CONNECT TO READING Encourage children to ask themselves these questions as they read *Tara and Tiree, Fearless Friends.*

- What am I reading, and what do I already know?
- What do the words and pictures tell me about what might happen next?

Read the story. **Look** at the pictures.
Write I, 2, 3, 4 to show the right order.

My dog, Sandy, scratched at the door. I went outside with her. Sandy ran across the yard. She barked and barked until I followed. Sandy led me to a cliff. At last, I saw why Sandy led me here. There was a hurt hiker! I ran home to get help.

Write a sentence that tells what might happen next.

Possible answer: People climbed down to get the hiker.

School + Home **Home Activity** Your child identified the sequence of events in a story about a child helping others. Work with your child to write about helping a person in trouble. Ask your child to describe the best procedure to follow when helping others.

▲ **Practice Book 2.1** p. 55, Sequence

Build Background

DISCUSS HEROES Display a picture of someone doing something heroic, such as helping someone out of a dangerous situation. Initiate discussion by asking children what they know about heroes.

- Have you ever heard or read about a hero?
- Who are some people who help when others are in danger?
- How do heroes provide a service for a community?

BACKGROUND BUILDING AUDIO Have children listen to the CD and share the new information they learned about animal heroes.

**Sing with Me/
Background Building Audio**

COMPLETE A T-CHART Draw a T-Chart or display Graphic Organizer 25. Label the left column "Hero" and the right column "Not a Hero." Ask children to suggest characteristics of heroes and non-heroes and complete the chart.

Hero	Not a Hero
helpful	afraid
brave	selfish
courageous	

▲ **Graphic Organizer 25**

CONNECT TO SELECTION Connect background information to *Tara and Tiree, Fearless Friends.*

Sometimes people get into dangerous situations and need help. We're going to read a story about two dogs that rescue someone from a dangerous situation. Dogs can be heroes too!

Activate Prior Knowledge Ask children to share personal experiences related to heroes. Remind them that they can talk about heroes or heroic things they've seen, heard about, or read about.

Words to Read

family
pull
listen
once
heard
break

Read the Words

Tag is our family pet. He is a good dog. He will pull on my pants leg until I take him for a walk. He will listen and do what I say. Once he heard me call and came running so fast that I thought he would break a leg.

Genre: Narrative Nonfiction
Narrative nonfiction tells the story of a true event. Next you will read a true story about two dogs that saved their owner.

_____ r-Controlled ar, or, ore   high-frequency/tested vocabulary

High-Frequency Words

OBJECTIVE

● Recognize high-frequency words.

Nondecodable Words

ROUTINE

1 **Say and Spell** Point to the first word. This word is family, *f-a-m-i-l-y*, family. What is this word? What are the letters in this word?

2 **Identify Familiar Letter-Sounds** Point to the first letter in *family*. What is this letter? What is the sound for this letter? (f/f/)

3 **Demonstrate Meaning** Tell me a sentence using this word. Repeat the routine with the other Words to Read. Have children identify these familiar letter-sounds and word parts: *once* (c/s/), *pull* (p/p/, l/l/), *listen* (blend the syllables: *lis, ten*), *heard* (h/h/, d/d/), *break* (br/br/, k/k/).

Have children read aloud the sentences on p. 165 and point to the Words to Read. Add the words to the Word Wall. **Word Wall**

Use Vocabulary Transparency 6 to review this week's words.

• Point to a word. Say and spell it.

• Have children say and spell the word.

• Ask children to identify familiar letter-sounds.

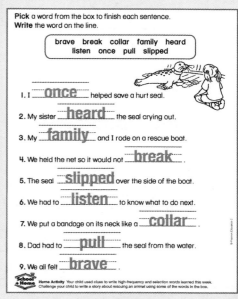

Pick a word from the box to finish each sentence.
Write the word on the line.

| brave break collar family heard |
| listen once pull slipped |

1. I __once__ helped save a hurt seal.
2. My sister __heard__ the seal crying out.
3. My __family__ and I rode on a rescue boat.
4. We held the net so it would not __break__.
5. The seal __slipped__ over the side of the boat.
6. We had to __listen__ to know what to do next.
7. We put a bandage on its neck like a __collar__.
8. Dad had to __pull__ the seal from the water.
9. We all felt __brave__.

 Home Activity Your child used clues to write high-frequency and selection words learned this week. Challenge your child to write a story about rescuing an animal using some of the words in the box.

▲ **Practice Book 2.1** p. 56, High-Frequency Words and Selection Words

Monitor Progress | **Check High-Frequency Words**

Point to the following words on the Word Wall and have individuals read them.

| family | break | once | pull | listen | heard |
| afraid | loved | water | warm | very | learn |

If… children cannot read these words,

then… have them practice in pairs with word cards before reading the selection. Monitor their fluency with these words during reading, and provide additional practice opportunities before the Day 5 Assessment.

SUCCESS PREDICTOR

| **Day 1** Check Word Reading | ▶**Day 2 Check High-Frequency Words** | **Day 3** Check Retelling | **Day 4** Check Fluency | **Day 5** Assess Progress |

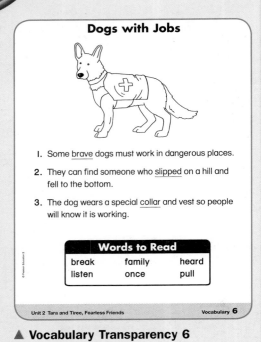

Dogs with Jobs

1. Some <u>brave</u> dogs must work in dangerous places.

2. They can find someone who <u>slipped</u> on a hill and fell to the bottom.

3. The dog wears a special <u>collar</u> and vest so people will know it is working.

Words to Read		
break	family	heard
listen	once	pull

Unit 2 Tara and Tiree, Fearless Friends   Vocabulary **6**

▲ **Vocabulary Transparency 6**

Vocabulary

SELECTION WORDS

Use Vocabulary Transparency 6 to introduce the selection words.

- Read each sentence as you track the print.
- Frame each underlined word. Explain the word's meaning.

  collar a band that a dog wears around its neck

  slipped slid without meaning to

  brave showing no fear of dangerous things

- Ask children to identify familiar letter-sounds and word parts: *slipped* (point out the base word plus the ending: *slip, ed), collar* (blend the syllables: *col, lar), brave* (b/b/, r/r/, a/ā/, v/v/).
- Have children read each sentence aloud with you.
- To encourage discussion using the selection words, ask children what they might see if a brave dog wearing a collar was trying to help someone who had slipped.

Group Time

On-Level	Strategic Intervention	Advanced
Read *Tara and Tiree, Fearless Friends.* • Use pp. 166–181.	**Read** SI Decodable Reader 6. • Read or listen to *Tara and Tiree, Fearless Friends.* • Use the **Routine** on p. DI·16.	**Read** *Tara and Tiree, Fearless Friends.* • Use the **Routine** on p. DI·17.

ELL Place English language learners in the groups that correspond to their reading abilities in English.

(i) Independent Activities

Independent Reading See p. 162j for Reading/Library activities and suggestions.

Journal Writing Write about an animal you know or heard of who helped someone. Share writing.

Literacy Centers To provide experiences with *Tara and Tiree, Fearless Friends,* you may use the Listening Center on p. 162j.

Practice Book 2.1 Sequence, p. 55; High-Frequency Words and Selection Words, p. 56; Character and Setting, p. 57

ELL

Access Content Use the vocabulary strategies and word cards in the ELL Teaching Guide, pp. 38–39.

Break into small groups after Vocabulary and before Writing.

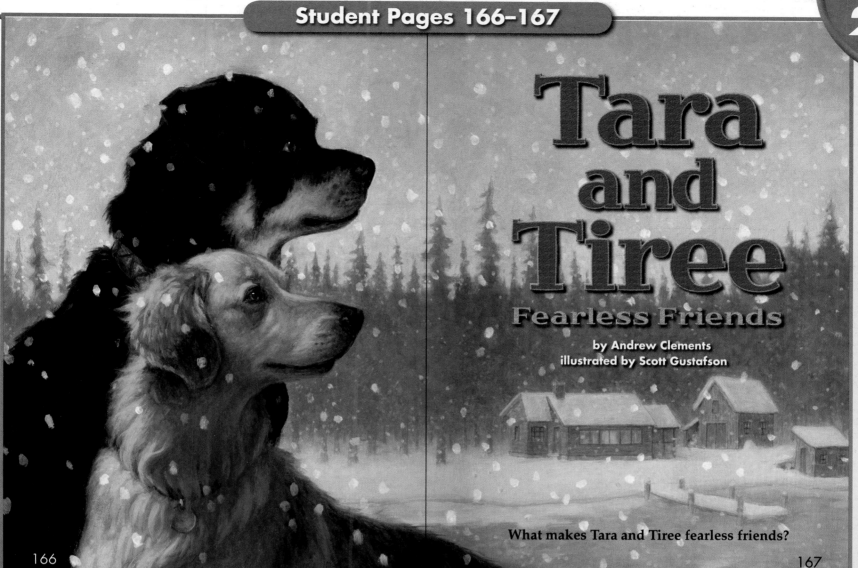

Tara and Tiree
Fearless Friends
by Andrew Clements
illustrated by Scott Gustafson

What makes Tara and Tiree fearless friends?

166

167

Read
Prereading Strategies

AudioText

PREVIEW AND PREDICT Have children read the title of the story. Read aloud the names of the author and the illustrator. Ask children who they think is shown in the picture. Do a picture walk of pp. 166–171 and ask what children think the story will be about.

DISCUSS NARRATIVE NONFICTION Read the definition of narrative nonfiction on p. 165 of the Student Edition. Remind children that selections that tell about real events are called nonfiction. Explain that narrative nonfiction tells us things that really happened, but reading it feels like reading a story.

SET PURPOSE Read the question on p. 167. Ask what children would like to find out about Tara and Tiree as they read the story.

ELL

Access Content Before reading, review the story summary in English and/or the home language. See the ELL Teaching Guide, pp. 40–42.

When Jim was a boy in Canada, his family had dogs. Jim loved those dogs. They were like part of his family.

When Jim grew up, he still loved dogs. He learned how to train them. He helped dogs learn to be good.

He always said, "There is no such thing as a bad dog." Training dogs became Jim's job.

168

169

▲ **Pages 168–169**
Have children look at the picture. Ask them to read to find out how Jim felt about his dogs when he was a boy.

EXTEND SKILLS

Details and Facts

For instruction in details and facts, discuss the following:

• The author gives small bits of information about Jim's relationship with dogs.

• What important details did you read about?

Assess Have children look for other important details on the next page.

Guiding Comprehension

Details • Literal

• **How did Jim feel about dogs when he was a child?**
He loved them.

Sequence • Literal

• **What happened next when Jim grew up?**
Jim still loved dogs. He learned how to train them.

Cause and Effect • Inferential

• **What effect did Jim's feelings for dogs have on his choice of a job?**
Because Jim loved dogs and believed they could all learn to be good, he decided to become a dog trainer.

_____ r-Controlled *ar, or, ore*   high-frequency/tested vocabulary

Jim had two dogs named <u>Tara</u> and Tiree.
<u>Tara</u> was mostly black. Tiree was mostly gold.
Jim loved them both, and they loved him, too.
Jim and his dogs liked the <u>winter</u> time.

170

They had good coats to keep warm. They
played in the snow. They went <u>for</u> long walks.
They liked going out, but they liked going back
in, too. It was good to sit by the fire and listen to
the wind.

171

Guiding Comprehension

Draw Conclusions • Inferential

• **What kind of life do Tara and Tiree have with Jim?**
They have a good life. They are happy, and Jim takes care of them.

Cause and Effect • Literal

• **How do Tara and Tiree stay warm when they're outside?**
They have good coats.

Analyze • Critical

• *Question the Author* **Does the author give you enough information about
what Tara and Tiree are like? What other information might you want the
author to give you?**
Possible response: Children may say they want to know how Jim trained Tara
and Tiree.

▲ **Pages 170–171**
Ask children to imagine what kind
of life the dogs have with Jim. Have
them read to find out.

Monitor Progress	
High-Frequency Words	
If... children have a problem reading a new high-frequency word,	**then...** use the High-Frequency Routine on p. 165a to reteach the problematic word.

Jim's house was by a lake. Every winter there was ice on it. One day Jim went for a walk out on the lake. Tara and Tiree went too. The dogs loved to run across the ice.

It was very cold. Jim was ready to go back home. Then all at once the ice broke. Jim fell into the cold, cold water.

Jim called for help. No one was near. No one could hear him. But Tara and Tiree heard Jim and came running. Jim wanted the dogs to stay away. He was afraid for them.

172

173

▲ **Pages 172–173**
Have children look at the pictures. Ask them to read to find out what happens to Jim and how Tara and Tiree react.

TIME FOR Science

Natural Hazards

If the temperature stays below freezing for many days, a layer of ice can form on lakes. This can be very beautiful, but it can also be very dangerous. You cannot tell by looking at the ice how thick and strong it is. You should never walk on a frozen surface without an adult.

Strategies in Context

⊙ PREDICT

- **What do you think Tara and Tiree will do next?**
  They will probably try to help Jim get out of the water.

Monitor Progress	**Predict**	
If... children have difficulty answering the question,		**then...** model how to make a prediction.

 Think Aloud

MODEL I know that Jim loves his dogs, and they love him. I can see that Jim is in trouble. He has fallen through the ice. Tara and Tiree come running up to him. In the picture, they look worried. The words and the pictures help me guess that Tara and Tiree will try to help Jim get out of the cold water.

ASSESS Have children read p. 174 and predict what will happen next. (Possible response: Tara will help pull Jim out of the water.)

_____ r-Controlled ar, or, ore   high-frequency/tested vocabulary

But Tiree loved Jim. She wanted to help. When she came near the hole, the ice broke again. Tiree fell into the water with Jim.

The water was so cold. Jim knew he did not have much time. Jim tried to help Tiree get out. But the ice broke <u>more</u> and <u>more</u>.

174

Jim hoped <u>Tara</u> would run away. He did not want her to fall in the water too. But <u>Tara</u> did not run away. She wanted to help.

First <u>Tara</u> got down low. Then she came closer, little by little. The ice did not <u>break</u>.

175

Skills in Context

↻ SEQUENCE

- **What did Tara do first? What did Tara do next?**
  First, Tara got down low. Next, she moved toward Jim.

Monitor Progress	Sequence
If... children have difficulty answering the question,	**then...** model how to recognize sequence.

Think Aloud

MODEL When I think about the order of events, I look for clue words. I see the word *first* in the sentence "First Tara got down low." I see the clue word *then* in the next sentence, which says "Then she came closer, little by little."

ASSESS Have children look at the previous page and tell the order of events. (Jim walks out on the frozen lake, the ice breaks, Jim falls in the water, Jim calls for help, the dogs run to him.) Remind children that there will not always be clue words.

▲ **Pages 174–175**
Have children read to find out what Tara and Tiree do next.

Monitor Progress	
Decoding	
If... children come to a word they don't know,	**then...** remind them to: 1. Blend the word. 2. Decide if the word makes sense. 3. Look in a dictionary for more help.

Then Tiree did something very smart. She walked on Jim's back—up and out of the water! Tiree was cold, but she was safe! Did she run off the ice? No. She loved Jim too much to run away.

Jim put out his hand. Tara got very close. Then Jim got hold of Tara's collar. Jim held on. Tara pulled back, but Jim was too big. He was still in the cold water.

176

177

▲ **Pages 176–177**
Have children read to find out what happens after Tiree falls in the water.

Strategy Self-Check

Have children ask themselves these questions to check their reading.

Decoding Words
- Do I look at the beginning, middle, and ending sounds of the word to blend it?
- Do I reread to be sure the new word makes sense in the story?

Predict
- Do I think about what I've read and what I know as I read?
- Do I look at the words and pictures for clues to decide what might happen next?

Guiding Comprehension

Summarize • Inferential
- **What has happened in the story so far?**
  Jim breaks through ice and falls into cold water. His dogs run to help. When Tiree gets too close to the hole, she falls in the water too.

Draw Conclusions • Inferential
- **Why do you think Tara backs up when Jim grabs her collar?**
  She is trying to pull him out of the water.

Make Inferences • Critical
- **One reason Tiree crawls up Jim's back is to get out of the cold water. What do you think is another reason?**
  Children will probably suggest that she knows she needs to be on the ice in order to help Jim.

_____ r-Controlled ar, or, ore   high-frequency/tested vocabulary

Tiree got down on her belly like Tara. She got close to Jim. Jim held out his other hand. And he grabbed on to Tiree's collar!

The two dogs pulled back hard. They slipped, but they didn't stop. Slowly they pulled Jim up onto the ice. He was safe.

178   179

Skills in Context

REVIEW CHARACTER AND SETTING

- **What do you know about Tara and Tiree?**
Tara and Tiree love Jim. They want to help him when he is in trouble, and they are very brave.

Monitor Progress	**Character and Setting**
If... children have difficulty answering the question,	**then...** model how to recognize characters and setting.

 Think Aloud

MODEL To find out what Tara and Tiree are like, what they feel, and why they do what they do, I look at the words and pictures. The words tell me that Tara and Tiree love Jim and want to help him. The pictures show how dangerous it is to walk on the broken ice and show me that the dogs must be very brave.

ASSESS Have children look at a previous story and tell something about the characters and the setting. Remind children that characters are people or animals who take part in the story.

▲ **Pages 178–179**
Have children look at the picture and read to find out more about Tara and Tiree.

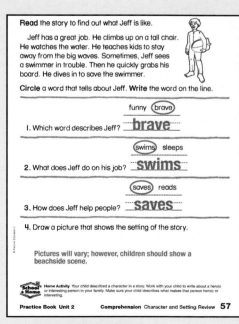

Read the story to find out what Jeff is like.

Jeff has a great job. He climbs up on a tall chair. He watches the water. He teaches kids to stay away from the big waves. Sometimes, Jeff sees a swimmer in trouble. Then he quickly grabs his board. He dives in to save the swimmer.

Circle a word that tells about Jeff. **Write** the word on the line.

            funny (brave)
1. Which word describes Jeff? **brave**

            (swims) sleeps
2. What does Jeff do on his job? **swims**

            (saves) reads
3. How does Jeff help people? **saves**

4. Draw a picture that shows the setting of the story.

    Pictures will vary; however, children should show a beachside scene.

School Home Home Activity Your child described a character in a story. Work with your child to write about a heroic or interesting person in your family. Make sure your child describes what makes that person heroic or interesting.

Practice Book Unit 2   **Comprehension** Character and Setting Review   **57**

▲ **Practice Book 2.1** p. 57, Character and Setting

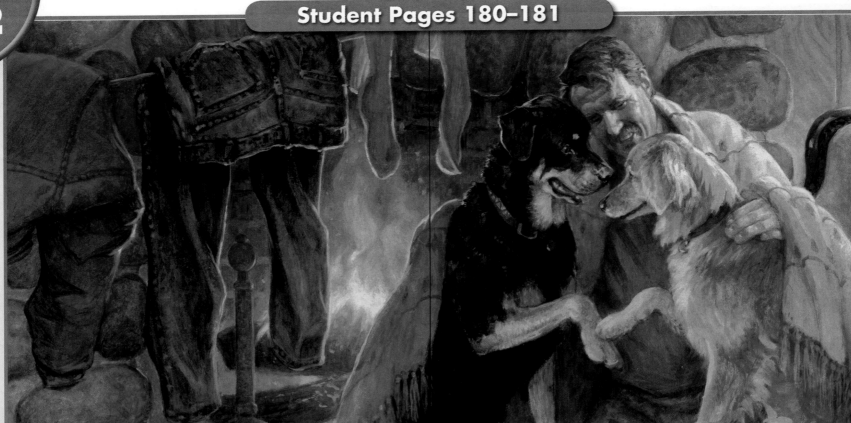

Tara and Tiree had saved his life! Soon they were all back in the house. They sat by the fire until they were warm again.

Jim always said, "There is no such thing as a bad dog."

180

Now Jim says something else, too: "There is such a thing as a brave and wonderful dog!"

Jim is sure of this, because he has two of them—Tara and Tiree.

181

▲ **Pages 180–181**
Ask children to read to find out how the story ends.

Service Dogs

Time for SOCIAL STUDIES

Some dogs are trained to help people in need. Rescue dogs learn to find missing people. Other dogs are trained to help people with disabilities. These dogs can turn on lights, pick up dropped objects, open doors, and guide people who cannot see.

Guiding Comprehension

Compare and Contrast • Inferential

- **What do Tara and Tiree have in common?**
They love Jim, they are smart, and they are brave.

Analyze • Critical

- **How do you think Jim feels at the end of the story?**
Jim probably feels proud, relieved, and tired.

Categorize • Critical

- *Text to Text* **What other stories do you know about animals helping people?**
Children will recall various stories, but they should all involve animals helping people.

Fluency

REREAD FOR FLUENCY

Paired Reading

ROUTINE

1. **Reader 1 Begins** Children read the entire book, switching readers at the end of each page.

2. **Reader 2 Begins** Have partners reread; now the other partner begins.

3. **Reread** For optimal fluency, children should reread three or four times.

4. **Provide Feedback** Listen to children read and provide corrective feedback regarding their oral reading and their use of the blending strategy.

Interactive Writing

WRITE Notes

BRAINSTORM Use the story *Tara and Tiree, Fearless Friends* to encourage a discussion about what to do in times of danger. Picture walk through the book and ask children to identify how the dogs react when Jim falls through the ice.

SHARE THE PEN Have children participate in writing notes about how the dogs save Jim. Remind children that notes are short sentences to remind them of what happened in the story. To begin, have a child say what happens first in the story. Have the class repeat it. Write the sentence, reminding individuals to use the rules they've learned about sentences. Ask questions such as:

- What does the sentence start with? (capital letter)
- What kind of sentence is it? (statement)
- What does the sentence end with? (period)

Continue to have individuals make contributions. Frequently reread what has been written while tracking the print.

READ THE NOTES Read the completed notes aloud, having children echo you.

Tara and Tiree Notes

Jim falls into the lake.

Tiree tries to help Jim.

She falls into the lake too.

Tara tries to pull Jim out.

Tiree climbs up Jim's back and onto the ice.

Tara and Tiree get close to Jim.

Jim grabs the dogs' collars.

The dogs pull him out of the lake.

INDEPENDENT WRITING

WRITE NOTES Have children write their own notes from a previously read story. Let children illustrate their writing.

Grammar

DEVELOP THE CONCEPT Nouns

IDENTIFY NOUNS Write *dog* and *ice* on the board. Point to each word as you read it. Ask children to identify whether the noun is a person, place, thing, or animal. *(animal, thing)* Continue with *man* and *outside.*

Names for people, places, animals, and things are called nouns. Can nouns be found in more than one place in a sentence? If so, where? (Yes, they can be in the subject and the predicate.)

PRACTICE

USE NOUNS IN SENTENCES Gather several pictures of people, animals, places, and things. Display a picture. Model using the noun in a sentence.

MODEL This is a man. **Write** *man.* I'll think of a sentence that uses the noun *man.* The man is walking. Write the sentence.

Have children suggest sentences using nouns as you show other pictures. Write the sentences children provide.

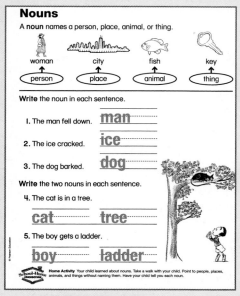

Nouns

A **noun** names a person, place, animal, or thing.

woman	city	fish	key
person	place	animal	thing

Write the noun in each sentence.

1. The man fell down. **man**
2. The ice cracked. **ice**
3. The dog barked. **dog**

Write the two nouns in each sentence.

4. The cat is in a tree.
   cat tree
5. The boy gets a ladder.
   boy ladder

Home Activity Your child learned about nouns. Take a walk with your child. Point to people, places, animals, and things without naming them. Have your child tell you each noun.

▲ **Grammar and Writing Practice Book** p. 21

PREVIEW Day 3

Tell children that tomorrow they will hear about another dog with an important job.

Wrap Up Your Day!

 HIGH-FREQUENCY WORDS Write the following sentences. *Once, I saw a family pull a rope. Then I heard sticks and bushes break. I stayed to watch and to listen for a while. Finally, I saw a huge gray animal at the other end of the rope.* Ask children to read the sentences and identify the high-frequency words *family, once, pull, listen, heard, break.*

 PREDICT Point to the last sentence and ask children to predict what the animal at the end of the rope was (elephant).

LET'S TALK ABOUT IT Recall the selection *Tara and Tiree, Fearless Friends.* Ask: Did Jim solve his dangerous problem by himself? (No, his dogs saved him.) Encourage children to add to the graphic organizer started in the Day 1 Build Background lesson.

Day 3
AT A GLANCE

Share Literature
Snoop, the Search Dog

Phonics and Spelling
REVIEW Consonant Diagraphs

Spelling: Words with *r*-Controlled *ar, or, ore*

High-Frequency Words
family   once   pull   **Word Wall**

listen   heard   break

Vocabulary
Position and Direction Words

Fluency
Read with Accuracy/Appropriate Rate

Independent Writing
Respond to Literature

Grammar
Nouns

Materials

- *Sing with Me Big Book*
- *Read Aloud Anthology*
- *Student Edition 182–183*

Morning Warm~Up!

Today we will read about Snoop. Snoop is a brave dog who searches for lost people. When would people need to use a dog like Snoop?

QUESTION OF THE DAY Encourage children to sing "To the Rescue!" from the *Sing with Me Big Book* as you gather. Write and read the message and discuss the question.

REVIEW SYNONYMS

- Point to *searches* in the message. Ask children to name a synonym, or a word that means the same thing. *(looks)*
- Reread the second sentence. Ask children to name synonyms for *brave (courageous)* and *lost (missing)*.

Build Background Use the Day 3 instruction on ELL Poster 6 to support children's use of English to communicate about lesson concepts.

ELL Poster 6

Share Literature

LISTEN AND RESPOND

REVIEW ILLUSTRATIONS Have children look at the photographs in "Snoop, the Search Dog." Review that photos are often used with nonfiction. They show real people and animals in action.

BUILD ORAL VOCABULARY Review that yesterday the class read the selection to find out when search dogs are used, such as during an emergency like an avalanche. They found out how the dogs find people. Rescuers rely on the search dogs being calm and not **skittish**. Ask that children listen today to find out what qualities are needed in a good search dog.

Read Aloud Anthology
Snoop, the Search Dog

MONITOR LISTENING COMPREHENSION

- When dogs use their sense of smell to find things, what are they relying on? (**instincts**)

- What are some traits of a good search dog? (not **skittish**, courageous, eager to please people)

- Why does a search dog need to be courageous? (Possible response: Search dogs have to work among many hazards such as earthquakes, mudslides, and tornadoes.)

- How does a search dog probably feel after it rescues someone? How do you know? (The dog feels excited or happy. I know because even if the dog doesn't find or rescue someone during a search, a team member will hide so that the dog can find him or her.)

OBJECTIVES

- Identify illustrations as a feature of nonfiction.
- Set purpose for listening.
- Build oral vocabulary.

Amazing Words to build oral vocabulary

Amazing Words	**MONITOR PROGRESS**
courageous hazard rescue avalanche **instinct** **skittish**	**If...** children lack oral vocabulary experiences about the concept Working Together, **then...** use the Oral Vocabulary Routine on pp. DI·1–DI·3 to develop the Amazing Words.

Listen and Respond Help children describe and demonstrate the actions conveyed by the word *scent* in "Snoop, the Search Dog." Contrast its meaning with its homophone, *sent*. As two children stand beside the words written on the board, one might sniff the air while the other might pretend to mail a letter.

3

OBJECTIVES

- Review consonant digraphs *ch, tch, sh, th, wh.*
- Apply decoding strategies: blend, preview words.
- Recognize high-frequency words.
- Spell words with *ar, or, ore.*

Say the word for each picture.
Write ch, tch, sh, th, or wh to finish each word.

1.	2.	3.	4.
__sh__ eep	__wh__ eel	__ch__ ips	ba __th__
5.	6.	7.	8.
pea __ch__	__sh__ orts	__th__ ink	fe __tch__

Find the word that has the same beginning sound as the picture.
Mark the space to show your answer.

9. ⬭ cheek 10. ⬛ chain ✓
⬛ shine   ⬭ green
⬭ sip   ⬭ plane

Home Activity Your child reviewed words that begin or end with ch, tch, sh, th, or wh, as in chest, itch, ship, thorn, and wheel. Ask your child to read aloud the above words that begin or end with these letters. Together, write a story using some of these words.

▲ **Practice Book 2.1** p. 58, Consonant Digraphs

Review Phonics

REVIEW CONSONANT DIGRAPHS

READ WORDS WITH DIGRAPHS Write *batch* and *sash.* Look at these words. You can read these words because you know how to read words with digraphs. What sounds do *tch* and *sh* stand for? **(They stand for the /tch/ and /sh/ sounds.)** What are the words?

INDIVIDUALS MAKE WORDS WITH DIGRAPHS Write *batch* and have the class blend it. Have children spell *batch* with letter tiles. Repeat with *that.* Monitor work and provide feedback.

- Change the *tch* in *batch* to *th.* What is the new word?

- Change the *th* in *bath* to *sh.* What is the new word?

- Change the *b* in *bash* to *w.* What is the new word?

- Change the first *t* in *that* to *w.* What is the new word?

| w | h | a | t |

- Change the *a* in *what* to *e,* and the *t* to *n.* What is the new word?

| w | h | e | n |

- Change the *n* in *when* to *r,* and add *e.* What is the new word?

| w | h | e | r | e |

High-Frequency Words

PRACTICE

RIDDLE CLUES Provide clues such as the following. Have children find the word on the Word Wall that fits each clue. **Word Wall**

- The word begins with *f* and tells about a group that may have a mom, dad, brother, and sister. What is it? **(family)**
- The word is the opposite of *push*. What is it? **(pull)**
- The word begins with *b*, and you don't want it to happen to a vase, a plate, or a toy. What is it? **(break)**
- The word comes before "upon a time." What is it? **(once)**
- The word begins with *l*, and you do it with your ears. What is it? **(listen)**
- The word begins with *h*, and you do it with your ears. What is it? **(hear)**

Spelling

PRACTICE *r*-Controlled *ar, or, ore*

RHYMING WORDS Have children practice by writing the spelling words that

- rhyme with *harm*, with *torch*, with *lard*, with *course* (*farm, porch, hard, horse*)
- rhyme with *chart*, with *horn* (*part, smart; born, corn*)
- rhyme with *door* (*before, more, chore, score, therefore*)

HOMEWORK Spelling Practice Book, p. 23

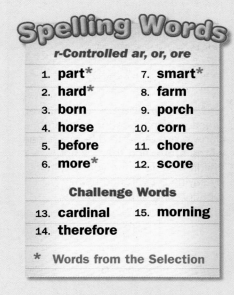

▲ **Practice Book 2.1** p. 59, High-Frequency Words

Spelling Words

r-Controlled ar, or, ore

1. **part***	7. **smart***
2. **hard***	8. **farm**
3. **born**	9. **porch**
4. **horse**	10. **corn**
5. **before**	11. **chore**
6. **more***	12. **score**

Challenge Words

13. **cardinal**	15. **morning**
14. **therefore**	

* **Words from the Selection**

▲ **Spelling Practice Book** p. 23

Strategic Intervention

Have children use old magazines to find pictures that show the location and direction words listed on the board. Ask them to label each picture with the appropriate direction or location word.

Advanced

Have children write a short story about a rescue. Tell them to use at least three direction and location words in their stories.

Extend Language Help children practice using location and direction words. Move to different areas of the room, and then call on children to describe your position by saying a sentence using location and direction words.

Vocabulary

POSITION AND DIRECTION WORDS

DISCUSS POSITION AND DIRECTION WORDS Have children recall that Jim and his dogs, Tara and Tiree, live by a lake. Explain that some words like the word *by* tell where something is located or which direction something is moving. Write the following sentence and have children fill in the blank with different position and direction words.

Jim walks ___ the ice.

EXPAND MEANING Write the following words on the board: *out, in, by, across, into, near, away, down (low), close(r), back, on, up, off, onto, far, farther.* Show children pictures from the book. Provide an example sentence that uses position and direction words and describes the action in one of the pictures. Have children volunteer to say a sentence using position and direction words for other pictures in the book. There can be several sentences for each picture.

Group Time

 DAY 3

On-Level

Read *Tara and Tiree, Fearless Friends.*

- Use pp. 166–183.

Strategic Intervention

Read or listen to *Tara and Tiree, Fearless Friends.*

- Use the **Routine** on p. DI·18.

Advanced

Read *Tara and Tiree, Fearless Friends.*

- Use the **Routine** on p. DI·19.

ELL Place English language learners in the groups that correspond to their reading abilities in English.

ⓘ Independent Activities

Independent Reading See p. 162j for Reading/Library activities and suggestions.

Journal Writing Write a journal entry about a dangerous situation you've heard about or read about. Use position and direction words in your entry. Share writing.

Literacy Centers To provide experiences with *Tara and Tiree, Fearless Friends,* you may use the Writing Center on p. 162k.

Practice Book 2.1 Consonant Digraphs, p. 58 High-Frequency Words, p. 59

Break into small groups after Vocabulary and before Writing.

Fluency

READ WITH ACCURACY / APPROPRIATE PACE

MODEL READING WITH ACCURACY AND APPROPRIATE PACE Use *Tara and Tiree, Fearless Friends.*

- Point to the first page of text on p. 168. When I see a word I don't know, I sound it out by syllables. When I come to the word *Canada*, I break it down into syllables, *Can-a-da.*

- Ask children to follow along as you read the page with accuracy.

- Have children read the page after you. Encourage them to read with both accuracy and appropriate pacing. Continue in the same way with pp. 170–171.

REREAD FOR FLUENCY

Choral Reading

ROUTINE

1 **Select a Passage** For *Tara and Tiree, Fearless Friends,* use pp. 168–171.

2 **Divide into Groups** Assign each group a part to read. For this story, have each group read a paragraph.

3 **Model** Have children track the print as you read.

4 **Read Together** Have children read along with you.

5 **Independent Readings** Have the groups read aloud without you. Monitor progress and provide feedback. For optimal fluency, children should reread three to four times.

Monitor Progress	Fluency
If... children have difficulty reading with accuracy,	**then...** prompt: Are there words you do not understand? If so, sound them out by syllables.
If... the class cannot read fluently without you,	**then...** continue to have them read along with you.

OBJECTIVE

- Read aloud fluently with accuracy and appropriate pace.

Options for Choral Reading

Use *Tara and Tiree, Fearless Friends* or one of the following Leveled Readers.

On-Level

Emergency

Strategic Intervention

Dogs to the Rescue

Advanced

Amazing Animals

E L L

Use *Sandy to the Rescue!* or *Tara and Tiree, Fearless Friends.* Model reading sections of the text with accuracy and appropriate pace. Point out words that may be unfamiliar, such as *Tiree.* Sound them out and practice saying them correctly so English language learners will know how to pronounce these new words.

Fluency Coach CD To develop fluent readers, use Fluency Coach.

Think and Share

TALK ABOUT IT Model a response. I think the most exciting part of the story is when the two dogs help Jim out of the water. It's exciting because they have to work hard to save him from danger.

1. **RETELL** Have children use the pictures across the bottom to retell the story. See Monitor Progress below.

2. **SEQUENCE** First, Tara got down low. Then she moved forward slowly until Jim could reach her collar.

3. **PREDICT** Possible response: I predicted that Jim would be saved by his dogs, so I was right. I also predicted that they would all go inside together to get warm.

LOOK BACK AND WRITE See Independent Writing, TE p. 183a. [Rubric 4 3 2 1]

Selection Test To assess with *Tara and Tiree, Fearless Friends,* use Selection Tests, pp. 21–24.

Monitor Progress | Check Retelling [Rubric 4 3 2 1]

If... children have difficulty retelling the story,

then... use the Scoring Rubric for Retelling below to help them move toward fluent retelling.

SUCCESS PREDICTOR

Day 1 Check Word Reading · **Day 2** Check High-Frequency Words · ▶**Day 3 Check Retelling** · **Day 4** Check Fluency · **Day 5** Assess Progress

---

Retelling Plan

☑ **This week assess Strategic Intervention students.**

☐ Week 2 assess Advanced students.

☐ Week 3 assess Strategic Intervention students.

☐ Week 4 assess On-Level students.

☐ Week 5 assess any students you have not yet checked during this unit.

Scoring Rubric | Narrative Retelling

[Rubric 4 3 2 1]	4	3	2	1
Connections	Makes connections and generalizes beyond the text	Makes connections to other events, stories, or experiences	Makes a limited connection to another event, story, or experience	Makes no connection to another event, story, or experience
Author's Purpose	Elaborates on author's purpose	Tells author's purpose with some clarity	Makes some connection to author's purpose	Makes no connection to author's purpose
Characters	Describes the main characters(s) and any character development	Identifies the main character(s) and gives some information about them	Inaccurately identifies some characters or gives little information about them	Inaccurately identifies the characters or gives no information about them
Setting	Describes the time and location	Identifies the time and location	Omits details of time or location	Is unable to identify time or location
Plot	Describes the events in sequence using rich detail	Tells the plot with some errors in sequence that do not affect meaning	Tells parts of plot with gaps that affect meaning	Retelling has no sense of story

Assessment Before retelling, help children name the characters and items shown. For more ideas on assessing comprehension, see the ELL and Transition Handbook.

Test Practice

Think and Share

Talk About It Choose the most exciting part of this story. What makes it exciting? Read it.

1. Use the pictures below to retell the story.

2. Tara seemed to know what to do when Jim fell into the water. What did she do first? What happened next?

3. What did you predict would happen to Jim? Were you right? What other predictions did you make?

Look Back and Write Look back at pages 176 and 177. Tiree did something smart and something kind. What did she do? Use details from the selection in your answer.

Meet the Author

Andrew Clements

Andrew Clements says, "Every good writer I know started off as a good reader." When he was growing up, he loved to read. He remembers a school librarian who made him feel he was the "owner" of every book he read. He says, "That's one of the greatest things about reading a book—read it, and you own it forever."

Read two more books by Andrew Clements.

Mr. Clements once taught school. Because he believes books make a difference, he read to his students in the classroom and to his four sons at home.

Retelling Strip

182

183

Retelling

SUCCESS PREDICTOR

OBJECTIVE

● Write a response.

DAILY FIX-IT

5. The dog has a jub?
The dog has a j**o**b**.**

6. he is berave.
He is **b**rave.

Writer's Checkup

✔ The first letter in a sentence begins with a capital letter. Did I do that?

✔ Nouns name a person, place, thing, or animal. Did I use at least one noun in each sentence?

✔ A sentence should end with the correct punctuation. Did I do that?

Independent Writing

Look Back and Write

RESPOND TO LITERATURE Read the writing prompt on p. 182 in the Student Edition and model your thinking. Then have children write their responses.

MODEL I'll look back at pp. 176 and 177 and read that part of the story again. I'll look for something smart and something kind that Tiree did. Then I'll write my response.

Tiree walks up Jim's back and out of the water. Tiree stays close to Jim instead of running away.

Scoring Rubric | Written Response

Rubric 4 3 2 1	4	3	2	1
Focus/Ideas	Clearly focuses on something smart and something kind that Tiree does	Focuses on something smart and something kind that Tiree does	Attempts to focus on something smart or something kind that Tiree does	Does not focus on something smart or something kind that Tiree does
Word Choice	Uses clear, exact words	Uses some good words	Uses same or dull words	Uses wrong words
Sentences	Uses all complete sentences	Mostly uses complete sentences	Uses some incomplete sentences	Uses all incomplete sentences
Conventions	Uses correct capital letters and end marks in all sentences	Generally uses correct capital letters and end marks in sentences	Does not use correct capital letters and end marks in some sentences	Does not use correct capital letters and end marks in any sentences

ELL

Support Writing Have children look at the illustration on pp. 176 and 177. Ask children what ideas the illustration gives them that will help answer the prompt.

Assess See the ELL and Transition Handbook for guidance on assessing writing at various levels of English proficiency.

Share Literature

CONNECT CONCEPTS

ACTIVATE PRIOR KNOWLEDGE Recall the dogs Tara and Tiree and Snoop and how they helped people who were in trouble. Explain that you will read another selection about someone who helps to save lives—"Porpoise Savers" by Elizabeth Schleichert.

Read Aloud Anthology
Porpoise Savers

BUILD ORAL VOCABULARY Read the first paragraph. Explain that the children and the scientists are working on a **blustery**, or windy, day and that their work is **fast-paced.** Ask children to listen to find out why everyone must work quickly.

MONITOR LISTENING COMPREHENSION

- Do you think you would be comfortable if you were in a boat on a cold, blustery day? Why or why not? (Possible response: No, I think I would be uncomfortable if it were cold and windy.)

- What do the divers do with the porpoises? (They get them out of the net and put them into the boat.)

- Why do you think the work is **fast-paced**? Explain. (Possible response: The work is **fast-paced** because the porpoises need to get back into the water quickly. Also, all of the people who are helping are probably working quickly to help them stay warm.)

Amazing Words to build oral vocabulary

	MONITOR PROGRESS
courageous **hazard** **rescue** **avalanche** **instinct** **skittish** **blustery** **fast-paced**	**If...** children lack oral vocabulary experiences about the concept Working Together, **then...** use the Oral Vocabulary Routine on pp. DI·1–DI·3 to develop the Amazing Words.

Connect Concepts Explain to children that porpoises are a type of small whale. Although they live in water, they are mammals and not fish. They are warm-blooded and they breathe air. They come to the surface of the water and take in air through a blowhole located on top of their head.

4

Spiral REVIEW

- Reviews inflected endings.
- Reviews *a* and *o* in CVC and CVCe words.
- Reviews high-frequency words *together, very, learn, often, though, gone,* and *pieces.*

Sentence Reading

REVIEW WORDS IN CONTEXT

READ DECODABLE AND HIGH-FREQUENCY WORDS IN CONTEXT Write these sentences. Call on individuals to read a sentence. Then randomly point to words and have them read. To help you monitor word reading, high-frequency words are underlined and decodable words are circled.

The (spacecraft)(orbited)(for) a <u>very</u> long time.

The (sharp) <u>pieces</u> of the (vase) are <u>gone</u>.

(Carl) often (blamed) (Mark).

Did you <u>learn</u> how to (bake)(those)(pork)(chops)?

The (spotted)(dog) and (black)(horse)(ate) <u>together</u>.

He is (picking) up the (order)(for) you, <u>though</u>.

Monitor Progress	Word Reading
If... children are unable to read an underlined word,	**then...** read the word for them and spell it, having them echo you.
If... children are unable to read a circled word,	**then...** have them use the blending strategy they have learned for that word type.

Support Phonics For additional review, see the phonics activities in the ELL and Transition Handbook.

Spelling

PARTNER REVIEW *r*-Controlled *ar, or, ore*

READ AND WRITE Supply pairs of children with index cards on which the spelling words have been written. Have one child read a word while the other writes it. Then have children switch roles. Have them use the cards to check spelling.

HOMEWORK Spelling Practice Book, p. 24

OBJECTIVE
● Spell words with /är/ and /ôr/.

Spelling Words

r-Controlled ar, or, ore

1.	part*	7.	smart*
2.	hard*	8.	farm
3.	born	9.	porch
4.	horse	10.	corn
5.	before	11.	chore
6.	more*	12.	score

Challenge Words

13.	cardinal	15.	morning
14.	therefore		

* Words from the Selection

Group Time

On-Level	Strategic Intervention	Advanced
Read *Rescue Dogs.*	**Read** or listen to *Rescue Dogs.*	**Read** *Rescue Dogs.*
• Use pp. 184–187.	• Use the **Routine** on p. DI·20.	• Use the **Routine** on p. DI·21.

ELL Place English language learners in the groups that correspond to their reading abilities in English.

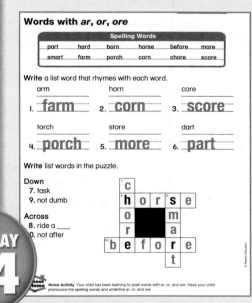

Words with *ar, or, ore*

Spelling Words

part	hard	born	horse	before	more
smart	farm	porch	corn	chore	score

Write a list word that rhymes with each word.

arm	horn	core
1. farm	2. corn	3. score

torch	store	dart
4. porch	5. more	6. part

Write list words in the puzzle.

Down
7. task
9. not dumb

Across
8. ride a ___
10. not after

Home Activity Your child has been learning to spell words with ar, or, and ore. Have your child pronounce the spelling words and underline ar, or, and ore.

▲ **Spelling Practice Book** p. 24

DAY 4

(i) Independent Activities

Fluency Reading Pair children to reread *Tara and Tiree.*

Journal Writing Write about a time when you helped someone who needed it. Share writing.

Spelling Partner Review

Independent Reading See p. 162j for Reading/Library activities and suggestions.

Literacy Centers To provide listening opportunities, you may use the Listening Center on p. 162j. To extend social studies concepts, you may use the Social Studies Center on p. 162k.

Break into small groups after Spelling and before Fluency.

Rescue Dogs

by Rena Moran

Do you know that dogs can be trained to save lives? These dogs are called rescue dogs. When people are in danger, rescue dogs are ready to help them.

Who do they help?

Rescue dogs find lost hikers and campers. They find people who are trapped after an earthquake or an avalanche. When people get lost in a snowstorm, rescue dogs search for them. Some dogs can even save people from drowning.

184

What kinds of dogs make good rescue dogs?

Good rescue dogs must be strong and smart. They also must listen to the people who train and handle them. Saint Bernards have been working as rescue dogs for many years. They help rescue people who get lost in snowstorms or get trapped under deep snow.

Bloodhounds, Labrador retrievers, and German shepherds are good at following the trails of lost people. German shepherds also are good at finding people who are trapped under snow. Newfoundlands do a great job with water rescues.

185

AudioText

Time for SOCIAL STUDIES

Hereos

"Hero" can be defined in different ways, but many people agree that a hero is someone who risks his or her own safety in order to help someone else. Name some jobs that might make people heroes. (firefighter, police officer, soldier, etc.)

Read Social Studies in Reading

PREVIEW AND PREDICT Read the title and author's name. Have children preview the article and describe the headings. (They are all questions.) Ask them where they think they will find the answers to the headings. (in the text below the heading) Then ask them to predict whether "Rescue Dogs" tells a story or provides information. Have children read how dogs can help people in dangerous situations.

INFORMATIONAL TEXT Review that selections about real people and real events are called nonfiction. Point out that the headings in this article let the reader know where to read in order to find specific information, such as how rescue dogs help others.

VOCABULARY/POSITION AND DIRECTION WORDS Review that some words describe position, or direction. Have children locate *in* and *under* on p. 185. What do these position words tell us about Saint Bernards? What are other position or direction words that could describe what rescue dogs do?

How do they do their jobs?

Like all dogs, rescue dogs have a very good sense of smell. They use their sense of smell to find a lost person. First, the dog sniffs something with the person's scent on it. This could be a hat or a blanket. Then, the dog follows the scent trail the person has left.

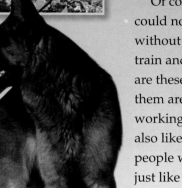

Rescue dogs do not always look for just one person. Often, they try to find the scent of any person in a certain spot. This is useful when more than one person is lost.

Of course, rescue dogs could not do their jobs without the people who train and handle them. Who are these people? Most of them are people who love working with dogs. They also like to help rescue people who are in danger— just like their dogs do!

186

187

BUILD CONCEPTS

Details and Facts • Inferential

- **What are some of the dangerous situations dogs can help people out of?**
  earthquake, avalanche, snowstorm, drowning, getting lost

Main Idea • Inferential

- **What is the selection mostly about?**
  dogs that help people who are in trouble

CONNECT TEXT TO TEXT

READING ACROSS TEXTS

Tara and Tiree helped Jim when he was in trouble. Do you think they could be trained to be full-time rescue dogs? If so, who do you think would train them?

Possible response: I think Tara and Tiree could be trained to be full-time rescue dogs because they seem to like helping people in trouble.

TIME FOR Science

Earthquake!
Earthquakes are one of the most damaging events in nature. They occur when energy is released in the rocks inside the earth. Earthquakes destroy roads and buildings and cause landslides and fires. Sometimes, rescue dogs are used to find the people who have been trapped in the rubble.

ELL

Activate Prior Knowledge Ask: Which breeds of rescue dogs have you seen or heard about before? Supply the names/pictures of breeds if children do not know them.

Fluency

READ WITH ACCURACY/APPROPRIATE PACE

MODEL READING WITH ACCURACY AND APPROPRIATE PACE Use *Tara and Tiree, Fearless Friends.*

- Point to the text on p. 173. When I see a word I don't know, I sound it out by syllables. When I come to the word *Tiree,* I break it down into syllables, Ti-ree.

- Ask children to follow along as you read the page with accuracy.

- Have children read the page after you. Encourage them to read with both accuracy and appropriate pacing. Continue in the same way with pp. 174–175.

REREAD FOR FLUENCY

Choral Reading

ROUTINE

1 **Select a Passage** For *Tara and Tiree,* use pp. 176–181.

2 **Divide Into Groups** Assign each group a part to read. For this story, have each group read a paragraph.

3 **Model** Have children track the print as you read.

4 **Read Together** Have children read along with you.

5 **Independent Readings** Have the groups read aloud without you. Monitor progress and provide feedback. For optimal fluency, children should reread three to four times.

Monitor Progress | **Check Fluency WCPM**

As children reread, monitor their progress toward their individual fluency goals. Current Goal: 58–68 words correct per minute. End-of-Year Goal: 90 words correct per minute.

If... children cannot read fluently at a rate of 58–68 words per minute,

then... make sure children practice with text at their independent level. Provide additional fluency practice, pairing nonfluent readers with fluent readers.

If... children already read fluently at 90 words per minute,

then... they do not need to reread three to four times.

SUCCESS PREDICTOR

| **Day 1** Check Word Reading | **Day 2** Check High-Frequency Words | **Day 3** Check Retelling | **▶ Day 4 Check Fluency** | **Day 5** Assess Progress |

Writing Across the Curriculum

WRITE List

DISCUSS Have children discuss what a hero is. What does a hero do? How is a hero different from anyone else? Encourage them to use oral vocabulary, such as *courageous*.

SHARE THE PEN Have children participate in creating a list. To begin, write a list of numbers on the board and explain that the class will work together to write words or phrases that tell what a hero is. Explain that the list is a series of descriptive words. Have the children copy the list on their own paper. Call on an individual to name a descriptive word and have the class repeat it. Write the word, inviting individuals to help spell the word by writing familiar letter-sounds. Ask questions, such as the following:

- What is the vowel sound you hear in the word *smart*? (/är/)
- What letters stand for that sound? *(ar)* Have a volunteer write *ar.*
- What is the ending sound you hear in the word *smart*? (/t/)
- What letter stands for that sound? *(t)* Have a volunteer write *t.*

Continue having individuals contribute to writing words on the list. Frequently reread the descriptive words.

Have children write a sentence at the bottom of their list, answering the question "Who is a hero you know or have read about?"

What Is a Hero?

1 smart
2 courageous
3 brave
4 kind
5 helpful

OBJECTIVE

● Create a list.

Advanced

Encourage children to write another list of heroes, using nouns (such as *fireman*, etc.).

Home Language Connection
Invite children to find out the descriptive words for a hero in their home languages. List the names on a multilingual diagram. Resources for home-language words may include parents, bilingual staff members, or bilingual dictionaries.

4

DAILY FIX-IT

7. I want two see the dog play.
   I want <u>to</u> see the dog <u>play</u>.

8. he is naping on the porch.
   <u>He</u> is nap<u>p</u>ing on the porch.

Nouns

Mark the letter of the word that completes each sentence.

1. Mike wants a ____.
   ○ A eat
   ⊗ B pet
   ○ C where

2. He got a ____.
   ⊗ A puppy
   ○ B nice
   ○ C when

3. They walk in the ____.
   ○ A here
   ○ B tell
   ⊗ C park

4. They play ____ in the yard.
   ○ A with
   ○ B feed
   ⊗ C games

5. The puppy is a ____ for Mike.
   ○ A then
   ⊗ B friend
   ○ C count

Home Activity Your child prepared for taking tests on nouns. Read a book together. Point out several simple sentences. Have your child identify the nouns in the sentences.

▲ **Grammar and Writing Practice Book** p. 23

Grammar

REVIEW Nouns

DEFINE NOUNS

- What are names for people, places, animals, and things called? (nouns)
- Can nouns appear more than once in a sentence? If so, where? (Yes, in the subject and in the predicate)

PRACTICE

CLASSIFY NOUNS Write *People, Places, Animals,* and *Things* to head four columns. Have individuals supply nouns to be written in each column.

People	Places	Animals	Things
man	lake	dog	ice

Speaking and Listening

NARRATE IN SEQUENCE

OBJECTIVES

● Speak to communicate story in sequence.
● Listen to understand story.

MODEL SPEAKING AND LISTENING Remind children of appropriate speaking and listening behaviors for storytelling, such as speakers facing the group and speaking clearly and listeners sitting quietly and listening to what is said. Then ask children to think about these behaviors as they take turns telling stories about rescues from dangerous situations.

• When you narrate in sequence or tell a story, you start at the beginning.

• Then you tell the middle of the story, or what happened next.

• Finally, you tell what happened last. This is the end of the story.

TELL A STORY Ask children to tell a story in proper order. Allow children the opportunity to complete Graphic Organizer 7 before taking their turn speaking to the class.

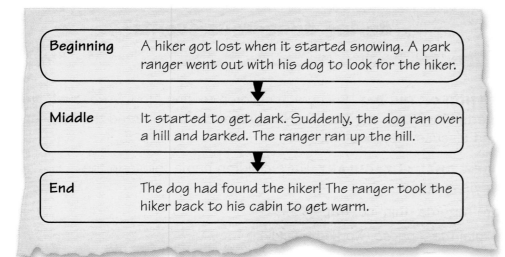

Beginning	A hiker got lost when it started snowing. A park ranger went out with his dog to look for the hiker.
Middle	It started to get dark. Suddenly, the dog ran over a hill and barked. The ranger ran up the hill.
End	The dog had found the hiker! The ranger took the hiker back to his cabin to get warm.

▲ **Graphic Organizer 7**

Wrap Up Your Day!

✓ **TEXT TO WORLD** What are some other ways that dogs can help people? (They can lead the blind, notify the deaf of sounds, serve as guard dogs, or just be kind companions.) Call on individuals to provide different answers.

LET'S TALK ABOUT IT Display the graphic organizer from Day 1. Ask children to identify some dangerous situations rescue dogs face and record answers in the "Dangerous Situations" column. Then have children suggest things rescue dogs and rescuers should do in these situations and record answers in the "What We Should Do" column.

PREVIEW Day 5

Remind children that they heard a story about how to help porpoises that have gotten trapped. Tell them that tomorrow they will hear more about how to help these animals.

Materials

- *Sing with Me Big Book*
- *Read Aloud Anthology*
- Reproducible Pages TE 188f–188g
- Student Edition 188–189

Morning Warm~Up!

This week we read about dogs that help a man who fell through thin ice, dogs that rescue, and dolphins that got caught in a traps. The rescuers worked together quickly to save lives. How can we help during dangerous events?

QUESTION OF THE DAY Encourage children to sing "To the Rescue!" from the *Sing with Me Big Book* as you gather. Write and read the message and discuss the question.

REVIEW ORAL VOCABULARY Have children name things in the message that

- are hazards (thin ice, traps)
- explain *fast-paced* (worked quickly)

ELL

Assess Vocabulary Use the Day 5 instruction on ELL Poster 6 to monitor children's progress with oral vocabulary.

ELL Poster 6

Share Literature

LISTEN AND RESPOND

USE PRIOR KNOWLEDGE Review that yesterday the class listened to find out why rescuers must work fast. Suggest that today the class listen to find out what the children did to help the porpoises.

Read Aloud Anthology
Porpoise Savers

MONITOR LISTENING COMPREHENSION

- What did the children do to help? (They splashed water on the porpoises while the porpoises were in the boat to keep them cool and wet.)

- What happened first during the rescue? (Divers caught the porpoises and handed them to the people in the boat.) What happened next? (Scientists gathered information about the animals, and the children kept them cool by splashing water on them.) What happened last? (The porpoise was set free.)

BUILD ORAL VOCABULARY

POSITION AND DIRECTION WORDS Read the first paragraph under the heading "Porpoises on Board!" Have children find position and direction words that describe what the divers did with the porpoises. ("The divers had grabbed the porpoises and now were handing them *up*, one at a time, *onto* the boat.") Write *up* and *onto*. Ask children to find other words that tell position and direction and list them. Position and direction words tell where something is located or how it is moving. Challenge children to use the words in sentences.

on	**onto**
in	**over**
into	**beyond**
up	

r-Controlled *ar, or, ore*

REVIEW

IDENTIFY *ar, or,* AND *ore* WORDS Write these sentences. Have children read each one aloud. Call on individuals to name and underline the *ar, or,* and *ore* words and identify the vowel sounds.

Her <u>mark</u> was <u>far</u> from the <u>target</u>.

I will <u>start</u> weeding the <u>garden</u> <u>before</u> <u>dark</u>.

Place your <u>order</u> <u>before</u> he rides to the <u>store</u>.

She rode the <u>horse</u> to <u>market</u> after her <u>chores</u>.

High-Frequency Words

REVIEW

SAY AND SPELL WORDS Read the rhyme. Ask children to complete each line with one of the Words to Know from p. 164. Have children say, spell, and locate the word on the Word Wall. Then read the rhyme together. **Word Wall**

There are six children in my _____. (family)

But Mom makes time to _____ to me. (listen)

Not _____ , but twice I fell out of a tree. (once)

Mom _____ me cry and ran to see. (heard)

"You did not _____ a bone or cut your knee. (break)

So _____ off your socks and come sit with me." (pull)

Vocabulary For additional practice with the high-frequency words, use the vocabulary strategies and word cards in the ELL Teaching Guide, pp. 38–39.

Spelling

TEST *r-Controlled ar, or, ore*

DICTATION SENTENCES Use these sentences to assess this week's spelling words.

1. Take <u>part</u> of my plum.
2. It was <u>hard</u> to get up.
3. What day were you <u>born</u>?
4. Did he ride the <u>horse</u>?
5. Look <u>before</u> you cross the street.
6. He wants <u>more</u> for lunch.
7. He is nice and <u>smart</u>.
8. I spent all day at the <u>farm</u>.
9. Tim and I sat on the <u>porch</u>.
10. The <u>corn</u> is so tall!
11. Dad has a <u>chore</u> for me.
12. What is the <u>score</u> of the game so far?

CHALLENGE WORDS

13. The <u>cardinal</u> sat on the branch.
14. The sun comes up in the <u>morning</u>.
15. You worked hard and, <u>therefore</u>, got good grades.

Group Time

ASSESS

● Spell words with *r*-controlled *ar, or,* and *ore.*

Spelling Words

r-Controlled ar, or, ore

1.	**part***	7.	**smart***
2.	**hard***	8.	**farm**
3.	**born**	9.	**porch**
4.	**horse**	10.	**corn**
5.	**before**	11.	**chore**
6.	**more***	12.	**score**

Challenge Words

13.	**cardinal**	15.	**morning**
14.	**therefore**		

* Words from the Selection

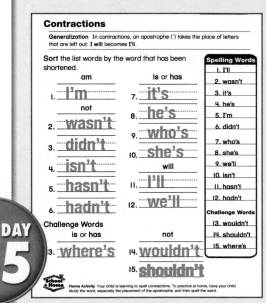

▲ **Spelling Practice Book** p. 25

On-Level

Read Set B Sentences.
● Use pp. 188e–188g.

Strategic Intervention

Read Set A Sentences.
● Use pp. 188e–188g.
● Use the **Routine** on p. DI·22.

Advanced

Read Set C Sentences and the Story.
● Use pp. 188e–188g.
● Use the **Routine** on p. DI·23.

 Place English language learners in the groups that correspond to their reading abilities in English.

DAY 5

ⓘ Independent Activities

Fluency Reading Children reread selections at their independent level.

Journal Writing Write about a time when you helped someone who needed it. Share writing.

Independent Reading See p. 162j for Reading/Library activities and suggestions.

Literacy Centers You may use the Technology Center on p. 162k to support this week's concepts and reading.

Practice Book 2.1 Glossary: Guide Words, p. 60

Break into small groups after Spelling and before Grammar and Writing.

ASSESS

- Decode *r*-Controlled *ar, or,* and *ore* words.
- Read high-frequency words.
- Read aloud with appropriate speed and accuracy.
- Recognize story sequence.
- Retell a story.

Differentiated Assessment

On-Level
Set B

Strategic Intervention
Set A

Advanced
Set C

Fluency Assessment Plan

☑ **This week assess Advanced students.**

☐ Week 2 assess Strategic Intervention students.

☐ Week 3 assess On-Level students.

☐ Week 4 assess Strategic Intervention students.

☐ Week 5 assess any students you have not yet checked during this unit.

Set individual fluency goals for children to enable them to reach the end-of-year goal.

- Current Goal: 58–68 wcpm
- End-of-Year Goal: 90 wcpm
- **ELL** For guidance in evaluating fluency, see the ELL and Transition Handbook.

SENTENCE READING

ASSESS *r*-CONTROLLED *ar, or, ore,* AND HIGH-FREQUENCY WORDS Use one of the reproducible lists on p. 188f to assess children's ability to read words with *r*-controlled *ar, or, ore,* and high-frequency words. Call on individuals to read two sentences aloud. Have each child in the group read different sentences. Start over with sentence one if necessary.

RECORD SCORES Use the Sentence Reading Chart for this unit on p. 313k.

Monitor Progress	*r*-Controlled *ar, or, ore*
If... children have trouble reading the *r*-Controlled *ar, or,* and *ore* words,	**then...** use the Reteach Lessons on p. DI·64.
High-Frequency Words	
If... children cannot read a high-frequency word,	**then...** mark the missed words on a high-frequency word list and send the list home for additional word reading practice or have the child practice with a fluent reader.

FLUENCY AND COMPREHENSION

ASSESS FLUENCY Take a one-minute sample of children's oral reading. See Monitoring Fluency, p. 313i. Have children read "Bart's Problem," the on-level fluency passage on p. 188g.

RECORD SCORES Record the number of words read correctly in a minute on the child's Fluency Progress Chart.

ASSESS COMPREHENSION Have the child read to the end of the passage. (If the child had difficulty with the passage, you may read it aloud.) Ask what happens last in the story and have the child retell the passage. Use the Retelling Rubric on p. 182g to evaluate the child's retelling.

Monitor Progress	Fluency
If... a child does not achieve the fluency goal on the timed reading,	**then...** copy the passage and send it home with the child for additional fluency practice or have the child practice with a fluent reader.
Sequence	
If... a child cannot tell the sequence of events,	**then...** use the Reteach Lesson on p. DI·64.

READ THE SENTENCES

Set A

1. My family went to a large farm.
2. I heard a dog bark from the north.
3. Once we saw corn by the barn.
4. Pull the cord before you go.
5. Listen to Carl give the order.
6. Art did not break his arm.

Set B

1. Barb said, "Once I went to see Martin."
2. I will have a party with my large family.
3. You must listen and do each chore in the army.
4. He heard me tell corny jokes to Mr. Marshall.
5. Did you see the farmer pull the short, fat pig in?
6. Do not break the vase with the border because I adore it.

Set C

1. Once they made the formula, they sold a portion.
2. It is an ordinary day, because I did not take a break from my boring work.
3. Listen and do not ignore me, or you will make things much harder.
4. The superstar will come and perform the songs for my family.
5. I heard him inform you that the artwork will go on sale in a day or two.
6. The gardener will pull up weeds by the ballpark.

Bart's Problem

Carla sat on the porch with her artwork.	8
"Do you want to help me pick corn?" asked Mom.	18
"Yes, I can help you with that chore," said Carla.	28
"It may storm so we need to be quick!" said Mom.	39
"We can walk past that flower border and go to the barn."	51
"May I ride Bart from the barn to the field?" asked Carla.	63
"That is not the best idea," said Mom.	71
"But Bart is a fast horse, and he can run farther than the others."	85
"I do not think that is smart, Carla. There is sort of a problem," said Mom.	101
"Bart can take us to the field before the storm hits," said Carla.	114
"I do not want to alarm you, but Bart cannot help," said Mom with a smile. "Bart has a bad habit. He likes to eat corn!"	140
"Oh, that is not the kind of help we need!" said Carla.	152

Monitor Progress | Fluency Passage

SUCCESS PREDICTOR

188g

Language Arts

Nouns

A **noun** names a person, place, animal, or thing.

The **boy** and his **dog** played with the **ball** in the **backyard.**

Boy names a person.

Dog names an animal.

Ball names a thing.

Backyard names a place.

Write Using Nouns

1. Choose a sentence from the selection. Write it. Underline the nouns.

2. Tara and Tiree are Jim's pets. Write a sentence about Tara and Tiree. Underline the nouns.

3. What would you teach a pet to do? Write some sentences telling about it. Underline the nouns in your sentences.

189

Grammar and Writing

WRITE USING NOUNS Read pp. 188–189 aloud. Guide children as they complete the items.

1. Possible response: <u>Tara</u> was mostly black.

2. Possible response: <u>Tara</u> and <u>Tiree</u> are brave <u>dogs</u>.

CONNECT TO UNIT WRITING Children write sentences.

3. Possible response:

My <u>dog</u> will learn new <u>tricks</u>.

My <u>dog</u> will catch a <u>ball</u>.

My <u>dog</u> will shake <u>hands</u>.

DAILY FIX-IT

9. what a good dog he is
   <u>W</u>hat a good dog he is<u>!</u>

10. will I see him later
    <u>W</u>ill I see him later<u>?</u>

Nouns

Circle the noun in each sentence.

1. The (ice) breaks.
2. The (dogs) walk together.
3. The (man) gets out.

Choose a noun in ( ) for each sentence.
Write the sentence.

4. The (where, water) feels cold.

   The water feels cold.

5. The (snow, ask) is deep.

   The snow is deep.

6. The (sing, fire) feels hot.

   The fire feels hot.

 **Home Activity** Your child reviewed nouns. Have your child write a letter to a relative and circle all the nouns.

▲ **Grammar and Writing Practice Book** p. 24

Tara and Tiree

● Use glossary: guide words.

Glossary: Guide Words
Look at the glossary pages. **Write** the answer to each question.

Glossary page 201	Glossary page 212
Canada · grape	slipped · trap
Canada (KANədə) Canada is a nation in northern North America: Some people speak French in Canada. *NOUN*	slipped (SLIPT) When you slip, you slide suddenly and unexpectedly: She slipped on the ice. *VERB*
fearless (FIR lis) A fearless person is afraid of nothing: Tom was fearless on the football field. *ADJECTIVE*	training (TRĀ ning) If you are training for a job, you are learning the skills of the trade: I am training my dog to sit. *NOUN*

1. What are the guide words for Glossary page 201?

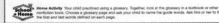
Canada, grape

2. What are the guide words for Glossary page 212?

slipped, trap

3. On what page would you find the word *collar*?

201

4. On what page might you find the word *stop*?

School + Home Home Activity Your child practiced using a glossary. Together, look at the glossary in a textbook or other nonfiction book. Choose a glossary page and ask your child to name the guide words. Ask him or her to find the first and last words defined on each page.

▲ **Practice Book 2.1** p. 60, Glossary

 **ELL**

Access Content Help English language learners understand what guide words are. Point out that *guide* means "to show the way" or "to lead." Explain that guide words in a glossary show a reader the way to the words that he or she is looking for information about.

Research/Study Skills

TEACH/MODEL Glossary: Guide Words

MODEL USING A GLOSSARY Create a simple glossary for *Tara and Tiree, Fearless Friends.* The glossary might include the words *Canada, collar, fearless, slipped,* and *training.* Include guide words at the top of the page. Explain that a glossary is an alphabetical listing of the words that appear in a particular story and their meanings. Then choose a word from the story, such as *fearless.* Read the guide words at the top of the page. Explain that they tell what the first and last words on the page are. Ask children if the word they are looking for (*fearless*) will be on that page. Ask them to explain how they know.

Model how to use guide words.

Think Aloud **MODEL** I can use the guide words in this glossary to figure out if the word I am looking for is on this page. First, I look at the first guide word. It tells me that the first word on the page is *Canada.* Then I read the other guide word. It tells me that the last word on the page is *training.* I know that *fearless* comes between the letters *c* and *t,* so it will be on this page.

USE GUIDE WORDS Using another, bigger glossary, ask individuals to tell what the guide words are on each page. Name a vocabulary word and ask if it would be found on that page.

PRACTICE

DEMONSTRATE USING A GLOSSARY Give students copies of a glossary. Assign a different word to each individual. On a separate sheet of paper, have them write the two guide words located on the page where their word is found, as well as the word's definition.

Wrap Up Your Week!

LET'S TALK ABOUT Working Together

QUESTION OF THE WEEK Recall this week's question.

• What can we do in a dangerous situation?

Display the Dangerous Situation/What We Should Do chart. Help children identify what would happen next in each situation.

Dangerous Situation	What We Should Do
An animal is stuck in a pipe.	Call animal workers.
A man falls into a lake.	Toss a life preserver.
A person gets lost.	Use search dogs and people to find the lost person.
There is a fire.	Get out of the building and call 911.
There is a tornado.	Seek shelter.

CONNECT Use questions such as these to prompt a discussion.

• A person who helps someone in danger is courageous. When might courageous people work as a team?

• An example of a hazard that occurs in nature is an avalanche. Snow or rock rushes down the side of a mountain. What are some hazards that one might encounter in fast-paced sports?

Build Background Use ELL Poster 6 to support the Preview activity.

PREVIEW Tell children that next week they will read about working together on a team.

PREVIEW
Next Week

Ronald Morgan Goes to Bat

ONLINE CLASSROOM

For the Teacher

PLAN  My Lesson Planner ONLINE

TEACH  Teacher's Edition ONLINE

ASSESS  Success Tracker ONLINE

For the Student

READ  Read It ONLINE

 Leveled Reader Database ONLINE

EXPLORE Take It to the NET ONLINE

PRACTICE Fluency Coach

Phonics Activities

Preview Your Week

What makes a team?

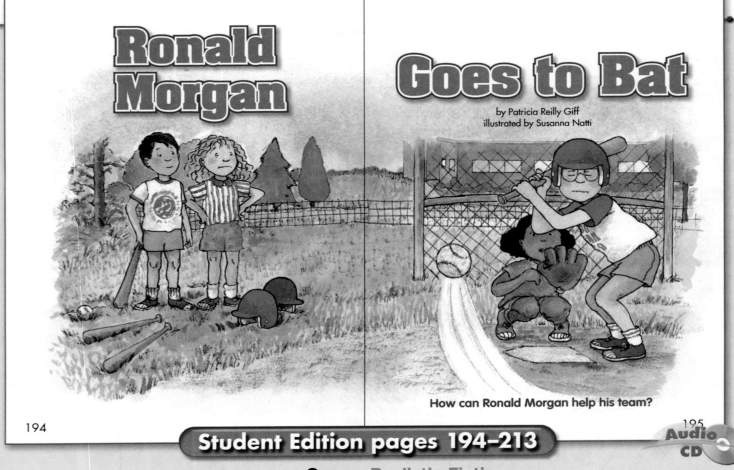

Ronald Morgan
Goes to Bat
by Patricia Reilly Giff
illustrated by Susanna Natti

How can Ronald Morgan help his team?

194   195

Student Edition pages 194–213

Audio CD

Genre	Realistic Fiction
Phonics	Contractions
Comprehension Skill	Realism and Fantasy
Comprehension Strategy	Prior Knowledge

Time for SOCIAL STUDIES

Paired Selection

Reading Across Texts
Compare Characters

Genre
Poetry

Text Features
Lines That Rhyme and
Have Rhythm

Poetry

Spaceball
by Brod Bagert
illustrated by Tedd Arnold

Last night I had a funny dream—
My brain's a mysterious place.
I dreamed about some aliens
Who lived in outer space.

I watched them play a game
That seemed a lot like baseball.
They played with bats and floppy hats,
But the aliens called it Spaceball.

Jupiter was the pitcher's mound,
Saturn was third base,
And the little alien kid at bat
Had a serious look on his face.

"Full count, bottom of the ninth,"
I heard the announcer say.
"This batter's trying to hit the ball
Clean out of the Milky Way."

Then I saw the ball was planet Earth!
Oh, how could it possibly be?
If he hits *that* ball, it's the end of us all,
That means . . . THE END OF ME!

I heard a shout: "STRIKE THREE, YOU'RE OUT!"
And space was filled with cheers.
But the little alien batter's eyes
Filled up with alien tears.

My dreams are strange, but last night's dream
Was the strangest dream of all.
Earth was saved by an alien
Who couldn't hit the ball.

214

Student Edition pages 214–215

Audio CD

Read It
ONLINE
sfsuccessnet.com

- Student Edition
- Leveled Readers
- Decodable Reader

Leveled Readers

🎯 **Skill** Realism and Fantasy

🎯 **Strategy** Prior Knowledge

Lesson Vocabulary

Below-Level

On-Level

Advanced

ELL Reader

- Concept Vocabulary
- Text Support
- Language Enrichment

Decodable Readers

Apply Phonics

- Jem Wasn't Happy

Time for
SOCIAL STUDIES

Integrate Social Studies Standards

- Cultural Heritage
- Production of Goods
- Self Direction
- Personal Responsibility
- Cooperation, Teamwork

✓ **Read**

Ronald Morgan Goes to Bat pp. 194–213

"Spaceball" pp. 214–215

✓ **Read**

Leveled Readers

Below-Level   **On-Level**   **Advanced**

- Support Concepts
- Develop Concepts
- Extend Concepts
- Social Studies Extension Activity

✓ **Read**

ELL Reader

✓ **Build Concept Vocabulary**
Working Together, pp. 190r, 190–191

✓ **Teach Social Studies Concepts**
Baseball Bats, pp. 198–199
Teamwork, pp. 206–207

✓ **Explore Social Studies Center**
Write Rules, p. 190k

Ronald Morgan **190c**

Planner

My Lesson Planner
ONLINE
sfsuccessnet.com

THIS WEEK
CHILDREN WILL LEARN
Phonics Contractions *n't, 's, 'll, 'm*
Comprehension Skill Realism and Fantasy
Comprehension Strategy Prior Knowledge

DAY 1

DAY 2

Oral Language *10–15 minutes*
- Build Concepts
- Share Literature

Oral Language 190l–190m
QUESTION OF THE WEEK *What makes a team?*
Share Literature
Sing with Me Big Book, 7

Oral Language 192a–192b
QUESTION OF THE DAY *What are some ways that individuals can help a team?*
Share Literature
Big Book *From Me to You*

Word Work *25–30 minutes*
- Phonics
- Spelling
- High-Frequency Words

Word Work 190n–190p
Phonics
Introduce Contractions *n't. 's, 'll, 'm* **T**

Spelling Pretest

Word Work 192c–192d, 192–193a
Phonics
Contractions *n't, 's, 'll, 'm* **T**

Spelling Dictation
High-Frequency Words T
Introduce *laugh, great, you're, either, certainly, second, worst*

Reading *60–75 minutes*
- Vocabulary
- Comprehension
- Fluency

- Cross-Curricular Connections

- Independent Reading

Reading 190q–191b
Vocabulary
Decodable Word Meaning
Read Decodable Reader 7
Comprehension Check
Fluency
Oral Rereading
Build Background
Let's Talk About Working Together
Comprehension
Realism and Fantasy **T**

SOCIAL STUDIES Concept Chart

Leveled Readers, LR10–18
Self-Selected Reading, TR22–23

Reading 192e–192f, 194a–211
Vocabulary
Introduce *terrific, spirit, clutched*
Comprehension
Realism and Fantasy **T**
Prior Knowledge
Read *Ronald Morgan Goes to Bat,* 194–211
REVIEW **Comprehension Skill**
Sequence

SOCIAL STUDIES Baseball Bats, Teamwork
SOCIAL STUDIES Concept Chart

Leveled Readers, LR10–18
Self-Selected Reading, TR22–23

Language Arts *20–30 minutes*
- Writing
- Grammar
- Speaking, Listening, Viewing
- Research/Study Skills

Language Arts 191c–191d
Shared Writing
List
DAILY WRITING
List sports in which people can compete.
Grammar
Introduce Proper Nouns **T**

Language Arts 211a–211b
Interactive Writing
Outline
DAILY WRITING
Write about a time you were part of a team.
Grammar
Practice Proper Nouns **T**

Monitor Progress

Daily **SUCCESS PREDICTORS** for
Adequate Yearly Progress

Day 1 Check 190o
Check Word Reading
Spiral REVIEW Phonics

Phonics

Day 2 Check 193a
Check High-Frequency Words
Spiral REVIEW High-Frequency Words

Fluency

190d

Vocabulary | **Check Oral Vocabulary** See p. DI·2.

Student Edition 194–213

Leveled Readers

Student Edition 214–215

DAY 3

Oral Language 212a–212b

QUESTION OF THE DAY *Why might a letter make him feel better?*

Share Literature
Big Book *From Me to You*

Word Work 212c–212d

Phonics
REVIEW r-Controlled *ar, or, ore*

Spelling Practice

High-Frequency Words T
Practice *laugh, great, you're, either, certainly, second, worst*

Reading 194–211, 212e–213

Vocabulary
Synonyms

Comprehension
Read *Ronald Morgan Goes to Bat,* 194–213

Think and Share

Fluency
Choral Reading

SOCIAL STUDIES Concept Chart

Leveled Readers, LR10–18
Self-Selected Reading, TR22–23

Language Arts 213a–213b

Independent Writing
Respond to Literature

DAILY WRITING
Write a journal entry about a time when you were part of a team.

Grammar
Write with Proper Nouns **T**

DAY 4

Oral Language 214a–214b

QUESTION OF THE DAY *What makes a team?*

Share Literature
Read Aloud Anthology "Flying a Kite, 1899"

Word Work 214c–214d

Phonics
REVIEW Sentence Reading

Spelling Partner Review

High-Frequency Words T
Practice *laugh, great, you're, either, certainly, second, worst*

Reading 214e–215a

Vocabulary
Descriptive Words

Comprehension
Read "Spaceball," 214–215
Social Studies in Reading
Reading Across Texts

Fluency
Choral Reading

SOCIAL STUDIES Cultural Heritage, Teamwork
SOCIAL STUDIES CENTER Write Rules

Leveled Readers, LR10–18
Self-Selected Reading, TR22–23

Language Arts 215b–215d

Writing Across the Curriculum
Chart

DAILY WRITING
List fun things to do for recreation.

Grammar
Review Proper Nouns **T**

Speaking and Viewing
Types of Media

DAY 5

Oral Language 216a–216b

QUESTION OF THE DAY *What makes a team?*

Share Literature
Read Aloud Anthology "Flying a Kite, 1899"

Word Work 216c–216f

Phonics
🎯 Review Contractions *n't, 's, 'll, 'm*

Spelling Test

High-Frequency Words T
Review *laugh, great, you're, either, certainly, second, worst*

Reading 216b, 216e–216g

Vocabulary
Descriptive Words

Monitor Progress
Read the Sentences
Read the Story

SOCIAL STUDIES Concept Chart

Leveled Readers, LR10–18
Self-Selected Reading, TR22–23

Language Arts 216–217a

Grammar and Writing
Use Proper Nouns **T**

Connect to Unit Writing
How-to Report

DAILY WRITING
Write about what you contribute to family.

Research/Study Skills
Newspaper and Periodicals

KEY

🎯 = Target Skill
T = Tested Skill

THIS WEEK'S RESOURCES

Practice Book pp. 61–70

Spelling Practice Book pp. 25–28

Grammar and Writing Practice Book pp. 25–28

Selection Test pp. 25–28

Fresh Reads for Differentiated Test Practice pp. 37–42

Phonics Songs and Rhymes Chart 7

Day 3 Check 212g
Check Retelling

Comprehension

Day 4 Check 215a
Check Fluency WCPM
Spiral REVIEW Phonics, High-Frequency Words

Fluency

Day 5 Check 216e
Contractions *n't, 's, 'll, 'm*
High-Frequency Words
Fluency
Comprehension

SUCCESS PREDICTOR

Resources for Differentiated Instruction

LEVELED READERS

▶ **Comprehension**
- 🎯 **Skill** Realism and Fantasy
- 🎯 **Strategy** Prior Knowledge

▶ **Lesson Vocabulary**

High-Frequency Words

laugh	you're
great	
either	certainly
second	worst

▶ **Social Studies Standards**
- **Cultural Heritage**
- **Production of Goods**
- **Self-Direction**
- **Personal Responsibility**
- **Cooperation**

Leveled Reader Database ONLINE

sfsuccessnet.com

Use the Online Database of over 600 books to

- Download and print additional copies of this week's leveled readers
- Locate more titles at various levels to practice this week's skill—realism and fantasy
- Search for more titles focused on this week's topic and content

---

On-Level

Social Studies

Warm and Fuzzy

by Kristin Cashore
illustrated by Rick Ewigleben

On-Level Reader

Realism and Fantasy

Think about the story *Warm and Fuzzy*. Then answer the questions below.

1. If the characters were people instead of animals, would the story be a realistic story or a fantasy?

   fantasy

2. If the character Geraldine was a sheep, would the story be a realistic story or a fantasy?

   fantasy

3. If Kenny was a boy, would the story be a realistic story or a fantasy?

   fantasy

4–5. What parts of the story are similar to real life? *possible responses given*

   Sheep have wool. People make the wool into yarn. People use the yarn to knit things like scarves.

🎯 **On-Level Practice** TE p. LR14

Vocabulary

Draw a line to match the word to its meaning.

1. certainly — a. one of two things
2. either — b. surely
3. great — c. a sound made by someone when something is funny
4. laugh — d. you are
5. second — e. the next after first
6. you're — f. very good

Antonyms are words that have opposite meanings. Draw a line to match the antonyms.

7. either — a. best
8. great — b. bad
9. laugh — c. both
10. worst — d. cry

🎯 **On-Level Practice** TE p. LR15

Strategic Intervention

Social Studies

Let's Play Baseball!

by Jessica Quilty

illustrated by
Chad Thompson

Below-Level Reader

Realism and Fantasy

Think about the story *Let's Play Baseball*. Then, answer the questions below.

1. If the character Sam was a rabbit, would the story be a realistic story or a fantasy?

   fantasy

2. If the character Ann hit a home run, would the story be a realistic story or a fantasy?

   realistic story

3. If the children played baseball on the moon, would the story be a realistic story or a fantasy?

   fantasy

4. If Sam's team lost the game, would the story be a realistic story or a fantasy?

   realistic story

5. If they played baseball while riding elephants, would the story be a realistic story or a fantasy?

   fantasy

🎯 **Below-Level Practice** TE p. LR11

Vocabulary

Draw a line to match the word to its meaning.

1. certainly — a. similarly; as well
2. either — b. to be sure
3. great — c. a sound made when something is funny
4. laugh — d. you are
5. second — e. the next after first
6. you're — f. very good
7. worst — g. the most bad

Synonyms are words that have the same meaning. Draw a line to match the synonyms.

8. laugh — h. surely
9. great — i. giggle
10. certainly — j. terrific

🎯 **Below-Level Practice** TE p. LR12

Advanced

Advanced Reader

Realism and Fantasy
Read the story titles below. Decide if the story is a realistic story or a fantasy. Circle your answer. Then, explain your answer.

1. Title: *The First Big Game in Space*
   realistic story   (fantasy story)
2. How do you know?

People do not play baseball in
space.

3. Title: *The First Big Game Played by Monkeys*
   realistic story   (fantasy story)
4. How do you know?

Monkeys do not play baseball.

5. Write your own title for a realistic story about baseball.

The First Night Game

Advanced Practice TE p. LR17

Vocabulary
Draw a line to match the word parts and make a whole word.

1. con   a. creation
2. com   b. tribute
3. re   c. pete

Use the words below in a sentence.   Possible responses given.

4. compete

In baseball, two teams
compete.

5. recreation

When you play with friends,
it is recreation.

Advanced Practice TE p. LR18

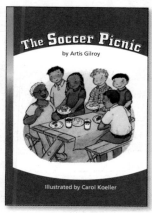

ELL Reader

ELL Poster 7

Teacher's Edition Notes
ELL notes throughout this lesson support instruction and reference additional resources at point of use.

Teaching Guide
pp. 43–49, 224–225

- Multilingual summaries of the main selection
- Comprehension lesson
- Vocabulary strategies and word cards
- ELL Reader 7 lesson

ELL and Transition Handbook

Ten Important Sentences

- Key ideas from every selection in the Student Edition
- Activities to build sentence power

More Reading

Reader's Theater Anthology
- Fluency practice
- Five scripts to build fluency
- Poetry for oral interpretation

Leveled Trade Books

- Extend reading tied to the unit concept
- Lessons in Trade Book Library Teaching Guide

Homework
- Family Times Newsletter
- ELL Multilingual Selection Summaries

Take-Home Books
- Decodable Readers
- Leveled Readers

Ronald Morgan   **190g**

Weekly Plan for Group Time
Differentiated Instruction

DAILY PLAN

WHOLE GROUP

- Morning Warm-Up
- Share Literature
- Phonics
- Spelling
- Vocabulary

DAILY GROUP TIME

1
2
3
4
5

- **Reading Support**
- **Skill Support**
- **Fluency Practice**

WHOLE GROUP

- Fluency
- Writing
- Grammar
- Wrap Up Your Day

Look for the ⓘ
Independent Activities

See Group Time pp. 190p, 194a, 212e, 214d, 216d.

✓ **Fluency Reading**
Choral Reading

✓ **Journal Writing**
See the Planner for daily writing prompts, pp. 190d–190e.

✓ **Homework**
Practice Book, pp. 61–70
Spelling Practice Book, pp. 25–28
Grammar and Writing Practice Book, pp. 25–80

✓ **Literacy Centers**
pp. 190j–190k
- Listening
- Reading/Library
- Word Work
- Writing
- Social Studies
- Technology

DAY 1

On-Level	Strategic Intervention	Advanced
Page 190q	**Page DI•24**	**Page DI•25**
• Read Decodable Reader 7	• Read Decodable Reader 7	• Read Advanced Selection 7
• Reread for Fluency	• Blend Words with Contractions	• Extend Word Reading
	• Reread for Fluency	• Introduce Concept Inquiry

DAY 2

On-Level	Strategic Intervention	Advanced
Pages 194–211	**Page DI•26**	**Page DI•27**
• Read *Ronald Morgan Goes to Bat*	• Read SI Decodable Reader 7	• Read *Ronald Morgan Goes to Bat*
• Reread for Fluency	• Read or Listen to *Ronald Morgan Goes to Bat*	• Continue Concept Inquiry
	• Blend Words with Contractions	

DAY 3

On-Level	Strategic Intervention	Advanced
Pages 194–213	**Page DI•28**	**Page DI•29**
• Reread *Ronald Morgan Goes to Bat*	• Reread *Ronald Morgan*	• Self-Selected Reading
	• Read Words and Sentences	• Continue Concept Inquiry
	• Review Realism and Fantasy and Prior Knowledge	
	• Reread for Fluency	

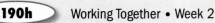

On-Level

Pages 214–215
- Read "Spaceball"

Strategic Intervention

Page DI•30
- Read or Listen to "Spaceball"
- Reread for Fluency
- Build Concepts

Advanced

Page DI•31
- Read "Spaceball"
- Expand Vocabulary
- Continue Concept Inquiry

DAY 4

On-Level

Pages 216e–216g
- Sentence Reading, Set B

Set B
1. Kim's first in line, but who's second?
2. It's certainly the worst storm she's seen.
3. Mom doesn't laugh when the room isn't clean.
4. He'll be a great help if the work hasn't been done.
5. Here's when I'll have to know if you're staying with us.
6. There's either juice or milk that's here to drink.

Strategic Intervention

Page DI•32
- Practice Word Reading
- Sentence Reading, Set A
- Monitor Fluency and Comprehension

Set A
1. He's funny, but Joan didn't laugh.
2. We'll see if there's a great place to park.
3. I'm glad you're happy and aren't sad.
4. He'll either be here by noon, or he isn't coming.
5. She'll find out if they'll be in second place.
6. It certainly wasn't the worst game that she will play.

Advanced

Page DI•33
- Sentence Reading, Set C
- Share Concept Inquiry

Set C
1. The great big hill wasn't easy to climb up, and it can't be hard to get down.
2. They'll either go on a picnic, or I'll meet them at the zoo on Friday.
3. I'm sure you'll laugh when you see how funny the show is.
4. It's certainly the worst trip that we'll ever make.
5. Mom isn't sure if you're going to visit your grandmother's house this summer.
6. That's the second letter that he's written to his pen pal in China.

DAY 5

Grouping Place English language learners in the groups that correspond to their reading abilities in English.

ELL

Use the appropriate Leveled Reader or other text at children's instructional level.

TIP Send home the appropriate Multilingual Summary of the main selection on Day 1.

MORE READING FOR
Group Time

Below-Level

On-Level

Advanced

Take It to the NET™
ONLINE
sfsuccessnet.com

Sharon Vaughn
For ideas and activities for English language learners, see the article "Storybook Reading" by P. Hickman, S. Pollard-Durodola, and Scott Foresman author S. Vaughn.

TEACHING TIP Create a learning community in your classroom.
Have children bring in books on a topic they're interested in. Ask a child who enjoyed a book to recommend it to another child. Respect each other as learners.

TEACHER TALK

Fluency is the ability to read words and connected text rapidly, accurately, and smoothly. Fluency may be measured in words correct per minute.

Be sure to schedule time for children to work on the unit inquiry project "Organize a Club.". This week children should organize a club to address the need of the school or community.

Looking Ahead

Literacy Centers

Listening

Let's Read Along

MATERIALS `SINGLES`
CD player, headphones, print copies of recorded pieces

LISTEN TO LITERATURE As children listen to the following recordings, have them follow along or read along in the print version.

AudioText
"Spaceball"
Ronald Morgan Goes to Bat

Sing with Me/Background Building Audio
"Teamwork"

Phonics Songs and Rhymes Audio
"I'm on the Team"

I'm on the Team

I'm a member of a great team.
We all love to play.
We don't miss a single practice.
We'll be there every day.

When it's time to play the big game,
No matter how it ends,
We'll keep helping one another.
We'll always be good friends.

Audio CD **Phonics Songs and Rhymes Chart 7**

Reading/Library

Read It Again!

MATERIALS `SINGLES` `PAIRS` `GROUPS`
collection of books for self-selected reading, reading logs

REREAD BOOKS Have children select previously read books from the appropriate book box and record titles of books they read in their logs. Use these books:

- **Decodable Readers**
- **Leveled Readers**
- **ELL Readers**
- **Stories written by classmates**
- **Books from the library**

TEN IMPORTANT SENTENCES Have children read the Ten Important Sentences for *Ronald Morgan Goes to Bat* and locate the sentences in the Student Edition.

BOOK CLUB Use p. 213 of the Student Edition to find out about the author of the book. Encourage a group to write letters to the author telling her what they liked best about the book.

Word Work

Contraction Match

MATERIALS `PAIRS` `GROUPS`
word cards

CONTRACTIONS *n't, 's, 'll, 'm* Have pairs or small groups play a card game in which they match contractions with the two words that make up the contraction.

1. Make a card for each contraction and a card for the two words that make up the contraction.
2. The cards should be placed facedown in rows.
3. Children take turns turning over two cards to make a match. Children read each card aloud. If the cards match, the player keeps them. If the cards do not match, they are turned facedown and the next player takes a turn.
4. Play continues until all the cards have been matched.

 Phonics Activities CD This interactive CD provides additional practice.

I'll   I will

can't

can not

Scott Foresman Reading Street Centers Survival Kit

Use the *Ronald Morgan Goes to Bat* materials from the
Scott Foresman Centers Survival Kit to organize
this week's centers.

Writing

Let's Play

MATERIALS `SINGLES`
index cards, pencils

WRITE DIRECTIONS Recall that Ronald Morgan learned to play baseball.

1. Have children think of a game they want to teach someone to play.
2. Then have them write directions for playing the game on an index card.
3. Then have children exchange cards and discuss their directions.

LEVELED WRITING Encourage children to write at their own ability level. Some may write directions using only words and phrases. Others will be able to write simple step-by-step directions. Your best writers will write clear directions with greater detail and more attention to mechanics and spelling.

Play Baseball

1. The pitcher throws the ball.
2. The batter hits the ball.
3. The batter runs to first base.
4. The pitcher throws to the next batter.

Social Studies

Go Team!

MATERIALS `PAIRS`
posterboard, markers

WRITE RULES Have children think about how to act during a sporting event.

1. Ask children to discuss proper behavior for sports fans.
2. Have partners write their own "Rules for Sports Fans."
3. Then have them share their lists.

Rules for Sports Fans

1 Do not boo.
2 Do not litter.
3 Do not yell rude things.
4 Cheer for your team.

Technology

Class Games

MATERIALS `SINGLES`
computer, printer

TYPE DIRECTIONS Have individuals type the directions they wrote for their games in the Writing Center.

1. Children turn on the computer and open a word processing program.
2. Children type the directions they wrote in the Writing Center. If they did not complete the activity, they should type directions to a game they know how to play.
3. Children then print out their directions. Encourage them to illustrate the page.
4. Compile printouts into a stapled book called "Class Games."

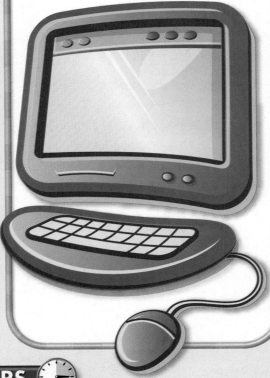

ALL CENTERS

Day 1
AT A GLANCE

Share Literature
"Teamwork" 7

Phonics and Spelling
 Contractions
Spelling Pretest:
  Words with Contractions

Read Apply Phonics [Word Wall]
Group Time < Differentiated Instruction

Build Background
Let's Talk About Working Together

Listening Comprehension
Skill Realism and Fantasy

Shared Writing
List

Grammar
Proper Nouns

Materials

- *Sing with Me Big Book*
- Letter Tiles
- Decodable Reader 7
- Student Edition 190–191
- Graphic Organizer 15
- Writing Transparency 7
- Grammar Transparency 7

Take It to the NET
ONLINE
Professional Development
To learn more about intervention, go to sfsuccessnet.com and read "Catch Them Before They Fall" by J. Torgesen.

Morning Warm-Up!

A team is like a family. It's important that each person supports the others. What makes a team?

QUESTION OF THE WEEK Tell children they will talk, sing, read, and write about what makes a team. Write and read the message and discuss the question.

CONNECT CONCEPTS Ask questions to connect to other Unit 2 selections.

- There is an example of teamwork in *Tara and Tiree, Fearless Friends*. What is it?

- How did Tara, Tiree, and Jim contribute to their team?

REVIEW HIGH-FREQUENCY WORDS

- Circle the high-frequency word *family* in the message.

- Have children say and spell the word as they write it in the air.

Build Background Use the Day 1 instruction on ELL Poster 7 to assess knowledge and develop concepts.

ELL Poster 7

Share Literature

BUILD ORAL VOCABULARY Display p. 7 of the *Sing with Me Big Book*. Tell children that the class is going to sing a song about working as a team. Read the title. Ask children to listen for the Amazing Words **compete, contribute,** and **recreation** as you sing. Then sing the song again and encourage children to sing along with you. Have children demonstrate their understanding of *compete, contribute,* and *recreation* by asking:

- What type of sports can you compete in?
- What sorts of things can you contribute to a picnic basket?
- What do you like to do for recreation?

Sing with Me/
Background Building Audio

Teamwork

Come on, teammates, let's go play!
We've got a team to beat.
Our pumped-up spirit helps us win.
We know how to compete.

We all contribute to the team—
Skill and inspiration.
And even though we work real hard,
For us it's recreation.

Sing with Me Big Book

OBJECTIVE

- Build oral vocabulary.

Amazing Words to build oral vocabulary

compete contribute recreation	**MONITOR PROGRESS**
	If... children lack oral vocabulary experiences about the concept Working Together, **then...** use the Oral Vocabulary Routine on pp. DI·1–DI·2, DI·4, to develop the Amazing Words.

Access Content Explain to children that the English word *beat* is a multiple-meaning word. Tell them that its meaning in "Teamwork" is *defeat* or *overcome*.

OBJECTIVES

- Use structural cues to decode contractions.
- Blend, read, and build contractions.

Skills Trace

Contractions

Introduce/Teach	TE: 2.2 190n–o
Practice	TE: 2.2 190q, DR7, 192c–d; PB: 2.1 63, 78
Reteach/Review	TE: 2.2 216c, 243c, DI-65
Assess/Test	TE: 2.2 216e–g; Benchmark Test, Unit 2

Generalization

Contractions A contraction is a shortened form of two words. An apostrophe appears where letters have been dropped from the original words.

Strategic Intervention

Use **Monitor Progress,** p. 190o during Group Time after children have had more practice with contractions.

Advanced

Use **Monitor Progress,** p. 190o as a preassessment to determine whether or not this group of children would benefit from this instruction on contractions.

Support Phonics Some languages such as the Romance languages include contractions. If possible, provide some examples of contractions in the home language. (In Spanish, *a* + *el* = *al*; in Portuguese, *de* + *as* = *das*.) Explain that in English, contractions use an apostrophe to replace the missing letters.

See the Phonics Transition Lessons in the ELL and Transition Handbook.

⟳ Contractions

TEACH/MODEL

Blending Strategy

ROUTINE

1 Connect Write *does not.* What are these words? Today we'll learn about combining two words like these to make a contraction.

2 Model Write *doesn't* below *does not.* *Doesn't* is a contraction, a short way of saying and writing two words. An apostrophe takes the place of letters that have been left out. If we compare these words, we see that the apostrophe takes the place of the letter *o.* Many contractions are made from Word Wall words. What two words make the contraction *doesn't*? *(does and not)* When you see a contraction, you know it is a short way of writing two words. **Model blending *doesn't.***

3 Group Practice Together form and read contractions for these words: *you will, I will, was not, she is, could not.*

4 Review What do you know about reading contractions? A contraction is a short way to say or write two words. An apostrophe takes the place of letters that are left out.

BLEND WORDS

INDIVIDUALS BLEND WORDS Call on individuals to read *who's, we'll, hadn't, isn't, wasn't, it's.* Have them tell which two words make up each contraction and what letters were left out. For feedback, refer to step four of the Blending Strategy Routine.

BLEND WORDS

READ LONGER WORDS Write the contractions shown below in the left column. Call on children to read the contractions and name the words that form them. Write the words and have them identify which letter or letters were left out to form the contraction. Have all the contractions reread.

can't	can not
she's	she is
hasn't	has not
they'll	they will
I'm	I am
we'll	we will

Pick the contraction that is formed from each pair of words. **Write** the contraction on the line.

It is happy.
It's happy.

can't   hasn't   he's   I'm
she's   they'll   we'll   who's

1. had + not **hasn't**	2. I + am **I'm**
3. can + not **can't**	4. they + will **they'll**
5. who + is **who's**	6. we + will **we'll**

Pick a word from the box to finish each sentence. **Write** the word on the line. **Begin** with a capital letter.

7. **He's** her little brother.

8. **She's** his big sister.

Home Activity Your child practiced forming contractions, such as hasn't, she's, we'll, and I'm. Read one of the contractions shown in the box above. Ask your child to tell you the words that make the word pair. Work with your child to practice the contractions shown on the page.

▲ **Practice Book 2.1** p. 63, Contractions

Monitor Progress | Check Word Reading Contractions

Write the following words and have individuals read them.

who's	there's	hadn't	it's	wasn't
we'll	I'll	I'm	she'll	he'll
weren't	he's	they'll	aren't	isn't

If... children cannot blend contractions at this point,

then... continue to monitor their progress using other instructional opportunities during the week so that they can be successful with the Day 5 Assessment. See the Skills Trace on p. 190n.

SUCCESS PREDICTOR

Spiral **REVIEW**

● Reviews high-frequency words.

▶ **Day 1 Check** Word Reading | **Day 2 Check** High-Frequency Words | **Day 3 Check** Retelling | **Day 4 Check** Fluency | **Day 5 Assess** Progress

Word Reading

SUCCESS PREDICTOR

- Segment word parts to spell words.
- Spell contractions.

Spelling Words

Contractions

1. I'll*	7. who's
2. wasn't	8. she's
3. it's	9. we'll*
4. he's	10. isn't
5. I'm*	11. hasn't
6. didn't	12. hadn't

Challenge Words

13. wouldn't	15. where's
14. shouldn't	

* Words from the Selection

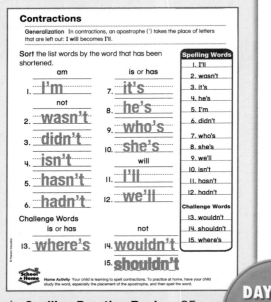

▲ **Spelling Practice Book** p. 25

Support Spelling Before giving the spelling pretest, clarify the meaning of each spelling word with examples, such as saying *I'm* (writing on the board) while writing on the board, and gesturing *no* to illustrate *isn't*.

Spelling

PRETEST Contractions

MODEL WRITING FOR WORD PARTS Each spelling word is a contraction. Before administering the spelling pretest, model how to segment contractions to spell them.

- You can spell contractions by thinking about the two words that make up the contraction. What words make up *can't*? *(can and not)*
- How do you spell *can*? Write *can* or have children spell it.
- What comes next? **(the apostrophe)** The apostrophe takes the place of *no* in *not*.
- After the apostrophe add the rest of the letter(s). What is the letter? *(t)* Write *t* after the apostrophe.
- When you spell contractions, make sure to put the apostrophe in the right place.
- Repeat with *you'll.*

PRETEST Dictate the spelling words. Segment the words for children if necessary. Have children check their pretests and correct misspelled words.

HOMEWORK Spelling Practice Book, p. 25

Group Time

On-Level	Strategic Intervention	Advanced
Read Decodable Reader 7.	**Read** Decodable Reader 7.	**Read** Advanced Selection 7.
• Use pp. 190q.	• Use the **Routine** on p. DI·24.	• Use the **Routine** on p. DI·25.

DAY 1

ELL Place English language learners in the groups that correspond to their reading abilities in English.

ⓘ Independent Activities

Fluency Reading Pair children to reread Leveled Readers or the ELL Reader from the previous week or other text at children's independent level.

Journal Writing List sports in which people can compete. Share writing.

Independent Reading See p. 190j for Reading/Library activities and suggestions.

Literacy Centers To practice contractions, you may use Word Work, p. 190j.

Practice Book 2.1 Contractions, p. 63 Realism and Fantasy, p. 64

Break into small groups after Spelling and before Build Background.

Decodable Reader 7

Jem Wasn't Happy
Written by Stephen Lewis
Illustrated by Ann Mitcham

Phonics Skill
Contractions *n't, 's, 'll, 'm*

Apply Phonics

◉ PRACTICE Contractions

HIGH-FREQUENCY WORDS Review *does, friends,* and *have.*

READ DECODABLE READER 7

- Pages 50–51 Read aloud quietly with the group.
- Pages 52–53 Have the group read aloud without you.
- Pages 54–56 Select individuals to read aloud.

CHECK COMPREHENSION AND DECODING Have children retell the story to include characters, setting, and events. Then have children locate contractions in the story. Review contraction spelling patterns *n't, 's,* and *'ll.* Sort words according to their spelling patterns. Point out that *let's* is a contraction for *let us.* What letter is left out of *let's? (u)*

n't	*'s*	*'ll*
didn't	let's	it'll
isn't		
wasn't		

HOMEWORK Take-Home Decodable Reader 7

REREAD FOR FLUENCY

Oral Rereading

ROUTINE

1 **Read** Have children read the entire selection orally.

2 **Reread** To achieve optimal fluency, children should reread the text three or four times.

3 **Provide Feedback** Listen as children read and provide corrective feedback regarding their oral reading and their use of the blending strategy.

Monitor Progress

Decoding

If... children have difficulty decoding a word,	**then...** prompt them to blend the word.
	• What is the new word?
	• Is the new word a word you know?
	• Does it make sense in the story?

E L L

Access Content

Beginning Preview *Jem Wasn't Happy,* identifying *vet* and *pups* in the pictures and print. Have children repeat the words as they point to the pictures of the vet and the pups.

Intermediate Preview *Jem Wasn't Happy,* explaining contractions such as *wasn't* and *it'll.* Facilitate a discussion, using these words to build conversational fluency.

Advanced After reading *Jem Wasn't Happy,* have partners take turns retelling the first few pages of the story.

OBJECTIVES

- Build background and oral vocabulary.
- Speak to share ideas.

Strategic Intervention

Have children use old magazines to find pictures of team members working together.

Advanced

Have children write a short story about a team working together to reach a goal.

Build Background Point out the running track to children. Explain that in organized track events, the runner who breaks through the finish line tape first is the winner.

Build Background

LET'S TALK ABOUT Working Together

GENERATE DISCUSSION Read the title and ask questions to generate language. Encourage children to respond in complete sentences.

- What games or activities are these children playing?
- How are they working together?

BUILD ORAL VOCABULARY Lead the class in a discussion that focuses on concepts and today's Amazing Words, *contribute, compete, recreation.*

Look at the soccer players. The two teams compete against each other. Soccer is a fun type of recreation. Each player contributes to the team in an effort to score a goal. How are the children in the other pictures competing? Look at the boy baseball player. His name is Ronald. This week we will read about how Ronald contributes to his baseball team.

VOCABULARY

CONCEPT CHART Remind children of the question of the week.

- What makes a team?

  Display Graphic Organizer 15. Label the center circle "What makes a team?" Using the pictures on the student page as a starting point, help children identify what makes a team. Encourage children to think of times they have been on a team and the things that made that fun for them. Display the chart for use throughout the week.

- Do team members work for their own goals or for the team's goals? (team's goals)

- What might the swim team in the picture want to accomplish? (winning the swim event, having fun, getting exercise)

Build Background

Let's Talk About
Working Together

190

191

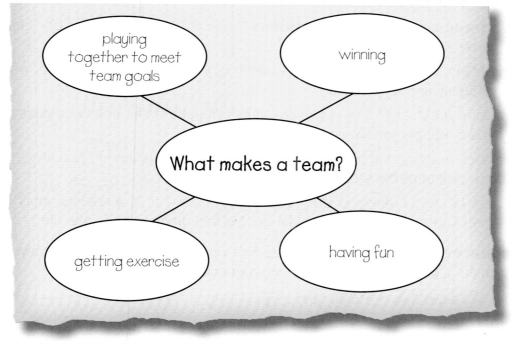

▲ **Graphic Organizer 15**

playing together to meet team goals

winning

What makes a team?

getting exercise

having fun

Take It to the NET™
ONLINE

For a Web site that tells more about baseball and other sports that kids play, do an Internet search using the keywords *kid sports.*

ELL

Access Content To prepare children for reading *Ronald Morgan Goes to Bat,* send home the story summary in English and/or the home language. See the ELL Teaching Guide, pp. 47–49.

Ronald Morgan **190–191**

◎ Distinguish realism and fantasy.

Skills Trace
◎ **Realism and Fantasy**

Introduce/Teach	TE: 2.1 129a–b, 130e; 2.2 191a–b, 192e; 2.5 264r, 264–265
Practice	PB: 2.1 27, 44–45, 64–65, 77, 87; 2.2 94–96
Reteach/Review	TE: 2.1 134–135, DI·68; 2.2 240–241, 266–267, DI·65; 2.5 DI·68
Assess/Test	TE: 2.1 17–20; 2.2 25–28; 2.5 97–100; Benchmark Test, Unit 2

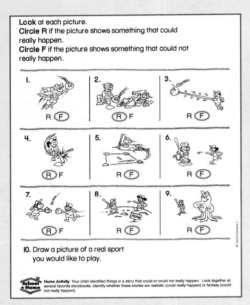

Look at each picture.
Circle R if the picture shows something that could really happen.
Circle F if the picture shows something that could not really happen.

10. Draw a picture of a real sport you would like to play.

 **Home Activity** Your child identified things in a story that could or could not really happen. Look together at several favorite storybooks. Identify whether these stories are realistic (could really happen) or fantasy (could not really happen).

▲ **Practice Book 2.1** p.64, Realism and Fantasy

ELL

Access Content For a Picture It! lesson on realism and fantasy, see the ELL Teaching Guide, pp. 43–44.

Listening Comprehension

◎ TEACH/MODEL Realism and Fantasy

DEFINE REALISM AND FANTASY
- A realistic story tells about something that could happen in real life.
- A fantasy is a make-believe story. It could not happen in real life.
- Good readers look for clues that tell them if a story is realism or fantasy.

READ ALOUD Read aloud "The Elephant Team" and model how to distinguish between realism and fantasy.

 MODEL The elephants in this story talk to one another. That is a clue that tells me that this story is a fantasy because elephants can't talk to one another in real life.

PRACTICE

CLUES TO REALISM AND FANTASY Ask children what other clues tell that this story is make-believe. (An elephant doesn't watch television. An elephant can't throw, catch, or hold a bat with its trunk.)

DISTINGUISH REALISM AND FANTASY Have children recall the story *Tara and Tiree, Fearless Friends*.
- Do Tara and Tiree act like dogs might in real life? How? (Yes, they love to run and play and take walks.)
- Does Jim act like a real person? How? (Yes, he trains dogs and goes for walks like a real person would.)
- Does anything happen in this story that couldn't happen in real life? (No, all the events of the story could really happen.)
- Is this story a realistic story or a fantasy? Why? (It is a realistic story because the people and animals act like people and animals do in real life.)

CONNECT TO READING Tell children that when they read any story, they should think about whether the story could or could not really happen.

The Elephant Team

Elmer Elephant loved baseball. He watched the players play every night on television. Watching baseball on TV was great recreation. But what Elmer really wanted to do was play baseball himself. He wanted to compete. He wanted to play in a big game!

Elmer looked for his friends. Certainly they could get a team of their own to play the game! He saw Freddie and asked him to play. Freddie said, "How can I contribute? I don't know how to play!"

Elmer showed Freddie how to hold the bat with his trunk. He pitched a few balls, and soon Elmer was hitting them well!

Elmer told Freddie, "It takes nine players to make a baseball team. Now we need to find seven more players."

Elmer and Freddie saw Elinor. They gave her a glove and taught her how to catch the ball. Then the three elephants went in search of other players. Before long, they had a field full of elephants. Elmer counted them. He saw eight players! They were hitting balls. They were catching. They were pitching.

Elmer said, "We still need nine players! I only count eight!"

Freddie said, "Don't forget to count yourself!"

Freddie was right. They had a team!

Then Elinor asked, "Who will play us? Don't we need a team to compete against?"

Elmer thought a minute and said, "That's a good point. But first things first. Today, we formed our team. Tomorrow, we will find a team to play against!"

Ronald Morgan

Shared Writing

WRITE List

OBJECTIVE
● Write list.

DAILY FIX-IT

1. we want to play baseball
   We want to play baseball.

2. its a fun game.
   It's a fun game.

This week's practice sentences appear on Daily Fix-It Transparency 7.

Strategic Intervention

Children who are not able to write independently may copy the sentences about what one of the animals can and cannot do and add an illustration.

Advanced

Have children write a list of the most athletic animals, including the animal's athletic traits.

Support Writing Let beginning English speakers look at pictures in nonfiction books about animals so they will better understand how a certain type of animal could or could not contribute as a baseball player.

GENERATE IDEAS Ask children what makes a good baseball player (ability to run, hit, catch, throw). Tell them to imagine that they are choosing animals to play on a baseball team. Which animals would they choose? Why?

WRITE A LIST Explain that the class will make a list of animals and decide whether or not the animals have any of the skills needed to play on a fantasy baseball team.

COMPREHENSION SKILL Have children think about a fantasy team—a team that could never happen.

- Display Writing Transparency 7 and read the title and the headings of the two columns.
- Ask children to read the item listed under number 1.
- Ask children to complete the list using other animals and their abilities and shortcomings.

HANDWRITING While writing, model the letter forms as shown on pp. TR18–TR21.

READ THE LIST Have children read the completed list aloud as you track the print.

A Fantasy Team

Animal	What It Can and Cannot Do
1. octopus	It can catch, throw, and hit.
Possible answers:	It cannot run.
2. horse	It can run.
	It cannot catch, throw, or hit.
3. monkey	It can run and hit.
	It cannot catch or throw.
4. fish	It cannot run or hit.
	It cannot catch or throw.
5. dog	It can catch and run.
	It cannot hit or throw.

Unit 2 Ronald Morgan Goes to Bat   Writing Model 7

▲ Writing Transparency 7

INDEPENDENT WRITING

WRITE LIST Have children write their own list about animal teammates playing a game other than baseball. Encourage them to use words from the Word Wall and the Amazing Words board. Let children illustrate their writing. You may have children volunteer to read their lists to the class.

Grammar

TEACH/MODEL Proper Nouns

REVIEW NOUNS Remind children that a noun is a word that names a person, place, animal, or thing.

IDENTIFY PROPER NOUNS Display Grammar Transparency 7. Read the definition aloud.

● *Alicia Ortiz* is a girl's first and last name. *July* is the name of a month. Special names for people, places, animals, and things are called proper nouns.

● Proper nouns begin with capital letters. *Alicia* and *Ortiz* are proper nouns, so each name begins with a capital letter. *July* is a proper noun, so it begins with a capital letter.

Continue modeling with items 2–5.

PRACTICE

SUGGEST NAMES Have children name other proper nouns. Write the names.

● Name a person or animal we have read about.

● What is the name of our town?

● Think of a name of a pet.

Proper Nouns

Proper nouns are special names for people, places, animals, and things. They begin with capital letters. **Days of the week,** months **of the year,** and **holidays** also begin with capital letters. **Titles** for people begin with capital letters. Many titles end with a **period (.)**.

 Mr. Morgan threw the ball. **Ronald** swung at it.

He got his first hit on **Tuesday, May** 10.

Underline the proper nouns. **Write** each proper noun correctly on the line.

1. alicia ortiz broke her arm in the game on july 1.
   Alicia Ortiz, July

2. dr. lee told her no more baseball until labor day.
   Dr. Lee, Labor Day

3. On friday alicia was back at pioneer park.
   Friday, Alicia, Pioneer Park

4. Her team, the patton panthers, was playing the terry tigers.
   Patton Panthers, Terry Tigers

5. "Go, roberto! Come on, cindy!" shouted alicia.
   Roberto, Cindy, Alicia

Unit 2 Ronald Morgan Goes to Bat   Grammar **7**

▲ **Grammar Transparency 7**

Wrap Up Your Day!

 CONTRACTIONS Write *wasn't* and ask children what the apostrophe takes the place of. (o) Repeat with *it's, I'm,* and *we'll.*

 SPELLING CONTRACTIONS Have children spell the contractions *hasn't, who's, I'll,* and *I'm.* Ask them to identify the missing letter or letters in each word.

 REALISM AND FANTASY To help children distinguish between realism and fantasy, ask: Could the story "The Elephant Team" have really happened? Why not?

LET'S TALK ABOUT IT Recall that Elmer really wanted to have a team so he could play baseball. What did Elmer focus on when he was building his team? (finding the right number of players, showing the players how to play)

 HOMEWORK Send home this week's Family Times newsletter.

PREVIEW Day 2

Tell children that tomorrow the class will read about a boy who loves baseball.

Day 2
AT A GLANCE

Share Literature
From Me to You

Phonics and Spelling
Contractions
Spelling: Words with Contractions

Comprehension
Skill Realism and Fantasy
Strategy Prior Knowledge

Build Background
Team Spirit

High-Frequency Words
laugh   great   you're   Word Wall
either   certainly   second   worst

Vocabulary
Selection Words
terrific   spirit   clutched

Read
Group Time < Differentiated Instruction

Ronald Morgan Goes to Bat

Interactive Writing
Outline

Grammar
Proper Nouns

Materials
- *Sing with Me Big Book*
- Big Book *From Me to You*
- Student Edition 192–211
- Phonics Songs and Rhymes Chart 7
- Background Building Audio CD
- Graphic Organizer 15
- Tested Word Cards
- Vocabulary Transparency 7

Morning Warm~Up!
Today we will read about
Ronald Morgan and his baseball team.
Ronald isn't a very good player, but he's
still an important part of the team.
What are some ways that
individuals can help a team?

QUESTION OF THE DAY Encourage children to sing "Teamwork" from the *Sing with Me Big Book* as you gather. Write and read the message and discuss the question.

REVIEW CONTRACTIONS

- Read the second sentence of the message.
- Have children raise their hands when they hear a contraction. *(isn't, he's)*

Build Background Use the Day 2 instruction on ELL Poster 7 to preview high-frequency words.

ELL Poster 7

Share Literature

BUILD CONCEPTS

FICTION Have children read the title. Identify the author. Review that books about make-believe characters and events are fiction. Fiction books often have illustrations as this book does.

BUILD ORAL VOCABULARY Ask children what they know about friendship and letting friends know how they feel about them. Point out that a friend is a person who is known and liked by another. Explain that friends **deserve** to know how others feel about them. Suggest that as you read, children listen to find out how characters in the story feel when they get a note from a friend.

Big Book

- Why does someone who is a good friend **deserve** to be told how his friends feel about him? (Possible answers: It will probably make him feel good. It will probably make him want to make others feel good.)

- How can you contribute to a friend's happiness? (Possible answers: by spending time with the friend, by telling the friend how much you like him or her)

MONITOR LISTENING COMPREHENSION

- What kind of recreation did Rat get in the story? (He walked a lot.)

- How does Frog's broken leg probably affect her? (Possible response: It keeps her from getting much recreation. It prevents her from competing in races.)

- Do you think Rat felt he **deserved** his letter at first? Explain your answer. (Possible response: Rat thought he had never been a true friend to anyone and didn't **deserve** the letter.)

OBJECTIVES
- Discuss characteristics of fiction.
- Set purpose for listening.
- Build oral vocabulary.

to build oral vocabulary

MONITOR PROGRESS
compete	**If...** children lack oral vocabulary experiences about the concept Working Together, **then...** use the Oral Vocabulary Routine on pp. DI·1–DI·2, DI·4 to develop the Amazing Words.
contribute
recreation
deserve

Build Concepts Being a good friend is a main theme in *From Me to You.* Have children demonstrate their understanding of this concept by showing or telling what good friends do, such as treat each other with kindness, invite friends to do fun things, hug each other, and so on.

OBJECTIVES

- Review contractions.
- Build contractions.
- Preview words before reading them.
- Spell contractions.

Strategic Intervention

Use **Strategic Intervention Decodable Reader 7** for more practice with contractions.

E L L

Support Phonics Invite children to act out what happens in "I'm on the Team" as you replay the Phonics Songs and Rhymes Audio CD.

Contractions

TEACH/MODEL

Fluent Word Reading

ROUTINE

1 **Connect** Write *I'll.* You can read this word because you know how to read contractions. What two words form *I'll?* (*I* and *will*)

2 **Model** When you come to a contraction, you know it is a short way of writing two words. An apostrophe takes the place of letters that were left out. **Model** reading *hadn't, can't, we'll, she's, isn't.*

3 **Group Practice** Write *hasn't, wouldn't, he's, who's, shouldn't, I'm.* Read these words. Look at the word, say the word to yourself, and then read the word aloud. **Allow 2–3 seconds previewing time.**

WORD READING

PHONICS SONGS AND RHYMES CHART 7 Frame each of the following words on Phonics Songs and Rhymes Chart 7. Call on individuals to read them. Guide children in previewing.

don't   it's   we'll   I'm

Sing "I'm on the Team" to the tune of "I've Been Workin' on the Railroad," or play the CD. Have children follow along on the chart as they sing. Then have individuals take turns locating contractions on the chart.

 **Phonics Songs and Rhymes Audio**

I'm on the Team

I'm a member of a great team.
We all love to play.
We don't miss a single practice.
We'll be there every day.

When it's time to play the big game,
No matter how it ends,
We'll keep helping one another.
We'll always be good friends.

Phonics Songs and Rhymes Chart 7

BUILD WORDS

INDIVIDUALS MAKE CONTRACTIONS List the word pairs shown below at the left. Have children name the contraction from the Phonics Songs and Rhymes chart that is made from *we will*. Write *we'll*. Have children complete the activity on paper by writing the contractions made from the word pairs. Ask individuals to read the contractions. Provide feedback as necessary.

we will	we'll
it is	it's
I am	I'm
do not	don't

Spelling

PRACTICE Contractions

WRITE DICTATION SENTENCES Have children write these sentences. Repeat words slowly, allowing children to hear each sound. Children may use the Word Wall to help with spelling high-frequency words. Word Wall

I'll ask Ann if it's her pen.
I'm going to ask who's coming.
I didn't find the ball he's asking for.
That doll wasn't the one she's talking about.

HOMEWORK Spelling Practice Book, p. 26

Spelling Words

Contractions

1. I'll*		7. who's	
2. wasn't		8. she's	
3. it's		9. we'll*	
4. he's		10. isn't	
5. I'm*		11. hasn't	
6. didn't		12. hadn't	

Challenge Words

13. wouldn't   15. where's
14. shouldn't

* **Words from the Selection**

Contractions

Spelling Words

I'll	wasn't	it's	he's	I'm	didn't
who's	she's	we'll	isn't	hasn't	hadn't

Write the contraction that can be made from the underlined words.

1. The turtle <u>has not</u> come up for air.   **hasn't**
2. It <u>is not</u> snowing.   **isn't**
3. Do you know <u>who is</u> riding the bus today?   **who's**
4. I think <u>she is</u> at the nature center.   **she's**
5. Tomorrow <u>we will</u> be at home.   **we'll**
6. The bird <u>was not</u> in the nest.   **wasn't**

Write the contractions for the words below.

7. it is   **it's**   8. did not   **didn't**
9. had not   **hadn't**   10. I will   **I'll**
11. he is   **he's**   12. I am   **I'm**

Home Activity Your child wrote contractions. Have your child name the words that were combined to make each contraction.

▲ **Spelling Practice Book** p. 26

Comprehension

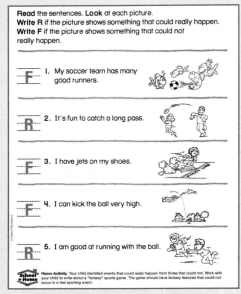

▲ **Practice Book 2.1,** p. 65,
Realism and Fantasy

⦿ SKILL Realism and Fantasy

RECOGNIZE REALISM AND FANTASY Review that a realistic story tells about something that could actually happen, while a fantasy is a make-believe story about something that could not happen in real life. Have children tell whether previously read stories were realism or fantasy.

CONNECT TO READING

- As you read, ask yourself if the things that happen could occur in real life.
- Notice clues from the pictures that tell if the story is realism or fantasy.

⦿ STRATEGY Prior Knowledge

INTRODUCE THE STRATEGY Tell children that prior knowledge is what they already know. Using prior knowledge as they read can help them to figure out the story, as well as help them to guess what might happen next.

MODEL When I read a story, I use information I already know to figure out different parts of the story. I think about what I would do if the events I read about happened to me. For example, if I read about a character hearing his doorbell ring, I would guess that he was going to go and open the door because I know that is what people do in real life.

CONNECT TO READING Encourage children to ask themselves these questions as they read *Ronald Morgan Goes to Bat.*

- How does this remind me of something I know?
- How does this remind me of something I've read?

Build Background

DISCUSS TEAM SPIRIT Display a picture showing team spirit or support for fellow team members. Initiate discussion by asking children what they know about team spirit.

- Have you ever shown team spirit? Explain when and how.
- What are some ways people can show team spirit?
- How does it feel to be part of a team with team spirit?

BACKGROUND BUILDING AUDIO Have children listen to the CD and share the new information they learned about team spirit.

**Sing with Me/
Background Building Audio**

COMPLETE A WEB Draw a web or display Graphic Organizer 15. Write *Team Spirit* in the center. Ask children to suggest different ways team spirit can be shown.

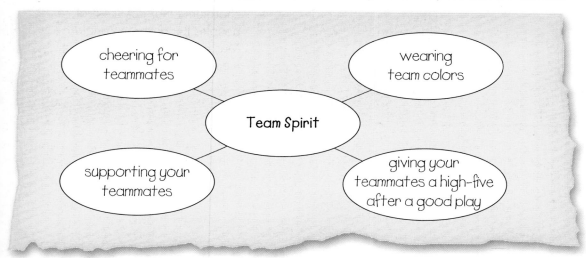

▲ **Graphic Organizer 15**

CONNECT TO SELECTION Connect background information to *Ronald Morgan Goes to Bat.*

Each person on a team offers something special. Some people are very strong. Some people are very smart. Some people are very spirited. Ronald Morgan is a character in the story we are about to read. We'll find out what Ronald offers his team.

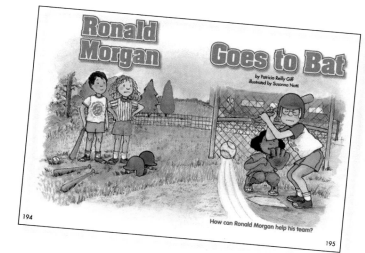

E L L

Activate Prior Knowledge Ask children to share home-language words related to team spirit.

Words to Read

you're
second
great
either
laugh
certainly
worst

192

Read the Words

You're invited to our second ball game of the year!

Come out and have a great time.

You will either laugh or cry, but you certainly will have fun.

We may have been the worst team last year, but this year will be our best ever!

Genre: Realistic Fiction
Realistic fiction has made-up characters that act like real people. Read about Ronald Morgan, who is an important member of his baseball team.

193

Pick a word from the box to match each clue.
Write the word on the line.

> certainly clutched either great laugh
> second spirit terrific worst you're

1. huge and important
great

2. after first
second

3. you are
you're

4. chuckle loudly
laugh

5. most bad
worst

6. one or the other
either

7. surely
certainly

8. grabbed tightly
clutched

9. wonderful
terrific

10. state of mind
spirit

Home Activity Your child used high-frequency and selection words to match clues. Write sentences using one of the words from the box, but leave a blank for the word. Have your child use one of the words to complete the sentence.

▲ **Practice Book 2.1** p. 66, High-Frequency Words and Selection Words

High-Frequency Words

Nondecodable Words

ROUTINE

1 **Say and Spell** Point to the first word. This word is *laugh*, *l-a-u-g-h*, *laugh*. What is this word? What are the letters in this word?

2 **Identify Familiar Letter-Sounds** Point to the first letter in *laugh*. What is this letter? What is the sound for this letter? (/l/)

3 **Demonstrate Meaning** Tell me a sentence using this word. Repeat the routine with the other Words to Read. Have children identify these familiar letter-sounds and word parts: *great* (gr/gr/, t/t/), *you're* (What letter does the apostrophe take the place of? (*a*)) *either* (blend the syllables: *ei-ther*), *certainly* (blend the syllables: *cer-tain-ly*), *second* (blend the syllables: *sec-ond*), *worst* (w/w/, st/st/).

Have children read aloud the sentences on p. 193 and point to the Words to Read. Add the words to the Word Wall. **Word Wall**

Use Vocabulary Transparency 7 to review this week's words.

- Point to a word. Say and spell it.
- Have children say and spell the word.
- Ask children to identify familiar letter-sounds.

Monitor Progress | Check High-Frequency Words

Point to the following words on the Word Wall and have individuals read them.

laugh	great	you're	either	certainly
second	worst	mother	father	eyes
opened	before	every	great	

If... children cannot read these words,

then... have them find each word on the Word Wall, chant its meaning, and then write it before reading the selection. Monitor their fluency with these words during reading, and provide additional practice opportunities before the Day 5 Assessment.

SUCCESS PREDICTOR

Day 1 Check Word Reading

▶**Day 2 Check High-Frequency Words**

Day 3 Check Retelling

Day 4 Check Fluency

Day 5 Assess Progress

SUCCESS PREDICTOR

A Great Catch

1. My school played baseball against a terrific team.

2. My friend clutched his mitt and jumped to catch the ball.

3. We cheered for him with a lot of spirit!

Words to Read			
certainly	either	great	laugh
second	worst	you're	

Unit 2 Ronald Morgan Goes to Bat   Vocabulary **7**

▲ **Vocabulary Transparency 7**

Vocabulary

SELECTION WORDS

Use Vocabulary Transparency 7 to introduce the selection words.

- Read each sentence as you track the print.
- Frame each underlined word. Explain the word's meaning.

  clutched held tightly
  terrific very good
  spirit energy

- Ask children to identify familiar letter-sounds and word parts: *terrific* (blend the syllables: *ter, rif, ic*), *spirit* (blend the syllables: *spir, it*), *clutched* (point out the base word and the ending: *clutch, ed*)

- Have children read each sentence aloud with you.

- To encourage discussion using the selection words, ask children to use the word in a personal context. Tell me about something you might *clutch*. Use *clutch* when you tell about it. Name a time when you felt a lot of *spirit*. What makes you feel *terrific*?

Group Time

DAY 2

On-Level

Read *Ronald Morgan Goes to Bat.*

- Use pp. 194–211.

Strategic Intervention

Read SI Decodable Reader 7.

- Read or listen to *Ronald Morgan Goes to Bat.*
- Use the **Routine** on p. DI·26.

Advanced

Read *Ronald Morgan Goes to Bat.*

- Use the **Routine** on p. DI·27.

ELL Place English language learners in the groups that correspond to their reading abilities in English.

(i) Independent Activities

Independent Reading See p. 190j for Reading/Library activities and suggestions.

Journal Writing Write about a time you were part of a team. Share writing.

Literacy Centers To provide experiences with *Ronald Morgan Goes to Bat,* you may use the Listening Center on p. 190j.

Practice Book 2.1 Realism and Fantasy, p. 65; High-Frequency Words, p. 66; Sequence, p. 67

ELL

Access Content Use the vocabulary strategies and word cards in the ELL Teaching Guide, pp. 45–46.

Break into small groups after Vocabulary and before Writing.

Ronald Morgan

Goes to Bat

by Patricia Reilly Giff
illustrated by Susanna Natti

How can Ronald Morgan help his team?

194

195

Read

Prereading Strategies

PREVIEW AND PREDICT Have children read the title of the story. Identify Ronald as the batter in the picture. Identify the author and illustrator. Do a picture walk of pp. 194–199. Ask children what they think this story will be about.

DISCUSS REALISTIC FICTION Reread the definition of realistic fiction on p. 193 of the Student Edition. Explain that realistic fiction is a made-up story about things that could really happen. Ask if Ronald is a real boy. Make sure children understand that Ronald is a made-up character who does things a real boy can do.

SET PURPOSE Read the question on p. 195. Ask children what they would like to find out as they read this story.

AudioText

Access Content Before reading, review the story summary in English and/or the home language. See the ELL Teaching Guide, pp. 47–49.

Baseball started today. Mr. Spano said everyone could play.

"Even me?" I asked.

And Tom said, "You're letting Ronald Morgan play? He can't hit, he can't catch. He can't do anything."

Mr. Spano looked at me.

"Everyone," he said.

196

"Yahoo!" I yelled. I pulled on my red and white shirt, the one that says GO TEAM GO, and ran outside to the field.

"Two things," Mr. Spano told us. "Try hard, and keep your eye on the ball."

Then it was time to practice. Michael was up first. He smacked the ball with the bat. The ball flew across the field.

"Good," said Mr. Spano.

"Great, Slugger!" I yelled. "We'll win every game."

197

▲ **Pages 196–197**
Have children look at the pictures and read to find out if the story is realistic or a fantasy.

EXTEND SKILLS

Idioms

For instruction in idioms, discuss the following:

• An idiom is a saying that can't be understood just by understanding the meaning of the words in the saying.

• Mr. Spano tells the team, "Keep your eye on the ball." He doesn't mean for them to really put their eyes on the ball. He means they need to watch carefully for where the ball is.

Assess Give children an example of another idiom in context, such as "Mary tried to get her mom to buy her the toy, but she struck out." Have children explain what the idiom means.

Skills in Context

REALISM AND FANTASY

• **Are these realistic characters? Why or why not?**
They are realistic because they do things that real people do. They play baseball on a team, and they have a coach who encourages them.

Monitor Progress	**Realism and Fantasy**
If... children are unable to identify whether the characters are realistic,	**then...** model how to use the text and pictures to identify realistic events.

 Think Aloud

MODEL I read that the kids are playing baseball, which could really happen. Ronald is not a very good player, but he helps the team because he has spirit. This could really happen too. So I think the characters are realistic.

ASSESS Have children find more clues that tell them the story is realistic. (Possible clues: The coach says that everyone can play. He's fair like a real coach. The people in the picture are dressed like kids in real life might dress.)

____ Contractions   high-frequency/tested vocabulary

It was my turn next. I put on the helmet and stood at home plate.

"Ronald Morgan," said Rosemary. "You're holding the wrong end of the bat."

Quickly I turned it around. I clutched it close to the end.

198

Whoosh went the first ball.
Whoosh went the second one.
Wham went the third. It hit me in the knee.

"Are you all right?" asked Michael.

But I heard Tom say, "I knew it. Ronald Morgan's the worst."

199

Guiding Comprehension

Draw Conclusions • Inferential
- **What do the kids think of Ronald?**
They think he is a terrible player.

Predict • Inferential
- **Do you think Ronald will find a way to help the team? Why or why not?**
Possible response: Ronald will find a way to help the team because the story is about him playing baseball.

Realism and Fantasy • Critical
- **Some of the players try to help Ronald, and some are upset with him. Is this realistic? Explain.**
Possible response: Yes, this is realistic. Some people just want to play for fun, so they might want to help him. Some people want to win, so they get angry.

▲ **Pages 198–199**
Ask children to read in order to find out what the other kids think about Ronald.

Monitor Progress

High-Frequency Words

| If... children have a problem reading a new high-frequency word, | then... use the High-Frequency Routine on p. 193a to reteach the problematic word. |

Baseball Bats

Many wooden baseball bats are made from ash trees. This wood is very straight and strong. Some players spread a sticky liquid on their bat handles to help them hold the bats more tightly.

Ronald Morgan **198–199**

At snack time, we told Miss Tyler about the team.

"I <u>don't</u> hit very well," I said.

And Rosemary said, "The ball hits him instead."

Everybody laughed, even me. I shook my head. "I hope it <u>doesn't</u> happen again."

Miss Tyler gave me some raisins. "You have to hit the ball before it hits you," she said.

200

We played every day. I tried hard, but the ball came fast. I closed my eyes and swung.

"If only he could hit the ball once," Rosemary said.

And Billy shook his head.

I <u>couldn't</u> tell them I was afraid of the ball. "Go, team, go," I whispered.

201

▲ **Pages 200–201**
Have children read to find out how Ronald does when he goes to bat.

Monitor Progress

Decoding

If... children come to a word they don't know,	**then...** remind them to:
	1. Blend the word.
	2. Decide if the word makes sense.
	3. Look in a dictionary for more help.

Strategies in Context

🔄 PRIOR KNOWLEDGE

- **How do you think Ronald will do when he goes to bat?**
  Ronald will try hard because he has team spirit, but he'll probably miss the ball because he's not good at baseball.

Monitor Progress	**Prior Knowledge**
If... children have difficulty predicting how Ronald will do,	**then...** model how to use what they already know to make a prediction.

 Think Aloud **MODEL** To figure out how Ronald will do when he goes to bat, I think back to what I already know about Ronald. I know he cares about his team, so I guess he will try hard. However, I also know he isn't good at baseball, so I think he will probably miss the ball.

ASSESS Have children predict how Ronald could get better at baseball. (Possible response: The story says that Ronald is afraid of the ball. He should learn not to be afraid. I also know from the words and the pictures that he closes his eyes when he's at bat. He should keep them open.)

_____ Contractions ▨ high-frequency/tested vocabulary

One day, the team sat on the grass. We watched the third grade play. They were big, they were strong, they were good. Johnny hit a home run, and Joy tagged a man out.

202

"We'll never hit like that," said Tom. And Rosemary said, "We'll never catch like that either."

But I said, "Our team is the best."

Mr. Spano nodded. "That's the spirit, Ronald."

203

Guiding Comprehension

Character • Literal

- **What does Mr. Spano tell Ronald?**
  He tells him he has good spirit.

Summarize • Inferential

- **What has happened in the story so far?**
  Ronald starts playing baseball, even though he's not very good. He cheers for his teammates. He tries hard, even though he is scared of the ball.

Main Idea • Inferential

- **What is the main idea so far?**
  Possible response: Ronald always believes in his team.

▲ **Pages 202–203**
Have children read to find out what Mr. Spano says to Ronald.

Strategy Self-Check

Have children ask themselves these questions to check their reading.

Decoding Words

- Do I use what I know about word parts to read a new word?
- Does the new word make sense in the story?

Prior Knowledge

- Does this remind me of something I know?
- Does this remind me of something I read?

Mr. Spano told us, "Now we'll run the bases. Rosemary, you can go first."

Rosemary went fast. She raced for first base.

"Terrific, Speedy!" I yelled.

204

"Let me go next," I said. "I can do that, too."

But the field was muddy. My sneaker came off.

Jimmy said, "That kid's running bases the wrong way."

And Tom yelled, "Ronald Morgan. You're heading for third base."

205

▲ **Pages 204–205**
Have children read to find out what happens after Ronald starts running the bases.

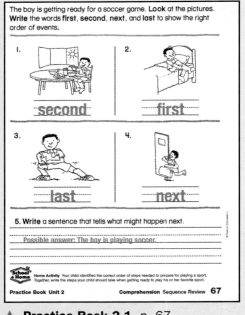

The boy is getting ready for a soccer game. **Look** at the pictures. **Write** the words **first, second, next,** and **last** to show the right order of events.

1. second
2. first
3. last
4. next

5. Write a sentence that tells what might happen next.

Possible answer: The boy is playing soccer.

 Home Activity Your child identified the correct order of steps needed to prepare for playing a sport. Together, write the steps your child should take when getting ready to play his or her favorite sport.

Practice Book Unit 2　　**Comprehension Sequence Review 67**

▲ **Practice Book 2.1** p. 67,
Sequence

Skills in Context

(REVIEW) **SEQUENCE**

• **What happens after Ronald starts running the bases?**
Ronald's shoe comes off, and he runs the wrong way.

Monitor Progress	Sequence
If... children have difficulty answering the question,	**then...** model how to determine the sequence of events.

Think Aloud **MODEL** To understand what I read, I keep track of the order in which things happen. I read that Ronald asks to run the bases. Then I read that his sneaker comes off in the mud and he runs the wrong way. That's what happens after he starts running.

ASSESS Have children tell what happens after Rosemary raced for first base. (Ronald yells, "Terrific, Speedy!")

The next day, we worked on catching. I was out in left field. While I waited, I found a stick, and started to scratch out the mud. I wrote G for go. I wrote G for great. Our team is the best, I thought. Then I wrote H for hit. H for home run. If only I could do that.

206

Just then I heard yelling. Someone had hit the ball.

"Catch it, Ronald!" Tom shouted.

I put down the stick. I put up my mitt. Too late. The ball sailed into the trees.

Mr. Spano took us for ice cream. "You deserve it for trying," he said. "Our team is really good."

I had a chocolate cone.

207

Guiding Comprehension

Character • Inferential

- **How does Ronald feel about his team?**
  He thinks his team is the best and wishes he could help them win.

Character • Inferential

- **What kind of person is Mr. Spano? Explain.**
  Mr. Spano is kind and supportive. He says the team deserves ice cream for trying.

Author's Purpose • Inferential

- *Question the Author* **How does the author show that Tom is excited and speaking loudly?**
  The author uses an exclamation point.

▲ **Pages 206–207**
Have children read to find out how Ronald feels about his team.

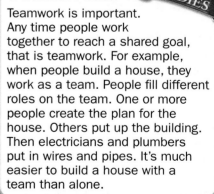

Teamwork

Time for SOCIAL STUDIES

Teamwork is important. Any time people work together to reach a shared goal, that is teamwork. For example, when people build a house, they work as a team. People fill different roles on the team. One or more people create the plan for the house. Others put up the building. Then electricians and plumbers put in wires and pipes. It's much easier to build a house with a team than alone.

Ronald Morgan **206–207**

2

Michael's a slugger, I thought. And Rosemary can really run. But I'm still afraid of the ball.

On the way home, we saw some kids playing ball.

"Want to hit a few?" Michael asked.

I shook my head. "Maybe I won't play ball anymore."

Michael said, "We need you. You have spirit. You help the team feel good."

"But how can we win?" I asked. "I can't even hit the ball."

208

I saw my father and ran to catch up.

"See you, Michael," I said.

My father asked, "How's the champ?"

"I'm the worst," I said.

"I was the worst, too," said my father. "But then. . . ."

"What?"

My father laughed. "I stopped closing my eyes when I swung."

"Maybe that's what I do."

209

▲ **Pages 208–209**
Have children read to find out what Ronald and the other characters do next.

EXTEND SKILLS

Type Formats

For instruction in type formats, discuss the following:

• The author uses different kinds of type in the story. Sometimes she uses italics, and sometimes she uses all capital letters.

• Find the word *crack* on p. 210. The word is italicized to show us that it is a sound.

Assess Have children find other examples of words in this story that are italicized or written in all caps. Have them explain why the author used the different type formats.

Guiding Comprehension

Paraphrase • Inferential

• **In your own words, describe what happens on these pages.**
Ronald feels badly because he can't hit the balls. His father tells him he learned to stop closing his eyes when he swung. Ronald wonders if he has the same problem.

Compare and Contrast • Inferential

• **How is Ronald like his father?**
His father was a bad baseball player too.

Classify • Critical Analysis

• *Text to Text* **What are other stories you know about people, animals, or things who keep trying?**
Possible response: In *The Little Engine that Could* and *Mike Mulligan and His Steam Shovel*, the characters have problems, but they work until they succeed.

"How about a little practice?" he asked.

We went into the yard. My father threw me some balls.

I missed the first one. . . . I missed the second. And then. . . . I opened my eyes and swung. *Crack* went the ball.

"Ouch!" went my father. "You hit me in the knee."

"Home run!" yelled my mother.

"Sorry," I said. "Hey, I did it!"

My father rubbed his knee. "You certainly did," he said.

I ran to pick up the ball. "See you later," I said.

My father smiled. "Where are you going?"

I grabbed the bat. "Some kids are playing ball. I think I'll hit a few."

I looked back. "And you know what else? I guess I'll stay on the team. I have spirit . . . and sometimes I can hit the ball. Mike was right. I think they need me."

210

211

Guiding Comprehension

Cause and Effect • Inferential

- **What effect does hitting the ball have on Ronald?**
  It makes him feel confident.

Draw Conclusions • Inferential

- **How does Ronald probably feel at the end of the story?**
  Ronald feels proud about his team spirit and hopeful that he can sometimes hit the ball.

Make Judgments • Critical

- *Text to World* **What are some other ways people can make a team strong?**
  Possible response: A good leader is helpful. It's important to have people who are willing and able to follow the leader's directions. It's also good to have team members who are cheerful even when things look bad.

▲ **Pages 210–211**
Have children read to find out what happens when Ronald practices with his dad.

Reread For Fluency ROUTINE

1 **Reader 1 Begins** Children read the entire book, switching readers at the end of each page.

2 **Reader 2 Begins** Have partners reread; now the other partner begins.

3 **Reread** For optimal fluency, children should reread three or four times.

4 **Provide Feedback** Listen to children read and provide corrective feedback regarding their oral reading and their use of blending.

Ronald Morgan **210–211**

Interactive Writing

WRITE Outline

DISCUSS Use the story *Ronald Morgan Goes to Bat* to encourage a discussion about what makes a team. Picture walk through the book and ask children to identify when Ronald looks happy and when he looks unhappy.

SHARE THE PEN Have children write an outline about what is needed to make a team. Remind children that an outline is a type of list with main headings and subheadings. To begin, have a child name one important element that is needed to make a team. (for example, *people who try hard*) Have the class repeat it. Write the example, inviting individuals to write familiar letter-sounds, word parts, and high-frequency words. Ask questions such as:

• What is the first sound you hear in the word *hard?* (/h/)
• What letter stands for that sound? *(h)* Have a volunteer write *h.*
• What is the second sound you hear in the word *hard?* (/är/)
• What letters stands for that sound? *(ar)* Have a volunteer write *ar.*

Continue to have individuals make contributions. Frequently reread what has been written while tracking the print.

READ THE OUTLINE Read the completed outline aloud, having children echo you.

Outline

   I. What a team needs

      A. The right number of players

      B. People who try hard

      C. People who can play well

INDEPENDENT WRITING

WRITE OUTLINE Have children write their own outline about what makes a team. Let children illustrate their writing.

Strategic Intervention

Children who are not able to write independently may copy one of the examples from the outline about what makes a team and add an illustration.

Advanced

Have children who are able to write complete sentences independently write their own sentence outline about building a strong team without mentioning anything about athletic skills.

Support Writing Before children begin writing, remind them that Ronald Morgan was not a very skilled player, but he was still an important part of the team. Explain that each person on a team adds something special to the team.

Beginning Provide children with a word bank that they can use while writing their outline.

Intermediate Help children create a word list to use in their writing assignment.

Advanced Encourage children to write and read aloud their outlines.

Support Grammar Ask children to write someone's name in their home languages. Use examples to show that in English and many other languages, people's names begin with capital letters. See the Grammar Transition lessons in the ELL and Transition Handbook.

Grammar

DEVELOP THE CONCEPT Proper Nouns

IDENTIFY PROPER NOUNS Write *month* and *July* on the board. Point to each word as you read it. Ask children to identify the proper noun. *(July)* Continue with *holiday* and *Thanksgiving*.

Special names for people, places, animals, and things are called proper nouns. How do proper nouns begin? (with capital letters)

PRACTICE

IDENTIFY HOLIDAYS WITH PROPER NOUNS Gather several pictures of holidays. Display a picture. Model giving the noun a special name.

Think Aloud

MODEL This is a holiday. Write *holiday.* People are eating turkey, and I see fall colors. This must be Thanksgiving. Thanksgiving is a proper noun, so it begins with a capital letter. Write *Thanksgiving.*

Have children suggest proper nouns (special names) for the other pictures and identify the first letter in each name. Write the names children provide.

DAILY FIX-IT

3. Whos going to play.
   Who's going to play?

4. When will we stat.
   When will we start?

Proper Nouns

Proper nouns are special names for people, places, animals, and things. They begin with capital letters. **Days of the week, months of the year,** and **holidays** also begin with capital letters. **Titles** for people begin with capital letters. Many titles end with a **period (.).**

Ronald Morgan plays baseball. **Mr. Spano** is the coach. The first game is at **Hull School** on **Saturday, April 28.**

Write the proper nouns in each sentence on the line.

1. Mrs. Spano gives snacks to the Carver Cougars.
   <u>Mrs. Spano, Carver Cougars</u>
2. Michael plays baseball every Tuesday and Friday.
   <u>Michael, Tuesday, Friday</u>
3. Miss Tyler lives in Tomah, New Mexico.
   <u>Miss Tyler, Tomah, New Mexico</u>
4. The next game is on Memorial Day.
   <u>Memorial Day</u>

Home Activity Your child learned about proper nouns. Go through a piece of mail with your child and have him or her point out all the proper nouns in the addresses.

▲ **Grammar and Writing Practice Book** p. 25

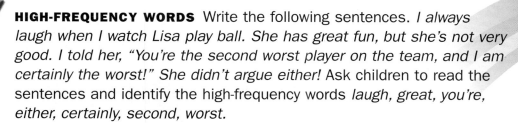

Wrap Up Your Day!

 HIGH-FREQUENCY WORDS Write the following sentences. *I always laugh when I watch Lisa play ball. She has great fun, but she's not very good. I told her, "You're the second worst player on the team, and I am certainly the worst!" She didn't argue either!* Ask children to read the sentences and identify the high-frequency words *laugh, great, you're, either, certainly, second, worst.*

PRIOR KNOWLEDGE Point to the sentences and ask children to use prior knowledge to predict what Lisa is like as a friend..

LET'S TALK ABOUT IT Recall the Big Book *From Me to You.* Ask: What did Rat do that would make him a good team member? (He worked hard to help his friends and make them feel better.) Display Graphic Organizer 15 from Day 1. Have children check to see that Rat's qualities are included.

PREVIEW Day 3

Tell children that tomorrow they will hear about Rat and his friends.

Day 3

AT A GLANCE

Share Literature
From Me to You

Phonics and Spelling
REVIEW *r*-Controlled *ar, or, ore*
Spelling: Words with Contractions

High-Frequency Words
laugh   great   you're   **Word Wall**
either   certainly   second
worst

Vocabulary
Descriptive Words: Verbs

Fluency
Read with Expression

Independent Writing
Respond to Literature

Grammar
Proper Nouns

Materials

- *Sing with Me Big Book*
- Big Book *From Me to You*
- Student Edition 212–213

Morning Warm~Up!

Today we will read about Rat.
Rat is a make-believe character who
feels lonely until he gets a letter.
Why might a letter make him feel better?

QUESTION OF THE DAY Encourage children to sing "Teamwork" from the *Sing with Me Big Book* as you gather. Write and read the message and discuss the question.

REVIEW MULTIPLE-MEANING WORDS

- Point to the word *letter* in the message. Ask children to explain what *letter* means in the message.

- Review that *letter* can also mean a symbol used in the alphabet.

Build Background Use the Day 3 instruction on ELL Poster 7 to support children's use of English to communicate about lesson concepts.

ELL Poster 7

Share Literature

LISTEN AND RESPOND

REVIEW FICTION Remind children that fiction is a made-up story while nonfiction is about real people and real events. Ask if the story is fiction or nonfiction.

BUILD ORAL VOCABULARY Review that yesterday the class read the book to find out about how friends should treat each other. Ask that children listen today to find out about different feelings.

MONITOR LISTENING COMPREHENSION

- When someone **mopes**, they feel sad and sorry for themselves. Why does Rat **mope** at the beginning of the story? (He is sad and lonely, and he doesn't have anything to do.)

- How does receiving a letter contribute to Rat's feelings of happiness? (He knows that someone cares about him.)

- Do you think Rat will stay at home and **mope** in the future? Explain your answer. (Possible response: No, I don't think Rat will **mope** any more. If he starts feeling sad again, he will go see his friends or find something fun to do. He learns a big lesson about being a good friend in this story.)

Big Book

OBJECTIVES

- Identify features of fiction.
- Set purpose for listening.
- Build oral vocabulary.

Amazing Words
to build oral vocabulary

	MONITOR PROGRESS
compete contribute recreation deserve mope	**If...** children lack oral vocabulary experiences about the concept Working Together, **then...** use the Oral Vocabulary Routine on pp. DI·1–DI·2, DI·4 to develop the Amazing Words.

Listen and Respond Help children describe and demonstrate the actions conveyed by the words *slunk* and *skipped* in *From Me to You*. Ask children how someone who *slunk* and someone who *skipped* would probably be feeling (sad, happy).

3

OBJECTIVES

- Review *r*-controlled vowels.
- Blend, read, and build words with *r*-controlled vowels.
- Recognize high-frequency words.
- Spell words with contractions.

▲ **Practice Book 2.1** p. 68, *r*-Controlled Vowels

Review Phonics

REVIEW *r*-Controlled *ar, or, ore*

READ *r*-CONTROLLED VOWEL WORDS Write *barn, sort,* and *before.* You can read these words because you know that *ar, or,* and *ore* stand for the /är/ and /ôr/ vowel sounds. What sounds do *ar, or,* and *ore* make? (The letters *ar* stand for /är/; the letters *or* and *ore* stand for /ôr/.) What are the words?

BUILD WORDS Have children spell *chore* with letter tiles. Monitor work and provide feedback.

- Change the *ch* in *chore* to *st.* What is the new word?
- Change the *e* in *store* to *k.* What is the new word?
- Change the *st* in *stork* to *f.* What is the new word?
- Change the *k* in *fork* to *m.* What is the new word?
- Change the *o* in *form* to *a.* What is the new word?
- Change the *f* in *farm* to *ch.* What is the new word?

High-Frequency Words

PRACTICE

STORY CLUES Read the following story to children. Have children find the word on the Word Wall that fits each blank in the story. **Word Wall**

Ben loved baseball, but he had never played. He wanted to try out for the team, but he was afraid. "What if I can't hit the ball and they _____ (laugh) at me?" said Ben. "I'm not a _____ (great) player like you, Dad."

Dad let out a big _____. (laugh) "Now wait one _____ (second), Ben," Dad chuckled. "I _____ (certainly) didn't start out that way. At first, I felt like the _____ (worst) player on my team."

Dad explained to Ben how hard he practiced. "Then I got better and better. I didn't want to give up."

Ben thought for a moment. "I don't want to give up _____! (either) Let's practice!"

Spelling

PRACTICE Contractions

GIVE CLUES Have children practice by writing the spelling words that

- rhyme with *stairs (where's)*
- are a rhyming pair *(wouldn't, shouldn't)*
- rhyme with *shoes (who's)*
- tell about only one person or thing *(I'll, it's, he's, I'm, she's)*
- include the word *not (wasn't, didn't, isn't, hasn't, hadn't)*
- tell about more than one person *(we'll)*

HOMEWORK Spelling Practice Book, p. 27

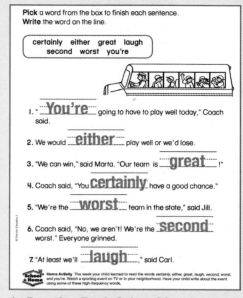

▲ **Practice Book 2.1** p. 69,
High-Frequency Words

Spelling Words

Contractions

1.	I'll*	7.	who's
2.	wasn't	8.	she's
3.	it's	9.	we'll*
4.	he's	10.	isn't
5.	I'm*	11.	hasn't
6.	didn't	12.	hadn't

Challenge Words

13.	wouldn't	15.	where's
14.	shouldn't		

* **Words from the Selection**

▲ **Spelling Practice Book** p. 27

OBJECTIVES

- Discuss descriptive verbs.
- Use descriptive verbs in sentences.

Strategic Intervention

Offer children a verbal alternative to written response. Support students by allowing them to dictate to you.

Advanced

Have children write a story about a sport they like. Tell them they must use at least three descriptive verbs.

Access Content Tell children that *clutched* means *held tightly*. Ask them what else Ronald might clutch.

Vocabulary

DESCRIPTIVE WORDS: VERBS

DISCUSS DESCRIPTIVE WORDS: VERBS Have children recall that Ronald loves baseball, but he is scared of the ball. Explain that verbs are words that tell what is happening. Write the following sentence and have children fill in the blank with different verbs.

Ronald ___ the ball.

EXPAND MEANING Discuss with children that verbs can help the reader to imagine what is happening. Provide an example using the word *clutched*. (Ronald clutched his father's hand.) Have children work with partners to write sentences using the following verbs: *smacked, whispered, raced.* Invite volunteers to share their sentences.

Group Time

On-Level	Strategic Intervention	Advanced
Read *Ronald Morgan Goes to Bat.*	**Read** or listen to *Ronald Morgan Goes to Bat.*	**Read** *Ronald Morgan Goes to Bat.*
• Use pp. 194–213.	• Use the **Routine** on p. DI·28.	• Use the **Routine** on p. DI·29.

DAY 3

 Place English language learners in the groups that correspond to their reading abilities in English.

(i) Independent Activities

Independent Reading See p. 190j for Reading/Library activities and suggestions.

Journal Writing Write a journal entry about a time when you were part of a team. Share writing.

Literacy Centers To provide experiences with *Ronald Morgan Goes to Bat,* you may use the Writing Center on p. 190k.

Practice Book 2.1 *r*-Controlled *ar, or, ore,* p. 68; High-Frequency Words, p. 69

Break into small groups after Vocabulary and before Writing.

Fluency

READ WITH EXPRESSION

MODEL READING DIALOGUE Use *Ronald Morgan Goes to Bat.*

- Point to the quotation marks on p. 196. Quotation marks show that someone is talking. I try to read the part in the quotation marks the way the character would say it.

- Ask children to follow along as you read the page with expression.

- Have children read the page after you. Encourage them to read the way the different characters would speak. Continue in the same way with pp. 197–199.

REREAD FOR FLUENCY

Choral Reading

ROUTINE

1 Select a Passage For *Ronald Morgan Goes to Bat,* use pp. 200–203.

2 Divide into Groups Assign each group a part to read. For this story, assign these parts: a narrator, Rosemary, Michael, Tom, Ronald, Miss Tyler.

3 Model Have children track the print as you read.

4 Read Together Have children read along with you.

5 Independent Readings Have the groups read aloud without you. Monitor progress and provide feedback. For optimal fluency, children should reread three to four times.

Monitor Progress	Fluency
If... children have difficulty reading dialogue,	**then...** prompt: • Are those sentences inside quotation marks? • Who is speaking? • Try to read the sentences the way the characters might say them.
If... the class cannot read fluently without you,	**then...** continue to have them read along with you.

OBJECTIVE

- Read aloud fluently with accuracy and appropriate pace.

Options for Choral Reading

Use *Ronald Morgan Goes to Bat* or one of the following Leveled Readers.

On-Level

Warm and Fuzzy

Strategic Intervention

Let's Play Baseball

Advanced

The First Big Game

ELL

Use *The Soccer Picnic* or *Ronald Morgan Goes to Bat.* Model reading sections of text with correct expression and intonation. Look for sentences that end with exclamation points and have English language learners echo you as you read with expression.

Fluency Coach CD To develop fluent readers, use Fluency Coach.

Think and Share

TALK ABOUT IT Model a response. I would tell Ronald to keep his eyes open and to just keep trying.

1. **RETELL** Have children use the pictures across the bottom to retell the story. See Monitor Progress below.

2. **REALISM AND FANTASY** *Ronald Morgan Goes to Bat* is a realistic story because it is about things that could really happen.

3. **PRIOR KNOWLEDGE** Possible response: I know that some people are good at one thing and not so good at another, just like Ronald. I understand that Ronald could end up helping his team.

LOOK BACK AND WRITE See Independent Writing, TE p. 213a. **Rubric** `4 3 2 1`

Selection Test To assess with *Ronald Morgan Goes to Bat*, use Selection Tests, pp. 25–28.

Monitor Progress — Check Retelling `Rubric 4 3 2 1`

If... children have difficulty retelling the story,

then... use the Scoring Rubric for Retelling below to help them move toward fluent retelling.

SUCCESS PREDICTOR

| **Day 1** Check Word Reading | **Day 2** Check High-Frequency Words | ▶**Day 3 Check Retelling** | **Day 4** Check Fluency | **Day 5** Assess Progress |

Retelling Plan

☑ Week 1 assess Strategic Intervention students.

☑ **This week assess Advanced students.**

☐ Week 3 assess Strategic Intervention students.

☐ Week 4 assess On-Level students.

☐ Week 5 assess any students you have not yet checked during this unit.

Assessment Before retelling, help children name the characters and items shown. For more ideas on assessing comprehension, see the ELL and Transition Handbook.

Scoring Rubric — Narrative Retelling

Rubric `4 3 2 1`	**4**	**3**	**2**	**1**
Connections	Makes connections and generalizes beyond the text	Makes connections to other events, stories, or experiences	Makes a limited connection to another event, story, or experience	Makes no connection to another event, story, or experience
Author's Purpose	Elaborates on author's purpose	Tells author's purpose with some clarity	Makes some connection to author's purpose	Makes no connection to author's purpose
Characters	Describes the main character(s) and any character development	Identifies the main character(s) and gives some information about them	Inaccurately identifies some characters or gives little information about them	Inaccurately identifies the characters or gives no information about them
Setting	Describes the time and location	Identifies the time and location	Omits details of time or location	Is unable to identify time or location
Plot	Describes the events in sequence using rich detail	Tells the plot with some errors in sequence that do not affect meaning	Tells parts of plot with gaps that affect meaning	Retelling has no sense of story

Think and Share

Talk About It What would you say to Ronald Morgan to help him play baseball?

1. Use the pictures below to retell the story. Tell what might come after the last picture. Draw a picture.

2. Is *Ronald Morgan at Bat* a realistic story or a fantasy? How do you know?

3. What do you know about playing sports? How did that help you as you read?

 Look Back and Write Look back at page 209. What did Ronald's father say that was helpful? Why was it helpful? Use information from the selection to support your answer.

Meet the Author

Patricia Reilly Giff

Books are important to Patricia Reilly Giff. She says, "While the rest of the kids were playing hide and seek, I sat under the cherry tree reading." She also says, "I wanted to write—always."

Ms. Giff got married, had three children, and taught school. Then she decided to follow her dream. She began writing. Some books come from her experiences. Others come from stories students told her.

Read more books by Patricia Reilly Giff.

Retelling Strip

212

213

Fresh Reads for Differentiated Test Practice

Fresh Reads, pp. 39–40

On-Level

Read the selection. Then answer the questions that follow.

A Pig Knows

Jimmy lost his yellow ball in the tall grass. He could not find his | 14
ball by himself. First he asked a bird to help him. "Bird, could you | 28
please help me find my ball?" The bird flew over the field and looked | 42
for the ball but could not find it. | 50

Then Jimmy asked a dog to help him. "Dog, could you please help | 63
me find my ball?" The dog ran around the field but saw a squirrel and | 78
forgot all about the ball. | 83

Finally, Jimmy asked a pig to help him. "Pig, could you please help | 96
me find my ball?" | 100

"Sure thing," said the pig. "I will use my nose." | 110

The pig put his nose in the grass and snuffled all over the field. He | 125
worked hard trying to find the ball. "Here's your ball!" the pig cried at | 139
last. | 140

"Thanks!" said Jimmy. | 143

Fresh Reads, pp. 37–38

Strategic Intervention

Read the selection. Then answer the questions that follow.

The Hill and the River

The hill said to the river, "You are very long." | 10
"Thank you," said the river. "You are very tall." | 19
"Thank you," said the hill. | 24
"What do you see?" the hill asked. | 31
"I see grass and the sky," said the river. | 40
"What do you see?" the river asked. | 47
"I see grass and the sky," said the hill. | 56
The hill is tall. The river is long. They both see grass and the sky. | 71

Fresh Reads, pp. 41–42

Advanced

Read the selection. Then answer the questions that follow.

A Helping Hand

"Howdy, neighbor," said the rabbit, as he hopped over to the | 11
birdhouse. "My name is Carl." | 16

"My name is Kevin, and I'm pleased to meet you," said the bird. | 29

"You sure have your hands full with this old birdhouse. No one has | 42
lived in it for many, many years," said Carl. | 51

"Well, I am a woodpecker, so I should have it fixed in no time," | 65
Kevin said as he flew inside. For the next several weeks, Kevin worked | 78
day and night. But each time he fixed something, another thing would | 90
break. | 91

One day there was a knock on Kevin's door. Kevin opened it and | 104
saw ten other rabbits with Carl. "We came to assist, neighbor," Carl | 116
said. They worked for a week. When they were finished, the house was | 129
beautiful. As Kevin thanked them, Carl said, "That is what friends are | 141
for." | 142

Retelling

SUCCESS PREDICTOR

OBJECTIVE

● Write a response.

DAILY FIX-IT

5. I'm made that it is rainning.
   I'm <u>mad</u> that it is <u>raining</u>.

6. I hop it does not last long
   I hop<u>e</u> it does not last long<u>.</u>

Writer's Checkup

✔ Each sentence should have a subject and a predicate. Did I do that?

✔ Proper nouns are special names. Did I use any proper nouns?

✔ Proper nouns start with a capital letter. Did I capitalize my proper nouns?

Independent Writing

Look Back and Write

RESPOND TO LITERATURE Read the writing prompt on p. 212 in the Student Edition and model your thinking. Then have children write their responses.

MODEL I'll look back at p. 209 and read that part of the story again. I'll look for something helpful that Ronald's father says. Then I'll write my response.

Ronald's father says he was the worst player on his team until he stopped closing his eyes when he swung the bat. This was helpful to Ronald because he hadn't realized before that he does the same thing.

Scoring Rubric — Written Response

Rubric 4 3 2 1	4	3	2	1
Focus/Ideas	Clearly focuses on what Ronald's father said and why it was helpful	Focuses on what Ronald's father said and why it was helpful	Attempts to focus on what Ronald's father said or why it was helpful	Does not focus on what Ronald's father said or why it was helpful
Voice	Careful selection of nouns, verbs, adjectives, and adverbs	Careful selection of most words	Careful selection of some words	Words are vague and/or misused
Sentences	Uses at least two complete sentences to address the two questions	Uses one or more complete sentences	Uses one or more incomplete sentences	Uses all incomplete sentences
Conventions	Uses correct capital letters and end marks in all sentences	Generally uses correct capital letters and end marks in sentences	Does not use correct capital letters and end marks in some sentences	Does not use correct capital letters and end marks in any sentences

ELL

Support Writing Have children look at the illustrations and read the text on p. 209 with a partner. Have pairs discuss how they will respond to the prompt.

Assess See the ELL and Transition Handbook for guidance on assessing writing at various levels of English proficiency.

Grammar

APPLY TO WRITING Proper Nouns

IMPROVE WRITING WITH PROPER NOUNS Have children recall the proper nouns for the character they just wrote about. Explain that giving Ronald a name lets the reader know exactly who the writer is talking about. Remind children to use proper nouns in their own writing.

Write *teacher, dentist, month, holiday.* Have children supply the proper noun for their teacher, dentist, a month, and a holiday. Ask how each proper noun should begin.

teacher	dentist	month	holiday
Ms. Bell	**Dr. Sims**	**January**	**Flag Day**

PRACTICE

WRITE WITH PROPER NOUNS Have children write sentences about holidays, naming the month in which they occur. Ask how to begin each holiday and month name.

▲ **Grammar and Writing Practice Book** p. 26

Wrap Up Your Day!

 REALISM AND FANTASY Have children recall whether the events in *Ronald Morgan Goes to Bat* are realistic or if they are a fantasy. (Ronald Morgan loves to play baseball. He's not very good. He runs the wrong way. He also closes his eyes when he bats because he's scared of the ball. These are all things that could happen in real life, so the story is realistic.) Could the events in the story be a fantasy? Why not?

FLUENCY Write *"I want to play on the team," said Ben.* Point out the quotation marks. What do quotation marks mean? (someone is talking) Call on individuals to read the sentence with expression.

LET'S TALK ABOUT IT Recall *Ronald Morgan Goes to Bat.* Ask: Did Ronald quit the team after playing poorly? (No, he kept trying to get better, and he kept encouraging his teammates.) Display Graphic Organizer 15 from Day 1. Talk about what makes Ronald Morgan a good team member.

PREVIEW Day 4

Tell children that tomorrow they will read about a weird baseball game.

Share Literature
Flying a Kite, 1899

Phonics and Spelling

Contractions
Spelling: Words with Contractions

Read

Group Time < Differentiated Assessment

"Spaceball"

Fluency
Read with Expression

Writing Across the Curriculum
Chart

Grammar
Proper Nouns

Speaking and Listening
Types of Media

Materials

- *Sing with Me Big Book*
- Read Aloud Anthology
- Student Edition 214–215

Morning Warm~Up!

Sports such as baseball require teams. What makes a team? Today we will read about how creatures in outer space play a game just like people do!

QUESTION OF THE DAY Encourage children to sing "Teamwork" from the *Sing with Me Big Book* as you gather. Write and read the message and discuss the question.

REVIEW END MARKS

- Ask children how many different end marks are used in the message. (three)
- Have children name each end mark and provide sentences that use each one.

Extend Language Use the Day 4 instruction on ELL Poster 7 to extend and enrich language.

ELL Poster 7

Share Literature

CONNECT CONCEPTS

ACTIVATE PRIOR KNOWLEDGE Recall Ronald Morgan's baseball team and how Rat and his friends work as a team. Explain that you will read another selection about people who work as a team—"Flying a Kite, 1899" by Stephen Krensky.

BUILD ORAL VOCABULARY Read the first paragraph. Explain that the kite is **aloft**, or flying, and it is **actuated**, or put into action, by the wind. Explain that the Wright brothers **tinker** with the kite in order to learn more about flight. Ask children to listen to find out what the brothers learn about flying from the kite.

Read Aloud Anthology
Flying a Kite, 1899

MONITOR LISTENING COMPREHENSION

- Where is the kite? When is it **aloft**? (It is **aloft**, or in the air.)

- Why does the kite need wind to be **actuated**? (A kite does not fly unless there is wind to move it.)

- Why do you think the Wright brothers like to **tinker** with things? Explain. (Possible response: They enjoy using their hands. They like to understand how things work.)

OBJECTIVES

- Set purpose for listening.
- Build oral vocabulary.

Amazing Words to build oral vocabulary

	MONITOR PROGRESS
contribute **compete** **recreation** **deserve** **mope** **aloft** **tinker** **actuate**	**If...** children lack oral vocabulary experiences about the concept Working Together, **then...** use the Oral Vocabulary Routine on pp. DI·1–DI·2, DI·4 to develop the Amazing Words.

Connect Concepts Wilbur and Orville Wright invented the airplane. "Flying a Kite, 1899" tells about their lives and how they first became interested in flight.

Spiral REVIEW

- Reviews consonant digraphs.
- Reviews short *e: ea.*
- Reviews high-frequency words *break, family, heard, listen, once, pull.*

Sentence Reading

REVIEW WORDS IN CONTEXT

READ DECODABLE AND HIGH-FREQUENCY WORDS IN CONTEXT Write these sentences. Call on individuals to read a sentence. Then randomly point to words and have children read them. To help you monitor word reading, high-frequency words are underlined and decodable words are circled.

She'll give bread to that family when it's ready.

They'll tell me if they heard the whir of crickets in the shady meadow.

I'm going to pull that thin white thread off the dark fabric.

I didn't break that gingerbread dish on the shelf.

I think he'll help Dad once in a while.

We'll listen to that pleasant music Uncle Chuck plays.

Monitor Progress	Word Reading
If... children are unable to read an underlined word,	**then...** read the word for them and spell it, having them echo you.
If... children are unable to read a circled word,	**then...** have them use the blending strategy they have learned for that word type.

Support Phonics For additional review, see the phonics activities in the ELL and Transition Handbook.

Spelling

PARTNER REVIEW Contractions

READ AND WRITE Supply pairs of children with index cards on which the spelling words have been written. Have one child read a word while the other writes it. Then have children switch roles. Have them use the cards to check their spelling.

HOMEWORK Spelling Practice Book, p. 28

OBJECTIVE

● Spell contractions.

Spelling Words

Contractions

1.	I'll*	7.	who's
2.	wasn't	8.	she's
3.	it's	9.	we'll*
4.	he's	10.	isn't
5.	I'm*	11.	hasn't
6.	didn't	12.	hadn't

Challenge Words

13.	wouldn't	15.	where's
14.	shouldn't		

* **Words from the Selection**

Contractions
Circle the correct word. Write it.
1. Do you think its (it's) spicy?
   it's
2. He had'nt (hadn't) finished.
   hadn't
3. I think wel'l (we'll) buy it.
   we'll
4. Do you know (who's) whos coming?
   who's

Circle the hidden list word. Write the word.
5. t m w a s n' l e' t r — **wasn't**
6. e' d i d n' t o o s — **didn't**
7. m e' r d h a s n' t — **hasn't**
8. l' m m e x' l l n l — **I'm**
9. s b d' e d I' l l b — **I'll**
10. f h i s n' l e d' s — **isn't**

Spelling Words	
I'll	who's
wasn't	she's
it's	we'll
he's	isn't
I'm	hasn't
didn't	hadn't

School + Home Home Activity Your child has been learning to spell contractions. Can your child think of other contractions that are not on the spelling list?

▲ **Spelling Practice Book** p. 28

Group Time

On-Level	Strategic Intervention	Advanced
Read "Spaceball."	**Read** or listen to "Spaceball."	**Read** "Spaceball."
• Use pp. 214–215.	• Use the **Routine** on p. DI·30.	• Use the **Routine** on p. DI·31.

DAY 4

ELL Place English language learners in the groups that correspond to their reading abilities in English.

(i) Independent Activities

Fluency Reading Pair children to reread *Ronald Morgan Goes to Bat.*

Journal Writing List fun things to do for recreation. Share writing.

Spelling: Partner Review

Independent Reading See p. 190j for Reading/Library activities and suggestions.

Literacy Centers To provide listening opportunities, you may use the Listening Center on p. 190j. To extend social studies concepts, you may use the Social Studies Center on p. 190k.

Break into small groups after Spelling and before Fluency.

4

AudioText

Cooperation

Cooperation means working together with others. It is one of the most basic elements of teamwork. People who cannot cooperate will find it very difficult, if not impossible, to reach a goal together.

Read Poetry

PREVIEW AND PREDICT Read the title and author's name. Have children preview the poem and describe the pictures. (They show silly cartoon monsters playing ball.) Then ask them to predict whether "Spaceball" is serious or amusing. Have children read about these imaginary teams.

POETRY Review that poetry is an arrangement of words in lines that use rhythm. Some poems, such as this one, also use rhyme. Point out that the second and fourth lines in each stanza end with rhyming words.

VOCABULARY/DESCRIPTIVE WORDS Review that authors use descriptive words to help us understand ideas. Have children locate the words *mysterious* and *strange*. What do these words describe? Find another descriptive word in the poem. *(floppy)*

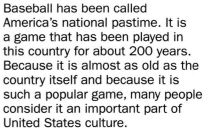

Poetry

Spaceball

by Brod Bagert
illustrated by Tedd Arnold

Last night I had a funny dream—
My brain's a mysterious place.
I dreamed about some aliens
Who lived in outer space.

I watched them play a game
That seemed a lot like baseball.
They played with bats and floppy hats,
But the aliens called it Spaceball.

Jupiter was the pitcher's mound,
Saturn was third base,
And the little alien kid at bat
Had a serious look on his face.

"Full count, bottom of the ninth,"
I heard the announcer say.
"This batter's trying to hit the ball
Clean out of the Milky Way."

Then I saw the ball was planet Earth!
Oh, how could it possibly be?
If he hits *that* ball, it's the end of us all,
That means . . . THE END OF ME!

I heard a shout: "STRIKE THREE, YOU'RE OUT!"
And space was filled with cheers.
But the little alien batter's eyes
Filled up with alien tears.

My dreams are strange, but last night's dream
Was the strangest dream of all.
Earth was saved by an alien
Who couldn't hit the ball.

214   215

BUILD CONCEPTS

Setting • Literal
- **What is the setting?**
outer space

Cause and Effect • Inferential
- **What would have happened if the alien had hit the ball?**
Responses may vary: Earth would be destroyed; the speaker would wake up.

CONNECT TEXT TO TEXT

How are Ronald Morgan and the little alien kid at bat alike?

Help children determine that both Ronald Morgan and the alien kid are not very good batters.

Cultural Heritage

Time for SOCIAL STUDIES

Baseball has been called America's national pastime. It is a game that has been played in this country for about 200 years. Because it is almost as old as the country itself and because it is such a popular game, many people consider it an important part of United States culture.

Activate Prior Knowledge Ask: Have you ever had a funny dream? What was it about?

Ronald Morgan   **214–215**

Options for Oral Reading

Use "Spaceball" or one of the following Leveled Readers.

On-Level

Warm and Fuzzy

Strategic Intervention

Let's Play Baseball

Advanced

The First Big Game

Use *The Soccer Picnic* or "Spaceball." For guidance in assessing the reading fluency of English language learners, see the ELL and Transition Handbook.

To develop fluent readers, use Fluency Coach.

Fluency

READ WITH EXPRESSION

MODEL READING DIALOGUE Use "Spaceball."

- Point to the quotation marks on p. 214. Quotations marks show that a character is talking. I try to read the part in the quotation marks the way the character would say it.
- Ask children to follow along as you read the page with expression.
- Have children read the page after you. Encourage them to read the way the different characters might speak. Continue in the same way with p. 215.

REREAD FOR FLUENCY

Choral Reading

ROUTINE

1. **Select a Passage** For "Spaceball," use pp. 214–215.

2. **Divide into Groups** Assign each group a part to read. For this poem, assign each group a stanza.

3. **Model** Have children track the print as you read.

4. **Read Together** Have children read along with you.

5. **Independent Readings** Have the groups read aloud without you. Monitor progress and provide feedback. For optimal fluency, children should reread three to four times.

Monitor Progress | Check Fluency

As children reread, monitor their progress toward their individual fluency goals. Current Goal: 58–68 words correct per minute. End-of-Year Goal: 90 words correct per minute.

If... children cannot read fluently at a rate of 58–68 words per minute,

then... make sure children practice with text at their independent level. Provide additional fluency practice, pairing nonfluent readers with fluent readers.

If... children already read fluently at 90 words per minute,

then... they do not need to reread three to four times.

SUCCESS PREDICTOR

| **Day 1** Check Word Reading | **Day 2** Check High-Frequency Words | **Day 3** Check Retelling | ▶ **Day 4 Check Fluency** | **Day 5** Assess Progress |

Writing Across the Curriculum

WRITE Chart

BRAINSTORM Have children think about what baseball players do and how these activities keep them healthy.

SHARE THE PEN Have children participate in creating a chart. To begin, draw a two-column chart on the chalkboard and explain that the class will work together to complete it. Explain that the chart is a way to show information in rows and columns. The first column is labeled *What Baseball Players Do* and the second is labeled *Why This Is Healthy*. Have the children copy the chart on their own paper. Call on an individual to name a healthy activity that baseball players do. Write the word, and then invite individuals to write a sentence explaining why this is healthy. Ask questions, such as the following:

- What is the beginning sound you hear in the word *run*? (/r/) Have a volunteer write *r*.

- What is the vowel sound you hear in the word *run*? (/u/)

- What letter stands for that sound? *(u)* Have a volunteer write *u.*

- What is the ending sound you hear in the word *run*? *(n)* Have a volunteer write *n.*

Continue having individuals contribute to filling in the chart. Frequently reread the answers.

Have children write a sentence at the bottom of their chart, answering the question "Why is baseball good for you?"

What Baseball Players Do	Why It Is Healthy
Run	Running makes you fast.
Hit	Hitting makes you powerful.
Throw	Throwing makes your arms strong.

Running, hitting, and throwing make you stronger.

OBJECTIVE

- Create a chart.

Advanced

Encourage children to create another chart about activities in a different sport and why they are healthy.

Support Writing Since many sports will have similar or identical activities, point out the pattern of the table to children. Do an oral language activity using the same pattern before children write.

DAILY FIX-IT

7. it didnt rain much.

It didn't rain much.

8. Can john be on my team.

Can John be on my team?

Proper Nouns

Mark the letter of the word or words that correctly complete each sentence.

1. Ronald's last name is ____.
   ○ A morgan
   ○ B spano
   ⊗ C Morgan

2. Ronald goes to school with ____.
   ○ A Rosemary and tom
   ⊗ B Rosemary and Tom
   ○ C rosemary and Tom

3. Ronald's father is ____.
   ○ A Mr. morgan
   ○ B mr. morgan
   ⊗ C Mr. Morgan

4. Ronald's nickname is ____.
   ○ A slugger
   ⊗ B Slugger
   ○ C SLUGGER

5. The team played on ____
   ○ A tuesday
   ⊗ B Tuesday
   ○ C TuesDay

Home Activity Your child prepared for taking tests on proper nouns. Read a story together. Have your child identify the proper nouns on a page.

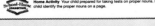

▲ **Grammar and Writing Practice Book** p. 27

Grammar

(REVIEW) PROPER NOUNS

DEFINE PROPER NOUNS

• What are special names for people, places, animals, and things called? (proper nouns)

• How do proper nouns always begin? (with a capital letter)

PRACTICE

CLASSIFY PROPER NOUNS Write *People, Places, Animals* to head three columns. Have individuals supply proper nouns to be written in each column.

People	Places	Animals
Ronald Morgan	Texas	Tiree

Speaking and Viewing

USE DIFFERENT TYPES OF MEDIA

OBJECTIVES

- Speak to communicate information through different types of media.
- View to understand a variety of techniques used in media presentations.

MODEL SPEAKING AND VIEWING Remind children of appropriate viewing and speaking behaviors for different types of media, such as viewing quietly and speaking clearly. Then ask children to think about these behaviors as they take turns using different techniques in a variety of media presentations.

- You can present information through a variety of media, such as tape recordings, video recordings, radio, and television.

- With different types of media, you communicate in different ways. If you were making an audio cassette, you would want to use lots of expression in your voice because your audience won't be able to see the expression on your face or any movements you are making.

- If you were making a videotape, you might want to use gestures and visual aids, such as charts, to get your point across.

USING MEDIA Ask children to present information about what makes a team or how teams work together. Provide them the opportunity to either audiotape or videotape their presentation and then share it with the class.

Wrap Up Your Day!

✓ **Text to Self** Have you ever felt sad or angry after not playing a game as well as you wanted to? Provide an example. (Possible response: I felt angry after I struck out in kickball last week.) Call on individuals to provide different answers.

LET'S TALK ABOUT IT Recall the Read Aloud selection, "Flying a Kite, 1899." Ask: How were Orville and Wilbur Wright a team? (They worked together to experiment with flying machines.) What do you think they did that helped them work together? (They shared what they learned and supported each other.) Display Graphic Organizer 15 from Day 1 and add these qualities.

PREVIEW Day 5

Remind children that they heard a story about two brothers and their invention. Tell them that tomorrow they will hear about the Wright brothers again.

Share Literature
Flying a Kite, 1899

Phonics and Spelling
 REVIEW Contractions

High-Frequency Words
laugh   great   you're   either
certainly   second   worst

Monitor Progress
Spelling Test: Words with
Contractions

Group Time < Differentiated
Assessment

Grammar and Writing
Proper Nouns

Research and Study Skills
Newspapers and Periodicals

Materials
- *Sing with Me Big Book*
- Read Aloud Anthology
- Reproducible Pages TE 216f–216g
- Student Edition 216–217

Morning Warm~Up!
This week we read about
people working and playing together.
Teams are formed for recreation and
for working. People contribute to teams
and compete with other teams.
What makes a team?

QUESTION OF THE DAY Encourage children to sing "Teamwork" from the *Sing with Me Big Book* as you gather. Write and read the message and discuss the question.

REVIEW ORAL VOCABULARY Have children explain what *contribute*, *recreation*, and *compete* mean. Then have children name

- teams that are formed for recreation
- teams that are formed to compete
- things that people contribute to these

ELL

Assess Vocabulary Use the Day 5 instruction on ELL Poster 7 to monitor children's progress with oral vocabulary.

ELL Poster 7

Share Literature

LISTEN AND RESPOND

USE PRIOR KNOWLEDGE Review that yesterday the class listened to find out what the Wright brothers learned about flight from the kite. Suggest that today the class listen to find out why the Wright brothers made a good team.

Read Aloud Anthology
Flying a Kite, 1899

MONITOR LISTENING COMPREHENSION

- How do you know the Wright brothers made a good team? Explain. (Possible response: They worked together, they built things together, they had the same interests, and they were very close.)

- Do you think it would have been easier if only one of the Wright brothers was trying to figure out how to build an airplane? Explain your answer. (Possible response: It would have been harder because by working together, they were able to work more quickly. Each brother offered his unique ideas and strengths to the project.)

BUILD ORAL VOCABULARY

DESCRIPTIVE WORDS: VERBS Read the third paragraph of "Flying a Kite, 1899." Have children find descriptive verbs. (twisted, curved) Write *twisted* and *curved* on the board. Ask children to find other descriptive verbs in the story and write them. Verbs that describe an action are called descriptive verbs. Challenge children to use the descriptive verbs from the story in original sentences.

twisted	**twisting**
curved	**warping**
tinker	

OBJECTIVES

- Set purpose for listening.
- Build oral vocabulary.

E L L

Extend Language Tell children that descriptive verbs provide the reader with a clearer picture of what's happening. For instance, you might say *He ate the candy.* However, a more descriptive sentence would be *He gobbled the candy* if he ate it very quickly. You might say *He nibbled the candy* if he only tasted it.

Contractions

REVIEW

IDENTIFY CONTRACTIONS Write these sentences. Have children read each one aloud. Call on individuals to name and underline contractions and identify the word parts.

She's telling them I'll be late.
There's no time. We can't ride today.
Who's watching the dogs while I'm at the store?
Didn't Mom say he's at the park?

High-Frequency Words

REVIEW

MEANING CLUES Read the following clues for children. Have children write a review word from p. 192 for each clue. Then reread clues and check answers together.

This means "you are." (you're)
This means the opposite of best. (worst)
This means the opposite of cry. (laugh)
Complete the following: first, _____, third. (second)
This means the same as wonderful. (great)
You may pick _____ this or that. (either)
This means "of course." (certainly)

Vocabulary For additional practice with high-frequency words, use the vocabulary strategies and word cards in the ELL Teaching Guide, pp. 45–46.

SPELLING TEST Contractions

DICTATION SENTENCES Use these sentences to assess this week's spelling words.

1. <u>I'm</u> walking to school.
2. <u>I'll</u> go to the store.
3. <u>Who's</u> coming over?
4. He <u>hasn't</u> done his chores.
5. We <u>didn't</u> have time to eat lunch.
6. <u>We'll</u> be sure to say thank you.
7. <u>He's</u> my big brother.
8. It <u>wasn't</u> time to go yet.
9. I <u>hadn't</u> visited my grandma in a long time.
10. <u>She's</u> my friend Jan.
11. It <u>isn't</u> a school day today.
12. <u>It's</u> cold outside!

CHALLENGE WORDS

13. I <u>wouldn't</u> go to the park in the dark.
14. <u>Where's</u> my snack?
15. He <u>shouldn't</u> take that pen from the desk.

ASSESS

● Spell contractions.

Spelling Words

Contractions

1.	I'll*	7.	who's
2.	wasn't	8.	she's
3.	it's	9.	we'll*
4.	he's	10.	isn't
5.	I'm*	11.	hasn't
6.	didn't	12.	hadn't

Challenge Words

13.	wouldn't	15.	where's
14.	shouldn't		

* Words from the Selection

Group Time

On-Level	Strategic Intervention	Advanced
Read Set B Sentences.	**Read** Set A Sentences and the Story.	**Read** Set C Sentences.
• Use pp. 216e–216g.	• Use pp. 216e–216g.	• Use pp. 216e–216g.
	• Use the **Routine** on p. DI·32.	• Use the **Routine** on p. DI·32.

DAY 5

 Place English language learners in the groups that correspond to their reading abilities in English.

(i) Independent Activities

Fluency Reading Children reread selections at their independent level.

Journal Writing Write about something you contribute to your family. Share writing.

Independent Reading See p. 190j for Reading/Library activities and suggestions.

Literacy Centers You may use the Technology Center on p. 190k to support this week's concepts and reading.

Practice Book 2.1 Newspaper/Periodicals, p. 70

Break into small groups after Spelling and before Grammar and Writing.

ASSESS

- Decode contractions *n't, 's, 'll, 'm.*
- Read high-frequency words.
- Read aloud with appropriate speed and accuracy.

- Distinguish realism and fantasy.
- Retell a story.

Differentiated Assessment

On-Level

Set B

Strategic Intervention

Set A

Advanced

Set C

Fluency Assessment Plan

☑ Week 1 assess Advanced students.

☑ **This week assess Strategic Intervention students.**

☐ Week 3 assess On-Level students.

☐ Week 4 assess Strategic Intervention students.

☐ Week 5 assess any students you have not yet checked during this unit.

Set individual fluency goals for children to enable them to reach the end-of-year goal.

- Current Goal: 58–68 wcpm
- End-of-Year Goal: 90 wcpm
- **ELL** For guidance in evaluating fluency, see the ELL and Transition Handbook.

SENTENCE READING

ASSESS CONTRACTIONS AND HIGH-FREQUENCY WORDS Use one of the reproducible lists on p. 216f to assess children's ability to read words with contractions and high-frequency words. Call on individuals to read two sentences aloud. Have each child in the group read different sentences. Start over with sentence one if necessary.

RECORD SCORES Use the Sentence Reading Chart for this unit on p. 313k.

Monitor Progress	Contractions
If... children have trouble reading contractions *n't, 's, 'll, 'm,*	**then...** use the Reteach Lessons on p. DI·65.
High–Frequency Words	
If... children cannot read a high-frequency word,	**then...** mark the missed words on a high-frequency word list and send the list home for additional word reading practice or have the child practice with a fluent reader.

FLUENCY AND COMPREHENSION

ASSESS FLUENCY Take a one-minute sample of children's oral reading. See Monitoring Fluency, p. 313i. Have children read "Dora Can't Skate," the on-level fluency passage on p. 216g.

RECORD SCORES Record the number of words read correctly in a minute on the child's Fluency Progress Chart.

ASSESS COMPREHENSION Have the child read to the end of the passage. (If the child had difficulty with the passage, you may read it aloud.) Ask questions about what could really happen and what could not really happen and have the child retell the passage. Use the Retelling Rubric on p. 212g to evaluate the child's retelling.

Monitor Progress	Fluency
If... a child does not achieve the fluency goal on the timed reading,	**then...** copy the passage and send it home with the child for additional fluency practice or have the child practice with a fluent reader.
Realism and Fantasy	
If... a child cannot distinguish realism and fantasy,	**then...** use the Reteach Lesson on p. DI·65.

READ THE SENTENCES

Set A

1. He's funny, but Joan didn't laugh.
2. We'll see if there's a great place to park.
3. I'm glad you're happy and aren't sad.
4. He'll either be here by noon, or he isn't coming.
5. She'll find out if they'll be in second place.
6. It certainly wasn't the worst game that she'll play.

Set B

1. Kim's first in line, but who's second?
2. It's certainly the worst storm she's seen.
3. Mom doesn't laugh when the room isn't clean.
4. He'll be a great help if the work hasn't been done.
5. Here's when I'll have to know if you're staying with us.
6. There's either juice or milk that's here to drink.

Set C

1. The great big hill wasn't easy to climb up, and it can't be hard to get down.
2. They'll either go on a picnic, or I'll meet them at the zoo on Friday.
3. I'm sure you'll laugh when you see how funny the show is.
4. It's certainly the worst trip that we'll ever make.
5. She's a great friend, when I don't know what to do.
6. That's the second letter that he's written to his pen pal in China.

Monitor Progress | Contractions
High-Frequency Words

SUCCESS PREDICTOR

Dora Can't Skate

Dora put on her skates and stepped on the ice.   10
"This isn't going to work," she said to her friend   20
Amy. "I'll never learn to skate."   26

"You'll have to let go of the rail," said Amy.   36

"I'll fall if I let go. I'm just too scared." Then   47
Dora's brother glided past her. "He's such a good   56
skater," said Dora.   59

"Let go of the rail," he said as he zoomed by   70
Dora.   71

Then Dora saw a lady helping other skaters.   79
"Who's that?" Dora asked.   83

"She's a skating teacher. I'm sure she'll help   91
you. Let's ask her," said Amy.   97

"You'll have to let go of the rail if you want to   109
learn to skate," she said.   114

Dora tried to be brave. She let go and began   124
to glide around the ice. She did fall, but it wasn't   135
so bad. "I'm a skater!" she said to herself.   144

"I guess I can't hold on to things that aren't going   155
to help."   157

Monitor Progress | Fluency Passage

216g

Proper Nouns

Proper nouns are special names for people, places, animals, and things. They begin with capital letters.

Ronald took his dog **Tramp** to **Fisher Park**.

Days of the week, months of the year, and **holidays** also begin with capital letters.

We played a ball game on **Memorial Day**, the fourth **Monday** in **May**.

Titles for people begin with capital letters. Many titles end with a **period (.)**.

Our coach, **Mr. Morgan**, taught us to throw the ball.

216

Write Using Proper Nouns

1. Write a sentence from the story that has more than one proper noun. Underline the proper nouns.

2. Write a sentence about Ronald Morgan and his friends. Use proper nouns in your sentence. Underline the proper nouns.

3. Write some sentences about a game you like to play at school or at home. Tell the name of the game. Tell when and where you play it. Tell how you play it. Underline the proper nouns in each sentence.

217

Grammar and Writing

WRITE USING PROPER NOUNS Read pp. 216–217 aloud. Guide children as they complete the items.

1. Possible response: And <u>Tom</u> said, "You're letting <u>Ronald Morgan</u> play?"
2. Possible response: <u>Rosemary</u> hopes <u>Ronald</u> hits the ball.

CONNECT TO UNIT WRITING Children write sentences underlining proper nouns.

3. Possible response:

GAME I like to play dodgeball.

WHEN I play dodgeball on <u>Monday</u>.

WHERE I play during gym class at <u>Dawson School</u>.

HOW You throw the ball at the other team. If it hits them, they're out. If they catch it, you are out.

DAILY FIX-IT

9. I hit the ball had
   I hit the ball ha<u>r</u>d.

10. What a fun gam this is
    What a fun gam<u>e</u> this is<u>!</u>

Proper Nouns

Write the sentences.
Capitalize the proper nouns.

1. ronald goes to carver elementary school.

   Ronald goes to Carver Elementary School.

2. He plays baseball every tuesday.

   He plays baseball every Tuesday.

3. ronald played four games in april.

   Ronald played four games in April.

4. mr. morgan throws balls to ronald.

   Mr. Morgan throws balls to Ronald.

5. The last game is on wednesday, august 26.

   The last game is on Wednesday, August 26.

6. That date is near labor day.

   That date is near Labor Day.

 Home Activity Your child reviewed proper nouns. Write your child a letter. Do not capitalize the proper nouns. Ask your child to circle the words that should be capitalized and write the words with capital letters.

▲ **Grammar and Writing Practice Book** p. 28

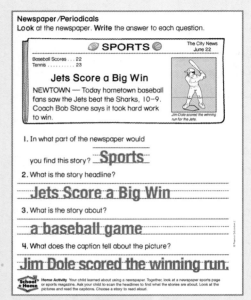

Newspaper/Periodicals
Look at the newspaper. **Write** the answer to each question.

🌐 SPORTS 🌐 — The City News June 22

Baseball Scores . . . 22
Tennis 23

Jets Score a Big Win

NEWTOWN — Today hometown baseball fans saw the Jets beat the Sharks, 10–9. Coach Bob Stone says it took hard work to win.

Jim Dole scored the winning run for the Jets.

1. In what part of the newspaper would you find this story? **Sports**

2. What is the story headline?
Jets Score a Big Win

3. What is the story about?
a baseball game

4. What does the caption tell about the picture?
Jim Dole scored the winning run.

Home Activity Your child learned about using a newspaper. Together, look at a newspaper sports page or sports magazine. Ask your child to scan the headlines to find what the stories are about. Look at the pictures and read the captions. Choose a story to read aloud.

▲ **Practice Book 2.1** p. 70,
Newspapers and Periodicals

Research/Study Skills

TEACH/MODEL Newspapers and Periodicals

MODEL USING A NEWSPAPER Show a newspaper to the class. Point out that the front page has a small box that tells how to find different sections of information in the paper. Read aloud the different sections. Ask children which section would have information about baseball. Remind them that most newspaper articles are written in order of importance.

Model how to find the sports page.

Think Aloud **MODEL** I can use this box on the front page to find information about baseball. Since baseball is a sport, I think I'll find information about it in the sports section. I look at the box to find out where the sports pages are. When I read a sports article from this section, I notice that the most important facts are mentioned first.

FIND DIFFERENT SECTIONS OF THE NEWSPAPER Call on individuals to find the following sections of the newspaper by using the box on the front page: national news, weather, classified ads.

PRACTICE

DEMONSTRATE USING A NEWSPAPER Label four boxes with the following newspaper categories: *national news, local news, classified ads, comics.* Have students look through newspapers and cut out sections that they will place in the appropriate box. Assign one box to each of four groups of children. Have them discuss their choices.

Acess Content Flip through the sections of a newspaper and identify each for English language learners. For example: *This is the sports section. It will give you information about different sports teams and the people who play on the teams.*

Wrap Up Your Week!

LET'S TALK ABOUT Working Together

QUESTION OF THE WEEK Recall this week's question.

- What makes a team?

Display the What Makes a Team web. Help children identify different kinds of teams (for example, soccer, baseball, swim, track, tug-of-war).

CONNECT Use questions such as these to prompt a discussion.

- Players on different teams compete against each other. Is it possible to share when you are competing?

- Baseball is one form of recreation. Do all kinds of recreation require sharing?

Build Background Use ELL Poster 7 to support the Preview activity.

PREVIEW Tell children that next week they will read about a beaver that does not want to work together or share a pond with a turtle.

PREVIEW Next Week

Working Together · Week 2

Turtle's Race with Beaver

ONLINE CLASSROOM

For the Teacher

PLAN
My Lesson Planner ONLINE

TEACH
Teacher's Edition ONLINE

ASSESS
Success Tracker ONLINE

For the Student

READ
Read It ONLINE

Leveled Reader Database ONLINE

EXPLORE
Take It to the NET ONLINE

PRACTICE
Fluency Coach

Phonics Activities

Preview Your Week

When does sharing make sense?

Student Edition pages 222–245

Turtle's Race with Beaver

as told by Joseph Bruchac and James Bruchac
illustrated by Jose Aruego and Ariane Dewey

Why are Turtle and Beaver racing, and who will win?

222 / 223

Audio CD

Genre Folktale

Phonics *r*-Controlled Vowels *-er, -ir, -ur*

Comprehension Skill Sequence

Comprehension Strategy Summarize

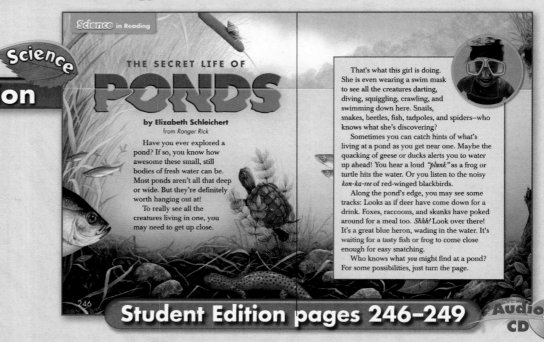

Paired Selection

Reading Across Texts
Compare Pictures

Genre
Diagram: Science

Text Features
Diagram

Science in Reading

THE SECRET LIFE OF
PONDS

by Elizabeth Schleichert
from Ranger Rick

Have you ever explored a pond? If so, you know how awesome these small, still bodies of fresh water can be. Most ponds aren't all that deep or wide. But they're definitely worth hanging out at!

To really see all the creatures living in one, you may need to get up close.

That's what this girl is doing. She is even wearing a swim mask to see all the creatures darting, diving, squiggling, crawling, and swimming down here. Snails, snakes, beetles, fish, tadpoles, and spiders—who knows what she's discovering?

Sometimes you can catch hints of what's living at a pond as you get near one. Maybe the quacking of geese or ducks alerts you to water up ahead! You hear a loud *"plunk"* as a frog or turtle hits the water. Or you listen to the noisy *kon-ka-ree* of red-winged blackbirds.

Along the pond's edge, you may see some tracks: Looks as if deer have come down for a drink. Foxes, raccoons, and skunks have poked around for a meal too. *Shhh!* Look over there! It's a great blue heron, wading in the water. It's waiting for a tasty fish or frog to come close enough for easy snatching.

Who knows what *you* might find at a pond? For some possibilities, just turn the page.

246

Student Edition pages 246–249

Audio CD

Read It
ONLINE
sfsuccessnet.com
- Student Edition
- Leveled Readers
- Decodable Reader

TIME FOR Science

Integrate Science Standards
- Physical Environment
- Survival
- Habitat
- Ecosystems

✓ **Read**

Turtle's Race with Beaver
pp. 222–242

"The Secret Life of Ponds"
pp. 246–249

✓ **Read**

Leveled Readers

Leveled Readers

Skill Sequence

Strategy Summarize

Lesson Vocabulary

Below-Level

On-Level

Advanced

Below-Level | On-Level | Advanced
- Support Concepts
- Develop Concepts
- Extend Concepts
- Science Extension Activity

✓ **Read**

ELL Reader

ELL Reader
- Concept Vocabulary
- Text Support
- Language Enrichment

Summer Returns to the Pond
by Fiona Killorin
Illustrated by Janice Skivington

✓ **Build Concept Vocabulary**
Working Together,
pp. 218r, 218–219

✓ **Teach Science Concepts**
Turtles, pp. 228–229
Beavers, pp. 232–233
Survival, pp. 246–247

Decodable Readers

Apply Phonics
- *Herb Helps Out*

Decodable Reader 8
Herb Helps Out
Written by Shanna Marcus
Illustrated by Ken Furlie

✓ **Explore Science Center**
Make a Survival List, p. 218k

Turtle's Race with Beaver **218c**

Planner

My Lesson Planner
ONLINE
sfsuccessnet.com

DAY 1

DAY 2

Oral Language 10-15 minutes
- Build Concepts
- Share Literature

Oral Language 218l–218m
QUESTION OF THE WEEK *When does sharing make sense?*
Share Literature
Sing with Me Big Book, 8

Oral Language 220a–220b
QUESTION OF THE DAY *What are some times you have been in a race?*
Share Literature
Read Aloud Anthology "A Ducky Day"

Word Work 25-30 minutes
- Phonics
- Spelling
- High-Frequency Words

Word Work 218n–218p
Phonics
Introduce *r*-Controlled Vowels *er, ir, ur* **T**
Spelling Pretest

Word Work 220c–220d, 220–221a
Phonics
r-Controlled *er, ir, ur* **T**
Spelling Dictation
High-Frequency Words **T**
Introduce *enough, toward, above, ago, word, whole*

Reading 60-75 minutes
- Vocabulary
- Comprehension
- Fluency

- Cross-Curricular Connections

- Independent Reading

Reading 218q–219b
Vocabulary
Decodable Word Meaning
Read Decodable Reader 8
Comprehension Check
Fluency
Paired Reading
Build Background
Let's Talk About Working Together
Comprehension
Sequence **T**

SCIENCE Concept Chart
Leveled Readers, LR19–27
Self-Selected Reading, TR22–23

Reading 220e–220f, 222a–242
Vocabulary
Introduce *challenge, lodge, embarrassed, buried, dam, halfway*
Comprehension
Sequence **T**
Summarize
Read *Turtle's Race with Beaver,* 222–242
REVIEW **Comprehension Skill**
Realism and Fantasy

SCIENCE Turtles, Beavers
SCIENCE Concept Chart
Leveled Readers, LR19–27
Self-Selected Reading, TR22–23

Language Arts 20-30 minutes
- Writing
- Grammar
- Speaking, Listening, Viewing
- Research/Study Skills

Language Arts x219c–219d
Shared Writing
Plan
DAILY WRITING
List ways people can solve a conflict.
Grammar
Introduce Singular and Plural Nouns **T**

Language Arts 242a–242b
Interactive Writing
Paragraph
DAILY WRITING
Write about a time you had a disagreement with someone.
Grammar
Practice Singular and Plural Nouns **T**

Monitor Progress

Daily **SUCCESS PREDICTORS** for **Adequate Yearly Progress**

Day 1 Check 218o
Check Word Reading
Spiral REVIEW Phonics
Phonics

Day 2 Check 221a
Check High-Frequency Words
Spiral REVIEW High-Frequency Words
Fluency

218d

 Vocabulary Check Oral Vocabulary See p. DI·2.

DAY 3

Oral Language 243a–243b
QUESTION OF THE DAY *Why might the baby ducks be skittish?*
Share Literature
Read Aloud Anthology "A Ducky Day"

Word Work 243c–243d
Phonics
REVIEW Contractions *n't, 's, 'll, 'm*

Spelling Practice
High-Frequency Words T
Practice *enough, toward, above, ago, word, whole*

Reading 222–242, 243e–245
Vocabulary
Time Order Words for Sequence
Comprehension
Read *Turtle's Race with Beaver,* 222–245
Think and Share
Fluency
Choral Reading

SCIENCE Concept Chart

Leveled Readers, LR19–27
Self-Selected Reading, TR22–23

Language Arts 245a–245b
Independent Writing
Respond to Literature
DAILY WRITING
Write a journal entry about a time when you shared something.
Grammar
Write with Singular and Plural Nouns T

DAY 4

Oral Language 246a–246b
QUESTION OF THE DAY *What other things live in ponds?*
Share Literature
Read Aloud Anthology "Harry Shares His Room"

Word Work 246c–246d
Phonics
REVIEW Sentence Reading

Spelling Partner Review
High-Frequency Words T
Practice *enough, toward, above, ago, word, whole*

Reading 246–249a
Vocabulary
Descriptive Words
Comprehension
Read "The Secret Life of Ponds," 246–249
Science in Reading
Reading Across Texts
Fluency
Choral Reading

SCIENCE Physical Environment, Survival, Habitat, Ecosystems
SCIENCE CENTER Write About Sharing

Leveled Readers, LR19–27
Self-Selected Reading, TR22–23

Language Arts 249b–249d
Writing Across the Curriculum
Venn Diagram
DAILY WRITING
List animals that inhabit your neighborhood.
Grammar
Review Singular and Plural Nouns T
Speaking and Listening
Follow and Give Directions

DAY 5

Oral Language 250a–250b
QUESTION OF THE DAY *How do you feel when you share?*
Share Literature
Read Aloud Anthology "Harry Shares His Room"

Word Work 250c–250f
Phonics
🎯 Review *r*-Controlled *er, ir, ur*

Spelling Test
High-Frequency Words T
Review *enough, toward, above, ago, word, whole*

Reading 250b, 250e–250g
Vocabulary
Time and Order Words
Monitor Progress
Read the Sentences
Read the Story

SCIENCE Concept Chart

Leveled Readers, LR19–27
Self-Selected Reading, TR22–23

Language Arts 250–251a
Grammar and Writing
Use Singular and Plural Nouns T
Connect to Unit Writing
How-to Report
DAILY WRITING
Write about when you resolved a conflict.
Research/Study Skills
Alphabetical Order

KEY
🎯 = Target Skill
T = Tested Skill

THIS WEEK'S RESOURCES
Practice Book pp. 71–80
Spelling Practice Book pp. 29–32
Grammar and Writing Practice Book pp. 29–32
Selection Test pp. 29–32
Fresh Reads for Differentiated Test Practice pp. 43–48
Phonics Songs and Rhymes Chart 8

Day 3 Check 243g
Check Retelling

Comprehension

Day 4 Check 249a
Check Fluency WCPM
Spiral REVIEW Phonics, High-Frequency Words

Fluency

Day 5 Check 250e
r-Controlled *er, ir, ur*
High-Frequency Words
Fluency
Comprehension

SUCCESS PREDICTOR

Resources for
Differentiated Instruction

▶ **Comprehension**

🎯 **Skill** Sequence

🎯 **Strategy** Summarize

▶ **Lesson Vocabulary**

High-Frequency Words

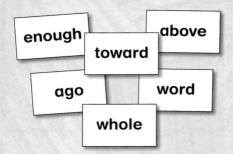

enough · above · toward · ago · word · whole

▶ **Science Standards**

• **Physical Environment**

• **Survival**

• **Habitat**

• **Ecosystems**

Leveled Reader Database ONLINE
sfsuccessnet.com

Use the Online Database of over 600 books to

• Download and print additional copies of this week's leveled readers

• Locate more titles at various levels to practice this week's skill—sequence

• Search for more titles focused on this week's topic and content

On-Level

Life Science
The Busy, Lively, Sleepy, and Quiet Pond
by Kim Borland   Illustrated by Bradley Clarke

On-Level Reader

Sequence
Read the passage. The beavers did things in a certain order. Underline the clue words that help you know that order.

Beavers have strong, sharp teeth. First, they use their teeth to cut down trees.
Next, they cut off the branches. Then they strip off the bark. The beavers then carry the logs toward the river.

spring   spring

fall   winter

On-Level Practice TE p. LR23

Vocabulary
Use words from the box to complete the paragraph.

Words to Know					
above	ago	enough	toward	whole	word

In the spring, the animals return to the pond. If you look **above** you in the sky, you might see ducks flying **toward** the pond. Then, in the summer, the **whole** pond is full of life. In the fall the beavers make sure that they gather **enough** food for the winter. When winter comes, there are few animals that live near or on the pond. Some are resting, but others have left for warmer places quite some time **ago**

On-Level Practice TE p. LR 24

Strategic Intervention

Life Science
Busy Beavers
by Jessica Quilty

Below-Level Reader

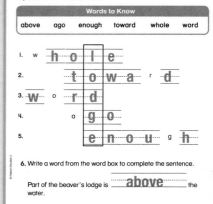

Sequence
Read the passage. The beavers did things in a certain order. Underline the clue words that help you know that order.

Beavers have strong, sharp teeth. First, they use their teeth to cut down trees.
Next, they cut off the branches. Then they strip off the bark. The beavers then carry the logs toward the river.

1. First **Beavers cut down trees with their teeth.**

2. Next **They cut off the branches.**

3. Next **They strip off the bark.**

4. Last **They carry the logs toward the river.**

Below-Level Practice TE p. LR20

Vocabulary
Write the words from the box that fit. Some letters have been done for you. When you are finished, the letters in the boxes will spell an important word from the book.

Words to Know					
above	ago	enough	toward	whole	word

1. w **h o l e**
2. **t o w a** r **d**
3. **w** o **r d**
4. a **g o**
5. **e n o u** g **h**

6. Write a word from the word box to complete the sentence.
Part of the beaver's lodge is **above** the water.

Below-Level Practice TE p. LR21

Advanced

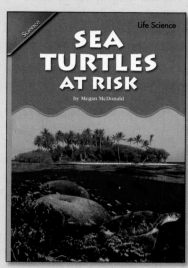

Advanced Reader

Sequence
Read the passage.

The tiny eggs develop in the warm sand. When they hatch, the baby sea turtles, called hatchlings, all pour out of the nest at once. They make a dash for the water. Once in the water, they must also watch out for sharks and fish.

Write what happens first, next, and last on the lines below.

1. First **The turtle eggs develop.**

2. Next **The eggs hatch.**

3. Next **Hatchlings pour out of the nest.**

4. Next **They make a dash for the water.**

5. Last **They watch out for sharks and fish.**

Advanced Practice TE p. LR26

Vocabulary
Write a word from the box that best completes each sentence. You may use a word more than once.

Words to Know		
conflict	inhabit	resolve

1. It takes **resolve** to break our old polluting habits.

2. To protect sea turtles, humans should make sure that their needs do not **conflict** with the turtles' needs.

3. Sharks and sea turtle hatchlings are in **conflict**] because the hatchlings are food for sharks.

4. Sea turtles **inhabit** the beach when it is time to lay eggs.

5. Shrimp fishermen should **resolve** to use special nets that let sea turtles escape.

Advanced Practice TE p. LR27

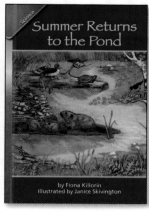

ELL Reader

ELL Poster 8

Teacher's Edition Notes

ELL notes throughout this lesson support instruction and reference additional resources at point of use.

Teaching Guide pp. 50–56, 226–227

- Multilingual summaries of the main selection
- Comprehension lesson
- Vocabulary strategies and word cards
- ELL Reader 8 lesson

ELL and Transition Handbook

Ten Important Sentences

- Key ideas from every selection in the Student Edition
- Activities to build sentence power

More Reading

Reader's Theater Anthology

- Fluency practice
- Five scripts to build fluency
- Poetry for oral interpretation

Leveled Trade Books

Below-Level

On-Level

Advanced

- Extend reading tied to the unit concept
- Lessons in Trade Book Library Teaching Guide

Homework

- Family Times Newsletter
- ELL Multilingual Selection Summaries

Take-Home Books

- Decodable Readers
- Leveled Readers

Weekly Plan for Group Time
Differentiated Instruction

DAILY PLAN

WHOLE GROUP

- Morning Warm-Up
- Share Literature
- Phonics
- Spelling
- Vocabulary

DAILY GROUP TIME

1
2
3
4
5

- **Reading Support**
- **Skill Support**
- **Fluency Practice**

WHOLE GROUP

- Fluency
- Writing
- Grammar
- Wrap Up Your Day

Look for the ⓘ
Independent Activities

See Group Time pp. 218p, 222a, 243e, 246d, 250d.

✓ **Fluency Reading**
Choral Reading

✓ **Journal Writing**
See the Planner for daily writing prompts, pp. 218d–218e.

✓ **Homework**
Practice Book, pp. 71–80
Spelling Practice Book, pp. 29–32
Grammar and Writing Practice Book, pp. 29–32

✓ **Literacy Centers**
pp. 218j–218k
- Listening
- Reading/Library
- Word Work
- Writing
- Science
- Technology

DAY 1

On-Level

Page 218q
- Read Decodable Reader 8
- Reread for Fluency

Strategic Intervention

Page DI•34
- Read Decodable Reader 8
- Blend Words with *r*-Controlled *er, ir, ur*
- Reread for Fluency

Advanced

Page DI•35
- Read Advanced Selection 8
- Extend Word Reading
- Introduce Concept Inquiry

DAY 2

On-Level

Pages 222–242
- Read *Turtle's Race with Beaver*
- Reread for Fluency

Strategic Intervention

Page DI•36
- Read SI Decodable Reader 8
- Read or Listen to *Turtle's Race with Beaver*
- Blend Words with *r*-Controlled *er, ir, ur*

Advanced

Page DI•37
- Read *Turtle's Race with Beaver*
- Continue Concept Inquiry

DAY 3

On-Level

Pages 222–245
- Reread *Turtle's Race with Beaver*

Strategic Intervention

Page DI•38
- Reread *Turtle's Race with Beaver*
- Read Words and Sentences
- Review Sequence and Summarize
- Reread for Fluency

Advanced

Page DI•39
- Self-Selected Reading
- Continue Concept Inquiry

On-Level

Pages 246–249
- Read "The Secret Life of Ponds"

Strategic Intervention

Page DI•40
- Read or Listen to "The Secret Life of Ponds"
- Reread for Fluency
- Build Concepts

Advanced

Page DI•41
- Read "The Secret Life of Ponds"
- Expand Vocabulary
- Continue Concept Inquiry

DAY 4

On-Level

Pages 250e–250g
- Sentence Reading, Set B
- Monitor Comprehension and Fluency

Strategic Intervention

Page DI•42
- Practice Word Reading
- Sentence Reading, Set A

Advanced

Page DI•43
- Sentence Reading, Set C
- Share Concept Inquiry

DAY 5

Grouping Place English language learners in the groups that correspond to their reading abilities in English.

Use the appropriate Leveled Reader or other text at children's instructional level.

TIP Send home the appropriate Multilingual Summary of the main selection on Day 1.

MORE READING FOR
Group Time

Below-Level

On-Level

Advanced

Take It to the NET
ONLINE
sfsuccessnet.com

Jeanne Paratore
For ideas on using repeated readings for diverse groups, see the article "Using Repeated Readings to Promote Reading Success . . ." by J. Turpie and Scott Foresman author J. Paratore.

TEACHING TIP Design your room for success.
Set up areas for whole-class instruction and small-group work; work stations; noisy and quiet areas spaced far from each other; places for children to store their things; and so on.

TEACHER TALK

A **syllable** is a unit of pronunciation that contains one vowel sound.

Be sure to schedule time for children to work on the unit inquiry project "Organize a Club." This week children should decide on officers to elect and hold an election.

Looking Ahead

Literacy Centers

Listening

Let's Read Along

MATERIALS `SINGLES`
CD player, headphones, print copies of recorded pieces

LISTEN TO LITERATURE As children listen to the following recordings, have them follow along or read along in the print version.

AudioText
Turtle's Race with Beaver
"The Secret Life of Ponds"

Sing with Me/Background Building Audio
"Turtle, Turtle"

Phonics Songs and Rhymes Audio
"Sisters Who Share"

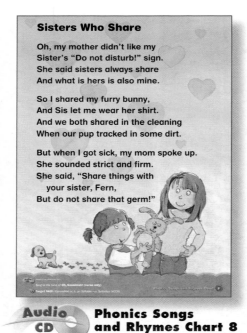

Sisters Who Share

Oh, my mother didn't like my
Sister's "Do not disturb!" sign.
She said sisters always share
And what is hers is also mine.

So I shared my furry bunny,
And Sis let me wear her shirt.
And we both shared in the cleaning
When our pup tracked in some dirt.

But when I got sick, my mom spoke up.
She sounded strict and firm.
She said, "Share things with
   your sister, Fern,
But do not share that germ!"

Audio CD **Phonics Songs and Rhymes Chart 8**

Reading/Library

Read It Again!

MATERIALS `SINGLES` `PAIRS` `GROUPS`
collection of books for self-selected reading, reading logs

REREAD BOOKS Have children select previously read books from the appropriate book box and record titles of books they read in their logs. Use these previously read books:

- **Decodable Readers**
- **Leveled Readers**
- **ELL Readers**
- **Stories written by classmates**
- **Books from the library**

TEN IMPORTANT SENTENCES Have children read the Ten Important Sentences for *Turtle's Race with Beaver* and locate the sentences in the Student Edition.

BOOK CLUB Use p. 240 of the Student Edition to read about folktales. Encourage a group to find more information about the genre.

Word Work

Once Upon a Time...

MATERIALS `GROUPS`
index cards

r*-CONTROLLED *er*, *ir*, *ur Have groups of children play a storytelling game using r-controlled words with *er*, *ir*, and *ur*.

1. Write r-controlled words with *er*, *ir*, and *ur* on index cards.
2. Stack the cards facedown.
3. Children take turns picking a card and reading the word. After reading the word aloud, the child provides a sentence using the word. The next child chooses another card and continues the story idea from the previous sentence.
4. Play continues until all the cards have been drawn.

 Phonics Activities CD This interactive CD provides additional practice.

circus
person
gerbil
burning
stirrup
church

Scott Foresman Reading Street Centers Survival Kit
Use the *Turtle's Race with Beaver* materials
from the Reading Street Centers Survival Kit
to organize this week's centers.

Writing

Write a How-to Report

MATERIALS
paper, pencils

`SINGLES`

WRITE A HOW-TO REPORT Recall how Beaver built a dam in *Turtle's Race with Beaver.*

1. Ask children to think of something they built or made.
2. Have them write a how-to report listing the steps they took to make or build their item.
3. Urge them to number their steps.

LEVELED WRITING Urge children to write at their own ability level. Some may write very simple reports with phrases. Others will be able to write organized reports containing simple sentences with some attention to mechanics and spelling. Your best writers will write well-organized reports containing sentences with greater detail and more attention to mechanics and spelling.

How to Make a Fort

1. Cut a door in the side of a cardboard box.
2. Put two chairs by the sides of the door.
3. Put a blanket over the backs of the two chairs and the box.

Science

Share and Survive

MATERIALS
paper, pencils

`PAIRS`
`GROUPS`

WRITE ABOUT SHARING Remind children that Beaver wouldn't share his home.

1. Have children think of things we need.
2. Have them pick one thing to share with someone.
3. Have children write about how and with whom they will share the item.

I need my red blanket because it's cold outside. I would share it with my best friend Janice.

Technology

Focus on Phonics

MATERIALS
computer, Phonics Practice Activities CD-ROM

`PAIRS`

USE A CD-ROM Have pairs of children use a CD-ROM.

1. Have children turn on the computer and open the Phonics Practice Activities CD-ROM.
2. Pairs complete one of the CD-ROM activities.

Phonics Activities CD

This interactive CD provides additional practice.

ALL CENTERS

Turtle's Race 218k

Day 1
AT A GLANCE

Share Literature
"Turtle, Turtle" 8

Phonics and Spelling
🔊 *r*-Controlled *er, ir, ur*
Spelling Pretest:
  Words with *er, ir, ur*

Read Apply Phonics

Group Time < Differentiated Instruction

Build Background
Let's Talk About Working Together

Listening Comprehension
🔊 **Skill** Sequence

Shared Writing
Plan

Grammar
Singular and Plural Nouns

Materials

- *Sing with Me Big Book*
- Letter Tiles
- Decodable Reader 8
- Student Edition 218–219
- Graphic Organizer 25
- Writing Transparency 8
- Grammar Transparency 8

Take It to the NET
ONLINE
Professional Development
For analysis of think-aloud studies and comprehension strategies, see a summary of *Verbal Protocols of Reading* by M. Pressley and Peter Afflerbach.

Morning Warm~Up!

People either live alone or with others. Animals usually share their space. When does sharing make sense?

QUESTION OF THE WEEK Tell children they will talk, sing, read, and write about when sharing makes sense. Write and read the message and discuss the question.

CONNECT CONCEPTS Ask questions to connect to other Unit 2 selections.

- Who shares the home mentioned in *Tara and Tiree: Fearless Friends*?
- Who shares Ronald's home in *Ronald Morgan Goes to Bat*?

REVIEW HIGH-FREQUENCY WORDS

- Circle the high-frequency word *either* in the message.
- Have children say and spell the word as they write it in the air.

Build Background Use the Day 1 instruction on ELL Poster 8 to assess knowledge and develop concepts.

ELL Poster 8

Share Literature

BUILD ORAL VOCABULARY Display p. 8 of the *Sing with Me Big Book.* Tell children that the class is going to sing a song about sharing a place to live. Read the title. Ask children to listen for the Amazing Words **conflict, inhabit,** and **resolve** as you sing. Then sing the song again and encourage children to sing along with you, demonstrating their understanding of *conflict, inhabit,* and *resolve.*

• What kinds of conflicts can we have with friends?

• What sort of places do people inhabit?

• How would you resolve a fight with a sibling about sharing a bike?

**Sing with Me/
Background Building Audio**

Turtle, Turtle
Turtle, Turtle, please respond.
Who can inhabit your small pond?
Is there room enough to share
With Beaver, Chipmunk, Fox, and Hare?
Resolve the conflict. Please respond.
Yes, you all can share my pond.

Sing with Me Big Book

Amazing Words to build oral vocabulary

	MONITOR PROGRESS
conflict inhabit resolve	**If...** children lack oral vocabulary experiences about the concept Working Together, **then...** use the Oral Vocabulary Routine on pp. DI·1–DI·2, DI·5 to develop the Amazing Words.

Access Content Help children recognize the meaning of the English word *respond* in "Turtle, Turtle" by asking them to please *respond* to a basic question, such as, "What color is your shirt?"

1

OBJECTIVES

- Associate the sound /ėr/ with the *er*, *ir*, and *ur* spelling patterns.
- Blend, read, and build *er*, *ir*, and *ur* words.

Skills Trace

r-Controlled *er*, *ir* *ur*

Introduce/Teach	TE: 2.1 218n–o
Practice	TE: 2.2 218q, DR8, 220c–d; PB: 2.1 73, 88
Reteach/Review	TE: 2.2 250c, 274c, DI-66
Assess/Test	TE: 2.2 250e–g Benchmark Test, Unit 2

Generalizations

r-Controlled *er*, *ir*, *ur* A single vowel followed by the letter *r* has a sound that is neither short nor long, but *r*-controlled.

VC/CV If a word has two consonants together in the middle (other than digraphs), divide between them.

Strategic Intervention

Use **Monitor Progress**, p. 218o during Group Time after children have had more practice with *r*-controlled *er*, *ir*, *ur*.

Advanced

Use **Monitor Progress**, p. 218o as a preassessment to determine whether or not this group of children would benefit from this instruction on *r*-controlled *er*, *ir*, *ur*.

Support Phonics Spanish does not have a sound equivalent to /ėr/, so Spanish speakers may pronounce *dirt* as *deert* or *paper* as *pa-pair*. Help children practice saying and writing words, such as *her*, *bird*, and *turn*.
Speakers of monosyllabic languages, such as Cantonese, Hmong, Khmer, Korean, and Vietnamese may pronounce a two-syllable word as two separate words.

See the Phonics Transition Lessons in the ELL and Transition Handbook.

r-Controlled *er, ir, ur*

TEACH/MODEL

ROUTINE

Blending Strategy

1 **Connect** Write *barn, sport,* and *chore.* What do you know about the vowel sounds in these words? **(They are *r*-controlled vowels.)** Today we'll learn about *r*-controlled *er*, *ir*, and *ur* and the sounds they stand for.

2 **Use Sound-Spelling Card** Display Card 11. This is *Earth.* *Earth* has the sound /ėr/ at the beginning. The letters *er*, *ir*, and *ur* can stand for the vowel sound /ėr/. /ėr/ is the *r*-controlled sound of *e*, *i*, and *u*. Say it with me: /ėr/.

er, ir, ur

Sound-Spelling Card 11

3 **Model** Write *burn.* When the letter *u* is followed by *r*, the *u* usually has an *r*-controlled sound. Listen as I blend this word. **Blend the sounds continuously across the word.** Let's blend this word together: /bėrn/, *burn.* Have children compare vowel sounds in *barn* and *burn.* Repeat steps 2 and 3 with *fern* and *dirt.*

Write *enter.* You can blend longer words with /ėr/ by dividing them into smaller parts. We usually divide words between two consonants. Read one syllable at a time and then blend them together. Model blending *enter.* Let's blend together: *en/ter, enter.*

4 **Group Practice** Blend these words together. Continue with *third, hurt, clerk, birth, nurse, verse, summer, corner, tender.*

5 **Review** What do you know about reading these words? (The letters *er*, *ir*, and *ur* stand for /ėr/.)

BLEND WORDS

INDIVIDUALS BLEND *er*, *ir*, AND *ur* WORDS Call on individuals to blend *chirp, surf, perch, first, urge, twirl, winter, person, survive.* Have them tell what they know about each word before reading it. For feedback, refer to step five of the Blending Strategy Routine.

BUILD WORDS

ch d e h i p s sh t u

INDIVIDUALS MAKE *er, ir,* AND *ur* WORDS Write *hurt* and have the class blend it. Have children spell *hurt* with letter tiles. Monitor work and provide feedback.

- Change the *hu* in *hurt* to *di,* What is the new word?

- Change the *d* in *dirt* to *sh.* What is the new word?

- Change the *sh* in *shirt* to *sp,* and change the *ir* to *ur.* What is the new word?

- Remove the *s* in *spurt* and change the *u* to *e.* What is the new word?

- Change the *t* in *pert* to *ch,* What is the new word?

d i r t

sh i r t

s p u r t

p e r t

p e r ch

Vocabulary TIP

You may wish to explain the meanings of these words.

border place where something begins or ends

herd a group of large animals that stay together

stern strict or harsh

tuck to put the edge of something into place

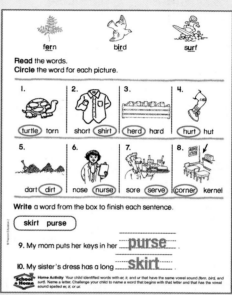

▲ **Practice Book 2.1** p. 73, *r*-Controlled *er, ir,* and *ur*

Monitor Progress | **Check Word Reading** *r*-Controlled *er, ir, ur*

Write the following words and have individuals read them.

germ	burn	stern	curb	girl
herd	carport	border	turn	first
sherbet	circus	tuck	curler	thick

If... children cannot blend words with *er, ir,* and *ur* at this point,

then... continue to monitor their progress using other instructional opportunities during the week so that they can be successful with the Day 5 Assessment. See the Skills Trace on p. 218n.

SUCCESS PREDICTOR

Spiral REVIEW

- Row 2 contrasts *ar, or, ore* with *er, ir, ur.*
- Row 3 contrasts short *e, i,* and *u* with *er, ir, ur.*

▶ **Day 1 Check Word Reading** : **Day 2** Check High-Frequency Words : **Day 3** Check Retelling : **Day 4** Check Fluency : **Day 5** Assess Progress

Word Reading

SUCCESS PREDICTOR

OBJECTIVES

- Segment sounds to spell words.
- Spell words with *r*-controlled *er, ir,* and *ur.*

Spelling Words

r-Controlled *er, ir, ur*

1.	her*	7.	serve
2.	person	8.	curb
3.	nurse	9.	curl
4.	dirt	10.	skirt
5.	turn*	11.	purse
6.	birth	12.	turtle*

Challenge Words

13.	hamburger	15.	perfect
14.	surface		

* Words from the Selection

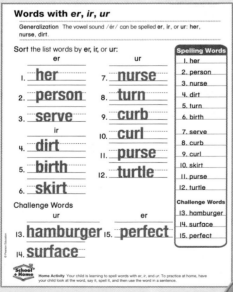

Words with *er, ir, ur*

Generalization The vowel sound /ėr/ can be spelled **er**, **ir**, or **ur**: her, nurse, dirt.

Sort the list words by **er**, **ir**, or **ur**:

er	ur
1. her	7. nurse
2. person	8. turn
3. serve	9. curb
ir	10. curl
4. dirt	11. purse
5. birth	12. turtle
6. skirt	

Spelling Words
1. her
2. person
3. nurse
4. dirt
5. turn
6. birth
7. serve
8. curb
9. curl
10. skirt
11. purse
12. turtle

Challenge Words
13. hamburger
14. surface
15. perfect

Challenge Words
ur	er
13. hamburger	15. perfect
14. surface	

Home Activity Your child is learning to spell words with *er, ir,* and *ur.* To practice at home, have your child look at the word, say it, spell it, and then use the word in a sentence.

▲ **Spelling Practice Book** p. 29

Support Spelling Before giving the spelling pretest, clarify the meaning of each spelling word with examples, such as saying a *skirt* is something you can wear, and pointing to a girl to illustrate *her.*

Spelling

PRETEST *r*-Controlled *er, ir, ur*

MODEL WRITING FOR SOUNDS Each spelling word has an /ėr/ vowel sound. Before administering the spelling pretest, explain that since *er, ir,* and *ur* all have the same sound, they'll have to remember the correct vowel for each spelling word.

- What sounds do you hear in *shirt?* (/sh/ /ėr/ /t/)
- What are the letters for /sh/? Write *sh.*
- Do you remember what letters stand for /ėr/ in *shirt? (ir)* Continue with *t* /t/.

- Repeat with *perk* and *turn.* Remind children that /ėr/ can also be spelled *er, ir,* or *ur.* Tell them that in *perk,* it is spelled *er,* and in *turn,* it is spelled *ur.*

PRETEST Dictate the spelling words. Segment the words for children if necessary. Have children check their pretests and correct misspelled words.

HOMEWORK Spelling Practice Book, p. 29

Group Time

Ned's Turtles

Ned was only eight years old, but he already knew a lot about turtles. He knew that female turtles lay more than a hundred eggs in nests they make in the dirt, and that only a few eggs grow up to become adults. He knew that most turtle eggs and baby turtles become food for other animals, and that is why many eggs are laid at one time.

He knew that different kinds of turtles inhabit different areas. Some live in and around ponds, while others live near the sea. He knew how to tell different kinds of turtles apart by what they looked like. He knew that snapping turtles won't attack people unless they are cornered and pushed into conflict. Ned knew a lot about turtles.

Ned had books about turtles and pictures of turtles on his

Decodable Reader 8

Herb Helps Out

Written by Thomas Mercer
Illustrated by Ken Forbis

On-Level	Strategic Intervention	Advanced
Read Decodable Reader 8.	**Read** Decodable Reader 8.	**Read** Advanced Selection 8.
• Use p. 218q.	• Use the **Routine** on p. DI·34.	• Use the **Routine** on p. DI·35.

ELL Place English language learners in the groups that correspond to their reading abilities in English.

(i) Independent Activities

Fluency Reading Pair children to reread Leveled Readers or the ELL Reader from the previous week or other text at children's independent level.

Journal Writing List ways people can resolve a conflict. Share writing.

Independent Reading See p. 218j for Reading/Library activities and suggestions.

Literacy Centers To practice *r*-controlled *er, ir, ur,* you may use Word Work, p. 218j.

Practice Book 2.1 *r*-Controlled *er, ir, ur,* p. 73; Sequence, p. 74

Break into small groups after Spelling and before Build Background.

Apply Phonics

⟳PRACTICE *r-Controlled er, ir, ur*

HIGH-FREQUENCY WORDS Review *from, there,* and *too* on the Word Wall. **Word Wall**

READ DECODABLE READER 8

- Pages 58–59 Read aloud quietly with the group.
- Pages 60–61 Have the group read aloud without you.
- Pages 62–64 Select individuals to read aloud.

CHECK COMPREHENSION AND DECODING Ask children the following questions:

- Who are the characters in the story? (Herb, Mom, a girl)
- Where does the story take place? (at many stores)
- Why does Herb need to find butter? (His mom needs it to make a cake.)

Then have children locate *er, ir,* and *ur* words in the story. Review the sound of *er, ir,* and *ur.* Sort words according to their spelling.

er	ir	ur
after	bird	turned
butter	first	
batter	stir	
better	shirt	
her	third	
Herb	stirred	
Herb's	stirring	

HOMEWORK Take-Home Decodable Reader 8

REREAD FOR FLUENCY

Paired Reading

ROUTINE

1. **Reader 1 Begins** Children read the entire selection, switching readers at the end of each page.

2. **Reader 2 Begins** Have partners reread; now the other partner begins.

3. **Reread** For optimal fluency, children should reread three or four times.

4. **Provide Feedback** Listen to children read and provide corrective feedback regarding their oral reading and their use of the blending strategy.

OBJECTIVES

- Apply knowledge of letter-sounds and word parts to decode unknown words when reading.
- Use context with letter-sounds and word parts to confirm the identification of unknown words.
- Practice fluency in paired reading.

Monitor Progress

Decoding

If...	then... prompt
children have difficulty decoding a word,	them to blend the word. • What is the new word? • Is the new word a word you know? • Does it make sense in the story?

ELL

Access Content

Beginning Lead children on a noun walk through *Herb Helps Out,* identifying people, places, and things in the pictures and print.

Intermediate Preview *Herb Helps Out,* explaining *er, ir,* and *ur* words, such as *entered* and *curb.*

Advanced Have children use sequence words *first, next, then,* and *last,* to retell the sequence of events in *Herb Helps Out.*

Strategic Intervention

Offer children a verbal alternative to written responses. Allow children to dictate their answers to you. You might want to elaborate on their responses to help them.

Advanced

Have children write a letter to a friend about a time they shared something.

Activate Prior Knowledge
Have children tell about a time they shared with someone or someone else shared with them. Ask how it made them feel.

Build Background

LET'S TALK ABOUT Working Together

GENERATE DISCUSSION Read the title and ask questions to generate language. Encourage children to respond in complete sentences.

- What are the bears doing?
- What are they sharing?

BUILD ORAL VOCABULARY Lead the class in a discussion that focuses on concepts and today's Amazing Words, *conflict, inhabit, resolve.*

Look at the bears. They inhabit the same area. Sometimes this causes conflicts because one bear will want what another bear has. How do you think bears resolve their conflicts? Why would they need to share the same space? Look at the picture of the turtle and beaver swimming together. This week we will read about how Turtle and Beaver try to resolve their conflict.

VOCABULARY

CONCEPT CHART Remind children of the question of the week.

- When does sharing make sense?

Display Graphic Organizer 25. Label the columns "When does sharing make sense?" and "When does sharing not make sense?" Using the pictures on the student page as a starting point, help children identify appropriate responses that fit each category. Encourage children to think of other examples of good and bad times to share. Display the chart for use throughout the week.

- What would happen if animals did not share the land or water where they lived? (Many animals would not survive.)
- Can you think of an example when sharing does not make sense? (when you're taking a test)

Build Background

Let's Talk About Working Together

218

219

When does sharing make sense?	When does sharing not make sense?
When you have something others need to survive	When you're taking a test at school
When space is scarce but there are lots of people, like on a crowded bus	When doing so would hurt you or someone else
When doing so will mean that others will later share with you	

▲ **Graphic Organizer 25**

Take It to the NET™ ONLINE

For a Web site that tells more about animals and things that live in ponds, do an Internet search using the keywords *pond life*.

ELL

Access Content To prepare children for reading *Turtle's Race with Beaver*, send home the story summary in English and/or the home language. See the ELL Teaching Guide, pp. 54–56.

OBJECTIVE

Identify sequence.

Skills Trace	
Sequence	
Introduce/Teach	TE: 2.2 163a–b, 164e; 219a–b, 220e; 2.5 180r, 180–181
Practice	PB: 2.1 54–55, 67, 74–75, 107; 2.2 64–65, 77
Reteach/Review	TE: 2.2 204–205, DI-64 DI-66; 2.3 330–331; 2.5 216–217, DI-65;
Assess/Test	TE: 2.2 21–24, 29–32; 2.5 85–88; Benchmark Test, Unit 2

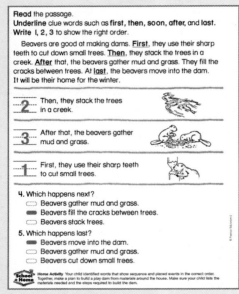

Read the passage.
Underline clue words such as **first, then, soon, after,** and **last.**
Write 1, 2, 3 to show the right order.

Beavers are good at making dams. **First**, they use their sharp teeth to cut down small trees. **Then**, they stack the trees in a creek. **After** that, the beavers gather mud and grass. They fill the cracks between trees. At **last**, the beavers move into the dam. It will be their home for the winter.

__2__ Then, they stack the trees in a creek.

__3__ After that, the beavers gather mud and grass.

__1__ First, they use their sharp teeth to cut small trees.

4. Which happens next?
   ◯ Beavers gather mud and grass.
   ⬤ Beavers fill the cracks between trees.
   ◯ Beavers stack trees.

5. Which happens last?
   ⬤ Beavers move into the dam.
   ◯ Beavers gather mud and grass.
   ◯ Beavers cut down small trees.

School + Home Home Activity Your child identified words that show sequence and placed events in the correct order. Together, make a plan to build a play dam from materials around the house. Make sure your child lists the materials needed and the steps required to build the dam.

▲ **Practice Book 2.1** p.74, Sequence

Access Content For a Picture It! lesson on sequence, see the ELL Teaching Guide, pp. 50–51.

Listening Comprehension

TEACH/MODEL Sequence

DEFINE SEQUENCE

- Sequence is the order in which things happen.
- When you read, think about what happens first, next, and last in a story. Look for clue words like *while, soon, after, then,* and *before* to help you understand when things are happening.
- When you retell a story, use words like *first, next,* and *last* to show the sequence.

READ ALOUD Read "Frog's Lily Pad" and model how to identify the sequence.

 MODEL As I read, I think about the order in which things happen. First, Turtle climbs up on Frog's lily pad. Then the lily pad sinks. Next, Frog decides that they can share a log instead.

PRACTICE

CLUES TO SEQUENCE Ask children to order the other events in the selection. (Frog doesn't want to tell Turtle that he is too heavy for the lily pad. Frog tells Turtle that the lily pad is just too small. Frog invites Turtle to join her on the log. Frog and Turtle sit on the log together.)

IDENTIFY SEQUENCE Have children recall the story *Tara and Tiree, Fearless Friends.*

- What was the first thing that happened to Jim after the ice broke? (He fell into the water and called for help.)
- What happened next? (Tiree came toward Jim and fell in too.) Then what happened? (Tara came close and Jim held onto her collar.) What happened after that? (Tiree climbed over on Jim's back to safety.)
- What happened last in the story? (Tara pulled Jim to safety.)

CONNECT TO READING Tell children that when they read any story, they should think about the order of events so they can keep track of what happens.

Frog's Lily Pad

Frog sat on her favorite lily pad. She liked her lily pad because she had a good view of the pond. She could easily catch flies whenever she was hungry. She could easily jump off the lily pad if she saw an animal coming that might want to eat her.

Then one day Turtle decided that he liked Frog's lily pad too. Turtle hopped up on the lily pad and sat right next to Frog. After a while, the lily pad sank slowly, ever so slowly. Soon both Frog and Turtle were under water.

"What happened?" Turtle asked. "Why did we sink?"

Frog didn't know what to say. She knew that Turtle was just too heavy to sit on the lily pad with her, but she didn't want to say so. That might hurt Turtle's feelings. That might cause a conflict. Frog needed to think of a way to resolve the problem.

Finally Frog said, "Can we both inhabit the same place? Yes, but we both can't share the lily pad. It sinks each time a friend comes to visit."

Frog swam over to a nearby log. It was a large log, and she could easily catch flies there. She had a good view of the pond, and she could easily jump off the log if she saw an animal coming after her.

Frog climbed up on the log and said, "I think this is a much better place for us. We can share this log."

Turtle slowly swam over and crawled onto the log too. He smiled at Frog and said, "Yes, it's quite comfortable. Thank you! Sharing is good, isn't it?"

Shared Writing

WRITE Plan

GENERATE IDEAS Have children think of someone they know who is very different from them. Ask them what they could do to get along with this person.

WRITE A PLAN Tell children they have to share a room with the person. Explain that they will write a plan to help them get along with the person.

COMPREHENSION SKILL Have children think of the order of items in their plan. Have them list the most important part of the plan first.

- Display Writing Transparency 8 and read the title.
- Ask children to read the item listed by the first bullet.
- Ask children to complete the list with other suggestions, reminding them to put the most important suggestion first and the least important suggestion last.

HANDWRITING While writing, model the letter forms as shown on pp. TR18–21.

READ THE PLAN Have children read the completed plan aloud as you track the print.

Our Plan

• We will be patient and not get angry.
   Possible answers:
• We will **be friendly** _____

• We will **say "please" and "thank you."**

• We will **keep our things on our side of the room**
• We will **keep our side of the room clean**

Unit 2 Turtle's Race with Beaver   Writing Model **8**

▲ **Writing Transparency 8**

INDEPENDENT WRITING

WRITE PLAN Have children write their own plan about sharing something other than a room with a person who is very different from them. Encourage them to use words from the Word Wall and the Amazing Words board. Let children illustrate their writing. Display the illustrated plans on poster board in the classroom.

Grammar

TEACH/MODEL Singular and Plural Nouns

REVIEW PROPER NOUNS Remind children that a proper noun is a special name for a person, place, animal, or thing.

IDENTIFY SINGULAR AND PLURAL NOUNS Display Grammar Transparency 8. Read the definitions aloud.

• Look at the picture above number 1. There is one thing, a tree. *Tree* is a singular noun, so nothing is added to the word.

Continue modeling with items 2–6.

PRACTICE

MAKE SINGULAR NOUNS PLURAL Have children change singular nouns into plural nouns. Write the following nouns on the chalkboard: *fox, desk, bench, horse, dress.* Children should write the correct plural nouns on their paper.

Singular and Plural Nouns

A **singular noun** names one person, place, animal, or thing. A noun that names more than one is called a **plural noun**.

bear (one)   turtles (more than one)

You add **-s** to most nouns to show more than one. If a noun ends in **s, ch, sh,** or **x**, add **-es** to the noun to show more than one.

rabbits (add -s)   foxes (add -es)

Add **-s** or **-es** if the noun should be plural. **Do not** add anything if the noun should be singular.

1. tree **tree**   4. box **box**

2. bus **buses**   5. lamp **lamp**

3. shoe **shoes**   6. dish **dishes**

Unit 2 Turtle's Race with Beaver   Grammar **8**

▲ **Grammar Transparency 8**

Wrap Up Your Day!

r-CONTROLLED *er, ir, ur* Write *dirt* and ask children what sound the *ir* in *dirt* has. (/ėr/) Repeat with *her* and *turn*.

SPELLING *r*-CONTROLLED *er, ir, ur* Have children name and write the letters for each sound in *dirt*. Continue with *her* and *turn*.

SEQUENCE To help children determine the order of events, have them look for clue words such as *while, soon, after, then*, and *before*. Then ask students: What is the second event that happens in the story?

LET'S TALK ABOUT IT Recall that Frog wants to share her space with Turtle. How does she do this after Turtle makes her lily pad sink? (She finds a log that will be strong enough for both of them to sit on.)

 HOMEWORK Send home this week's Family Times newsletter.

PREVIEW Day 2

Tell children that tomorrow the class will read about a turtle and a beaver that need to share a pond.

Day 2
AT A GLANCE

Share Literature
A Ducky Day

Phonics and Spelling
 r-Controlled er, ir, ur
Spelling: Words with r-Controlled er, ir, ur

Comprehension
Skill Sequence
Strategy Summarize

Build Background
Pond Ecosystems

High-Frequency Words
enough   toward   above
ago   word   whole

Word Wall

Vocabulary
Selection Words
challenge   lodge   embarrassed
buried   dam   halfway

Read

 **Group Time** < Differentiated Instruction

Turtle's Race with Beaver

Interactive Writing
Paragraph

Grammar
Singular and Plural Nouns

Materials

- Sing with Me Big Book
- Read Aloud Anthology
- Student Edition 220–242
- Phonics Songs and Rhymes Chart 8
- Background Building Audio CD
- Graphic Organizer 25
- Tested Word Cards
- Vocabulary Transparency 8

Morning Warm~Up!

Today we will read about Turtle and Beaver. We will read about how they compete in a race that is not just for recreation. What are some times you have been in a race?

QUESTION OF THE DAY Encourage children to sing "Turtle, Turtle" from the Sing with Me Big Book as you gather. Write and read the message and discuss the question.

REVIEW ORAL VOCABULARY

- Read the second sentence of the message.
- Have children explain what the words compete and recreation mean.

 **ELL**

Build Background Use the Day 2 instruction on ELL Poster 8 to preview high-frequency words.

ELL Poster 8

Share Literature

BUILD CONCEPTS

CAPITALIZATION AND PUNCTUATION Have children read the second paragraph in "A Ducky Day." Help them to find all of the capitalized words. Review that sentences and proper nouns always begin with capital letters. Punctuation marks include periods and commas. They tell the reader when to pause or when a sentence is complete.

Read Aloud Anthology
A Ducky Day

BUILD ORAL VOCABULARY Ask children what they know about ducks and their babies. Point out that sometimes animals have to **coax** their babies to try something new because the new activity might be scary to the babies. Explain that a **ramp** is a sloping walkway that is used to help someone get up or over something. Suggest that as you read, children listen to find out how the baby ducks got into the house.

- Why did the people try to **coax** the mother duck into the house? (They wanted her to go to the back deck so that she and her babies could get through its openings and go to the pond.)

- What do the people make to help the ducks get into the house? (a **ramp**)

MONITOR LISTENING COMPREHENSION

- What is the problem in the story? (The ducks cannot get off the enclosed deck.)

- How do the people resolve the conflict? (They make a **ramp** from some wood and set it up leading into the front door.)

- How does the mother duck **coax** her babies? (She walks up and down the ramp quacking until the babies follow her.)

- How do you think the people in the house felt when they watched the ducks going to the pond? (Possible response: proud, happy, maybe a little bit sad that they were leaving)

OBJECTIVES

- Discuss characteristics of capitalization and punctuation.
- Set purpose for listening.
- Build oral vocabulary.

Amazing Words to build oral vocabulary

	MONITOR PROGRESS
conflict inhabit resolve coax ramp	**If...** children lack oral vocabulary experiences about the concept Working Together, **then...** use the Oral Vocabulary Routine on pp. DI·1–DI·2, DI·5 to develop the Amazing Words.

Build Concepts Most of the action in "A Ducky Day" takes place on a deck. Explain to children that a *deck* is an area without a roof that is attached to a house. Have children demonstrate their understanding by drawing a house with a deck.

2

OBJECTIVES

- Review *r*-controlled *er, ir,* and *ur* words.
- Sort *r*-controlled *er, ir,* and *ur* words.
- Preview words before reading them.
- Spell *r*-controlled *er, ir,* and *ur* words.

Strategic Intervention

Use **Strategic Intervention Decodable Reader 8** for more practice with words with *er, ir, ur.*

ELL

Support Phonics Invite children to act out what happens in "Sisters Who Share" as you replay the Phonics Songs and Rhymes Audio CD.

r-Controlled *er, ir, ur*

TEACH/MODEL

Fluent Word Reading *ROUTINE*

1 Connect Write *squirt.* You can read this word because you know how to read words with *r*-controlled vowels. What sounds do the letters *ir* stand for in this word? (/ėr/) What's the word? *(squirt)* Do the same with *verb* and *purse.*

2 Model When you come to new word, look at the letters from left to right and think about the vowel sounds. Say the sounds in the word to yourself and then read the word. **Model reading** *winter, circus, murmur.* When you come to a new word, what are you going to do?

3 Group Practice Write *nerve, first, burden, confirm, Thursday, clerk, birthday.* Read these words. Look at the letters, think about the vowel sounds, say the sounds to yourself, and then read the word aloud together. Allow 2–3 seconds previewing time.

WORD READING

PHONICS SONGS AND RHYMES CHART 8 Frame each of the following words on Phonics Songs and Rhymes Chart 8. Call on individuals to read them. Guide children in previewing.

hers	shirt	disturb	germ
Fern	furry	dirt	firm

Sing "Sisters Who Share" to the tune of "Oh, Susannah (verse only)," or play the CD. Have children follow along on the chart as they sing. Then have individuals take turns locating *er, ir,* and *ur* words on the chart.

 **Phonics Songs and Rhymes Audio**

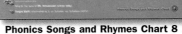

Sisters Who Share

Phonics Songs and Rhymes Chart 8

SORT WORDS

INDIVIDUALS SORT *er, ir,* AND *ur* WORDS Have all children complete the activity on paper. Write *er, ir,* and *ur* as headings. Have individuals write *er, ir,* and *ur* words from the Phonics Chart under the appropriate headings and circle the letters that stand for /ėr/. Ask individuals to read the completed lists. Provide feedback as necessary.

er	ir	ur
hers	shirt	disturb
germ	dirt	furry
Fern	firm	

Spelling

PRACTICE *r*-Controlled *er, ir, ur*

WRITE DICTATION SENTENCES Have children write these sentences. Repeat words slowly, allowing children to hear each sound. Children may use the Word Wall to help with spelling high-frequency words. **Word Wall**

She held the purse next to her skirt.

A nurse is a good person to help you.

Watch the turtle walk across the dirt path.

HOMEWORK Spelling Practice Book, p. 30

Spelling Words

r-Controlled er, ir, ur

1. her*		7. serve	
2. person		8. curb	
3. nurse		9. curl	
4. dirt		10. skirt	
5. turn*		11. purse	
6. birth		12. turtle*	

Challenge Words

13. hamburger   15. perfect
14. surface

* Words from the Selection

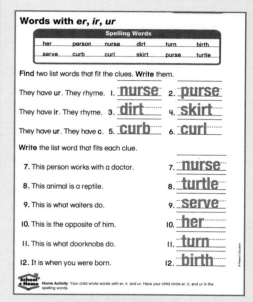

▲ **Spelling Practice Book** p. 30

The class will help to save the pond.
Read sentences from the class journal.
Underline clue words such as **before, then, soon, after,** and **last.**
Write 1, 2, 3, 4, 5 to show the right order.

2 **Then**, a few kids walked into the water and started picking up trash.

4 **After** lunch, we filled jars with water. We will test to see if the pond water is clean.

1 **First**, we put on rubber boots before we got in the water.

5 The **last** thing we did was to pick up our jars and trash. The pond looks much better now!

3 **Soon**, it was lunchtime. Our class had been working all morning.

Home Activity Your child identified words that show sequence and placed events in the correct order. Together, write a plan for cleaning your child's bedroom. Make sure your child places the steps for your plan in the correct order.

▲ **Practice Book 2.1** p. 75, Sequence

Comprehension

➲ SKILL Sequence

RECOGNIZE SEQUENCE Review that sequence is the order in which things happen. Remind children to think about what happens first, next, and last. Review that clue words can help you understand when things are happening. Have children tell the sequence of several previously read stories.

CONNECT TO READING

- Notice clues from the pictures that tell about the order of events.
- As you read, look for clue words such as *while*, *before*, and *then*.

➲ STRATEGY Summarize

INTRODUCE THE STRATEGY Tell children that a summary is a brief retelling of the main points of a story. Summarizing as they read can help them remember the main events in a story.

 Think Aloud

MODEL When I read a story, I sum up the main events in my own words. I ask myself what the characters want, what the problem is, and how the problem is solved.

CONNECT TO READING Encourage children to ask themselves these questions as they read *Turtle's Race with Beaver*.

- Do I know what this story is mostly about?
- Do I know what Turtle wants? Do I know what Beaver wants?
- Do I know how they are going to solve their problem?

Build Background

DISCUSS POND ECOSYSTEMS Display a picture of a pond ecosystem. Initiate discussion by asking children what they know about pond ecosystems.

- What are some of the plants that live in or around a pond?
- What are some of the animals that live in or around a pond?
- How do plants help some of the animals that live in or around a pond?

BACKGROUND BUILDING AUDIO Have children listen to the CD and share the new information they learned about ecosystems.

Sing with Me/Background Building Audio

COMPLETE A WEB Draw a web or display Graphic Organizer 15. Write *Ecosystem* in the center. Ask children to share information they learned about ecosystems. Add their responses to the web.

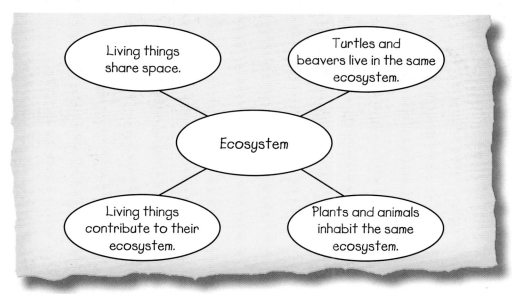

▲ **Graphic Organizer 15**

CONNECT TO SELECTION Connect background information to *Turtle's Race with Beaver.*

Plants and animals that live close to one another can help each other in different ways. However, they must share their space. Beaver is a character in the story we are about to read. We'll find out what Beaver learns about sharing.

Activate Prior Knowledge Ask children to share home-language words related to pond ecosystems. They might give the name in their home-language for *beaver*, *turtle*, and *pond*.

Turtle's Race **220f**

Words to Read

toward
ago
word
whole
above
enough

220

Read the Words

Beaver walked slowly toward the finish line. He had lost the race. Grandfather had told him long ago to always do his best. Beaver gave his word that he would. The whole forest had been cheering for him, but Turtle had won. Above all, Beaver had disappointed Grandfather. "Enough," Beaver told himself. "I will be a good sport and be happy for Turtle."

Genre: Folk Tale

A folk tale is a story that has been handed down from one generation to the next. Now you will read about Turtle and Beaver, who work out a problem by having a race.

221

High-Frequency Words

Nondecodable Words

ROUTINE

1 **Say and Spell** Point to the first word. This word is *enough, e-n-o-u-g-h, enough.* What is this word? What are the letters in this word?

2 **Identify Familiar Letter-Sounds** Point to the first letter in *enough.* What is this letter? What is the sound for this letter? (*e/ē/*)

3 **Demonstrate Meaning** Tell me a sentence using this word. Repeat the routine with the other Words to Read. Have children identify these familiar letter-sounds and word parts: *toward* (*t/t/*, *d/d/*), *above* (blend the syllables: *a-bove*), *ago* (blend the syllables: *a-go*), *word* (*w/w/*, *d/d/*), *whole* (*wh/h/*, *o/ō/*, *l/l/*).

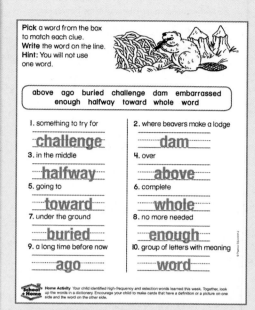

Pick a word from the box to match each clue.
Write the word on the line.
Hint: You will not use one word.

| above | ago | buried | challenge | dam | embarrassed |
| enough | halfway | toward | whole | word | |

1. something to try for
   __challenge__
2. where beavers make a lodge
   __dam__
3. in the middle
   __halfway__
4. over
   __above__
5. going to
   __toward__
6. complete
   __whole__
7. under the ground
   __buried__
8. no more needed
   __enough__
9. a long time before now
   __ago__
10. group of letters with meaning
    __word__

School + Home **Home Activity** Your child identified high-frequency and selection words learned this week. Together, look up the words in a dictionary. Encourage your child to make cards that have a definition or a picture on one side and the word on the other side.

▲ **Practice Book 2.1** p. 76
High-Frequency Words and Selection Words

Have children read aloud the sentences on p. 221 and point to the Words to Read. Add the words to the Word Wall. **Word Wall**

Use Vocabulary Transparency 8 to review this week's words.
- Point to a word. Say and spell it.
- Have children say and spell the word.
- Ask children to identify familiar letter-sounds.

Monitor Progress | Check High-Frequency Words

Point to the following words on the Word Wall and have individuals read them.

| **enough** | **toward** | **above** | **ago** | **word** | **whole** |
| **beautiful** | **work** | **build** | **bear** | **animals** | **though** |

If...children cannot read these words,

then...have them practice in pairs with word cards before reading the selection. Monitor their fluency with these words during reading, and provide additional practice opportunities before the Day 5 Assessment.

SUCCESS PREDICTOR

| **Day 1** Check Word Reading | ▶**Day 2 Check High-Frequency Words** | **Day 3** Check Retelling | **Day 4** Check Fluency | **Day 5** Assess Progress |

High-Frequency Words

SUCCESS PREDICTOR

More than One Way to Win

1. My friend <u>challenged</u> me to a race.

2. She wanted to run all the way to the beaver <u>lodge</u>.

3. We raced past a <u>dam</u> made of rocks.

4. I stopped when I saw something almost <u>buried</u> in the mud.

5. I was <u>embarrassed</u> when my friend raced past me.

6. I raced only <u>halfway</u>, but I found a big prize— a gold rock!

Words to Read		
above	ago	enough
toward	whole	word

▲ **Vocabulary Transparency 8**

Vocabulary

SELECTION WORDS

Use Vocabulary Transparency 8 to introduce the selection words.

- Read each sentence as you track the print.
- Frame each underlined word. Explain the word's meaning.

  buried covered
  dam something that blocks the flow of water
  lodge a beaver's den
  challenge to invite someone to take part in a game or an argument
  halfway in the middle
  embarrassed uncomfortable or ashamed

- Ask children to identify familiar letter-sounds and word parts: *challenge* (blend the syllables: *chal, lenge*), *lodge* (l/l/, o/o/ dge/j/), *embarrassed* (blend the syllables: *em, bar, rassed*), *buried* (blend the syllables: *bur, ied*), *dam* (d/d/, a/a/, m/m/), *halfway* (blend the words: *half, way*)
- Have children read each sentence aloud with you.
- To encourage discussion using the selection words, ask children for reasons and examples. What is an example of a time you felt embarrassed? What is an example of a time you challenged someone to do something? Continue with the rest of the words.

Group Time

DAY 2

On-Level	Strategic Intervention	Advanced
Read *Turtle's Race with Beaver.* • Use pp. 222–242.	**Read** SI Decodable Reader 8. • Read or listen to *Turtle's Race with Beaver.* • Use the **Routine** on p. DI·36.	**Read** *Turtle's Race with Beaver.* • Use the **Routine** on p. DI·37.

ELL Place English language learners in the groups that correspond to their reading abilities in English.

ⓘ Independent Activities

Independent Reading See p. 218j for Reading/Library activities and suggestions.

Journal Writing Write about a time you had a disagreement with someone. Share writing.

Literacy Centers To provide experiences with *Turtle's Race with Beaver*, you may use the Listening Center on p. 218j

Practice Book 2.1 Sequence, p. 75; High-Frequency Words and Selection Words, p. 76; Realism/Fantasy, p.77

ELL

Access Content Use the vocabulary strategies and word cards in the ELL Teaching Guide, pp. 52–53.

Break into small groups after Vocabulary and before Writing.

Turtle's Race with Beaver

as told by Joseph Bruchac and James Bruchac
illustrated by Jose Aruego and Ariane Dewey

Why are Turtle and Beaver racing, and who will win?

222

223

Read
Prereading Strategies

PREVIEW AND PREDICT Have children read the title of the story. Identify Turtle and Beaver in the picture. Identify the author and illustrator. Do a picture walk of pp. 222–227. Ask children what they think this story will be about.

DISCUSS FOLK TALES Reread the definition of folk tale on p. 221 of the Student Edition. Explain that a folk tale is a story that was made up a long time ago and spoken aloud for many generations before it was finally written down. Tell children that this is a Native American tale. Folk tales usually have a good character and a bad character. Make sure children understand that Turtle and Beaver are made up characters whose story teaches a lesson.

SET PURPOSE Read the question on p. 223. Ask children what they would like to find out as they read this story.

AudioText

ELL

Access Content Before reading, review the story summary in English and/or the home language. See the ELL Teaching Guide, pp. 54–56.

Long ago, Turtle lived in a beautiful little pond.

224

She was very happy because this pond had everything a turtle needed. The water was just deep enough, there was plenty of food to eat, and there were lots of nice rocks just above the water for Turtle to sun herself on.

225

▲ **Pages 224–225**
Have children read to find out how Turtle feels about her pond.

Monitor Progress
Decoding

If...children come to a word they don't know,	**then**...remind them to:
	1. Blend the word.
	2. Decide if the word makes sense.
	3. Look in a dictionary for more help.

Guiding Comprehension

Setting • Inferential
• **What is the setting of this story?**
a beautiful little pond

Cause and Effect • Inferential
• **Why does Turtle feel happy about her pond?**
She is happy because her beautiful pond has everything she needs—just enough water, plenty of food, and rocks to sun on.

_____ *r*-Controlled *er, ir, ur*   high-frequency/tested vocabulary

One day, as happens every year in the north, winter began to come to the land. As she had done year after year, Turtle swam to the bottom of the pond and buried herself in the thick mud.

While Turtle slept for the winter, another animal came walking along. It was Beaver, who had been looking for a new home.

"This will be perfect," said Beaver, "once I make some changes."

Soon he began doing one of the things beavers do so well. *Chomp! Chomp!* went Beaver as he took down one tree after another to build a big dam.

226

227

Guiding Comprehension

▲ **Pages 226–227**
Have children read to find out why Turtle buries herself in the mud.

Draw Conclusions • Critical

• **Why does Turtle bury herself in the mud?**
It keeps her warm and safe during the winter.

Cause and Effect • Inferential

• **What effect will Beaver's new home have on the pond?**
Since he is building a dam, it will stop the flow of water.

Compare and Contrast • Inferential

• **How are Turtle and Beaver alike?**
They both need to live in or near water. They both like the pond.

Monitor Progress

High-Frequency Words

| **If**…children have a problem reading a new high-frequency word, | **then**…use the High-Frequency Routine on p. 221a to reteach the problematic word. |

He worked hard for many days. And as he did, the water got deeper and deeper.

After finishing his dam, Beaver made himself a fine lodge of mud and sticks, then settled in for the rest of the winter. He was very happy.

The moons came and went, and spring returned once more to the land. The birds sang and the ice melted away. Then Turtle woke up. Crawling out from under the mud, she began to swim toward the surface of the water. But she had to swim higher, and higher, and higher, and higher.

228

By the time Turtle made it to the surface, she realized that the water was four times as deep as before! Her pond didn't look the same at all. All of the rocks she loved to sun herself on were under water. On one side the pond stretched as far as her eyes could see. On the other stood a huge dam. Not too far from that was a big round lodge.

229

▲ **Pages 228–229**
Have children read to find out what happens to Turtle and Beaver.

EXTEND SKILLS

Figurative Language

For instruction discuss the following:

• Sometimes an author uses words to tell the reader something different from what the words really say.

• On p. 228, the author says, "The moons came and went," meaning that time passed and the season changed from winter to spring.

Assess Have children explain what the author means on p. 232 when he says the race will take place "at first light."

Strategies in Context

🔁 SUMMARIZE

• **In your own words, tell what happens in this part of the story.**
Beaver works hard and finishes the dam and the lodge. Spring returns, and Turtle wakes up. She has to swim a long time to reach the top because Beaver's work has made the pond very deep.

Monitor Progress	**Summarize**
If... children have difficulty telling what happens in this part of the story,	**then...** model how to use the text and pictures to summarize events.

Think Aloud

MODEL I see Turtle looks scared as she's swimming. When I read, I find out that she has to swim a long way to get to the surface because Beaver's dam made the pond so deep.

ASSESS Have children complete a T-chart to summarize events related to Beaver and events related to Turtle.

_____ r-Controlled er, ir, ur   high-frequency/tested vocabulary

Then Turtle heard a loud *Whack!* She turned to see where the sound had come from. A strange animal was swimming toward her. It was Beaver.

"Who are you?" asked Beaver. "What are you doing here?"

"I am Turtle," Turtle said. "This is my pond. I have lived here my whole life."

"*Your* pond!" said Beaver. "This is *my* pond! Look at my wonderful dam and my splendid lodge. This is a beaver's pond."

"Yes," Turtle said, "I can see that you've done lots of work. Couldn't we just share the pond? There's plenty of room."

230

"Ha!" Beaver laughed. "I will not share my pond with any little turtle. But I *will* challenge you to a race. Whoever wins can stay, whoever loses must go find a new home."

Turtle didn't really want to race. She could see that Beaver, with his big flat tail, was probably a much faster swimmer. But this pond was the only home she knew.

"I agree," Turtle said. "We will race."

231

Guiding Comprehension

Compare and Contrast • Inferential

- **How are Turtle and Beaver different?**
Turtle is kind and wants to share. Beaver doesn't want to share.

Classify • Critical

- *Text to Text* **What are some other stories you've heard about animals or people who have a problem with each other? What happened?**
Possible response: In the story about the three little pigs, the pigs have a problem with the wolf. He wants to eat them, and they don't want to be eaten. He blows down two of their houses, but they all move into the strong brick house and are safe.

Summarize • Inferential

- **What has happened in the story so far?**
Beaver moves into Turtle's pond and changes it. Turtle offers to share the pond, but Beaver refuses. He and Turtle agree to race across the pond to see if they will share the pond.

▲ **Pages 230–231**
Have children read to find out how Turtle and Beaver are different.

Strategy Self-Check

Have children ask themselves these questions to check their reading.

Decoding Words

- Do I look at other words in the sentence to figure out the meaning of a new word?
- Does the new word make sense in the story?

Summarize

- Do I know what the story is mostly about?
- Do I know what Turtle wants? Do I know what Beaver wants?
- Do I know how they are going to solve their problem?

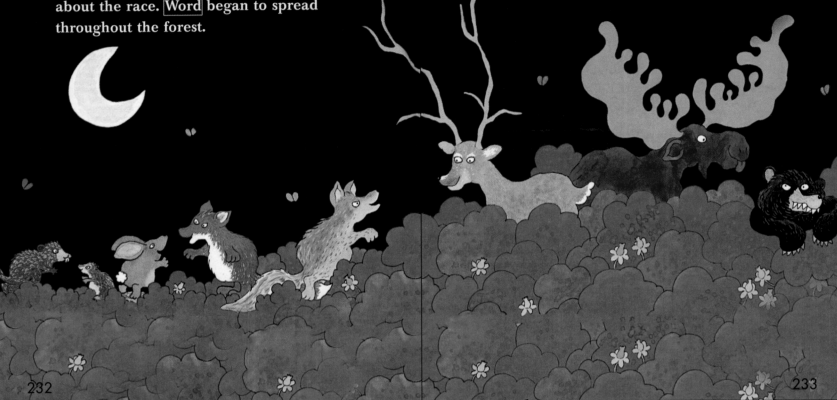

It was decided that the race would take place the next morning at first light. The two would meet on one side of the pond and race to the other.

That night, Beaver told other animals about the race. Word began to spread throughout the forest.

Squirrel told Rabbit, Rabbit told Fox, Fox told Wolf, Wolf told Deer, Deer told Moose, Moose told Bear. Soon every animal in the forest knew.

232

233

▲ **Pages 232–233**
Have children read to find out how the animals found out about the race.

TIME FOR Science

Beavers

Beavers spend a lot of their time swimming. They can close their noses and ears underwater. They also have see-through eyelids to protect their eyes while they swim. Their waterproof hair helps them stay warm.

Beavers build a lodge that has underwater entrances. This protects them from other animals. The main room of the lodge is above water. This is where the beavers sleep. They eat mostly bark, wood, and leaves. They store extra food underwater by the lodge.

Guiding Comprehension

Cause and Effect • Literal
- **How do other animals find out about the race?**
  Beaver tells them. Then each animal tells another animal, so word spreads quickly.

Make Inferences • Inferential
- **Why do you think Beaver tells the other animals about the race?**
  Possible response: He thinks he's going to win and wants to show off.

_____ *r*-Controlled *er, ir, ur*   high-frequency/tested vocabulary

Before first light came to the land, all of the animals of the forest gathered around the pond. As they waited for Turtle and Beaver to arrive, many chose sides. Most of the smaller animals, such as Mouse, Chipmunk, and Rabbit, sided with Turtle. Most of the bigger animals, such as Wolf, Moose, and Bear, sided with Beaver.

As they waited, they began to sing:
TURTLE! BEAVER! TURTLE!
BEAVER! TURTLE! BEAVER!

They sang even louder when Beaver came swimming over from his lodge and Turtle popped up from under the water.
TURTLE! BEAVER! TURTLE!
BEAVER! TURTLE! BEAVER!

234

235

Skills in Context

○ SEQUENCE

• **When did the animals go to the pond? What happened next?**
The animals go to the pond very early in the morning. After they get there, they decide which animal to cheer for.

Monitor Progress	Sequence
If... children are unable to identify sequence,	**then...** model how to use the text to determine order of events.

Think Aloud

MODEL To sequence the events, I think about the order in which things happen. First, the animals gather at the pond. Then they choose sides. Next they begin to sing.

ASSESS Have children find clue words that tell the order of events. *(Before, as)*

▲ **Pages 234–235**
Have children read to find out the order of events.

E L L

Access Content Point out that "before first light came to the land" means "before the sun rises."

Turtles
Freshwater turtles swim a lot. They rest on rocks, land, or floating logs. Some turtles like fast-moving water, and others like quiet ponds. Turtles eat bugs, plants, and fish.

Turtle and Beaver took their positions on the shore.

Bear lifted his big paw in the air. "On your mark. . . get set. . . **GO!**"

SPLASH! went Beaver, leaping off from the shore.

236

He was certain he would leave Turtle far behind. But Turtle had gotten an idea. Before Beaver hit the water, Turtle stretched out her long neck, opened her mouth, and bit into the end of Beaver's tail.

FLAP! FLAP! FLAP! went Beaver, swimming as fast as he could. But as fast as he went, Turtle was right behind, holding on as hard as she could.

The other animals kept cheering, but now some of the bigger animals were cheering for Turtle instead of Beaver.

TURTLE! BEAVER! TURTLE!
BEAVER! TURTLE! *TURTLE!*

237

▲ **Pages 236–237**
Have children look at the pictures and read to understand more about Beavers.

Extend Language Have students name synonyms for *positions*, such as *places* or *seats*.

Guiding Comprehension

Character • Inferential
- **What can you tell about Beaver from the words and pictures?**
  He swims as fast as he can and is sure he will beat turtle. In the pictures, he looks mean.

Sequence • Literal
- **What happens before Beaver enters the water?**
  Turtle bites his tail and holds on.

_____ *r*-Controlled *er, ir, ur*   high-frequency/tested vocabulary

Soon Beaver was halfway across the pond. Even though Turtle was still holding on, it looked as if Beaver would win for sure. Then Turtle bit a little harder into Beaver's tail.

FLAP! FLAP! FLAP! Beaver swam even faster. Turtle still held on. Now more of the animals were cheering for Turtle.

TURTLE! BEAVER! TURTLE!
TURTLE! TURTLE! TURTLE!

Now they were almost to the other side. Beaver seemed sure to win. But Turtle bit as hard as she could into Beaver's tail. *CRUNCH!*

238

"YEEEE-OWWWW!" yelled Beaver. He flipped his big flat tail up and out of the water. When his tail reached its highest point, Turtle let go.

"Weeee!" sang Turtle as she flew through the air right over Beaver's head.

KA-THUNK! Turtle landed on the far shore and crawled across the finish line. Turtle had won the race. All the animals cheered.

TURTLE! TURTLE! TURTLE!
TURTLE! TURTLE! TURTLE!

239

Guiding Comprehension

▲ **Pages 238–239**
Have children read to find out why Turtle bites Beaver so hard.

Cause and Effect • Inferential
• **Why does Turtle bite Beaver's tail so hard?**
She knows it will hurt him and that he will fling his tail. That way she'll be thrown across the finish line first.

Character • Inferential
• **What are some of Turtle's qualities?**
She is smart and determined.

Author's Purpose • Critical
• *Question the Author* **Why does the author use all capital letters for some words?**
Using all capital letters lets the reader know these words or sounds in the story are loud.

Turtle's Race **238–239**

2

Turtle was very pleased. But she could see how sad Beaver was. "I would still be happy to share my pond," she said.

But Beaver was so embarrassed that he left without another word.

Over time Beaver's dam fell apart and the water got shallower and shallower. Turtle had back all her wonderful rocks to sun herself on.

As for Beaver, he did find a new home in a pond not too far away. In that pond, though, there also lived a turtle.

"Can I share your pond with you?" Beaver asked.

"Of course," that other turtle said.

240

241

▲ **Pages 240–241**
Have children look at pictures and read to find out if the story is realistic or a fantasy.

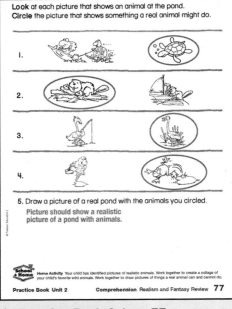

Look at each picture that shows an animal at the pond. Circle the picture that shows something a real animal might do.

1.
2.
3.
4.

5. Draw a picture of a real pond with the animals you circled.
Picture should show a realistic picture of a pond with animals.

Home Activity: Your child has identified pictures of realistic animals. Work together to create a collage of your child's favorite wild animals. Work together to draw pictures of things a real animal can and cannot do.

Practice Book Unit 2   Comprehension Realism and Fantasy Review **77**

▲ **Practice Book 2.1** p. 77, Realism and Fantasy

Skills in Context

REVIEW **REALISM AND FANTASY**

- **Is the story realistic, or is it a fantasy? How do you know?**
  The story is a fantasy because animals don't really talk and the events are not things that could really happen.

Monitor Progress	**Realism and Fantasy**
If... children are unable to identify whether the story is realism or fantasy,	**then...** model how to use the text and pictures to identify fantastic events.

Think Aloud **MODEL** I know that the story is a fantasy because in real life animals cannot talk. In real life, animals do not behave like people. These animals make faces, talk about their problems, and plan a race.

ASSESS Have children look back to find other clues that tell them the story is a fantasy. (In real life, a turtle probably couldn't figure out that a beaver's dam was ruining her pond. Also, in real life animals probably wouldn't cheer and sing for two racing animals.)

____ r-Controlled er, ir, ur   high-frequency/tested vocabulary

And so the two of them lived there happily through all the seasons to come.

242

◀ **Page 242**
Have children read to find out what happens to Beaver.

Reread For Fluency ROUTINE

1 **Reader 1 Begins** Children read the entire book, switching readers at the end of each page.

2 **Reader 2 Begins** Have partners reread; now the other partner begins.

3 **Reread** For optimal fluency, children should reread three or four times.

4 **Provide Feedback** Listen to children read and provide corrective feedback regarding their oral reading and their use of blending.

Guiding Comprehension

Make Inferences • Inferential

- **What lesson does Beaver learn?**
Beaver learns to share with another turtle.

Character • Inferential

- **What can you tell from Beaver's face?**
He is happy.

Make Judgments • Critical

- *Text to World* **How do you think Turtle and Beaver should have solved their problem? Why?** Beaver should have agreed to share the pond.

Strategic Intervention

Children who are not able to write independently may copy one of the sentences from the paragraph and add an illustration.

Advanced

Have children who are able to write independently complete their own paragraph about a time they shared something.

Support Writing Before writing, children might share ideas in their home languages.

Beginning Provide children with a word writing framework that they can copy, filling in missing words.

Intermediate Have children talk with you about what they want to write. Then clarify and restate one of their key ideas in conventional English to guide their writing.

Advanced Encourage children to work in small groups to discuss what they will write as one group member takes notes. Children can refer to these notes when they write.

Support Grammar Tell children that some languages use articles before nouns that change depending on whether the noun is singular or plural. Use examples to show that in English the article "the" stays the same for both singular and plural nouns. See the Grammar Transition lessons in the ELL and Transition Handbook.

Interactive Writing

WRITE Paragraph

DISCUSS Use the story *Turtle's Race with Beaver* to encourage a discussion about sharing. Picture walk through the selection and ask children to identify how Turtle and Beaver's facial expressions change when they share and when they don't.

SHARE THE PEN Have children participate in writing a paragraph about why it is good to share. Remind children that a paragraph is a group of complete sentences about a single topic. The paragraph should be indented. To begin, have a child say a sentence naming one reason why it is good to share. Have the class repeat it. Write the example, inviting individuals to write familiar letter-sounds, word parts, and high-frequency words. Ask questions such as:

● What is the first sound you hear in the word *nice*? (/n/)
● What letter stands for that sound? *(n)* Have a volunteer write *n*.
● What is the second sound you hear in the word *nice*? (/ī/)
● What letter stands for that sound? *(i)* Have a volunteer write *i*.

Continue to have individuals make contributions. Frequently reread what has been written while tracking the print.

READ THE PARAGRAPH Read the completed paragraph aloud, having children echo you.

Why It Is Good to Share

It is good to share because you can help someone. It is also good to share because you might have something someone else needs. When you share something, you get to be with other people too. You might even make a new friend!

INDEPENDENT WRITING

WRITE PARAGRAPH Have children write their own paragraph about why sharing is good. Let children illustrate their writing.

333

Grammar

DEVELOP THE CONCEPT
Singular and Plural Nouns

IDENTIFY SINGULAR AND PLURAL NOUNS Write *dog* and *foxes* on the board. Point to each word as you read it. Ask children to identify the singular noun. *(dog)* Ask children to identify the plural noun. *(foxes)*

A singular noun describes one person, place, animal, or thing. A plural noun describes more than one person, place, animal, or thing. How do you make a singular noun into a plural noun? (Add an *-s* to most singular nouns to make them plural; if the noun ends in *x, ch, sh, s,* or *ss,* add an *-es* to make it plural.)

PRACTICE

MAKE NOUNS SINGULAR OR PLURAL List a mixture of singular and plural nouns in the first column of a three-column chart: *floor, taxes, face, glasses, brush, watch, books.* Label the second column *Singular Nouns* and the third column *Plural Nouns.* Model changing the singular nouns to plural and plural nouns to singular.

 MODEL The first noun is *floor.* That is a singular noun, so I will write it in the column labeled *Singular Nouns.* To make *floor* plural, I have to add an *-s,* so I will write *floors* in the column labeled *Plural Nouns.*

Have children complete the chart.

DAILY FIX-IT

3. They were siting in the dert.
They were sitting in the dirt.

4. turtle took a purse
Turtle took a purse.

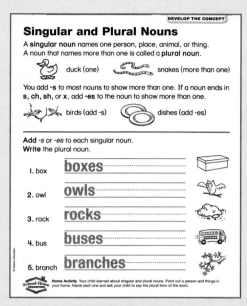

Singular and Plural Nouns

A **singular noun** names one person, place, animal, or thing. A noun that names more than one is called a **plural noun**.

duck (one)   snakes (more than one)

You add **-s** to most nouns to show more than one. If a noun ends in **s, ch, sh,** or **x,** add **-es** to the noun to show more than one.

birds (add -s)   dishes (add -es)

Add **-s** or **-es** to each singular noun. **Write** the plural noun.

1. box — **boxes**
2. owl — **owls**
3. rock — **rocks**
4. bus — **buses**
5. branch — **branches**

▲ **Grammar and Writing Practice Book** p. 29

PREVIEW Day 3

Tell children that tomorrow they will hear about a duck family that needs help.

Wrap Up Your Day!

✓ **HIGH-FREQUENCY WORDS** Write the following sentences. *A long time ago, I saved enough money to buy a whole cake to share with friends. I went to the grocery store. There was a sign above the door with the word "Closed" on it. After I saw the sign, I started walking toward the bakery.* Ask children to read the sentences and identify the high-frequency words *enough, toward, above, ago, word, whole.*

✓ **SUMMARIZE** Help children summarize the events in *Turtle's Race with Beaver.* (Turtle and Beaver race to decide who can stay in their pond. Turtle wins. Beaver moves to another pond and learns to share.)

LET'S TALK ABOUT IT Recall the story *Turtle's Race with Beaver.* Ask: Does Beaver look happier when he is sharing or when he is not sharing? (when he is sharing)

Share Literature
A Ducky Day

Phonics and Spelling
REVIEW Contractions
Spelling: Words with *r*-Controlled *er, ir, ur*

High-Frequency Words
enough	toward	above
ago	word	whole

Vocabulary
Time and Order Words for Sequence

Fluency
Express Characterization

Independent Writing
Respond to Literature

Grammar
Singular and Plural Nouns

Materials

- *Sing with Me Big Book*
- *Read Aloud Anthology*
- Student Edition 243–245

Morning Warm~Up!

Today we will read about a duck
who lays her eggs in an odd place.
The mother duck wants to protect
her babies from hazards.
Why might the baby ducks be skittish?

QUESTION OF THE DAY Encourage children to sing "Turtle, Turtle" from the *Sing with Me Big Book* as you gather. Write and read the message and discuss the question.

REVIEW ORAL VOCABULARY

- Point to the second sentence in the message. Ask children to explain what *hazard* means. (something that could cause injury)
- Point to the third sentence in the message. Ask children to explain what *skittish* means. (easily frightened)

ELL

Build Background Use the Day 3 instruction on ELL Poster 8 to support children's use of English to communicate about lesson concepts.

ELL Poster 8

3

Share Literature

LISTEN AND RESPOND

REVIEW TEXT AS A MEANS OF GAINING INFORMATION
Explain that before reading a selection, a reader may be able to predict the topic due to the title. Explain that text is a means of gathering information. Review that illustrations provide some information about the selection as well.

Read Aloud Anthology
A Ducky Day

BUILD ORAL VOCABULARY Review that yesterday the class read the story to find out how the ducks got into the house. Ask that children listen today to find out what happens next.

MONITOR LISTENING COMPREHENSION

• A guest did not know the duck was real, and she was **startled** when the duck moved. Who else was **startled** in the story? (The baby ducks were **startled** when the people tried to herd them through the doorway.)

• The mother duck inhabits a nest in a flowerpot on a deck beside a house. What is another place a duck might inhabit? (a nest beside a pond)

• What is a likely reason the mother duck wants to take her babies to the pond? (Possible response: She wants to take them to the pond because it will be easier for them to find food and water and learn to swim there.)

OBJECTIVES
● Identify features of text as a source of information.
● Set purpose for listening.
● Build oral vocabulary.

Amazing Words
to build oral vocabulary

	MONITOR PROGRESS
conflict **inhabit** **resolve** **coax** **ramp** **startle**	**If...** children lack oral vocabulary experiences about the concept Working Together, **then...** use the Oral Vocabulary Routine on pp. DI·1–DI·2, DI·5 to develop the Amazing Words.

Listen and Respond Explain that *waddled* describes a duck's movements and *quacked* describes a noise a duck would make. Help children describe and demonstrate the actions conveyed by these words in "A Ducky Day."

OBJECTIVES

- ◎ Review contractions *n't, 's, 'll, 'm.*
- ● Build, blend, and read contractions *n't, 's, 'll, 'm.*
- ● Recognize high-frequency words.
- ● Spell *r*-controlled *er, ir, ur* words.

Write the contraction that is formed from each pair of words on the line.

I <u>will</u> ride in the race.
I'<u>ll</u> ride in the race.

1. they will
they'll

2. was not
wasn't

3. she will
she'll

4. has not
hasn't

5. I am
I'm

6. we will
we'll

Pick a word from the box to finish each sentence. **Write** the word on the line.

| haven't | it's |

7. I **haven't** been in a race before.

8. Now **it's** time to start.

School Home **Home Activity** Your child reviewed contractions such as *wasn't, it's, we'll,* and *I'm.* As you read with your child, point out contractions. Ask your child to say the two words used to make each contraction. Have your child write the contraction and the two words that were used to form it.

▲ **Practice Book 2.1** p. 78, Contractions

Review Phonics

REVIEW Contractions

READ CONTRACTIONS Write *he's.* This word is a contraction, a short way of saying and writing two words. An apostrophe takes the place of letters that are left out. Write *he is* under *he's.* If we compare these words, we see that the apostrophe takes the place of the letter *i.* What's the contraction? (*he's*)

Write *can't.* The contraction *can't* is short for *can not.* Write *can not* under *can't.* Which letter or letters have been left out of *can't?* (*n* and *o*) Have children read *can't.* Repeat with *we'll (we will)* and *I'm (I am).*

BUILD WORDS List the contractions shown below. Have individuals write the two words that make up the contraction.

doesn't	does not
who's	who is
she's	she is
I'll	I will
I'm	I am
shouldn't	should not

High-Frequency Words

PRACTICE

WRITE A CLASS STORY Have children use this week's high-frequency words *above, ago, enough, toward, whole,* and *word* to write a class story about a race.

- Write *above, ago, enough, toward, whole,* and *word* on the chalkboard.
- Have children dictate a class story about a race, using at least one of the high-frequency words in each sentence.
- Record the class story on the board or chart paper.
- Chorally read the story with children and circle each high-frequency word as it is read by the class.

Spelling

PRACTICE *r-Controlled er, ir, ur*

PANTOMIME AND SPELL WORDS Have children practice by writing spelling words that have been pantomimed.

- Write each spelling word on a paper and put it in a bag.
- Have children take turns choosing a word from the bag and acting out the meaning of the word.
- Have the child who guesses the word spell it.
- Repeat the game until all words have been chosen and spelled.

HOMEWORK Spelling Practice Book, p. 31

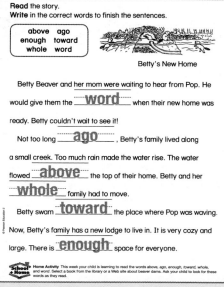

Read the story.
Write in the correct words to finish the sentences.

above	ago
enough	toward
whole	word

Betty's New Home

Betty Beaver and her mom were waiting to hear from Pop. He would give them the **word** when their new home was ready. Betty couldn't wait to see it!

Not too long **ago**, Betty's family lived along a small creek. Too much rain made the water rise. The water flowed **above** the top of their home. Betty and her **whole** family had to move.

Betty swam **toward** the place where Pop was waving.

Now, Betty's family has a new lodge to live in. It is very cozy and large. There is **enough** space for everyone.

Home Activity This week your child is learning to read the words above, ago, enough, toward, whole, and word. Select a book from the library or a Web site about beaver dams. Ask your child to look for these words as they read.

▲ **Practice Book 2.1** p. 79, High-Frequency Words

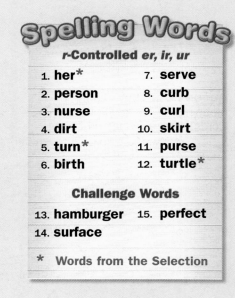

Spelling Words

r-Controlled er, ir, ur

1.	her*	7.	serve
2.	person	8.	curb
3.	nurse	9.	curl
4.	dirt	10.	skirt
5.	turn*	11.	purse
6.	birth	12.	turtle*

Challenge Words

13.	hamburger	15.	perfect
14.	surface		

* Words from the Selection

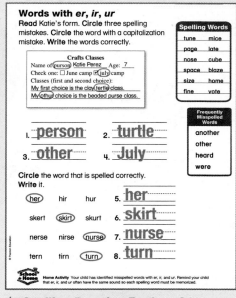

Words with *er, ir, ur*
Read Katie's form. **Circle** three spelling mistakes. **Circle** the word with a capitalization mistake. **Write** the words correctly.

Spelling Words	
tune	mice
page	late
nose	cube
space	blaze
size	home
fine	vote

Crafts Classes
Name of (purson) Katie Perez Age: _7_
Check one: ☐ June camp ☒ (july) camp
Classes (first and second choice):
My first choice is the clay (tertle) class.
My (othur) choice is the beaded purse class.

1. **person**   2. **turtle**
3. **other**   4. **July**

Frequently Misspelled Words
another
other
heard
were

Circle the word that is spelled correctly.
Write it.

(her)	hir	hur	5.	**her**
skert	(skirt)	skurt	6.	**skirt**
nerse	nirse	(nurse)	7.	**nurse**
tern	tirn	(turn)	8.	**turn**

Home Activity Your child has identified misspelled words with er, ir, and ur. Remind your child that er, ir, and ur often have the same sound so each spelling word must be memorized.

▲ **Spelling Practice Book** p. 31

Turtle's Race **243d**

Strategic Intervention

Children who are not able to write independently may copy one of the sentences from the board and add an illustration.

Advanced

Have children write a short story with animals as characters. Tell them they must use at least three time and order words in their stories.

Access Content Clarify meanings of any multiple-meaning words, such as *long* and *spring*.

Vocabulary

TIME AND ORDER WORDS FOR SEQUENCE

DISCUSS TIME AND ORDER WORDS FOR SEQUENCE Have children recall that Turtle and Beaver do things in a certain order. Explain that sequence is the order in which things happen and that clue words can help readers understand when things are happening. Write the following sentences and have children identify the time and order words.

One day, Turtle and Beaver raced across the pond.

Beaver was gone the next morning.

EXPAND MEANING Discuss with children that all stories have a beginning, a middle, and an end. Remind them that time and order words help us understand the story's sequence. Write the following words on the chalkboard: *long ago, every year, many days, that night, spring, winter.* Provide example sentences using some of the words and write them on the board. (Turtle took a vacation each spring.) Have children write sentences using the other words. Invite volunteers to share their sentences.

Group Time

DAY 3

On-Level	Strategic Intervention	Advanced
Read *Turtle's Race with Beaver.*	**Read** or listen to *Turtle's Race with Beaver.*	**Read** *Turtle's Race with Beaver.*
• Use pp. 222–245.	• Use the **Routine** on p. DI·38.	• Use the **Routine** on p. DI·39.

 Place English language learners in the groups that correspond to their reading abilities in English.

(i) Independent Activities

Independent Reading See p. 218j for Reading/Library activities and suggestions.

Journal Writing Write a journal entry about a time when you shared something. Share writing.

Literacy Centers To provide experiences with *Turtle's Race with Beaver,* you may use the Writing Center on p. 218k.

Practice Book 2.1 Contractions *n't, 's, 'll,* p. 78, High-Frequency Words, p. 79

Break into small groups after Vocabulary and before Writing.

Fluency

EXPRESS CHARACTERIZATION

MODEL EXPRESSING CHARACTERIZATION Use *Turtle's Race with Beaver.*

- Point to the quotation marks on p. 227. Quotations marks let us know a character is talking. Sometimes we learn what a character is like by what he or she says. From the quotation, I can tell that Beaver has his own ideas about what makes a perfect home.

- Ask children to follow along as you read p. 227 aloud.

- Have children read p. 227 after you. Encourage them to read the way Beaver would speak. Continue in the same way with pp. 224–227.

REREAD FOR FLUENCY

Choral Reading

ROUTINE

1 Select a Passage For *Turtle's Race with Beaver,* use pp. 228–233.

2 Divide into Groups Assign each group a part to read. For this story, have each group read a paragraph.

3 Model Have children track the print as you read.

4 Read Together Have children read along with you.

5 Independent Readings Have the groups read aloud without you. Monitor progress and provide feedback. For optimal fluency, children should reread three to four times.

Monitor Progress	**Fluency**
If... children have difficulty expressing characterization,	**then...** prompt: • What do the pictures tell us about each character? Does the character look happy or sad? • Determine who is speaking each time you come across quotation marks. • Notice if there are italics, words written in all capital letters, or exclamation points. These all indicate that a word or sentence should be read with emphasis. Then, continue to have them read along with you.
If... the class cannot read fluently without you,	**then...** continue to have them read along with you.

Options for Choral Reading

Use *Turtle's Race with Beaver* or one of the following Leveled Readers.

On-Level

The Busy, Quiet, Lively, Sleepy Pond

Strategic Intervention

Building a Dam

Advanced

Sea Turtles at Risk

ELL

Use *Summer Returns to the Pond* or *Turtle's Race with Beaver.* Model expressing characterization while reading sections of text. Read each character's dialogue with correct expression, showing how dialogue should be read differently from the narration. Invite English language learners to copy you.

 To develop fluent readers, use Fluency Coach

Think and Share

TALK ABOUT IT Model a response. Beaver learned that it's important to share. I would say that sharing makes sense because it's a good way to make friends.

1. **RETELL** Have children use the pictures across the bottom to retell the story. See Monitor Progress below.

2. **SEQUENCE** Possible response: My favorite part of the story was when Turtle bit Beaver really hard. Just before that, Beaver was probably going to win the race. After that, Beaver flipped his tail, which threw Turtle across the finish line.

3. **SUMMARIZE** It looked like Beaver was going to win the race. Even though Turtle was holding Beaver's tail, Beaver was in front, and he was the faster swimmer. But then Turtle thought to bite Beaver really hard, and she won the race because Beaver threw her.

LOOK BACK AND WRITE See Independent Writing, TE p. 245a. `Rubric 4 3 2 1`

Selection Test To assess with *Turtle's Race with Beaver*, use Selection Tests, pp. 29–32.

Monitor Progress | **Check Retelling** `Rubric 4 3 2 1`

If... children have difficulty retelling the story,

then... use the Scoring Rubric for Retelling below to help them move toward fluent retelling.

SUCCESS PREDICTOR

| Day 1 Check Word Reading | Day 2 Check High-Frequency Words | ▶ Day 3 Check Retelling | Day 4 Check Fluency | Day 5 Assess Progress |

Retelling Plan

- ☑ Week 1 assess Strategic Intervention students.
- ☑ Week 2 assess Advanced students.
- ☑ **This week assess Strategic Intervention students.**
- ☐ Week 4 assess On-Level students.
- ☐ Week 5 assess any students you have not yet checked during this unit.

Assessment Before retelling, help children name the characters and items shown. For more ideas on assessing comprehension, see the ELL and Transition Handbook.

Scoring Rubric | Narrative Retelling

`Rubric 4 3 2 1`	**4**	**3**	**2**	**1**
Connections	Makes connections and generalizes beyond the text	Makes connections to other events, stories, or experiences	Makes a limited connection to another event, story, or experience	Makes no connection to another event, story, or experience
Author's Purpose	Elaborates on author's purpose	Tells author's purpose with some clarity	Makes some connection to author's purpose	Makes no connection to author's purpose
Characters	Describes the main character(s) and any character development	Identifies the main character(s) and gives some information about them	Inaccurately identifies some characters or gives little information about them	Inaccurately identifies the characters or gives no information about them
Setting	Describes the time and location	Identifies the time and location	Omits details of time or location	Is unable to identify time or location
Plot	Describes the events in sequence using rich detail	Tells the plot with some errors in sequence that do not affect meaning	Tells parts of plot with gaps that affect meaning	Retelling has no sense of story

Reader Response

Think and Share

Talk About It What lesson did Beaver learn? How would you explain the lesson to a friend?

1. The pictures below show what happened at the beginning of the story. Tell what happened in the middle and at the end.

2. What was your favorite part of this story? What happened before and after that part?

3. Think about the race. How did it go? Summarize the part about the race.

Look Back and Write Look back at pages 241 and 242. Did Beaver learn a lesson? How do you know? Use details from the story in your answer.

Retelling Strip

Meet the Authors
Joseph and James Bruchac

Read more books by Joseph or James Bruchac.

Joseph Bruchac retells Native American stories to share with children. Mr. Bruchac says the best stories teach important lessons, but they also must be fun. Mr. Bruchac and his son James often write together.

James Bruchac says, "Stories about animals are by far my favorites. Our animal brothers and sisters are always teaching us things." James Bruchac is a wilderness expert. He runs the Ndakinna Wilderness Project in Greenfield Center, New York, where he teaches classes on animal tracking, hiking, and the natural world.

243 | 244

Fresh Reads for Differentiated Test Practice

On-Level
Fresh Reads, pp. 45–46

Read the selection. Then answer the questions that follow.

Helping Shoes

One day Juan's mother made him go shopping with her. They went | 12
to buy shoes. Juan hated shopping for shoes. | 20

At the store Juan saw a lot of shoes. First he saw a pair of black | 36
shoes. Then he saw a shiny pair of green shoes. "Can we just get those | 51
and go home?" he asked. | 56

When he wore the green shoes to school, everyone laughed at him. | 68
Suddenly the shoes started walking to the playground! Juan had to go | 80
with the shoes. | 83

When he got to the playground, he saw Lily on the ground. She was | 97
hurt! The shoes took her to the nurse. | 105

"How did you know Lily was hurt?" the nurse asked. | 115

"I did not know," said Juan. "My shoes knew!" | 124

Now Juan loved his green shoes. His shoes took him to people who | 137
needed his help. | 140

Strategic Intervention
Fresh Reads, pp. 43–44

Read the selection. Then answer the questions that follow.

Apple Cake

Hiroshi and his grandfather are hungry. They want to make an apple | 12
cake. Hiroshi and his grandfather mix the cake. They put it in a pan. | 26
Then they cut up apples. They put the apples on top. Then they cook | 40
the cake. They wait and wait. It smells great. At last, the apple cake is | 55
ready. Hiroshi and his grandfather eat the whole cake. It is very, very | 68
good. | 69

Advanced
Fresh Reads, pp. 47–48

Read the selection. Then answer the questions that follow.

The Catch of the Day

"I want to go too," I said to Dan, my older brother. | 12

"Fishing is only for big kids," Dan snapped. | 20

I walked away with my head down. "Why the sad face, Mark?" | 32
asked Mr. Sloan, who lived next door. | 39

"Do you know how to fish?" I asked. | 47

"I sure do," he said. | 52

First, Mr. Sloan told me how to select a good location. Next, he | 65
showed me how to position a worm on the hook. I closed my eyes the | 80
first time. Then he showed me how to cast the hook. With practice, it | 94
went twenty yards! Finally, he said, "Be patient." | 102

We went to the lake, and I cast my hook into the water. "I got one!" | 118
I yelled. I caught a huge fish. Dan and his friends stared with their | 132
mouths open. Mr. Sloan smiled. | 137

Retelling

SUCCESS PREDICTOR

DAILY FIX-IT

5. he was nammed Beaver.
   <u>H</u>e was <u>named</u> Beaver.

6. Turtle gav him a mint?
   Turtle gav<u>e</u> him a mint<u>.</u>

Writer's Checkup

✔ Sentences should include a variety of nouns, verbs, adjectives, and adverbs. Did I do that?

✔ Singular nouns name one person, place, thing, or animal. Did I use my singular nouns correctly?

✔ Plural nouns name more than one person, place, thing, or animal. Did I use my plural nouns correctly?

Independent Writing

Look Back and Write

RESPOND TO LITERATURE Read the writing prompt on p. 243 in the Student Edition and model your thinking. Then have children write their responses.

MODEL I'll look back at pp. 241–242 and read that part of the story again. I'll read to see whether or not Beaver learned a lesson. Then I'll write my response.

Beaver learns a lesson. I know this because he goes to another pond and asks the turtle there if he can share the pond. At the end of the story, Beaver and the new turtle are sharing a little island and smiling.

Scoring Rubric — Written Response

Rubric 4 3 2 1	4	3	2	1
Focus/Ideas	Clearly focuses on the lesson Beaver learned	Focuses on the lesson Beaver learned	Attempts to focus on the lesson Beaver learned	Does not focus on the lesson Beaver learned
Organization/ Paragraphs	Includes information in the correct order	Includes most of the information in the correct order	Includes some information in the correct order	Does not include information in the correct order
Word Choice	Uses clear, exact words	Uses some good words	Uses same or dull words	Uses all wrong words
Conventions	Uses correct capital letters and end marks in all sentences	Generally uses correct capital letters and end marks in sentences	Does not use correct capital letters and end marks in some sentences	Does not use correct capital letters and end marks in any sentences

ELL

Support Writing The prompt asks if Beaver learned a lesson. Explain to children that in this sentence the word "lesson" means something learned by experience.

Assess See the ELL and Transition Handbook for guidance on assessing writing at various levels of English proficiency.

Grammar

APPLY TO WRITING Singular and Plural Nouns

IMPROVE WRITING WITH SINGULAR AND PLURAL NOUNS Have children recall the nouns they used in the answer they wrote for *Look Back and Write*. Explain that it is important to use singular nouns when you're talking about one person, place, animal, or thing and plural nouns when you're talking about more than one person, place, animal, or thing. Doing so makes the writing clear. Remind children to use singular and plural nouns correctly in their own writing.

Write *The cats played with the balls. The dog chewed the stick.* Have children change the singular nouns to plural and the plural nouns to singular.

The cat played with the ball.
The dogs chewed the sticks.

PRACTICE

WRITE WITH SINGULAR AND PLURAL NOUNS Have children write sentences that include both singular and plural nouns. Ask what the difference is between a singular noun and a plural noun.

APPLY TO WRITING

Singular and Plural Nouns

Write sentences about the story *Turtle's Race with Beaver.*
Underline the singular nouns you use.
Circle the plural nouns you use.

Possible answer: The turtle
liked the rocks. The beaver
cut down trees. The animals
had a race.

Home Activity Your child learned about how to use singular and plural nouns in writing. Have your child help you make a grocery list. Ask him or her to tell you which things on the list are singular nouns and which are plural.

▲ **Grammar and Writing
Practice Book** p. 30

Wrap Up Your Day!

✓ **SEQUENCE** Have children recall the order of events in *Turtle's Race with Beaver*. (Beaver moves into the pond. He refuses to share the pond with Turtle. They race to see who gets to stay in the pond. Turtle wins the race and Beaver moves away, but he agrees to share the pond he moves to.) Could the events in the story have occurred in a different order? Why or why not?

✓ **FLUENCY** Discuss with children the characters of Turtle and Beaver. Model how to read dialogue from *Turtle's Race with Beaver* with expression. Have children take turns reading dialogue in the way they think each character would speak.

LET'S TALK ABOUT IT Display Graphic Organizer 25 from Day 1. Is the story *Turtle's Race with Beaver* about a time when sharing makes sense or a time when sharing does not make sense? (sharing makes sense) Give an example. (Beaver learns to share the pond with others so everyone can live together in peace.) Add other examples to the Graphic Organizer.

**PREVIEW
Day 4**

Tell children that tomorrow they will read a selection about ponds.

Day 4
AT A GLANCE

Share Literature
Harry Shares His Room

Phonics and Spelling

r-Controlled er, ir, ur
Spelling: Words with er, ir, ur

Read
Group Time < Differentiated Instruction
"The Secret Life of Ponds"

Fluency
Express Characterization

Writing Across the Curriculum
Venn Diagram

Grammar
Singular and Plural Nouns

Speaking and Listening
Follow and Give Directions

Materials

- *Sing with Me Big Book*
- Read Aloud Anthology
- Student Edition 246–249

Morning Warm~Up!

Turtles and beavers live in ponds.

What other things live in ponds?

Today we will read about things that live near ponds as well as things that live under the surface of ponds.

QUESTION OF THE DAY Encourage children to sing "Turtle, Turtle" from the *Sing with Me Big Book* as you gather. Write and read the message and discuss the question.

REVIEW *r*-CONTROLLED *er, ir, ur*

- Reread the first sentence in the message. Ask children what word is *r*-controlled *er, ir,* or *ur.* (turtle)

- Reread the third sentence in the message. Ask children what word is *r*-controlled *er, ir,* or *ur.* (surface)

Extend Language Use the Day 4 instruction on ELL Poster 8 to extend and enrich language.

ELL Poster 8

Share Literature

CONNECT CONCEPTS

ACTIVATE PRIOR KNOWLEDGE Recall that Turtle, Beaver, and the duck all live in or near ponds and that these animals share their ponds with other living things. Explain that you will read another story about someone who shares his living space when you read "Harry Shares His Room" by Judy Delton.

Read Aloud Anthology
Harry Shares His Room

BUILD ORAL VOCABULARY Read the first paragraph. Explain that Harry's aunt is vacationing in Mexico now but that she will soon stop by Harry's house to visit. Ask children to listen to find out how Harry feels about sharing his room with his aunt.

MONITOR LISTENING COMPREHENSION

- What conflict does Harry face? **(He doesn't want to share his room with his aunt.)**

- Do you think Harry was startled when his aunt started a pillow fight? Explain your answer. **(Children will probably agree that Harry was surprised because adults don't usually have pillow fights.)**

- What does Harry's aunt give him? How does he feel about it at first? **(She gives him a serape. At first, he doesn't like it.)**

- How does Harry's aunt feel about him? Explain your answer. **(Possible response: She loves him and enjoys his company. She brings him a gift, spends time with his friends, and hugs Harry tightly.)**

to build oral vocabulary

	MONITOR PROGRESS
conflict **inhabit** **resolve** **coax** **ramp** **startle** **serape** **vacation**	**If…** children lack oral vocabulary experiences about the concept Working Together, **then…** use the Oral Vocabulary Routine on pp. DI·1–DI·2, DI·5 to develop the Amazing Words.

Connect Concepts Aunt Elsie is moving into a new home in "Harry Shares His Room." Her home is a *condo* or a *condominium*. Explain to children that this is a building with individual apartments that are owned by the people that live there.

4

Sentence Reading

REVIEW WORDS IN CONTEXT

READ DECODABLE AND HIGH-FREQUENCY WORDS IN CONTEXT Write these sentences. Call on individuals to read a sentence. Then randomly point to words and have them read. To help you monitor word reading, high-frequency words are underlined and decodable words are circled.

You're getting dirty from planting the birches, firs, and other trees.

Uncle Herb is going to buy that great big farm, the tractor, and the horses before winter.

The day I missed the bus, forgot my art project, and dropped the urn was the worst day ever.

You may pick either the dark red purse or the purple skirt for the wedding.

I had to laugh when the large perch ate the worm from the fishing line and flopped back into the water!

This is the second time this summer that Carla and Bert will be working at our family store.

Monitor Progress	Word Reading
If... children are unable to read an underlined word,	**then...** read the word for them and spell it, having them echo you.
If... children are unable to read a circled word,	**then...** have them use the blending strategy they have learned for that word type.

Support Phonics For additional review, see the phonics activities in the ELL and Transition Handbook.

Spelling

PARTNER REVIEW *r*-Controlled *er, ir, ur*

READ AND WRITE Supply pairs of children with index cards on which the spelling words have been written. Have one child read a word while the other writes it. Then have children switch roles. Have them use the cards to check their spelling.

HOMEWORK Spelling Practice Book, p. 32

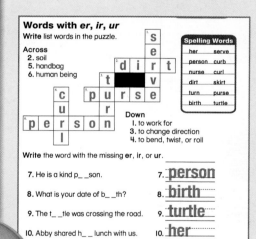

OBJECTIVE

● Spell words with *er, ir, ur.*

Spelling Words

r-Controlled *er, ir, ur*

1. her*	7. serve
2. person	8. curb
3. nurse	9. curl
4. dirt	10. skirt
5. turn*	11. purse
6. birth	12. turtle*

Challenge Words

13. hamburger	15. perfect
14. surface	

* Words from the Selection

Group Time

On-Level	Strategic Intervention	Advanced
Read "Secret Life of Ponds."	**Read** or listen to "Secret Life of Ponds."	**Read** "Secret Life of Ponds."
• Use pp. 246–249.	• Use the **Routine** on p. DI·40.	• Use the **Routine** on p. DI·41.

DAY 4

Words with *er, ir, ur*
Write list words in the puzzle.

Across
2. soil
5. handbag
6. human being

Down
1. to work for
3. to change direction
4. to bend, twist, or roll

Spelling Words	
her	serve
person	curb
nurse	curl
dirt	skirt
turn	purse
birth	turtle

Write the word with the missing *er, ir,* or *ur.*

7. He is a kind p_ _son. — 7. **person**
8. What is your date of b_ _th? — 8. **birth**
9. The t_ _tle was crossing the road. — 9. **turtle**
10. Abby shared h_ _ lunch with us. — 10. **her**
11. Did you get a t_ _n? — 11. **turn**
12. I helped s_ _ve lunch. — 12. **serve**

Home Activity Your child has been learning to spell words with *er, ir,* and *ur.* Look for these letter combinations in words in schoolbooks and library books.

▲ **Spelling Practice Book** p. 32

ELL Place English language learners in the groups that correspond to their reading abilities in English.

(i) Independent Activities

Fluency Reading Pair children to reread *Turtle's Race.*

Journal Writing List animals that inhabit your neighborhood. Share writing.

Spelling: Partner Review

Independent Reading See p. 218j for Reading/Library activities and suggestions.

Literacy Centers To provide listening opportunities, you may use the Listening Center on p. 218j. To extend science concepts, you may use the Science Center on p. 218k.

Break into small groups after Spelling and before Fluency.

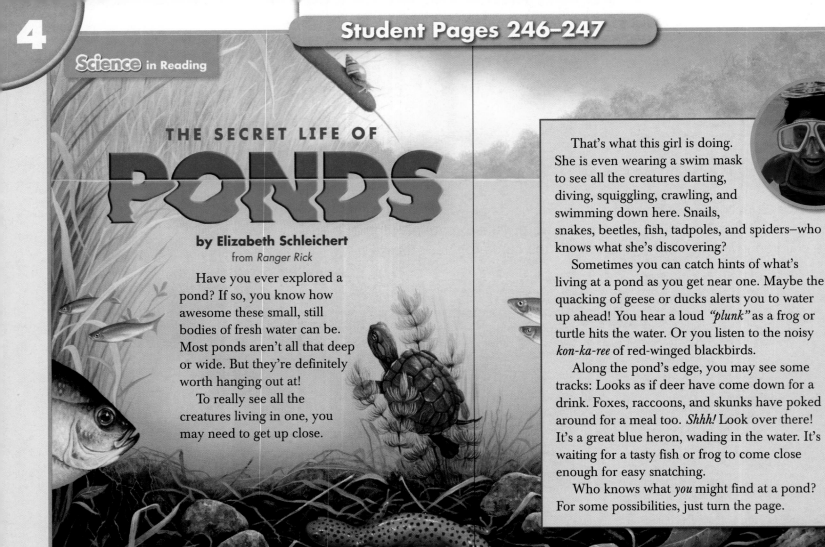

THE SECRET LIFE OF
PONDS

by Elizabeth Schleichert
from *Ranger Rick*

Have you ever explored a pond? If so, you know how awesome these small, still bodies of fresh water can be. Most ponds aren't all that deep or wide. But they're definitely worth hanging out at!

To really see all the creatures living in one, you may need to get up close.

That's what this girl is doing. She is even wearing a swim mask to see all the creatures darting, diving, squiggling, crawling, and swimming down here. Snails, snakes, beetles, fish, tadpoles, and spiders—who knows what she's discovering?

Sometimes you can catch hints of what's living at a pond as you get near one. Maybe the quacking of geese or ducks alerts you to water up ahead! You hear a loud *"plunk"* as a frog or turtle hits the water. Or you listen to the noisy *kon-ka-ree* of red-winged blackbirds.

Along the pond's edge, you may see some tracks: Looks as if deer have come down for a drink. Foxes, raccoons, and skunks have poked around for a meal too. *Shhh!* Look over there! It's a great blue heron, wading in the water. It's waiting for a tasty fish or frog to come close enough for easy snatching.

Who knows what *you* might find at a pond? For some possibilities, just turn the page.

246   247

Audio CD   **AudioText**

Read
Science in Reading

PREVIEW AND PREDICT Read the title and author's name. Have children preview the article and match the labels to the pictures. Then ask them to predict whether "The Secret Life of Ponds" tells a story or provides information. Have children read to learn how many types of plants and animals share the space around or in a pond.

INFORMATIONAL TEXT Review that selections that provide information about the real world are called nonfiction. Point out that the picture of the plants and animals in the pond has numbers on it and that the numbers match the list of numbers with accompanying text that names each object.

VOCABULARY/DESCRIPTIVE WORDS Review how descriptive words can paint a vivid image in the reader's mind. Have children reread the first paragraph on p. 247 and notice the words *darting, diving, squiggling,* and *crawling*. Ask them to describe the images these words call to mind and to pantomime the actions with their hands.

OBJECTIVE

● Recognize text structure: nonfiction.

TIME FOR Science

Survival
Survival is when something continues to live. In order to survive, animals need food and water. They also must be able to fight off or escape from other animals. Survival also depends on where an animal chooses to live. Many animals try to remain hidden.

What's Here?

The painting shows a pond in the Midwest or Northeast. You might not see all of these plants and animals in one pond. But you'll most likely see some.

1. fragrant water lily
2. green frog
3. sunfish
4. cattail
5. damselflies
6. water scorpion
7. orb snail
8. pickerel
9. leech
10. red-spotted newt
11. dragonfly
12. whirligig beetles
13. red-eared slider
14. shiner
15. giant water bug
16. bullhead

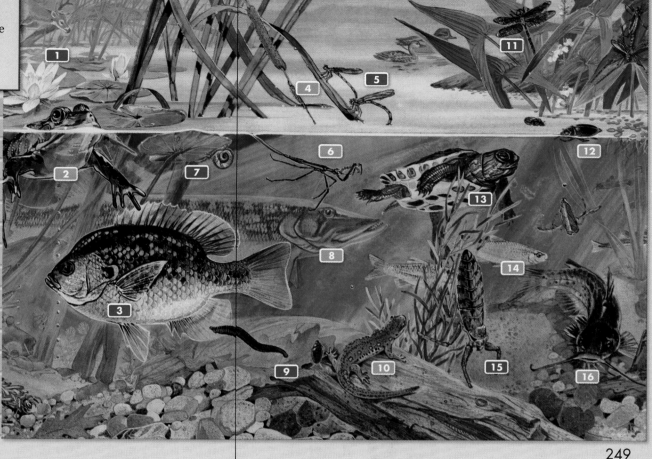

248

249

BUILD CONCEPTS

Graphic Sources • Inferential

- **How does the picture relate to what you read?**
  It shows what you might see in a pond.

Draw Conclusions • Critical

- **What is a likely reason that the article is called "The Secret Life of Ponds"?**
  Sample response: There is more going on in a pond than can be seen with a quick glance. There is life in and around the water that we have to look closely to find. It seems secret because it's hidden.

CONNECT TEXT TO TEXT

READING ACROSS TEXTS

Some of the same animals and plants are shown in the ponds in both stories. Look at the pictures and tell what you find in both stories.

Have children determine which plants and animals are similar in the two stories, such as turtle, deer, dragonflies, water lilies, underwater plants, fish.

E L L

Access Content Ask: Do you know what the phrase "worth hanging out at" means? If children do not understand the idiom, explain its meaning.

Turtle's Race **248–249**

OBJECTIVE

- Read aloud fluently while expressing characterization.

Options for Oral Reading

Use *Turtle's Race with Beaver* or one of the following Leveled Readers.

On-Level

The Busy, Quiet, Lively, Sleepy Pond

Strategic Intervention

Building a Dam

Advanced

Sea Turtles at Risk

ELL

Use *Summer Returns to the Pond* or "The Secret Life of Ponds." For guidance in assessing the reading fluency of English language learners, see the ELL and Transition Handbook.

Fluency Coach CD To develop fluent readers, use Fluency Coach.

Fluency

EXPRESS CHARACTERIZATION

MODEL EXPRESSING CHARACTERIZATION Use *Turtle's Race with Beaver.*

- Point to the quotation marks on p. 240. Quotations marks let us know someone is talking. To be able to talk like the character, I need to pay attention to information about the character.

- Have children read p. 240 after you. Encourage them to read the way Turtle would speak. Continue in the same way with pp. 241–242, reminding them that they will be reading the way both Beaver and Turtle would speak.

REREAD FOR FLUENCY

Choral Reading

ROUTINE

1 **Select a Passage** For *Turtle's Race,* use pp. 234–242.

2 **Divide Into Groups** Have children read, switching reads at the end of each page.

3 **Model** Have children track the print as you read.

4 **Read Together** Have children read along with you.

5 **Independent Readings** Have the groups read aloud without you. Monitor progress and provide feedback. For optimal fluency, children should reread three to four times.

Monitor Progress | Check Fluency

As children reread, monitor their progress toward their individual fluency goals. Current Goal: 58–68 words correct per minute. End-of-Year Goal: 90 words correct per minute.

If... children cannot read fluently at a rate of 58–68 words per minute,

then... make sure children practice with text at their independent level. Provide additional fluency practice, pairing nonfluent readers with fluent readers.

If... children already read fluently at 90 words per minute,

then... they do not need to reread three to four times.

SUCCESS PREDICTOR

| **Day 1** Check Word Reading | **Day 2** Check High-Frequency Words | **Day 3** Check Retelling | ▶ **Day 4** Check Fluency | **Day 5** Assess Progress |

Writing Across the Curriculum

WRITE Venn Diagram

BRAINSTORM Have children think about real turtles and beavers. How are they alike? How are they different? Encourage children to use oral vocabulary, such as *inhabit*.

SHARE THE PEN Have children participate in creating a Venn diagram. To begin, draw a Venn diagram on the chalkboard and explain that one circle will be for turtles, one for beavers, and the intersecting circle will be the things the two animals have in common. Tell the class they will work together to complete it. Have children copy the diagram on their own paper. Call on an individual to name something that is different about turtles and beavers. Write the word, phrase, or sentence in the appropriate circle, and have the class repeat it. Invite individuals to help spell contractions by writing familiar letter-sounds. Ask questions, such as the following:

- What is the beginning sound you hear in the word *it's*? (/i/) Write *i*. Continue with the sounds /t/ and /s/.

- What are the two words that make *it's*? *(it is)*

- Where does the apostrophe go? What letter does the apostrophe take the place of in *it's*? *(i)*

Continue having individuals contribute to the diagram. Frequently reread the answers.

Have children write a sentence at the bottom of their Venn diagram, answering the question "What is one way turtles and beavers are alike?"

Fill in the Venn diagram and include the word *it's*.

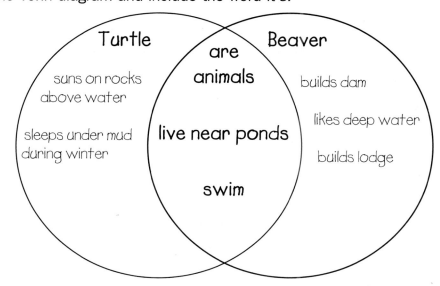

Turtles and beavers both need to live near a pond.

OBJECTIVE
● Create a Venn diagram.

Advanced

Encourage children to create another Venn diagram comparing and contrasting two other types of animals.

Support Writing Create a word list for children with content-area words they might not know, such as *reptile, mammal,* and so on. Discuss the terms orally before children write together.

4

DAILY FIX-IT

7. His kids hade a new hom.

His kids <u>had</u> a new hom<u>e</u>.

8. he asked if she wanted it?

<u>H</u>e asked if she wanted it<u>.</u>

TEST PREPARATION

Singular and Plural Nouns

Mark the letter of the word that correctly completes each sentence.

1. A beaver chops down two ____.
   - ○ A tree
   - ⊗ B trees
   - ○ C treeses

2. Beavers eat leaves from some ____.
   - ⊗ A bushes
   - ○ B bush
   - ○ C bushs

3. Some ____ can live together.
   - ○ A animales
   - ○ B animal
   - ⊗ C animals

4. Four ____ live in a den.
   - ○ A fox
   - ⊗ B foxes
   - ○ C foxs

5. Turtles have ____.
   - ⊗ A shells
   - ○ B shelles
   - ○ C shell

Home Activity Your child prepared for taking tests on singular and plural nouns. Read a book together. Have your child find plural nouns that add -s or -es.

▲ **Grammar and Writing Practice Book** p. 31

Grammar

REVIEW Singular and Plural Nouns

DEFINE SINGULAR AND PLURAL NOUNS

- What do singular nouns name? (one person, place, animal, or thing)
- What do plural nouns name? (more than one person, place, animal, or thing)

PRACTICE

CLASSIFY SINGULAR AND PLURAL NOUNS Write a list of singular and plural nouns on the chalkboard. Have individuals classify the nouns as either singular or plural.

Singular	Plural
cat	roads
bike	pedals

Speaking and Listening

FOLLOW AND GIVE DIRECTIONS

MODEL SPEAKING AND LISTENING Remind children of appropriate speaking and listening behaviors for giving and following directions, such as speaking clearly and listening carefully. Then ask children to think about these behaviors as they take turns giving and following directions (some directions will not be able to be followed in class).

- When you give directions, you tell someone how to do something. You always start with the first step.

- Then you tell the second step. The steps should be short and clear.

- Then you tell the final step. Sometimes directions will have more than three or four steps.

- When you listen to directions, you follow the steps one at a time in the order given.

GIVING DIRECTIONS Ask children to give directions, using three or four simple steps. Allow children the opportunity to complete a steps in a process chart or Graphic Organizer 23 before taking their turn speaking to the class.

Wrap Up Your Day!

✓ **Text to Self** Have you ever explored a pond? What did you see? (Possible response: I have explored a pond in my neighborhood. I've seen ducks and turtles and fish in it.) Call on individuals to provide different answers.

LET'S TALK ABOUT IT Recall the Read Aloud selection "Harry Shares His Room." Ask: Why did sharing make sense in this story? (Harry's aunt needed a place to stay, and Harry had room.) Display Graphic Organizer 25 from Day 1 and add this example.

PREVIEW Day 5

Remind children that they heard a story about a boy who learns to share. Tell them that tomorrow they will hear about Harry again.

Share Literature
Harry Shares His Room

Phonics and Spelling

Review *r*-Controlled *er, ir, ur*;
Syllable *-er*

High-Frequency Words
enough   toward   above
ago   word   whole

Word Wall

Monitor Progress
Spelling Test: Words with *er, ir, ur*

Group Time < Differentiated Assessment

Grammar and Writing
Singular and Plural Nouns

Research and Study Skills
Alphabetical Order: Second Letter

Materials

- *Sing with Me Big Book*
- Read Aloud Anthology
- Reproducible Pages
  TE 250f–250g
- Student Edition 250–251

Morning Warm-Up!

This week we read about
animals and people who didn't want
to share their
ponds, decks, and rooms.
Then things usually got easier.

How do you usually feel when you share?

QUESTION OF THE DAY Encourage children to sing "Turtle, Turtle" from the *Sing with Me Big Book* as you gather. Write and read the message and discuss the question.

REVIEW ORAL VOCABULARY Have children name things in the message that

- people or animals inhabit (ponds, decks, rooms)
- might cause a conflict (sharing)

ELL

Assess Vocabulary Use the Day 5 instruction on ELL Poster 8 to monitor children's progress with oral vocabulary.

ELL Poster 8

Share Literature

LISTEN AND RESPOND

USE PRIOR KNOWLEDGE Review that yesterday the class listened to find out how Harry felt about sharing his room with his aunt. Suggest that today the class listen to find out why Harry's feelings changed.

MONITOR LISTENING COMPREHENSION

* What were some of Harry's complaints about having Aunt Elsie in his room? (She smelled like flowers, her clock was loud, and she snored.)

* When do you think Harry changed his mind about having his aunt inhabit his room with him? (Possible response: I think Harry realized how much fun Aunt Elsie was and how much he enjoyed her company when she brought in snacks and started a pillow fight.)

Read Aloud Anthology
Harry Shares His Room

LISTEN AND RESPOND

TIME AND ORDER WORDS FOR SEQUENCE Read the first page of "Harry Shares His Room." Have children find time and order words that tell sequence (the next day, on Tuesday morning). Write *the next day* and *on Tuesday morning*. Ask children to find other time and order words in the story that tell sequence and list them. Time and order words tell when things happened. Challenge children to use the time and order words for sequence in sentences.

the next day	**after supper**
on Tuesday morning	**at bedtime**
on Thursday	**the next morning**
tomorrow	**that night**
in the morning	**on Sunday**
at noon	**on Saturday**

OBJECTIVES

* Set purpose for listening.
* Build oral vocabulary.

Extend Language Help children list other time and order words (*yesterday, one day, every spring, first, then, next,* and so on). Have children use the words in short stories or conversations.

r-Controlled *er, ir, ur*

REVIEW

IDENTIFY *er, ir,* and *ur* WORDS Write these sentences. Have children read each one aloud. Call on individuals to name and underline the *er, ir,* and *ur* words and identify the vowel sounds.

> **The <u>first</u> <u>nurse</u> was <u>stern</u>.**
> **The <u>clerk</u> in the <u>purple</u> <u>shirt</u> sold us the <u>skirt</u>.**
> **The <u>water</u> began to <u>swirl</u> and <u>churn</u>.**
> **Did you <u>hear</u> the crickets <u>whir</u> and <u>chirp</u> in the <u>ferns</u>?**

High-Frequency Words

REVIEW

COMPLETE THE RHYME Write the rhyme, leaving blanks for missing words. Ask children to complete each line with one of the Words to Know from p. 220. Then read the rhyme together.

In a kingdom long, long _____, (ago)

high _____ the mountains and snow, (above)

lived a king with a _____ lot of seeds—and so, (whole)

he gave his _____ to the people below, (word)

that he would give them _____ seeds to plant and grow. (enough)

Then he threw the seeds _____ the people below! (toward)

SPELLING TEST *r*-Controlled *er, ir, ur*

DICTATION SENTENCES Use these sentences to assess this week's spelling words.

1. They will <u>serve</u> the pizza.
2. Will you help me <u>curl</u> my hair?
3. I like that pretty <u>skirt</u>!
4. That <u>nurse</u> was nice to me.
5. Which <u>person</u> gave Dad that gift?
6. Mom gave me her old <u>purse</u>.
7. My dog likes to dig in the <u>dirt</u>.
8. When will it be my <u>turn</u>?
9. Do not step off the <u>curb</u>!
10. We have a new pet <u>turtle</u>.
11. I have not seen <u>her</u> for a long time.
12. The cat gave <u>birth</u> to six kittens.

CHALLENGE WORDS

13. I ate a <u>hamburger</u> for dinner.
14. The <u>surface</u> of the pond is calm.
15. My teacher said my paper was <u>perfect</u>!

ASSESS

● Spell *er, ir, ur* words.

Spelling Words

r-Controlled *er, ir, ur*

1. **her***	7. **serve**
2. **person**	8. **curb**
3. **nurse**	9. **curl**
4. **dirt**	10. **skirt**
5. **turn***	11. **purse**
6. **birth**	12. **turtle***

Challenge Words

13. **hamburger**	15. **perfect**
14. **surface**	

* Words from the Selection

Group Time

On-Level	Strategic Intervention	Advanced
Read Set B Sentences and the Story.	**Read** Set A Sentences.	**Read** Set C Sentences.
• Use pp. 250e–250g.	• Use pp. 250e–250g.	• Use pp. 250e–250g.
	• Use the **Routine** on p. DI·42.	• Use the **Routine** on p. DI·43.

DAY 5

E L L Place English language learners in the groups that correspond to their reading abilities in English.

i Independent Activities

Fluency Reading Children reread selections at their independent level.

Journal Writing Write about a time when you resolved a conflict. Share Writing.

Independent Reading See p. 218j for Reading/Library activities and suggestions.

Literacy Centers You may use the Technology Center on p. 218k to support this week's concepts and reading.

Practice Book 2.1 Alphabetical Order: Second Letter, p. 80

Break into small groups after Spelling and before Grammar and Writing.

ASSESS

- ⦿ Decode *r*-controlled *er, ir, ur.*
- Read high-frequency words.
- Read aloud with appropriate speed and accuracy.
- ⦿ Recognize story sequence.
- Retell a story.

Differentiated Assessment

On-Level
Set B

Strategic Intervention
Set A

Advanced
Set C

Fluency Assessment Plan

- ☑ Week 1 assess Advanced students.
- ☑ Week 2 assess Strategic Intervention students.
- ☑ **This week assess On-Level students.**
- ☐ Week 4 assess Strategic Intervention students.
- ☐ Week 5 assess any students you have not yet checked during this unit.

Set individual fluency goals for children to enable them to reach the end-of-year goal.

- Current Goal: 58–68 wcpm
- End-of-Year Goal: 90 wcpm
- **ELL** For guidance in evaluating fluency, see the ELL and Transition Handbook.

SENTENCE READING

ASSESS *r*-CONTROLLED *er, ir, ur* AND HIGH-FREQUENCY WORDS Use one of the reproducible lists on p. 250f to assess children's ability to read words with *r*-controlled *er, ir, ur* and high-frequency words. Call on individuals to read two sentences aloud. Have each child in the group read different sentences. Start over with sentence one if necessary.

RECORD SCORES Use the Sentence Reading Chart for this unit on p. 313k.

Monitor Progress	*r*-Controlled *er, ir, ur*
If… children have trouble reading *r*-controlled *er, ir, ur,*	**then…** use the Reteach Lessons on p. DI·66.
High-Frequency Words	
If… children cannot read a high-frequency word,	**then…** mark the missed words on a high-frequency word list and send the list home for additional word reading practice or have the child practice with a fluent reader.

FLUENCY AND COMPREHENSION

ASSESS FLUENCY Take a one-minute sample of children's oral reading. See Monitoring Fluency, p. 313i. Have children read "The Purple Shirt," the on-level fluency passage on p. 250g.

RECORD SCORES Record the number of words read correctly in a minute on the child's Fluency Progress Chart.

ASSESS COMPREHENSION Have the child read to the end of the passage. (If the child had difficulty with the passage, you may read it aloud.) Ask questions about the sequence of events and have the child retell the passage. Use the Retelling Rubric on p. 243g to evaluate the child's retelling.

Monitor Progress	Fluency
If… a child does not achieve the fluency goal on the timed reading,	**then…** copy the passage and send it home with the child for additional fluency practice or have the child practice with a fluent reader.
Sequence	
If… a child cannot recognize the sequence of events,	**then…** use the Reteach Lesson on p. DI·66.

READ THE SENTENCES

Set A

1. The girl ate enough perch for lunch.
2. The bird and turtle walked toward pond.
3. What is the first word on her list?
4. The whole herd was in the third pen.
5. Dad fixed the curb by the fir tree a long time ago.
6. The surf was above Kirk's head.

Set B

1. The dog's whole head was full of curly fur.
2. Plant the fern toward the curve of the garden.
3. The robin chirped in the birch tree above us.
4. The nurse lost her purse and hat a long time ago.
5. Stir the pancake batter enough, but do not hurry.
6. She tried to offer a kind word to her hurt friend.

Set C

1. Have they served enough water to drink, or are you still thirsty?
2. We walked toward the clerk who was behind the shirt counter.
3. The teacher said to turn the paper over and write one spelling word in the circle.
4. A long time ago, the circus came to our city and set up a huge purple tent.
5. The river rose above its banks and flooded the church with swirling water.
6. Dad cooked a whole turkey with stuffing and didn't burn it!

Monitor Progress | *r*-Controlled *er, ir, ur*
High-Frequency Words

SUCCESS PREDICTOR

The Purple Shirt

Fox and Turkey sat in the sun and waited for   10
Turtle. "What do you want for your birthday?"   18
asked Fox when he saw Turtle.   24

"I would like a purple shirt," said Turtle. "I do   34
not like my dark green shell. You have red fur,   44
Fox. And your feathers are beautiful, Turkey.   51
Purple is better than any other color."   58

Later, Fox and Turkey went to a little pond.   67
First, they got purple plums and mashed them up.   76
They put the plums in the water. Next, they put the   87
shirt in and stirred it up. They left the shirt in the   99
pond so it would turn purple.   105

Before long, Turtle came to the pond. It was a   115
hot day, so he went for a swim.   123

The next day, Turtle asked, "Did you get me a   133
purple shirt?"   135

Fox and Turkey looked at him and laughed.   143
"You do not need a purple shirt! You are purple!"   153

Turtle was not upset. He loved it! He was the   163
only purple turtle in the whole woods!   170

SUCCESS PREDICTOR

250g

Singular and Plural Nouns

A **singular noun** names one person, place, animal, or thing.

Turtle rested on the **rock**.

A noun that names more than one is called a **plural noun**.

Turtle could not find any of his **rocks**.

You add **–s** to most nouns to show more than one. If a noun ends in **s, ch, sh,** or **x,** add **–es** to the noun to show more than one.

Two **foxes** watched the race from the **bushes**.

250

Write Using Singular and Plural Nouns

1. Find some singular nouns in the story. Make them plural. Write them.

2. Write a sentence to Beaver about why he should share the pond with Turtle. Use a singular and a plural noun. Underline them.

3. What food would you make for a picnic at the big race? Write how to make it. Use singular and plural nouns.

251

Grammar and Writing

WRITE USING SINGULAR AND PLURAL NOUNS Read pp. 250–251 aloud. Guide children as they complete the items.

1. Possible response: pond/ponds, animal/animals, dam/dams
2. Possible response: You and Turtle can race past the <u>rocks</u> each <u>week</u>.

CONNECT TO UNIT WRITING Children write sentences about how to make food for a picnic. They should use both singular and plural nouns.

3. Possible response:

I would make fruit <u>salad</u>. First I would cut up some <u>bananas</u>. Then I would add <u>apples</u>. I would slice one <u>pineapple</u> and add it too. Then I would stir in some <u>yogurt</u>.

DAILY FIX-IT

9. They walkked to the dame.
 They <u>walked</u> to the <u>dam</u>.

10. turtle likked it very much.
 <u>Turtle</u> <u>liked</u> it very much.

CUMULATIVE REVIEW

Singular and Plural Nouns
Underline the singular noun in each sentence. Circle the plural noun.

1. The (rabbits) came to the race.

2. The bear cheered for the (teams).

3. The turtle saved the (trees) too.

Choose the correct plural noun in ( ). **Write** the sentence.

4. Fish swim in (lakeses, lakes).

 Fish swim in lakes.

5. Bears live in (forestes, forests).

 Bears live in forests.

6. Cats sleep in (boxs, boxes).

 Cats sleep in boxes.

Home Activity Your child reviewed singular and plural nouns. Together make a list of objects in the room. Have your child write the plural forms of the words on the list.

▲ **Grammar and Writing Practice Book** p. 32

Turtle's Race **250–251**

- Use alphabetical order: second letter.

Dictionary
Look at the dictionary page. **Write** the answer to each question.

> **race • rye**
> **race** (rās) *NOUN.* a contest of speed.
> **reach** (rēch) *VERB.* to arrive.
> **rice** (ris) *NOUN.* the grain from a grass that grows in warm places.
> **rust• y** (rus' tē) *ADJECTIVE.* covered with rust.

1. What are the guide words for this page?

race, rye

2. What does *reach* mean?

to arrive

3. What do the letters in ( ) mean?

how to say the word

4. How is *reach* used in a sentence?

It is a verb.

5. If the entry word *rocket* were on this page, between which two words would it fall? **rice and rusty**

Home Activity Your child learned how to read a dictionary entry. Name a word, such as *turtle*. Ask your child how to find it in a dictionary and what the dictionary would tell about the word. If possible, have your child use a dictionary to find the entry.

▲ **Practice Book 2.1** p. 80, Alphabetical Order: Second Letter

Access Content The alphabets from some first languages may be different from the English alphabet. Review the English alphabet with English language learners and give them practice alphabetizing by first letter before having them start alphabetizing by second letter.

Research/Study Skills

TEACH/MODEL Alphabetical Order: Second Letter

MODEL USING ALPHABETICAL ORDER: SECOND LETTER Look at the picture of the pond in "Secret Life of Ponds." Tell students you will be putting some of the names in alphabetical order. Explain that alphabetical order is helpful because it makes information easier to find. Remind them that alphabetical order is used in dictionaries, glossaries, and encyclopedias. Ask children to put these words in alphabetical order: *leech, water lily, cattail*.

Tell children that sometimes they will need to alphabetize words that start with the same letter. Model how to put names in alphabetical order according to the second letter.

Think Aloud **MODEL** I see two names that start with *g*. One is *green frog*, and the other is *giant water bug*. Since they both start with the same letter *g*, I will look at the second letter in each name to tell me which name should come first. The second letter in *green frog* is *r*, and the second letter in *giant water bug* is *i*. Since *i* comes before *r*, *giant water bug* would come before *green frog*.

DEMONSTRATE ALPHABETIZING Put children into small groups. Call on individuals to alphabetize the first names of the children in their group. They can write their list on the board.

PRACTICE

DEMONSTRATE USING ALPHABETICAL ORDER: SECOND LETTER Divide children into small groups. Give each child in each group a piece of paper with a word written in large letters. All of the words used in one group should start with the same letter. Have children arrange their words in alphabetical order. They can either lay the pages in alphabetical order on the ground, or they can hold the pages and arrange themselves in alphabetical order according to each word.

Wrap Up Your Week!

LET'S TALK ABOUT Working Together

QUESTION OF THE WEEK Recall this week's question.

• When does sharing make sense?

Display the sharing chart. Help children identify other situations in which sharing does or doesn't make sense.

When does sharing make sense?	When does sharing not make sense?
When you have something others need to survive	When you're taking a test at school
When space is scarce but there are lots of people	When doing so would hurt you or someone else
When you have more than you need	

CONNECT Use questions such as these to prompt a discussion.

• Characters have a conflict when they disagree or want different things. What characters do you know who wanted different things? Would working together have solved their problem?

• We inhabit, or live, in our homes. How can people or animals who inhabit the same place work together?

Build Background Use ELL Poster 8 to support the Preview activity.

PREVIEW Tell children that next week they will read more about working together when a group of animals decides to do just that.

PREVIEW Next Week

The Bremen Town Musicians

ONLINE CLASSROOM

For the Teacher

PLAN — My Lesson Planner ONLINE

TEACH — Teacher's Edition ONLINE

ASSESS — Success Tracker™ ONLINE

For the Student

READ — Read It ONLINE

Leveled Reader Database ONLINE

EXPLORE — Take It to the NET™ ONLINE

PRACTICE — Fluency Coach

Phonics Activities

Preview Your Week

When should we work together? When should we work alone?

The Bremen Town **Musicians**

retold as a play by Carol Pugliano
illustrated by Jon Goodell

Who are the Bremen Town Musicians?

256 257

Audio CD

Student Edition pages 256–275

Genre	Fairy Tale
Phonics	Plural
Comprehension Skill	Author's Purpose
Comprehension Strategy	Story Structure

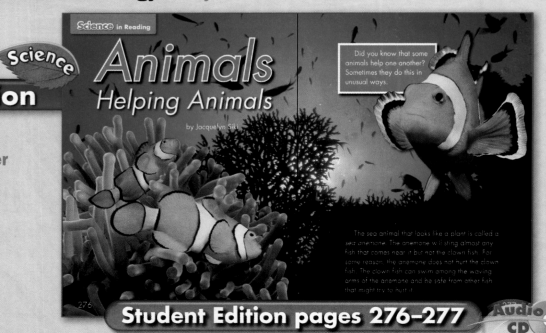

Science in Reading

Science

Animals Helping Animals

by Jacquelyn Siki

Paired Selection

Reading Across Texts
Recall Working Together

Genre
Photo Essay

Text Features
Photographs

Did you know that some animals help one another? Sometimes they do this in unusual ways.

The sea animal that looks like a plant is called a sea anemone. The anemone will sting almost any fish that comes near it but not the clown fish. For some reason, the anemone does not hurt the clown fish. The clown fish can swim among the waving arms of the anemone and be safe from other fish that might try to hurt it.

276

Student Edition pages 276–277

Audio CD

Read It
ONLINE
sfsuccessnet.com

- Student Edition
- Leveled Readers
- Decodable Reader

Leveled Readers

🔵 **Skill** Author's Purpose

🔵 **Strategy** Story Structure

Lesson Vocabulary

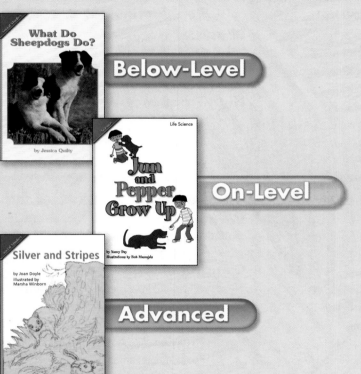

Below-Level

On-Level

Silver and Stripes
by Joan Doyle
illustrated by Marsha Winborn

Advanced

ELL Reader

- Concept Vocabulary
- Text Support
- Language Enrichment

Decodable Readers

Apply Phonics

- *Fletch and Fran*

Integrate Science Standards

- Interdependence
- Survival
- Living Things
- Environment

✓ **Read**

The Bremen Town Musicians pp. 256–275

"Animals Helping Animals," pp. 276–279

✓ **Read**

Leveled Readers

- **Below-Level**
- **On-Level**
- **Advanced**

- Support Concepts
- Develop Concepts
- Extend Concepts
- Science Extension Activity

✓ **Read**

ELL Reader

✓ **Build Concept Vocabulary**
Working Together,
pp. 252r, 252–253

✓ **Teach Science Concepts**
Donkeys, pp. 260–261
Aging Pets, pp. 268–269
Interdependence, pp. 276–277

✓ **Explore Science Center**
Imagine Life Without Plants,
p. 252k

Bremen Town Musicians **252c**

Planner

My Lesson Planner
ONLINE
sfsuccessnet.com

DAY 1

DAY 2

Oral Language · 10-15 minutes

- **Build Concepts**
- **Share Literature**

Oral Language 252l-252m

QUESTION OF THE WEEK *When should we work together? When should we work alone?*

Share Literature
Sing with Me Big Book, 9

Oral Language 254a-254b

QUESTION OF THE DAY *When have you worked with others?*

Share Literature
Big Book *From Me to You*

Word Work · 25-30 minutes

- **Phonics**
- **Spelling**
- **High-Frequency Words**

Word Work 252n-252p

Phonics
Introduce Plurals –s, -es, -ies **T**

Spelling Pretest

Word Work 254c-254d, 254-255a

Phonics
Plurals –s, -es, -ies **T**

Spelling Dictation

High-Frequency Words T
Introduce *people, sign, shall, bought, probably, pleasant, scare*

Reading · 60-75 minutes

- **Vocabulary**
- **Comprehension**
- **Fluency**

- **Cross-Curricular Connections**

- **Independent Reading**

Reading 252q-253b

Vocabulary
Decodable Word Meaning

Read Decodable Reader 9

Comprehension Check

Fluency
Oral Rereading

Build Background
Let's Talk About Working Together

Comprehension
Author's Purpose **T**

SCIENCE Concept Chart

Leveled Readers, LR28–36
Self-Selected Reading, TR22–23

Reading 254e-254f, 256a-273

Vocabulary
Introduce *mill, excitement, musician, robbers, monsters*

Comprehension
Author's Purpose **T**
Story Structure

Read *The Bremen Town Musicians,* 256–273

REVIEW **Comprehension Skill**
Realism and Fantasy

SCIENCE Donkeys, Older Pets
SCIENCE Concept Chart

Leveled Readers, LR28–36
Self-Selected Reading, TR22–23

Language Arts · 20-30 minutes

- **Writing**
- **Grammar**
- **Speaking, Listening, Viewing**
- **Research/Study Skills**

Language Arts 253c-253d

Shared Writing
Poster

DAILY WRITING
Write about why partnerships are important.

Grammar
Introduce Plural Nouns That Change Spelling **T**

Language Arts 273a-273b

Interactive Writing
Questions

DAILY WRITING
Write about a time when you worked closely with another person.

Grammar
Practice Plural Nouns That Change Spelling **T**

Monitor Progress

Daily **SUCCESS PREDICTORS** for
Adequate Yearly Progress

Day 1 Check 252o
Check Word Reading
Spiral REVIEW Phonics

Phonics

Day 2 Check 255a
Check High-Frequency Words
Spiral REVIEW High-Frequency Words

Fluency

252d Vocabulary Check Oral Vocabulary See p. DI·2.

Student Edition 256–275   **Leveled Readers**   **Student Edition** 276–279

DAY 3

Oral Language 274a–274b

QUESTION OF THE DAY *What might make Bat feel better?*

Share Literature
Big Book *From Me to You*

Word Work 274c–274d

Phonics
REVIEW *r-*Controlled *er, ir, ur*

Spelling Practice

High-Frequency Words T
Practice *people, sign, shall, bought, probably, pleasant, scared*

Reading 256–273, 274e–275

Vocabulary
Homophones

Comprehension
Read *The Bremen Town Musicians*, 256–275

Think and Share

Fluency
Reader's Theater

SCIENCE Concept Chart

Leveled Readers, LR28–36
Self-Selected Reading, TR22–23

Language Arts 275a–275b

Independent Writing
Respond to Literature

DAILY WRITING
Write about a time when you worked with someone else to accomplish something.

Grammar
Write with Plural Nouns that Change Spelling T

DAY 4

Oral Language 276a–276b

QUESTION OF THE DAY *What things might an animal need help with?*

Share Literature
Read Aloud Anthology "How Fletcher Was Hatched!"

Word Work 276c–276d

Phonics
REVIEW Sentence Reading

Spelling Partner Review

High-Frequency Words T
Practice *people, sign, shall, bought, probably, pleasant, scared*

Reading 276–279a

Vocabulary
Homophones

Comprehension
Read "Animals Helping Animals," 276–279
Science in Reading
Reading Across Texts

Fluency
Reader's Theater

SCIENCE Interdependence, Environment
SCIENCE Make a Book

Leveled Readers, LR28–36
Self-Selected Reading, TR22–23

Language Arts 279b–279d

Writing Across the Curriculum
Math Story

DAILY WRITING
List ways animals help each other.

Grammar
Review Plural Nouns That Change Spelling T

Speaking and Viewing
Compare and Contrast Characters

DAY 5

Oral Language 280a–280b

QUESTION OF THE DAY *Why is it often better to work with others?*

Share Literature
Read Aloud Anthology "How Fletcher Was Hatched!"

Word Work 280c–280f

Phonics
🔄 Review Plurals *-s, -es, -ies*

Spelling Test

High-Frequency Words T
Review *people, sign, shall, bought, probably, pleasant, scared*

Reading 280b, 280e–280g

Vocabulary
Homophones

Monitor Progress
Read the Sentences
Read the Story

SCIENCE Concept Chart

Leveled Readers, LR28–36
Self-Selected Reading, TR22–23

Language Arts 280–281a

Grammar and Writing
Use Plurals That Change Spelling T

Connect to Unit Writing
How-to Report

DAILY WRITING
Write a story with a problem and solution.

Research/Study Skills
Poster

KEY

🔄 = Target Skill

T = Tested Skill

THIS WEEK'S RESOURCES
Practice Book pp. 81–90

Spelling Practice Book pp. 33–36

Grammar and Writing Practice Book pp. 33–36

Selection Test pp. 33–36

Fresh Reads for Differentiated Test Practice pp. 49–54

Phonics Songs and Rhymes Chart 9

Day 3 Check 274g
Check Retelling
Comprehension

Day 4 Check 279a
Check Fluency WCPM
Spiral REVIEW Phonics, High-Frequency Words
Fluency

Day 5 Check 280e
Plurals *-s, -es, -ies*
High-Frequency Words
Fluency
Comprehension

SUCCESS PREDICTOR

Resources for Differentiated Instruction

LEVELED READERS

▶ **Comprehension**

🎯 **Skill** Author's Purpose

🎯 **Strategy** Story Structure

▶ **Lesson Vocabulary**

High-Frequency Words

people	sign	shall
bought		probably
pleasant		scared

▶ **Science Standards**

• Interdependence

• Survival

• Living Things

• Environment

Leveled Reader Database

ONLINE

sfsuccessnet.com

Use the Online Database of over 600 books to

• Download and print additional copies of this week's leveled readers

• Locate more titles at various levels to practice this week's skill—author's purpose

• Search for more titles focused on this week's topic and content

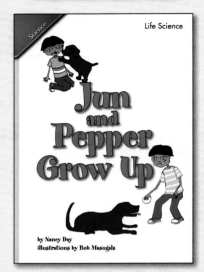

On-Level Reader

Jun and Pepper Grow Up
by Nancy Day
illustrations by Bob Masugals
Life Science

Author's Purpose

Read the text below. Then circle the best answer for each question.

> Jun learned to give Pepper his food and keep his water dish filled. The big puppy followed Jun everywhere. Now Jun didn't mind so much. He even thought it was pleasant and bought puppy treats.

1. Why did the author write about Jun taking care of Pepper?
   a. to teach ⟵
   b. to be funny
   c. to be sad

2. What is another reason the author wrote about Jun and Pepper?
   a. so that you will like the author
   b. so that you will not like dogs
   c. so that you will like the story ⟵

3. How does the author want you to feel about taking care of dogs?
   a. that it is hard and dirty
   b. that it is bad and sad
   c. that it is work and fun ⟵

4–5. Write a sentence that tells what you think about taking care of a dog after reading *Jun and Pepper Grow Up*.

On-Level Practice TE p. LR32

Vocabulary

Circle the silent letters in the words below.

1. people   3. bought
2. sign   4. pleasant

Circle the word that best completes each sentence, and write the word on the line.

5. Dad _____ a puppy and took it home.
   bought   scared

6. Jun didn't like dogs jumping on him, because he was _____ of dogs.
   sign   scared

7. Pepper learned not to jump up on _____
   people   pleasant

8. Pepper's tongue felt a little rough to Jun, but _____
   probably   pleasant

9. Mom asked, "_____ we take Pepper to the park?"
   Shall   Bought

10. When Pepper licked Jun, it was a _____ that Pepper liked him.
   sign   shall

On-Level Practice TE p. LR33

Below-Level Reader

What Do Sheepdogs Do?
by Jessica Quilty
Social Studies

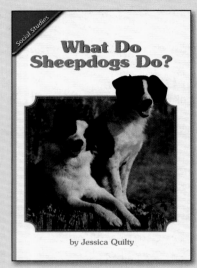

Author's Purpose

Read the text below. Then circle the best answer for each question.

> Sheepdogs love to work. They also like to run and play. They have a good time. It is probably lots of fun for them to live and work on the farm!

1. Why did the author write about what sheepdogs like to do?
   a. to teach ⟵
   b. to be funny
   c. to be sad

2. What is another reason the author wrote about what sheepdogs like to do?
   a. so that you will like the story ⟵
   b. so that you will like the author
   c. so that you will not like sheepdogs

3. How does the author want you to feel about a sheepdog's life?
   a. that it is hard
   b. that it is bad
   c. that it is fun ⟵

4–5. Write a sentence that tells what you think about sheepdogs after reading the book. Answers will vary.

Below-Level Practice TE p. LR29

Vocabulary

Circle the silent letters in the words below.

1. people
2. sign
3. bough
4. pleasant

Draw a line to match the word to its meaning.

5. bought   a. nice, pleasing
6. sign   b. afraid
7. shall   c. got something by paying money
8. probably   d. likely to happen or be true
9. pleasant   e. a helping verb used to ask a question
10. scared   f. a symbol or hand movement that means something

Below-Level Practice TE p. LR30

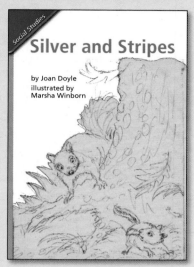

Advanced Reader

Silver and Stripes
by Joan Doyle
illustrated by Marsha Winborn

Author's Purpose

Read the text below. Then circle the best answer for each question.

> **Tiny:** Well, hold on a minute! A true partnership works better if there are more members to help.
> **Silver:** Really? Do you think we should ask Tess to join us?
> **Tiny:** Yes. Tess needs to get food for the winter too, and then she would not have to take it. . . .
> **Tess:** I've got it! If you let me join your partnership, I can help carry sticks and stones too. You can use them to make your homes warmer and stronger for the winter.

1. Why did the author write about Tess and the partnership?
   a. to teach ⟵
   b. to be funny
   c. to be sad

2. What is another reason the author wrote about Tess and the partnership?
   a. so that you will like the author
   b. so that you will like the story ⟵
   c. so that you will not like badgers

3. How does the author want you to feel about having a partnership?
   a. that it is unfair
   b. that it is too hard
   c. that it is good ⟵

4–5. Write a sentence that tells what you think about working with other children after reading the story. Answers will vary.

Advanced Practice TE p. LR35

Vocabulary

Say each word aloud. Then draw a line between each syllable.

Words to Know		
partnership	solution	survival

1. partnership
2. solution
3. survival

Choose a word from the Word Box that best completes each sentence.

4. Charing is a great **solution** to many problems at playtime.

5. Some animals in a forest must gather food before the winter for their **survival** .

6. A **partnership** is when people work together to get something done.

7–10. Write a sentence that tells how your family is one kind of partnership.

Advanced Practice TE p. LR36

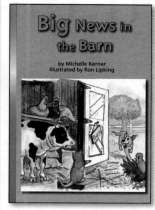

ELL Reader

Big News in the Barn
by Michelle Kerner
Illustrated by Ron Lipking

ELL Poster 9

Teacher's Edition Notes

ELL notes throughout this lesson support instruction and reference additional resources at point of use.

Teaching Guide pp. 57–63, 228–229
- Multilingual summaries of the main selection
- Comprehension lesson
- Vocabulary strategies and word cards
- ELL Reader 9 lesson

ELL and Transition Handbook

Ten Important Sentences
- Key ideas from every selection in the Student Edition
- Activities to build sentence power

More Reading

Reader's Theater Anthology
- Fluency practice
- Five scripts to build fluency
- Poetry for oral interpretation

Leveled Trade Books

- Extend reading tied to the unit concept
- Lessons in Trade Book Library Teaching Guide

School + Home

Homework
- Family Times Newsletter
- ELL Multilingual Selection Summaries

Take-Home Books
- Decodable Readers
- Leveled Readers

Weekly Plan for Group Time
Differentiated Instruction

DAILY PLAN

WHOLE GROUP
- Morning Warm-Up
- Share Literature
- Phonics
- Spelling
- Vocabulary

1 2 3 4 5

DAILY GROUP TIME
- **Reading Support**
- **Skill Support**
- **Fluency Practice**

WHOLE GROUP
- Fluency
- Writing
- Grammar
- Wrap Up Your Day

Independent Activities

See Group Time pp. 252p, 256a, 274e, 276d, 280d.

✓ **Fluency Reading**
Reader's Theater

✓ **Journal Writing**
See the Planner for daily writing prompts, pp. 252d–252e.

✓ **Homework**
Practice Book, pp. 81–90
Spelling Practice Book, pp. 33–36
Grammar and Writing Practice Book, pp. 33–36

✓ **Literacy Centers**
pp. 252j–252k
- Listening
- Reading/Library
- Word Work
- Writing
- Science
- Technology

DAY 1

On-Level	Strategic Intervention	Advanced
Page 252q	**Page DI·34**	**Page DI·45**
• Read Decodable Reader 9	• Read Decodable Reader 9	• Read Advanced Selection 9
• Reread for Fluency	• Blend Words with Plurals	• Extend Word Reading
	• Reread for Fluency	• Introduce Concept Inquiry

DAY 2

On-Level	Strategic Intervention	Advanced
Pages 256–275	**Page DI·46**	**Page DI·47**
• Read *The Bremen Town Musicians*	• Read SI Decodable Reader 9	• Read *The Bremen Town Musicians*
• Reread for Fluency	• Read or Listen to *The Bremen Town Musicians*	• Continue Concept Inquiry
	• Blend Words with Plurals	

DAY 3

On-Level	Strategic Intervention	Advanced
Pages 256–275	**Page DI·48**	**Page DI·49**
• Reread *The Bremen Town Musicians*	• Reread *The Bremen Town Musicians*	• Self-Selected Reading
	• Read Words and Sentences	• Continue Concept Inquiry
	• Review Author's Purpose and Story Structure	
	• Reread for Fluency	

On-Level

Pages 276–279

- Read "Animals Helping Animals"

Strategic Intervention

Page DI•50

- Read or Listen to "Animals Helping Animals"
- Reread for Fluency
- Build Concepts

Advanced

Page DI•51

- Read "Animals Helping Animals"
- Expand Vocabulary
- Continue Concept Inquiry

DAY 4

On-Level

Pages 280e–280g

- Sentence Reading, Set B

Strategic Intervention

Page DI•52

- Practice Word Reading
- Sentence Reading, Set A
- Monitor Fluency and Comprehension

Advanced

Page DI•53

- Sentence Reading, Set C
- Share Concept Inquiry

DAY 5

Set B
1. Bess brought the gray sand pail to the beach.
2. The train may be here any minute now.
3. We promise to make you a plain vase from the clay later.
4. Ray was sorry he didn't pay the bill on time.
5. Hang the apron on the nail behind the door.
6. Which way did everybody go after class today?

Set A
1. Mark brought the mail and paper inside.
2. Everybody was sorry Jay couldn't stay longer.
3. We will wait by the trail for one more minute.
4. I promise to clean the tray before I play.
5. Do not put hay away behind the barn door.
6. A chain keeps the main door shut.

Set C
1. We promise to call and say hello the minute we sail into town.
2. The clouds brought so much rain that all the grain got soaked.
3. We are sorry we could not paint the fence, but we will do it in April.
4. The maid sprayed the room and closed the door when she was finished cleaning.
5. Everybody in the club will fly to Spain for a holiday trip.
6. Jada's dog strayed from behind her home.

Grouping Place English language learners in the groups that correspond to their reading abilities in English.

Use the appropriate Leveled Reader or other text at children's instructional level.

TIP Send home the appropriate Multilingual Summary of the main selection on Day 1.

MORE READING FOR Group Time

What Do Sheepdogs Do? — Below-Level

Jun and Pepper Grow Up — On-Level

Silver and Stripes — Advanced

Take It to the NET ONLINE
sfsuccessnet.com

Connie Juel

For activities to build oral vocabulary, see the article "Walking with Rosie" by Scott Foresman author Connie Juel and others.

TEACHING TIP **Invite children to bring in current events to post.** Each day, ask children to share current event items. It could be family news (the birth of a sibling), a community event, or a national or world event.

TEACHER TALK

High-frequency words are words commonly found in everyday reading, such as *the, of,* or *two.* Some high-frequency words may be taught as **sight words,** words immediately recognized as a whole.

Looking Ahead

Be sure to schedule time for children to work on the unit inquiry project "Organize a Club." This week children should hold a club meeting to discuss problems and begin planning how to address the identified need.

Literacy Centers

Listening

Let's Read
Along

MATERIALS [SINGLES]
CD player, headphones, print copies of recorded pieces

LISTEN TO LITERATURE As children listen to the following recordings, have them follow along or read along in the print version.

AudioText
The Bremen Town Musicians
"Animals Helping Animals"

Sing with Me Background Building Audio
"A Partnership With You"

Phonics Songs and Rhymes Audio
"Buddies Helping You"

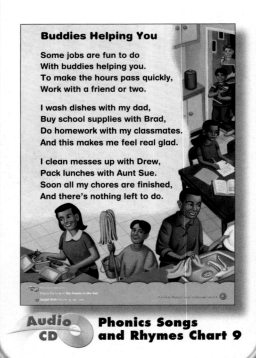

Buddies Helping You

Some jobs are fun to do
With buddies helping you.
To make the hours pass quickly,
Work with a friend or two.

I wash dishes with my dad,
Buy school supplies with Brad,
Do homework with my classmates.
And this makes me feel real glad.

I clean messes up with Drew,
Pack lunches with Aunt Sue.
Soon all my chores are finished,
And there's nothing left to do.

Audio CD **Phonics Songs and Rhymes Chart 9**

Reading/Library

Read It
Again!

MATERIALS [SINGLES] [PAIRS] [GROUPS]
collection of books for self-selected reading, reading logs

REREAD BOOKS Have children select previously read books from the appropriate book box and record titles of books they read in their logs. Use these previously read books:

- **Decodable Readers**
- **Leveled Readers**
- **ELL Readers**
- **Stories written by classmates**
- **Books from the library**

TEN IMPORTANT SENTENCES Have children read the Ten Important Sentences for *The Bremen Town Musicians* and locate the sentences in the Student Edition.

BOOK CLUB Hold a book discussion with a group of classmates. Have each classmate summarize his or her book.

Word Work

More Than
One

MATERIALS [SINGLES] [PAIRS] [GROUPS]
index cards, paper, pencils

PLURALS -s, -es, -ies Have children play a matching game using words and numbers.

1. Make two sets of cards. One set will have a number on each card. The other set will have a singular noun on each card.
2. Place the cards facedown in two stacks, one with the numbers and one with the words.
3. Children pick one card from each pile and write a sentence using the number and the word. For example, if a child drew "two" and "penny," the child might write, "I have two pennies."
4. Play continues until all cards have been used.

Phonics Activities CD This interactive CD provides additional practice.

penny

two

I have two pennies.

Scott Foresman Reading Street Centers Survival Kit

Use *The Bremen Town Musicians* materials
from the Reading Street Centers Survival Kit
to organize this week's centers.

Writing

Science

Technology

Working Together

MATERIALS — SINGLES
paper, pencils, crayons

WRITE A PARAGRAPH Recall how the animals in *The Bremen Town Musicians* work together.

1. Have children write a paragraph about animals working together. The paragraph can be based on the story or on their own ideas.
2. Then have them draw a picture to accompany their writing.

LEVELED WRITING Encourage children to write at their own ability level. Some may write only sentence fragments. Others will be able to write simple sentences with some attention to mechanics and spelling. Your best writers will write sentences with greater detail and more attention to mechanics and spelling.

Huskies work together to pull sleds in the snow. One or two dogs are in the front. They lead the others. All of the dogs pull together.

What If?

MATERIALS — SINGLES
writing and art supplies, paper, magazines, glue, stapler

MAKE A BOOK Remind children that animals depended on each other in *The Bremen Town Musicians*. In real life, people depend on plants in the same way.

1. Have children imagine what would happen if there were no longer any plants.
2. Have them draw and/or find pictures in magazines of things they would have to live without, such as apples and flowers.
3. Children can paste their pictures on a sheet of paper and write a caption for each.
4. Compile the pictures into a book titled "What if there were no plants?"

I wouldn't have flowers to smell.

I wouldn't have apples to eat.

Animals with Jobs

MATERIALS — GROUPS
computer, printer

PRINT A LIST Have groups of children use the computer to create and print out lists of animals that work with people.

1. Have children turn on the computer and create and save a word processing file named "Animals with Jobs."
2. Have them type a list of at least three kinds of animals that have jobs.
3. Have groups print out their lists and present them to the class, explaining how the animals on the list help people.

1. Guide dogs guide people who can't see.
2. Search and rescue dogs find lost people.
3. Horses and donkeys can carry heavy things.
4. Cows and oxen help farmers plow their fields.

ALL CENTERS

Share Literature
"A Partnership With You" 9

Phonics and Spelling
 Plurals

Spelling Pretest:
Plurals

Read Apply Phonics [Word Wall]

(Group Time) < Differentiated Instruction

Build Background
Let's Talk About Working Together

Listening Comprehension
Skill Author's Purpose

Shared Writing
Poster

Grammar
Plural Nouns That Change Spelling

Materials
- *Sing with Me Big Book*
- Letter Tiles
- Decodable Reader 9
- Student Edition 252–253
- Graphic Organizer 14
- Writing Transparency 9
- Grammar Transparency 9

Take It to the NET
ONLINE
Professional Development
To learn more about story retelling, go to sfsuccessnet. com and read the article "Story Retelling" by L. Morrow.

Morning Warm~Up!
Sometimes we need help when we're working toward a goal or trying to solve a problem. When should we work together? When should we work alone?

QUESTION OF THE WEEK Tell children they will talk, sing, read, and write about Working Together. Write and read the message and discuss the question.

CONNECT CONCEPTS Ask questions to connect to other Unit 2 selections.

- In *Tara and Tiree, Fearless Friends*, how did the two dogs work together?
- Why did things change for Beaver when he moved into the second pond in *Turtle's Race with Beaver*?

REVIEW HIGH-FREQUENCY WORDS

- Circle the high-frequency word *toward* in the message.
- Have children say and spell the word as they write it in the air.

Build Background Use the Day 1 instruction on ELL Poster 9 to assess knowledge and develop concepts.

ELL Poster 9

Share Literature

BUILD ORAL VOCABULARY Display p. 9 of the *Sing with Me Big Book.* Tell children that the class is going to sing a song about working with others. Read the title. Ask children to listen for the Amazing Words **partnership, solution,** and **survival** as you sing. Then sing the song again and encourage children to sing with you, demonstrating their understanding of *partnership, solution,* and *survival.*

Sing with Me/
Background Building Audio

A Partnership with You

Had a problem,
Had a problem.
Tried to solve it on my own.
Couldn't find a good solution,
So I called you on the phone.

Solved my problem,
Solved my problem.
Thank you, Friend, for all you do.
What is good for my survival
Is a partnership with you.

Sing with Me Big Book

Amazing Words to build oral vocabulary

	MONITOR PROGRESS
partnership **solution** **survival**	**If...** children lack oral vocabulary experiences about the concept Working Together, **then...** use the Oral Vocabulary Routine on pp. DI·1–DI·2, DI·6 to develop the Amazing Words.

Access Content Help children recognize the meaning of the English words *problem* and *solution* in "A Partnership With You" by asking them which comes first.

- Use structural cues to decode plurals *-s, -es, -ies.*
- Blend, read, and build plurals *-s, -es, -ies.*

Skills Trace

Plurals

Introduce/Teach	TE: 2.2 252n–o
Practice	TE: 2.2 252q, DR9, 254c–d; PB: 2.1 83, 98
Reteach/Review	TE: 2.2 280c, 303c, DI-67
Assess/Test	TE: 2.2 280e–g; Benchmark Test, Unit 2

Generalization

For base words ending with consonant-*y*, the *y* changes to *i* before adding *-es, -ed, -er, -est.*

Strategic Intervention

Use **Monitor Progress**, p. 252o during Group Time after children have had more practice with plurals *-s, -es, -ies.*

Advanced

Use **Monitor Progress**, p. 252o as a preassessment to determine whether or not this group of children would benefit from this instruction on plurals.

Support Phonics In Chinese, Hmong, and Vietnamese, nouns do not have a plural form. Instead, adjectives indicate whether a noun is singular or plural. Speakers of these languages may need additional practice with plural word endings in English.

See the Phonics Transition Lessons in the ELL and Transition Handbook.

Plurals *-s, -es, -ies*

TEACH/MODEL

Blending Strategy

ROUTINE

1 **Connect** Write *flagged* and *skating*. What do you know about reading these words? (Both have a base word, an ending, and a spelling change.) Read the words together. What are the base words? What are the endings? What are the spelling changes? (The final consonant was doubled; the *e* was dropped.) Today you'll learn about endings for plurals, words that mean "more than one."

2 **Model** Write *stars* and *wishes.* To make words mean "more than one," the ending *-s* or *-es* is added. *-s* is added to most words; *-es* is added to words that end in *sh, ch, tch, s, ss,* or *x*. This is how I blend these words. Cover the ending, read the base word, uncover and read the ending. Blend the two parts. Let's blend these words together: *star, s—stars; wish, es—wishes.*

w i s h e s

Write *cities.* The base word is *city.* Cover the ending *-es.* The *y* in *city* changed to *i* in *cities.* Uncover the ending. To blend this word, I read one part at a time and then I blend the parts together: *cit, ies—cities.* Have children blend the word with you.

c i t i e s

3 **Group Practice** First, see if *y* changed to *i* in the base word. Then read the base word, read the ending, and blend the two parts together. Continue with *patches, dishes, boxes, pennies, farms, ranches, buddies, glasses.*

4 **Review** What do you know about reading plural words? See if *y* changed to *i* in the base word. Read the base word, read the ending, and then blend the two parts.

BLEND WORDS

INDIVIDUALS BLEND WORDS Call on children to blend *parties, lunches, messes, foxes, skirts, candies, sashes, bodies, ponies.* Have them tell what they know about each word before reading it. (Blend the base word and ending to read the whole word.) For feedback, refer to step four of the Blending Strategy Routine.

BUILD WORDS

READ LONGER WORDS Write *-s, -es,* and *-ies* as headings for a three-column chart. Write these base words: *expert, basket, order, dancer, bench, scratch, kiss, circus, baby, lady, buddy, candy.* Have children form plurals by adding *-s, -es,* or changing *y* to *i* and adding *-es* and place each word under the correct heading. Then have them read the plurals.

-s	-es	-ies
experts	benches	babies
baskets	scratches	ladies
orders	kisses	buddies
dancers	circuses	candies

Vocabulary Tip

You may wish to explain the meanings of these words.

gerbils small animals that look like mice.

lilies plants with tall, thin stems and large bell-shaped flowers

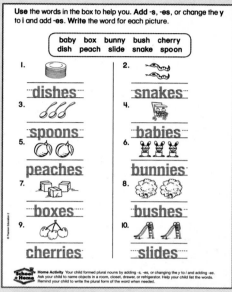

Use the words in the box to help you. Add *-s, -es,* or change the *y* to *i* and add *-es.* Write the word for each picture.

| baby | box | bunny | bush | cherry |
| dish | peach | slide | snake | spoon |

1. dishes
2. snakes
3. spoons
4. babies
5. peaches
6. bunnies
7. boxes
8. bushes
9. cherries
10. slides

Home Activity Your child formed plural nouns by adding -s, -es, or changing the y to i and adding -es. Ask your child to name objects in a room, closet, drawer, or refrigerator. Help your child list the words. Remind your child to write the plural form of the word when needed.

▲ **Practice Book 2.1** p. 83, Plurals

Monitor Progress | Check Word Reading Plurals

Write the following words and have individuals read them.

mixes	hitches	dishes	lilies	puppies
corners	stories	perches	armies	buses
germs	roses	centers	gerbils	cents

If… children cannot blend plurals at this point,

then… continue to monitor their progress using other instructional opportunities during the week so that they can be successful with the Day 5 Assessment. See the Skills Trace on p. 252n.

SUCCESS PREDICTOR

Spiral REVIEW

- Row 2 reviews *r*-controlled vowels.
- Row 3 reviews *c* /s/, *g* /j/, *s/z/*.

▶ **Day 1 Check Word Reading** : **Day 2 Check High-Frequency Words** : **Day 3 Check Retelling** : **Day 4 Check Fluency** : **Day 5 Assess Progress**

Word Reading

SUCCESS PREDICTOR

OBJECTIVES

- Segment sounds and word parts to spell words.
- Spell plurals with -s, -es, -ies.

Spelling Words

Plurals

1. note
2. notes
3. lunch
4. lunches
5. story
6. stories
7. tune
8. tunes*
9. switch*
10. switches*
11. baby
12. babies

Challenge Words

13. crumbs
14. supplies
15. centuries

* Words from the Selection

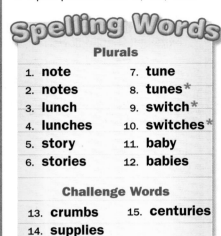

Adding -s and -es

Generalization Add -s to most words; add -es to words that end in ch, sh, or x; and change y to i and add -es to most words that end with y: notes, switches, stories.

Sort according to how the plural is formed.

-s	Change y to i add -es	Spelling Words
1. note	9. story	1. note
2. notes	10. stories	2. notes
3. tune	11. baby	3. lunch
4. tunes	12. babies	4. lunches
-es	**Challenge Words**	5. story
5. lunch	**-s**	6. stories
6. lunches	13. crumbs	7. tune
7. switch	14. holidays	8. tunes
8. switches	Change y to i add -es	9. switch
	13. crumbs	10. switches
	14. supplies	11. baby
	15. supplies	12. babies
		Challenge Words
		13. crumbs
		14. supplies
		15. holidays

Home Activity Your child is learning to spell words with and without -s and -es. To practice at home, have your child say the word, write it, and then check it.

▲ **Spelling Practice Book** p. 33

ELL

Support Spelling Before giving the spelling pretest, clarify the meaning of each spelling word with examples, such as saying *lunches* are meals people eat midday, and pointing to a story book to illustrate *stories*.

Spelling

PRETEST Plurals -s, -es, -ies

MODEL WRITING FOR WORD PARTS Each spelling word has the ending -s, -es, or -ies. Before administering the spelling pretest, model how to segment base words and endings to spell them.

- You can spell these words by thinking about the base words and endings. What base word and ending make up *votes?* (*vote* and -s)
- Start with the sounds in the base word: *vote*. What letters spell /vōt/? Write *vote*.
- Now add -s. Add *s*.
- Now spell *votes*.
- Repeat with *wishes and ladies*.

PRETEST Dictate the spelling words. Segment the words for children if necessary. Have children check their pretests and correct misspelled words.

HOMEWORK Spelling Practice Book, p. 33

Group Time

Helping Hands

Animals can be trained to assist disabled people. You may have seen service dogs assisting disabled people. Monkeys can be trained to assist people too. Quadriplegics are people who can't move their arms, hands, and legs. One major problem faced by quadriplegics is not being able to do simple everyday tasks for themselves.

On-Level	Strategic Intervention	Advanced
Read Decodable Reader 9.	**Read** Decodable Reader 9.	**Read** Advanced Selection 9.
• Use pp. 252q.	• Use the **Routine** on DI·44.	• Use the **Routine** on p. DI·45.

ELL Place English language learners in the groups that correspond to their reading abilities in English.

(i) Independent Activities

Fluency Reading Pair children to reread Leveled Readers or the ELL Reader from the previous week or other text at children's independent level.

Journal Writing Write about why partnerships are important. Share writing.

Independent Reading See p. 252j for Reading/Library activities and suggestions.

Literacy Centers To practice Plurals, you may use Word Work, p. 252j.

Practice Book 2.1 Plurals, p. 83 Author's Purpose, p. 84

DAY 1

Break into small groups after Spelling and before Build Background.

Apply Phonics

🔁 PRACTICE Plurals *-s, -es, -ies*

HIGH-FREQUENCY WORDS Review *about*, *they*, and *together*.

READ DECODABLE READER 9

- Pages 66–67 Read aloud quietly with the group.
- Pages 68–69 Have the group read aloud without you.
- Pages 70–72 Select individuals to read aloud.

CHECK COMPREHENSION AND DECODING Have children retell the story to include characters, setting, and plot. Then have children locate plurals in the story. Review plural spellings *-s, -es,* and *-ies.* Sort words according to their plural endings.

-s		-es	-ies
bases	rocks	classes	berries
crafts	snacks	lunches	puppies
lots	stands		
notes	things		
places	tunes		
races			

HOMEWORK Take-Home Decodable Reader 9

REREAD FOR FLUENCY

Oral Rereading

ROUTINE

1 **Read** Have children read the entire story orally.

2 **Reread** To achieve optimal fluency, children should reread the text three or four times.

3 **Provide Feedback** Listen as children read and provide corrective feedback regarding their oral reading and their use of the blending strategy.

OBJECTIVES

- Apply knowledge of letter-sounds and word parts to decode unknown words when reading.
- Use context with letter-sounds and word parts to confirm the identification of unknown words.
- Practice fluency in oral rereading.

Monitor Progress

Decoding

If...	then...
children have difficulty decoding a word,	prompt them to blend the word. • What is the new word? • Is the new word a word you know? • Does it make sense in the story?

Access Content

Beginning Preview the story *Fletch and Fran*, identifying *Fletch*, *Fran*, and *lunches* in the pictures and print.

Intermediate Preview *Fletch and Fran*, explaining the meanings of plural words such as *bases*, *crafts*, and *snacks*. Have children point them out in the pictures.

Advanced After reading *Fletch and Fran*, have partners take turns retelling the first few pages of the story.

Strategic Intervention

Have children copy the question from the web, and then have them draw a picture to illustrate their answer.

Advanced

Have children write a story about working together.

Extend Language Write the word *partnership* on the board. Identify the suffix *(-ship),* and then cross off the word on the board. Have children discuss the meaning of the word *partner.* Ask children if they know any other words that end in *-ship.*

Build Background

LET'S TALK ABOUT Working Together

GENERATE DISCUSSION Read the title and ask questions to generate language. Encourage children to respond in complete sentences.

- How are the people in the pictures working together?
- How are the bees working together?

BUILD ORAL VOCABULARY Lead the class in a discussion that focuses on concepts and today's Amazing Words *partnership, survival, solution.*

Look at the boys in the canoe. They have established a partnership. They are all working together to move the canoe with their paddles. Look at the people crossing the stream. They have formed a human chain to cross the dangerous water. If one person stumbles, the other people guarantee their survival. Forming the human chain is the solution to crossing the water. Have you ever been in a partnership in which you offered a solution to a problem? Look at the picture of the animals. This week we will read about how these animals form a partnership for their survival.

VOCABULARY

CONCEPT CHART Remind children of the question of the week.

- When should we work together? When should we work alone?

Display Graphic Organizer 14. Label the middle circle "When should we work together?" Using the pictures on the student page as a starting point, help children identify appropriate responses and fill in the blank spaces on the graphic organizer. Encourage children to think of other examples of times people should work together. Display the chart for use throughout the week.

- Think of a time you worked with someone else. Why did you work together? (Possible response: I worked with my father and my friends to build a tree house. This way, we finished faster, and my father helped us make the tree house safe.)

Build Background

Let's Talk About
Working Together

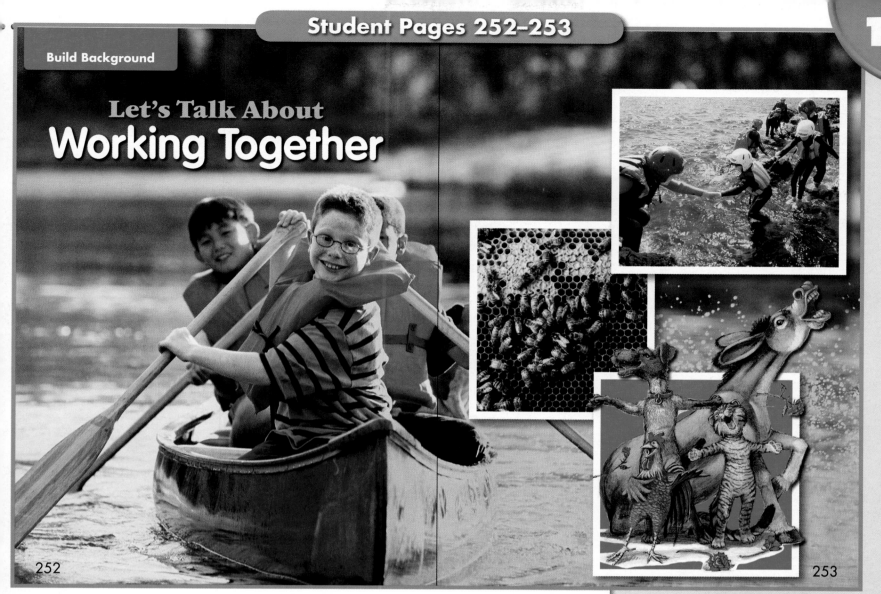

252

253

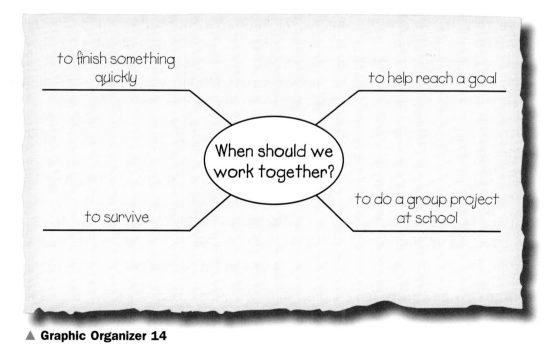

to finish something
quickly

to help reach a goal

When should we work together?

to survive

to do a group project
at school

▲ Graphic Organizer 14

Take It to the NET™
ONLINE

For a Web site that tells more about musicians and instruments, do an Internet search using the keywords *musical instruments*.

Access Content To prepare children for reading *The Bremen Town Musicians*, send home the story summary in English and/or the home language. See the ELL Teaching Guide, pp. 61–63.

OBJECTIVE

Identify author's purpose.

Skills Trace

Author's Purpose

Introduce/Teach	TE: 2.2 253a-b, 254e; 2.3 317a-b, 318e; 2.5 234r, 234-235
Practice	PB: 2.1 84-85, 97, 104-105, 117; 2.2 57, 84-85, 97
Reteach/Review	TE: 2.1 56-57; 2.2 296-297, DI·67; 2.3 362-363, DI·64; 2.5 168-169, 278-279, DI·67
Assess/Test	TE: 2.2 33-36; 2.3 41-44; 2.5 93-96; Benchmark Test, Unit 5

Read the story. **Look** at the picture. **Follow** the directions.

The Ant and the Grasshopper
by Aesop

On a hot summer day, Ant was working. She was storing food to eat in winter. Ant passed Grasshopper as she worked. Grasshopper was taking a nap. Grasshopper laughed at Ant. He did not worry about winter. When winter did come, Grasshopper was not laughing. He was hungry!

1. What is the author's name? **Aesop**

2. Circle the word that tells what Ant was doing.
   sleeping (working)

3. Circle the word that tells what Grasshopper did when he saw Ant.
   (laughed) napped

4. Underline the sentence that tells why Ant was working.

5. Why do you think the author wrote this story?
   Answers will vary but should include either to entertain or to teach a lesson about planning for the future.

School + Home Home Activity Your child answered questions about a fable and told why the author wrote it. Read a fable or another story with your child. Ask your child to identify who wrote the story and why the writer might have written it.

▲ **Practice Book 2.1** p.84, Author's Purpose

Access Content For a Picture It! lesson on author's purpose, see the ELL Teaching Guide, pp. 57–58.

Listening Comprehension

TEACH/MODEL Author's Purpose

DEFINE AUTHOR'S PURPOSE

- An author has a reason for writing.
- An author can write to inform or explain something.
- An author can write to entertain.
- An author can write to describe something.
- An author can write to convince the reader to think or act in a certain way.

READ ALOUD Read "The Mango Tree" and model how to identify author's purpose.

MODEL When I read, I think about why an author writes a story. Parts of this story made me laugh. I think that the author chose monkeys as the main characters because monkeys are funny and do silly things. I think the author wrote this story to entertain me.

PRACTICE

CLUES TO AUTHOR'S PURPOSE Ask children to identify other clues that tell about the author's purpose. What was the story about? (It was about a monkey who built a raft to get to some mangoes.) Was this story funny, serious, or sad? Why do you think so? (It was funny because Marlee built a raft when all she needed to do was to cross a bridge.)

IDENTIFY AUTHOR'S PURPOSE Have children recall the story *Ronald Morgan Goes to Bat*.

- Was this story funny, serious, or sad? Why do you think so? (It was funny, because the characters did and said funny things.)
- What was funny about this story? (Ronald did funny things. He ran the bases the wrong way and closed his eyes when he batted. He also said funny things.)
- What do you think was the author's purpose? (She wanted to tell a funny story.)

CONNECT TO READING Tell children that when they read any story, they should think about who wrote the story and why.

The Mango Tree

Marlee Monkey had a problem. She was so hungry, and the ripe, juicy mangoes on the tree across the river looked so good. But how could she get to the mangoes? Marlee thought hard until she found a solution. She would build a raft.

Marlee worked all day collecting logs. She tied them together with vines and made a very large raft.

But when Marlee tried to move the raft, nothing happened. She pushed and she pulled, and she pulled and she pushed, but the raft was too heavy to move.

It was at that moment that Maddie Monkey came swinging by. Maddie saw the raft and the mangoes, and she understood Marlee's problem. Together Marlee and Maddie pushed and pulled, but still the raft was too heavy to move.

"Wait here!" Maddie said and disappeared. When she returned, she had brought Malcolm, Murphy, Mary, and Mabel.

They said, "How about a little partnership? We've all come to help you!"

So all the little monkeys worked together to move the raft toward the water. Once it began to float, they all jumped on.

Finally the raft reached the other side. All the little monkeys jumped ashore and began to eat mangoes.

"That was a lot of hard work, but it was worth it!" Marlee said happily.

Just then they spotted Max on the other side of the river.

"It's too bad you weren't here before!" Marlee called to Max. "You could have ridden on the raft with us. Now we are too tired and full of mangoes to come get you."

"That's okay," Max said. "There is a bridge just down the river. I will cross that way."

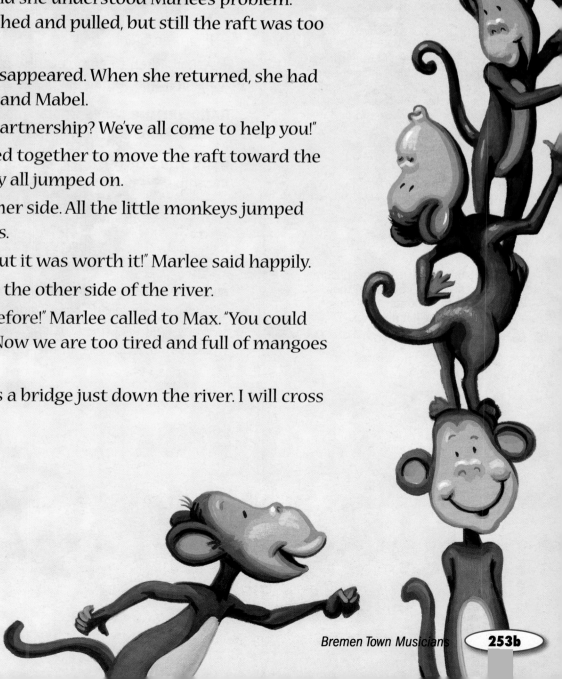

Read ALOUD

1

OBJECTIVE

• Write a poster.

DAILY FIX-IT

1. The donkey didnt have
   any food

The donkey didn't have any food.

2. He mised his lunchs.

He missed his lunches.

This week's practice sentences appear on Daily Fix-It Transparency 9.

Strategic Intervention

Have children use old magazines to find pictures that illustrate the who, what, where, and why listed on the poster. Ask them to label each picture with the appropriate heading.

Advanced

Have children make a poster that persuades people to take care of their aging pets.

Support Writing Allow children to dictate the information they want on their poster to a more proficient English speaker.

Shared Writing

WRITE Poster

GENERATE IDEAS Encourage children to think about a group they would like to form. Ask them what the group would do, why they think people should join the group, and how they would get people to join.

MAKE A POSTER Explain that the class will make a poster to tell people about the group and to try to persuade them to join.

 COMPREHENSION SKILL Have children think about their purpose for writing a poster—to persuade others to join their group.

• Display Writing Transparency 9 and read the title.

• Ask children to read the first heading and fill in the blank.

• Ask children to complete the poster by filling in the remaining blank spaces.

HANDWRITING While writing, model the letter forms as shown on pp. TR18–TR21.

READ THE POSTER Have children read the completed poster aloud as you track the print.

Join Our Group!

Possible answers:

Name of Group **Good Book Group**

What the Group Does **We get together to talk about good books we have read.**

Where the Group Meets **We meet at 4:00 P.M. on Tuesday afternoons in Room 210.**

Why You Should Join the Group **You will find out about good books, meet new people, and have fun.**

Unit 2 The Bremen Town Musicians   Writing Model **9**

▲ **Writing Transparency 9**

INDEPENDENT WRITING

MAKE A POSTER Have children make their own poster providing information about a new group they want to form. Encourage them to use words from the Word Wall and the Amazing Words board. Let children illustrate their writing. Display the posters in the classroom.

Grammar

TEACH/MODEL Plural Nouns That Change Spelling

REVIEW SINGULAR AND PLURAL NOUNS Remind children that a singular noun names one person, place, animal, or thing. Remind children that a plural noun names more than one person, place, animal, or thing.

IDENTIFY PLURAL NOUNS THAT CHANGE SPELLING Display Grammar Transparency 9. Read the definition aloud.

• Look at the picture above *man*. There is one person, a man. Look at the picture above the blank. There are three people. Find the plural noun in the box that goes with the picture.

Continue modeling with items 2–6.

PRACTICE

MATCH SINGULAR NOUNS AND PLURAL NOUNS THAT CHANGE SPELLING Have children match singular nouns with their plurals. Write the following words in a column on the chalkboard: *goose, ox, wife, loaf*. Write the following words in another column on the chalkboard: *wives, geese, loaves, oxen*. Children should write the correct pairs on their paper.

OBJECTIVE

● Identify plural nouns that change spelling.

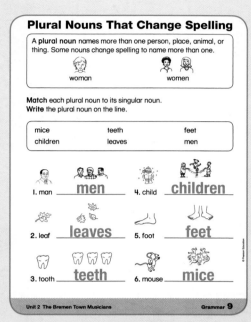

Plural Nouns That Change Spelling

A **plural noun** names more than one person, place, animal, or thing. Some nouns change spelling to name more than one.

woman   women

Match each plural noun to its singular noun.
Write the plural noun on the line.

mice	teeth	feet
children	leaves	men

1. man **men**   4. child **children**

2. leaf **leaves**   5. foot **feet**

3. tooth **teeth**   6. mouse **mice**

Unit 2 The Bremen Town Musicians   Grammar 9

▲ **Grammar Transparency 9**

Wrap Up Your Day!

 PLURALS -s, -es, -ies Write *baby* and ask children to spell the plural of the word (babies). Repeat with *note* and *switch*.

 SPELLING PLURALS -s, -es, -ies Have children explain why they spelled *babies, notes, switches* the way they did.

 AUTHOR'S PURPOSE To help children determine why the author wrote *The Mango Tree*, have them decide what lesson the author wanted them to learn. (It's important to work together.)

LET'S TALK ABOUT IT Recall that Marlee wants to cross the river and eat mangoes. When is it wise for us to work with others? (It is wise to work with others when a team can more easily reach the goal.)

 HOMEWORK Send home this week's Family Times newsletter.

PREVIEW Day 2

Tell children that tomorrow the class will read about the adventures of a group of animals.

Day 2
AT A GLANCE

Morning Warm~Up!

Today we will read about some animals traveling to Bremen Town. We will read about how and why they work together. When have you worked with others?

QUESTION OF THE DAY Encourage children to sing "A Partnership with You" from the *Sing with Me Big Book* as you gather. Write and read the message and discuss the question.

REVIEW GRAMMAR AND MECHANICS

- Read all three sentences of the message.

- Have children explain why certain words are capitalized. Also have them explain why two periods and one question mark are used as end punctuation.

Build Background Use the Day 2 instruction on ELL Poster 9 to preview high-frequency words.

ELL Poster 9

Share Literature

BUILD CONCEPTS

Big Book

CAPITALIZATION AND PUNCTUATION Have children look at p. 17. Review that the first word in a sentence is always capitalized. Also remind children that proper nouns are capitalized. Punctuation marks, such as commas, question marks, and periods, make sentences clear and let readers know how sentences should be read.

BUILD ORAL VOCABULARY Ask children what they know about different feelings. Point out that Rat feels **miserable** at the beginning of the story. Explain that when someone is **miserable**, he or she is very unhappy. Suggest that as you read, children listen to find out how Rat's feelings change.

• Why does Rat feel **miserable**? (Possible answer: He is bored and lonely.)

• How does receiving a letter affect Rat? (Possible answer: It makes him feel happy and excited and full of energy.)

MONITOR LISTENING COMPREHENSION

• When Rat goes to see Mouse, the two animals form a partnership to fix something. What do they fix? (They work together all day to fix Mouse's damaged roof.)

• How does Rat arrive at the solution that Frog did not write the letter? (He compares her handwritten shopping list to the writing on the envelope.)

• Who probably sent the letter to Rat? Explain your answer. (Possible response: I think either Mouse or Frog sent it. They wink at each other when they're talking to Rat about the letter, as if they share a secret.)

OBJECTIVES

● Discuss characteristics of capitalization and punctuation.
● Set purpose for listening.
● Build oral vocabulary.

Amazing Words to build oral vocabulary

	MONITOR PROGRESS
partnership **survival** **solution** **miserable**	**If…** children lack oral vocabulary experiences about the concept Working Together, **then…** use the Oral Vocabulary Routine on pp. DI·1–DI·2, DI·6 to develop the Amazing Words.

Build Concepts Two characters feel lonely in *From Me to You*. When someone is lonely, he or she is unhappy because he or she is not with other people. Have children determine the root (*lone*) and then name other words with the same root (*alone, lonesome*).

Plurals -s, -es, -ies

OBJECTIVES

- Review plurals *-s, -es, -ies.*
- Sort and read plurals *-s, -es, -ies.*
- Preview words before reading them.
- Spell plurals *-s, -es, -ies.*

Strategic Intervention

Use **Strategic Intervention Decodable Reader 9** for more practice with plural words.

ELL

Support Phonics Explain that *chores* is another name for *jobs.* Then invite children to name the things pictured in the art for "Buddies Helping You" as you replay the Phonics Songs and Rhymes Audio CD.

TEACH/MODEL

Fluent word reading

ROUTINE

1 **Connect** Write *flies.* You can read this word because you know how to read plural words. What is the base word? **What is the word? Do the same with** *ducks* and *wishes.*

2 **Model** When you come to a plural word, figure out the base word and ending and then read it. Model reading *papers, stores, batches, lashes, daddies.* When you come to a new plural word, what are you going to do?

3 **Group Practice** Write *pockets, spices, patches, brushes, purses, mommies, mixes.* Read these words. Look at the word; say the word to yourself, and then read the word aloud. Allow 2–3 seconds previewing time.

WORD READING

PHONICS SONGS AND RHYMES CHART 9 Frame each of the following words on Phonics Songs and Rhymes Chart 9. Call on individuals to read them. Guide children in previewing.

jobs	buddies	hours
dishes	supplies	chores
classmates	messes	lunches

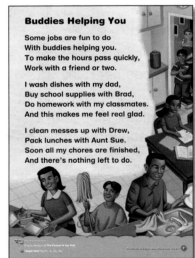

Buddies Helping You

Some jobs are fun to do
With buddies helping you.
To make the hours pass quickly,
Work with a friend or two.

I wash dishes with my dad,
Buy school supplies with Brad,
Do homework with my classmates.
And this makes me feel real glad.

I clean messes up with Drew,
Pack lunches with Aunt Sue.
Soon all my chores are finished,
And there's nothing left to do.

Sing "Buddies Helping You" to the tune of "The Farmer in the Dell," or play the CD. Have children follow along on the chart as they sing. Then have individuals take turns pointing to and reading plurals on the chart. Identify *hours* if necessary.

 **Phonics Songs and Rhymes Audio**

Phonics Songs and Rhymes Chart 9

SORT WORDS

INDIVIDUALS SORT -s, -es, AND -ies WORDS Write -s, -es, and -ies as headings. Have individuals write -s, -es, and -ies words from the Phonics Chart under the appropriate headings and circle the plural endings. Have all children complete the activity on paper. Ask individuals to read the completed lists and identify the base words. Provide feedback as necessary.

-s	-es	-ies
jobs	dishes	buddies
hours	messes	supplies
classmates	lunches	
chores		

Spelling

PRACTICE Plurals -s, -es, -ies

WRITE DICTATION SENTENCES Have children write these sentences. Repeat words slowly, allowing children to hear each sound. Children may use the Word Wall to help with spelling high-frequency words. **Word Wall**

> **The tunes had many notes.**
> **I will read the stories to the baby.**
> **We did not switch lunches.**
> **The babies like hearing the same story.**

HOMEWORK Spelling Practice Book, p. 34

Spelling Words

Plurals

1.	note	7.	tune
2.	notes	8.	tunes*
3.	lunch	9.	switch*
4.	lunches	10.	switches*
5.	story	11.	baby
6.	stories	12.	babies

Challenge Words

13.	crumbs	15.	centuries
14.	supplies		

* Words from the Selection

Adding -s and -es

Spelling Words

note	lunch	story	tune	switch	baby
notes	lunches	stories	tunes	switches	babies

Write the missing list words.

1. I will eat my **lunch** now.
2. She told a **story** about a lost prince.
3. We packed **lunches** to eat on the hike.
4. My sister wrote two **stories**.
5. Your **baby** loves to eat bananas.
6. The **babies** can play in the shade.

Write the list word that rhymes. Then write the word adding -s or -es.

dune	ditch	vote
7. **tune**	8. **switch**	9. **note**
10. **tunes**	11. **switches**	12. **notes**

School + Home **Home Activity** Your child wrote words with and without -s and -es. Name a singular word and have your child explain how the plural is formed.

▲ **Spelling Practice Book** p. 34

Read the text. Follow the directions.

 The Bee Dance
by Buzz Flyer

Did you know that bees dance? They don't dance for fun. A bee dances to show other bees where to find food. First, a bee finds a good patch of flowers. Then it flies back to the beehive. The bee jumps and crawls and spins. Its dance tells the other bees where to find good food.

1. What is the author's name? **Buzz Flyer**

2. Which word below tells about the story?
   (bees) flowers flying

3. Underline three words in the story that tell how the bee dances.

4. Circle the word that tells where bees get the food.

5. Why do you think the author wrote this story?

   to tell the reader about why bees dance

Home Activity Your child wrote about a nonfiction text and why the author wrote it. Select an article from a newspaper or magazine to read together. Ask your child to identify who wrote the text and why the writer might have written it.

▲ **Practice Book 2.1** p.85,
Author's Purpose

Comprehension

SKILL Author's Purpose

RECOGNIZE AUTHOR'S PURPOSE Review that an author has a reason for writing. He or she might write to explain or inform, entertain, express feelings, or convince the reader to think or act a certain way. Have children tell what the author's purpose was in previously read stories.

CONNECT TO READING

• As you read, ask yourself what the story is about and why the author might have written it.

• Notice if the story is funny, serious, or sad.

STRATEGY Story Structure

INTRODUCE THE STRATEGY Tell children that story structure is how the story is put together. It includes setting, plot, and characters. Each piece of the story is needed to make it whole. Paying attention to story structure as they read helps them to understand the story.

Think Aloud **MODEL** When I read a story, I think about its different parts. I notice where and when the story takes place. I notice who the characters are and how they act. I pay attention to what is happening.

CONNECT TO READING Encourage children to ask themselves these questions as they read *The Bremen Town Musicians*.

• Where does this story take place?

• What happens in the beginning, middle, and end of this story?

• Who are the characters in this story, and what do they do?

Build Background

DISCUSS WORK DONE BY FARM ANIMALS Display a picture of a donkey, cat, dog, or rooster doing work on a farm. Initiate discussion by asking children what they know about the type of work these farm animals do.

- Have you ever been on a farm?
- What kind of animals did you see?
- What kind of work did the animals do?

BACKGROUND BUILDING AUDIO Have children listen to the CD and share the new information they learned about farm animals.

**Sing with Me/
Background Building Audio**

COMPLETE A WEB Draw a web or display Graphic Organizer 14. Write *Work done by farm animals* in the center. Ask children to think about the animals from the story and then have them suggest different types of work that these farm animals provide.

▲ **Graphic Organizer 14**

CONNECT TO SELECTION Connect background information to *The Bremen Town Musicians*.

Farm animals work hard. There are four farm animals in the story we are about to read. We'll find out what happens to them when they grow old and when their owners no longer need them.

Activate Prior Knowledge Ask children to share personal experiences related to farm animals and their work.

Words to Read

people
sign
bought
scared
probably
shall
pleasant

Read the Words

People waited for hours to get tickets for the big concert. One man made a sign asking for extra tickets! Some wise fans bought their tickets months ago. They were scared by all the talk that the concert would probably be sold out.

"I shall do my best," one singer said. "I think this will be a very pleasant concert."

The Bremen Town Musicians

Genre: Fairy Tale
A fairy tale usually takes place long ago and far away and has fantastic characters. Next you will read about four animals that become friends and travel to a faraway town.

254

255

Read the story.
Write in the correct words to finish the sentences.

bought	people
pleasant	probably
scared	shall

Carlos crept up to the old mill. There was a **sign** that said "Keep Out!" But Carlos wanted to see if there were really monsters inside. Would they think there were robbers breaking in?

Just as Carlos got close, he heard a racket. Carlos was **scared**. He would **probably** be eaten.

But what would **people** say if he turned back? Carlos stepped inside.

And what was inside? It was an old man playing a horn! The excitement was gone.

"What was that horrid sound?" asked Carlos.

"I don't know what you mean," the musician sniffed.

"I just **bought** this horn. I think my playing is very **pleasant**. Wait! I **shall** play you another tune!"

Home Activity Your child completed sentences in a story using high-frequency and selection words learned this week. Work with your child to write a suspenseful fantasy story using these words.

▲ **Practice Book 2.1** p. 86, High-Frequency Words and Selection Words

_____ Plurals -s, -es, -ies   [ ] high-frequency/tested vocabulary

High-Frequency Words

Nondecodable Words

ROUTINE

① **Say and Spell** Point to the first word. The word is *people, p-e-o-p-l-e, people.* What is this word? What are the letters in this word?

② **Identify Familiar Letter-Sounds** Point to the first letter in *people.* What is this letter? What is the sound for this letter? (*p*/p/)

③ **Demonstrate Meaning** Tell me a sentence using this word. Repeat the routine with the other Words to Read. Have children identify these familiar letter-sounds and word parts: *sign* (s/s/, i/ī/, n/n/), *shall* (sh/sh/, a/a/, l/l/) *bought* (b/b/, t/t/), *probably* (blend the syllables: *prob-a-bly*), *pleasant* (blend the syllables: *pleas-ant*), *scared* (sc/sk/, d/d/).

Have children read aloud the sentences on p. 255 and point to the Words to Read. Add the words to the Word Wall. **Word Wall**

Use Vocabulary Transparency 9 to review this week's words.

• Point to a word. Say and spell it.

• Have children say and spell the word.

• Ask children to identify familiar letter-sounds.

Monitor Progress | Check High-Frequency Words

Point to the following words on the Word Wall and have individuals read them.

people	sign	shall	bought	probably	pleasant	scared
friend	love	full	stood	door	never	sure

If... children cannot read these words,

then... have them find each word on the Word Wall, chant its meaning, and then write it before reading the selection. Monitor their fluency with these words during reading, and provide additional practice opportunities before the Day 5 Assessment.

SUCCESS PREDICTOR

Day 1 Check Word Reading : **▶Day 2 Check High-Frequency Words** : **Day 3** Check Retelling : **Day 4** Check Fluency : **Day 5** Assess Progress

High-Frequency Words

SUCCESS PREDICTOR

A Dream Come True

1. Donkey was tired of working at the <u>mill</u>.

2. One day three furry <u>monsters</u> scared Donkey and stole all the grain.

3. "Oh, no! Those <u>robbers</u> took everything!" Donkey cried.

4. Donkey was surprised when his owner danced with <u>excitement</u>.

5. "Now we don't have to work, and we can become <u>musicians</u>!" said Donkey's owner.

Words to Read			
brought	people	pleasant	sign
probably	scared	shall	

Unit 2 The Bremen Town Musicians — Vocabulary **9**

▲ **Vocabulary Transparency 9**

Vocabulary

SELECTION WORDS

Use Vocabulary Transparency 9 to introduce the selection words.

- Read each sentence as you track the print.
- Frame each underlined word. Explain the word's meaning.

  mill a building where grain is crushed into flour

  musician someone who plays music

  excitement a feeling of being very happy

  robbers people who steal

  monsters scary creatures

- Ask children to identify familiar letter-sounds and word parts: *mill* (m/m/, i/i/, ll/l/), *excitement* (blend the base word and ending: *excite, ment*), *musician* (blend the syllables: *mu, si, cian*), *robbers* (blend the syllables: *rob, bers*), *monsters* (blend the syllables: *mon, sters*).

- Have children read each sentence aloud with you.

- To encourage discussion using the selection words, have children use the words in a personal context. Tell about a time you felt *excitement*. Use *excitement* when you tell about it. Continue with the other words.

Group Time

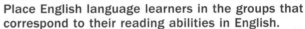

DAY **2**

On-Level	Strategic Intervention	Advanced
Read *The Bremen Town Musicians.* • Use pp. 256–273.	**Read** SI Decodable Reader 9. • Read or listen to *The Bremen Town Musicians.* • Use the **Routine** on p. DI·46.	**Read** *The Bremen Town Musicians.* • Use the **Routine** on p. DI·47.

ELL Place English language learners in the groups that correspond to their reading abilities in English.

ⓘ Independent Activities

Independent Reading See p. 252j for Reading/Library activities and suggestions.

Journal Writing Write about a time when you worked closely with another person. Share writing.

Literacy Centers To provide experiences with *The Bremen Town Musicians,* you may use the Listening Center on p. 252j.

Practice Book 2.1 Author's Purpose, p. 85 High-Frequency Words and Selection Words, p. 86 Realism/Fantasy, p. 87

Access Content Use the vocabulary strategies and word cards in the ELL Teaching Guide, pp. 59–60.

Break into small groups after Vocabulary and before Writing.

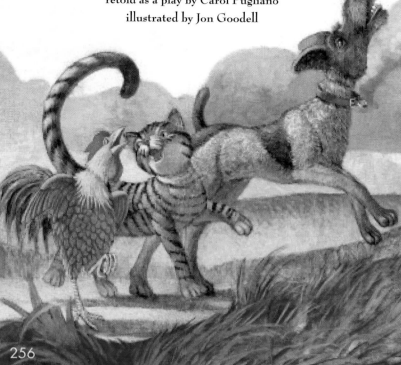

The Bremen Town Musicians

retold as a play by Carol Pugliano
illustrated by Jon Goodell

256

Who are the Bremen Town Musicians?

257

Read

Prereading Strategies

PREVIEW AND PREDICT Have children read the title of the story. Identify the different animals in the picture. Identify the author and illustrator. Do a picture walk of pp. 256–263. Ask children what they think this story will be about.

DISCUSS FAIRY TALE Reread the definition of fairy tale on p. 255 of the Student Edition. Explain that a fairy tale is a story with magical or fantastic characters and events. Ask children who they think the characters are in this story.

SET PURPOSE Read the question on p. 257. Ask children what they would like to find out as they read this story.

AudioText

ELL

Access Content Before reading, review the story summary in English and/or the home language. See the ELL Teaching Guide, pp. 61–63.

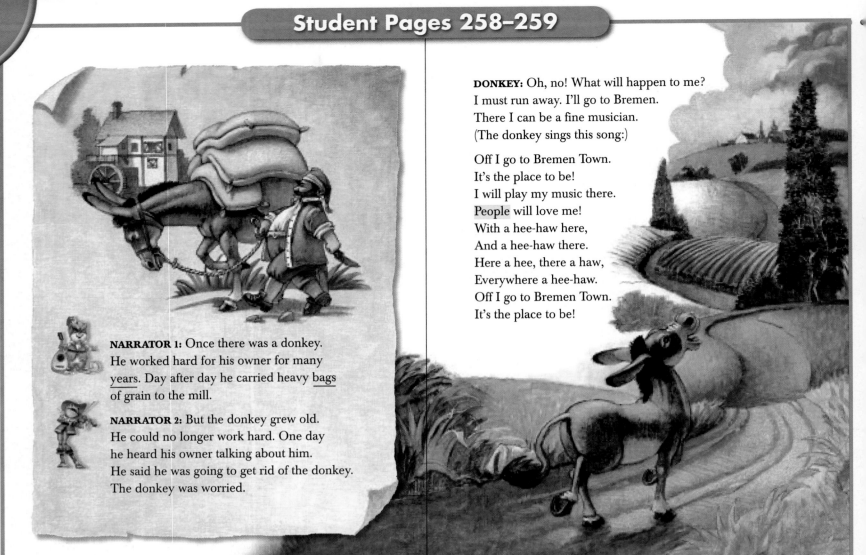

NARRATOR 1: Once there was a donkey. He worked hard for his owner for many years. Day after day he carried heavy bags of grain to the mill.

NARRATOR 2: But the donkey grew old. He could no longer work hard. One day he heard his owner talking about him. He said he was going to get rid of the donkey. The donkey was worried.

DONKEY: Oh, no! What will happen to me? I must run away. I'll go to Bremen. There I can be a fine musician. (The donkey sings this song:)

Off I go to Bremen Town.
It's the place to be!
I will play my music there.
People will love me!
With a hee-haw here,
And a hee-haw there.
Here a hee, there a haw,
Everywhere a hee-haw.
Off I go to Bremen Town.
It's the place to be!

258

259

▲ **Pages 258-259**
Have children look at the pictures and read to find out who is speaking.

Monitor Progress

Decoding

If...children come to a word they don't know,	**then**...remind them to:
	1. Blend the word.
	2. Decide if the word makes sense.
	3. Look in a dictionary for more help.

Skills in Context

🎯 AUTHOR'S PURPOSE

- **The author has narrators and animal characters talk in the play. Why do you think the author uses both?**
The author uses the narrators to explain things to the audience. She uses the animals to tell their own stories. This makes the play more interesting.

Monitor Progress | **Author's Purpose**

If... children are unable to answer the question,	**then...** model how to identify author's purpose.

Think Aloud

MODEL As I read, I find that there are both narrators and animal speakers. First the narrators talk about the donkey's past. They talk directly to the audience to explain things. Then the donkey talks, asking what will become of him. The donkey tells its own story. This makes the play more interesting.

ASSESS Have children read to find out what the narrators discuss. (They explain what happens in the past and describe the action when the animals aren't talking.)

____ Plurals -s, -es, -ies   high-frequency/tested vocabulary

NARRATOR 1: So the donkey left that night. He had not gone far when he saw a dog lying on the ground.

NARRATOR 2: The dog looked weak. He also looked sad. The donkey knelt down to speak to the dog.

DONKEY: What is the matter, my friend?

DOG: Ah, me. Now that I am old and weak, I can no longer hunt. My owner wants to get rid of me. I got scared, so I ran away. Now I don't know what I will do.

DONKEY: You can come with me to Bremen. I am going to be a musician. Will you join me?

DOG: I'd love to! I can bark very pleasant tunes.

DOG AND DONKEY: Off we go to Bremen Town. It's the place to be! We will play our music there. We'll be filled with glee!

DONKEY: With a hee-haw here, and a hee-haw there. Here a hee, there a haw, everywhere a hee-haw.

DOG: With a bow-wow here and a bow-wow there. Here a bow, there a wow, everywhere a bow-wow.

DOG AND DONKEY: Off we go to Bremen Town. It's the place to be!

260

261

Guiding Comprehension

Draw Conclusions • Inferential

- **Why does the donkey invite the dog to join him?**
  Possible response: Both animals were no longer wanted by their owners. They are better off together.

Cause and Effect • Inferential

- **Why do the dog and donkey speak together in rhyme?**
  Possible response: They are singing.

▲ **Pages 260–261**
Have children read to find out what the donkey is saying to the dog.

Monitor Progress
High-Frequency Words

If...children have a problem reading a new high-frequency word,	then...use the High-Frequency Routine on p. 255a to reteach the problematic word.

Donkeys

TIME FOR Science

Donkeys are good pack animals because they are strong. They can be trained to protect sheep and goats. Sometimes they are placed with hurt animals to help calm them.

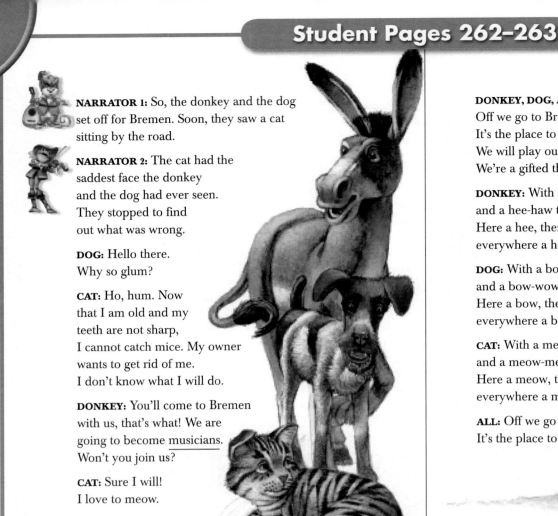

NARRATOR 1: So, the donkey and the dog set off for Bremen. Soon, they saw a cat sitting by the road.

NARRATOR 2: The cat had the saddest face the donkey and the dog had ever seen. They stopped to find out what was wrong.

DOG: Hello there. Why so glum?

CAT: Ho, hum. Now that I am old and my teeth are not sharp, I cannot catch mice. My owner wants to get rid of me. I don't know what I will do.

DONKEY: You'll come to Bremen with us, that's what! We are going to become <u>musicians</u>. Won't you join us?

CAT: Sure I will! I love to meow.

DONKEY, DOG, AND CAT:
Off we go to Bremen Town.
It's the place to be!
We will play our music there.
We're a gifted three!

DONKEY: With a hee-haw here, and a hee-haw there. Here a hee, there a haw, everywhere a hee-haw.

DOG: With a bow-wow here, and a bow-wow there. Here a bow, there a wow, everywhere a bow-wow.

CAT: With a meow-meow here, and a meow-meow there. Here a meow, there a meow, everywhere a meow-meow.

ALL: Off we go to Bremen Town. It's the place to be!

262

263

▲ **Pages 262–263**
Have children read to find out what problem all of the animals have.

EXTEND SKILLS

Repetition
For instruction in repetition, discuss the following:

- The author uses repetition to be humorous in the story.
- Look at how the animals repeat each other on p. 263. By repeating parts of the song, the other animals can add their own parts to it.

Assess Have children find other examples of repetition in the story. Have them explain what changes each time a different animal repeats the same verse.

Strategies in Context

STORY STRUCTURE

- **What problem do the animals share?**
  They have all grown old, so their owners no longer want them.

Monitor Progress	Story Structure
If... children have difficulty determining what problem the animals have,	**then...** model how to use the text to determine elements of story structure, such as plot.

Think Aloud **MODEL** I read that the donkey and the dog and the cat are all old, and their owners no longer want them. This makes the animals sad. They all decide they will go to Bremen Town together to be musicians.

ASSESS What problem do the animals have on p. 268 and how do they solve it? (The animals are tired and hungry. They find a house with robbers in it and solve their problem by scaring the robbers into leaving. Then the animals can eat the food in the house and there.)

_____ Plurals *-s, -es, -ies*   high-frequency/tested vocabulary

NARRATOR 1: The three musicians walked along some more. They came to a farmyard. There they heard a rooster crowing sadly.

ROOSTER: Cock-a-doodle-doo! Cock-a-doodle-doo!

DONKEY: My, you sound so sad. What is wrong?

ROOSTER: I used to crow to wake up the farmer each morning. But he just bought an alarm clock. Now he doesn't need my crowing so he wants to get rid of me. Now I'm a cock-a-doodle-*don't!* Oh, what will I do?

DOG: Come with us to Bremen. We're going to be musicians.

CAT: With your fine crowing, we'll make a wonderful group!

ROOSTER: I cock-a-doodle-*do* think that's a wonderful idea! Let's go!

264

265

Guiding Comprehension

⊙ **Story Structure • Inference**

- **Where does the story take place? How do you know?**
  Possible response: The story takes place in the countryside. The animals could all live on farms. When they were younger, they did work that would be done in the countryside: carrying bags to a mill, hunting, catching mice, and waking a farmer. The pictures show a road and plants and only a few buildings.

Draw Conclusions • Inferential

- **Why do you think the animals want to become musicians?**
  Possible response: They can all sing, even though they are old.

Summarize • Inferential

- **What has happened in the story so far?**
  The donkey, dog, cat, and rooster have all found one another. They are all growing older, so their owners no longer want or need them. The animals agree to go to Bremen Town to be musicians.

▲ **Pages 264–265**
Have children look at the pictures and read to find out the setting of the story.

Strategy Self-Check

Have children ask themselves these questions to check their reading.

Decoding Words
- Do I try to use the word in a new sentence?
- Does the new word make sense in the story?

Story Structure
- Do I think about where this story takes place?
- Do I think about what happens in the beginning, middle, and end of this story?
- Do I think about who the characters are and what they do?

DONKEY, DOG, CAT, AND ROOSTER:
Off we go to Bremen Town. It's the place to be!
We will play our music there. We're a sight to see!

DONKEY: With a hee-haw here, and a hee-haw there.
Here a hee, there a haw, everywhere a hee-haw.

DOG: With a bow-wow here, and a bow-wow there.
Here a bow, there a wow, everywhere a bow-wow.

CAT: With a meow-meow here, and a meow-meow
there. Here a meow, there a meow, everywhere a
meow-meow.

ROOSTER: With a cock-a-doodle here, and a
cock-a-doodle there. Here a doodle, there a doodle,
everywhere a cock-a-doodle.

ALL: Off we go to Bremen Town. It's the place to be!

266

267

▲ **Pages 266–267**
Have children look at pictures and
read to find out if the story is
realistic or fantasy.

▲ **Practice Book 2.1** p. 87,
Realism and Fantasy

Skills in Context

(REVIEW) REALISM AND FANTASY

• **Is the play realistic or is it a fantasy? How do you know?**
The play is a fantasy because the events could not really happen.

Monitor Progress	Realism and Fantasy
If... children have difficulty answering the question,	**then...** model how to use the text and pictures to determine if the play is realism or fantasy.

Think Aloud — **MODEL** I know the play is a fantasy because it is full of characters and events that could not really happen in real life. For example, animals don't talk or worry about what to do when their owners want to get rid of them. They also don't make plans together.

ASSESS Have children find more clues that tell them the play is a fantasy. (The animals are singing together, which is something that would not happen in real life.)

____ Plurals -s, -es, -ies   high-frequency/tested vocabulary

NARRATOR 2: The four musicians walked until it got dark. Finally, they saw a sign that said Bremen Town. They danced with excitement, but they were also very tired. They wanted to rest.

NARRATOR 1: They saw light coming from a little house up the road. They walked up to the window, but none of the animals were tall enough to see inside. So, the dog stood on the donkey's back, the cat stood on the dog's back, and the rooster stood on the cat's back and peeked inside.

DOG: What do you see, rooster?

ROOSTER: I think there are three robbers in there! They are sitting at a table full of delicious-looking food!

CAT: Food? I'm starving! What shall we do? We must get them out of that house!

ROOSTER: I have a plan. Listen closely.

NARRATOR 2: The rooster whispered his plan to the others.

268

NARRATOR 1: All of a sudden, the four began singing. They made quite a noise. When the robbers heard the animals, they ran out of the house screaming!

NARRATOR 2: The four musicians went inside the house. There they ate and ate until they were full. Then, it was time for bed.

269

Guiding Comprehension

Cause and Effect • Literal

- **What happens when the animals sing outside the window of the house?**
  The robbers run out of the house screaming.

Classify • Critical

- *Text to Text* **How is this play like *Turtle's Race with Beaver*?**
  Possible response: In both stories, good characters have to trick bad characters. In *Turtle's Race with Beaver*, Turtle knows she is not as fast as Beaver, so she won't win the race across the pond on her strength alone. Instead, she bites Beaver's tail, and he throws her across the finish line.

Predict • Inferential

- **What do you think the robbers will do next?**
  Possible response: I think the robbers will come back to the house.

▲ **Pages 268–269**
Have children look at pictures and read to find out what happened when the animals sang.

Older Pets

TIME FOR Science

Pets change as they grow older. They might want to play less and sleep more. They might not see or hear as well. People need to pay attention to their pets' changing needs. If an animal does not see as well, it is important to keep things, such as water and food bowls and bedding, in the same place. Also, as animals age they don't want to run as much. People should make sure their pets don't gain too much weight. Can you think of other changes that you might notice in an aging pet?

NARRATOR 1: The donkey slept in the soft grass in the yard. The dog slept behind the front door. The cat slept near the warmth of the fireplace. And the rooster slept high on a bookshelf.

NARRATOR 2: After a while, the robbers returned to finish eating their feast.

ROBBER 1: That noise was probably just the wind. Besides, I can't wait to eat the rest of that roast beef!

ROBBER 2: I can taste those mashed potatoes now!

ROBBER 3: I'll go first just to make sure it's safe.

NARRATOR 1: So the robber went inside. He was cold, so he went to the fireplace to warm himself. There he surprised the cat, who scratched his face.

NARRATOR 2: The robber ran to the front door. The dog was startled and bit his leg. The robber ran outside. He tripped over the donkey, who kicked him.

270

271

▲ **Pages 270–271**
Have children read to find out if the robbers do what they predicted.

EXTEND SKILLS

Paraphrase

For instruction in paraphrase, discuss the following:

- You can retell part of a story in your own words to show you understand it.

- To retell what happens on p. 271, I think about what the author is trying to say. Then I retell it in my own words: The robbers decide what scared them was the wind, so they come back to finish eating. The first robber goes in to see if it is safe and gets scratched, bit, and kicked by the animals.

Assess Have children paraphrase what happens on p. 270.

Guiding Comprehension

Confirm Predictions • Inferential

- **What do the robbers do? Is this what you predicted?**
  The robbers return. Children may have predicted this.

Sequence • Inferential

- **What happened to the robber after he went inside?**
  He was scratched and bitten and kicked.

◉ **Author's Purpose • Inferential**

- *Question the Author* **Why did the author write this play—to entertain the reader or to inform the reader?**
  Possible response: The author wrote this play to entertain because it is interesting to read about animals who want to be musicians and can trick robbers.

____ Plurals *-s, -es, -ies*   ▭ high-frequency/tested vocabulary

NARRATOR 1: All this noise woke the rooster up. He started screeching, "Cock-a-doodle-doo!" The robber ran back to his friends.

ROBBER 3: There are four horrible monsters in there! One scratched me with its long nails. Another bit me. Another kicked me. And the fourth one screamed, "Coming to get yooouuuuu!"

ROBBER 1: Four monsters! Let's get out of here!

NARRATOR 2: And the robbers ran off, never to be heard from again.

272

NARRATOR 1: But the four musicians stayed there. They sang every night in Bremen, where they became the famous Bremen Town Musicians!

273

Guiding Comprehension

Main Idea • Inferential

- **What is the main idea of the story?**
  Old animals can still be useful and enjoy life.

Cause and Effect • Critical

- **Why does the robber think the animals are monsters?**
  Possible response: It is nighttime, so it is dark. He can't see what the animals really are. Also, he is very scared, so his thoughts are not clear.

Compare and Contrast • Critical

- *Text to Self* **Have you ever had or known an old pet? How was it different from when it was younger?**
  Possible response: I had a dog that was very old. He started sleeping more. He grew gray hair on his face. He didn't want to walk as far.

▲ **Pages 272–273**
Have children read to find out what the robber thinks about the animals.

Reread For Fluency   ROUTINE

1. **Reader 1 Begins**
   Children read the entire book, switching readers at the end of each page.

2. **Reader 2 Begins** Have partners reread; now the other partner begins.

3. **Reread** For optimal fluency, children should reread three or four times.

4. **Provide Feedback** Listen to children read and provide corrective feedback regarding their oral reading and their use of blending.

Bremen Town Musicians **272–273**

OBJECTIVES

● Write questions.
● Identify plural nouns that change spelling.

Interactive Writing

WRITE Questions

DISCUSS Use the story *The Bremen Town Musicians* to encourage a discussion about when it is good to work with others. Picture walk through the story and ask children to identify times the animals worked together.

SHARE THE PEN Have children participate in writing questions (and answers) about when it is good to work with others. To begin, have a child ask a question. Have the class repeat it. Write the question, reminding individuals to use the rules they've learned about sentences. Ask questions such as:

* What does the question start with? (capital letter)
* What does the question end with? (question mark)
* What does the answer end with? (period)

Continue to have individuals make contributions. Frequently reread what has been written while tracking the print.

READ THE QUESTIONS Read the questions and answers aloud, having children echo you.

Questions and Answers

Is it good to work together when you all want the same thing? (Yes)

It is good to work together when you all don't want the same thing? (No)

Is it good to work together when you all know what you are doing? (Yes)

Is it good to work together when you all don't know what you are doing? (No)

INDEPENDENT WRITING

WRITE QUESTIONS Have children write their own questions and answers about when it is good to work with others. Let children illustrate their writing.

Strategic Intervention

Children who are not able to write independently may dictate their questions and answers to a more proficient writer.

Advanced

Have children who are able to write independently complete their own questions and answers about working with others.

Support Writing Before having children begin, reread the class writing product (questions and answers) and point out key words that children might want to use in their own writing,

Beginning Pair children with more proficient English speakers who can help them write their ideas.

Intermediate Teach a useful language pattern that children can use in the writing assignment. Remind children that they might want to begin questions with the words *who, what, when, where, why,* or *how*. Tell them that questions always end with a question mark.

Advanced Encourage children to do a "think-aloud" with a partner to discuss what they are planning to write.

Support Grammar For children who speak Russian, Polish, and some other languages, forming plurals in various ways will not be new. For more support, see the grammar lessons in the ELL and Transition Handbook.

Grammar

DEVELOP THE CONCEPT
Plural Nouns That Change Spelling

IDENTIFY PLURAL NOUNS THAT CHANGE SPELLING Write *child* and *mouse* on the board. Point to each word as you read it. Ask children to identify the plural of each word. *(children, mice)*

A plural noun names more than one person, place, or thing. Some nouns change to a different word when they are made plural. What is an example of a singular noun that changes spelling when it is made plural? (wolves)

PRACTICE

USE PLURAL NOUNS THAT CHANGE SPELLING IN A SENTENCE Gather several pictures of nouns that change spelling when made plural, such as *man, tooth,* and *foot.* Display a picture. Model using the noun in a sentence. Then model using the plural noun in a sentence.

MODEL This is a man. Write *man.* I'll think of a sentence that uses the singular noun *man. The man is tall.* Write the sentence. These are men. Write *men.* I'll think of a sentence that uses the plural noun *men. The men are talking.* Write the sentence.

Have children suggest sentences for the other pictures. Write the sentences children provide.

DAILY FIX-IT

3. He at good food on the fam.
   He ate good food on the farm.

4. But he was'nt at the farm now
   But he wasn't at the farm now.

Plural Nouns That Change Spelling
A **plural noun** names more than one person, place, animal, or thing. Some nouns change spelling to name more than one.

Singular	Plural	Singular	Plural
child	children	leaf	leaves
man	men	wolf	wolves
woman	women	mouse	mice
tooth	teeth	goose	geese
foot	feet		

Choose the correct plural noun in ( ).
Write the noun on the line.

1. A bird has two (foots, feet).
feet
2. The bugs crawl through the (leaves, leafs).
leaves
3. All the (children, childs) listen to the music.
children
4. The (gooses, geese) are noisy.
geese

Home Activity Your child learned about plural nouns that change spelling. Together look through several of your child's favorite books. Have your child point out plural nouns that change spelling.

▲ **Grammar and Writing Practice Book** p. 33

Wrap Up Your Day!

HIGH-FREQUENCY WORDS Write the following sentences. *The people were probably happy after they bought the new pet. I bet things were pleasant for a while. But, as the saying goes, all things shall change. I think the people are scared now. I saw a sign in their yard that said "Monster for Sale–Cheap!"* Ask children to read the sentences and identify the high-frequency words *people, sign, shall, bought, probably, pleasant, scared.*

STORY STRUCTURE Ask children to tell why Donkey decides to run away to Bremen. (his owner was trying to get rid of him, so he decides to go to become a musician)

LET'S TALK ABOUT IT Recall the selection *The Bremen Town Musicians.* Ask: Do the animals seem happier when they are alone or together? (together)

PREVIEW Day 3

Tell children that tomorrow they will learn about some friends and their special party.

Day 3
AT A GLANCE

Share Literature
From Me to You

Phonics and Spelling
REVIEW *r*-Controlled *er, ir, ur*
Spelling: Words with Plurals

High-Frequency Words

people	sign	**Word Wall**
shall	bought	
probably	pleasant	scared

Vocabulary
Homophones

Fluency
Read with Appropriate Phrasing

Independent Writing
Respond to Literature

Grammar
Plural Nouns That Change Spelling

Materials

- *Sing with Me Big Book*
- Big Book *From Me to You*
- Student Edition 274–275

Morning Warm~Up!

**Today we will read about Bat.
Bat is alone and sad.
What might make Bat feel better?**

QUESTION OF THE DAY Encourage children to sing "A Partnership with You" from the *Sing with Me Big Book* as you gather. Write and read the message and discuss the question.

REVIEW SYNONYMS AND ANTONYMS

- Point to *sad* in the message. Ask children to name a synonym, or word with a similar meaning. (unhappy)
- Ask children to name antonyms, or words with the opposite meaning for sad. (happy, joyful)

Build Background Use the Day 3 instruction on ELL Poster 9 to support children's use of English to communicate about lesson concepts.

ELL Poster 9

Share Literature

LISTEN AND RESPOND

REVIEW WORDS ABOUT FEELINGS Ask children what *From Me to You* is mostly about. (friendship) Go through the book and list words that tell about feelings and friends. (happy, miserable, blues, mope, sighing, sad, curious, kind, delighted)

From Me to You

Anthony France   illustrated by Tiphanie Beeke

Big Book

BUILD ORAL VOCABULARY Review that yesterday the class read the book to find out how Rat felt. Ask that children listen today to find out how Bat feels.

MONITOR LISTENING COMPREHENSION

• How does Bat feel when Rat goes to see him? Explain your answer. (Possible answer: Bat is miserable. I know this because he doesn't want to talk to Rat. He is also still wearing his bathrobe, even though it's daytime.)

• Why is Rat **struggling** to help Bat? (He knows how Bat feels, and he wants to help him.)

• What do you think will happen after Bat reads his mail? (Possible response: I think Bat will be happy. I think he will probably write a friendly note to someone else.)

Amazing Words to build oral vocabulary

	MONITOR PROGRESS
partnership survival solution miserable **struggle**	**If...** children lack oral vocabulary experiences about the concept Working Together, **then...** use the Oral Vocabulary Routine on pp. DI·1–DI·2, DI·6 to develop the Amazing Words.

 ELL

Listen and Respond Help children describe and demonstrate the actions conveyed by the words *knocked* and *winked* in *From Me to You*.

3

- Review *r*-Controlled *er, ir, ur* words.
- Blend, read, and sort *r*-Controlled *er, ir, ur* words.
- Spell *r*-Controlled *er, ir, ur* words.
- Preview words before reading them.

Say each word.
Circle 7 words that have the same vowel sound as **shirt**.
Write those words on the lines.

shirt

1. her	2. turn
her	turn

3. stir	4. warm
stir	

5. burn	6. start
burn	

7. fur	8. perch
fur	perch

9. wore	10. skirt
	skirt

Home Activity Your child identified words that contain the vowel sound in shirt. Think of a letter. Challenge your child to name a word that begins with that letter and has the same vowel sound as shirt spelled with er, ir, or ur.

▲ **Practice Book 2.1** p. 88, *r*-Controlled *er, ir, ur*

Review Phonics

r-CONTROLLED *er, ir, ur*

READ *r*-CONTROLLED *er, ir, ur* WORDS Write *jerk, dirt,* and *fur.* You can read these words because you know the sounds that *er, ir,* and *ur* stand for. What sounds can *er, ir,* and *ur* stand for? (/ėr/) What are the words?

INDIVIDUALS SORT *r*-CONTROLLED *er, ir, ur* WORDS Distribute word cards with words containing *er, ir,* and *ur.* Write *er, ir,* and *ur* as headings for a three-column chart. Have children read their words and place their word cards under the appropriate heading. Have all children copy the completed chart and circle the letters that stand for /ėr/. Have children use the words in sentences to demonstrate meaning.

er	*ir*	*ur*
herself	firm	burn
perch	birth	curl
clerk	stir	purse
modern	birdbath	survive

High-Frequency Words

PRACTICE

CHOOSE AN EXAMPLE Provide children with two examples. Ask them to decide which example illustrates a Word Wall word and explain why. **Word Wall**

- Which is a pleasant dream—a dream about going on a picnic or a dream about a monster?
- Which happens when you are scared—you smile or your heart beats quickly?
- Which will probably happen—you will see a unicorn or you will see a dog?
- Which might be bought at a store every week—a dance or a loaf of bread?
- Which will most people choose to drink—a cup of oil or a cup of water?
- Which might you see on a sign—"35 miles per hour" or snowflakes?
- Which is something you shall do later today—homework or grade tests?

Spelling

PRACTICE PLURALS *-s, -es, -ies*

WRITE A SPELLING STORY Have children practice the spelling words by writing a spelling story.

- Have pairs write a story using all the spelling words.
- Have children circle the spelling words in their stories.
- Have stories read aloud to the class.
- Place the stories in the Reading/Library Center for children to reread.

HOMEWORK Spelling Practice Book, p. 35

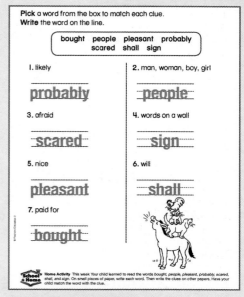

Pick a word from the box to match each clue.
Write the word on the line.

| bought | people | pleasant | probably |
| scared | shall | sign | |

1. likely **probably**
2. man, woman, boy, girl **people**
3. afraid **scared**
4. words on a wall **sign**
5. nice **pleasant**
6. will **shall**
7. paid for **bought**

Home Activity This week Your child learned to read the words bought, people, pleasant, probably, scared, shall, and sign. On small pieces of paper, write each word. Then write the clues on other papers. Have your child match the word with the clue.

▲ **Practice Book 2.1** p. 89,
High-Frequency Words

Spelling Words

Plurals

1. note	7. tune
2. notes	8. tunes*
3. lunch	9. switch*
4. lunches	10. switches*
5. story	11. baby
6. stories	12. babies

Challenge Words

| 13. crumbs | 15. centuries |
| 14. supplies | |

* Words from the Selection

Adding -s and -es
Read the journal entry. **Circle** three spelling mistakes. **Circle** the word with a capitalization mistake. **Write** the words correctly.

Spelling Words

note	tune
notes	tunes
lunch	switch
lunches	switches
story	baby
stories	babies

My Journal
Monday
I ate lunch with my (friends). Then Mrs. (perez) read a story about a mother raccoon and her (babys). I like (storys).

1. **friends** 2. **babies**
3. **stories** 4. **Perez**

Frequently Misspelled Words

friends
presents

Fill in the circle to show the correctly spelled word.

5. The ● baby ○ beby ○ babys is crying.
6. Can we ○ switche ● switch ○ swich desks?
7. Dad whistled some ● tunes ○ tunies ○ tuns.
8. We can eat our ○ lunchs ● lunches ○ lunchies outside.
9. He wrote a ● note ○ not ○ noties to his friend.
10. She ○ switchies ○ switchs ● switches on the light.

Home Activity Your child has identified misspelled words with and without -s and -es. Ask your child to explain why -es is added to lunch and switch. (The words end with ch.)

▲ **Spelling Practice Book** p. 35

- Discuss homophones.
- Use homophones in sentences.

Strategic Intervention

Children who are not able to write independently may copy one of the homophone pairs from the chalkboard and illustrate each word.

Advanced

Provide children with an additional list of homophone pairs such as *sun/son, wood/would, by/buy.* Have them write sentences using these words.

ELL

Access Content Have children act out meanings of various homophone pairs while others guess what the word is.

Vocabulary

HOMOPHONES

DISCUSS HOMOPHONES Have children recall that the animal characters are growing old and their owners think they are weak. Explain that *weak* is a homophone, or a word that sounds the same as another word, but has a different meaning and/or spelling. Write the following sentence pair and discuss the two meanings of *weak* and *week*—"not strong" and "a period of seven days." Then have children think of more sentences using each meaning.

The dog felt weak.

The dog walked for a week.

EXPAND MEANING Discuss with children the two meanings of each of the following homophone pairs: *know/no, be/bee, here/hear, there/their, ate/eight, aunt/ant, see/sea.* Provide an example for each meaning. Have children work with partners to write sentences for each meaning of each word. Invite volunteers to share their sentences.

Group Time

DAY 3

On-Level	Strategic Intervention	Advanced
Read *The Bremen Town Musicians.*	**Read** or listen to *The Bremen Town Musicians.*	**Read** *The Bremen Town Musicians.*
• Use pp. 256–275.	• Use the **Routine** on p. DI·48.	• Use the **Routine** on p. DI·49.

ELL Place English language learners in the groups that correspond to their reading abilities in English.

ⓘ Independent Activities

Independent Reading See p. 252j for Reading/Library activities and suggestions.

Journal Writing Write a journal entry about a time when you worked with someone else to accomplish something. Share writing.

Literacy Centers To provide experiences with *The Bremen Town Musicians,* you may use the Writing Center on p. 252k.

Practice Book 2.1 *r*-Controlled *er, ir, ur,* p. 88 High-Frequency Words, p. 89

Break into small groups after Vocabulary and before Writing.

Fluency

READ WITH APPROPRIATE PHRASING

MODEL GROUPING WORDS APPROPRIATELY Use *The Bremen Town Musicians.*

- Point to the fourth paragraph on p. 260. Commas and periods are types of punctuation that let us know we need to pause or stop briefly. They are also clues about how to group words as you read, rather than reading word-by-word.
- Ask children to follow along as you read the page with appropriate phrasing.
- Have children read the page after you. Encourage them to pause as they read when they encounter a comma or a period. Continue in the same way with pp. 258–259.

REREAD FOR FLUENCY

Reader's Theater

ROUTINE

1. **Select a Passage** For *The Bremen Town Musicians,* use pp. 261–265.

2. **Assign** Assign children the following roles: Narrator 1, Narrator 2, Donkey, Dog, Cat.

3. **Rehearse** Have children practice their assigned parts silently. For optimal fluency, encourage children to attend to punctuation marks.

4. **Provide Feedback** Suggest ways to improve fluency of reading, emphasizing grouping words.

5. **Read Aloud** Have children read their assigned parts aloud. Monitor progress and provide feedback.

Monitor Progress	**Fluency**
If… children have difficulty reading with appropriate phrasing,	**then…** prompt: • What do you do when you see a comma? • What do you do when you see a period?
If… the class cannot read fluently without you,	**then…** continue to have them read along with you.

OBJECTIVE

- Read aloud fluently with appropriate phrasing.

Options for Choral Reading

Use *The Bremen Town Musicians* or one of the following Leveled Readers.

On-Level

Jun and Pepper Grow Up

Strategic Intervention

What Do Sheepdogs Do?

Advanced

Silver and Stripes

E L L

Fluency Use *Big News in the Bath* or *The Bremen Town Musicians.* Model reading sections of the text with appropriate phrasing. Have English language learners echo you as you read Donkey's song, pausing after each line.

Fluency Coach CD To develop fluent readers, use Fluency Coach.

Think and Share

TALK ABOUT IT Model a response. The musicians were amazing. They sang songs like I'd never heard before! It was great fun.

1. **RETELL** Have children use the pictures across the bottom to retell the story. See Monitor Progress below.

2. **AUTHOR'S PURPOSE** The author is telling us that even when animals grow old, they are still useful.

3. **STORY STRUCTURE** The animals are no longer wanted by their owners. They solve the problem by becoming musicians.

LOOK BACK AND WRITE See Independent Writing, TE p. 275a. Rubric 4 3 2 1

Selection Test To assess with *Turtle's Race with Beaver*, use Selection Tests, pp. 33–36.

Monitor Progress — Check Retelling   Rubric 4 3 2 1

If... children have difficulty retelling the story,

then... use the Scoring Rubric for Retelling below to help them move toward fluent retelling.

SUCCESS PREDICTOR

| **Day 1** Check Word Reading | **Day 2** Check High-Frequency Words | ▶**Day 3 Check Retelling** | **Day 4** Check Fluency | **Day 5** Assess Progress |

Retelling Plan

☑ Week 1 assess Strategic Intervention students.

☑ Week 2 assess Advanced students.

☑ Week 3 assess Strategic Intervention students.

☑ **This week assess On-Level students.**

☐ Week 5 assess any students you have not yet checked during this unit.

Assessment Before retelling, help children name the characters and items shown. For more ideas on assessing comprehension, see the ELL and Transition Handbook.

Scoring Rubric — Narrative Retelling

Rubric 4 3 2 1	**4**	**3**	**2**	**1**
Connections	Makes connections and generalizes beyond the text	Makes connections to other events, stories, or experiences	Makes a limited connection to another event, story, or experience	Makes no connection to another event, story, or experience
Author's Purpose	Elaborates on author's purpose	Tells author's purpose with some clarity	Makes some connection to author's purpose	Makes no connection to author's purpose
Characters	Describes the main characters(s) and any character development	Identifies the main character(s) and gives some information about them	Inaccurately identifies some characters or gives little information about them	Inaccurately identifies the characters or gives no information about them
Setting	Describes the time and location	Identifies the time and location	Omits details of time or location	Is unable to identify time or location
Plot	Describes the events in sequence using rich detail	Tells the plot with some errors in sequence that do not affect meaning	Tells parts of plot with gaps that affect meaning	Retelling has no sense of story

Think and Share

Talk About It You have seen the Bremen Town Musicians perform. Tell about the show they put on for you.

1. Put the pictures below in order to tell the story of the Bremen Town Musicians.

2. What do you think the author is trying to tell us with this story?

3. This play has a beginning, middle, and end. The characters also have a problem. What is it and how is it solved?

Look Back and Write Why are the three robbers afraid of the animals? Look back at page 272. Use details from the story in your answer.

Meet the Author
Carol Pugliano-Martin

Here are two books by Carol Pugliano-Martin with plays you may want to perform.

Carol Pugliano-Martin has written many plays for school children to perform. Some of her plays are about real Americans. Others tell about the heroes of American folk tales. Ms. Pugliano-Martin lives in White Plains, New York.

Retelling Strip

274

275

Fresh Reads for Differentiated Test Practice

OBJECTIVE

● Write a response.

DAILY FIX-IT

5. He red a dog storie.
   He re<u>a</u>d a dog stor<u>y</u>.

6. He new other storys too.
   He <u>k</u>new other stor<u>ies</u> too.

Writer's Checkup

✔ Sentences should begin with capital letters. Did I do that?

✔ Sentences should end with correct punctuation. Did I do that?

✔ Some plural nouns change spelling. Did I use my plural nouns correctly?

Independent Writing

Look Back and Write

RESPOND TO LITERATURE Read the writing prompt on p. 274 in the Student Edition and model your thinking. Then have children write their responses.

Think Aloud

MODEL I'll look back at p. 272 and read that part of the story again. I'll look for the reason why the robbers are afraid of the animals. Then I'll write my response.

The robbers are afraid of the animals because they think they are monsters. One robber goes inside to see if it is safe. He is scratched by the cat. Then he is bitten by the dog. Then he is kicked by the donkey. When the rooster crows, the robber thinks the noise he hears is someone saying "coming to get you." He runs away and tells the other robbers about the four monsters that attacked him. So they all leave.

Scoring Rubric | Written Response

Rubric 4 3 2 1	4	3	2	1
Focus/Ideas	Clearly focuses on why the robbers are afraid of the animals	Focuses on why the robbers are afraid of the animals	Attempts to focus on why the robbers are afraid of the animals	Does not focus on why the robbers are afraid of the animals
Organization/ Paragraphs	Includes information in the correct order	Includes most of the information in the correct order	Includes some information in the correct order	Does not include information in the correct order
Word Choice	Uses clear, exact words	Uses some good words	Uses same or dull words	Uses all wrong words
Sentences	Uses varied, interesting, connected sentences	Uses varied, connected sentences	Uses simple sentences with few errors	Uses simple sentences with many errors

ELL

Support Writing Have children look at the illustrations on the cited pages. Ask children what ideas the illustrations give them that will help answer the prompt.

Assess See the ELL and Transition Handbook for guidance on assessing writing at various levels of English proficiency.

Grammar

APPLY TO WRITING
Plural Nouns That Change Spelling

IMPROVE WRITING WITH PLURAL NOUNS THAT CHANGE SPELLING Have children recall the plural nouns they used in the answer they wrote for Look Back and Write. Explain that it is important to spell plural nouns correctly. Remind children that some plural nouns change spelling. Remind children to use plural nouns that change spelling correctly in their own writing.

Write sentences as follows. Have children change the underlined singular noun to a plural noun. Ask how the noun's spelling changes from singular to plural.

> ### The mouse ate the cheese.
> ### The woman smiled.

PRACTICE

WRITE WITH PLURAL NOUNS THAT CHANGE SPELLING Have children write sentences that include plural nouns that change spelling. Ask what the difference is between the singular noun and the plural noun.

Plural Nouns That Change Spelling

Write the plural noun for each singular noun.

1. wolf

   wolves

2. man

   men

3. tooth

   teeth

Write a sentence that uses each plural noun above. Use words from the box or your own words to describe each noun.

| gray | shiny | tall |

Possible answers:

Gray wolves howl.

We saw two tall men.

She has shiny teeth.

▲ **Grammar and Writing Practice Book** p. 34

Wrap Up Your Day!

 AUTHOR'S PURPOSE Have children determine why the author wrote *The Bremen Town Musicians*. What did the author want us to learn from the story? (We can work together to accomplish a goal.)

 **READ WITH APPROPRIATE PHRASING** Have children read a paragraph from *The Bremen Town Musicians*, pausing when they encounter commas and periods.

LET'S TALK ABOUT IT When do the animals in *The Bremen Town Musicians* work together? (They work together to form a singing group, to see inside the house where the burglars are, and to scare the burglars away.)

PREVIEW Day 4

Tell children that tomorrow they will listen to a story about a dog whose animal friends work together to help him.

Share Literature

How Fletcher Was Hatched!

Phonics and Spelling

Plurals

Spelling: Words with Plurals

Read

Group Time < Differentiated Instruction

"Animals Helping Animals"

Fluency

Read with Appropriate Phrasing

Writing Across the Curriculum

Math Story

Grammar

Plural Nouns That Change Spelling

Speaking and Listening

Compare and Contrast Characters

Materials

• *Sing with Me Big Book*
• Read Aloud Anthology
• Student Edition 276–279

Morning Warm-Up!

Some animals work as teams.

What things might an animal need help with?

Today we will read about how some animals work together.

QUESTION OF THE DAY Encourage children to sing "A Partnership with You" from the *Sing with Me Big Book* as you gather. Write and read the message and discuss the question.

REVIEW PLURALS

• Ask children how many plural nouns they see in the message.
• Have them hold up that many fingers. (4)

ELL

Extend Language Use the Day 4 instruction on ELL Poster 9 to extend and enrich language.

ELL Poster 9

Share Literature

CONNECT CONCEPTS

ACTIVATE PRIOR KNOWLEDGE Recall the Bremen Town musicians and Rat and his friends. They all work together and help one another. Explain that you will read another story about someone who gets help from his friends in *How Fletcher Was Hatched!* by Wende and Harry Devlin.

BUILD ORAL VOCABULARY Read the first page. Explain that Fletcher is **faithful** to his owner, but he has some **misgivings,** or concerns, about her interest in a baby chick. Fletcher's friends come up with a plan. Ask children to listen to find how Fletcher uses the **occasion** to get his owner's attention.

MONITOR LISTENING COMPREHENSION

- What is the **occasion** that makes Fletcher sad? (His owner is not paying attention to him because she is interested in a new baby chick.)

- Why do you think Fletcher has **misgivings** about being sealed up in an egg? (Children will probably agree that dogs don't belong in eggs. Fletcher doesn't know what to expect so he is suspicious and doubtful.)

- How would a dog act if it were **faithful** to his owner? (Possible response: It would stay close by its owner. It would want to please its owner.)

Read Aloud Anthology
How Fletcher Was Hatched!

OBJECTIVES

- Set purpose for listening.
- Build oral vocabulary.

Amazing Words to build oral vocabulary

	MONITOR PROGRESS
partnership survival solution miserable struggle faithful misgivings occasion	**If...** children lack oral vocabulary experiences about the concept Working Together, **then...** use the Oral Vocabulary Routine on pp. DI·1–DI·2, DI·6 to develop the Amazing Words.

Connect Concepts Explain that some baby animals *hatch,* or come out of eggs. Birds and reptiles are two examples. However, mammals, such as dogs and people, do not break out of eggs.

Spiral REVIEW

- Reviews contractions *n't, 's, 'll, 'm.*
- Reviews consonant digraphs.
- Reviews high-frequency words *above, ago, enough, toward, whole, word.*

Sentence Reading

REVIEW WORDS IN CONTEXT

READ DECODABLE AND HIGH-FREQUENCY WORDS IN CONTEXT Write these sentences. Call on individuals to read a sentence. Then randomly point to words and have children read them. To help you monitor word reading, high-frequency words are underlined and decodable words are circled.

(I'm) putting (vases) on a (shelf) <u>above</u> the (dishes).

(Don't) go <u>toward</u> (those) (bushes) (where) the (puppies) play.

(She'll) have to spell the <u>whole</u> <u>word</u>.

(They'll) dig <u>enough</u> (holes) to plant (crops).

The (cages) are full of a (bunch) of (bunnies).

(She's) making (dresses) like (those) from long <u>ago</u>.

Monitor Progress	Word Reading
If... children are unable to read an underlined word,	**then...** read the word for them and spell it, having them echo you.
If... children are unable to read a circled word,	**then...** have them use the blending strategy they have learned for that word type.

Support Phonics For additional review, see the phonics activities in the ELL and Transition Handbook.

Spelling

PARTNER REVIEW Plurals -s, -es, -ies

READ AND WRITE Supply pairs of children with index cards on which the spelling words have been written. Have one child read a word while the other writes it. Then have children switch roles. Have them use the cards to check their spelling.

HOMEWORK Spelling Practice Book, p. 36

▲ **Spelling Practice Book** p. 36

Group Time

On-Level

Read "Animals Helping Animals."

• Use pp. 276–279.

Strategic Intervention

Read or listen to "Animals Helping Animals."

• Use the **Routine** on p. DI·50.

Advanced

Read "Animals Helping Animals."

• Use the **Routine** on DI·51.

 Place English language learners in the groups that correspond to their reading abilities in English.

DAY 4

ⓘ Independent Activities

Fluency Reading Pair children to reread *The Bremen Town Musicians.*

Journal Writing List ways animals help each other.

Spelling: Partner Review

Independent Reading See p. 252j for Reading/Library activities and suggestions.

Literacy Centers To provide listening opportunities, you may use the Listening Center on p. 252j. To extend science concepts, you may use the Science Center on p. 252k.

Break into small groups after Spelling and before Fluency.

4

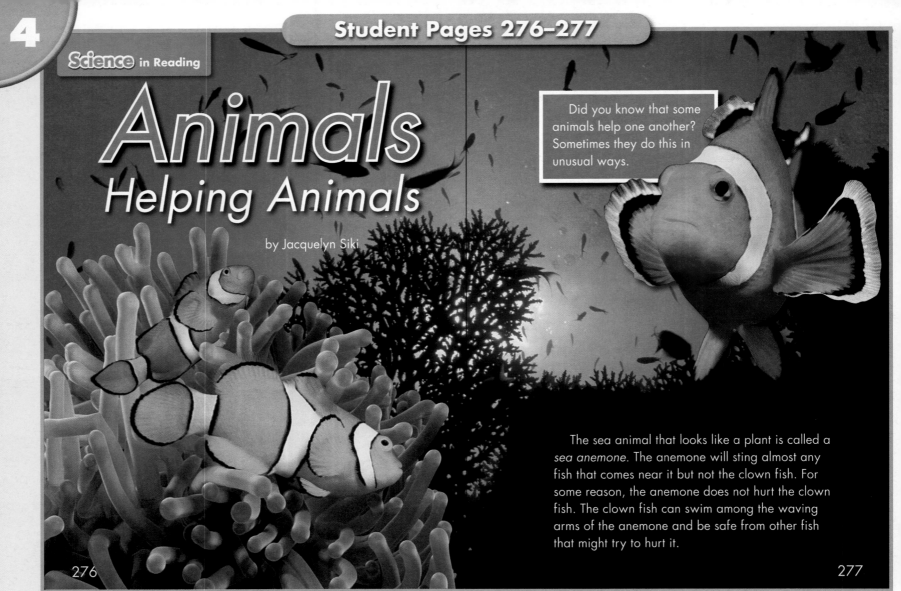

Animals
Helping Animals

by Jacquelyn Siki

Did you know that some animals help one another? Sometimes they do this in unusual ways.

The sea animal that looks like a plant is called a *sea anemone*. The anemone will sting almost any fish that comes near it but not the clown fish. For some reason, the anemone does not hurt the clown fish. The clown fish can swim among the waving arms of the anemone and be safe from other fish that might try to hurt it.

276

277

Audio CD AudioText

TIME FOR **Science**

Interdependence

All living things are interdependent. This means that they all work together or depend on each other in some way. For example, an aphid eating a plant leaf is eaten by a grasshopper. The grasshopper hops to the pond, where it is eaten by a frog. This food chain is an example of interdependence.

Read
Science in Reading

PREVIEW AND PREDICT Read the title and author's name. Have children preview the article and look at the pictures. Then ask them to predict whether "Animals Helping Animals" tells a story or provides information. Have children read to learn how animals work together.

INFORMATIONAL TEXT Review that selections that provide information about the real world are called nonfiction. Point out that the pictures show the animal pairs discussed in the text, and most of the pictures show how the animals work together to help one another.

VOCABULARY/HOMOPHONES Review that homophones are two or more words that sound alike but have different meanings and spellings. Have children locate *know* and *sea* on p. 277. What is the homophone that goes with *know*? What is the homophone that goes with *sea*? What is the meaning of each of the words?

Watch out! Has this crocodile found its lunch? No! This plover is a bird that helps keep the crocodile's mouth clean. It cleans the crocodile's teeth and mouth just like a dentist cleans your teeth.

This bird, called a *honey guide*, leads a *ratel*, or honey badger, to a beehive. The honey guide likes honey, and so does the badger. But the honey guide needs the badger's help to break open the hive. Then both animals can enjoy a treat!

What is this little cowbird doing? It's not getting a free ride. It's cleaning the insects off of the cow. The bird gets a meal. The cow gets clean.

These animals help each other too. When they are at a water hole together, baboons and impalas warn one another of danger. Baboons will even try to drive the danger away!

Like people, many animals help one another. They do this so that they can live together and survive.

278

279

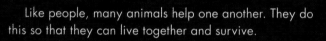

BUILD CONCEPTS

Cause and Effect • Inferential

- **What happens when a clown fish swims among the arms of an anemone?**
  The clown fish is safe from other animals because the anemone stings everything except the clown fish.

Draw Conclusions • Critical

- **Why do the animals discussed in the selection work together?**
  Possible response: Both animals in each pair get something from the relationship. They help each other because it is good for both of them.

CONNECT TEXT TO TEXT

The donkey, dog, cat, and rooster worked together when they climbed up on one another's backs to look in the window. How else did they work together?

Possible response: Another way they worked together was by scaring away the robbers. That way, they could eat all the food in the house.

Environment

Environment is the air, water, and land that surrounds us. An animal's needs must be met for it to survive in a certain environment. For example, a fish cannot survive on land because its need to be in water would not be met. Therefore, certain animals will be found only in certain environments.

Extend Language A sentence in the selection says "[The bird is] cleaning the insects off of the cow." What is a synonym for the word *insects?*

Bremen Town Musicians **278–279**

Fluency

READ WITH APPROPRIATE PHRASING

MODEL GROUPING WORDS APPROPRIATELY Use *The Bremen Town Musicians*.

- Point to the text on p. 263. Commas and periods are types of punctuation that let us know we need to pause or stop briefly.
- Ask children to follow along as you read the page with appropriate phrasing.
- Have children read the page after you. Encourage them to pause as they read when they encounter a comma or a period. Continue in the same way with pp. 264–267.

REREAD FOR FLUENCY

Reader's Theater

ROUTINE

1. **Select a Passage** For *The Bremen Town Musicians,* use pp. 258–263.

2. **Assign** Assign children the following roles: Narrator 1, Narrator 2, Donkey, Dog, Cat.

3. **Rehearse** Have children practice their assigned parts silently. For optimal fluency, encourage children to attend to punctuation marks.

4. **Provide Feedback** Suggest ways to improve fluency of reading, emphasizing grouping words.

5. **Read Aloud** Have children read their assigned parts aloud. Monitor progress and provide feedback.

Monitor Progress | Check Fluency

As children reread, monitor their progress toward their individual fluency goals. Current Goal: 58–68 words correct per minute. End-of-Year Goal: 90 words correct per minute.

If... children cannot read fluently at a rate of 58–68 words per minute,

then... make sure children practice with text at their independent level. Provide additional fluency practice, pairing nonfluent readers with fluent readers.

If... children already read fluently at 90 words per minute,

then... they do not need to reread three to four times.

SUCCESS PREDICTOR

Day 1 Check Word Reading	**Day 2** Check High-Frequency Words	**Day 3** Check Retelling	▶ **Day 4 Check Fluency**	**Day 5** Assess Progress

---

Writing Across the Curriculum

WRITE Math Story

DISCUSS Have children discuss the number of animals and robbers in the story. How many animals are there? How many robbers are there? Why do you think the animals and the robbers are in groups? Encourage children to use oral vocabulary such as *partnership* and *solution*.

SHARE THE PEN Have children participate in creating a math story. Ask the class to create a math story using numbers of objects, events, or characters found in the story. Call on an individual to read the story aloud. Write the sentences on the board, and have the class solve the problem. Ask questions, such as the following:

- What does a sentence start with? (capital letter)
- What does a sentence end with? (appropriate end punctuation, such as period, question mark, or exclamation point)
- What are two things a sentence has to have? (subject and verb)

Ask other individuals to share their stories. Continue having the class solve the math stories.

There were once four animals traveling together—one donkey, one dog, one cat, and one rooster. They came upon a house where there were three robbers. The animals decided to scare away the robbers. If one animal scared away one robber, how many animals would it take to scare away all three robbers? (three)

OBJECTIVE
- Create a math story.

Advanced

Encourage children to create another math story using a different subject and different numbers.

Support Writing If children suggest sentences that do not reflect conventional English, respond positively and restate the sentence without the errors.

OBJECTIVE

● Identify plural nouns that change spelling.

DAILY FIX-IT

7. The donkey blue the hurn.
   The donkey <u>blew</u> the h<u>o</u>rn.

8. The dog stated to hum a tun.
   The dog sta<u>r</u>ted to hum a tun<u>e</u>.

Plural Nouns That Change Spelling

Mark the letter of the word that correctly completes each sentence.

1. A flock of ___ flew by.
   ○ A goose
   ○ B geeses
   ⊗ C geese

2. All the ___ ate the cheese.
   ⊗ A mice
   ○ B mices
   ○ C mouse

3. The three ___ wear hats.
   ⊗ A men
   ○ B man
   ○ C mens

4. People tapped their ___.
   ○ A foots
   ⊗ B feet
   ○ C feets

5. Men and ___ danced.
   ⊗ A women
   ○ B woman
   ○ C womans

6. Does a rooster have ___?
   ○ A tooth
   ○ B tooths
   ⊗ C teeth

Home Activity Your child prepared for taking tests on plural nouns that change spelling. Have your child look through a newspaper or magazine article and find plural nouns that change spelling. Ask him or her to circle the words.

▲ **Grammar and Writing Practice Book** p. 35

REVIEW Plural Nouns That Change Spelling

DEFINE PLURAL NOUNS THAT CHANGE SPELLING

- What do plural nouns name? (more than one person, place, animal, or thing)
- What happens to some nouns when they are changed from singular to plural? (Their spelling changes.)

PRACTICE

LIST PLURAL NOUNS THAT CHANGE SPELLING Write a list of singular nouns that change spelling when made plural on the chalkboard. Have individuals copy the list, adding the correct plural form of the noun. Have children share their work in a group.

Singular	Plural
man	
tooth	
mouse	

Speaking and Viewing

COMPARE AND CONTRAST

OBJECTIVES

- View to gain information from multimedia presentation.
- Speak to compare and contrast people, places, or events from the media and from stories read in class.

MODEL SPEAKING AND VIEWING Remind children of appropriate viewing and speaking behaviors such as viewing attentively and speaking directly to one's audience. Then ask children to think about these behaviors as they take turns comparing and contrasting characters, places, or events in the media.

- When you watch multimedia presentations, you listen for facts and ideas.
- Choose one character, place, or event from *The Bremen Town Musicians* and one character, place, or event from the multimedia presentation you view. You will discuss how they are alike and different.

COMPARING AND CONTRASTING Ask children to tell how two characters, places, or events they chose from the story and from the multimedia presentation are alike and different. Allow children the opportunity to complete Graphic Organizer 18 before taking their turn speaking to the class.

> Central Issues
> The donkey from **Shrek** and the donkey from **The Bremen Town Musicians**

> Alike
> They are both donkeys. They are both smart. They both talk. They both sing.

> Different
> The donkey from Shrek is happy and carefree, while the donkey from the story has run away because his owner was going to get rid of him.

> Conclusions
> The two characters are alike in many ways. Their biggest difference is that one is happy and the other is worried. However, by the end of the story, the second donkey is happy too.

▲ **Graphic Organizer 18**

Wrap Up Your Day!

✓ **Text to Self** What are some other stories you know about animals helping each other? (Possible response: I know a story about a dog who raised a kitten after the kitten's mother got hurt.) Call on individuals to provide different answers.

LET'S TALK ABOUT IT Recall the Read Aloud Anthology story *How Fletcher Was Hatched.* Ask: How did the animals in this story need to work together? (Fletcher needed their help to get Alexandra's attention, so they built him an egg to hatch from.) Display the "When should we work together?" Graphic Organizer from Day 1. Ask children to think of times when they have needed help and add those to the organizer. (doing difficult homework, building something large)

PREVIEW Day 5

Remind children that they heard a story about a jealous dog who hatches like a chicken to get attention. Tell them that tomorrow they will hear again about how this dog's animal friends help him with his plan.

Share Literature
How Fletcher Was Hatched!

Phonics and Spelling

Review Plurals
Spelling: Words with Plurals

High-Frequency Words

people	sign	**Word Wall**
shall	bought	
probably	pleasant	scared

Monitor Progress
Spelling Test: Adding -s, -es, -ies

Group Time < Differentiated Assessment

Grammar and Writing
Plural Nouns That Change Spelling

Research and Study Skills
Advertisement/Poster

Materials

- *Sing with Me Big Book*
- Read Aloud Anthology
- Reproducible Pages TE 280f–280g
- Student Edition 280–281

Morning Warm~Up!

This week we read about animals helping each other to live and enjoy life.

Some formed a singing group, some cheered up unhappy friends, and some kept each other safe and clean.

Why is it often better to work with others?

QUESTION OF THE DAY Encourage children to sing "A Partnership with You" from the *Sing with Me Big Book* as you gather. Write and read the message and discuss the question.

REVIEW ORAL VOCABULARY Have children name things in the message that

- summarize what is necessary for survival (keeping safe)
- are ways to form a partnership (helping each other)
- mean the same as *miserable* (unhappy)
- are ways of being faithful to a friend (cheering up or keeping the friend safe)

Assess Vocabulary Use the Day 5 instruction on ELL Poster 9 to monitor children's progress with oral vocabulary.

ELL Poster 9

Share Literature

LISTEN AND RESPOND

OBJECTIVES

- Set purpose for listening.
- Build oral vocabulary.

USE PRIOR KNOWLEDGE Review that yesterday the class listened to find out how Fletcher got his owner's attention. Suggest that today the class listen to find out who else paid attention to Fletcher.

MONITOR LISTENING COMPREHENSION

- Who came to see the big egg? (the custodian, school children, the science teacher, a professor from the university, and the principal)

- What is a likely reason that the author wrote about such an unlikely event? (Possible response: The author probably wanted to entertain the readers.)

Read Aloud Anthology
How Fletcher Was Hatched!

BUILD ORAL VOCABULARY

HOMOPHONES Read the third paragraph of *How Fletcher Was Hatched!* Have children recall how Alexandra describes the chick. (dear) Write *dear.* Ask children to think of another word that sounds the same as *dear* but is spelled differently and has a different meaning. (deer) Point out other words in the story such as *reed, hole,* and *two* and ask children to name their homophones. Words that sound alike but have different meanings and spellings are called *homophones.* Challenge children to use the homophones in sentences.

dear   **hole**

reed   **two**

ELL

Extend Language Tell children that homophones are not always found in pairs. Sometimes there are three words that are homophones. Examples include *their, there, they're* and *to, two, too.*

OBJECTIVES

- Review plurals -s, -es, -ies.
- Review high-frequency words.

Plurals -s, -es, -ies

REVIEW

IDENTIFY PLURALS -s, -es, -ies Write these sentences. Have children read each one aloud. Call on individuals to name and underline the plural words with -s, -es, and -ies endings.

The **ladies** ate **grapes** and **jellies**.

I put away the **dishes**, **plates**, and **cups**.

He gave the **babies** their **lunches** and **drinks**.

The **bunnies** ran through the **bushes**.

High-Frequency Words

REVIEW

MEANING CLUES Read the following clues aloud. Have children write a word from Words to Know on p. 254 for each clue. Then read clues and answers to check responses.

This is another word for nice. (pleasant)

This is the opposite of sold. (bought)

These are men, women, boys, and girls. (people)

This is another word for afraid. (scared)

This is something you read. (sign)

This means aout the same as will. (shall)

This is another word for most likely. (probably)

ELL

Vocabulary For additional practice with the high-frequency words, use the vocabulary strategies and word cards in the ELL Teaching Guide, pp. 59–60.

SPELLING TEST Plurals -s, -es, -ies

DICTATION SENTENCES Use these sentences to assess this week's spelling words.

1. The <u>baby</u> is napping.
2. We will eat <u>lunch</u>.
3. Did you read the <u>notes</u>?
4. He liked her <u>stories</u>.
5. She can hum the <u>tunes</u>.
6. Those <u>babies</u> are cute!
7. Dad will tell me a <u>story</u>.
8. The <u>switches</u> were all shut off.
9. I like that <u>tune</u>.
10. I have a <u>note</u> for you.
11. Did you hand out the <u>lunches</u>?
12. Turn on the light <u>switch</u>.

CHALLENGE WORDS

13. Will you pick up those <u>crumbs</u>?
14. I have lots of school <u>supplies</u>.
15. Her brothers were born in different <u>centuries</u>.

ASSESS

● Spell plurals -s, -es, -ies.

Spelling Words

Plurals

1. note
2. notes
3. lunch
4. lunches
5. story
6. stories
7. tune
8. tunes*
9. switch*
10. switches*
11. baby
12. babies

Challenge Words

13. crumbs
14. supplies
15. centuries

* Words from the Selection

Group Time

On-Level

Read Set B Sentences.

• Use pp. 280e–280g.

Strategic Intervention

Read Set A Sentences and the Story.

• Use pp. 280e–280g.

• Use the **Routine** on p. DI·52.

Advanced

Read Set C Sentences.

• Use pp. 280e–280g.

• Use the **Routine** on p. DI·53.

 Place English language learners in the groups that correspond to their reading abilities in English.

DAY
5

ⓘ Independent Activities

Fluency Reading Children reread selections at their independent level.

Journal Writing Write a story with a problem and a solution. Share Writing

Independent Reading See p. 252j for Reading/Library activities and suggestions.

Independent Reading You may use the Technology Center on p. 252k to support this week's concepts and reading.

Practice Book 2.1 Advertisement/Poster, p. 90

Break into small groups after Spelling and before Grammar and Writing.

ASSESS

- Decode plurals.
- Read high-frequency words.
- Read aloud with appropriate speed and accuracy.
- Recognize the author's purpose.
- Retell a story.

Differentiated Assessment

On-Level
Set B

Strategic Intervention
Set A

Advanced
Set C

Fluency Assessment Plan

- ☑ Week 1 assess Strategic Intervention students.
- ☑ Week 2 assess Advanced students.
- ☑ Week 3 assess Strategic Intervention students.
- ☑ **This week assess On-Level students.**
- ☐ Week 5 assess any students you have not yet checked during this unit.

Set individual fluency goals for children to enable them to reach the end-of-year goal.

- Current Goal: 58–68 wcpm
- End-of-Year Goal: 90 wcpm
- **ELL** For guidance in evaluating fluency, see the ELL and Transition Handbook.

SENTENCE READING

ASSESS PLURALS AND HIGH-FREQUENCY WORDS Use one of the reproducible lists on p. 280f to assess children's ability to read plurals and high-frequency words. Call on individuals to read two sentences aloud. Have each child in the group read different sentences. Start over with sentence one if necessary.

RECORD SCORES Use the Sentence Reading Chart for this unit on p. 313k.

Monitor Progress	Plurals
If... children have trouble reading plurals	**then...** use the Reteach Lessons on p. DI·67.
High-Frequency Words	
If... children cannot read a high-frequency word,	**then...** mark the missed words on a high-frequency word list and send the list home for additional word reading practice or have the child practice with a fluent reader.

FLUENCY AND COMPREHENSION

ASSESS FLUENCY Take a one-minute sample of children's oral reading. See Monitoring Fluency, p. 313i. Have children read "Animal Wishes," the on-level fluency passage on p. 280g.

RECORD SCORES Record the number of words read correctly in a minute on the child's Fluency Progress Chart.

ASSESS COMPREHENSION Have the child read to the end of the passage. (If the child had difficulty with the passage, you may read it aloud.) Ask why the author wrote the story and have the child retell the passage. Use the Retelling Rubric on p. 274g to evaluate the child's retelling.

Monitor Progress	Fluency
If... a child does not achieve the fluency goal on the timed reading,	**then...** copy the passage and send it home with the child for additional fluency practice or have the child practice with a fluent reader.
Author's Purpose	
If... a child cannot recognize the author's purpose,	**then...** use the Reteach Lesson on p. DI·67.

READ THE SENTENCES

Set A

1. The sign said there were dogs and kitties for sale.
2. Shall we dry the glasses and dishes?
3. There are probably pennies and dimes on the shelf.
4. The roses and pansies had a pleasant smell.
5. The bunnies were scared of the cats.
6. Most people bought lunches in boxes.

Set B

1. The people on the stages sang pleasant tunes.
2. Jane used brushes to paint the letters on the sign.
3. Shall I read stories to the classes?
4. Mike bought kites to fly on the beaches.
5. We will probably ride buses in the cities.
6. The thunder scared the horses and puppies.

Set C

1. Some people will probably ride mules into the canyon, but others will hike.
2. Our families enjoyed a pleasant day of picking peaches at the farm.
3. Shall we make copies of all the pages for everybody?
4. At the fair, Dad bought ice cream cones and slices of watermelon for us to eat.
5. The sign told us that the paint on the benches and swings was still wet.
6. A snake scared Aunt Barb while we were planting daisies and lilies.

Monitor Progress   Plurals
High-Frequency Words

SUCCESS PREDICTOR

Animal Wishes

Owl asked all his friends to gather together. 8

"Now that summer is almost here, I would like to 18
know what your wishes are." 23

"Bees, what do you wish for?" Owl asked. 31

"We wish for lots of pansies and other flowers. 40
We can make honey for other animals and build 49
big hives." 51

"Turtles, what do you wish for?" Owl asked. 59

"We wish for lots of rain. The rain will fill the 70
ponds and lakes. Then all the animals will have 79
water to drink. And we will have places to swim." 89

"Birds, what do you wish for?" Owl asked. 97

"We wish for lots of berry bushes. Then all the 107
birds will have plenty of berries to eat. We will 117
chirp all day. The animals like to listen to birds 127
chirping." 128

Then one little bird asked, "What is your wish, 137
Owl?" 138

Owl said, "I wish all of your wishes come true." 148

Plural Nouns That Change Spelling

A **plural noun** names more than one person, place, animal, or thing. Some nouns change spelling to name more than one.

Cat saw one **mouse** in the house.

Cat saw two **mice** by the door.

Singular	Plural
leaf	leaves
tooth	teeth
foot	feet
man	men
woman	women
goose	geese

280

Write Using Plural Nouns That Change Spelling

1. Write this sentence so that the singular noun *man* is plural.

The man heard the rooster crowing.

2. Choose an animal from the play. Write a sentence about that animal. Use a plural noun that changes spelling. Underline the plural noun.

3. Write some sentences telling the animals how to get to Bremen Town. Use plural nouns from the chart on page 280 in your sentences.

281

Grammar and Writing

WRITE USING PLURAL NOUNS THAT CHANGE SPELLING Read pp. 280–281 aloud. Guide children as they complete the items.

1. The men heard the rooster crowing.

2. Possible response: The donkey said his <u>feet</u> hurt.

CONNECT TO UNIT WRITING Children write sentences telling animals how to get to Bremen Town. They should use plural nouns from the chart on p. 280.

3. Possible response:

The animals should walk past the tree with yellow leaves. They should walk around the sharp rocks so that they don't make their feet hurt. When the animals see lots of geese dancing in the grass, they will know they are in Bremen Town.

DAILY FIX-IT

9. donkey humed with Dog.
   Donkey hum**m**ed with Dog.

10. what fun they had.
    What fun they had**!**

Plural Nouns That Change Spelling

Circle the plural nouns in each sentence.

1. The (horses) made noise with their (feet).
2. (Geese) can swim with the (ducks).
3. (Mice) come into the (houses) in winter.

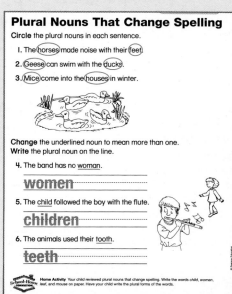

Change the underlined noun to mean more than one. Write the plural noun on the line.

4. The band has no <u>woman</u>.

women

5. The <u>child</u> followed the boy with the flute.

children

6. The animals used their <u>tooth</u>.

teeth

Home Activity Your child reviewed plural nouns that change spelling. Write the words *child, woman, leaf,* and *mouse* on paper. Have your child write the plural forms of the words.

▲ **Grammar and Writing Practice Book** p. 36

Bremen Town Musicians **280–281**

Research/Study Skills

TEACH/MODEL Poster

MODEL MAKING A POSTER Draw a poster for the animals' first performance in *The Bremen Town Musicians.* Explain that posters announce events. Read the poster and ask children what it tells them about the Bremen Town Musicians.

Model how to make a poster.

MODEL I can make a poster that will tell people about the Bremen Town Musicians' first show. I will want to include important information. I'll tell who they are, when they will perform, where they will perform, and how much it costs to hear them. I'll include photos or drawings and large print on my poster.

DISCUSS INFORMATION IN A POSTER Call on individuals to discuss why each part of the poster is needed: *who, when, where, how much.*

PRACTICE

DEMONSTRATE MAKING A POSTER Have partners make their own poster announcing an event that they make up. Remind them to include all information that readers would need to know.

Who: **The Bremen Town Musicians**

When: **Saturday, May 6, 7 P.M.**

Where: **Town Square at Freedom Hall**

How Much: **Free!**

Wrap Up Your Week!

LET'S TALK ABOUT Working Together

QUESTION OF THE WEEK Recall this week's question.

- When should we work together? When should we work alone?

Display the When Should We Work Together web. Have children tell about times in the classroom that they've all worked together (for example, when they practiced for a play).

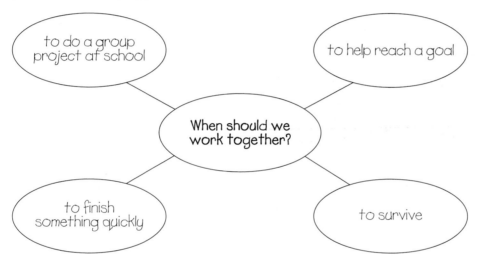

CONNECT Use questions such as these to prompt a discussion.

- The animals from *The Bremen Town Musicians* form a partnership. When have you worked in a partnership to celebrate something special?

- The animals in the story sang together on many occasions. Do you sing with others on special occasions?

Build Background Use ELL Poster 10 to support the Preview activity.

PREVIEW Tell children that next week they will read more about working together and contributing to a celebration.

PREVIEW Next Week

A Turkey for Thanksgiving

Preview Your Week

How can we contribute to a celebration?

A Turkey for Thanksgiving

by Eve Bunting
illustrated by Diane de Groat

What will Mr. Moose do with a turkey for Thanksgiving?

286   287

Student Edition pages 286–305

Audio CD

Genre	Animal Fantasy
Phonics	Long *a: a, ai, ay*
Comprehension Skill	Draw Conclusions
Comprehension Strategy	Visualize

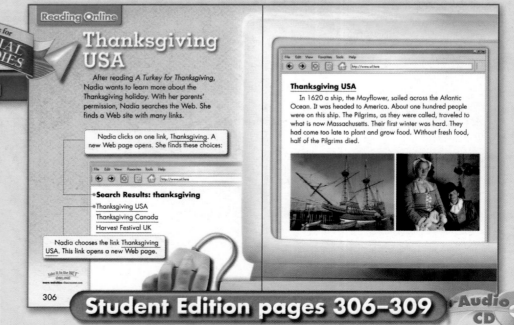

Paired Selection

Reading Across Texts
Research Thanksgiving

Genre
Web Page

Text Features
Captions

Thanksgiving USA

After reading *A Turkey for Thanksgiving*, Nadia wants to learn more about the Thanksgiving holiday. With her parents' permission, Nadia searches the Web. She finds a Web site with many links.

Nadia clicks on one link, Thanksgiving. A new Web page opens. She finds these choices:

Search Results: thanksgiving
- Thanksgiving USA
- Thanksgiving Canada
- Harvest Festival UK

Nadia chooses the link Thanksgiving USA. This link opens a new Web page.

306

Thanksgiving USA

In 1620 a ship, the Mayflower, sailed across the Atlantic Ocean. It was headed to America. About one hundred people were on this ship. The Pilgrims, as they were called, traveled to what is now Massachusetts. Their first winter was hard. They had come too late to plant and grow food. Without fresh food, half of the Pilgrims died.

Student Edition pages 306–309

Audio CD

Read It
ONLINE
sfsuccessnet.com
• Student Edition
• Leveled Readers
• Decodable Reader

Leveled Readers

🎯 **Skill** Draw Conclusions
🎯 **Strategy** Visualize
Lesson Vocabulary

Below-Level

On-Level

Advanced

ELL Reader
• Concept Vocabulary
• Text Support
• Language Enrichment

Decodable Readers

Apply Phonics

· *Bert Does Not Like Bugs*

Time for SOCIAL STUDIES

Integrate Social Studies Standards

• National Celebrations
• Patriotism
• Traditions

✓ Read

A Turkey for Thanksgiving
pp. 286–305

"Thanksgiving USA"
pp. 306–309

✓ Read

Leveled Readers

Below-Level **On-Level** **Advanced**

• Support Concepts
• Develop Concepts
• Extend Concepts
• Social Studies Extension Activity

✓ Read

ELL Reader

✓ **Build Concept Vocabulary**
Working Together,
pp. 282r, 282–283

✓ **Teach Social Studies Concepts**
Thanksgiving History,
pp. 298–299
Thanksgiving Foods, pp. 290–291
National Celebrations,
pp. 306–307

✓ **Explore Social Studies Center**
Invite a Thanksgiving Guest,
p. 282k

Planner

My Lesson Planner
ONLINE
sfsuccessnet.com

DAY 1

DAY 2

Oral Language 10-15 minutes

- Build Concepts
- Share Literature

Oral Language 282l-282m
QUESTION OF THE WEEK *How can we contribute to a celebration?*
Share Literature
Sing with Me Big Book, 10

Oral Language 284a-284b
QUESTION OF THE DAY *What do you usually do on Thanksgiving?*
Share Literature
Read Aloud Anthology "My First Chinese New Year"

Word Work 25-30 minutes

- Phonics
- Spelling
- High-Frequency Words

Word Work 282n-282p
Phonics
Introduce Long *a: a, ai, ay* **T**

Spelling Pretest

Word Work 284c-284d, 284-285a
Phonics
Long *a: a, ai, ay* **T**

Spelling Dictation
High-Frequency Words T
Introduce *door, behind, brought, minute, promise, sorry, everybody*

Reading 60-75 minutes

- Vocabulary
- Comprehension
- Fluency

- Cross-Curricular Connections

- Independent Reading

Reading 282q-283b
Vocabulary
Decodable Word Meaning
Read Decodable Reader 10
Comprehension Check
Fluency
Paired Reading
Build Background
Let's Talk About Working Together
Comprehension
Draw Conclusions **T**

SOCIAL STUDIES Concept Chart

Leveled Readers, LR37–45
Self-Selected Reading, TR22–23

Reading 284e-284f, 286a-302
Vocabulary
Introduce *Thanksgiving, lumbered, riverbank, hooves*
Comprehension
Draw Conclusions **T**
Visualize
Read *A Turkey for Thanksgiving,* 286-302
REVIEW **Comprehension Skill**
Author's Purpose

SOCIAL STUDIES Thanksgiving Food, Thanksgiving History
SOCIAL STUDIES Concept Chart

Leveled Readers, LR37–45
Self-Selected Reading, TR22–23

Language Arts 20-30 minutes

- Writing
- Grammar
- Speaking, Listening, Viewing
- Research/Study Skills

Language Arts 283c-283d
Shared Writing
Invitation
DAILY WRITING
List friends you would like to dine with.
Grammar
Introduce Possessive Nouns **T**

Language Arts 302a-302b
Interactive Writing
List
DAILY WRITING
Write about your favorite holiday.
Grammar
Practice Possessive Nouns **T**

Monitor Progress

Daily **SUCCESS PREDICTORS** for
Adequate Yearly Progress

Day 1 Check 282o
Check Word Reading
Spiral **REVIEW** Phonics

Phonics

Day 2 Check 285a
Check High-Frequency Words
Spiral **REVIEW** High-Frequency Words

Fluency

282d   Vocabulary   Check Oral Vocabulary See p. DI·2.

Student Edition 286–305   **Leveled Readers**   **Student Edition** 306–309

DAY 3

QUESTION OF THE DAY *When do you think the holiday is celebrated?*
Share Literature
Read Aloud Anthology "My First Chinese New Year"

Word Work 303c–303d
Phonics
REVIEW Plurals -s, -es, -ies

Spelling Practice
High-Frequency Words T
Practice *door, behind, brought, minute, promise, sorry, everybody*

Reading 286–302, 303e–305
Vocabulary
Similes

Comprehension
Read *A Turkey for Thanksgiving,* 286–305

Think and Share
Fluency
Silent Reading

SOCIAL STUDIES Concept Chart

Leveled Readers, LR37–45
Self-Selected Reading, TR22–23

Language Arts 305a–305b
Independent Writing
Respond to Literature
DAILY WRITING
Write about a holiday celebration.
Grammar
Write with Possessive Nouns **T**

DAY 4

Oral Language 306a–306b
QUESTION OF THE DAY *What other ways can we learn about things?*
Share Literature
Read Aloud Anthology "The Blizzard"

Word Work 306c–306d
Phonics
REVIEW Sentence Reading

Spelling Partner Review
High-Frequency Words T
Practice *door, behind, brought, minute, promise, sorry, everybody*

Reading 306–309a
Vocabulary
Position and Direction Words

Comprehension
Read *Thanksgiving USA,* 306–309
Social Studies in Reading
Reading Across Texts

Fluency
Silent Reading

SOCIAL STUDIES National Celebrations, Traditions
SOCIAL STUDIES CENTER Write a Description

Leveled Readers, LR37–45
Self-Selected Reading, TR22–23

Language Arts 309b–309d
Writing Across the Curriculum
List
DAILY WRITING
Write about a special holiday.
Grammar
Review Possessive Nouns **T**
Speaking and Listening
Make Introductions

DAY 5

Oral Language 310a–310b
QUESTION OF THE DAY *How can we add to a celebration?*
Share Literature
Read Aloud Anthology "The Blizzard"

Word Work 310c–310f
Phonics
⊙ Review Long *a: a, ai, ay*

Spelling Test
High-Frequency Words T
Review *door, behind, brought, minute, promise, sorry, everybody*

Reading 310b, 310e–310g
Vocabulary
Similes

Monitor Progress
Read the Sentences
Read the Story

SOCIAL STUDIES Concept Chart

Leveled Readers, LR37–45
Self-Selected Reading, TR22–23

Language Arts 310–311a
Grammar and Writing
Use Possessive Nouns **T**
Connect to Unit Writing
How-to Report
DAILY WRITING
List activities during a holiday.
Research/Study Skills
Reading a Web Page

KEY

⊙ = Target Skill
T = Tested Skill

THIS WEEK'S RESOURCES
Practice Book pp. 91–100
Spelling Practice Book pp. 37–40
Grammar and Writing Practice Book pp. 37–40
Selection Test pp. 37–40
Fresh Reads for Differentiated Test Practice pp. 55–60
Phonics Songs and Rhymes Chart 10

Day 3 Check 303g
Check Retelling

Comprehension

Day 4 Check 309a
Check Fluency WCPM
Spiral REVIEW Phonics, High-Frequency Words

Fluency

Day 5 Check 310e
Long *a: a, ai, ay*
High-Frequency Words
Fluency
Comprehension

SUCCESS PREDICTOR

Resources for Differentiated Instruction

LEVELED READERS

▶ **Comprehension**
- 🔄 **Skill** Draw Conclusions
- 🔄 **Strategy** Visualize

▶ **Lesson Vocabulary**

High-Frequency Words

door	brought

behind

minute	promise

sorry	everybody

▶ **Social Studies Standards**
- **National Celebrations**
- **Patriotism**
- **Traditions**

Leveled Reader Database

ONLINE

sfsuccessnet.com

Use the Online Database of over 600 books to

- Download and print additional copies of this week's leveled readers
- Locate more titles at various levels to practice this week's skill—draw conclusions
- Search for more titles focused on this week's topic and content

On-Level

Social Studies

Giving Thanks Around the World

by Christine Wolf

On-Level Reader

Draw Conclusions

Think about what you read in *Giving Thanks Around the World*. Then think about what you already know about Thanksgiving Day. Circle the phrase that best completes each conclusion below.

1. Many people celebrate and give thanks in autumn because
   a. people like to carve pumpkins.
   b. many crops are harvested in autumn.
   c. they like to be outdoors.

2. The Chinese celebrate the Moon Festival
   a. in the morning.
   b. in the afternoon.
   c. at night.

3. By making offerings to the rain and the sun, southern Indian villagers hope
   a. there will be sun and rain next year.
   b. there will be no rain next year.
   c. there will be no sun next year.

4–5. What more do you know about giving thanks around the world? Write your own conclusion on the line below. *Possible response given.*

People are thankful for the food they eat.

🔄 **On-Level Practice** TE p. LR41

Vocabulary

Choose a word from the Word Box to complete the sentences below.

Words to Know
behind brought door everybody
minute promise sorry

1. behind — a. each and every person
2. brought — b. toward the back
3. door — c. feel sadness or regret
4. everybody — d. to give your word
5. minute — e. the barrier at the entrance of a building or room
6. promise — f. carried or taken with you
7. sorry — g. 60 seconds

8. She made a promise to clean up her room.
9. She opened the door so her dog could go out.
10. Ben brought his books to school in his backpack.

🔄 **On-Level Practice** TE p. LR42

Strategic Intervention

Social Studies

Together for Thanksgiving

by Jessica Quilty
illustrated by April Hartman

Below-Level Reader

Draw Conclusions

Think about the story *Together for Thanksgiving*. Then think about what you already know about Thanksgiving Day. Circle the phrase that best completes each conclusion below.

1. People go by car, plane, or train to Thanksgiving dinner, so
   a. some live nearby and some live far away.
   b. everyone lives far away.
   c. they do not like to travel.

2. Everyone brings a dish, so
   a. there is not enough food.
   b. there is lots of food.
   c. there is no dessert.

3. Everyone helps clean up, so
   a. it goes by fast.
   b. it takes a long time.
   c. they do not want to play.

4–5. What more do you know about Thanksgiving Day? Write your own conclusion on the line below. *Possible response given.*

Thanksgiving Day is a day to share.

🔄 **Below-Level Practice** TE p. LR38

Vocabulary

Choose the word from the box that best fits into each sentence.

Words to Know
behind brought door everybody
minute promise sorry

1. John was sorry he broke the window.
2. The guests knocked on the front door.
3. Everybody ate some turkey.
4. My aunt brought pumpkin pie.
5. We made a promise to help clean up.
6. Dinner will be ready in a minute.
7. Yummy smells came from behind the kitchen door.

🔄 **Below-Level Practice** TE p. LR39

Advanced

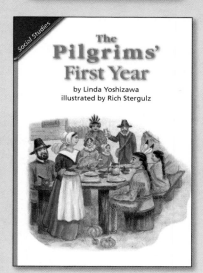

The Pilgrims' First Year
by Linda Yoshizawa
illustrated by Rich Stergulz

Social Studies

Advanced Reader

Fact and Opinion

Think about what you read in *The Pilgrims' First Year*. Then think about what you already know about Pilgrims and Native Americans. Circle the phrase that best completes each conclusion below.

1. The Wampanoag sewed clothes from deer and elk skins, so
   a. deer and elk roamed nearby.
   b. they must have liked deer and elk the most.
   c. they must have only eaten clams.

2. The Wampanoag spent the winter in the forest because
   a. they grew different crops in the winter.
   b. trees sheltered them from the winter weather.
   c. it was too muddy by the shore.

3. The Pilgrims did not know a lot about hunting because
   a. they only ate vegetables.
   b. they were taught as children.
   c. they did not hunt as much in England.

4–5. What more do you know about the Pilgrim's first year? Write your own conclusion on the line below. Possible response given.

~~The Wampanoags helped the~~
~~Pilgrims survive.~~

Advanced Practice TE p. LR44

Vocabulary

Choose a word from the Word Box to complete the sentences below.

Words to Know			
dine	faith	fertilizer	holiday
participate	resources	traditions	

1. The Pilgrims invited the Wampanoag to **dine** with them.
2. Thanksgiving is now a national **holiday**.
3. The Pilgrims brought many **tradition** from England.
4. Squanto taught the Pilgrims to use fish for **fertilizer**.
5. The Pilgrims wanted to practice their **faith**.
6. The Wampanoag used the **resources** around them.
7. Everyone had to **participate** in doing chores.

Advanced Practice TE p. LR45

A Thanksgiving Party
by Rosa García

Illustrated by Susan Spellman

ELL Reader

ELL Poster 10

Teacher's Edition Notes

ELL notes throughout this lesson support instruction and reference additional resources at point of use.

Teaching Guide
pp. 64–70, 230–231

- Multilingual summaries of the main selection
- Comprehension lesson
- Vocabulary strategies and word cards
- ELL Reader 10 lesson

ELL and Transition Handbook

Ten Important Sentences

- Key ideas from every selection in the Student Edition
- Activities to build sentence power

More Reading

Reader's Theater Anthology

- Fluency practice
- Five scripts to build fluency
- Poetry for oral interpretation

Leveled Trade Books

- Extend reading tied to the unit concept
- Lessons in Trade Book Library Teaching Guide

School + Home

Homework
- Family Times Newsletter
- ELL Multilingual Selection Summaries

Take-Home Books
- Decodable Readers
- Leveled Readers

Family Times

You are your child's first and best teacher!

This week we're
Reading A Turkey for Thanksgiving

Talking About How we can contribute to a celebration
Learning About Long o: a, ai, ay
Draw Conclusions

Weekly Plan for Group Time
Differentiated Instruction

DAILY PLAN

WHOLE GROUP

- Morning Warm-Up
- Share Literature
- Phonics
- Spelling
- Vocabulary

DAILY GROUP TIME

1 2 3 4 5

- **Reading Support**
- **Skill Support**
- **Fluency Practice**

WHOLE GROUP

- Fluency
- Writing
- Grammar
- Wrap Up Your Day

Look for the
ⓘ

Independent Activities

See Group Time pp. 282p, 286e, 303e, 306d, 310d.

✓ **Fluency Reading**
Silent Reading

✓ **Journal Writing**
See the Planner for daily writing prompts, pp. 282d–282e.

✓ **Homework**
Practice Book, pp. 91–100
Spelling Practice Book, pp. 37–40
Grammar and Writing Practice Book, pp. 37–40

✓ **Literacy Centers**
pp. 282j–282k
- Listening
- Reading/Library
- Word Work
- Writing
- Social Studies
- Technology

DAY 1

On-Level
Page 282q
- Read Decodable Reader 10
- Reread for Fluency

Strategic Intervention
Page DI•54
- Read Decodable Reader 10
- Blend Words with Long *a: a, ai, ay*
- Reread for Fluency

Advanced
Page DI•55
- Read Advanced Selection 10
- Extend Word Reading
- Introduce Concept Inquiry

DAY 2

On-Level
Pages 286–303
- Read *A Turkey for Thanksgiving*
- Reread for Fluency

Strategic Intervention
Page DI•56
- Read SI Decodable Reader 10
- Read or Listen to *A Turkey for Thanksgiving*
- Blend Words with Long *a: a, ai, ay*

Advanced
Page DI•57
- Read *A Turkey for Thanksgiving*
- Continue Concept Inquiry

DAY 3

On-Level
Pages 286–305
- Reread *A Turkey for Thanksgiving*

Strategic Intervention
Page DI•58
- Reread *A Turkey for Thanksgiving*
- Read Words and Sentences
- Review Draw Conclusions and Visualize
- Reread for Fluency

Advanced
Page DI•59
- Self-Selected Reading
- Continue Concept Inquiry

On-Level

Pages 306–309
- Read "Thanksgiving USA"

Strategic Intervention

Page DI•60
- Read or Listen to "Thanksgiving USA"
- Reread for Fluency
- Build Concepts

Advanced

Page DI•61
- Read "Thanksgiving USA"
- Expand Vocabulary
- Continue Concept Inquiry

 DAY 4

On-Level

Pages 310e–310g
- Sentence Reading, Set B
- Monitor Fluency and Comprehension

Set B
1. Bess brought the gray sand pail to the beach.
2. The train may be here any minute now.
3. We promise to make you a plain vase from the clay later.
4. Ray was sorry he didn't pay the bill on time.
5. Hang the apron on the nail behind the door.
6. Which way did everybody go after class today?

Strategic Intervention

Page DI•62
- Practice Word Reading
- Sentence Reading, Set A
- Monitor Fluency and Comprehension

Set A
1. Mark brought the mail and paper inside.
2. Everybody was sorry Jay couldn't stay longer.
3. We will wait by the trail for one more minute.
4. I promise to clean the tray before I play.
5. Do not put hay away behind the barn door.
6. A chain keeps the main door shut.

Advanced

Page DI•63
- Sentence Reading, Set C
- Monitor Fluency and Comprehension
- Share Concept Inquiry

Set C
1. We promise to call and say hello the minute we sail into town.
2. The clouds brought so much rain that all the grain got soaked.
3. We are sorry we could not paint the fence, but we will do it in April.
4. The maid sprayed the room and closed the door when she was finished cleaning.
5. Everybody in the club will fly to Spain for a holiday trip.
6. Jada's dog strayed from behind her home.

DAY 5

Grouping Place English language learners in the groups that correspond to their reading abilities in English.

Use the appropriate Leveled Reader or other text at children's instructional level.

TIP Send home the appropriate Multilingual Summary of the main selection on Day 1.

MORE READING FOR Group Time

Below-Level On-Level Advanced

Take It to the NET ONLINE
sfsuccessnet.com

Donald Leu
For ideas and activities to build new literacies, see the article "The New Literacies" by Scott Foresman author Donald Leu.

TEACHING TIP **A class message board is a great way to share classroom news.** Divide the board into three areas: Dates I Need to Know, We're Proud of You! (student accomplishments), and We Have News (classroom events).

TEACHER TALK

Phonemic awareness is the understanding that spoken words are made up of speech sounds (phonemes) and the ability to segment these sounds and blend them together to make words.

Be sure to schedule time for children to work on the unit inquiry project "Organize a Club." This week children should present their plan to the class.

Looking Ahead

Literacy Centers

Listening

Let's Read
Along

MATERIALS | SINGLES
CD player, headphones, print copies of recorded pieces

LISTEN TO LITERATURE As children listen to the following recordings, have them follow along or read along in the print version.

AudioText
A Turkey for Thanksgiving
"Thanksgiving USA"

Sing with Me Background Building Audio
"Holidays"

Phonics Songs and Rhymes Audio
"A Party Plan"

A Party Plan

I say let's plan a party.
Everyone gets a job.
Bring me some paper. I'll write a list.
Do not be lazy. We all must assist.
Cousin Ray will mail invitations.
Gail will help all she can.
When we work together like this,
It's a party plan.

Audio CD **Phonics Songs and Rhymes Chart 10**

Reading/Library

Read It
Again!

MATERIALS | SINGLES / PAIRS / GROUPS
collection of books for self-selected reading, reading logs

REREAD BOOKS Have children select previously read books from the appropriate book box and record titles of books they read in their logs. Use these previously read books:

- Decodable Readers
- Leveled Readers
- ELL Readers
- Stories written by classmates
- Book from the library

TEN IMPORTANT SENTENCES Have children read the Ten Important Sentences for *A Turkey for Thanksgiving* and locate the sentences in the Student Edition.

BOOK CLUB Use pp. 304–305 of the Student Edition to set up an "Illustrator Study" of Diane de Groat.

Word Work

Long a
Match-Up

MATERIALS | SINGLES / PAIRS / GROUPS
index cards, word endings list

LONG *a*: *a*, *ai*, *ay* Have children make words with long *a*.

1. Make a list with the following long a patterns: *ate*, *ain*, *ail*, and *ay*.
2. Make a stack of cards with initial sounds or blends, such as *p*, *pl*, *br*, *tr*, *st*.
3. Children take turns picking a card and trying to make a word with the long *a* word patterns. Children can write down any words they make.
4. Play continues until all cards have been used.

 This interactive CD provides additional practice.

br
pl
tr
st

ain
ate
ail
ay

brain
plate
trail
stay

Scott Foresman Reading Street Centers Survival Kit

Use *A Turkey for Thankgiving* materials
from the Reading Street Centers Survival Kit
to organize this week's centers.

Writing

Helping with Dinner

MATERIALS | SINGLES
paper, pencils

WRITE A HOW-TO REPORT Review how the characters in *A Turkey for Thanksgiving* get ready for dinner.

1. Ask children to think of a time when their parents asked them to help prepare for dinner or a celebration.
2. Have them list the steps they performed to help their families get ready. Suggest they use order words like *once* and *after* to organize their steps.
3. Urge children to number their lists.

LEVELED WRITING Urge children to write at their own ability level. Some may write simple lists with phrases. Others will be able to write simple sentences with some attention to mechanics and spelling. Your best writers will write sentences with greater detail and more attention to mechanics and spelling.

How To Set the Table
1. Put plates on the table.
2. Put glasses on the table.
3. Make sure everyone has a spoon, fork, and knife.
4. Put napkins on the table.

Social Studies

Holiday Guest

MATERIALS | SINGLES
paper, pencils | GROUPS

WRITE A DESCRIPTION Remind children that the characters in *A Turkey for Thanksgiving* celebrate a holiday.

1. Have children think of a real or a make-believe guest to invite to Thanksgiving dinner.
2. Have children write a description of their dinner with the guest.
3. Children may illustrate their stories.
4. Encourage volunteers to share their writing with the group.

I would invite my favorite football player for Thanksgiving dinner. He would probably eat a lot!

Technology

Holiday Tune

MATERIALS | SINGLES
computer with Internet access, | PAIRS
paper, pencils | GROUPS

LEARN ABOUT HOLIDAYS Have children study a Web site for information about different holidays.

1. Have children turn on the computer and access a Web site about holiday traditions.
2. Ask children to use the site to find facts about one holiday.
3. Have them record the most interesting facts and share them.

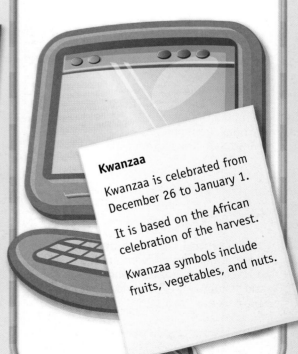

Kwanzaa

Kwanzaa is celebrated from December 26 to January 1.

It is based on the African celebration of the harvest.

Kwanzaa symbols include fruits, vegetables, and nuts.

 **ALL CENTERS**

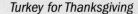

Day 1

AT A GLANCE

Share Literature
"Holiday" 10

Phonics and Spelling
🔊 Long *a: a, ai, ay*
Spelling Pretest:
   Words with *a, ai, ay*

Read Apply Phonics [Word Wall]

(**Group Time**) < Differentiated Instruction

Build Background
Let's Talk About Thanksgiving Celebration

Listening Comprehension
🔊 **Skill** Draw Conclusions

Shared Writing
Invitation

Grammar
Possessive Nouns

Materials

- *Sing with Me Big Book*
- Sound-Spelling Card 2
- Letter Tiles
- Decodable Reader 10
- Student Edition 282–283
- Graphic Organizer 15
- Writing Transparency 10
- Grammar Transparency 10

Take It to the NET
ONLINE
Professional Development
To learn more about word study, go to sfsuccessnet.com and read "Grapheme–Phoneme Knowledge..." by L. Ehri.

Morning Warm-Up!

Holidays are a pleasant time when people gather together to celebrate. How can we contribute to a celebration?

QUESTION OF THE WEEK Tell children they will talk, sing, read, and write about contributing to a celebration. Write and read the message and discuss the question.

CONNECT CONCEPTS Ask questions to connect to other Unit 2 selections.

- What does Mr. Spano do for the baseball team to celebrate their hard work in *Ronald Morgan Goes to Bat?*

- How do the animals of the forest celebrate the race in *Turtle's Race with Beaver*

REVIEW HIGH-FREQUENCY WORDS

- Circle the high-frequency words *pleasant* and *people* in the message.

- Have children say and spell the words as they write them in the air.

Build Background Use the Day 1 instruction on ELL Poster 10 to assess knowledge and develop concepts.

ELL Poster 10

Share Literature

BUILD ORAL VOCABULARY Display p. 10 of the *Sing with Me Big Book.* Tell children that the class is going to sing a song about contributing to a celebration. Read the title. Ask children to listen for the Amazing Words **dine, holiday,** and **participate** as you sing. Then sing the song again and encourage children to sing along with you. Have children demonstrate their understanding of *dine, holiday,* and *participate* by asking:

- When you dine at a restaurant, what types of things do you order?

- What holidays do some people celebrate in the winter?

- In what ways do you participate in class?

Holidays

Every holiday
Is fun to celebrate.
Our friends and family
gather 'round.
We all participate.

Everyone brings food.
The table's set to dine.
We share good times
and laughter too,
Holidays are fine.

Sing with Me Big Book

**Sing with Me/
Background Building Audio**

OBJECTIVE

- Build oral vocabulary.

 **to build oral vocabulary**

	MONITOR PROGRESS
dine **holiday** **participate**	**If...** children lack oral vocabulary experiences about the concept Working Together, **then...** use the Oral Vocabulary Routine on pp. DI·1–DI·2, DI·7 to develop the Amazing Words.

Access Content Point out the word *table's* in "Holidays." Ask children what letter the apostrophe takes the place of.

Long *a: a, ai, ay*

TEACH/MODEL

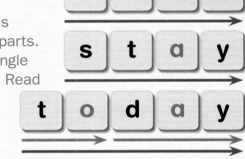

Sound-Spelling Card 2

Blending Strategy

ROUTINE

1 **Connect** Write *late.* What do you know about reading this word? (The *a* in *late* makes a long *a* vowel sound and the *e* is silent.) Today we'll learn about *ai* and *ay* words that also stand for the long *a* sound.

2 **Use Sound-Spelling Card** Display Card 2. This is *apron. Apron* has the sound /ā/ at the beginning. Say it with me: /ā/.

3 **Model** Write *laid.* When the letters *ai* appear together in a word or syllable, the *a* stands for its long vowel sound and the *i* is silent. Listen as I blend this word. Blend the sounds continuously across the word. Let's blend this word together: /lād/, *laid.* Repeat steps 2 and 3 with *stay.*

Write *today.* You can blend longer words with /ā/ by dividing them into smaller parts. When a word or syllable ends with a single vowel, the vowel sound is usually long. Read one syllable at a time and then blend them together. Model blending *today.* Let's blend together: *to/day, today.*

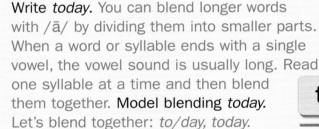

4 **Group Practice** Blend these words together. Continue with *snail, gray, braid, clay, sprain, sway, paint.*

5 **Review** What do you know about reading these words? The letters *ai* and *ay* stand for /ā/.

BLEND WORDS

INDIVIDUALS BLEND *ai* AND *ay* WORDS Call on individuals to blend *aim, hay, claim, pray, gain, way, faint.* Have them tell what they know about each word before reading it. For feedback, refer to step five of the Blending Strategy Routine.

BUILD WORDS

| a | b | d | i | n | o | r | t | y |

INDIVIDUALS MAKE ai AND ay WORDS Write *rain* and have the class blend it. Have children spell *rain* with letter tiles. Monitor work and provide feedback.

- Add *b* to *rain*.
  What is the new word?

  | b | r | a | i | n |

- Change the *b* in *brain* to *t*.
  What is the new word?

  | t | r | a | i | n |

- Change the *ai* in *train* to *ay*, and drop the *n*.
  What is the new word?

  | t | r | a | y |

- Drop the *t* in *tray*.
  What is the new word?

  | r | a | y |

- Change the *r* in *ray* to *d*.
  What is the new word?

  | d | a | y |

- Add *to* in front of *day*.
  What is the new word?

  | t | o | d | a | y |

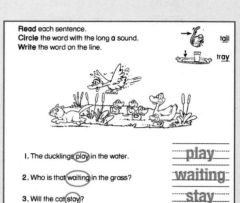

Read each sentence.
Circle the word with the long a sound.
Write the word on the line.

tail
tray

1. The ducklings play in the water. — play
2. Who is that waiting in the grass? — waiting
3. Will the cat stay? — stay
4. The big ducks are not afraid of the cat. — afraid
5. The cat runs away as fast as it can. — away

Home Activity Your child identified words in which the long a sound is spelled ai or ay (tail, tray). Have your child read sentences to find words with the long a sound. Ask your child to tell how the long a sound is spelled in each word.

▲ **Practice Book 2.1** p. 93, Long *a: a, ai, ay*

Monitor Progress — Check Word Reading Long *a: a, ai, ay*

Write the following words and have individuals read them.

rain	say	pail	fray	afraid
bake	plate	maze	race	date
farm	crack	slap	parched	match

If... children cannot blend words with *ai* and *ay* at this point,

then... continue to monitor their progress using other instructional opportunities during the week so that they can be successful with the Day 5 Assessment. See the Skills Trace on p. 282n.

SUCCESS PREDICTOR

Spiral REVIEW

- Row 2 reviews long *a*, CVCe.
- Row 3 contrasts short *a* and *r*-controlled *ar*.

▶ **Day 1** Check Word Reading
Day 2 Check High-Frequency Words
Day 3 Check Retelling
Day 4 Check Fluency
Day 5 Assess Progress

Word Reading

SUCCESS PREDICTOR

OBJECTIVES

- Segment sounds to spell words.
- Spell words with long *a*: *a*, *ai*, *ay*.

Spelling Words

Long a

1. **tail***	7. **raise***
2. **main**	8. **brain**
3. **wait***	9. **paint**
4. **say**	10. **stay**
5. **away***	11. **today**
6. **play**	12. **tray**

Challenge Words

13. **holiday**	15. **raisin**
14. **daily**	

* Words from the Selection

Long a: ai, ay

Generalization Sometimes long a is spelled ai or ay: pail, day.

Sort the list words according to ai and ay.

ai
1. tail
2. main
3. wait
4. raise
5. brain
6. paint

ay
7. say
8. away
9. play
10. stay
11. today
12. tray

Challenge Words

ai
13. daily
14. raisin

ay
15. holiday

Spelling Words
1. tail
2. main
3. wait
4. say
5. away
6. play
7. raise
8. brain
9. paint
10. stay
11. today
12. tray

Challenge Words
13. holiday
14. daily
15. raisin

School + Home Home Activity Your child is learning to spell words with long a spelled ai and ay. To practice at home, have your child read each word to you. Say each word and ask your child to write the word on a piece of paper.

▲ **Spelling Practice Book** p. 37

DAY 1

ELL

Support Spelling Before giving the spelling pretest, clarify the meaning of each spelling word with examples, such as saying a horse has a *tail* and pointing to your head to illustrate a *brain*.

Spelling

PRETEST Long *a*: *a*, *ai*, *ay*

MODEL WRITING FOR SOUNDS Each spelling word has an /ā/ vowel sound. Before administering the spelling pretest, model how to segment *ai* and *ay* words to spell them.

- What sounds do you hear in *day*? (/d/ /ā/)
- What is the letter for /d/? Write *d*. Continue with the *ay* /ā/.
- What letters stand for /ā/? (*ay*)
- Repeat with *plain*. Remind children that /ā/ can be spelled *a*, *ai*, or *ay*, and tell them that in *plain*, it is spelled *ai*.

PRETEST Dictate the spelling words. Segment the words for children if necessary. Have children check their pretests and correct misspelled words.

HOMEWORK Spelling Practice Book, p. 37

Thanksgiving Day

It was the morning of Thanksgiving Day, and Nicholas was excited about the holiday. His mother had just finished preparing the turkey and was ready to put it in the oven.

"Can I help you?" asked Nicholas, reaching for the roasting pan.

"No, dear, this is too heavy for you," said his mother, lifting the full roasting pan into the oven.

Nicholas saw his father slicing apples. "Can I help you?" Nicholas asked, reaching for the knife.

"No, thank you, Nicholas," said his father. "This knife is very sharp and you might accidentally cut yourself."

Nicholas felt left out. He wanted to participate, but it seemed as though there was nothing for him to do.

"—but you could help me with the cranberry sauce," suggested his father. Nicholas opened the can of cranberry sauce...

Bert Does Not Like Bugs
Written by Julie Welsh
Illustrated by Carmen Billings

Decodable Reader 10

Group Time

On-Level	Strategic Intervention	Advanced
Read Decodable Reader 10. • Use p. 282q.	**Read** Decodable Reader 10. • Use the **Routine** on p. DI·54.	**Read** Advanced Selection 10. • Use the **Routine** on p. DI·55.

 Place English language learners in the groups that correspond to their reading abilities in English.

(*i*) Independent Activities

Fluency Reading Pair children to reread Leveled Readers or the ELL Reader from the previous week or other text at children's independent level.

Journal Writing List friends you would like to dine with. Share writing.

Independent Reading See p. 282j for Reading/Library activities and suggestions.

Literacy Centers To practice long *a*: *a*, *ai*, *ay*, you may use Word Work, p. 282j.

Practice Book 2.1 Long *a*, *a*, *ai*, *ay* p. 93

Break into small groups after Spelling and before Build Background.

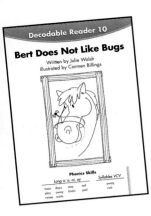

Decodable Reader 10

Bert Does Not Like Bugs
Written by Julie Walsh
Illustrated by Carmen Billings

Apply Phonics

🎯 PRACTICE Long *a: a, ai, ay*

HIGH-FREQUENCY WORDS Review *about*, *does*, and *wants*
on the Word Wall. **Word Wall**

READ DECODABLE READER 10

- Pages 74–75 Read aloud quietly with the group.
- Pages 76–77 Have the group read aloud without you.
- Pages 78–80 Select individuals to read aloud.

CHECK COMPREHENSION AND DECODING Have children retell the story to
include characters, setting, and plot. Then ask children the following questions:

- Who are the characters in the story? (Bert the horse, bugs)
- Where does the story take place? (Bert's barn)
- How does Bert solve his problem? (He swings his tail hard at the pail, and the
bugs get wet and go away.)

Then have children locate *ai* and *ay* words in the story. Review *ai* and *ay*
spelling patterns. Sort words according to their spelling patterns.

ai	*ay*
brain	away
main	days
pail	play
raises	stay
tail	
waits	

HOMEWORK Take-Home Decodable Reader 10

REREAD FOR FLUENCY

Paired Reading   ROUTINE

1 **Reader 1 Begins** Children read the entire book, switching readers
at the end of each page.

2 **Reader 2 Begins** Have partners reread; now the other partner begins.

3 **Reread** For optimal fluency, children should reread three or four times.

4 **Provide Feedback** Listen to children read and provide corrective feedback
regarding their oral reading and their use of the blending strategy.

OBJECTIVES

- Apply knowledge of letter-sounds and word parts to decode unknown words when reading.
- Use context with letter-sounds and word parts to confirm the identification of unknown words.
- Practice fluency in paired reading.

Monitor Progress

Decoding

If... children have difficulty decoding a word,	**then...** prompt them to blend the word.
	• What is the new word?
	• Is the new word a word you know?
	• Does it make sense in the story?

ELL

Access Content

Beginning Lead children on a noun
walk through *Bert Does Not Like Bugs*,
identifying Bert, bugs, and other things
in the pictures and print.

Intermediate Preview *Bert Does Not
Like Bugs* and explain that *scram* is an
expression that means "go away!" Ask
children why Bert wants the bugs to go
away.

Advanced Point out that Bert uses
his brain to come up with a plan. Have
children tell how they use their brains.
Guide children using the sentence
frame: *I use my brain to _____.*

Strategic Intervention

Have children illustrate a way to contribute to a celebration.

Advanced

Have children search the Internet or the library for information about how people celebrate other holidays.

Activate Prior Knowledge
Invite children who share a home language to identify things in the pictures in that language and in English.

Build Background

LET'S TALK ABOUT Working Together

GENERATE DISCUSSION Read the title and ask questions to generate language. Encourage children to respond in complete sentences.

- What are these people doing?
- What is alike in all of the pictures?

BUILD ORAL VOCABULARY Lead the class in a discussion that focuses on concepts and today's Amazing Words, *participate, holiday, dine.*

Look at the people. They are celebrating different occasions. One thing many people do on holidays is dine with friends and family. How do you participate in celebrating different holidays? Look at the picture of the turkey sitting at the table. This week we will read about Turkey and what he does on Thanksgiving.

VOCABULARY

CONCEPT CHART Remind children of the question of the week.

- How can we contribute to a celebration?

Display Graphic Organizer 15. Label the center circle "Contributing to a Celebration." Using the pictures on the student page as a starting point, help children identify appropriate responses to add to the other circles. Display the chart for use throughout the week.

- What is one way you contribute to a Thanksgiving celebration? (share typical Thanksgiving food)
- What is one way you contribute to a birthday celebration? (give a birthday gift)

Build Background

Let's Talk About
Working Together

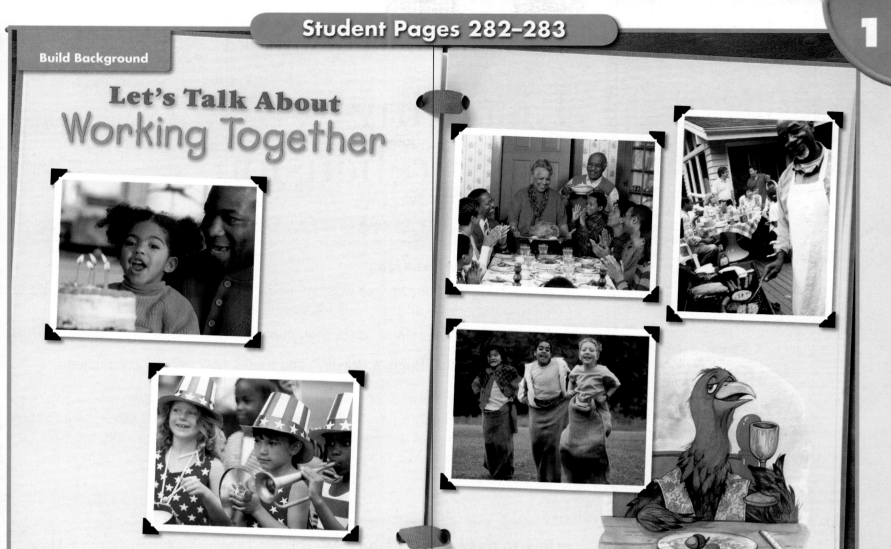

▲ **Graphic Organizer 15**

Take It to the **NET**
ONLINE

For a Web site that tells more about Thanksgiving, do an Internet search using the keywords *Thanksgiving celebrations.*

Access Content To prepare children for reading *A Turkey for Thanksgiving,* send home the story summary in English and/or the home language. See the ELL Teaching Guide, pp. 68–70.

Turkey for Thanksgiving **282–283**

Read the story. **Ask** yourself what is happening. **Answer** each question.

My name is Greg. Tomorrow, Grandma will bring Max to Thanksgiving dinner. I will be happy to see Max. I am going to make a special meal for him. First, he can chew on some bones. Then he will get a bowl of ground turkey. For dessert, Max can have some cheese treats. It will be a real feast!

1. Who is bringing Max to dinner? __**Grandma**__

2. Write a sentence that tells how Greg feels about Max.

   Greg likes Max.

3. Who do you think Max is? __**a dog**__

4. What things in the story tell you about Max?

   Answer should include: Max likes to chew bones and eat ground turkey and cheese treats.

5. Why do you think Max will enjoy the feast?

   Possible response: Max will enjoy the feast because Greg is making him a special meal.

Home Activity Your child read a story and draw conclusions from information in the story. Read aloud a portion of a story or article your child has not read. Work together to draw conclusions about a character or event in the text.

▲ **Practice Book 2.1** p. 94, Draw Conclusions

Access Content For a Picture It! lesson on drawing conclusions, see the ELL Teaching Guide, pp. 64–65.

Listening Comprehension

◎TEACH/MODEL Draw Conclusions

DEFINE DRAW CONCLUSIONS

- To draw conclusions, we use what we know about real life and what we read to figure out more about the characters and what happens in the story.

- Good readers ask themselves if their conclusions make sense.

READ ALOUD Read "Happy's Holiday" and model how to draw conclusions.

MODEL The author of this story doesn't tell me why everyone wants to come to Happy's party. All the other animals are really excited about the party and want to bring food. I like parties, and most people do. So I think the animals are excited about going to a party they might enjoy.

PRACTICE

CLUES TO DRAW CONCLUSIONS Ask children to use clues in the story to draw conclusions. Frances the Cat decides to have a National Cat Holiday. Why do you think she does that? (She had a good time at Happy's holiday party, so she wants one of her own.) Happy the Dog gave everyone a bone for a present. Why do you think he did that? (Dogs like bones, so Happy thought the other animals would enjoy a bone too.) Do you think the other animals appreciated the presents? Why or why not? (probably not, because cats, hamsters, and parrots don't like bones like dogs do)

DRAW CONCLUSIONS Have children recall the story *The Bremen Town Musicians.*

- Why did the animals get so excited when they saw the sign for Bremen Town? (Possible response: They knew that they were close to being where they could start a new life.)

- Why did the robbers run out of the house screaming? (Possible response: The singing made such a horrible noise that the robbers thought something horrible was outside the house.)

CONNECT TO READING Tell children that when they read any story, they should think about what they know and what they have read to draw conclusions.

Happy's Holiday

Happy the Dog was putting up balloons and decorations around his house. Frances the Cat walked by and stopped to chat.

"What are you doing?" asked Frances.

"I'm getting ready for my holiday. It's a special day, and it's tomorrow."

"What holiday?" Frances asked. She had not heard that tomorrow was a holiday.

"It's National Dog Day," he said. "Would you like to celebrate it with me? Come to my house and dine tomorrow at two!"

"Okay!" Frances said. Frances loved holidays, and she was glad to participate.

Frances went to the grocery store. She bought bread and cheese for the celebration. She saw Herman the Hamster. He was buying some pine chips for his burrow.

"Nice turkey!" Herman said.

"It's for National Dog Day tomorrow! I'm going to a party at Happy the Dog's house. Would you like to come too?"

"Sure!" Herman said. And so he picked up a cake for the party.

Pam the Parrot saw Herman the Hamster buying the cake and asked him why he was buying such a huge dessert.

"It's National Dog Day!" he said. "Do you want to go to a party? It's at Happy the Dog's house.

"Sure!" Pam the Parrot said. "I just happen to have a few crackers hanging around my cage. I'll bring them, and I'll make some soup too!"

So the next day, Frances the Cat, Herman the Hamster, and Pam the Parrot met at Happy the Dog's house for a holiday celebration. Happy the Dog gave everyone a huge bone for a present, and then the animals dined on the wonderful food that everyone had brought.

Frances the Cat said, "Who made up this holiday anyway?"

"I did," said Happy the Dog. "I thought that dogs needed a day of their own to celebrate."

Everyone agreed with Happy. Then Frances the Cat said, "Now that I think about it, I believe that one day next week is National Cat Day."

"Really?" asked Happy the Dog. "That's good. Then we can have another party!"

1

● **LANGUAGE ARTS** ● ● ● ● ● ● ● ● ● ● ● ● ● ● ●

DAILY FIX-IT

1. The dog had pant on his tal.
   The dog had pa_i_nt on his tai_l_.

2. He wantted to wash it awae.
   He _wanted_ to wash it awa_y_.

This week's practice sentences appear
on Daily Fix-It Transparency 10.

Strategic Intervention

Children who are not able to write
independently may dictate their
responses. Elaborate on their
responses in order to help them
complete the invitation.

Advanced

Have children make an invitation
to their favorite holiday celebration.
Also have them write a plan for the
celebration—including food and
activities.

Support Writing Have children
do a "think-aloud" with a partner
to discuss the specific items they
will include on their invitations.

Shared Writing

WRITE Invitation

GENERATE IDEAS Have children recall a holiday meal, or party, or special time
they have shared with others. Ask them what made this occasion special.

WRITE AN INVITATION Explain that the class will write an invitation asking other
people to come to a class party.

COMPREHENSION SKILL Have children
draw conclusions about what the invitation
should say—based on what they've read
about parties and what they've
experienced in real life.

- Display Writing Transparency 10 and read
  the title.
- Ask children to read the first line and
  provide an answer.
- Ask children to complete the invitation by
  filling in the remaining blank spaces.

HANDWRITING While writing, model the
letter forms as shown on pp. TR18–21.

READ THE INVITATION Have children read
the completed invitation aloud as you
track the print.

▲ **Writing Transparency 10**

INDEPENDENT WRITING

MAKE AN INVITATION Have children make their own invitation for another
occasion. Encourage them to use words from the Word Wall and the Amazing
Words board. Let children illustrate their writing. Display the invitations
in the classroom.

Grammar

TEACH/MODEL Possessive Nouns

REVIEW PLURAL NOUNS THAT CHANGE SPELLING Remind children that plural nouns name more than one person, place, animal, or thing. Remind children that some nouns change spelling when they become plural.

IDENTIFY POSSESSIVE NOUNS Display Grammar Transparency 10. Read the definition aloud.

- Look at the picture above *horse*. There is one horse, so the noun is singular. Look at the blank space. Write the possessive form of the singular noun *horse* to complete the item.

Continue modeling with items 2–5.

PRACTICE

USE POSSESSIVE NOUNS Have children look at five sentences on the board. Each sentence contains a possessive noun—some are correct and others are incorrect. Children should number their papers one through five. For each correct sentence, they should write *correct* on their paper, and for each incorrect sentence, they should write the correct possessive noun.

Possessive Nouns

A noun that shows who or what owns something is a **possessive noun**. To show ownership, add an **apostrophe** (') and **-s** when the noun is singular. Add just an **apostrophe** (') when the noun is plural.

   the turkey's tail   the rabbits' tails

Add **'s** or **'** to each noun. Write the possessive noun on the line.

1. horse   the ___**horse's**___ head
2. goats   the ___**goats'**___ legs
3. lion   the ___**lion's**___ mane
4. bear   the ___**bear's**___ fur
5. animals   the ___**animals'**___ dinner

Unit 2 A Turkey for Thanksgiving   Grammar **10**

▲ **Grammar Transparency 10**

Wrap Up Your Day!

 LONG a: a, ai, ay Write *say* and ask children what sound the *ay* in *say* has. (/ā/) Repeat with *main* and *favorite*.

 SPELLING PLURALS LONG a: -a, -ai, -ay Have children name and write the letters for each sound in *play, brain,* and *agent*.

 DRAW CONCLUSIONS To help children draw conclusions about *Happy's Holiday*, have them use what they already know from real life and what they just read in *Happy's Holiday*. Then ask: Why do you think Herman the Hamster bought a big cake?

LET'S TALK ABOUT IT Recall that Frances, Herman, and Pam go to Happy's house to celebrate. How do they contribute to the celebration? (Everyone brings something to eat.)

 HOMEWORK Send home this week's Family Times newsletter.

PREVIEW Day 2

Tell children that tomorrow the class will read about a group of animals who are celebrating Thanksgiving.

Share Literature
My First Chinese New Year

Phonics and Spelling
Long *a: a, ai, ay*
Spelling: Words with Long *a*

Comprehension
Skill Draw Conclusions
Strategy Visualize

Build Background
Thanksgiving Celebrations

High-Frequency Words
door   behind   brought   **Word Wall**
minute   promise   sorry
everybody

Vocabulary
Selection Words
Thanksgiving   lumbered
riverbank   hooves

Read

Group Time < Differentiated Instruction

A Turkey for Thanksgiving

Interactive Writing
List

Grammar
Possessive Nouns

Materials

- *Sing with Me Big Book*
- Read Aloud Anthology
- Phonics Songs and Rhymes Chart 10
- Background Building Audio CD
- Graphic Organizer 15
- Student Edition 284–302
- Tested Word Cards
- Vocabulary Transparency 10

Morning Warm~Up!

Today we will read about a holiday celebration. We will read about what a group of animals does on Thanksgiving day. What do you usually do on Thanksgiving?

QUESTION OF THE DAY Encourage children to sing "Holidays" from the *Sing with Me Big Book* as you gather. Write and read the message and discuss the question.

REVIEW LONG *a: a, ai, ay*

- Read the first and second sentences of the message.
- Have children raise their hands when they hear a word with long *a*. (*today, holiday, celebration, Thanksgiving, day*). Then have volunteers circle the letters that stand for /ā/.

Build Background Use the Day 2 instruction on ELL Poster 10 to preview high-frequency words.

ELL Poster 10

Share Literature

BUILD CONCEPTS

REALISTIC FICTION Have children read the title. Identify the author. Review that books about make-believe characters or events in realistic situations are called realistic fiction. The characters act like people in real life might act.

BUILD ORAL VOCABULARY Ask children what they know about holidays. Explain that sometimes people **decorate** their homes to celebrate holidays. Suggest that as you read, children listen to find out how people prepare to celebrate Chinese New Year.

Read Aloud Anthology
My First Chinese New Year

- How does the family **decorate** for Chinese New Year? (They put cut red paper on the walls.)

MONITOR LISTENING COMPREHENSION

- What are other ways the family participates in this holiday? (They sweep away bad luck, buy plum blossoms, make an altar, wear new clothes, get haircuts, cook, share a big meal, give gifts of money, and go to a parade.)

- Why do you think the character in the story is excited about Chinese New Year? (Possible response: It is a time of new beginnings, good luck, and happiness.)

OBJECTIVES

- Discuss characteristics of realistic fiction.
- Set purpose for listening.
- Build oral vocabulary.

to build oral vocabulary

	MONITOR PROGRESS
participate **holiday** **dine** **decorate**	**If...** children lack oral vocabulary experiences about the concept Working Together, **then...** use the Oral Vocabulary Routine on pp. DI·1–DI·2, DI·7 to develop the Amazing Words.

Build Concepts Chinese New Year is the most important holiday in China. Have children demonstrate their understanding of the holiday by acting out some of the things that are done before and during the celebration (sweeping, getting a haircut, cooking, and so on).

OBJECTIVES

- Review long *a: a, ai* and *ay* words.
- Sort long *a: a, ai* and *ay* words.
- Preview words before reading them.
- Spell long *a: ai* and *ay* words.

Strategic Intervention

Use **Strategic Intervention Decodable Reader 10** for more practice with long *a*.

ELL

Support Phonics Explain that *assist* means to help out and then replay "A Party Plan" on the Phonics Songs and Rhymes Audio CD.

Long *a: a, ai, ay*

TEACH/MODEL

ROUTINE

Fluent Word Reading

1 **Connect** Write *claim*. You can read this word because you know how to read words with the /ā/ sound. What sound do the letters *ai* stand for in this word? (/ā/) What's the word? *(claim)* Do the same with *spray*.

2 **Model** When you come to a new word, look at the letters from left to right and think about the vowel sounds. Say the sounds in the word to yourself and then read the word. Model reading *detail* and *birthday*. When you come to a new word, what are you going to do?

3 **Group Practice** Write *afraid, haystack, remain, crayon, explain, maybe, obtain*. Read these words. Look at the letters, think about the vowel sounds, say the sounds to yourself, and then read the word aloud together. Allow 2–3 seconds previewing time.

WORD READING

PHONICS SONGS AND RHYMES CHART 10 Frame each of the following words on Phonics Songs and Rhymes Chart 10. Call on individuals to read them. Guide children in previewing.

say	**Ray**	**mail**
Gail	**paper**	**lazy**

Sing "A Party Plan" to the tune of "Take Me Out to the Ball Game," or play the CD. Have children follow along on the chart as they sing. Then have individuals take turns circling *ai* and *ay* words on the chart.

 **Phonics Songs and Rhymes Audio**

A Party Plan

I say let's plan a party.
Everyone gets a job.
Bring me some paper. I'll write a list.
Do not be lazy. We all must assist.
Cousin Ray will mail invitations.
Gail will help all she can.
When we work together like this,
It's a party plan.

Phonics Songs and Rhymes Chart 10

SORT WORDS

INDIVIDUALS SORT *ai* AND *ay* WORDS Distribute word cards with words containing *ai* and *ay*. Write *ai* and *ay* as headings for two columns. Have children read their words and place their word cards under the appropriate heading. Have all children copy the completed chart and circle the letters that stand for the sound /ā/. Have children use the words in sentences to demonstrate meaning.

ai	ay
mail	play
waist	spray
braid	hay
paint	today
stain	away

Spelling

PRACTICE Long *a: ai, ay*

WRITE DICTATION SENTENCES Have children write these sentences. Repeat words slowly, allowing children to hear each sound. Children may use the Word Wall to help with spelling high-frequency words. **Word Wall**

> **Will you stay and paint today?**
> **Did you say we will raise the tray?**
> **I can't wait to play over the holiday.**

HOMEWORK Spelling Practice Book, p. 38

▲ **Spelling Practice Book** p. 38

OBJECTIVES

- Recognize how to draw conclusions.
- Visualize.
- Build background.

Some friends are getting ready for Thanksgiving.
Read the sentences. **Follow** the directions.
Circle your answer.

1. Liz mixed some eggs in a bowl. Then she added milk and flour. She will bake it for an hour. What did Liz make?

   a salad   (a cake)

2. Ben got some greens from his garden. He chopped them and put them in a bowl. What did Ben make?

   (a salad)   a cake

Write your answer on the line.

3. Dan will cook the turkey. He thinks it is a great job. How does Dan feel about making the turkey?

   He likes it.

4. Teesha doesn't like to cook. She thinks that people might get thirsty while they eat. What did Teesha bring to dinner?

   something to drink: juice, milk, or soda

5. **Draw** a picture of other things the friends could eat for dinner.

   Children's pictures might include mashed potatoes, bread, or vegetables.

 Home Activity Your child read short passages and drew conclusions. Choose a favorite comic strip from the newspaper and cut off the last frame. Then read together the first portion of the comic strip. Draw conclusions about how the comic might end.

▲ **Practice Book 2. 1** p. 95, Draw Conclusions

Comprehension

🎯 SKILL Draw Conclusions

RECOGNIZE HOW TO DRAW CONCLUSIONS Review that drawing conclusions means using what you know about real life and what you read to figure out something about the characters and what happens in a story.

CONNECT TO READING

- As you read, look for clues that will help you draw sensible conclusions.
- Think about what you know in real life to help you draw conclusions about the story you're reading.

🎯 STRATEGY Visualize

INTRODUCE THE STRATEGY Tell children that when they visualize something, they can picture it in their minds. Paying attention to how something is described can help readers to imagine it and understand what they read.

 MODEL When I read a story, I pay attention to descriptions. By reading descriptions carefully, I can picture in my mind what the character or setting looks like or what is happening in the story.

CONNECT TO READING Encourage children to ask themselves these questions as they read *A Turkey for Thanksgiving*.

- How can I picture what is happening as I read?
- What do the pictures in my mind remind me of?
- What words help me imagine what is being described?

Build Background

DISCUSS THANKSGIVING CELEBRATIONS Display a picture showing a Thanksgiving celebration. Initiate discussion by asking children what they know about Thanksgiving celebrations.

- What does your family eat on Thanksgiving?
- Who does your family eat with on Thanksgiving?
- What else does your family do on Thanksgiving?

BACKGROUND BUILDING AUDIO Have children listen to the CD and share the new information they learned about Thanksgiving celebrations.

Sing with Me/Background Building Audio

COMPLETE A T-CHART Make a T-chart or display Graphic Organizer 25. Write *Thanksgiving* and *Independence Day* as headings. Ask children to list the foods and activities for each holiday.

Thanksgiving	Independence Day
turkey and dressing	hot dogs
sweet potatoes	hamburgers
cranberry sauce	corn
pumpkin pie	salad
watch parades	watch parades
watch football on TV	watch fireworks

▲ **Graphic Organizer 25**

CONNECT TO SELECTION Connect background information to *A Turkey for Thanksgiving*.

Americans have been celebrating Thanksgiving for hundreds of years. Different families celebrate in different ways, though many focus on sharing a meal that often includes turkey with relatives and friends. Mr. and Mrs. Moose are characters in the story we are about to read. We'll find out how they celebrate Thanksgiving.

Build Background Tell children that the first Thanksgiving celebration in the land that later became the United States took place almost 400 years ago. At this time, the Pilgrims and the Native Americans who had helped them survive in the New World feasted together. Ask children to share other information they know about Thanksgiving.

Words to Read

everybody
sorry
promise
minute
brought
behind
door

284

Read the Words

It was the night before the big dinner. Everybody was coming—everybody but Sheep. Mr. Moose was sorry about that. But he made a promise to invite Sheep another time. Now Mr. Moose had to get busy. He didn't like to wait until the last minute to do anything. He brought in firewood from behind the door and began cooking. Soon the feast was ready.

A Turkey for Thanksgiving

Genre: Animal Fantasy
The animal characters in an animal fantasy act like people. Read about Mr. Moose and how he finds a turkey for Thanksgiving.

285

____ Long *a: a, ai, ay*   high-frequency/tested vocabulary

High-Frequency Words

Nondecodable Words

ROUTINE

1 **Say and Spell** Point to the first word. This word is *everybody, e-v-e-r-y-b-o-d-y, everybody.* What is this word? What are the letters in this word?

2 **Identify Familiar Letter-Sounds** Point to the first letter in *everybody.* What is this letter? What is the sound for this letter? (*e/e/*)

3 **Demonstrate Meaning** Tell me a sentence using this word. Repeat the routine with the other Words to Read. Have children identify these familiar letter-sounds and word parts: *behind* (blend the syllables: *be-hind*), *brought* (*br/br/*, *t/t/*), *minute* (blend the syllables: *min-ute*), *promise* (blend the syllables: *prom-ise*), *sorry* (blend the syllables: *sor-ry*), *door* (*d/d/*, *r/r/*).

Have children read aloud the sentences on p. 285 and point to the Words to Read. Add the words to the Word Wall. **Word Wall**

Use Vocabulary Transparency 10 to review this week's words.

- Point to a word. Say and spell it.
- Have children say and spell the word.
- Ask children to identify familiar letter-sounds.

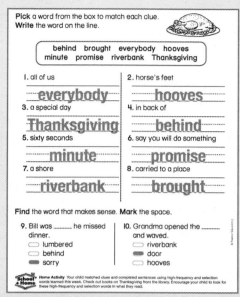

▲ **Practice Book 2.1** p. 96
High-Frequency Words and Selection
Words

Monitor Progress | Check High-Frequency Words

Point to the following words on the Word Wall and have individuals read them.

door	behind	brought	minute	promise
sorry	everybody	straight	saw	paper
want	friends	won't	show	

If... children cannot read these words,

then... have them practice in pairs with word cards before reading the selection. Monitor their fluency with these words during reading, and provide additional practice opportunities before the Day 5 Assessment..

SUCCESS PREDICTOR

SUCCESS PREDICTOR

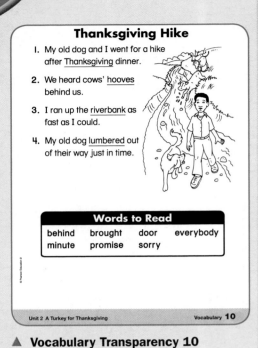

Thanksgiving Hike

1. My old dog and I went for a hike after Thanksgiving dinner.
2. We heard cows' hooves behind us.
3. I ran up the riverbank as fast as I could.
4. My old dog lumbered out of their way just in time.

Words to Read			
behind	brought	door	everybody
minute	promise	sorry	

Unit 2 A Turkey for Thanksgiving · Vocabulary 10

▲ **Vocabulary Transparency 10**

Vocabulary

SELECTION WORDS

Use Vocabulary Transparency 10 to introduce the selection words.

- Read each sentence as you track the print.
- Frame each underlined word. Explain the word's meaning.

 Thanksgiving a holiday for giving thanks
 hooves the hard bottom part of the feet of animals such as moose, deer, horses, and sheep
 riverbank the rising ground beside a river
 lumbered moved slowly and awkwardly

- Ask children to identify familiar letter-sounds and word parts: *Thanksgiving* (blend the words: *thanks, giving*), *lumbered* (blend the syllables: *lum, bered*), *riverbank* (blend the words: *river, bank*), *hooves* (h/h/, v/v, s/z/).
- Have children read each sentence aloud with you.
- To encourage discussion using the selection words, have children answer questions. Why might you lumber along after eating a big meal on Thanksgiving? Why might hooves be good for walking on a riverbank?

Group Time

DAY 2

On-Level	Strategic Intervention	Advanced
Read *A Turkey for Thanksgiving.* • Use pp. 286–302.	**Read** SI Decodable Reader 10. • Read or listen to *A Turkey for Thanksgiving.* • Use the **Routine** on p. DI·56.	**Read** *A Turkey for Thanksgiving.* • Use the **Routine** on p. DI·57.

ELL Place English language learners in the groups that correspond to their reading abilities in English.

(i) Independent Activities

Independent Reading See p. 282j for Reading/Library activities and suggestions.

Journal Writing Write about your favorite holiday. Share writing.

Literacy Centers To provide experiences with *A Turkey for Thanksgiving,* you may use the Listening Center on p. 282j.

Practice Book 2.1 Draw Conclusions, p. 95; High-Frequency Words, p. 96; Author's Purpose, p. 97

ELL

Access Content Use the vocabulary strategies and word cards in the ELL Teaching Guide, pp. 66–67.

 Break into small groups after Vocabulary and before Writing.

A Turkey for Thanksgiving

by Eve Bunting
illustrated by Diane de Groat

What will Mr. Moose do with a turkey for Thanksgiving?

286

287

AudioText

Read

Prereading Strategies

PREVIEW AND PREDICT Have children read the title of the story. Identify Mr. Moose in the picture. Identify the author and illustrator. Do a picture walk of pp. 286–295. Ask children what they think this story will be about.

DISCUSS ANIMAL FANTASY Reread the definition of animal fantasy on p. 285 of the Student Edition. Explain that an animal fantasy is a story with animal characters that dress and solve problems in the same ways that people do. Ask children what they think the problem in the story will be.

SET PURPOSE Read the question on p. 287. Ask children what they would like to find out as they read this story.

ELL

Access Content Before reading, review the story summary in English and/or the home language. See the ELL Teaching Guide, pp. 68–70.

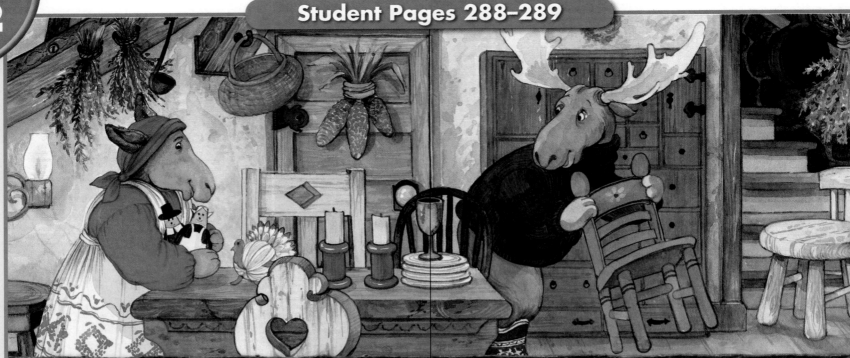

It was Thanksgiving morning. Mr. Moose helped Mrs. Moose set the Thanksgiving table.

"Sheep will sit here. He likes a chair that's straight up and down," Mr. Moose said. "Rabbit here. Porcupine here. Mr. and Mrs. Goat here." He smiled at his wife. "Isn't it nice to have friends to share Thanksgiving?"

288

Mrs. Moose set two paper pilgrims, one at each end of the table. She placed the paper turkey with its great fan of a tail between the candles, and stood back.

"They look good, my dear," Mr. Moose said.

Mrs. Moose sighed. "Yes. But I wish we had a real turkey. Everyone always has a turkey for Thanksgiving. Everyone but us."

289

▲ **Pages 288-289**
Have children look at the pictures and read to find out what Mr. and Mrs. Moose are doing and talking about.

Monitor Progress

Decoding

If... children come to a word they don't know,	**then...** remind them to:
	1. Blend the word.
	2. Decide if the word makes sense.
	3. Look in a dictionary for more help.

Skills in Context

➲ DRAW CONCLUSIONS

- **Mr. and Mrs. Moose are preparing for the Thanksgiving holiday. How does Mrs. Moose feel?**

Mrs. Moose enjoys Thanksgiving, as she is decorating her table. However, she is sad because they do not have a turkey.

Monitor Progress	**Draw Conclusions**
If... children are unable to identify how Mrs. Moose feels,	**then...** model how to use the text and what they already know to draw conclusions.

MODEL As I read, I learn that Mrs. Moose is busy decorating the table with paper pilgrims, a paper turkey, and candles. I think she must be excited about Thanksgiving. However, I don't think she's happy. She sighs and says she wishes they had a turkey.

ASSESS Have children describe how Mr. Moose feels. (Mr. Moose is excited about the holiday. He talks about how nice it is to share Thanksgiving with friends.)

Long *a: a, ai, ay*   high-frequency/tested vocabulary

Mr. Moose nuzzled Mrs. Moose's head. "Well, that won't do. I will go this minute and find you a turkey for Thanksgiving."

Mr. Moose put on his cap and went out.

Mist wandered through the bare trees. The cold made his nose water.

Rabbit poked his head from his rabbit hole. "Mr. Moose! Is it dinnertime?"

"Not quite yet. Mrs. Moose wants a turkey. I'm off to find one."

Rabbit joined him in three quick hops. "I'll come, too."

Moose's warm breath hung white in front of him. Snow crunched under his hooves and made little holes that Rabbit jumped over.

"I see the Goats," Rabbit said.

Mr. Goat raised his head and spat out the tin can he was chewing. "Is it dinnertime?" he called.

"Not till I find a turkey," Mr. Moose said.

"We saw one down by the river," Mrs. Goat told him, and Mr. Goat added, "A fat one."

290

291

Guiding Comprehension

◉ Draw Conclusions • Inferential

- **How does Mr. Moose feel about Mrs. Moose? How do you know?**
  Possible response: He probably loves her very much. He nuzzles her head and is willing to go out in the cold to find a turkey in order to make her happy.

Author's Purpose • Inferential

- *Question the Author* **How does the author show the reader what the weather is like?**
  The author talks about bare trees and snow. He mentions that the cold makes Mr. Moose's nose water. He also talks about how Mr. Moose's breath comes out as steam in the cold air.

▲ **Pages 290–291**
Have children read to find out how Mr. Moose feels about Mrs. Moose.

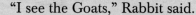

Monitor Progress

High-Frequency Words

If... children have a problem reading a new high-frequency word,	then... use the High-Frequency Routine on p. 285a to reteach the problematic word.

Time for **SOCIAL STUDIES**

Thanksgiving Food

Traditional Thanksgiving menus include turkey, dressing, cranberry sauce, sweet potatoes, green beans, and pumpkin or pecan pie. What does your family eat on Thanksgiving?

The Goats leaped down from their perch. "We'll show you."

Sheep was farther up the hillside, looking round as a fur ball in his winter coat. "Is it dinnertime?" he bellowed.

"First I have to find a turkey," Mr. Moose bellowed back.

"There's a turkey nest on the riverbank," Sheep called. "Wait for me."

292

The earth smelled of ice and moss as they crunched along. Above them a crow hung, black as a puff of wood smoke.

Porcupine was hiding in the underbrush. "It's you," he said and put his quills down.

"We're off to get a turkey for Mrs. Moose," Mr. Moose explained. "Do you want to come?"

"I'm slow," Porcupine said. "Pick me up on your way back."

"Who'd want to pick you up?" Sheep asked, and laughed his bleat of a laugh.

"I'll wait," Porcupine told Mr. Moose.

293

▲ **Pages 292–293**
Have children read to find descriptions of the animals.

EXTEND SKILLS

Personification

For instruction in personification, discuss the following:

- The author of this animal fantasy gives animals the characteristics of humans to make them seem like people.

- One example of how the animals in this story behave like humans is when on p. 295, Mr. Moose talks to Turkey in "his sweetest voice," like a person would.

Assess Have children find other examples of personification in the story.

Strategies in Context

🎯 VISUALIZE

- **What do the animals look like?**
  The sheep looks "round as a fur ball in his winter coat." The crow hangs in the air "black as a puff of wood smoke."

Monitor Progress	**Visualize**
If... children have difficulty describing what the animals look like,	**then...** model how to visualize.

Think Aloud

MODEL I've read that the sheep looks "round as a fur ball in his winter coat." I can picture that his coat is very full, and he looks fat and fluffy. When I read that the crow hangs in the air "black as a puff of wood smoke," I can picture that the crow must look very black in the air.

ASSESS Have children find other descriptions that help them visualize. (Sheep makes a joke about not wanting to pick up Porcupine. This helps me imagine Porcupine's sharp quills sticking out.)

Long *a: a, ai, ay*　　high-frequency/tested vocabulary

They saw Turkey's nest right <u>away</u>, and Turkey himself peering over the top of it.

"Turkey! Turkey!" Mr. Moose called in his sweetest voice.

"Aagh!" Turkey blundered from his nest and ran.

Mr. Moose lumbered after him. "Turkey! Don't run. We just want you for Thanksgiving dinner." Turkey ran faster.

294

295

Guiding Comprehension

Predict • Inferential

- **Do you think Mr. Moose will find a turkey to take home to Mrs. Moose? Why or why not?**
Possible response: Most children will probably say yes because Mr. Moose seems so determined and because of the story's title.

Classify • Critical

- *Text to Self* **What does your family do to celebrate Thanksgiving?**
Possible response: We think about things we're thankful for, eat a big meal, and watch football on television.

Summarize • Inferential

- **What has happened in the story so far?**
Mr. and Mrs. Moose have prepared their table for Thanksgiving. Mrs. Moose is sad about not having a turkey, so Mr. Moose goes out to find one. Many of his friends who are going to celebrate the holiday with him join in the hunt.

▲ **Pages 294–295**
Have children look at the pictures and read to find out if Mr. Moose finds a turkey.

Strategy Self-Check

Have children ask themselves these questions to check their reading.

Decoding Words

- Do I apply knowledge of letter-sound relationships to decode unfamiliar words when reading text?
- Does the new word make sense in the story?

Visualize

- Do I picture what happens as I read?
- Do the pictures in my mind remind me of something I've seen?
- What words help me imagine what is being described?

Mr. Moose saw the red and blue sheen of Turkey's neck. Turkey's tail brushed crumbs of snow behind him as he tried to fly.

"Too fat," Mr. Goat said.

Turkey's legs bent in the middle as he fell.

296

Mr. Moose put a booted hoof on his head and smiled his great, toothy smile. "I hope you don't have other plans for Thanksgiving, Turkey."

He helped Turkey up. "My wife won't mind that you're too fat," he said. "Let's go. It's getting close to dinnertime."

They marched Turkey in front. "I'm sorry about this, for I can see you don't want to come," Mr. Moose said. "But I must insist. A promise is a promise."

297

▲ **Pages 296-297**
Have children read to find out why the author wrote this story.

Read the journal. **Answer** the questions.

The Best Thanksgiving
by Lisa Black

This year was the best Thanksgiving ever. Mom made green beans with cheese! I ate a whole turkey leg. The apple pie that Aunt Jean made was great! All of the food was good. But that is not why this was the best Thanksgiving. The best thing was that my brother came home to be with us.

1. What is the author's name? <u>Lisa Black</u>

2. **Circle** the words in the story that tell what was for dinner.

3. **Circle** the name below of the person who made the pie.
Mom (Aunt Jean)

4. **Underline** the sentence in the story that tells what made this the best Thanksgiving.

5. **Write** a sentence that tells why you think the author wrote this story.

<u>Responses should include: To tell about something special.</u>
<u>To tell about a happy day.</u>

Home Activity Your child read a journal entry about Thanksgiving and told why the author wrote it. Together, choose a special day or event in your child's life. Have your child write about it and then tell why he or she chose to write about that day or event.

Practice Book Unit 2   Comprehension Author's Purpose Review **97**

▲ **Practice Book 2.1** p. 97, Author's Purpose

Skills in Context

(REVIEW) **AUTHOR'S PURPOSE**

• **Why do you think the author wrote this story?**
The author wrote this story to entertain readers.

Monitor Progress	**Author's Purpose**
If... children have difficulty answering the question,	**then...** model how to use the text and pictures to determine the author's purpose.

Think Aloud **MODEL** While reading, I think about why the author wrote the story. This story is silly and cute. Parts of it are funny. I think the author wrote it to entertain readers.

ASSESS Have children look for more clues that show that the author wrote the story to entertain. (The story has talking animals who are celebrating Thanksgiving.)

Long a: a, ai, ay   high-frequency/tested vocabulary

There was a wreath of dried fruit on the Mooses' door. Inside, the house was filled with Thanksgiving smells. Mr. Moose hid Turkey behind him.

"Look who I brought, Mrs. Moose," he said. "Sheep, the Goats, Rabbit, and Porcupine. And ta-da!" He pushed Turkey around in front of him. "For you. A turkey for Thanksgiving!"

Mrs. Moose clapped her hooves. "I'm *so* happy to have you, Turkey. Thank you, Mr. Moose. Now everything's perfect."

298

"Shall we sit?" Sheep asked, heading for the straight-up-and-down chair.

"Let's." Mrs. Moose pointed. "Rabbit here. Porcupine here. Mr. and Mrs. Goat here, and look! I brought a chair from the other room in hopes of Turkey."

"A . . . a *chair*?" Turkey stammered.

"Right next to me," Mrs. Moose said. "Light the candles, Mr. Moose."

299

Guiding Comprehension

Character • Inferential

- **What are some words that describe Mr. Moose?**
Considerate, polite, kind, happy, loving, patient.

Compare and Contrast • Inferential

- **How are the animals the same?**
They are all polite and well-mannered.

Confirm Predictions • Inferential

- **Did Mr. Moose bring home a turkey? Is this what you predicted would happen?**
He did bring home a turkey. Most children will have predicted this, but they might be surprised to see that Turkey is a guest.

▲ **Pages 298–299**
Have children look at pictures and read to find out what kind of character Mr. Moose is.

Time for SOCIAL STUDIES

Thanksgiving History

In the United States, Thanksgiving is celebrated the fourth Thursday of each November. Today's holiday celebrates a harvest festival that the Plymouth colony Pilgrims shared with the Native Americans in 1621. The Native Americans had helped the Pilgrims survive, doing such things as giving them seeds so they could grow corn.

Much later, a woman named Sarah Hale tried to get people to recognize Thanksgiving as a national holiday. President Abraham Lincoln supported her efforts, and the first national holiday took place in 1863.

There were bowls of <u>acorns</u> and alfalfa sprouts, dried since summer. There was willow bark and cured grasses and wild parsley. There were pressed leaves, thin and pale as new ice on a pond.

"I hope you find something here to your liking, Mr. Turkey," Mrs. Moose said. "I wasn't sure of your taste."

"You are so kind to worry about my taste," Turkey said. "I thought you'd be worrying about *how* I'd taste."

"Heavens, no!" Mr. Moose smiled his big-toothed smile and filled everyone's cup with cold spring water. "It's so nice to have friends around the <u>table</u> at Thanksgiving."

Turkey's wattles wobbled. "It's even nicer to be AT your <u>table</u> and not ON it," he said. "Happy Thanksgiving, everybody."

300

301

▲ **Pages 300–301**
Have children read to find out how Turkey feels about sitting at the Thanksgiving table.

Access Con tent Tell children that "cured grasses" are grasses that have been treated so that they will not rot.

Guiding Comprehension

Cause and Effect • Inferential
- **Why does Turkey say "You are so kind to worry about my taste"?**
  Turkey was worried that he was going to be eaten and that the other animals would be worrying about how Turkey tasted.

◉**Visualize • Inferential**
- **What do you picture when Turkey says he's glad he's not on the table?**
  Possible response: I picture him on a serving plate instead of sitting happily in his chair.

◉**Draw Conclusions • Critical**
- **Why do you think the animals' menu is so different from a traditional Thanksgiving menu?**
  Possible response: The animals' menu is full of things that plant-eating animals would enjoy.

Long *a: a, ai, ay*   high-frequency/tested vocabulary

"Happy Thanksgiving, Turkey."

302

◀ **Page 302**
Have children read to decide what the story is mostly about.

Guiding Comprehension

Main Idea • Inferential
• **What is the story mostly about?**
Possible response: It's nice to share holidays with friends.

Character • Inferential
• **How does Turkey feel at the end of the story?**
Relieved, happy, surprised, thankful.

Classify • Critical
• *Text to Text* **What are some other stories you know about celebrating holidays?**
Possible response: I read *How the Grinch Stole Christmas* about the Grinch, who learned that Christmas is about being with the people you love, not about presents.

Reread For Fluency ROUTINE

① **Reader 1 Begins**
Children read the entire book, switching readers at the end of each page.

② **Reader 2 Begins** Have partners reread; now the other partner begins.

③ **Reread** For optimal fluency, children should reread three or four times.

④ **Provide Feedback** Listen to children read and provide corrective feedback regarding their oral reading and their use of blending.

Interactive Writing

WRITE List

OBJECTIVES

⬤ Write a list.
⬤ Identify possessive nouns.

Strategic Intervention

Children who are not able to write independently may copy one of the examples from the list about ways to contribute to a celebration and add an illustration.

Advanced

Have children who are able to write independently complete their own list about ways they, or someone they know, has contributed to a celebration.

Support Writing Before having children begin, restate the prompt and explain that "contribute to a celebration" means "add to or help with a party, holiday, or festival."

Beginning Allow children to look at the story for visual support as they write.

Intermediate Have children work in small groups, discussing what they will write as one group member takes notes. Children can refer to these notes when they write their list.

Advanced Review children's writing and show them where they can make changes that will make the writing more informative or more interesting.

DISCUSS Use the story *A Turkey for Thanksgiving* to encourage a discussion about ways to contribute to a celebration. Picture walk through the story and ask children to identify how different animals contribute different things.

SHARE THE PEN Have children participate in writing a list about how to contribute to a celebration. To begin, have a child suggest one way to contribute to a celebration. Have the class repeat it. Write the example, reminding individuals to use the rules they've learned about sentences. Ask questions such as:

- What does the sentence start with? (capital letter)
- What does the sentence end with? (period)
- What are two things each sentence has in it? (subject, verb)

Continue to have individuals make contributions. Frequently reread what has been written while tracking the print.

READ THE LIST Read the list aloud, having children echo you.

Ways to Contribute to a Celebration

Take food to share.

Help the host decorate.

Take flowers for the host.

Help clean up.

INDEPENDENT WRITING

WRITE LISTS Have children look at the list and then write their own list about ways to contribute to a celebration. Remind children to write in complete sentences. Let children illustrate their writing.

ELL

Support Grammar In many languages, speakers show possession in phrases (like *of the cat*) rather than noun endings (like *cat's*). Help children see the difference between possessive and plural nouns. See the grammar lessons in the ELL and Transition Handbook.

Grammar

DEVELOP THE CONCEPT Possessive Nouns

IDENTIFY POSSESSIVE NOUNS Write *turkey's friends* and *dogs' friends* on the board. Point to each example as you read it. Ask children to identify which example is singular and which example is plural. *(turkey's, dogs')*

A possessive noun shows who or what owns something. It can be singular or plural. Add *'s* to a singular noun to show ownership. When do you just add an apostrophe to a noun to show ownership? (when the noun is plural)

PRACTICE

USE POSSESSIVE NOUNS Gather several pictures of noun pairs, such as *car/tire* and *girl/cat*. Display a picture pair. Model making one noun possessive while using the other noun as its possession. Then model using the pair in a sentence.

 Think Aloud **MODEL** This is a car. Write *car*. This is a tire. Write *tire.* I'll use the two nouns together, making one of them a possessive noun: the car's tire. Now I'll think of a sentence that uses the two nouns: The car's back tire is flat. Write the sentence.

Have children suggest sentences for the other pictures. Write the sentences children provide.

Possessive Nouns

A noun that shows who or what owns something is a **possessive noun**. To show ownership, add an **apostrophe** (') and **-s** when the noun is singular. Add just an **apostrophe** (') when the noun is plural.

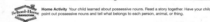

the goat's legs   the bears' paws

Add *'s* to each singular noun in ( ).
Write the words on the line.
1. the (turkey) chair
the turkey's chair
2. the (moose) coat
the moose's coat
Add *'* to each plural noun in ( ).
Write the words on the line.
3. the (rabbits) tails
the rabbits' tails
4. the (animals) plates
the animals' plates

Home Activity Your child learned about possessive nouns. Read a story together. Have your child point out possessive nouns and tell what belongs to each person, animal, or thing.

▲ **Grammar and Writing Practice Book** p. 37

Wrap Up Your Day!

✓ **HIGH-FREQUENCY WORDS** Write the following sentences. *Everybody was hiding behind the door. They had all brought gifts. After a few minutes, Sam walked into the room. Everyone jumped out and yelled. Sam jumped. Joe said, "I'm sorry we scared you, but we made a promise to make your birthday special!" Sam had a big grin on his face.* Ask children to read the sentences and identify the high-frequency words *door, behind, brought, minute, promise, sorry, everybody.*

✓ **VISUALIZE** Have children close their eyes and visualize a meal at a special celebration. Then have them write a description of that meal using complete sentences in their writing.

LET'S TALK ABOUT IT Recall the selection *A Turkey for Thanksgiving.* Ask: What did Mrs. Moose do to contribute to the celebration? (She decorated the table, she invited friends over, and she prepared food.)

PREVIEW Day 3

Tell children that tomorrow they will hear about a celebration from another country.

Share Literature
My First Chinese New Year

Phonics and Spelling
(Review) Plurals
Spelling: Words with Long *a*

High-Frequency Words
door   behind   brought Word Wall
minute   promise   sorry everybody

Vocabulary
Similes

Fluency
Read Silently with Fluency

Independent Writing
Respond to Literature

Grammar
Possessive Nouns

Materials

- *Sing with Me Big Book*
- Read Aloud Anthology
- Student Edition 303–305

Morning Warm~Up!

Today we will read about Chinese New Year. Everyone in the family contributes to the celebration. How have you contributed to your family celebrations?

QUESTION OF THE DAY Encourage children to sing "Holidays" from the *Sing with Me Big Book* as you gather. Write and read the message and discuss the question.

REVIEW ORAL VOCABULARY

- Read the second sentence of the message.
- Have children explain what the word *contributes* means. (gives to)

ELL

Build Background Use the Day 3 instruction on ELL Poster 10 to support children's use of English to communicate about lesson concepts.

ELL Poster 10

Share Literature

LISTEN AND RESPOND

REVIEW REALISTIC FICTION Recall what "My First Chinese New Year" is about. Ask if the story is fiction or nonfiction. Ask if it is realistic or a fantasy.

BUILD ORAL VOCABULARY Review that yesterday the class read the seleciton to find out how people prepare to celebrate Chinese New Year. Ask that children listen today to find out about the many types of food that are served during the **banquet,** which is a large meal served at a special occasion.

Read Aloud Anthology
My First Chinese New Year

MONITOR LISTENING COMPREHENSION

- Why do the characters start cooking a few days before the celebration? (They need time to make a lot of food.)

- What is served at the **banquet**? (soup, chicken, fish, rice pudding)

- How do you think the family feels after they dine? (Possible response: full, happy, lucky, grateful)

Amazing Words — to build oral vocabulary

	MONITOR PROGRESS
participate holiday dine decorate **banquet**	**If...** children lack oral vocabulary experiences about the concept Working Together, **then...** use the Oral Vocabulary Routine on pp. DI·1–DI·2, DI·7 to develop the Amazing Words.

Listen and Respond Help children describe and demonstrate the actions associated with the words *wiggling* and *gobbles* in "My First Chinese New Year."

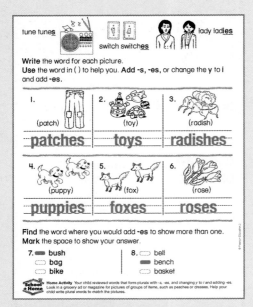

▲ **Practice Book 2.1** p. 98, Plurals

Review Phonics

REVIEW PLURALS

READ *-s, -es, -ies* WORDS Write *noses, ditches,* and *bunnies.* You can read these words because you know how to read plurals *-s, -es,* and *-ies.* You can cover the ending, read the base word, and then blend the base word and the ending to read the whole word. What are the words?

INDIVIDUALS SORT WORDS WITH *-s, -es, -ies* Distribute word cards with words containing plurals *-s, -es, -ies.* Write *-s, -es,* and *-ies* as headings for three columns. Have children read their words and place their word cards under the appropriate heading. Have all children copy the completed chart and circle the letters that make the plural endings. Have children use the words in sentences to demonstrate meaning.

-s	*-es*	*-ies*
notes	bunches	ladies
hopes	batches	babies
hands	ashes	buddies
heels	boxes	nannies

High-Frequency Words

PRACTICE

STORY CLUES Read the following story to children. Have children find the word on the Word Wall that fits each blank in the story. **Word Wall**

"I have a surprise for you!" said Mom as she walked through the _____. (door) "Close your eyes, Mia. If you peek, you'll be _____!" (sorry) she joked.

Mia covered her eyes. "Don't worry, Mom. I _____ (promise) not to peek." Mom was gone for only a _____. (minute) Then she came back into the room. She held something _____ (behind) her back. "I _____ (brought) you something from the pet store," said Mom.

Mia opened her eyes. "A new puppy!" she squealed. "Let's go show _____!" (everybody)

Spelling

PRACTICE Long *a: ai, ay*

WRITE A THANKSGIVING STORY Have children practice the spelling words by working together to write a Thanksgiving story that uses all the words.

• Divide children into pairs. Tell pairs to think about how Mr. Moose and Turkey celebrated Thanksgiving. Ask pairs to work together to think of a special kind of Thanksgiving they would like to have or someone they would like to invite for Thanksgiving.

• Tell one partner to use a spelling word to write the first sentence of their story. Have the second partner write the second sentence using another spelling word. Pairs can reuse the words as needed.

• Have pairs exchange stories and circle the spelling words.

• Collect stories in a class Thanksgiving book.

HOMEWORK Spelling Practice Book, p. 39

Pick a word from the box to finish each sentence. **Write** the word on the line. **Remember** to use a capital letter at the beginning of a sentence.

behind	brought	door	everybody
minute	promise	sorry	

1. **Everybody** will be at dinner tonight.

2. Father made sure we **brought** warm coats.

3. Our sled was pulled **behind** two fine horses.

4. My sister made me **promise** to be good.

5. We were all **sorry** that Grandpa was sick.

6. It took only a **minute** to ride up the path to the house.

7. There was Grandma, waving from the front **door**!

School + Home **Home Activity** Your child learned to read the words behind, brought, door, everybody, minute, promise, and sorry. Together, write an invitation for a Thanksgiving celebration at your home. Encourage your child to include some of these words.

▲ **Practice Book 2.1** p. 99, High-Frequency Words

Spelling Words

Long *a: ai, ay*

1. **tail***
2. **main**
3. **wait***
4. **say**
5. **away***
6. **play**
7. **raise***
8. **brain**
9. **paint**
10. **stay**
11. **today**
12. **tray**

Challenge Words

13. **holiday**
14. **daily**
15. **raisin**

* **Words from the Selection**

Long *a: ai, ay*
Read the poster. Circle three spelling mistakes. Write the words correctly. Then write the last sentence, using correct grammar.

Spelling Words	
tail	raise
main	brain
wait	paint
say	stay
away	today
play	tray

Fire Safety Tips
• Stay (away) from fires.
• Replace worn electric cords because (thay) can start fires.
• Store (paynt) away from heat.
• Don't never play with matches.

1. **away**
2. **they**
3. **paint**

Frequently Misspelled Words
favorite
they

4. **Don't play with matches.**

Circle the word in each pair that is spelled correctly. Write the word.

5. tial
   (tail) → **tail**

6. (main) / mian → **main**

7. (brain) / brian → **brain**

8. (raise) / rase → **raise**

  Home Activity Your child has been spelling words with long a spelled ai and ay. Have your child underline these letter combinations in the list words.

▲ **Spelling Practice Book** p. 39

Turkey for Thanksgiving **303d**

Strategic Intervention

Children who are not able to write independently may copy one of the sentences from the board and add an illustration.

Advanced

Provide children with a list of similes (as dry as a bone, as fat as a pig, as hard as a rock) and have them write sentences using these similes.

ELL

Access Content Have children look at pictures from the book and verbalize similes (Porcupine is as prickly as a cactus).

Vocabulary

SIMILES

DISCUSS SIMILES Remind children that the story used descriptive writing to help readers picture different characters and scenes. Explain that one type of descriptive writing in the story is the use of similes, or comparisons between two unlike things using the words *like* or *as*. Write the following sentences and discuss what two things are being compared in each. Then have children think of more sentences using similes.

Mr. Moose's smile was as bright as the sun.

Turkey cried like a baby.

EXPAND MEANING Write the following sentences from the story on the board: *Sheep was farther up the hillside, looking round as a fur ball in his winter coat. Above them a crow hung, black as a puff of wood smoke.* Explain that each is a simile, with the first comparing Sheep to a fur ball and the second comparing the crow to a puff of smoke. Have children work in groups to write sentences about the characters in the story using similes. Invite volunteers to share their sentences.

Group Time

DAY 3

On-Level	Strategic Intervention	Advanced
Read *A Turkey for Thanksgiving.*	**Read** or listen to *A Turkey for Thanksgiving.*	**Read** *A Turkey for Thanksgiving.*
• Use pp. 286–305.	• Use the **Routine** on p. DI·58.	• Use the **Routine** on p. DI·59.

ELL Place English language learners in the groups that correspond to their reading abilities in English.

(i) Independent Activities

Independent Reading See p. 282j for Reading/Library activities and suggestions.

Journal Writing Write a journal entry about a holiday celebration. Explain what you or your family added to the celebration. Share writing.

Literacy Centers To provide experiences with *A Turkey for Thanksgiving,* you may use the Writing Center on p. 282k.

Practice Book 2.1 Plurals *-s, -es, -ies,* p. 98; High-Frequency Words, p. 99

Break into small groups after Vocabulary and before Writing.

Fluency

READ SILENTLY WITH FLUENCY

MODEL READING SILENTLY WITH FLUENCY Use *A Turkey for Thanksgiving*.

- Have children turn to p. 288. When I see a word I don't know, I sound it out by syllables or word parts. When I come to the word *Thanks-giving*, I break it down into words, *Thanks-giving*.

- Ask children to follow along as you read the page with fluency.

- Have children read the page after you. Encourage them to self-correct when reading. Continue in the same way with pp. 289–290.

REREAD FOR FLUENCY

Reader's Theater

ROUTINE

1 **Select a Passage** For *A Turkey for Thanksgiving*, use pp. 291–293.

2 **Assign** Assign each child a short passage of text.

3 **Practice** Have children read their assigned passage 3–5 times silently.

4 **Independent Readings** Have children read aloud to you. Monitor progress and provide feedback. For optimal fluency, children should read at an appropriate pace.

Monitor Progress	Fluency
If... children have difficulty reading silently with fluency,	**then...** prompt: • Where did I get stuck? • Should I try sounding out a word by syllables or word parts?
If... the class cannot read fluently without you,	**then...** continue to have them read along with you.

OBJECTIVE

● Read silently with fluency.

Options for Choral Reading

Use *A Turkey for Thanksgiving* or one of the following Leveled Readers.

On-Level

Thanksgiving

Strategic Intervention

Together for Thanksgiving

Advanced

The Pilgrims' First Year

Use *A Thanksgiving Party* or *A Turkey for Thanksgiving*. Model reading sections of the text with fluency and self-correcting when necessary. Stumble over difficult words such as *thanksgiving* and *alfalfa* and go back to correct yourself before reading on. Have English language learners read similarly difficult passages and practice self-correcting.

To develop fluent readers, use Fluency Coach.

Think and Share

TALK ABOUT IT Model a response. I don't want to go to dinner at Mr. and Mrs. Moose's house because I don't want to be eaten!

Selection Test To assess with *Turtle's Race with Beaver*, use Selection Tests, pp. 37–40.

1. **RETELL** Have children use the pictures across the bottom to retell the story. See Monitor Progress below.

2. **DRAW CONCLUSIONS** Turkey thought he'd be eaten because many people eat turkeys on Thanksgiving. I thought he would be a guest.

3. **VISUALIZE** I imagine Turkey running scared and Moose chasing him with a confused expression on his face. Visualizing helps me keep track of what's happening.

LOOK BACK AND WRITE See Independent Writing, TE p. 305a. ⁴³²¹

Monitor Progress — Check Retelling ⁴³²¹

If... children have difficulty retelling the story,

then... use the Scoring Rubric for Retelling below to help them move toward fluent retelling.

SUCCESS PREDICTOR

Day 1 Check Word Reading • **Day 2** Check High-Frequency Words • ▶**Day 3** Check Retelling • **Day 4** Check Fluency • **Day 5** Assess Progress

Retelling Plan

☑ Week 1 assess Strategic Intervention students.

☑ Week 2 assess Advanced students.

☑ Week 3 assess Strategic Intervention students.

☑ Week 4 assess On-Level students.

☑ **This week assess any students you have not yet checked during this unit.**

Assessment Before retelling, help children name the characters and items shown. For more ideas on assessing comprehension, see the ELL and Transition Handbook.

Scoring Rubric — Narrative Retelling

Rubric ⁴³²¹	4	3	2	1
Connections	Makes connections and generalizes beyond the text	Makes connections to other events, stories, or experiences	Makes a limited connection to another event, story, or experience	Makes no connection to another event, story, or experience
Author's Purpose	Elaborates on author's purpose	Tells author's purpose with some clarity	Makes some connection to author's purpose	Makes no connection to author's purpose
Characters	Describes the main character(s) and any character development	Identifies the main character(s) and gives some information about them	Inaccurately identifies some characters or gives little information about them	Inaccurately identifies the characters or gives no information about them
Setting	Describes the time and location	Identifies the time and location	Omits details of time or location	Is unable to identify time or location
Plot	Describes the events in sequence using rich detail	Tells the plot with some errors in sequence that do not affect meaning	Tells parts of plot with gaps that affect meaning	Retelling has no sense of story

Reader Response

Think and Share

Talk About It Pretend you are Turkey. Tell why you are afraid to come to dinner.

1. The pictures below show the beginning, middle, and end of the story. Retell the story. Fill in the missing parts.

2. What conclusion did Turkey draw? Why would he think that?

3. Read page 295 again. What picture do you have in your mind as you read that page?

Look Back and Write Look back at page 300. Make a list of the foods Mrs. Moose served her guests. How do you think everyone enjoyed the dinner? What makes you think so?

Retelling Strip

303

Meet the Author

Eve Bunting

Read other books by Eve Bunting.

Eve Bunting does not eat turkey. She always thinks "poor turkey" when she sees a bird being put into the oven. That feeling is where she got the idea for *A Turkey for Thanksgiving*, one of her favorite books. Ms. Bunting grew up in Ireland. There they do not celebrate a holiday like Thanksgiving.

Ms. Bunting loves to write. She has written over two hundred books for children. She has written about giants and ogres and creatures with scales and fins. She has written about sharks and whales and giant squid. She has written about children growing up and men growing old. Writing an animal fantasy like *A Turkey for Thanksgiving* is her "fun and relaxing time."

304

Retelling

SUCCESS PREDICTOR

OBJECTIVE

● Write a response.

Independent Writing

DAILY FIX-IT

5. The cat find the sop.
   The cat f<u>ou</u>nd the so<u>a</u>p.

6. Sh'es a smat cat.
   She<u>'</u>s a sma<u>r</u>t cat.

Writer's Checkup

✔ Singular possessive nouns should have an apostrophe and *s*. Did I do that?

✔ Plural possessive nouns should have an apostrophe added. Did I do that?

✔ Proper nouns should begin with a capital letter. Did I do that?

Look Back and Write

RESPOND TO LITERATURE Read the writing prompt on p. 303 in the Student Edition and model your thinking. Then have children write their responses.

 MODEL I'll look back at p. 300 and read that part of the story again. I'll look for the foods that Mrs. Moose served her guests. Then I'll write my response.

Mrs. Moose's meal included:
acorns
alfalfa sprouts
willow bark
cured grasses
wild parsley
pressed leaves

I think everyone loved Mrs. Moose's dinner because the animals that were invited probably enjoy these kinds of plants.

ELL

Support Writing Have children look at the illustrations before and on the cited page. Ask children what ideas the illustrations give them that will help answer the prompt.

Assess See the ELL and Transition Handbook for guidance on assessing writing at various levels of English proficiency.

Scoring Rubric — Written Response

Rubric 4 3 2 1	4	3	2	1
Focus/Ideas	Clearly focuses on foods served and how the guests enjoyed them	Focuses on foods served and how the guests enjoyed them	Attempts to focus on foods served and how the guests enjoyed them	Does not focus on food or enjoyment
Organization/ Paragraphs	Includes information in the correct order	Includes most of the information in the correct order	Includes some information in the correct order	Includes little information in incorrect order
Sentences	Uses varied, interesting, connected sentences	Uses varied connected sentences	Uses simple sentences with few errors	Uses simple sentences with many errors
Conventions	No spelling or punctuation errors	Few spelling or punctuation errors	Some spelling and punctuation errors	Many spelling and punctuation errors

Grammar

APPLY TO WRITING Possessive Nouns

IMPROVE WRITING WITH POSSESSIVE NOUNS Have children recall the possessive nouns they used in the answer they wrote for Look Back and Write. Remind children that possessive nouns show ownership. Remind children to use possessive nouns correctly in their own writing.

Write phrases as follows. Have children rewrite the phrases using a possessive noun.

bike of one girl

books of two boys

PRACTICE

WRITE WITH POSSESSIVE NOUNS Have children write sentences that include possessive nouns. Ask what the difference is between making a singular noun possessive and making a plural noun possessive.

Possessive Nouns

Write about members of your family.
Tell about each person's favorite color, food, or game.
Use possessive nouns to show ownership.

Possible answer: My mom's favorite color is blue. My dad's favorite food is pizza. My two brothers' favorite game is baseball.

Home Activity Your child learned how to use possessive nouns in writing. Have your child use sticky notes to label things in your home and show the person whom they belong to. (Sandra's bedroom, Dad's chair)

▲ **Grammar and Writing Practice Book** p. 38

Wrap Up Your Day!

 DRAW CONCLUSIONS Have children draw conclusions about *A Turkey for Thanksgiving*. Why did Mrs. Moose want a turkey? (Mrs. Moose thought that Thanksgiving dinner should include turkey.) What do you think was Turkey's reason for feeling so thankful? (He thought he was supposed to be dinner, and he was happy they invited him to be a guest.)

READ SILENTLY WITH FLUENCY Have children read a paragraph from *A Turkey for Thanksgiving*, sounding out syllables for unfamiliar words and self-correcting as needed.

LET'S TALK ABOUT IT What other holidays do you celebrate? How do you contribute to these holidays? (Responses will vary. Children should name holidays in which they participate and tell how they celebrate.)

PREVIEW Day 4

Tell children that tomorrow they will listen to a story about a boy whose friends contribute to his birthday celebration.

Share Literature
The Blizzard

Phonics and Spelling
Long *a: a, ai, ay*
Spelling: Words with Long *a*

Read

(Group Time) < Differentiated Instruction

"Reading a Web Page"

Fluency
Read Silently with Fluency

Writing Across the Curriculum
List

Grammar
Possessive Nouns

Speaking and Listening
Make Introductions

Materials

- *Sing with Me Big Book*
- Read Aloud Anthology
- Student Edition 306-309

Morning Warm-Up!

We can read books when we want to learn something new.

What other ways can we learn about things?

QUESTION OF THE DAY Encourage children to sing "Holidays" from the *Sing with Me Big Book* as you gather. Write and read the message and discuss the question.

REVIEW SYNONYMS

- Read the first sentence in the message.
- Have children name synonyms for *learn.* (study, be taught, discover)

E L L

Extend Language Use the Day 4 instruction on ELL Poster 10 to extend and enrich language.

ELL Poster 10

Share Literature

CONNECT CONCEPTS

ACTIVATE PRIOR KNOWLEDGE Recall the selections about Thanksgiving and Chinese New Year. Explain that you will read another story about a celebration—*The Blizzard* by Betty Ren Wright.

BUILD ORAL VOCABULARY Read the seventh paragraph. Explain that as the fire burns the coals, the coals can **glimmer,** or make a faint light, and **flare,** or flame up briefly. The fire might make a **whispery** sound as it burns. Ask children to listen to find out about the big snow storm.

Read Aloud Anthology
The Blizzard

MONITOR LISTENING COMPREHENSION

- As the children walk through the heavy snow, what sounds might they hear? (Possible response: Their feet might crunch against the old snow. Their feet might make **whispery** sounds through the new soft snow.)

- What might the children see **glimmering** in the distance as they walk through the storm? (Possible response: They might see lights from Billy's house **glimmering** in the distance.)

- If the fire **flared** while the children were standing beside it, would that make them warmer or colder? Explain. (It would make them warmer because the flames would be burning strong and bright.)

Amazing Words to build oral vocabulary

MONITOR PROGRESS

participate holiday dine decorate banquet glimmer flare whispery	**If...** children lack oral vocabulary experiences about the concept Working Together, **then...** use the Oral Vocabulary Routine on pp. DI·1–DI·2, DI·7 to develop the Amazing Words.

Connect Concepts To show their understanding of *blizzard,* children can use the picture on the cover to point out the heavy snow and the blowing scarves. Have children explain why people *stumbled* through the snow, and have them demonstrate stumbling.

Spiral REVIEW

- Reviews *r*-controlled *er, ir, ur.*
- Reviews *r*-controlled *ar, or, ore* and syllables VCCV.
- Reviews high-frequency words *bought, people, please.*

Sentence Reading

REVIEW WORDS IN CONTEXT

READ DECODABLE AND HIGH-FREQUENCY WORDS IN CONTEXT Write these sentences. Call on individuals to read a sentence. Then randomly point to words and have them read. To help you monitor word reading, high-frequency words are underlined and decodable words are circled.

I was scared when I got lost in the park and forgot my way back to May's quaint farm.

Each day I shall wait by the sign to watch the birds perch on the birdbath.

Today I wait for the daily train with all the people.

One day I will probably be an artist or ride horses.

During the holidays I bought a purse, a shirt, and a darling skirt.

When the day is pleasant, I sit on the porch before dark.

Monitor Progress	Word Reading
If... children are unable to read an underlined word,	**then...** read the word for them and spell it, having them echo you.
If... children are unable to read a circled word,	**then...** have them use the blending strategy they have learned for that word type.

Support Phonics For additional review, see the phonics activities in the ELL and Transition Handbook.

Spelling

PARTNER REVIEW Long *a: ai, ay*

READ AND WRITE Supply pairs of children with index cards on which the spelling words have been written. Have one child read a word while the other writes it. Then have children switch roles. Have them use the cards to check their spelling.

HOMEWORK Spelling Practice Book, p. 40

OBJECTIVE

● Spell words with long *a: ai, ay*.

Spelling Words

Long *a: ai, ay*

1.	**tail***	7.	**raise***
2.	**main**	8.	**brain**
3.	**wait***	9.	**paint**
4.	**say**	10.	**stay**
5.	**away***	11.	**today**
6.	**play**	12.	**tray**

Challenge Words

13	**holiday**	15.	**raisin**
14.	**daily**		

* Words from the Selection

Group Time

On-Level	Strategic Intervention	Advanced
Read "Thanksgiving U.S.A."	**Read** or listen to "Thanksgiving U.S.A."	**Read** "Thanksgiving U.S.A."
• Use pp. 306–309.	• Use the **Routine** on p. DI·60.	• Use the **Routine** on p. DI·61.

DAY 4

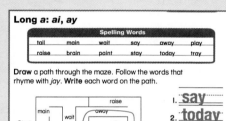

▲ **Spelling Practice Book** p. 40

ELL Place English language learners in the groups that correspond to their reading abilities in English.

(*i*) Independent Activities

Fluency Reading Pair children to reread *A Turkey for Thanksgiving.*

Journal Writing Write a paragraph about a special holiday. Share writing.

Spelling Partner Review

Independent Reading See p. 282j for Reading/Library activities and suggestions.

Literacy Centers To provide listening opportunities, you may use the Listening Center on p. 282j. To extend social studies concepts, you may use the Social Studies Center on p. 282k.

Break into small groups after Spelling and before Fluency.

Reading Online

Thanksgiving USA

After reading *A Turkey for Thanksgiving*, Nadia wants to learn more about the Thanksgiving holiday. With her parents' permission, Nadia searches the Web. She finds a Web site with many links.

Nadia clicks on one link, Thanksgiving. A new Web page opens. She finds these choices:

File   Edit   View   Favorites   Tools   Help

http://www.url.here

• **Search Results: thanksgiving**

• Thanksgiving USA

Thanksgiving Canada

Harvest Festival UK

Nadia chooses the link Thanksgiving USA. This link opens a new Web page.

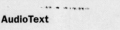

Take It to the NET
ONLINE
more activities sfsuccessnet.com

306

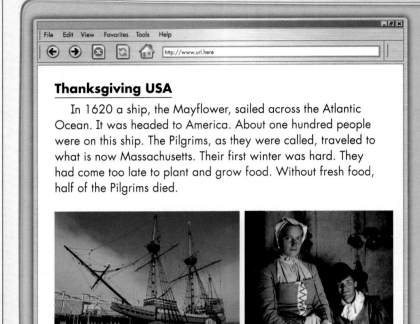

File   Edit   View   Favorites   Tools   Help

http://www.url.here

Thanksgiving USA

In 1620 a ship, the Mayflower, sailed across the Atlantic Ocean. It was headed to America. About one hundred people were on this ship. The Pilgrims, as they were called, traveled to what is now Massachusetts. Their first winter was hard. They had come too late to plant and grow food. Without fresh food, half of the Pilgrims died.

307

Audio CD **AudioText**

OBJECTIVE

● Recognize text structure: nonfiction.

Time for **SOCIAL STUDIES**

National Celebrations

There are many national celebrations in the U.S. On these days, most people do not have to go to work; they have the day off. National celebrations include Thanksgiving, Christmas, New Year's Day, the Fourth of July, and Martin Luther King Day, among others.

Read

Reading Online

PREVIEW AND PREDICT Read the title. Have children preview the article and find the captions (pp. 306 and 309). Then ask them to predict whether "Reading Online" gives information about the real world or tells a make-believe story. Have children read to learn about Web pages.

INFORMATIONAL TEXT Review that selections that provide information about the real world are called nonfiction. Point out that the captions give information about the images.

VOCABULARY/POSITION AND DIRECTION WORDS Remind children that some words describe position or direction. Have children locate *across* and *on* on p. 307. What does *across* tell about the Mayflower? What does *on* tell about the Pilgrims?

The following spring, the Iroquois Indians showed the Pilgrims how to grow corn and other plants. The Indians showed the Pilgrims how to hunt and fish. By the fall of 1621, the Pilgrims had grown a lot of food. They had much to be thankful for. They planned a huge day for giving thanks. They invited the Indian chief and 90 Indians. The Indians brought deer to roast and other foods. The Indians had taught the Pilgrims different ways to cook corn and squash. The Indians even brought popcorn to this first Thanksgiving.

308

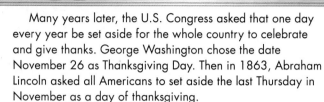

Nadia uses the scroll bar on the right-hand side of the Web page to find out more about Thanksgiving.

Many years later, the U.S. Congress asked that one day every year be set aside for the whole country to celebrate and give thanks. George Washington chose the date November 26 as Thanksgiving Day. Then in 1863, Abraham Lincoln asked all Americans to set aside the last Thursday in November as a day of thanksgiving.

Today, Thanksgiving falls on a different date every year, but it is always on the fourth Thursday of November.

309

BUILD CONCEPTS

Compare and Contrast • Inferential

• **How is reading information on a Web page the same as and different from reading information in a book?**
Possible response: They are the same because they both have information. They are different because one is electronic and the other is paper.

Author's Purpose • Critical

• **What is a likely reason that the author included pages from the Web?**
Possible response: The author used these pictures because they let the reader see what a Web page looks like on a computer screen.

CONNECT TEXT TO TEXT

How could Nadia's research on Thanksgiving help her understand *A Turkey for Thanksgiving?*

Responses will vary, but children's answers should demonstrate understanding that the Web is a valuable tool for research.

Traditions
Time for SOCIAL STUDIES

Traditions are customs which people have followed for a long time. The way that people celebrate holidays is one form of tradition. What traditions does your family observe on New Year's Day?

ELL

Access Content Ask: Do you know what a link is on a Web page? Explain that a link is a connection to another place on that page or site, or a connection to a different Web site. When children click on it, the particular location is displayed. A sample analogy would be to point to a title in a book's table of contents and having the book open to that chapter.

A Turkey for Thanksgiving **308–309**

OBJECTIVE

● Read silently with fluency.

Options for Oral Reading

Use *A Turkey for Thanksgiving* or one of the following Leveled Readers.

On-Level

Celebrating Thanksgiving

Strategic Intervention

Thanksgiving

Advanced

The Pilgrims' First Year

Use *A Thanksgiving Party* or "Thanksgiving USA." For guidance in assessing the reading fluency of English language learners, see the ELL and Transition handbook.

To develop fluent readers, use Fluency Coach.

Fluency

READ SILENTLY WITH FLUENCY

MODEL READING SILENTLY WITH FLUENCY Use *A Turkey for Thanksgiving*.

• Point to the text on pp. 292–293. When I see a word I don't know, I sound it out by syllables. When I come to the word *riverbank*, I break it down into two smaller words, *river-bank*.

• Ask children to follow along as you read the page with fluency.

• Have children read the page after you. Encourage them to self-correct when reading. Continue in the same way with pp. 294–295.

REREAD FOR FLUENCY

Silent Reading

ROUTINE

1 **Select a Passage** For *A Turkey for Thanksgiving,* use pp. 296–302.

2 **Assign** Assign each child a short passage of text.

3 **Practice** Have children read their assigned passage 3–4 times silently.

4 **Independent Readings** Have children read aloud to you. Monitor progress and provide feedback. For optimal fluency, children should read at an appropriate pace.

Monitor Progress Check Fluency WCPM

As children reread, monitor their progress toward their individual fluency goals. Current Goal: 58–68 words correct per minute. End-of-Year Goal: 90 words correct per minute.

If... children cannot read fluently at a rate of 58–68 words per minute,

then... make sure children practice with text at their independent level. Provide additional fluency practice, pairing nonfluent readers with fluent readers.

If... children already read fluently at 90 words per minute,

then... they do not need to reread three to four times.

SUCCESS PREDICTOR

Day 1 Check Word Reading	Day 2 Check High-Frequency Words	Day 3 Check Retelling	▶ **Day 4 Check** **Fluency**	Day 5 Assess Progress

Writing Across the Curriculum

WRITE List

DISCUSS Have children discuss holiday celebrations. Which one is their favorite? What does their family do to celebrate certain holidays? Encourage children to use oral vocabulary such as *participate, holiday,* and *dine.*

SHARE THE PEN Have children participate in creating a list. Explain that the class will work together to list holiday celebrations. Explain that each item on the list will include the name of a holiday and some phrases or sentences about how children's families celebrate these holidays. Have children copy the list as items are added. Write each phrase or sentence, inviting individuals to help spell the words by writing familiar letter-sounds. Ask questions, such as the following:

- What is the beginning sound you hear in the word *make?* (/m/)
- What is the vowel sound you hear in the word *make?* (/ā/)
- What is the ending sound you hear in the word *make?* (/k/)
- What letter stands for that sound? *(k)* Have a volunteer write *k.*
- What about the *e* at the end of *make?* (It makes the *a* long.)

Continue having individuals contribute to the list. Frequently reread the descriptive phrases and sentences.

Have children write a sentence at the bottom of their list, answering the question "How do you contribute when celebrating your favorite holiday?"

Holiday Celebrations

Thanksgiving	**We eat a big meal and think of things we're thankful for.**
July 4th	**We watch a parade and fireworks.**
New Year's Day	**We watch football and make resolutions for the new year.**

Fluency

SUCCESS PREDICTOR

OBJECTIVE

● Identify possessive nouns.

DAILY FIX-IT

7. she washed the dogs tail.
She washed the dog's tail.

8. That mad him happy
That made him happy.

Possessive Nouns

Mark the letter of the word that completes each sentence.

1. The ____ chair was waiting for him.
   ○ A turkey
   ○ B turkeys'
   ⊗ C turkey's

2. The first Thanksgiving was the ____ idea.
   ○ A Pilgrims's
   ○ B Pilgrim
   ⊗ C Pilgrims'

3. We ate dinner at the ____ house.
   ○ A Chins
   ⊗ B Chins'
   ○ C Chin's

4. Both ____ ears began to twitch.
   ⊗ A rabbits'
   ○ B rabbits
   ○ C rabbit's

5. One ____ breath showed in the cold air.
   ○ A moose
   ○ B mooses
   ⊗ C moose's

6. A ____ quills are very sharp.
   ⊗ A porcupine's
   ○ B porcupines'
   ○ C porcupines

Home Activity Your child prepared for taking tests on possessive nouns. Write the words goats, bear, turkeys, and porcupine on paper. Have your child add either 's or ' and something that could belong to the animals, for example, goats' food.

▲ **Grammar and Writing Practice Book** p. 39

Grammar

REVIEW Possessive Nouns

DEFINE POSSESSIVE NOUNS

• What does a possessive noun do? (shows ownership)
• How do you make a noun possessive? (Add 's to a singular noun and add ' to a plural noun.)

PRACTICE

WRITE POSSESSIVE NOUNS Write a list of phrases indicating possession on the board. Have individuals copy the list, using the correct possessive form of the noun in a sentence. Have children share their work in a group.

Phrase	Sentence
ears of one dog	The dog's ears are dirty.
tails of two cats	
shirt of one boy	
dogs of two girls	

Speaking and Listening

MAKE INTRODUCTIONS

MODEL SPEAKING AND LISTENING Remind children of appropriate speaking and listening behaviors such as speaking in a pleasant tone and listening carefully. Then ask children to think about these behaviors as they take turns introducing people.

- When you introduce people who have never met before, you should include their names and how you know them.

- If I want to introduce Jack and Jill, I'll say, "Jack, this is my friend Jill. Jill, this is my friend Jack."

- Remember to make eye contact and speak directly to the listener.

INTRODUCING PEOPLE Ask children to form groups of three. Each child will take a turn introducing the other two children to one another. Encourage them to make up different ways that they know one another.

Wrap Up Your Day!

TEXT TO SELF How are the things Billy and his friends did similar to or different than what you and your friends like to do to celebrate your birthday? (Possible response: I like to have my friends over to play, eat cake, and sing songs. I don't like to do chores on my birthday.)

LET'S TALK ABOUT IT Recall *The Blizzard*. Ask: How did Billy's school friends contribute to his birthday celebration? (They helped him with his chores, played with him, and sang with him, so he had a fun birthday.) Display the Contributing to a Celebration Graphic Organizer from Day 1. Have children add some of the things Billy's friends did to the organizer.

PREVIEW Day 5

Remind children that they heard a story about a boy who gets to celebrate his birthday with everyone from school. Tell them that tomorrow they will hear about Billy and his birthday celebration again.

Day 5
AT A GLANCE

Share Literature
The Blizzard

Phonics and Spelling
 Review Long *a: a, ai, ay*

High-Frequency Words
door	behind	brought
minute	promise	
sorry	everybody	

Monitor Progress
Spelling Test: Words with Long *a*

Group Time < Differentiated Assessment

Grammar and Writing
Possessive Nouns

Research and Study Skills
Reading a Web Page

Materials

- *Sing with Me Big Book*
- Read Aloud Anthology
- Reproducible Pages TE 310f–310g
- Student Edition 310–311

Morning Warm~Up!

This week we read about many celebrations.

Thanksgiving, Chinese New Year, and birthdays are all things to celebrate.

How can we add to a celebration?

QUESTION OF THE DAY Encourage children to sing "Holidays" from the *Sing with Me Big Book* as you gather. Write and read the message and discuss the question.

REVIEW ORAL VOCABULARY Have children name things in the message that

- they can participate in (celebrations)
- are holidays (Thanksgiving, Chinese New Year)
- require preparing food for a banquet at which people dine (Thanksgiving, Chinese New Year, birthdays)

Assess Vocabulary Use the Day 5 instruction on ELL Poster 10 to monitor children's progress with oral vocabulary.

ELL Poster 10

Share Literature

LISTEN AND RESPOND

USE PRIOR KNOWLEDGE Review that yesterday the class listened to find out about the blizzard. Suggest that today the class listen to find out about Billy's birthday celebration.

MONITOR LISTENING COMPREHENSION

- How do the schoolchildren participate in Billy's birthday? (They help Billy with his chores, they have snowball fights, they all eat together, and they sing.)

- What is served at the banquet? (ham, chicken, potatoes, beans, corn, canned beef, fresh milk, pie, and birthday cake)

- Why might the candles on Billy's birthday cake have **flared**? (Possible response: They might have flared because there are so many of them. They might have flared because of a draft in the room.)

Read Aloud Anthology
The Blizzard

BUILD ORAL VOCABULARY

SIMILES Have children recall that the size of the chocolate cookie in *The Blizzard* is compared to a saucer. Write *a chocolate cookie as big as a saucer.* Phrases that compare two unlike things using the words *like* or *as* are called *similes.* Help children find other similes in the story and list them. Challenge children to think of other similes that would fit the story.

> **chocolate cookie as big as a saucer**
>
> **Miss Bailey walked around the room like a general.**

Extend Language Tell children that similes describe one thing by comparing it to something else. Remind them that while the two things that are compared are unalike, they must have something in common. An example is describing someone's red face by saying "Her face was as red as a fire engine."

Long *a: a, ai, ay*

REVIEW

IDENTIFY *ai* AND *ay* WORDS Write these sentences. Have children read each one aloud. Call on individuals to name and underline the *ai* and *ay* words and identify the vowel sounds.

Mom <u>paid</u> the bills and put them in the <u>mail</u> <u>today</u>.

I like the <u>quaint</u> <u>painting</u> of the home by the <u>bay</u>.

The <u>snail</u> makes a <u>trail</u> as it inches its <u>way</u> along the sand.

It is a <u>gray</u> <u>day</u> because of the <u>rain</u>.

High-Frequency Words

REVIEW

CATEGORY CLUES Write the following category clues for children. Have children write the missing review word from p. 284 for each group. Then read clues and answers together.

forgive, regret, _____ (sorry)

bring, bringing, _____ (brought)

knob, lock, _____ (door)

all, everyone, _____ (everybody)

second, hour, _____ (minute)

above, in front, _____ (behind)

vow, pledge, _____ (promise)

SPELLING TEST Long *a: ai, ay*

DICTATION SENTENCES Use these sentences to assess this week's spelling words.

1. I will give <u>away</u> this old toy.
2. Dad put the food on a <u>tray</u>.
3. Can you hear what I <u>say</u>?
4. I will <u>stay</u> with Nan for two days.
5. Can you <u>play</u> after school?
6. I will <u>paint</u> my bed red.
7. You use your <u>brain</u> every day.
8. The dog wags its <u>tail</u> a lot.
9. <u>Today</u> is the first day of the year!
10. May will <u>raise</u> pigs on her farm.
11. Will you please <u>wait</u> for me?
12. This is the <u>main</u> path to the park.

CHALLENGE WORDS

13. Which <u>holiday</u> comes next?
14. I like to read the <u>daily</u> paper.
15. We made some <u>raisin</u> bread.

ASSESS

● Spell *ai, ay* words.

Spelling Words

Long *a: ai, ay*

1.	**tail**＊	7.	**raise**＊
2.	**main**	8.	**brain**
3.	**wait**＊	9.	**paint**
4.	**say**	10.	**stay**
5.	**away**＊	11.	**today**
6.	**play**	12.	**tray**

Challenge Words

13	**holiday**	15	**raisin**
14	**daily**		

＊ Words from the Selection

Group Time

On-Level	Strategic Intervention	Advanced
Read Set B Sentences and the Story for rechecking.	**Read** Set A Sentences and the Story for rechecking.	**Read** Set C Sentences and the Story for rechecking.
• Use pp. 310e–310g.	• Use pp. 310e–310g.	• Use pp. 310e–310g.
	• Use the **Routine** on p. DI·32.	• Use the **Routine** on p. DI·33.

DAY 5

 Place English language learners in the groups that correspond to their reading abilities in English.

(i) Independent Activities

Fluency Reading Children reread selections at their independent level.

Journal Writing List activities people can participate in during a holiday. Share writing.

Independent Reading See p. 282j for Reading/Library activities and suggestions.

Literacy Centers You may use the Technology Center on p. 282k to support this week's concepts and reading.

Practice Book 2.1 Read a Web page, p. 100

Break into small groups after Spelling and before Grammar and Writing.

ASSESS

- Decode long *a: a, ai, ay*.
- Read high-frequency words.
- Read aloud with appropriate speed and accuracy.
- Draw conclusions.
- Retell a story.

Differentiated Assessment

On-Level
Set B

Strategic Intervention
Set A

Advanced
Set C

Fluency Assessment Plan

☑ Week 1 assess Advanced students.

☑ Week 2 assess Strategic Intervention students.

☑ Week 3 assess On-Level students.

☑ Week 4 assess Strategic Intervention students.

☑ **This week assess any students you have not yet checked during this unit.**

Set individual fluency goals for children to enable them to reach the end-of-year goal.

- Current Goal: 58–68 wcpm
- End-of-Year Goal: 90 wcpm
- **ELL** For guidance in evaluating fluency, see the ELL and Transition Handbook.

SENTENCE READING

ASSESS LONG *a: a, ai, ay* AND HIGH-FREQUENCY WORDS Use one of the reproducible lists on p. 310f to assess children's ability to read long *a: a, ai, ay* and high-frequency words. Call on individuals to read two sentences aloud. Have each child in the group read different sentences. Start over with sentence one if necessary.

RECORD SCORES Use the Sentence Reading Chart for this unit on p. 313k.

Monitor Progress	Long *a: a, ai, ay*
If... children have trouble reading long *a: a, ai, ay*,	**then...** use the Reteach Lesson on p. DI·68.
High-Frequency Words	
If... children cannot read a high-frequency word,	**then...** mark the missed words on a high-frequency word list and send the list home for additional word reading practice or have the child practice with a fluent reader.

FLUENCY AND COMPREHENSION

ASSESS FLUENCY Take a one-minute sample of children's oral reading. See Monitoring Fluency, p. 313i. Have children read "The Day of the Mermaid," the on-level fluency passage on p. 310g.

RECORD SCORES Record the number of words read correctly in a minute on the child's Fluency Progress Chart.

ASSESS COMPREHENSION Have the child read to the end of the passage. (If the child had difficulty with the passage, you may read it aloud.) Ask the child to draw conclusions/make inferences about the story and have the child retell the passage. Use the Retelling Rubric on p. 303g to evaluate the child's retelling.

Monitor Progress	Fluency
If... a child does not achieve the fluency goal on the timed reading,	**then...** copy the passage and send it home with the child for additional fluency practice or have the child practice with a fluent reader.
Draw Conclusions	
If... a child cannot draw conclusions/make inferences,	**then...** use the Reteach Lesson on p. DI·68.

READ THE SENTENCES

Set A

1. Mark brought the mail and paper inside.
2. Everybody was sorry Jay couldn't stay longer.
3. We will wait by the trail for one more minute.
4. I promise to clean the tray before I play.
5. Do not put hay away behind the barn door.
6. A chain keeps the main door shut.

Set B

1. Bess brought the gray sand pail to the beach.
2. The train may be here any minute now.
3. We promise to make you a plain vase from the clay later.
4. Ray was sorry he didn't pay the bill on time.
5. Hang the apron on the nail behind the door.
6. Which way did everybody go after class today?

Set C

1. We promise to call and say hello the minute we sail into town.
2. The clouds brought so much rain that all the grain got soaked.
3. We are sorry we could not paint the fence, but we will do it in April.
4. The maid sprayed the room and closed the door when she was finished cleaning.
5. Everybody in the club will fly to Spain for a holiday trip.
6. Jada's dog strayed from behind her home.

Monitor Progress | Long *a: a, ai, ay*
High-Frequency Words

SUCCESS
PREDICTOR

The Day of the Mermaid

Gail and her brother David lived in a plain   9
house on a plain street. Each day was the same   19
for Gail. She wanted something different.   25

She could not wait for the big family trip. They   35
were going far away. Later that week, they took a   45
train to a lake. Then the family went sailing. Gail 55
looked into the water. "I can see a mermaid," she   65
said to David.   68

"You do not. There are no such things as   77
mermaids," said David. David saw a sad look in   86
Gail's eyes. So he decided to play along with the   96
game and put some excitement into the trip. "I   105
can see a whale that's 50 feet long!"   113

"I see it too," Gail said with glee. "Now I see a   125
squid with 20 arms! It's right next to a huge snail." 136

Gail and David laughed as they made up things   145
they saw in the water. Gail was having an amazing   155
day. And it was different from all the rest.   164

Monitor Progress | Fluency Passage

SUCCESS PREDICTOR

Possessive Nouns

A noun that shows who or what owns something is a **possessive noun.** To show ownership, add an **apostrophe** (') and **-s** when the noun is singular. Add just an **apostrophe** (') when the noun is plural.

The quills of the **porcupine** are sharp.

The **porcupine's** quills are sharp.

The **'s** shows that the quills belong to one porcupine.

The house of the **goats** is by the river.
The **goats'** house is by the river.

The **'** after the **s** shows that the house belongs to more than one goat.

310

Write Using Possessive Nouns

1. Rewrite these phrases using possessive nouns.

the long ears of two rabbits

the feathers of one turkey

2. Write a sentence that tells about Turkey. Use possessive nouns to show ownership.

3. Who would you invite for Thanksgiving dinner? Write some sentences to use as an invitation. Use possessive nouns to show ownership.

311

Grammar and Writing

WRITE USING POSSESSIVE NOUNS Read pp. 310–311 aloud. Guide children as they complete the items.

1. the rabbits' long ears; the turkey's feathers

2. Possible response: Turkey's family joined him for dinner.

CONNECT TO UNIT WRITING Children write sentences to use as an invitation. They should use possessive nouns to show ownership.

3. Possible response:

I would invite my cousins and my pets.

Bob, Susan, Quinn, Spot, and Lucky, I hope you can join my parents and me for Thanksgiving dinner. Dad's turkey dinner is good! Mom's pies are the best in the world! I will move all the pets' toys out of the way. Come eat with us!

DAILY FIX-IT

9. It wasnt' long befoe they left.
It wasn't long before they left.

10. What fune they had.
What fun they had!

Possessive Nouns
Add 's or ' to each noun in ( ).
Write the words on the line.

I. two (bears) houses

two bears' houses

2. the (turkey) gobble

the turkey's gobble

3. many (donkeys) laughter

many donkeys' laughter

Add 's or ' to the underlined word.
Write the sentence on the line.

4. Some <u>roosters</u> feathers are brown.

Some roosters' feathers are brown.

5. A <u>bear</u> fur is thick.

A bear's fur is thick.

6. <u>Rabbits</u> tails are fluffy.

Rabbits' tails are fluffy.

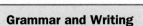 **Home Activity** Your child reviewed possessive nouns. Have your child look through a newspaper or magazine article and circle any possessive nouns that he or she finds. Then ask your child to explain how the possessive noun was made.

▲ **Grammar and Writing Practice Book** p. 40

Turkey for Thanksgiving   **310–311**

5

OBJECTIVE

● Use electronic sources: Web pages.

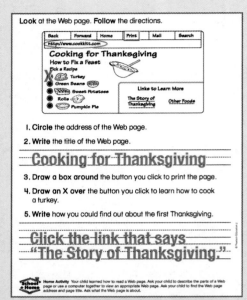

Look at the Web page. **Follow** the directions.

Cooking for Thanksgiving
How to Fix a Feast
Pick a Recipe
Turkey
Green Beans
Sweet Potatoes
Rolls
Pumpkin Pie

Links to Learn More
The Story of Thanksgiving   Other Foods

1. **Circle** the address of the Web page.
2. **Write** the title of the Web page.

Cooking for Thanksgiving

3. **Draw a box around** the button you click to print the page.
4. **Draw an X over** the button you click to learn how to cook a turkey.
5. **Write** how you could find out about the first Thanksgiving.

Click the link that says "The Story of Thanksgiving."

Home Activity Your child learned how to read a Web page. Ask your child to describe the parts of a Web page or use a computer together to view an appropriate Web page. Ask your child to find the Web page address and page title. Ask what the Web page is about.

▲ **Practice Book 2.1** p. 100, Web Page

Access Content Make sure English language learners understand the terms for the different parts of a Web page: URL, the scroll bar, and the search box. Explain that *URL* is another way of saying "address"; the *scroll bar* is the tool you use to scroll, or move up and down, a page on the screen; and the *search box* is the place where you enter what you want to search, or look for.

Research/Study Skills

TEACH/MODEL Reading a Web Page

MODEL READING A WEB PAGE Show children the artwork from "Reading a Web Page," or, if you have a computer with Internet access in your classroom, open an appropriate site. Point out different elements of the Web page, such as the URL, the scroll bar, and the search box. Explain that Web pages help you find information.

Model how to read a Web page.

 MODEL I can use this Web page to find information. First, I use the scroll bar to read all of the text on the page. There might also be links to related information. These links might be blue text or buttons. When I click on a link, it takes me to another page. The URL is the address for the site.

DISCUSS HOW TO READ A WEB PAGE Call on individuals to explain how to maneuver in a Web site.

PRACTICE

DEMONSTRATE READING A WEB PAGE Print out and provide copies of a Web page to children. Have children label the URL, scroll bar, and search box. If you have Internet access in your classroom, give partners time to explore different Web pages that you recommend.

Wrap Up Your Week!

LET'S TALK ABOUT Working Together

QUESTION OF THE WEEK Recall this week's question.

- How can we contribute to a celebration?

  Display the Celebration web. Have children name celebrations where they could help prepare, serve, entertain, or clean up.

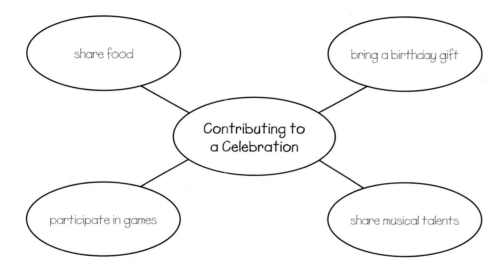

share food

bring a birthday gift

Contributing to a Celebration

participate in games

share musical talents

CONNECT Use questions such as these to prompt a discussion.

- You participate in celebrations by sharing meals with friends and family. How did Ronald participate with his baseball team in *Ronald Morgan Goes to Bat?*

- The characters in *A Turkey for Thanksgiving* dine together. If Jim in *Tara and Tiree* prepared a special meal for his dogs to dine on, what might it be?

Build Background Use ELL Poster 11 to support the Preview activity.

PREVIEW Tell children that next week they will read about how inventors work together to turn ideas into inventions.

PREVIEW Next Week

Unit 2
Wrap-Up

OBJECTIVES

- Discuss the unit theme.
- Connect content across selections.
- Combine content and skills in meaningful activities that build literacy.
- Respond to unit selections through a variety of modalities.

WORKING TOGETHER
Discuss the Big Idea

How can we work together?

Help children relate the theme question for this unit to the selections and their own experiences. Write the questions and prompt discussion with questions such as the following. Then assign the Wrap-Up activities.

- **How did the characters in the selections work together?** (Possible answers: *Tara and Tiree, Fearless Friends* The dogs and their owner worked together to save one another's lives. *Ronald Morgan Goes to Bat* Ronald Morgan helped his team by providing team spirit. *Turtle's Race with Beaver* Beaver learned the value of cooperation after losing a race with Turtle. *The Bremen Town Musicians* A team of animals worked together to overpower robbers. *A Turkey for Thanksgiving* Animals worked together to have a happy meal at Thanksgiving, including Turkey.)

- **Why does working together make solving a problem easier?** (Possible answer: When more than one person works on a problem, they can find a solution together and share the work.)

- **Which character would you like to work with if you had a problem?** (Answers will vary.)

Working Together Poster

Think about all the stories you read in this unit. What lessons did you learn from them? Work with a group. Make a list of rules for working together in school. Talk about what you learned from the stories as you make your list.

Rules for Working Together
1.
2.
3.
4.
5.

How can we work together?

Go Along, Get Along Sock Puppets

connect to **DRAMA**

Choose two characters from different stories in Unit 2. Make a sock puppet for each one. Have the two puppets talk to each other. They should tell about what happened to them and what they learned about working together with others.

Team Member Award

connect to **SOCIAL STUDIES**

Ronald Morgan was not a great hitter, but he was an important part of his team. Think about how you add something important to a group. Make an award for yourself. The award should show and tell about how you help the group as you work together.

Tony the Reading helper
I help other kids read hard books.

313

Unit Inquiry Project Rubric

4	3	2	1
• Child participates in planning and implementation of club. Works well within a group. Takes both leadership and participant roles as appropriate. • Actively discusses problems and way to address them. Takes active part in class presentation.	• Takes an active role, but sometimes holds back cooperation in group. Does not take a leadership role or, if so, does not delegate responsibility. • Child participates in club, but is not proactive. Participates in presentation but does not take major role.	• Participates in planning and implementation when asked, but does not volunteer. Does not always participate in discussion. • Child participates in club to a minimal degree. Participates only minimally in presentation to class.	• Refrains from adding to group brainstorming and club discussion. Does not work well with others in group. • Child does not participate in club or discussion.

Writing Workshop

How-to Report

OBJECTIVES

- Develop an understanding of expository writing.
- Explain the steps of a process in the correct order.
- Use processes and strategies that good writers use.

Key Features
How-to Report

A how-to report is written as step-by-step directions that others can easily follow.

- Explains a task fully
- Uses words such as *first* to show the order of steps
- Provides necessary information and details
- Has clear sentences to guide the reader

Connect to Weekly Writing

Writing Transparencies 6-10

Strategic Intervention

See Differentiated Instruction p. 313g.

Advanced

See Differentiated Instruction p. 313h.

ELL

See Differentiated Instruction p. 313h.

Writing Prompt: Working Together
Think about something that you can make or do, such as a craft or a game. Write an explanation for a friend of how to make or do this thing. Make sure the steps are clear and in order.
Purpose: Explain how to make or do something
Audience: A friend

READ LIKE A WRITER

Ask children to look back at *Tara and Tiree.* Discuss with the children the steps that the dogs take to save their owner's life. Point out why the order of these steps is important. Ask children to think of something that they can make or do in three or four steps. Tell them that they will be writing a how-to report.

SHOW THE MODEL AND RUBRIC

GUIDED WRITING Read the model aloud. Point out the time-order words. (*First, Next, Now, Then, Last*)

- Read the sentences that begin with time-order words. Point out that the writer uses these words to make the order of the steps clear.
- Point out that most of the sentences are commands, which are common in a how-to report because the writer is telling readers what to do.
- Discuss how the model reflects traits of good writing.

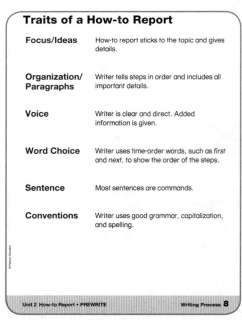

How to Make a Terrarium

Making a terrarium isn't hard. All you need are pebbles, charcoal chips, a glass container, and a plastic jar cover.

First, spread a layer of charcoal chips on the bottom. This will keep the terrarium smelling fresh. Next, spread pebbles over the chips. This will help water drain from the soil. Now put a layer of soil on the pebbles. Then poke holes in the soil and put in the plants. Last, put the cover over the container.

You can make your terrarium special. Add bugs, moss, and lizards.

Unit 2 How-to Report • PREWRITE   Writing Process **7**

Traits of a How-to Report

Focus/Ideas	How-to report sticks to the topic and gives details.
Organization/ Paragraphs	Writer tells steps in order and includes all important details.
Voice	Writer is clear and direct. Added information is given.
Word Choice	Writer uses time-order words, such as *first* and *next*, to show the order of the steps.
Sentence	Most sentences are commands.
Conventions	Writer uses good grammar, capitalization, and spelling.

Unit 2 How-to Report • PREWRITE   Writing Process **8**

▲ **Writing Transparency** WP7   ▲ **Writing Transparency** WP8

FINDING A TOPIC

MAKE A LIST Have children make a list of things they can make or do, such as foods they know how to make, games they know how to play, or crafts they know how to make.

NARROW THE CHOICE Have children ask questions about the ideas they have chosen. They might ask: How well do I know this topic? Is there too much information to explain? Would the topic interest my audience?

Think Aloud **MODEL** Most kids know how to play tag. Swimming is a big topic. I don't think I could explain it in three or four steps. I've made scratch-art pictures in class, and it was fun. I know I can give clear directions about how to do it.

PREWRITING STRATEGY

USE A HOW-TO CHART Use Writing Transparency WP9 to show how to organize the steps in a process.

Think Aloud **MODEL** The title tells what the writer is going to explain how to make. This tells readers exactly what the how-to report is about. Then the writer tells the steps in the process. The boxes help put the steps in the correct 1-2-3-4 order.

PREWRITING ACTIVITY Have children use the How-to Chart graphic organizer on Grammar and Writing Practice Book p. 164 to help them organize the steps in their process.

Topic Ideas

how to play tag
how to swim
how to make a scratch-art picture

How-to Chart

Fill out this how-to chart to help you organize your ideas.

Title: ___How to Make a Scratch-Art Picture___

Step 1
Color part of paper with a crayon.

⬇

Step 2
Switch crayons and keep coloring.

⬇

Step 3
Paint paper black.

⬇

Step 4
Scratch with toothpick.

Unit 2 How-to Report • PREWRITE   Writing Process **9**

▲ **Writing Transparency** WP9

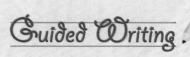

Guided Writing

Some children will need additional guidance as they plan and write their how-to reports. You might give these children the option of writing a group report under your supervision or pair them with a more able writer.

How-to Chart

Fill out this how-to chart to help you organize your ideas.

Title _____

Step 1   Answers will vary.

⬇

Step 2

⬇

Step 3

⬇

Step 4

▲ **Grammar and Writing Practice Book** p. 164

Writing Workshop

Think Like a Writer

Use Strong Verbs Explain that when you write directions, you need to use strong verbs so that the listener can clearly visualize the steps in the process. For example, if you write about a craft project, you may use words such as *press, paint,* or *glue.*

Support Writing Ask children to describe a few of their topic ideas. Help them narrow their topics to one that they are able to explain. Have children write an action verb for each of the steps in the process and then write sentences using these verbs.

WRITING THE FIRST DRAFT

GUIDED WRITING Have children review their How-to Charts to help them organize their steps as they write their first drafts. Remind them to do the following.

- Begin with an introduction that grabs the interest of their audience.
- Make sure directions are in order.
- Use time-order words.
- Use strong verbs that give specific directions.

Strong Words

cut

press

remove

attach

glue

USE STRONG WORDS Write the strong verbs on the board. Explain that each step in a how-to report tells an action and uses a verb. Show how verbs that are exact give readers a clear picture of what to do.

Weak Verb   Put the beans in the dirt.

Strong Verb   Press the beans in the dirt.

DRAFTING STRATEGIES

WRITE WHAT TO DO IN ORDER Suggest that children write a list of action verbs that tell what they do in each step of their how-to report. Then they can use this list to write sentences telling the steps in their report.

PRACTICE USING TIME-ORDER WORDS Have children use Grammar and Writing Practice Book p. 165 to practice using time-order words.

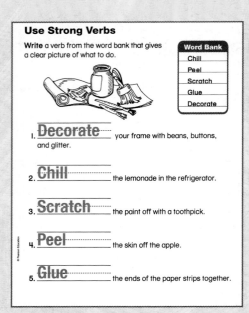

Use Strong Verbs

Write a verb from the word bank that gives a clear picture of what to do.

Word Bank
Chill
Peel
Scratch
Glue
Decorate

1. **Decorate** your frame with beans, buttons, and glitter.

2. **Chill** the lemonade in the refrigerator.

3. **Scratch** the paint off with a toothpick.

4. **Peel** the skin off the apple.

5. **Glue** the ends of the paper strips together.

▲ **Grammar and Writing Practice Book** p. 165

REVISING STRATEGIES

GUIDED WRITING Use Writing Transparency WP10 to model how to revise a how-to report.

MODEL The writer changed *it* to *the paper* to clearly identify what is being colored. She changed the verb *Color* to *Press*, which tells exactly what to do. She added the sentence, *keep switching until all the papers are colored,* signaling when to end the coloring.

How to Make a Scratch-Art Picture

Would you like to make a very different picture? Make scratch-art with your friends. Start by giving each person a sheet of paper and a different color of crayon First, color part of it. ^the paper

^Press
~~Color~~ hard so that the color is dark. Then swich crayons with another person and color another part of your paper. Next, paint the paper black. Keep switching crayons until the whole sheet is colored.

Last, when the paint is dry, take toothpicks. Scratch off some black paint so you can see the colors. Make a design or draw a picture.

Be creative!

Unit 2 How-to Report • REVISE   Writing Process **10**

▲ **Writing Transparency** WP10

WRITER'S CRAFT ORGANIZATION

ELABORATION Write the following sentences on the board. Ask children to put the sentences in order.

How to Meet a New Kid at School

Show the new person around the school.

Walk up to the new person.

Tell the new person your name.

TIP Adding time-order words to the sentences will make order clearer.

First, walk up to the new person.

Next, tell the new person your name.

Then show the new person around the school.

ADDITIONAL SUPPORT Point out how the revisions on Writing Transparency WP10 clarify what to do in the steps. Use Grammar and Writing Practice Book p. 166 to improve sentences by adding details.

APPLY WRITER'S CRAFT Have children examine organization in their writing.

- Write the Revising Checklist on the board or make copies to distribute. Children can use this checklist to revise their how-to reports.

Revising Checklist

✔ Does the how-to report tell how to make or do something?

✔ Have I put the steps in the correct order?

✔ Did I use time-order words?

✔ Do strong verbs tell readers exactly what to do?

ELL

Extend Language To help children add time-order words to their writing, work with them to make a list of time-order words. Begin with *first, next, then,* and *last*. Encourage them to find other time-order words in their reading and add the words to the list. (*now, later, second, third, finally*).

Writing Trait: Organization

Put the steps in the order they happened. Write a time-order word from the word bank to complete each step.

Word Bank
First
Next
Then
Last

How-to Make a Frozen Yogurt Sundae

Then _or_ Next, add your favorite fruit toppings.

First, take frozen yogurt out of the freezer.

Last, eat your delicious yogurt sundae.

Next or Then, scoop frozen yogurt into a dish.

▲ **Grammar and Writing Practice Book** p. 166

Writing Workshop

1 PREWRITE 2 DRAFT 3 REVISE 4 EDIT 5 PUBLISH

Editing Checklist

- ✔ Did I spell words correctly, including those that end with *ch, sh,* or *x*?

- ✔ Did I use the correct plural forms for nouns?

- ✔ Does each sentence begin with a capital letter and end with the correct punctuation mark?

Support Writing When reviewing a child's draft, focus on ideas more than errors. If you find consistent spelling errors, choose one or two skills for attention during editing. Reinforce the skills with the appropriate Phonics Transition lessons in the ELL and Transition Handbook.

EDITING STRATEGY

WORK WITH A PARTNER Have children work with a partner. Ask them to read each other's report and look for errors. They should circle possible errors and then discuss them with their partner. Model this strategy using Writing Transparency WP11.

 MODEL When I proofread, I look for missing or incorrect punctuation, misspelled words, and words that need capital letters. The word *crayon* ends a sentence, so the writer has added a period there. The sentence that begins with *First* begins the steps of the process, so she has started a new paragraph there. That's good. The word *swich* doesn't look right. It needs a *t.* The writer has fixed that.

Write the Editing Checklist on the board or make copies to distribute. Children can use this checklist to edit their how-to reports.

Tech Talk **OFFLINE** If children are using a computer to type their how-to reports, they may find these tips useful.

- If your program has a thesaurus, look up some of the verbs you use in your steps and see if you can find a better word.

- If your program has a print preview or a page layout feature, use this to show you how the work will appear on your page before you print it out.

Proofreading Marks

Add Period	⊙
Add	^
Spelling	◯
Paragraph	¶

How to Make a Scratch-Art Picture

Would you like to make a very different picture? Make scratch-art with your friends. Start by giving each person a sheet of paper and a different color of crayon First, color part of it. Press Color hard so that the color is dark. Then swich crayons with another person and color another part of your paper. Next, paint the paper black.

Last, when the paint is dry, take toothpicks. Scratch off some black paint so you can see the colors. Make a design or draw a picture.

Be creative!

Unit 2 How-to Report • EDIT   Writing Process **11**

▲ **Writing Transparency** WP11

SELF-EVALUATION

Prepare children to fill out a Self-Evaluation Guide. Display Writing Transparency WP12 to model the self-evaluation process.

Think Aloud

MODEL Steps are in the right order, and there are words that show this order. *Press, switch,* and *scratch* are strong verbs. I would mark *Yes* for numbers 1, 2, and 3. My favorite part is about scratching the paint off with toothpicks. If I wrote this how-to report again, I would list the materials you need at the beginning.

Assign Grammar and Writing Practice Book p. 167. Children can save their Self-Evaluation Guides and their work in a portfolio to monitor their development as writers. Encourage them to build on their skills and note areas to improve.

How to Make a Scratch-Art Picture

Would you like to make a very different picture? Make scratch-art with your friends. Start by giving each person a sheet of paper and a different color of crayon.

First, color part of the paper. Press hard so that the color is dark. Then switch crayons with another person and color another part of your paper. Keep switching crayons until the whole sheet is colored. Next, paint the paper black.

Last, when the paint is dry, take toothpicks and scratch off some black paint so you can see the colors. Make a design or draw a picture. Be creative!

Unit 2 How-to-Report • PUBLISH   Writing Process **12**

▲ **Writing Transparency** WP12

Ideas for Publishing

Demonstrations Children can take turns demonstrating the process they described in their how-to reports.

Class Products Children can illustrate or make their products. Display the products in the classroom.

Self-Evaluation Guide

Check *Yes* or *No* about organization and word choice in your report.

	Yes	No
1. I wrote the steps in the correct order.		
2. I used one or more time-order words to show the order.		
3. I used one or more strong verbs to tell what to do.		

Answer the questions.

4. What is the best part of your report?

Answers will vary.

5. What is one thing you would change about this report if you could write it again?

Answers will vary.

▲ **Grammar and Writing Practice Book** p. 167

Scoring Rubric   How-to Report

Rubric 4 3 2 1	4	3	2	1
Focus/Ideas	How-to report focused on topic; gives all important steps	How-to report generally focused on topic; gives most steps	How-to report not clearly focused; gives few steps	How-to report with no focus or steps
Organization/ Paragraphs	Steps organized in correct order	Steps mostly organized in correct order	Some steps not in order or missing	No order
Voice	Clear, knowledgeable voice	Fairly clear, knowledgeable voice	No clear voice	Uninvolved or indifferent
Word Choice	Uses time-order words and strong verbs	Uses some time-order words and strong verbs	Few time-order words or strong verbs	Incorrect or limited word choice
Sentences	Clear sentences; use of commands	Mostly clear sentences; some commands	Sentences unclear; few commands	Incoherent sentences; no commands
Conventions	Shows good understanding of writing conventions	Shows understanding of most writing conventions	Shows understanding of some writing conventions	Contains serious errors that detract from writing and may prevent understanding

For 6-, 5-, and 3-point Scoring Rubrics, see pp. TR1–5.

How-to Report
Differentiated Instruction

WRITING PROMPT: Working Together

Think about something that you can make or do, such as a craft or a game. Write an explanation for a friend of how to make or do this thing. Make sure the steps are clear and in order.

Purpose: Explain how to make or do something

Audience: A friend

MODIFY INSTRUCTION

Pick One

ALTERNATIVE PROMPTS

ALTERNATIVE PROMPT: Expository Writing

Strategic Intervention Think of something you know how to do, such as make your bed or brush your teeth. Write the steps in a list. Put a number next to each step. Make sure the steps are in the right order.

On-Level Explain a simple task, such as making a sandwich, to someone who doesn't know how to do it. Write the steps. Then pretend you are giving your how-to report as an oral report. Choose some visual aids that you can show to your audience as you explain the steps in the process.

Advanced Think of a craft or game that involves four-to-six steps. Write a how-to report that explains this activity. Include a brief introduction to involve your reader. Add a concluding sentence.

Strategic Intervention

MODIFY THE PROMPT

Help emerging writers choose a topic. Write the key words in the prompt on the board (craft or game, explanation, steps are clear, in order) and discuss them with children. Offer examples of what is meant by the key words.

PREWRITING SUPPORT

- As a class, discuss things that children know how to make or do. Tell children about things that you know how to make or do.

- Show children examples of how-to writing, such as game instructions, recipes, and manuals. Read aloud excerpts to children.

- Let children dictate to you the process they want to explain in their how-to report. Record their steps and circle key words or concepts. Ask them questions about these key elements. Help them write an opening sentence.

OPTIONS

- Give children the option of writing a group how-to report under your supervision.

CHECK PROGRESS Segment the assignment into manageable pieces. Check work at intervals, such as graphic organizers and first drafts, to make sure writing is on track.

MODIFY THE PROMPT

Expect advanced writers to produce writing that includes more details and steps. They should choose specific words, especially verbs, that give their writing a clear voice. Some writers may use compound and complex sentences. Require advanced writers to include an introduction and a conclusion.

APPLY SKILLS

- As children edit their work, have them consider some ways to improve it.

  Check that each sentence has a subject and a predicate.

  Make sure each sentence ends with the correct punctuation mark.

  Look up words in a dictionary to see whether they are spelled correctly.

OPTIONS

- Work with children to create their own class rubrics. Follow these steps.
  1. Read examples of class how-to reports and rank them 1–4, with 4 the highest.
  2. Discuss how they arrived at each rank.
  3. Isolate the six traits and make a rubric based on them.

CHECK PROGRESS Discuss children's Self-Evaluation Guides. Work with children to monitor their growth and identify their strengths and weaknesses as writers.

MODIFY THE PROMPT

Provide Beginning speakers with a framework of partial sentences that are pertinent to the writing assignment. Have children fill in the blanks.

BUILD BACKGROUND

- Point out that a report gives information. A how-to report gives information about how to make or do something. Discuss the list of Key Features of a how-to report that appears in the left column of p. 313a.

OPTIONS

- As children write their how-to reports, guide them toward books, magazines, or Web sites that provide comprehension support through features such as the following.

  instructions for games and activities

  recipes

  directions for crafts

  text in the home-language

- For more suggestions on scaffolding the Writing Workshop, see the ELL and Transition Handbook.

CHECK PROGRESS You may need to explain certain traits and help children fill out their Self-Evaluation Guides. Downplay conventions and focus more on ideas. Recognize examples of vocabulary growth and efforts to use language in more complex ways.

Monitoring Fluency

Ongoing assessment of student reading fluency is one of the most valuable measures we have of students' reading skills. One of the most effective ways to assess fluency is taking timed samples of students' oral reading and measuring the number of words correct per minute (WCPM).

How to Measure Words Correct Per Minute—WCPM

Choose a Text
Start by choosing a text for the student to read. The text should be:
- narrative
- unfamiliar
- on grade level

Make a copy of the text for yourself and have one for the student.

Timed Reading of the Text
Tell the student: As you read this aloud, I want you to do your best reading and to read as quickly as you can. That doesn't mean it's a race. Just do your best, fast reading. When I say *begin,* start reading.

As the student reads, follow along in your copy. Mark words that are read incorrectly.

Incorrect	Correct
• omissions	• self-corrections within 3 seconds
• substitutions	• repeated words
• mispronunciations	
• reversals	

After One Minute
At the end of one minute, draw a line after the last word that was read. Have the student finish reading but don't count any words beyond one minute. Arrive at the words correct per minute—WCPM—by counting the total number of words that the student read correctly in one minute.

Fluency Goals
Grade 2 End-of-Year Goal = 90 WCPM

Target goals by unit

Unit 1 50 to 60 WCPM	**Unit 4** 74 to 84 WCPM
Unit 2 58 to 68 WCPM	**Unit 5** 82 to 92 WCPM
Unit 3 66 to 76 WCPM	**Unit 6** 90 to 100 WCPM

More Frequent Monitoring
You may want to monitor some children more frequently because they are falling far below grade-level benchmarks or they have a result that doesn't seem to align with their previous performance. Follow the same steps above, but choose 2 or 3 additional texts.

Fluency Progress Chart Copy the chart on the next page. Use it to record each student's progress across the year.

Fluency Progress Chart, Grade 2

Name _____

	1	2	3	4	5	6	7	8	9	10	11	12	13	14	15	16	17	18	19	20	21	22	23	24	25	26	27	28	29	30
125																														
120																														
115																														
110																														
105																														
100																														
95																														
90																														
85																														
80																														
75																														
70																														
65																														
60																														
55																														
50																														
45																														
40																														
35																														
30																														

Timed Reading

Sentence Reading Chart
Unit 2

	Phonics		High-Frequency		Reteach ✓	Reassess: Words Correct
	Total Words	Words Correct	Total Words	Words Correct		
Week 1 *Tara and Tiree, Fearless Friends* A B C						
r-Controlled *ar, or, ore:* Syllables VCCV	4					
High-Frequency Words			2			
Week 2 *Ronald Morgan Goes to Bat* A B C						
Contractions *n't, 's, 'll, 'm*	4					
High-Frequency Words			2			
Week 3 *Turtle's Race with Beaver* A B C						
r-Controlled *er, ir, ur:* Syllables VCCV	4					
High-Frequency Words			2			
Week 4 *The Bremen Town Musicians* A B C						
Plurals -s, -es, -ies	4					
High-Frequency Words			2			
Week 5 *A Turkey for Thanksgiving* A B C						
Long *a: a, ai, ay;* Syllables VCV	4					
High-Frequency Words			2			
Unit Scores	**20**		**10**			

- **RECORD SCORES** Use this chart to record scores for the Day 5 Sentence Reading Assessment. Circle A, B, or C to record which set of sentences was used.
- **RETEACH PHONICS SKILLS** If the child is unable to read all the tested phonics words, then reteach the phonics skills using the Reteach lessons on pp. DI·64–DI·68.

- **PRACTICE HIGH-FREQUENCY WORDS** If the child is unable to read all the tested high-frequency words, then provide additional practice for the week's words. See pp. 188e, 216e, 250e, 280e, and 310e.
- **REASSESS** Use the same set of sentences or an easier set for reassessment.

Unit 2
Assess and Regroup

FYI In Grade 2 there are opportunities for regrouping every five weeks—at the end of Units 2, 3, 4, and 5. These options offer sensitivity to each child's progress although some teachers may prefer to regroup less frequently.

Regroup for Unit 3

To make regrouping decisions at the end of Unit 2, consider children's end-of-unit scores for

- Units 1 and 2 Sentence Reading (Day 5 Assessments)
- Fluency (WCPM)
- Units 1 and 2 Benchmark Tests

Group Time

On-Level	Strategic Intervention	Advanced
To continue On-Level or to move into the On-Level group, children should	**Children would benefit from Strategic Intervention if they**	**To move to the Advanced group, children should**
• score 80% or better on their cumulative Units 1 and 2 Scores for Sentence Reading for phonics and high-frequency words	• score 60% or lower on their cumulative Units 1 and 2 Scores for Sentence Reading for phonics and high-frequency words, regardless of their fluency scores	• score 100% on their cumulative Units 1 and 2 Scores for Sentence Reading for phonics and high-frequency words
• meet the current benchmark for fluency (58–68 WCPM), reading On-Level text such as Student Edition selections	• do not meet the current benchmark for fluency (58–68 WCPM)	• score 95% on the Units 1 and 2 Benchmark Tests
• score 80% or better on the Units 1 and 2 Benchmark Tests	• score below 80% on their cumulative Units 1 and 2 Scores for Sentence Reading for phonics and high-frequency words AND have fluency scores below the current benchmark of 58–68 WCPM	• read above grade-level material (58–68 WCPM) with speed, accuracy, and expression. You may try them out on one of the Advanced Selections.
• be capable of working in the On-Level group based on teacher judgment	• score below 60% on the Units 1 and 2 Benchmark Tests	• use expansive vocabulary and ease of language in retelling
	• are struggling to keep up with the On-Level group based on teacher judgment	• be capable of handling the problem solving and the investigative work of the Advanced group based on teacher judgment

QUESTIONS TO CONSIDER

- What types of test questions did the child miss? Are they specific to a particular skill or strategy?
- Does the child have adequate background knowledge to understand the test passages or selections for retelling?
- Has the child's performance met expectations for daily lessons and assessments with little or no reteaching?
- Is the child performing more like children in another group?
- Does the child read for enjoyment, different purposes, and with varied interests?

Benchmark Fluency Scores

Current Goal: 58–68 WCPM

End-of-Year Goal: 90 WCPM

Unit Scores for Sentence Reading

Phonics	High-Frequency Words
100% = **20**	100% = **10**
80% = **16**	80% = **8**
60% = **12**	60% = **6**

Glossary

Glossary

Aa

agriculture (ag ruh KUL cher) **Agriculture** is farming and growing crops. *NOUN*

amazing (uh MAY zing) Something that is **amazing** is very surprising: The hero made an **amazing** escape. *ADJECTIVE*

astronaut (ASS truh nawt) An **astronaut** is a person who has been trained to fly in a spacecraft. While in space, **astronauts** repair space stations and do experiments. *NOUN*

astronaut

Bb

brave (BRAYV) If you are **brave**, you are not afraid: The **brave** girl pulled her little brother away from the burning leaves. *ADJECTIVE*

buried (BAIR eed) If you have **buried** something, you have hidden or covered it up: It was so cold that she **buried** her head under the covers. *VERB*

Cc

cactus (KAK tuhss) A **cactus** is a plant with sharp parts but no leaves. Most **cactuses** grow in very hot, dry areas of North and South America. Many have bright flowers. *NOUN*

cactus

challenge (CHAL lunj) To **challenge** is to call or invite someone to a game or contest: The knight **challenged** his rival to fight a duel. *VERB*

chiles (CHIL ayz) **Chiles** are a green or red pepper with a hot taste. *NOUN*

climate (KLY mit) **Climate** is the kind of weather a place has. *NOUN*

clutched (KLUCHT) To **clutch** is to hold something tightly: I **clutched** the railing to keep from falling. *VERB*

collar (KOL er) A **collar** is a band that is put around the neck of a dog or other pet. **Collars** can be made of leather or plastic. *NOUN*

college (KOL ij) **College** is the school that you go to after high school: After I finish high school, I plan to go to **college** to become a teacher. *NOUN*

coyote (ky OH tee or KY oht) A **coyote** is a small animal that looks something like a wolf. **Coyotes** have light yellow fur and bushy tails. *NOUN*

coyote

Dd

dam (DAM) A **dam** is a wall built to hold back the water of a creek, lake, or river. *NOUN*

dangerous (DAYN jer uhss) Something that is **dangerous** is not safe: Skating on thin ice is **dangerous**. *ADJECTIVE*

delicious (di LISH uhss) When something is **delicious**, it tastes or smells very good: The cookies were **delicious**. *ADJECTIVE*

desert (DEZ ert) A **desert** is a place without water or trees but with a lot of sand. It is usually hot. *NOUN*

desert

drooled (DROOLD) To **drool** is to let saliva run from the mouth like a baby sometimes does. The dog **drooled** when it saw the bone. *VERB*

Ee

electricity (i lek TRISS uh tee) **Electricity** is a kind of energy that makes light and heat. **Electricity** also runs motors. **Electricity** makes light bulbs shine, radios and televisions play, and cars start. *NOUN*

embarrassed (em BAIR uhst) When you feel **embarrassed**, you feel that people are thinking of you badly because of something you said or did: When I realized that I had given the wrong answer, I was **embarrassed**. *ADJECTIVE*

envelope (EN vuh lohp) An **envelope** is a folded paper cover. An **envelope** is used to mail a letter or something else that is flat. *NOUN*

excitement (ek SYT muhnt) **Excitement** happens when you have very strong, happy feelings about something that you like. *NOUN*

experiment (ek SPAIR uh muhnt) An **experiment** is a test to find out something: We do **experiments** in science class. *NOUN*

experiment

482

Gg

gnaws (NAWS) When an animal **gnaws**, it is biting and wearing away by biting: The brown mouse **gnaws** the cheese. *VERB*

gravity (GRAV uh tee) **Gravity** is the natural force that causes objects to move toward the center of the earth. **Gravity** causes objects to have weight. *NOUN*

greenhouse (GREEN howss) A **greenhouse** is a building with a glass or plastic roof and sides. A **greenhouse** is kept warm and full of light for growing plants. *NOUN*

greenhouse

Hh

halfway (HAF WAY) to be **halfway** is to be in the middle: He was **halfway** through running the race. *ADJECTIVE*

harsh (HARSH) To be **harsh** is to be rough, unpleasant, and unfriendly. The **harsh** weather made us stay indoors. *ADJECTIVE*

483

hooves (HUVZ or HOOVZ) **Hooves** are the hard part of the feet of some animals. Horses, cattle, sheep, moose, deer, and pigs have hooves. *NOUN*

Jj

justice (JUHS tis) **Justice** happens when things are right and fair. *NOUN*

Ll

laboratory (LAB ruh tor ee) A **laboratory** is a room where scientists work and do experiments and tests. *NOUN*

ladder

ladder (LAD er) A **ladder** is a set of steps between two long pieces of wood, metal, or rope. **Ladders** are used for climbing up and down. *NOUN*

lantern

lanterns (LAN tern) **Lanterns** are portable lamps with coverings around them to protect them from wind and rain. *NOUN*

484

lazy (LAY zee) If a person is **lazy**, he or she does not want to work hard or to move fast: The **lazy** cat lay on the rug all day. *ADJECTIVE*

lodge (LOJ) A **lodge** is a den of an animal: The beavers built a **lodge**. *NOUN*

luckiest (LUHK ee est) The **luckiest** person is the one who has had the best fortune. *ADJECTIVE*

lumbered (LUHM berd) To **lumber** is to move along heavily and noisily: The old truck **lumbered** down the road. *VERB*

Mm

meadow (MED oh) A **meadow** is a piece of land where grass grows: There are sheep in the **meadow**. *NOUN*

meadow

mill (MIL) A **mill** is a building in which grain is ground into flour or meal. *NOUN*

485

Glossary

monsters (MON ster) **Monsters** are make-believe people or animals that are scary. In stories, some **monsters** are friendly, and others are not. Dragons are **monsters**. *NOUN*

musician (myoo ZISH uhn) A **musician** is a person who sings, plays, or writes music. *NOUN*

Nn

narrator (NAIR ayt or) A **narrator** is a person who tells a story or play. In a play, a **narrator** keeps the action moving. *NOUN*

Pp

persimmons (puhr SIM uhns) **Persimmons** are round, yellow and orange fruits about the size of plums. *NOUN*

persimmons

photograph (FOH tuh graf) A **photograph** is a picture you make with a camera. *NOUN*

Rr

relatives (REL uh tivs) Your **relatives** are the people who belong to the same family as you do. Your mother, sister, and cousin are all your **relatives**. *NOUN*

486

riverbank (RIV er bangk) A **riverbank** is the land on the side of a river or stream. *NOUN*

robbers (ROB ers) **Robbers** are people who rob or steal: The police chased the bank **robbers**. *NOUN*

robot (ROH bot or ROH BUHT) A **robot** is a machine that is run by a computer. **Robots** help people do work. **Robots** can look like people. *NOUN*

roller skate (ROH ler SKAYT) To **roller-skate** is to move by using **roller skates**, which are shoes that have wheels. *VERB*

roller skates

Ss

shivered (SHIV erd) To **shiver** is to shake with cold, fear, or excitement: I **shivered** in the cold wind. *VERB*

shuttle (SHUHT uhl) A **shuttle** is a spacecraft with wings, which can orbit the earth, land like an airplane, and be used again. *NOUN*

487

slipped (SLIPT) When you **slip** you slide suddenly and unexpectedly: She **slipped** on the ice. *VERB*

smudged (SMUDJ) If something is **smudged**, it is marked with a dirty streak. *ADJECTIVE*

snuggled (SNUHG uhld) To **snuggle** is to lie closely and comfortably together; cuddle: The kittens **snuggled** together in the basket. *VERB*

snuggled

spirit (SPIR it) To have **spirit** is to have enthusiasm, courage, and loyalty: My sister has team **spirit**. *NOUN*

Tt

telescope (TEL uh skohp) A **telescope** is something you look through to make things far away seem nearer and larger: We looked at the moon through a **telescope**. *NOUN*

488

terrific (tuh RIF ik) To be **terrific** means to be very good, wonderful. She is a **terrific** tennis player. *ADJECTIVE*

Thanksgiving (thangks GIV ing) **Thanksgiving** is a holiday in November. *NOUN*

tortillas (tor TEE uhs) **Tortillas** are thin, flat, round breads usually made of cornmeal. *NOUN*

trash (TRASH) **Trash** is anything of no use or that is worn out. **Trash** is garbage or things to be thrown away. *NOUN*

trash

Ww

wad (WOD) A **wad** is a small, soft ball or chunk of something: She stepped in a **wad** of chewing gum. *NOUN*

weave (WEEV) To **weave** is to form threads into cloth. *VERB*

489

Tested Words

Unit 1

Iris and Walter

someone
somewhere
friend
country
beautiful
front

Exploring Space with an Astronaut

everywhere
live
work
woman
machines
move
world

Henry and Mudge and the Starry Night

couldn't
love
build
mother
bear
father
straight

A Walk in the Desert

water
eyes
early
animals
full
warm

The Strongest One

together
very
learn
often
though
gone
pieces

Unit 2

Tara and Tiree, Fearless Friends

family
once
pull
listen
heard
break

Ronald Morgan Goes to Bat

laugh
great
you're
either
certainly
second
worst

Turtle's Race with Beaver

enough
toward
above
ago
word
whole

490

491

Acknowledgments

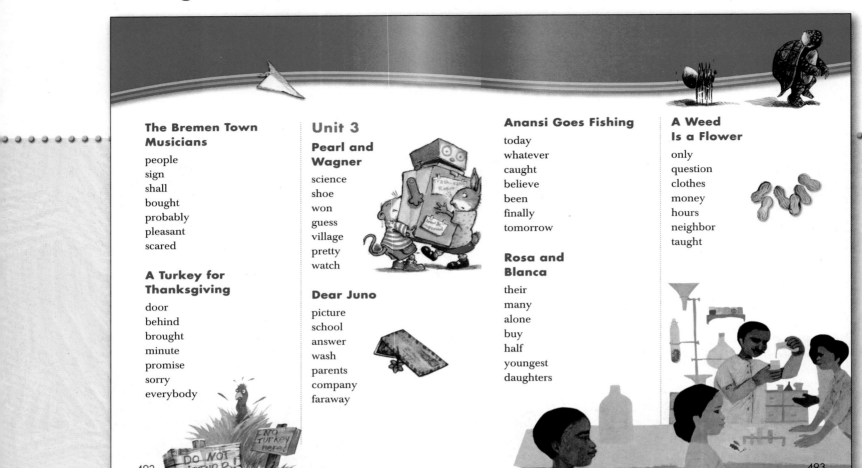

The Bremen Town Musicians

people
sign
shall
bought
probably
pleasant
scared

A Turkey for Thanksgiving

door
behind
brought
minute
promise
sorry
everybody

Unit 3

Pearl and Wagner

science
shoe
won
guess
village
pretty
watch

Dear Juno

picture
school
answer
wash
parents
company
faraway

Anansi Goes Fishing

today
whatever
caught
believe
been
finally
tomorrow

Rosa and Blanca

their
many
alone
buy
half
youngest
daughters

A Weed Is a Flower

only
question
clothes
money
hours
neighbor
taught

492

493

Acknowledgments

Text

Page 16: Text from *Iris And Walter*, copyright © 2000 by Elissa Haden Guest, reprinted by permission of Harcourt, Inc.

Pages 38–39: From *Poems for Small Friends* by Bobbi Katz, copyright © 1989 by Random House, Inc. Illustrations © 1989 by Gyo Fujikawa. Used by permission of Random House Children's Books, a division of Random House, Inc.

Page 46: *Exploring Space with an Astronaut* by Patricia J. Murphy, copyright © Enslow Publishers, Inc., Berkeley Heights, NJ. All rights reserved. Reprinted by permission.

Page 72: From *Henry and Mudge and the Starry Night*. Text copyright © 1998 by Cynthia Rylant. Illustrations copyright © 1998 by Sucie Stevenson. Reprinted with permission of Simon & Schuster for Young Readers, Simon & Schuster Children's Publishing Division. All rights reserved.

Page 100: From *A Walk in the Desert* by Caroline Arnold. Copyright © Alloy Entertainment and Al Jarcon. Reprinted by permission. All rights reserved.

Page 123: From *www.factmonster.com* from The Columbia Electronic Encyclopedia, 6E. Copyright © 2004 Columbia University Press. Licensed from Columbia University Press. All rights reserved. Reprinted by permission.

Page 132: "*The Strongest One*" (Text), from *Pushing Up The Sky* by Joseph Bruchac, copyright © 2000 by Joseph Bruchac, text. Used by permission of Dial Books for Young Readers, A Division of Penguin Young Readers Group, A Member of Penguin Group (USA) Inc., 345 Hudson Street, New York, NY 10014. All rights reserved.

Page 166: From *Tara and Tiree, Fearless Friends*. Text copyright © 2002 by Andrew Clements. Reprinted with permission of Simon & Schuster Books for Young Readers, Simon & Schuster Children's Publishing Division. All rights reserved.

Page 194: From *Ronald Morgan Goes to Bat* by Patricia Reilly Giff, copyright © 1988 by Patricia Reilly Giff. Used by permission of Viking Penguin, A Division of Penguin Young Readers Group, A Member of Penguin Group (USA) Inc., 345 Hudson Street, New York, NY 10014. All rights reserved.

Page 214: "*Spaceball*" from *Giant Children* by Brod Bagert. Copyright © 2002 by Brod Bagert, text. Copyright © by Tedd Arnold, pictures. Used by permission of Dial Books for Young Readers, A Division of Penguin Young Readers Group, A Member of Penguin Group (USA) Inc., 345 Hudson Street, New York, NY 10014. All rights reserved.

Page 222: *Turtle's Race with Beaver* by Joseph Bruchac & James Bruchac, illustrations by Jose Aruego & Ariane Dewey, Dial Books for Young Readers, 2003.

Page 246: From "*The Secret Life of Ponds*" by Elizabeth Schleichert, Illustrations by Frank Fretz. Reprinted from the June 2003 issue of Ranger Rick® magazine, with the permission of the publisher, the National Wildlife Federation. Copyright © 2003 by the National Wildlife Federation®. Illustrations reprinted by permission of Frank Fretz © 2003.

Page 256: From *Easy-To-Read Folk and Fairy Tale Plays* by Carol Pugliano. Copyright © 1997 by Carol Pugliano. Reprinted by permission of Scholastic Inc.

Page 286: From *A Turkey for Thanksgiving* by Eve Bunting, illustrated by Diane de Groat. Text copyright © 1991 by Eve Bunting. Illustrations copyright © 1991 by Diane de Groat. Reprinted by permission of Clarion Books, a division of Houghton Mifflin Company. All rights reserved.

Page 306: *www.vispa.com*

Page 320: *Pearl and Wagner, Two Good Friends* by Kate McMullan, Illustrations by R. W. Alley, Dial Books for Young Readers, 2003.

Page 340: "*Robots at Home*" from *Robots* by Clive Gifford, Kingfisher Publications, 2003.

Page 348: From *Dear Juno* by Soyung Pak, copyright © 1999 by Soyung Pak, text. Used by permission of Viking Penguin, A Division of Penguin Young Readers Group, A Member of Penguin Group (USA) Inc., 345 Hudson Street, New York, NY 10014. All rights reserved.

Page 368: From *Saying It Without Words: Signs and Symbols* by Arnulf K. & Louise A. Esterer, 1980. Reprinted by permission of Prentice Hall.

Page 376: From *Anansi Goes Fishing* by Eric A. Kimmel. Text copyright © 1992 by Eric A. Kimmel. Illustrations copyright © 1992 by Janet Stevens. All rights reserved. Reprinted by permission of Holiday House, Inc

Page 398: "*Do Spiders Stick to Their Own Webs*" (text) from *Where Fish Go in Winter and Other Great Mysteries* by Amy Goldman Koss, copyright © 1987 by Amy Goldman Koss, text. Used by permission of Dial Books for Young Readers, A Division of Penguin Young Readers Group, A Member of Penguin Group (USA) Inc., 345 Hudson Street, New York, NY 10014. All rights reserved.

Page 406: From *Rosa and Blanca* by Joe Hayes, Illustrated by José Ortega, 1993. Reprinted by permission of Joe Hayes.

Page 420: From *The Crow and the Pitcher* retold by Eric Blair, Illustrated by Dianne Silverman. Copyright © 2004 by Picture Window Books. All rights reserved. Reprinted by permission.

Page 430: From *A Weed is a Flower*. Copyright © 1998 by Aliki Brandenberg. Reprinted with permission of Simon & Schuster Books for Young Readers, Simon & Schuster Children's Publishing Division. All rights reserved.

Page 455: "*Products Made from Corn*" from Ohio Corn Marketing Program Web site, www.ohiocorn.org. Reprinted by permission of Ohio Corn Marketing Program.

Illustrations

Cover: © Scott Gustafson
Pages: 38–39, 420–423 Laura Ovresat
Pages: 128–151, 157 David Diaz
Page: 153 © Derek Grinnell
Pages: 163–183, 189 © Scott Gustafson
Pages: 191–213, 217 Susanna Natti
Page: 246–247 Russell Farrell
Pages: 253–275, 280–281 Jon Goodell
Pages: 312–318, 320–339, 342–343 Robert W. Alley
Pages: 344–345 Gideon Kendall
Pages: 373–395, 400–401 © Janet Stevens

Photographs

Every effort has been made to secure permission and provide appropriate credit for photographic material. The publisher deeply regrets any omission and pledges to correct errors called to its attention in subsequent editions.

Unless otherwise acknowledged, all photographs are the property of Scott Foresman, a division of Pearson Education.

Photo locators denoted as follows: Top (T), Center (C), Bottom (B), Left (L), Right (R), Background (Bkgd).

Page: 5 NASA
Page: 6 NASA
Page: 7 NASA
Page: 8 NASA
Page: 9 NASA
Page: 10 NASA
Page: 12 NASA, © Doug Armand/Getty Images, (CR) © Phil Schermeister/Corbis
Page: 13 NASA, (TR, CL) © Ariel Skelley/Corbis
Page: 15 NASA
Page: 18 NASA
Page: 19 NASA
Page: 20 NASA
Page: 22 NASA/Roger Ressmeyer/Corbis
Page: 42 (C) © Shilo Sports/Getty Images, NASA
Page: 43 (TR) © George Hall/Corbis, (CL) © Museum of Flight/Corbis
Page: 44 Corbis
Page: 45 Getty Images
Page: 60 Getty Images

Page: 63 Corbis, © Richard T. Nowitz/Corbis, © Joseph Sohm-ChromoSohm Inc./Corbis
Page: 64 © Richard T. Nowitz/Corbis
Page: 65 Getty Images, © Richard T. Nowitz/Corbis
Page: 66 © Lester Lefkowitz/Getty Images, © Cliff Beittel, © Peter Cade/Getty Images
Page: 68 © Jim Ballard/Getty Images, (CL) © Joe McDonald/Corbis
Page: 69 (CL) © Nigel J. Dennis/Gallo Images/Corbis, (TR) © Michael & Patricia Fogden/Corbis
Page: 92 Getty Images, © Roger Ressmeyer/Corbis
Page: 93 © Roger Ressmeyer/Corbis
Page: 96 © George H. H. Huey/Corbis, (CL) © Altrendo Nature/Getty Images, (BR) © Galen Rowell/Corbis, (BR) © Steve Maslowski/Visuals Unlimited
Page: 98 © David A. Northcott/Corbis, © Ralph Hopkins/Lonely Planet Images
Page: 99 © Tim Flach/Stone, © Arthur Tilley/Getty Images
Page: 102 Getty Images
Page: 104 © Paul McCormick/Getty Images
Page: 108 © Arthur S. Aubry/Getty Images
Page: 112 © Joe McDonald/Corbis
Page: 120 © Arthur Tilley/Getty Images
Page: 129 (TL) © Ron Watts/Corbis, (TR) © Martin Harvey/Peter Arnold, Inc.
Page: 152 © Tom Brakefield/Corbis
Page: 153 © Tom Brakefield/Corbis
Page: 154 © Roland Seitre/Peter Arnold, Inc., © John H. Hoffman/Bruce Coleman Inc.
Page: 155 © Theo Allofs/Corbis
Page: 163 (TL) © Matthew Polak/Corbis, (CR) © AFP/Getty Images, (BL) Getty Images
Page: 184 © Tim Davis/Corbis
Page: 185 © Andrea Comas/Corbis, © Jean-Bernard Vernier/Corbis, © Tom Nebbia/Corbis
Page: 186 © Owen Franken/Corbis, © Vaughn Youtz/Corbis, © Armando Arorizo/Corbis, © Shamil Zhumatov/Corbis
Page: 187 © Kai Pfaffenbach/Corbis, © Ralf-Finn Hestoft/Corbis
Page: 188 Getty Images
Page: 190 © Julia Fishkin/Getty Images
Page: 191 © CLEO Freelance/Index Stock Imagery
Page: 218 © Kennan Ward/Corbis
Page: 246 Getty Images

494

495

Leveled Readers

Table of Contents

Dogs to the Rescue

SEQUENCE

PREDICT/CONFIRM PREDICTIONS

LESSON VOCABULARY break, family, heard, listen, once, pull

SUMMARY Children learn how dogs can be more than just pets. A description of the typical training of a rescue dog provides children with practice identifying a sequence of events. Detailed photographs support children's comprehension.

INTRODUCE THE BOOK

BUILD BACKGROUND Discuss, as a class, the different dangers that people may need to be rescued from such as a flood, fire, or earthquake. Or discuss the unique characteristics of dogs such as their loyalty and sense of smell.

PREVIEW/USE TEXT FEATURES Ask children to look through the book at the photographs and captions. Ask: How do the photographs and captions help you to predict what the book will be about?

TEACH/REVIEW VOCABULARY Children can look at the sentence and surrounding sentences for clues to help them find the meaning of a word. Direct children to find the word *break* on page 4. Ask a volunteer to explain the meaning of the word. Then ask what surroundings words or sentences helped them find the meaning. Repeat the process with each vocabulary word.

TARGET SKILL AND STRATEGY

SEQUENCE Remind children that it is important to keep track of the *sequence,* or order of events when reading. As you read about rescue dogs and their training on pages 6 and 7, think about what they learn to do first, next, and last. Ask children to point to the sentence that tells them what the dogs learn first, next, then last. Point out that the words *once* and *when* are clues that tell the order of events.

PREDICT/CONFIRM PREDICTIONS Children can draw upon their prior knowledge to *predict* what will come next in the sequence of topics in a book. As children come to page 5, tell them to close their books and ask: What do you think will be next in the book? Write children's predictions on the board and let children open their book to *confirm* their predictions.

READ THE BOOK

Use the following questions to support comprehension.

PAGE 3 How do rescue workers help others? *(They bring people to safety.)*

PAGE 6 What do families that take in rescue dogs need to know? *(How to train a rescue dog.)*

PAGE 7 In you own words, when is a rescue dog ready to work? *(after it learns important commands)*

TALK ABOUT THE BOOK

THINK AND SHARE
1. Possible response: They are good listeners.
2. Possible response: They pull people from harm.
3. Possible response: rescue, workers, strong.
4. Possible response: Yes, because the dog would one day help others.

RESPONSE OPTIONS

WRITING Ask children to write one fact and one opinion of their own about rescue dogs.

ELL Lead a writing activity that uses sentence frames such as *Rescue dogs are* _____, *Rescue dogs can* _____, *and Rescue dogs have* _____. Direct each child to complete the sentences on their own paper.

CONTENT CONNECTIONS

SOCIAL STUDIES Children will want to find out more about how dogs help people everyday. Arrange with the librarian to have some books in the classroom about service dogs, sled dogs, and herding dogs.

Time for SOCIAL STUDIES

Name_____

Sequence

Sequence refers to the order of events in both fiction and nonfiction. Sequence can also refer to the steps in a process.

Read the story. Then, read what happened next. Put the sentences in order by writing the correct number between 1–5 next to each one.

Rachel went on a walk in the forest. She tripped and fell on a rock. Her ankle hurt so she could not walk back to her car. She used her mobile phone to call for help. A rescue worker named Miguel was sent to the forest to help Rachel.

_____ **1.** Miguel looks at Rachel's leg to see if it is broken.

_____ **2.** Next, Rachel smiles when she sees Miguel and Max.

_____ **3.** After Max picks up Rachel's smell, he follows a path into the woods.

_____ **4.** Then, Max stopped and held up his head. Max and Miguel hear Rachel cry for help.

_____ **5.** First, Miguel and his rescue dog Max found Rachel's car.

34

Name_____

Vocabulary

Unscramble each word below. Look at the words in the Word Box to help you. Write the word on the line. Say the word aloud. Count the number of syllables.

Words to Know
break   family   heard   listen   once   pull

1. ymifal _____ How many syllables? _____

2. draeh _____ How many syllables? _____

3. enltis _____ How many syllables? _____

4. lpul _____ How many syllables? _____

5. ceon _____ How many syllables? _____

6. akbre _____ How many syllables? _____

7-8. Write the meaning of the word *heard*.

_____

_____

9-10. Write the meaning of the word *listen*.

_____

_____

35

What To Do in an Emergency

What To Do in an Emergency
by Christine Wolf

◎ **SEQUENCE**

◎ **PREDICT/CONFIRM PREDICTIONS**

LESSON VOCABULARY break, family, heard, listen, once, pull

SUMMARY Children learn how to prepare themselves for various kinds of emergencies. The sequence of events are emphasized through lists. Photographs build children's knowledge of what to expect in an different emergencies.

INTRODUCE THE BOOK

BUILD BACKGROUND Discus what types of situations are an emergency. Ask children to recall people in the community that help others during emergencies such police officers, firefighters, and rescue persons.

ELL Invite ELLs to share content related words in their home language such as emergency, firefighter, ambulance, and help. Ask: Do you think there are firefighters and police officers all over the world?

PREVIEW/USE TEXT FEATURES As children look through the book have them look at the photographs and the section headings. Ask: How are the section headings similar? Do the section headings give you clues as to what the book is about? How do the photographs relate to the headings?

TEACH/REVIEW VOCABULARY Remind children that they can look at the sentence and surrounding sentences for clues to help them find the meaning of an unfamiliar word. Direct children to find the word *family* on page 3. Ask a volunteer to explain the meaning of the word. Then ask what surroundings words or sentences helped them find the meaning. Repeat the process with each vocabulary word

TARGET SKILL AND STRATEGY

◎ **SEQUENCE** Remind children that it is important to keep track of the *sequence,* or order, of events when reading about how to do something. When children come to page 5, point out the sentences with bullets. Explain that the group of sentences is a list. Ask children to point to the sentence that tells them what to do first, next, then last. Point out that a list is one type of clue that shows them the order of events.

◎ **PREDICT/CONFIRM PREDICTIONS** Children can draw upon their prior knowledge to *predict* what will come next in the sequence. As children come to page 7, tell them to close their books. Ask: What do think you should you do if you are lost indoors? Can you predict what the author says you should do first? Write children's predictions on the board and let children open their book to see if their predictions are correct.

READ THE BOOK

Use the following questions to support comprehension.

PAGE 5 What happens when you call 9-1-1? *(You talk to someone who can send help.)*

PAGE 8 What might happen if you stopped to take things with you? *(It would take time and you should get out as fast as you can.)*

PAGE 12 How could you check yourself for injuries? *(I would look for cuts where I felt pain.)*

TALK ABOUT THE BOOK

THINK AND SHARE
1. Possible response: it can keep you safe.
2. Possible response: they may call my home.
3. Possible response: if there was a fire you could tell people where the fire was happening.
4. Possible response: getting lost, getting out of a fire, and getting help in an accident.

RESPONSE OPTIONS

WRITING Have children write three things they can do today to prepare themselves for emergencies.

CONTENT CONNECTIONS

SOCIAL STUDIES Many community fire departments have educational programs on fire safety for children. Arrange a class trip to a fire station or a visit from a firefighter to the school.

Time for SOCIAL STUDIES

Name_____

Sequence

Sequence refers to the order of events in both fiction and nonfiction. Sequence can also refer to the steps in a process.

Read the steps on how to be safe in case of a fire. They are listed out of order. Put them in order by writing them on the correct line below.

- Break windows to get out if you must.
- Don't stop to take anything with you.
- First get down low. The air is easier to breathe.
- Next, check your clothes. If they are on fire, stop drop and roll.
- After you are out of danger, you can call 9-1-1.

---

1. _____

2. _____

3. _____

4. _____

5. _____

34

Name _____

Vocabulary

| Words to Know |
| break   family   heard   listen   once   pull |

Draw a line to match the word to its meaning.

1. break   **a.** people that are related to each other

2. family   **b.** to sense sounds through your ear

3. heard   **c.** a single time

4. listen   **d.** to hurt or damage

5. once   **e.** to pay attention to sounds

6. pull   **f.** to move by dragging or tugging

7-8. Write the meaning of the word *heard*.
_____
- -
_____

9-10. Wite the meaning of the word *listen*.
_____
- -
_____

35

Amazing Animals

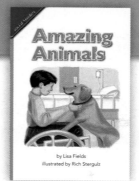

Amazing Animals

by Lisa Fields
illustrated by Rich Stergulz

🔁 **SEQUENCE**

🔁 **PREDICT**

LESSON VOCABULARY courageous, depends, groom, hazard, rescue, tasks, therapy

---

SUMMARY This nonfiction text describes the different ways that service animals can help humans.

INTRODUCE THE BOOK

BUILD BACKGROUND Engage children in a discussion of animals and how they can help people. Ask: What are some ways that people use horses? What are some other animals that are useful to people? Why are these animals important?

PREVIEW/TAKE A PICTURE WALK Invite children to preview the text by flipping through the pages and looking at the pictures. Encourage children to use what they see to make predictions about the text. Ask: How is the animal on this page helping this person?

TEACH/PREVIEW VOCABULARY Have children practice looking up the vocabulary words in the glossary to find the definitions. Have children write down the definitions on their own paper and help them write at least one sentence using each word.

TARGET SKILL AND STRATEGY

🔁 **SEQUENCE** As children read, encourage them to keep track of the *sequence* of information in the text in order to better understand and remember what they learn. Model for children how to keep a simple outline as they read.

🔁 **PREDICT** Prior to reading, have children to make predictions about the text. Ask: What animals do you think you will learn about in this book? What do you think you will learn about these animals and how they help people? What do you think you will learn about the people who need these animals to help them?

READ THE BOOK

Use the following questions to support comprehension.

PAGE 6 Why do you think therapy dogs are important to help people feel better? *(Responses will vary: make them feel happy, forget they are sick, help them not feel as badly about being in the hospital.)*

PAGE 8 What special things do you think search and rescue dogs can do better than humans? *(Responses will vary: can get into smaller spaces, can use their sense of smell to find people, may be more courageous than some people.)*

PAGE 13 How have therapy horses helped their special riders? *(learned how to walk by feeling how the horse walks, better balance by sitting steady in saddle)*

TALK ABOUT THE BOOK

THINK AND SHARE

1. First, the person and horse spend time together. Next, the person learns how to groom the horse. Last, the horse lets the person get on its back.

2. Possible response: Max will guide Peg home safely, following the same route.

3. Possible response: Traffic, uneven sidewalk, other people, shopping carts

4. The heading says Therapy Monkeys and the illustrations show a monkey turning a light switch on and off. These pages will be about how monkeys help people.

RESPONSE OPTIONS

WORD WORK Once children have located the highlighted vocabulary words in the book, help them think of synonyms for each word. Then read the sentences from the book and replace the vocabulary words with their synonyms.

CONTENT CONNECTIONS

SOCIAL STUDIES If possible, invite a community member to come speak to the class about service animals. This may be a person who uses a service animal or someone who trains them. Have children think of questions to ask your guest beforehand.

Time for **SOCIAL STUDIES**

Name_____

Sequence

Sequence refers to the order of events in both fictional and nonfiction. Sequence can also refer to the steps in a process.

Re-read pages 4 and 5 of *Amazing Animals*. Then number each of the sentences below to put them into the correct order.

_____

_____ **1.** Guide dogs like Max have special permission to enter the grocery stores to help their owners.

_____

_____ **2.** Peg trusts Max to know when it is safe to cross the street.

_____

_____ **3.** Peg holds on to Max's harness as he leads her safely down the steps and onto the sidewalk.

_____

_____ **4.** Max is Peg's guide dog.

_____

_____ **5.** Max lets Peg know when there is a hazard and leads her around the danger.

34

Name_____

Vocabulary

Complete each sentence below using the correct vocabulary word.

Words to Know
courageous   depends   groom hazard   rescue   tasks   therapy

1. Rescue dogs have to be very _____ .

2. Before riding on a therapy horse, the person learns how

   to _____ the horse.

3. A _____ dog visits children and adults in nursing homes and hospitals.

4. Therapy monkeys help their owners with many

   _____, such as turning lights on and off.

5. Some dogs are trained to _____ people who

   are lost in the snow or the woods.

6. A guide dog helps lead its owner around a _____.

7. An owner _____ on his or her service animal in many different ways.

35

Let's Play Baseball!

Let's Play Baseball!
by Jessica Quilty
illustrated by Chad Thompson

🔘 **REALISM AND FANTASY**

🔘 **PRIOR KNOWLEDGE**

LESSON VOCABULARY certainly, either, great, laugh, second, worst, you're

SUMMARY Read about an exciting baseball game. Boys and girls play together and show good sportsmanship. Readers' experiences playing sports brings this story to life.

INTRODUCE THE BOOK

BUILD BACKGROUND Review with children the basic rules and terms of baseball. Draw a baseball diamond on the board. Ask volunteers to help you fill out the names of positions and bases.

PREVIEW As children look through the book at the illustrations, guide them to get to know the characters. Ask: How many girls and boys are on the teams? How many coaches are there? What position does the coach play? Which characters seem happy? Which characters seem sad?

TEACH/REVIEW VOCABULARY Have children complete sentences using the vocabulary words. Write one sentence for each vocabulary word on the board such as: Our team came in _____ (second) place in the relay race. Next to the sentences in a different order write all of the vocabulary words. Ask volunteers to come up to the board and write the correct word in the line.

ELL Help children learn the many idiomatic expressions of baseball such as *home plate, strike out, up at bat,* and *home run.* Write each individual word on multiple cards and have children play a game similar to Go Fish. The object of the game is for children to use all of their cards by making idiomatic baseball expressions. Each child starts with five cards. The remaining cards are put in a stack in the center with one card turned over. Each child takes turns asking one other child if they have a specific card. If they do not have the card, the child must "go fish" from the stack in the center.

TARGET SKILL AND STRATEGY

🔘 **REALISM AND FANTASY** Remind children that fiction can be either a *realistic story* or a *fantasy.* A realistic story is something that could happen. A fantasy is something that could not happen. Ask children to look at the cover illus-tration to predict what type of story *Let's Play Baseball* is. Guide them to support their answers with specific details.

🔘 **PRIOR KNOWLEDGE** Discuss with children that their prior knowledge can help them figure out if a story is a *realistic* story or a *fantasy.* By comparing their prior knowledge to events and characters in the story they can identify the type of story it is. Prior knowledge can be from their own experiences, from reading, and/or from their feelings.

READ THE BOOK

Use the following questions to support comprehension.

PAGE 3 Where is second base? *(Possible response: behind the pitcher.)*

PAGE 4 Why did Jill make it to second base? *(Possible response: ball wasn't caught quickly.)*

PAGE 6 How many players have to strike out for the other team to be up at bat? *(three)*

TALK ABOUT THE BOOK

THINK AND SHARE
1. Possible response: this story is a realistic story because kids do play baseball.
2. Possible response: teams, pitcher, bases, home plate, equipment, and rules.
3. Possible response: let's you're, you'll, I'm, can't.
4. Possible responses: playing baseball is fun even if you don't win.

RESPONSE OPTIONS

WRITING Write two sentences describing what makes a good teammate.

CONTENT CONNECTIONS

SOCIAL STUDIES Have children go to the library and choose a book about their favorite sport. Have children present to class one fact they knew before they read the book and one fact they learned from the book.

Time for SOCIAL STUDIES

Name _____

Realism and Fantasy

Think about the story *Let's Play Baseball*. Then, answer the questions below.

1. If the character Sam was a rabbit, would the story be a realistic story or a fantasy?

_____

- -

_____

2. If the character Ann hit a home run, would the story be a realistic story or a fantasy?

_____

- -

_____

3. If the children played baseball on the moon, would the story be a realistic story or a fantasy?

_____

- -

_____

4. If Sam's team lost the game, would the story be a realistic story or a fantasy?

_____

- -

_____

5. If they played baseball while riding elephants, would the story be a realistic story or a fantasy?

_____

- -

_____

38

Name _____

Vocabulary

Draw a line to match the word to its meaning.

1. certainly   a. similarly; as well

2. either   b. to be sure

3. great   c. a sound made when something is funny

4. laugh   d. you are

5. second   e. the next after first

6. you're   f. very good

7. worst   g. the most bad

Synonyms are words that have the same meaning. Draw a line to match the synonyms.

8. laugh   h. surely

9. great   i. giggle

10. certainly   j. terrific

39

Unit 2 Week 2

◉ **REALISM AND FANTASY**

◉ **PRIOR KNOWLEDGE**

LESSON VOCABULARY certainly, either, great, laugh, second, worst, you're

Warm and Fuzzy

SUMMARY Cooperation and sharing are themes of this fantasy. Children can draw upon their prior knowledge as they read about how a scarf is made. Lively illustrations hold readers' attention.

INTRODUCE THE BOOK

BUILD BACKGROUND Start a discussion about wool and knitting by asking children what they wear when it is cold. Elicit them to answer scarves, mittens, and sweaters. Lead children to think about how these items are made.

ELL Invite children to share home language words that mean *warm, fuzzy, knitting, wool, sheep,* and *giraffe.* Encourage them to share similarities or differences between the natural cloth of their native country.

PREVIEW Have children look through the book at the illustrations. Invite them to get to know the characters by studying the illustrations. Ask: What kind of animals are most of the characters? How can you tell the sheep characters apart from each other? Are the characters mostly happy or sad in this story?

TEACH/REVIEW VOCABULARY Have children complete sentences using vocabulary words. Write a sentence for each vocabulary word on the board such as: Knock, knock jokes always make me _____ (laugh). Write all of the vocabulary words in a different order next to the sentences. Ask volunteers to come up to the board and write the correct word in the space provided.

TARGET SKILL AND STRATEGY

◉ **REALISM AND FANTASY** Before reading, remind children that fiction can be either a *realistic story* or a *fantasy.* A realistic story is something that could happen. A fantasy is something that could not happen. Ask children to look at the cover illustration for clues as to what type of story *Warm and Fuzzy* is. Guide them to support their answers with specific details.

◉ **PRIOR KNOWLEDGE** Review with children that their *prior knowledge* can help them figure out if a story is a realistic story or a fantasy. Guide them to recognize that what they already know about animals before they read is their prior knowledge. By comparing their prior knowledge to events and characters in the story they knew what type of story it was.

READ THE BOOK

Use the following questions to support comprehension.

PAGE 4 Which sheep is Kenny? How do you know? *(Possible response: Kenny is the sheep on the left. I know from the text and the illustration.)*

PAGE 7 What did the sheep do after they cut their wool? *(They brushed it.)*

PAGE 10 Why did Kenny knit such a long scarf? *(Possible response: because Geraldine has a very long neck.)*

TALK ABOUT THE BOOK

THINK AND SHARE
1. Possible response: fantasy because the animals act like people.
2. Responses will vary.
3. Possible response: you're, it's, don't, I'm, I'll, she'll.
4. Possible response: because at sometime during the story everyone is warm and fuzzy.

RESPONSE OPTIONS

WRITING Ask children to write two sentences about their favorite character in the story.

CONTENT CONNECTIONS

SOCIAL STUDIES Bring in samples of natural fabrics and the raw materials used to make them for children to touch and explore, such as silk, wool, and cotton. Arrange with your librarian to have books in the classroom about silkworms and cotton.

Name _____

Realism and Fantasy

Think about the story *Warm and Fuzzy*. Then answer the questions below.

1. If the characters were people instead of animals, would the story be a realistic story or a fantasy?

_____

- -

_____

2. If the character Geraldine was a sheep, would the story be a realistic story or a fantasy?

_____

- -

_____

3. If Kenny was a boy, would the story be a realistic story or a fantasy?

_____

- -

_____

4–5. What parts of the story are similar to real life?

_____

- -

_____

_____

- -

_____

_____

- -

_____

_____

- -

_____

38

Name _____

Vocabulary

Draw a line to match the word to its meaning.

1. certainly		**a.** one of two things
2. either		**b.** surely
3. great		**c.** a sound made by someone when something is funny
4. laugh		**d.** you are
5. second		**e.** the next after first
6. you're		**f.** very good

Antonyms are words that have opposite meanings. Draw a line to match the antonyms.

7. either		**a.** best
8. great		**b.** bad
9. laugh		**c.** both
10. worst		**d.** cry

39

The First Big Game

REALISM AND FANTASY

PRIOR KNOWLEDGE

LESSON VOCABULARY compete, contribute, recreation

SUMMARY In this historical-fiction story, in 1846 a young boy's father takes him to his first professional baseball game. The story supports and extends the lesson concept of what makes a team.

INTRODUCE THE BOOK

BUILD BACKGROUND Ask children to discuss what they know about playing baseball. Ask: When do you think the game of baseball was first invented?

ELL To support comprehension, use visual aids, such as pictures of baseball games and equipment, to help children build background before reading.

PREVIEW Have children preview the pictures and chapter headings. Ask: Who is the main character? Have children preview the heading and photos on page 16. Ask: Why did the author include this page?

TEACH/PREVIEW VOCABULARY Give children this sentence: I do soccer just for <u>fun</u>, but I <u>give</u> all I can to help my team <u>play</u> well. Have them replace each underlined word with a vocabulary word so that the meaning of the sentence does not change.

TARGET SKILL AND STRATEGY

REALISM AND FANTASY Remind children that a *realistic story* tells about something that could happen. A *fantasy* is a story about something that could not happen. Write this story on the chalkboard: The fairy waved her wand. Like magic, the frog became a prince. Write a second story: Mom used her mop. In no time at all, the floor was clean. Point out that one is a realistic story and the other is a fantasy. For each story, ask: Is this story a realistic story or a fantasy? Why? As they read, model questions to identify a realistic story: Could things in the story really happen? Fantasy: Are there things in this story that could not really happen? Near the end, ask: Is this a realistic story, or a fantasy?

PRIOR KNOWLEDGE Remind children that successful readers use what they already know to help them understand what they read. Model text-to-self connections

(page 3): This is how I felt on Saturdays when I was a child. Text-to-world connections (page 7): I wonder if "base ball" is like the baseball we play today. Text-to-text connections (page 5): Mama reminds me of the mother in the story we read yesterday. Encourage children as they read to pause and ask, "What does this remind me of?"

READ THE BOOK

Use the following questions to support comprehension.

PAGE 8 Why couldn't Robbie and Papa take a car or bus to New Jersey? *(There were none.)*

PAGE 10 Why did the players wear matching uniforms? *(Possible response: To know who was on each team. To show they were professionals.)*

PAGE 14 Robbie catches the ball. Does this make the story a realistic story, or a fantasy? Why? *(A realistic story, because it could happen.)*

TALK ABOUT THE BOOK

THINK AND SHARE
1. It is a realistic story, because everything in it could happen. Possible response: Clues are children playing and going to a ball game.
2. Possible response: Know: Baseball is played with a bat and ball. Learned: There was a baseball team called the New York Club.
3. Possible response: Answers may vary.
4. Possible response: People would dress and travel differently. Base ball would be one word.

RESPONSE OPTIONS

WRITING Have children name a favorite game or sport and explain its object or purpose.

CONTENT CONNECTIONS

SOCIAL STUDIES Provide information on the origins of basketball, volley ball, and football. Have children choose one sport and chart this data: inventor, date invented, number of players, and a simple description of basic play.

Name _____

Realism and Fantasy

Read the story titles below. Decide if the story is a realistic story or a fantasy. Circle your answer. Then, explain your answer.

I. Title: *The First Big Game in Space*

      realistic story   fantasy story

2. How do you know?

_____

_____

_____

3. Title: *The First Big Game Played by Monkeys*

      realistic story   fantasy story

4. How do you know?

_____

_____

_____

5. Write your own title for a realistic story about baseball.

_____

_____

_____

© Pearson Education 2

38

Name _____

Vocabulary

Draw a line to match the word parts and make a whole word.

1. con   a. creation

2. com   b. tribute

3. re   c. pete

Use the words below in a sentence.

4. compete

_____

_____

_____

5. recreation

_____

_____

_____

39

Busy Beavers

SUMMARY This nonfiction book describes how beavers live in a river that is shared with other animals. It extends the lesson concept of what we can share.

INTRODUCE THE BOOK

BUILD BACKGROUND Have children discuss what they know about what lives and grows in or along rivers. Have children also share anything they may know about beavers.

PREVIEW/TAKE A PICTURE WALK Have children look at the photos in the book before reading. Ask: What are the beavers doing in these photos?

TEACH/REVIEW VOCABULARY Give pairs of children a set of vocabulary word cards. Give them another set with these clues, but first read them aloud: If you have this, you don't need more. If you walk this way, you won't go away. It's not below. This means before. You find this in a sentence. Two halves make this. Have pairs play a memory game by revealing each word and its clue.

ELL Help children make word cards with a vocabulary word on one side and a translation in a common home language on the other side. Lay out the cards, translation side up, and have children capture cards by naming the vocabulary words.

TARGET SKILL AND STRATEGY

◎ **SEQUENCE** Remind children that as they read, they should think about what happens first, next, and last. Explain that clue words like *after* and *at last* can help them figure out the order of events. Point out the words *first, next,* and *then* on page 4. Explain that these clue words tell us the order of the steps that beavers use to prepare logs for building a lodge. Have children use a sequence ladder to map the sequence of events described on pages 4–5.

◎ **SUMMARIZE** Remind children that good readers are able to use their own words to tell the important things that happen in a book or what the book is about. Using their own words to retell is a way of showing that they have understood what they have read. Model page 4:

On this page, I read that beavers use their sharp teeth to cut down trees. Then they cut off the branches, strip the bark, and carry the logs to the river. To tell what happens in my own words, I ask, "What is this page mostly about?" I will use my own words to tell: Beavers use their teeth to make logs. As children read *Busy Beavers,* have them tell the main idea of each page by asking: What is this page mostly about?

READ THE BOOK

PAGE 5 What happens first, next, and last? *(First: Beavers cut reeds and ferns. Next: They use rocks. Next: They use mud. Last: The top of the home sticks out above the water.)*

PAGE 6 What must a beaver be able to do well? *(swim)*

PAGE 8 Why are turtles, fish, frogs, and beavers able to share the river? *(Possible response: They don't eat each other.)*

TALK ABOUT THE BOOK

THINK AND SHARE
1. Cut down trees, cut off branches, strip bark, move logs, cut reeds and ferns, use rocks, glue with mud.
2. Possible response: Beavers work together to build safe homes on the river.
3. beavers, river, first, ferns, beaver, water, under, turtles
4. Possible response: It keeps them dry. It is hard for other animals to get inside.

RESPONSE OPTIONS

WRITING Have children write one or two sentences that describe a beaver lodge.

CONTENT CONNECTIONS

SCIENCE Display information about where river turtles and frogs rest. Have children work in pairs to make charts for comparing beaver, turtle, and frog "homes."

TIME FOR Science

Name _____

Sequence

Read the passage. The beavers did things in a certain order.
Underline the clue words that help you know that order.

Beavers have strong, sharp teeth. First, they use their teeth to cut down trees.
Next, they cut off the branches. Then they strip off the bark. The beavers then carry the logs toward the river.

_____

I. First _____

_____

_____.

_____

2. Next _____

_____

_____.

_____

3. Next _____

_____

_____.

_____

4. Last _____

_____

_____.

© Pearson Education 2

42

Name _____

Vocabulary

Write the words from the box that fit. Some letters have been done for you. When you are finished, the letters in the boxes will spell an important word from the book.

Words to Know					
above	ago	enough	toward	whole	word

1. w _____

2. _____ r _____

3. _____ o _____

4. a _____

5. _____ g _____

6. Write a word from the word box to complete the sentence.

_____

Part of the beaver's lodge is _____ the water.

43

The Busy, Lively, Sleepy, Pond

Life Science
The Busy, Lively, Sleepy, and Quiet Pond
by Kim Borland Illustrated by Bradley Clarke

SEQUENCE

SUMMARIZE

LESSON VOCABULARY above, ago, enough, toward, whole, word

SUMMARY This nonfiction book describes how different animals spend the seasons on the same pond. It extends the lesson concept of what we can share.

INTRODUCE THE BOOK

BUILD BACKGROUND Have children discuss animal life on lakes and ponds. Have them also share what they know about seasonal changes.

PREVIEW/TAKE A PICTURE WALK Have children preview the pictures and labels. Ask: What kind of animals do you see? Do the pictures show that time is changing? How do you know?

ELL Use the pictures to help children identify the different animals that are described in the book. This will help them to understand the text by connecting a familiar image to an English word.

TEACH/REVIEW VOCABULARY Write this story on the chalkboard: A little while <u>ahead</u>, I needed a special coin to make my collection <u>half</u>. I finally saved <u>little</u> money, so I biked <u>away</u> the mall. I went to the store that had a sign <u>below</u> the door with the <u>number</u> Coins. Have children replace the underlined words with vocabulary words so the story makes sense.

TARGET SKILL AND STRATEGY

SEQUENCE Remind children that as they read, they should think about what happens first, next, and last. Explain that clue words like *after* and *at last* can help them figure out the order of events. Point out the word *now* on page 7. Explain: This clue word tells us that the ducklings learn to fly *after* a few months. Have children use a timeline to map the seasonal sequence of events described in the book. Have them label the timeline with the labels *Spring, Summer, Fall,* and *Winter.* Children should summarize the events that take place in each season.

SUMMARIZE Remind children that good readers are able to use their own words to tell the important things that happen in a book or what the book is about. Using their own words to retell is a way of showing that they have understood what they have read. Model page 6: I read that hot summer days warm the water. Ducks paddle around the pond, looking for food. Frogs sit on water lilies and catch insects with their long tongues. To tell what happens in my own words, I ask, "What is this page mostly about?" I will use my own words to tell: In the hot summer, the pond's ducks and frogs eat and take it easy. Have children tell the main idea of each page by asking: What is this page mostly about?

READ THE BOOK

PAGE 5 Why do animals come to the pond in the spring? *(Possible response: There will be food to eat.)*

PAGE 8 Why will the turtles spend the winter under the mud? *(Possible response: They will sleep and stay warm until spring comes.)*

PAGE 12 What happens before the animals return to the pond? *(Spring returns, and the ice melts.)*

TALK ABOUT THE BOOK

THINK AND SHARE

1. They crawl toward the water.
2. Responses will vary.
3. Possible response: Above: bird, tree. In or below: fish, cattail.
4. Responses will vary.

RESPONSE OPTIONS

WRITING Have children choose a season and write a summary of what happens on the pond.

CONTENT CONNECTIONS

SCIENCE Have children choose a plant or an animal described in the book. Have them do guided Internet research to find out about how that plant or animal lives in its habitat. Have children share their findings in small groups.

TIME FOR Science

Name _____

Sequence

Read the passage. The beavers did things in a certain order.
Underline the clue words that help you know that order.

> Beavers have strong, sharp teeth. First, they use their teeth to
> cut down trees.
> Next, they cut off the branches. Then they strip off the bark.
> The beavers then carry the logs toward the river.

42

Name _____

Vocabulary

Use words from the box to complete the paragraph.

Words to Know					
above	ago	enough	toward	whole	word

In the spring, the animals return to the pond. If you look

_____

_____ you in the sky, you might see

_____

----

ducks flying _____ the pond. Then,

_____

----

in the summer, the _____ pond is full

of life. In the fall the beavers make sure that they gather

_____

_____ food for the winter. When winter

comes, there are few animals that live near or on the pond.

Some are resting, but others have left for warmer places quite

_____

----

some time _____.

43

Sea Turtles at Risk

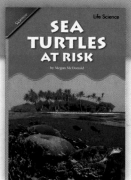

🔊 **SEQUENCE**

🔊 **SUMMARIZE**

LESSON VOCABULARY conflict, endangered, inhabit, predator, resolve, species

---

SUMMARY This nonfiction book gives information about sick and endangered sea turtles and the efforts to save them while coexisting. The book supports and extends the lesson concept of what we can share.

INTRODUCE THE BOOK

BUILD BACKGROUND Have children discuss anything they may know about sea turtles, such as where they live.

PREVIEW/TAKE A PICTURE WALK Have children preview the photos and captions. Ask: What do you think you may learn from reading this book?

TEACH/PREVIEW VOCABULARY Have children pair up. Have each partner write a cloze sentence for a vocabulary word. Ask them to exchange sentences and fill in the correct word. Have children repeat the activity until all the words have been used.

TARGET SKILL AND STRATEGY

🔊 **SEQUENCE** Remind children that as they read, they should think about what happens first, next, and last. Point out the words *after* and *then* on page 11. Explain: These clue words tell us that, first, the turtle lays eggs, second, the scientists move the eggs, and third, the scientists watch the eggs. Have children apply the skill to the first paragraph on page 7. Say: This paragraph describes how shrimp nets endanger sea turtles. What happens first, next, and last?

🔊 **SUMMARIZE** Remind children that successful readers can show that they understand what they have read by using their own words to tell the important things that happen in a book or what the book is about. Model page 6: I read a lot of things about the different ways that sea turtles face danger from humans. To tell what happens in my own words, I ask, "What is this paragraph mostly about?" I will use my own words: Humans have made all species of sea turtles endangered. As children read *Sea Turtles at Risk,* have them tell the main idea of each paragraph by asking: What is this paragraph mostly about?

ELL Have children start a KWL chart to use before, during, and after reading. During reading, have children summarize by listing the most important thing they learned on each page. After reading, have them write a sentence summarizing the book.

READ THE BOOK

Use the following questions to support comprehension.

PAGE 4 How are sea turtles different from fish? *(Possible response: They can't breathe under water. They can live on land.)*

PAGE 8 Besides bright lights, why is a crowded beach a problem for sea turtles? *(Possible response: There's no place to nest.)*

PAGE 10 Explain why chemicals in the ocean are a problem. Tell what happens first, next, and last. *(First: Chemicals pollute the water and make seaweed grow. Next: The seaweed attracts sea turtles. Last: Pollution makes the turtles sick.)*

TALK ABOUT THE BOOK

THINK AND SHARE
1. The female sea turtle digs a hole in the sand. She lays her eggs in the hole. She covers the hole with sand. She goes back to the sea.
2. Some people are trying to protect sea turtles. Examples: Countries pass laws to protect sea turtles. Scientists protect eggs and hatchlings.
3. to find a solution to a problem
4. Sea turtle eggs have soft shells.

RESPONSE OPTIONS

WRITING Have children write a paragraph to persuade others to help protect sea turtles.

CONTENT CONNECTIONS

SCIENCE Have children choose a species of sea turtle. Have them do guided Internet research to find the species' size, weight, diet, habitat, nesting pattern, and range of habitat. Have children share their findings.

Name _____

Sequence

Read the passage.

> The tiny eggs develop in the warm sand. When they hatch, the baby sea turtles, called hatchlings, all pour out of the nest at once. They make a dash for the water. Once in the water, they must also watch out for sharks and fish.

Write what happens first, next, and last on the lines below.

_____

I. First _____.

2. Next _____.

3. Next _____

_____.

4. Next _____

_____.

5. Last _____

_____.

© Pearson Education 2

42

Name _____

Vocabulary

Write a word from the box that best completes each sentence. You may use a word more than once.

Words to Know		
conflict	inhabit	resolve

1. It takes _____ to break our old polluting habits.

2. To protect sea turtles, humans should make sure that their needs do not _____ with the turtles' needs.

3. Sharks and sea turtle hatchlings are in _____] because the hatchlings are food for sharks.

4. Sea turtles _____ the beach when it is time to lay eggs.

5. Shrimp fishermen should _____ to use special nets that let sea turtles escape.

43

What Do Sheepdogs Do?

What Do Sheepdogs Do?

by Jessica Quilty

◉ **AUTHOR'S PURPOSE**

◉ **STORY STRUCTURE**

LESSON VOCABULARY bought, people, pleasant, probably, scared, shall, sign

SUMMARY Read about how sheepdogs keep the other farm animals in their place. The author chooses interesting facts to express their affection towards this breed. Descriptive text helps children to visualize the everyday life of a sheepdog.

INTRODUCE THE BOOK

BUILD BACKGROUND Invite children to talk about dogs and their special characteristics. Ask children if the dogs they know can do any tricks such as fetching a stick. Ask: How could a dog's ability to fetch help a dog's owner?

PREVIEW/TAKE A PICTURE WALK Remind children to browse through the book before reading and look at the pictures. Prompt children to predict what the book will be about. Ask: What other animals are shown in the photographs? Does the sheepdog seem friendly or threatening?

TEACH/REVIEW VOCABULARY Lead a synonym activity. First describe synonyms as words with same meaning. Group children in pairs and assign each pair of children a vocabulary word and its synonym: *people—humans, sign—signal, shall—will, bought—purchased, pleasant—nice, scared—frightened.* Have each pair of children write a sentence using the vocabulary word. Then have each pair read their sentence to the group once and a second time replacing the vocabulary word with its synonym.

TARGET SKILL AND STRATEGY

◉ **AUTHOR'S PURPOSE** Begin prompting children to identify the *author's purpose* by identifying the author. Ask the following questions before reading. Who wrote this book? What do you think the book will be about? Why? How do you think you will feel or think about Sheepdogs after reading this book? Do you think this book is funny, sad, serious, or exciting? Lead children to explain their answers to the questions by identifying facts in the text. Record children's answers to discuss after reading.

◉ **STORY STRUCTURE** Noticing the *story structure* can help children identify the author's purpose. Ask children what facts they learned about sheep dogs. Write each

fact on a piece of paper. Prompt children to put the facts in the correct order. Ask: Why do you think the author chose to write about these facts? How did learning about these facts make you feel about sheepdogs?

READ THE BOOK

Use the following questions to support comprehension.

PAGE 4 What are the dogs barking and nipping at? *(the sheep.)*

PAGE 6 Where do Sheepdogs that live with sheep stay? *(outdoors)*

PAGE 7 What is the sheepdog doing in the picture? *(Possible response: playing with the cat.)*

TALK ABOUT THE BOOK

THINK AND SHARE
1. Possible response: the author wanted to teach people about sheepdogs.
2. Possible response: by herding and protecting other animals.
3. Possible response: sheepdogs, leashes, puppies.
4. Possible response: both because they are friends and helpers to the farmer.

RESPONSE OPTIONS

WRITING Ask children to write two sentences that describe the sheepdogs' most import job on a farm.

ELL Have children draw a picture of farm. Then ask them to label the items in their drawing.

CONTENT CONNECTIONS

SOCIAL STUDIES Have your librarian suggest a selection of fables and myths based on the theme of animals helping people. Either have the books available for children to read independently or read a few to the class.

Time for SOCIAL STUDIES

Name _____

Author's Purpose

Read the text below. Then circle the best answer for each question.

> Sheepdogs love to work. They also like to run and play. They have a good time. It is probably lots of fun for them to live and work on the farm!

1. Why did the author write about what sheepdogs like to do?

   a. to teach

   b. to be funny

   c. to be sad

2. What is another reason the author wrote about what sheepdogs like to do?

   a. so that you will like the story

   b. so that you will like the author

   c. so that you will not like sheepdogs

3. How does the author want you to feel about a sheepdog's life?

   a. that it is hard

   b. that it is bad

   c. that it is fun

4–5.   Write a sentence that tells what you think about sheepdogs after reading the book.

_____
_____
_____
_____
_____

46

Name _____

Vocabulary

Circle the silent letters in the words below.

_____

1. people

2. sign

3. bought

4. pleasant

Draw a line to match the word to its meaning.

_____

5. bought

6. sign

7. shall

8. probably

9. pleasant

10. scared

a. nice, pleasing

b. afraid

c. got something by paying money

d. likely to happen or be true

e. a helping verb used to ask a question

f. a symbol or hand movement that means something

47

Jun and Pepper Grow Up

🔘 **AUTHOR'S PURPOSE**

🔘 **STORY STRUCTURE**

LESSON VOCABULARY bought, people, pleasant, probably, scared, shall, sign

SUMMARY Children read and find the similarities between how a boy and a dog grow up. Jun, scared of dogs at first, later learns that a dog can be a friend. The author's purpose is made clear through exploring the literary elements of the story.

INTRODUCE THE BOOK

BUILD BACKGROUND Compare the stages of both animal and human development. Ask: What are some of the first things a baby learns? What are some of the first things a puppy learns?

PREVIEW Remind children to browse through the book before reading and look at the pictures. Prompt children to look at the captions in the illustrations. Ask: How old is Jun in the beginning of the book? How old is Pepper at the end of the book?

TEACH/REVIEW VOCABULARY Lead a synonym activity. First describe synonyms as words with same meaning. Group children in pairs and assign each pair of children a vocabulary word and its synonym: *people—humans, sign—signal, shall—will, bought—purchased, pleasant—nice, scared—frightened.* Have each pair of children write a sentence using the vocabulary word. Then have each pair read their sentence to the group once and a second time ask them to replace the vocabulary word with its synonym.

TARGET SKILL AND STRATEGY

🔘 **AUTHOR'S PURPOSE** Begin prompting children to identify the *author's purpose* by identifying the author. Ask: Who wrote this book? Why? How do you think you will feel or think about dogs after reading this book? Why do you think the author compares the boy growing up to a dog growing up? Lead children to explain their answers to the questions by identifying facts in the text. Emphasize that authors can have more than one purpose.

🔘 **STORY STRUCTURE** Noticing the *story structure* can help children identify the author's purpose. Write each event on a piece of paper. Prompt children to put the events (pieces of paper) in the correct order. Ask: What

two things is the author comparing? How did the story make you feel about dogs as pets?

READ THE BOOK

Use the following questions to support comprehension.

PAGE 3 Who is Soo Mi? *(Jun's sister)*

PAGE 6 Why does the author tell you about Jun and Pepper going to school? *(Possible response: to show the similarities.)*

PAGE 9 What does the fact that Pepper run to Jun tell you? *(Possible response: that Pepper is loyal to Jun.)*

TALK ABOUT THE BOOK

THINK AND SHARE
1. Possible response: to teach something and to tell an interesting story.
2. Possible response: at first he was scared of pepper, and at the end he was very fond of pepper.
3. Possible response: puppies, paws, boxes. At the pet store, the puppies' paws poked out of their carrying boxes.
4. Possible response: I would like to have fish because they are colorful.

RESPONSE OPTIONS

WRITING Have children write a sentence describing one thing they have in common with Jun.

ELL Have children complete a simple Venn Diagram. Tell them to write three facts comparing and contrasting the events of Jun growing up and Pepper growing up.

CONTENT CONNECTIONS

SCIENCE Ask children to go to the library and pick out a book about their favorite animal. Ask them to present to the class one similarity and one difference between themselves and their favorite animal's young.

TIME FOR Science

Name _____

Author's Purpose

Read the text below. Then circle the best answer for each question.

> Jun learned to give Pepper his food and keep his water dish filled. The big puppy followed Jun everywhere. Now Jun didn't mind so much. He even thought it was pleasant and bought puppy treats.

1. Why did the author write about Jun taking care of Pepper?

a. to teach

b. to be funny

c. to be sad

2. What is another reason the author wrote about Jun and Pepper?

a. so that you will like the author

b. so that you will not like dogs

c. so that you will like the story

3. How does the author want you to feel about taking care of dogs?

a. that it is hard and dirty

b. that it is bad and sad

c. that it is work and fun

4–5. Write a sentence that tells what you think about taking care of a dog after reading *Jun and Pepper Grow Up*.

_____

==

_____

_____

46

Name _____

Vocabulary

Circle the silent letters in the words below.

1. people   3. bought

2. sign   4. pleasant

Circle the word that best completes each sentence, and write the word on the line.

5. Dad _____ a puppy and took it home.

                                                      bought   scared

6. Jun didn't like dogs jumping on him, because he was

_____ of dogs.

sign   scared

7. Pepper learned not to jump up on _____.

                                                             people   pleasant

8. Pepper's tongue felt a little rough to Jun, but _____.

                                                             probably   pleasant

9. Mom asked, "_____ we take Pepper to the park?"

                      Shall   Bought

10. When Pepper licked Jun, it was a _____ that Pepper liked him.

                                                                      sign   shall

© Pearson Education 2

47

Silver and Stripes

Silver and Stripes
by Joan Doyle
illustrated by
Marsha Winborn

◉ **AUTHOR'S PURPOSE**

◉ **STORY STRUCTURE**

LESSON VOCABULARY partnership, solution, survival

SUMMARY In this play, four woodland animals work together to survive the approaching winter. It supports and extends the lesson concept of when we need help.

INTRODUCE THE BOOK

BUILD BACKGROUND Discuss what children know about hibernation. They may know that bears sleep during the winter. Ask: In the forest, do you think you could find plants to eat when it snows?

PREVIEW Guide children to see how the headings show scene changes and how each change of speaker is shown. Explain the role of the narrator, which is to explain and comment on the action.

TEACH/PREVIEW VOCABULARY Have children use the vocabulary words to replace one word in each sentence to have it make sense: You need food for dying. You work together in a contest. You need a question to solve a problem.

TARGETED SKILL AND STRATEGY

◉ **AUTHOR'S PURPOSE** Do not use the term *author's purpose*. Instead, during the preview, ask children these questions: Who wrote this play? What do you think the play will be about? Do you think you will like the play? Why? During reading, ask follow-up questions, such as: Were you right about what the play is about? Ask questions about specific parts: On page 4, why does the author name the squirrel "Silver" and the chipmunk "Stripes"? Ask questions about the theme: Why does the author use four *different* animals as characters? Finally, ask: Why do you think the author wrote this play?

◉ **STORY STRUCTURE** Remind children that plays are stories, and stories are written from beginning to end. Each event in the story leads to the next event. As children read, have them look for a pattern in the play. To help children discover the pattern, give them a problem-and-solution graphic organizer to list each problem as it arises and how it is solved. Ask: What happens at the end of the play?

ELL Have children make a four-row chart. Help them summarize each scene so that they can see the problem/solution story structure of the play.

READ THE BOOK

Use the following questions to support comprehension.

PAGE 7 Why did Stripes listen to Silver and go away? *(Silver is bigger than Stripes.)*

PAGE 9 Was Tiny tricky, helpful, or lazy? *(helpful)*

PAGE 12 Silver, Stripes, and Tiny solved their problem by working together. What new problem did their solution cause? *(Tess ate the food they found.)*

PAGE 14 Why did the author use big animals and small animals as characters? *(She wants us to know that the weak can help the strong.)*

TALK ABOUT THE BOOK

THINK AND SHARE
1. to teach the reader that it is better to work together; to entertain (persuade also acceptable)
2. Possible response: Stage directions, narrator, scenes, character's name before dialogue.
3. part: a share of a whole thing. partner: one member of a team. ship: word ending meaning involved with, or a big boat. partnership: people working together.
4. The partners in the play must have the same goal so that they can share at the end.

RESPONSE OPTIONS

SPEAKING Have children perform a scene from this play for the class.

CONTENT CONNECTIONS

SCIENCE Have children choose an animal from the play. Have them do guided Internet research to find out how that animal survives the winter. Have children share their findings.

TIME FOR Science

Name _____

Author's Purpose

Read the text below. Then circle the best answer for each question.

Tiny: Well, hold on a minute! A true partnership works better if there are more members to help.

Silver: Really? Do you think we should ask Tess to join us?

Tiny: Yes. Tess needs to get food for the winter too, and then she would not have to take it. . . .

Tess: I've got it! If you let me join your partnership, I can help carry sticks and stones too. You can use them to make your homes warmer and stronger for the winter.

---

1. Why did the author write about Tess and the partnership?

   a. to teach

   b. to be funny

   c. to be sad

2. What is another reason the author wrote about Tess and the partnership?

   a. so that you will like the author

   b. so that you will like the story

   c. so that you will not like badgers

3. How does the author want you to feel about having a partnership?

   a. that it is unfair

   b. that it is too hard

   c. that it is good

4–5. Write a sentence that tells what you think about working with other children after reading the story.

_____

- -

_____

_____

- -

_____

46

Name _____

Vocabulary

Say each word aloud. Then draw a line between each syllable.

Words to Know		
partnership	solution	survival

1. partnership
2. solution
3. survival

Choose a word from the Word Box that best completes each sentence.

_____

4. Charing is a great _____ to many problems at playtime.

5. Some animals in a forest must gather food before the winter

   for their _____ .

6. A _____ is when people work together to get something done.

7–10. Write a sentence that tells how your family is one kind of partnership.

_____

_____

_____

_____

47

Together for Thanksgiving

Unit 2 Week 5

DRAW CONCLUSIONS

VISUALIZE

LESSON VOCABULARY behind, brought, door, everybody, minute, promise, sorry

SUMMARY This story describes a typical Thanksgiving Day. Relatives and friends gather for the feast, and everyone brings a different kind of food. Then dinner is served, and everyone says what they are thankful for. After dinner, everyone goes outside and plays ball. At the end of the day, everyone is sorry to go.

INTRODUCE THE BOOK

BUILD BACKGROUND Ask children to describe a typical Thanksgiving Day in their family. Discuss with children what their favorite dish is. What does their family serve for dessert? Do they have many guests, or is it just their family?

ELL Ask ELL children to describe their first Thanksgiving Day. What did they eat? What was their favorite dish? Do they have any day like Thanksgiving in their native country?

PREVIEW

TEACH/REVIEW VOCABULARY Go over the meaning of the vocabulary words. Tell children you have chosen a mystery word, and it is their job to guess what the word is, based on three clues about the word. Create mystery words for all other vocabulary words.

TARGET SKILL AND STRATEGY

DRAW CONCLUSIONS Remind children that *drawing conclusions* means to think about the facts and details that are presented and to decide something about them. Have children look at the cover illustration. Ask children what they imagine the people on the cover are doing, and ask them to support their answer with clues in the illustration.

VISUALIZE Remind children that to *visualize* is to create a picture in your mind. While the term visualize seems to only involve the sense of sight, visualizing includes all the senses so that the reader becomes truly involved with the scene. Encourage them to visualize as they read this story

READ THE BOOK

Use the following questions to support comprehension.

PAGE 3 How do people travel to get home to their families for Thanksgiving? *(by car, bus, train, and plane)*

PAGE 4 Where is the turkey roasting? *(in the oven)*

PAGE 6 The family and friends at the table say thanks before eating. If you were sitting with them, what would you be thankful for? *(Responses will vary.)*

TALK ABOUT THE BOOK

THINK AND SHARE
1. Possible response: They all enjoy Thanksgiving with family and friends. It says they all had fun. The illustrations show them having a good time.
2. Possible response: saw people sitting down at the table, heard them giving thanks, smelled dishes of food on the table
3. Possible responses: Thanks, giving, sing, tank, than, sting
4. Aunt Amy brought stuffing; Uncle Ralph brought cranberry sauce; Grandma brought yams and sweet potato pies; Mary Jo brought spinach and green beans.

RESPONSE OPTIONS

WRITING Have children visualize that their Thanksgiving Dinner is spread out on the table in front of them. Everyone has just gathered for the meal. Have children describe who is at the table and the different types of food that are on the table. Make sure they describe the smells and tastes of all of the dishes.

CONTENT CONNECTIONS

SOCIAL STUDIES Have children research the history of Thanksgiving, using either the library or the Internet. What did the Pilgrims eat at their first Thanksgiving? What were they thankful for? What kind of things did they learn from the Indians?

Together for Thanksgiving **LR37**

Name _____

Draw Conclusions

Think about the story *Together for Thanksgiving*. Then think about what you already know about Thanksgiving Day. Circle the phrase that best completes each conclusion below.

1. People go by car, plane, or train to Thanksgiving dinner, so

   a. some live nearby and some live far away.

   b. everyone lives far away.

   c. they do not like to travel.

2. Everyone brings a dish, so

   a. there is not enough food.

   b. there is lots of food.

   c. there is no dessert.

3. Everyone helps clean up, so
   a. it goes by fast.

   b. it takes a long time.

   c. they do not want to play.

4-5. What more do you know about Thanksgiving Day? Write your own conclusion on the line below.

_____

- -

_____

_____

- -

_____

50

Name _____

Vocabulary

Choose the word from the box that best fits into each sentence.

Words to Know
behind   brought   door   everybody
minute   promise   sorry

1. John was _____ he broke the window.

2. The guests knocked on the front _____ .

3. _____ ate some turkey.

4. My aunt _____ pumpkin pie.

5. We made a _____ to help clean up.

6. Dinner will be ready in a _____ .

7. Yummy smells came from _____ the kitchen door.

51

Giving Thanks Around the World

Giving Thanks Around the World

DRAW CONCLUSIONS

VISUALIZE

LESSON VOCABULARY behind, brought, door, everybody, minute, promise, sorry

SUMMARY This book describes harvest celebrations around the world. In African villages, people celebrate the yam harvest. The Chinese celebrate by watching the full moon rise. In Southern India, the rice harvest is celebrated. In America, people celebrate Thanksgiving with a big meal.

INTRODUCE THE BOOK

INTRODUCE THE TITLE AND AUTHOR Discuss with children the title and the author of *Giving Thanks Around the World.* Based on the title, ask children what kind of information they think this book will provide. Does the photo on the cover give them any additional clues?

PREVIEW Invite children to take a picture walk through the pictures in the book. Ask children how the pictures give clues as to what the book is about.

ELL Ask ELL children to describe their first Thanksgiving Day? What did they eat? What was their favorite dish? Do they have any day like Thanksgiving in their country?

TEACH/REVIEW VOCABULARY Go over the meaning of the vocabulary words. Tell children you have chosen a mystery word, and it is their job to guess what the word is, based on three clues about the word. Create mystery words for all other vocabulary words.

TARGET SKILL AND STRATEGY

DRAW CONCLUSIONS Remind children that *drawing conclusions* means to think about the facts and details that are presented and to decide something about them. Have children look at the map on page 4. Tell them that in Ghana and Nigeria in Africa, they celebrate their major crop. Have them draw conclusions about what that crop is based on the map illustration.

VISUALIZE Remind children that to *visualize* is to create a picture in your mind. Visualizing includes all the senses so that the reader becomes truly involved with the scene. Encourage them to visualize as they read this story. Remind them that visualizing not only includes the sense of sight, but can also involve the senses of smell, hearing, and taste.

READ THE BOOK

Use the following questions to support comprehension.

PAGE 3 Who celebrated the very first Thanksgiving? *(the pilgrims and Native Americans celebrated together)*

PAGE 4 Harvest celebrations tend to take place in which season of the year? *(in the fall)*

PAGE 5 Which vegetable is celebrated in Ghana and Nigeria? *(yams)*

TALK ABOUT THE BOOK

THINK AND SHARE
1. The Chinese celebrate the full moon at the harvest, so their cakes are shaped like little moons.
2. Possible responses: turkey, stuffing, sweet potatoes or yams
3. Possible responses: holiday, day, way, place, takes, cakes, parades
4. Responses will vary.

RESPONSE OPTIONS

WRITING Have children visualize the harvest celebrations in Nigeria, China, or India. Have them write a short paragraph describing how that country celebrates the harvest. They should write from the point of view that they are taking part in the celebration directly. What are the sights, sounds and smells that go along with this celebration? What special foods are eaten?

CONTENT CONNECTIONS

SOCIAL STUDIES Have children read the information on page 12. Have children research the turkey, using their library or the Internet. How many countries in the world have turkeys? What is the difference between a wild turkey and the kind of turkey we eat on Thanksgiving?

Time for SOCIAL STUDIES

Draw Conclusions

Think about what you read in *Giving Thanks Around the World*.
Then think about what you already know about Thanksgiving Day.
Circle the phrase that best completes each conclusion below.

1. Many people celebrate and give thanks in autumn because

   a. people like to carve pumpkins.

   b. many crops are harvested in autumn.

   c. they like to be outdoors.

2. The Chinese celebrate the Moon Festival

   a. in the morning.

   b. in the afternoon.

   c. at night.

3. By making offerings to the rain and the sun, southern Indian villagers hope

   a. there will be sun and rain next year.

   b. there will be no rain next year.

   c. there will be no sun next year.

4–5. What more do you know about giving thanks around the world? Write your own conclusion on the line below.

_____

_____

_____

_____

_____

© Pearson Education 2

50

Name _____

Vocabulary

Choose a word from the Word Box to complete the sentences below.

> **Words to Know**
>
> behind   brought   door   everybody
> minute   promise   sorry

1. behind   **a.** each and every person

2. brought   **b.** toward the back

3. door   **c.** feel sadness or regret

4. everybody   **d.** to give your word

5. minute   **e.** the barrier at the entrance of a building or room

6. promise   **f.** carried or taken with you

7. sorry   **g.** 60 seconds

8. She made a _____ to clean up her room.

9. She opened the _____ so her dog could go out.

10. Ben _____ his books to school in his backpack.

51

The Pilgrims' First Year

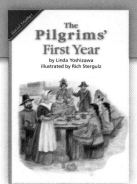

◉ DRAW CONCLUSIONS

◉ VISUALIZE

LESSON VOCABULARY dine, faith, fertilizer, holiday, participate, resources, traditions

---

SUMMARY This reader tells of the first year of the Pilgrims in America. Without the help of the Wampanoag people, they would not have survived. The Pilgrims and the Wampanoag worked closely together to plant crops and build their dwellings. Finally, after their first full year, they celebrated with a feast that became our Thanksgiving Day.

INTRODUCE THE BOOK

BUILD BACKGROUND Ask children to discuss what they know about the Pilgrims and the first Thanksgiving. Do they know which crops they planted? What was the name of the ship that brought them over from England?

PREVIEW Invite children to take a picture walk through the pictures in the book. Ask children how the pictures give clues as to what the book is about.

TEACH/PREVIEW VOCABULARY Go over the meaning of the vocabulary words. Tell children you have chosen a mystery word and it is their job to guess what the word is, based on three clues about the word. Create mystery words for all other vocabulary words.

ELL Give English learners a list of definitions and have them match the definition with the correct vocabulary word.

TARGET SKILL AND STRATEGY

◉ DRAW CONCLUSIONS Remind children that *drawing conclusions* means to think about the facts and details that are presented and to decide something about them. Have children look at the pictures on pages 4–5 and pages 8–9. The Native Americans built houses that could be easily picked up and moved. Ask: What conclusions can you draw about whether the Pilgrims houses could be moved?

◉ VISUALIZE Remind children that to *visualize* is to create a picture in your mind. Visualizing includes all the senses so that the reader becomes truly involved with the scene. Encourage them to visualize as they read this story.

READ THE BOOK

Use the following questions to support comprehension.

PAGE 4 During what season did the Wampanoag move to the shore? *(the spring)*

PAGE 5 Why did the Pilgrims set sail for America? *(to find religious freedom)*

PAGE 17 How long did the first Thanksgiving feast take? *(three days)*

TALK ABOUT THE BOOK

THINK AND SHARE

1. Possible responses: surprised, excited, thankful, at home
2. Responses can vary, but should include images of pilgrims crowded and hungry, traveling across the ocean.
3. Possible responses: The boys helped the older men hunt, fish, and trap animals. They made canoes, knives, bows and arrows. The Wampanoag girls helped their mother's farm, gather wild pants, make clothing and grass mats.
4. The first Thanksgiving was in October, not November.

RESPONSE OPTIONS

WRITING Have children imagine that they are crossing the ocean on the *Mayflower*. They should write a brief letter home to one of their friends telling them about the voyage, including the conditions on the ship, their hopes and dreams about the future, the sounds and smells of the sea.

CONTENT CONNECTIONS

Time for **SOCIAL STUDIES**

SOCIAL STUDIES Have children research Squanto on the Internet or in the library. They should try to find out as much information on his life before and after he met the Pilgrims. What eventually happened to Squanto? Did he continue to live with the Pilgrims?

Name _____

Fact and Opinion

Think about what you read in *The Pilgrims' First Year*. Then think about what you already know about Pilgrims and Native Americans. Circle the phrase that best completes each conclusion below.

1. The Wampanoag sewed clothes from deer and elk skins, so

    a. deer and elk roamed nearby.

    b. they must have liked deer and elk the most.

    c. they must have only eaten clams.

2. The Wampanoag spent the winter in the forest because

    a. they grew different crops in the winter.

    b. trees sheltered them from the winter weather.

    c. it was too muddy by the shore.

3. The Pilgrims did not know a lot about hunting because

    a. they only ate vegetables.

    b. they were taught as children.

    c. they did not hunt as much in England.

4–5. What more do you know about the Pilgrim's first year? Write your own conclusion on the line below.

_____

- -

_____

_____

- -

_____

50

Name _____

Vocabulary

Choose a word from the Word Box to complete the sentences below.

> **Words to Know**
>
> dine   faith   fertilizer   holiday
> participate   resources   holiday traditions

1. The Pilgrims invited the Wampanoag to _____ with them.

2. Thanksgiving is now a national _____.

3. The Pilgrims brought many _____ from England.

4. Squanto taught the Pilgrims to use fish for _____.

5. The Pilgrims wanted to practice their _____.

6. The Wampanoag used the _____ around them.

7. Everyone had to _____ in doing chores.

© Pearson Education 2

51

Answer Key for Below-Level Reader Practice

Dogs to the Rescue!   LR1

🎯 Sequence, LR2
1. 5 **2.** 4 **3.** 2 **4.** 3 **5.** 1

Vocabulary, LR3
1. family-3 **2.** heard-1 **3.** listen-2 **4.** pull-1 **5.** once-1 **6.** break-1
7–8. answer reflects their understanding **9–10.** answer reflects their understanding

Let's Play Baseball   LR10

🎯 Realism and Fantasy, LR11
1. fantasy **2.** realistic story **3.** fantasy **4.** realistic story **5.** fantasy

Vocabulary, LR12
1. b **2.** a **3.** f **4.** c **5.** e **6.** d **7.** g **8.** i **9.** j **10.** h

Busy Beavers   LR19

🎯 Sequence, LR20
1. Beavers cut down trees with their teeth. **2.** They cut off the branches. **3.** They strip off the bark. **4.** They carry the logs toward the river.

Vocabulary, LR21
ACROSS: **1.** -hole **2.** towa-d **3.** w-rd **4.** -go **5.** enou-h DOWN: lodge **6.** above

What Do Sheepdogs Do?   LR28

🎯 Author's Purpose, LR29
1. a **2.** a **3.** c **4–5.** Answers will vary.

Vocabulary, LR30
1. o **2.** g **3.** gh **4.** a **5.** c **6.** f **7.** e **8.** d **9.** a **10.** b

Together for Thanksgiving   LR37

🎯 Draw Conclusions, LR38
1. a **2.** b **3.** a **4–5.** Possible response given. Thanksgiving Day is a day to share.

Vocabulary, LR39
1. sorry **2.** door **3.** Everybody **4.** brought **5.** promise **6.** minute
7. behind

Answer Key for On-Level Reader Practice

What To Do in an Emergency   LR4

⊙ Sequence, LR5
1. First get down low… **2.** Next, check your clothes… **3.** Don't stop to take anything… **4.** Break windows to get out… **5.** Call 9-1-1!

Vocabulary, LR6
1. d **2.** a **3.** b **4.** e **5.** c **6.** f **7–8.** answer reflects their understanding **9–10.** answer reflects their understanding

Warm and Fuzzy   LR13

⊙ Realism/Fantasy, LR14
1. fantasy **2.** fantasy **3.** Fantasy **4–5.** Possible responses given. Sheep have wool. People make the wool into yarn. People use the yarn to knit things like scarves.

Vocabulary, LR15
1. b **2.** a **3.** f **4.** c **5.** e **6.** d **7.** c **8.** b **9.** d **10.** a

The Busy, Quiet, Lively, Sleepy Pond   LR22

⊙ Sequence, LR23
Clockwise from top left: spring, spring, fall, winter

Vocabulary, LR24
above, toward, whole, enough, ago

Jun and Pepper Grow Up   LR31

⊙ Author's Purpose, LR32
1. a **2.** c **3.** c

Vocabulary, LR33
1. o **2.** g **3.** gh **4.** A **5.** bought **6.** scared **7.** people **8.** pleasant **9.** Shall **10.** sign

Giving Thanks Around the World   LR40

⊙ Draw Conclusions, LR41
1. a **2.** c **3.** a **4–5.** Possible response given. People are thankful for the food they eat.

Vocabulary, LR42
1. b **2.** f **3.** e **4.** a **5.** g **6.** d **7.** c **8.** promise **9.** door **10.** brought

Answer Key for Advanced-Level Reader Practice

Amazing Animals   LR7

🎯 Sequence, LR8
1. 5 **2.** 3 **3.** 2 **4.** 1 **5.** 4

Vocabulary, LR9
1. courageous **2.** groom **3.** therapy **4.** tasks **5.** rescue **6.** hazard
7. depends

The First Big Game   LR16

🎯 Realism/Fantasy, LR17
1. fantasy story **2.** People do not play baseball in space. **3.** fantasy
story **4.** Monkeys do not play baseball. **5.** The First Night Game

Vocabulary, LR18
1. B **2.** C **3.** A **4.** In baseball, two teams compete. **5.** When you play
with friends, it is recreation.

Sea Turtles at Risk   LR25

🎯 Sequence, LR26
1. The turtle eggs develop. **2.** The eggs hatch. **3.** Hatchlings pour
out of the nest. **4.** They make a dash for the water. **5.** They watch out
for sharks and fish.

Vocabulary, LR27
1. resolve **2.** conflict **3.** conflict **4.** inhabit **5.** resolve

Silver and Stripes   LR34

🎯 Author's Purpose, LR35
1. a. to teach **2.** b. so that you will like the story **3.** c. that it is good
4–5. Answers will vary.

Vocabulary, LR36
1. part-ner-ship **2.** sol-u-tion **3.** sur-viv-al **4.** solution **5.** survival
6. partnership **7.** Answers will vary.

The Pilgrims' First Year   LR43

🎯 Fact and Opinion, LR44
1. A **2.** B **3.** C **4–5.** Possible responses given. The Wampanoags
helped the Pilgrims survive.

Vocabulary, LR45
1. dine **2.** holiday **3.** tradition **4.** fertilizer **5.** faith **6.** resources
7. participate

Differentiated Instruction

Table of Contents

Let's Learn Amazing Words

TEACH/MODEL

Use the Oral Vocabulary Routine along with the definitions, examples, letter-sounds, and word parts that are provided on the following pages to introduce each Amazing Word.

ROUTINE

Oral Vocabulary

1 **Introduce the Word** Relate the word to the song or story in which it appears. Supply a child-friendly definition. Have children say the word. Example:
- People who are courageous are very brave. If you help someone in trouble by calling 9-1-1, you are doing something courageous. Say the word courageous with me, courageous.

2 **Demonstrate** Provide familiar examples to demonstrate meaning. When possible, use gestures to help convey meaning. Examples:
- A firefighter who rescues someone from a burning building is courageous. Soldiers who fight in a war are courageous.

3 **Apply** Have children demonstrate understanding with a simple activity. Suggestions for step 3 activities appear on the next page. Example:
- Tell me which dog is courageous—one that sleeps all the time or one that growls and barks to protect its family from danger.

4 **Display the Word/Letter-Sounds** Write the word on a card and display it on a classroom Amazing Words board. Have children identify some familiar letter-sounds or word parts. Example:
- This word is courageous. What sound is at the beginning of the word? What letter stands for that sound? Find the word courage in courageous.

ACTIVITIES

To allow children to demonstrate understanding of the Amazing Words, use activities such as these in step 3 of the Routine.

ANSWER QUESTIONS Would you prefer to have a *festive* day or an *ordinary* day? Why?

CREATE EXAMPLES What is something a good *citizen* might do?

MAKE CHOICES If any of the things I name can *hatch*, say *hatch*; if not, say nothing: a train, a chicken, a jar of jam, a snake, a tadpole, a horse.

PANTOMIME Show me how an eagle *soars*, a rocket, an airplane.

PERSONAL CONTEXT Some people are *fond* of fishing. Tell about something you are *fond* of. Use the word *fond* when you tell about it.

SYNONYMS AND ANTONYMS Name a word that means the opposite of *genuine*; name a word that means about the same as *genuine*.

Monitor Progress | Check Oral Vocabulary

To monitor understanding of concepts and vocabulary that have been explicitly taught each week:

- Display the week's Build Background pages in the Student Edition.
- Remind the child of the concept that the class has been talking about that week.
- Ask the child to tell you about the Build Background illustrations using some of the week's Amazing Words.

If... a child has difficulty using the Amazing Words,

then... ask questions about the illustration using the Amazing Words. Note which questions the child can respond to. Reteach unknown words using the Oral Vocabulary Routine.

SUCCESS PREDICTOR

to build oral vocabulary

Definitions, **examples**, and **letter-sounds** to use with Oral Vocabulary Routine on p. DI•1

USE WITH

DAY 1

1 **HAZARD** A *hazard* is something dangerous.

2 **Examples:** The broken swing on the playground is a *hazard*. Be careful of the *hazard* where the sidewalk is tilted.

4 **Letter-Sounds:** Identify *h*/h/ and *z*/z/. Point out the final *rd*/rd/.

1 **RESCUE** If you *rescue* someone, you save that person from danger. If you saved someone, you made a *rescue*.

2 **Examples:** The firefighter *rescued* the child from the burning building. The lifeguard came to the *rescue* of the child who could not swim.

4 **Letter-Sounds:** Children can decode the first syllable. Point out the long u sound in the second syllable.

DAY 2

1 **AVALANCHE** An *avalanche* happens when a lot of snow suddenly slides down a mountain.

2 **Examples:** The huge *avalanche* last week buried lots of trees on the mountain. Some dogs are specially trained to find people lost in *avalanches*.

4 **Letter-Sounds:** Identify *a*/a/ in the first syllable and *ch*/ch/ at the end of the word.

DAY 3

1 **INSTINCT** An *instinct* is an ability an animal is born with that makes it act in a certain way.

2 **Examples:** *Instinct* tells animals how to hunt for their own food. Birds have an instinct for building their nests in a certain way.

4 **Letter Sounds:** Children can decode the syllable *in*. Identify *st*/st/ at the beginning of the second syllable.

1 **SKITTISH** *Skittish* means nervous and easily upset.

2 **Examples:** A *skittish* horse bolts when it hears an unusual noise. Our new puppy is so *skittish* it runs and hides whenever the door opens.

4 **Letter-Sounds:** Children can decode *skittish*.

DAY 4

1 **BLUSTERY** A storm is *blustery* when the wind blows hard and makes a lot of noise.

2 **Examples:** The wind and rain made the day so *blustery* that I was glad to get home. You can't really put up an umbrella when it's this *blustery* outside.

4 **Letter-Sounds:** Point out the initial *bl*/bl and the long e sound of final *y*.

1 **FAST-PACED** You know what *fast* means. *Pace* means the speed at which something happens. So something that is *fast-paced* is happening very quickly.

2 **Examples:** We had so much to do this morning that it was *fast-paced*. The baseball game was so *fast-paced* that it was over in an hour. (Step 3: Have children demonstrate *fast-paced* walking.)

4 **Word Parts:** Children can decode the parts *fast* and *paced*. Point out the hyphen that combines the words into a compound word.

Ronald Morgan Goes to Bat

Amazing Words

to build oral vocabulary

USE WITH

DAY 1

① **COMPETE** When you *compete*, you try very hard to win or you become part of a contest.

② **Examples:** Our team will *compete* with their team for the championship. Mark and Jenny are *competing* in the spelling bee.

④ **Letter-Sounds:** Identify *c*/k/ and have children decode the last syllable with its long e sound.

① **CONTRIBUTE** When you *contribute* to something, you help along with others.

② **Examples:** Everybody on the team contributes hard work. Let's *contribute* our own ideas for the party.

④ **Letter-Sounds:** Clap the three syllables *con-trib-ute*. Children can decode each one.

① **RECREATION** *Recreation* is fun or something you do to have a good time.

② **Examples:** We like to go to the beach for *recreation* in the summer. Tim's family goes camping for *recreation*.

④ **Letter-Sounds:** Identify *rec*/rek/ and the ending *-tion*/shon/.

DAY 2

① **MOPE** When you *mope*, you feel sad and sorry for yourself.

② **Examples:** The dog *moped* around the house when the children were in school. It's easy to mope when you don't have anyone to play with.

④ **Letter-Sounds:** Children can decode *mope*.

DAY 3

① **DESERVE** If you *deserve* something, you have a right to it or have earned it.

② **Examples:** You *deserve* a treat for cleaning your room. Sometimes a naughty child *deserves* punishment.

④ **Letter-Sounds:** Point out s/z/.

DAY 4

① **ACTUATE** When you *actuate* something, you get it started or put it into action.

② **Examples:** Many different steps are needed to *actuate* a spaceship. That toy is *actuated* by a wind-up spring.

④ **Word Parts:** Point out the base word *act* in *actuate*.

① **ALOFT** Something that is *aloft* is high up or up in the air.

② **Examples:** An airplane flies aloft. After the plane is aloft, passengers can get up and walk around.

④ **Letter-Sounds:** Identify final *ft*/ft/.

① **TINKER** When you *tinker* with something, you work at it and fool around with it.

② **Examples:** Sometimes a person invents something great when he or she is just *tinkering*. My dad *tinkered* with our old TV set and figured out how to fix it.

④ **Letter-Sounds:** Identify *nk*/nk/ at the end of the first syllable. Children can decode *tinker*.

Amazing Words to build oral vocabulary

Definitions, examples, and **letter-sounds** to use with Oral Vocabulary Routine on p. DI•1

USE WITH

DAY 1

1 **CONFLICT** A *conflict* is a struggle or fight, especially one that goes on for a long time.

2 **Examples:** My brother and I always have a *conflict* over whose turn it is to do the dishes. Sometimes a simple argument can develop into a real *conflict*.

4 **Word Parts:** Children can decode the syllables *con-flict.*

1 **INHABIT** When you inhabit a place, you live in it.

2 **Examples:** Lots of fish *inhabit* that lake. That big cactus is *inhabited* by many different desert animals.

4 **Word Parts:** Point out the syllables in *in-hab-it.*

1 **RESOLVE** If you *resolve* something, you make a decision or you solve or fix a problem.

2 **Examples:** We were arguing about what to do until my dad came and *resolved* the problem. I *resolved* to study harder for the next test.

4 **Word Parts:** Point out the base word *solve.*

DAY 2

1 **COAX** When you gently talk someone into doing something, you *coax* that person.

2 **Examples:** My brother *coaxed* me into letting him ride my bike. Mom sometimes has to *coax* the baby into eating. (Step 3: Have children *coax* you to do something in the classroom.)

4 **Letter-Sounds:** Point out that the long *o* sound of *oa* and decode the word with children.

1 **STARTLE** When you *startle* someone, you surprise and shock them very suddenly.

2 **Examples:** The huge boom of thunder startled me so that I dropped my glass. The dog's sharp bark *startled* the children.

4 **Letter-Sounds:** Children can decode *start* in *startle.*

DAY 3

1 **RAMP** A *ramp* is a slope or slant that connects two different levels.

2 **Examples:** Cars go down a *ramp* from the street to the parking garage. At the pool, you can slide down a *ramp* into the water. (Have children build a makeshift *ramp* to roll a pencil down.)

4 **Letter-Sounds:** Children can decode *ramp.*

DAY 4

1 **SERAPE** A *serape* is a shawl or blanket that people can wear over their shirts. *Serapes* are worn in Latin America and usually have bright colors, often stripes.

2 **Examples:** Mom got a *serape* in Mexico that she wears sometimes instead of a sweater. A girl at school has a *serape* with red and green and yellow stripes.

4 **Word Parts:** *Serape* is a Spanish word with three syllables: *se/ra/pe.* The last syllable has a long e sound.

1 **VACATION** A *vacation* is a time away from school or your usual duties. When you take a *vacation*, you can say you *vacation*.

2 **Examples:** Our family *vacationed* at the lake last summer. It was the first *vacation* we ever took away from home.

4 **Word Parts:** Point out the base word *vacate.* *Vacate* means to go away from something and leave it empty.

The Bremen Town Musicians

Definitions, **examples**, and **letter-sounds** to use with Oral Vocabulary Routine on p. DI·1

Amazing Words

to build oral vocabulary

USE WITH

DAY 1

① **PARTNERSHIP** A *partnership* happens when two or more people become partners and joint together to share something.

② **Examples:** My best friend and I have a real *partnership*—we do everything together. The *partnership* of those people has lasted for many years.

④ **Word Parts:** Point out the words *part* and *partner*. A partner is someone who shares a part with someone else.

① **SOLUTION** A *solution* is the process of solving a problem.

② **Examples:** The *solution* to that problem took a long time. Mom came up with the *solution* by promising to drive me to the game.

④ **Letter-Sounds:** Identify the letter-sounds s/s/, l/l/, and the final syllable *-tion*.

① **SURVIVAL** *Survival* means the act of living on or of surviving.

② **Examples:** The *survival* of the people in that fire depended on the firefighters. *Survival* in a harsh place like the desert is difficult.

④ **Letter-Sounds:** Children can decode *sur.*

DAY 2

① **STRUGGLE** If you *struggle*, you work hard to do something difficult. If you have a *struggle*, you have some very hard work to get something done.

② **Examples:** The swimmer *struggled* hard against the big waves. It is a *struggle* for me to save money from my allowance.

④ **Letter-Sounds:** Children can decode *strug.*

DAY 3

① **MISERABLE** If you are *miserable*, you are very, very unhappy. Something that is *miserable* causes great unhappiness.

② **Examples:** Pat was *miserable* about missing school that day. Sally has a *miserable* cold.

④ **Letter-Sounds:** Identify s/z/ in the syllable *mis..*

DAY 4

① **FAITHFUL** When you are *faithful*, you are loyal and you believe in someone or something.

② **Examples:** *Faithful* friends always like you and like to be with you. Our dog Tipper was *faithful* to everyone in the family.

④ **Word Parts:** Point out the base word *faith*, which means "a belief," and the suffix *-ful*.

① **MISGIVINGS** A *misgiving* is a feeling of doubt or worry.

② **Examples:** We had *misgivings* about traveling in the storm. I voted for Jane for class president with some *misgivings*.

④ **Word Parts:** Point out the base word give and the prefix *mis-*, meaning "bad."

① **OCCASION** An *occasion* is a certain time or a special event.

② **Examples:** The Fourth of July is an *occasion* of parades and fireworks. That big birthday party was a wonderful occasion.

④ **Letter-Sounds:** Identify cc/k/ and the long a sound of the second syllable.

Oral Vocabulary

SUCCESS PREDICTOR

to build oral vocabulary

Definitions, examples, and letter-sounds to use with Oral Vocabulary Routine on p. DI•1

USE WITH

DAY 1

1 **DINE** When you dine, you eat dinner.

2 **Examples:** We *dined* on a huge turkey on Thanksgiving Day. We will *dine* on hot dogs and potato salad at the picnic.

4 **Letter-Sounds:** Children can decode *dine*.

1 **HOLIDAY** A *holiday* is a day when people celebrate something special.

2 **Examples:** Thanksgiving is a *holiday* for people in the United States. The 4th of July is the *holiday* when we celebrate the birth of our country.

4 **Letter-Sounds:** Identify the letter-sound for *h*/h/ and the final syllable day.

1 **PARTICIPATE** When you participate in something, you join in.

2 **Examples:** The girls always *participate* in soccer. Gwen wants to *participate* in the singing contest.

4 **Letter-Sounds:** Identify the syllables *par* and *pate*.

DAY 2

1 **DECORATE** When you *decorate* something, you make it as pretty as you can.

2 **Examples:** My mom *decorated* my birthday cake with baseballs made of frosting. We *decorated* the Thanksgiving dinner table with little turkeys we made out of paper. (Ask children to *decorate* the bulletin board.)

4 **Letter-Sounds:** Decode *deco* and have children decode *rate.*

DAY 3

1 **BANQUET** A *banquet* is a very special dinner

2 **Examples:** Our school held a special *banquet* in the gym for all the parents. There was an awards *banquet* at the end of the season for all the teams.

4 **Word Parts:** Run your hand under *ban-quet* as you say the syllables.

DAY 4

1 **FLARE** When something *flares*, it flames or lights briefly and unsteadily.

2 **Examples:** The campfire *flared* up before it went out. Dad struck a match to light the birthday candles, and they *flared* up quickly.

4 **Letter-Sounds:** Children can decode *flare*.

1 **GLIMMER** A *glimmer* is an unsteady light. Something that *glimmers* shines with an unsteady light.

2 **Examples:** Stars twinkled and glimmered in the dark night sky. I saw a *glimmer* of light down the path.

4 **Letter-Sounds:** Children can decode *glimmer*.

1 **WHISPERY** When something is whispery, it sounds like a whisper with a soft, rustling sound.

2 **Examples:** The blowing snow was *whispery* against the windows. The wind was *whispery* in the dead leaves of the tree.

4 **Word Parts:** Identify the base word *whisper* and the ending *–y*.

Grade 2
Oral Vocabulary Words

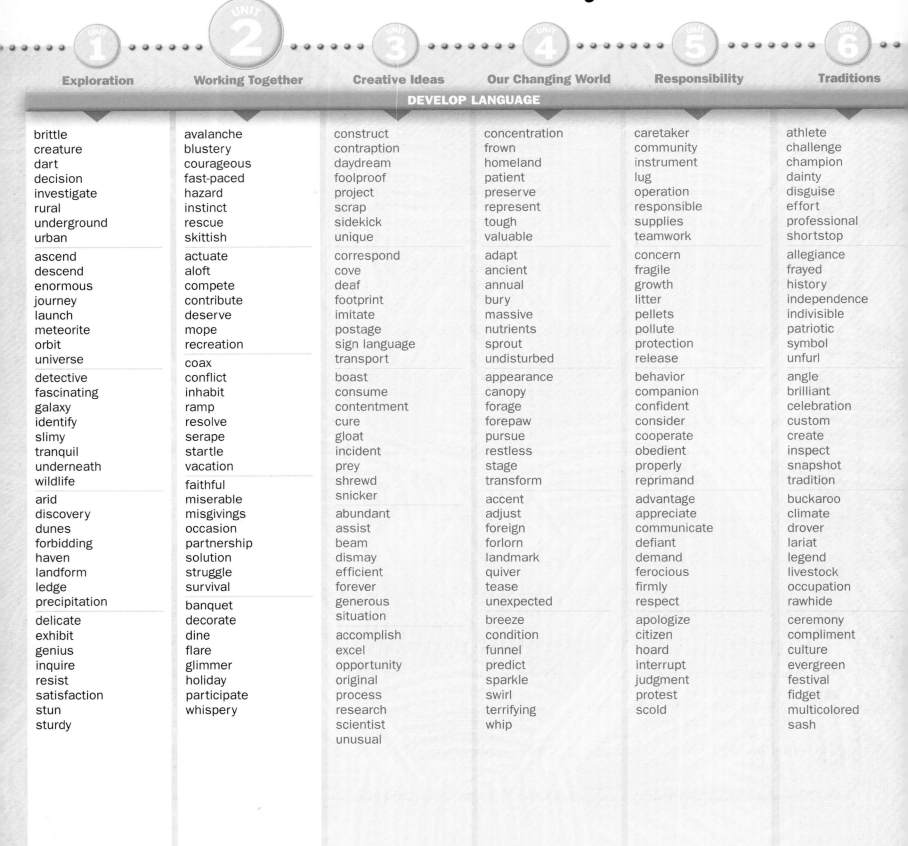

UNIT 1 Exploration	UNIT 2 Working Together	UNIT 3 Creative Ideas	UNIT 4 Our Changing World	UNIT 5 Responsibility	UNIT 6 Traditions

DEVELOP LANGUAGE

brittle	avalanche	construct	concentration	caretaker	athlete
creature	blustery	contraption	frown	community	challenge
dart	courageous	daydream	homeland	instrument	champion
decision	fast-paced	foolproof	patient	lug	dainty
investigate	hazard	project	preserve	operation	disguise
rural	instinct	scrap	represent	responsible	effort
underground	rescue	sidekick	tough	supplies	professional
urban	skittish	unique	valuable	teamwork	shortstop
ascend	actuate	correspond	adapt	concern	allegiance
descend	aloft	cove	ancient	fragile	frayed
enormous	compete	deaf	annual	growth	history
journey	contribute	footprint	bury	litter	independence
launch	deserve	imitate	massive	pellets	indivisible
meteorite	mope	postage	nutrients	pollute	patriotic
orbit	recreation	sign language	sprout	protection	symbol
universe	coax	transport	undisturbed	release	unfurl
detective	conflict	boast	appearance	behavior	angle
fascinating	inhabit	consume	canopy	companion	brilliant
galaxy	ramp	contentment	forage	confident	celebration
identify	resolve	cure	forepaw	consider	custom
slimy	serape	gloat	pursue	cooperate	create
tranquil	startle	incident	restless	obedient	inspect
underneath	vacation	prey	stage	properly	snapshot
wildlife	faithful	shrewd	transform	reprimand	tradition
arid	miserable	snicker	accent	advantage	buckaroo
discovery	misgivings	abundant	adjust	appreciate	climate
dunes	occasion	assist	foreign	communicate	drover
forbidding	partnership	beam	forlorn	defiant	lariat
haven	solution	dismay	landmark	demand	legend
landform	struggle	efficient	quiver	ferocious	livestock
ledge	survival	forever	tease	firmly	occupation
precipitation	banquet	generous	unexpected	respect	rawhide
delicate	decorate	situation	breeze	apologize	ceremony
exhibit	dine	accomplish	condition	citizen	compliment
genius	flare	excel	funnel	hoard	culture
inquire	glimmer	opportunity	predict	interrupt	evergreen
resist	holiday	original	sparkle	judgment	festival
satisfaction	participate	process	swirl	protest	fidget
stun	whispery	research	terrifying	scold	multicolored
sturdy		scientist	whip		sash
		unusual			

K-9 Paul, Police Dog

"Did you hear about today's special assembly?" Joe asked Nate. "There's going to be a police rescue dog." Nate was excited by this news. He loved dogs, and having a police dog visit school was much more fun than a math test.

Nate and Joe sat together for the assembly. They listened as the principal introduced Officer Reynolds and his four-footed partner, K-9 Paul, a big German shepherd.

"K-9 Paul looks friendly," Nate whispered.

"He probably looks different when he's chasing bad guys," Joe responded.

Nate listened closely to every word Officer Reynolds said. "Police dogs are smart and courageous," said Officer Reynolds. "They will face dangerous situations without hesitating. They can do some things human officers can't, like finding suspects by sniffing their scent. I trust K-9 Paul with my life." Officer Reynolds finished his speech and asked if there were any questions from the audience. Nate raised his hand.

"Where does the dog live?" Nate asked.

"He lives with me," answered the officer. "We live and work together as a team."

Nate had never thought about being a police officer when he grew up, but now it seemed like a good choice, as long as he could have a dog for a partner.

Little League

Do you like to play baseball? Some children are happy playing a pick-up game in the park for recreation, but other children want to wear real baseball uniforms and compete with children from other teams. These children join Little League.

Little League has its own World Series. The Little League World Series is held each year in Williamsport, Pennsylvania. Only the best Little League teams from the United States and around the world are invited to play in the Little League World series. Teams compete to see who will be that year's champion.

Little League began in 1939 with only three teams. It grew over the years, and now there are thousands of Little League teams in America and other countries all over the world. At first, Little League was only for boys, and girls weren't allowed to play. But now girls can play too.

Many major league players got their start in Little League, including players who are now in Baseball's Hall of Fame. Even President George W. Bush played Little League baseball.

So, if you want to play for the love of the sport or just for fun, what are you waiting for? If there are no Little League teams in your community, find out what it takes to get one started. Then get out there and hit a home run!

ADVANCED SELECTION 7   VOCABULARY: recreation, compete

Ned's Turtles

Ned is only eight years old, but he already knows a lot about turtles. He knows that female turtles lay more than a hundred eggs in nests they make in the dirt. He also knows that most turtle eggs and baby turtles become food for other animals.

Ned knows that different kinds of turtles inhabit different areas. Some live in and around ponds, while others live near the sea. He knows how to tell different kinds of turtles apart by what they look like. He knows that snapping turtles won't attack people unless they are cornered and pushed into conflict. Ned knows a lot about turtles.

Ned has books about turtles and pictures of turtles on his bedroom wall. He has models of turtles and a few toy turtles left over from when he was little.

Ned's friend Kelly once asked him why he didn't have a pet turtle. Ned said he liked turtles too much to keep one as a pet. He wanted the turtles to be free.

For his birthday, Ned's parents took him to a park where he could see turtles living in nature. He watched them for hours. Finally, the park was closing, and it was time to go. Though Ned was sorry to leave, he thought it was the best birthday he ever had.

ADVANCED SELECTION 8   VOCABULARY: inhabit, conflict

Helping Hands

Animals can be trained to assist disabled people. You may have seen service dogs assisting disabled people. Monkeys can be trained to assist people too.

Monkeys can be trained to assist quadriplegics. Quadriplegics are people who can't move their arms, hands, and legs. One major problem faced by quadriplegics is the inability to do simple, everyday tasks for themselves.

A psychologist, M. J. Willard, thought of a possible solution to the problem—a partnership between animals and people with disabilities. She thought that an animal with hands could do simple, everyday tasks for a quadriplegic.

The doctor decided to train Capuchin monkeys, whose hands are very much like human hands. These monkeys also have friendly dispositions and make good companions. The idea was a success.

Today, an organization called Helping Hands trains the monkeys. They train the monkeys to do a variety of tasks, such as brushing hair, turning lights on or off, and retrieving fallen objects. Some can even put food in a microwave oven and feed a person.

These monkey helpers make a difference, allowing their human companions to live more independent lives.

ADVANCED SELECTION 9   VOCABULARY: solution, partnership

Thanksgiving Day

It was the morning of Thanksgiving Day, and Nicholas was excited about the holiday. His mother had just finished preparing the turkey and was ready to put it in the oven.

"Can I help you?" asked Nicholas, reaching for the roasting pan.

"No, dear, this is too heavy for you," said his mother, lifting the full roasting pan into the oven.

Nicholas saw his father slicing apples. "Can I help you?" Nicholas asked, reaching for the knife.

"No, thank you, Nicholas," said his father. "This knife is very sharp and you might accidentally cut yourself" Nicholas felt left out. He wanted to participate, but it seemed as though there was nothing for him to do.

"You could help me with the cranberry sauce," suggested his father. Nicholas opened the can of cranberry sauce and carefully spooned it into a silver dish without spilling a drop.

"Now, you can set our Thanksgiving table," said Mom, "and don't forget to set places for Grandma and Grandpa. They'll be here soon."

Nicholas set the table for five to dine. He made place cards so everyone would know where to sit, and next to each name he drew a little turkey. Nicholas was happy to participate in his family's Thanksgiving celebration.

ADVANCED SELECTION 10 **VOCABULARY:** holiday, participate, dine

Group Time

DAY 1

Strategic Intervention

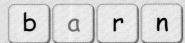

1 Word Work

PHONEMIC AWARENESS Write the word pairs below one at a time. Model segmenting and blending each word in the pair; have children repeat after you. Then have them isolate the vowel sound in each word.

pat—part   not—north   chop—chore   cat—cart

R-CONTROLLED *ar, or, ore* Reteach p. 162n. Additional words to blend:

charm   horn   more   art   tore

Then have children spell *bark* with letter tiles. Monitor their work.

- Change the *k* in *bark* to *n*.
  What is the new word?

b	a	r	n

- Change the *a* in *barn* to *o*.
  What is the new word?

b	o	r	n

- Change the *n* in *born* to e.
  What is the new word?

b	o	r	e

SPELLING Reteach p. 162p. Model spelling *hard* and *porch*. You may wish to give children fewer words to learn.

2 Read Decodable Reader 6

BEFORE READING Review the *ar, or,* and *ore* words on p. 162q and have children blend these story words: *before, grinned, Darling, jumped, patted, asked, horses, fixed.* Be sure children understand meanings of words such as *chores.*

Monitor Progress	Word and Story Reading
If... children have difficulty with any of these words,	**then...** reteach them by modeling. Have children practice the words, with feedback from you, until they can read them independently.
If... children have difficulty reading the story individually,	**then...** read a page aloud as children follow along. Then have the group reread the page. Continue reading in this way before children read individually.

3 Reread for Fluency

Use the Paired Reading Routine, p. 162q, and text at each child's independent reading level.

MORE READING FOR
Group Time

Use this Leveled Reader or other text at children's instructional level.

Reviews
- High-frequency words *break, family, heard, listen, once, pull*
- Sequence

Check this database for additional titles.

Leveled Reader
Database
ONLINE
sfsuccessnet.com

Advanced

1 Word Work

🔊 *r-Controlled ar, or, ore;* **Syllables VCCV** Practice with longer words. If children know the words on first read, they may need no further practice. Practice items:

border	darling	custard	ignorant	harpoon
pardon	fortunate	horrify	force	remarkable
argument	important	target	ordinary	marvelous

Have children put a box around the *ar, or,* or *ore* in these words. Then have individuals choose several words to use in a sentence.

2 Read Advanced Selection 6

BEFORE READING Have children identify this oral vocabulary word: *courageous*.

DURING READING Children may read silently. Provide guidance as needed.

AFTER READING Have children think about the bravery required of police officers and police dogs. Ask:

- Why do you think police dogs will face dangerous situations without hesitation?
- Do you think Nate decided he might become a police officer only because he could have a dog? Explain?

On the back of the selection page, have children write a paragraph about the type of police officer Nate would be.

K-9 Paul, Police Dog

DI•9

3 Extend Concepts Through Inquiry

IDENTIFY QUESTIONS Have children work with a partner and choose an assistance or service dog to research. During the week, they should learn more about their choice from reading, studying pictures, and talking with adults or older children. On Day 5 they will share what they learned. Guide children in brainstorming possible choices.

- What kinds of assistance or service dogs are there? What kind of training do they need? What is life like for these dogs?

Day **1**	2	3	4	5
Identify Questions	Investigate	Investigate	**Organize Information**	Communicate

MORE READING FOR
Group Time

Use this Leveled Reader or other text at children's instructional level.

Advanced

Reviews
- Concept vocabulary
- Sequence

Group Time

ROUTINE

DAY 2

1 Word Work

🔄 **r-CONTROLLED *ar, or, ore*** Reteach p. 164c. Additional words to blend:

carp	adore	order	market
fort	arch	lark	score

HIGH-FREQUENCY WORDS Reteach pp. 164–165. Have individuals practice reading the words from word cards.

2 Read Strategic Intervention Decodable Reader 6

BEFORE READING Before reading, review *begged, getting, darling, rocking, porch,* and *baskets* on the Word Wall. Point out question marks on p. 5 and explain that they are used when someone asks a question; in this case, Brett is wondering what Dad's gift might be.

AFTER READING Check comprehension by having children retell the story, including the characters, setting, and plot.

Have children locate *ar, or,* and *ore* words in the story. List words children name. Review the *ar, or,* and *ore* spelling patterns Have children sort the words they found below *car* and *for*.

<u>car</u>	<u>for</u>
darling	horse
hard	porch
jars	
close	

3 Read *Tara and Tiree, Fearless Friends*

BEFORE READING Have children practice the words below—first as a group and then individually. Then use Guiding Comprehension, pp. 166–181 to monitor understanding.

learned	training	winter	listen
broke	grabbed	saved	wonderful

Monitor Progress	Word and Story Reading
If... children have difficulty with any of these words,	**then...** vreteach them by modeling. Have children practice the words, with feedback from you, until they can read them independently.
If... children have difficulty reading the story individually,	**then...** have them follow along in their books as they listen to the AudioText. You may also have them read pages of the selection aloud together, first with you and then without you, before reading individually.

AudioText

ROUTINE

Advanced

1 Read *Tara and Tiree, Fearless Friends*

DURING READING Have children read silently to p. 176. Provide guidance as needed. Ask:

- How important is the setting to this story? Explain.
- What do you predict will happen in the rest of the story? Why?

Have children read silently to p. 182. Provide guidance as needed. Ask:

- Do you think Jim had trained Tara and Tiree to be rescue dogs? What makes you think so?

Sequence Have children think about the order in which things happened in the story. Discuss how the order is important to the reader of a story.

- What happens after Tara comes to the hole and fails to pull Jim to safety?
- How does what happens next build up suspense for the reader?

Predict Children can work with a partner to complete a Story Predictions Chart. Draw a chart or distribute copies of Graphic Organizer 6.

Story Predictions Chart
Title Tara and Tiree, Fearless Friends

What might happen?	What clues do I have?	What did happen?
[Answers will vary.]	[Answers will vary.]	Tara and Tiree pulled Jim to safety from the hole in the ice.

▲ **Graphic Organizer 6**

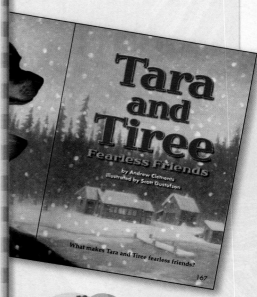

Audio CD   AudioText

RESPONSE Have students suppose they are Jim and write Tara and Tiree a letter of at least four sentences thanking and praising them for saving his life.

2 Extend Concepts Through **Inquiry**

INVESTIGATE Guide children in choosing material at their independent reading level to explore their topic. A book that may be helpful is *Assistance Dogs: In Special Service* by Elizabeth Ring or *Canine Companions* by Judith Janda Presnall. Continue to explain and model ways to research a topic.

Help children decide how they will present their information. Children may use a graphic organizer, a written format, drawings, or models.

1	**Day 2**	3	4	5
Identify Questions		Investigate	Organize Information	Communicate

Investigate

Group Time

AudioText

Strategic Intervention

ROUTINE

1 Word Work

REVIEW **CONSONANT DIGRAPHS** *ch, tch, sh, th, wh* Review p. 182c, using these additional words. Have children sort the words into *ch, tch, sh, th, wh* lists.

chase	shore	wish	which	with	whale
white	catch	bunch	those	shells	match

REVIEW **SENTENCE READING** Have individuals read these sentences to review decoding skills.

> I wish I could chase a whale and catch it!
> Which top will match those pants?
> I will pick up a bunch of shells on the shore.
> Those white roses are pretty!

2 Comprehension

SEQUENCE/PREDICT Reteach p. 164e. Have children respond to the Connect to Reading questions after completing step 3 Reread for Fluency.
- Now read the story again quietly. When you have finished, I'd like you to use pictures and clue words to tell what happens first, next, and last and what might happen next.

3 Reread for Fluency

READ WITH ACCURACY/APPROPRIATE PACE Teach p. 182f using text at children's independent level. Reading options include Student Edition selections, Decodable Readers, Strategic Intervention Decodable Readers, and Leveled Readers.

Monitor Progress	Fluency
If... children have difficulty reading with accuracy and appropriate pace,	**then...** discuss with them any words they do not understand and provide additional modeling. Have them listen to your model and then read aloud together, first with you and then without you, before reading individually.

MORE READING FOR
Group Time

Use this Leveled Reader or other text at children's instructional level.

Below-Level

Reviews
- High-frequency words *break, family, heard, listen, once, pull*
- Sequence

Advanced

ROUTINE

DAY 3

1 Read Self-Selected Reading

BEFORE READING Have children select a trade book or Leveled Reader to read independently. Guide children in selecting books of appropriate difficulty.

AFTER READING When they have finished, have each child choose their favorite passage to read aloud to a partner.

2 Extend Concepts Through Inquiry

INVESTIGATE Give children time to investigate the dog they are researching and to begin preparing their information. Help students with their chosen methods of presentation.

1	2	Day 3	4	5
Identify Questions	Investigate	Investigate	Organize Information	Communicate

Trade Books for Self-Selected Reading

A GUIDE PUPPY GROWS UP by Caroline Arnold, Harcourt, 1991

THE RIGHT DOG FOR THE JOB by Dorothy Patent, Walker & Company, 2004

MORE READING FOR Group Time

Use this Leveled Reader or other text at children's instructional level.

Advanced

Reviews
• Concept vocabulary
• Sequence

Group Time

Strategic Intervention

ROUTINE

1 Read "Rescue Dogs"

BEFORE READING Have children practice the words below—first as a group and then individually. Then use Social Studies in Reading, pp. 184–187.

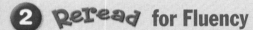

| rescue | drowning | danger | trapped | scent |

Monitor Progress	Word and Selection Reading
If... children have difficulty with any of these words,	**then...** have them practice in pairs reading word cards before reading the selection.
If... children have difficulty reading the selection individually,	**then...** have them follow along in their books as they listen to the AudioText. You may also have them read pages of the selection aloud together, first with you and then without you, before reading individually.

2 Reread for Fluency

Preteach p. 187a, using text at children's independent reading level. Reading options include Student Edition selections, Decodable Readers, Strategic Intervention Decodable Readers, and Leveled Readers.

3 Build Concepts

Use the Oral Vocabulary Routine, pp. DI•1–DI•3, and the Amazing Words on p. DI•8.

AudioText

MORE READING FOR
Group Time

Use this Leveled Reader or other text at children's instructional level.

Below-Level

Reviews
• High-frequency words *break, family, heard, listen, once, pull*
• Sequence

Advanced

1 Read "Rescue Dogs"

AFTER READING Ask:
- Why do you think rescue dogs need to be strong and smart?
- All the breeds of dogs mentioned are at least 55–60 pounds and several are much larger. Do you think rescue dogs need to be large? Why or why not?
- Can you think of a similar relationship between people and animals as there is between handler and rescue dog? Explain.

2 Vocabulary

Extend vocabulary with questions such as these:
- Do you think an *avalanche* is a *hazard*? Why or why not?
- Do you think a *skittish* dog would make a good *rescue* dog? Why or why not?
- Do you think *rescue* dogs have a natural *instinct* for their work? Why or why not?
- When a *rescue* dog is at work, would you call it a *fast-paced* job? Why or why not?

Encourage children to use the words in their writing.

3 Extend Concepts Through Inquiry

ORGANIZE INFORMATION Give children time to continue reading about their assistance or service dogs. Remind them that tomorrow they will share their information. By now they should have begun putting the information in a presentation format. Help those who need assistance.

What kinds of dogs make good rescue dogs?

Good rescue dogs must be strong and smart. They also must listen to the people who train and handle them. Saint Bernards have been working as rescue dogs for many years. They help rescue people who get lost in snowstorms or get trapped under deep snow.

Bloodhounds, Labrador retrievers, and German shepherds are good at following the trails of lost people. German shepherds also are good at finding people who are trapped under snow. Newfoundlands do a great job with water rescues.

185

Audio CD AudioText

1	2	3	Day 4	5
Identify Questions	Investigate	Investigate	**Organize Information**	Communicate

MORE READING FOR
Group Time

Use this Leveled Reader or other text at children's instructional level.

Advanced

Reviews
- Concept vocabulary
- Sequence

Group Time

DAY 5

1 Word Work

r-CONTROLLED *ar, or, ore* Have children read aloud as you track the print. Call on individuals to blend the underlined words.

> We drove our <u>car</u> <u>far</u> from the <u>border</u>.
> Do you want to <u>order</u> <u>more</u> <u>art</u>?
> My dog <u>barks</u> when I walk to the <u>corner</u>.
> We went into the <u>barn</u> <u>before</u> the <u>storm</u>.

HIGH-FREQUENCY WORDS Use pp. 164–165 to review *break, family, heard, listen, once, pull*

Monitor Progress	High-Frequency Words
If... children have difficulty with any of these words,	**then...** tell them the word and have them repeat it. Have children spell the word and tell what word they spelled. Have them practice in pairs with word cards.

2 Monitor Progress

SENTENCE READING SET A Use Set A on reproducible p. 188f to assess children's ability to read decodable and high-frequency words in sentences.

COMPREHENSION To assess comprehension, have each child read Strategic Intervention Decodable Reader 6 or other text at the child's independent level. Ask when and where the story takes place (setting), and have the child retell the story.

MORE READING FOR
Group Time

Use this Leveled Reader or other text at children's instructional level.

Below-Level

Reviews
- High-frequency words *break, family, heard, listen, once, pull*
- Sequence

Advanced

1 Monitor Progress

SENTENCE READING SET C Use Set C on reproducible p. 188f to assess children's ability to read decodable and high-frequency words in sentences. If you have any question about whether children have mastered this week's skills, have them read the Set B sentences.

COMPREHENSION Have each child read "Bart's Problem" on reproducible p. 188g. Ask what the sequence of events is in the story (sequence), and have the child retell the passage. Use the Retelling Rubric on p. 182g to evaluate the child's retelling.

2 Extend Concepts Through Inquiry

COMMUNICATE Have partners share their "special" dog project.

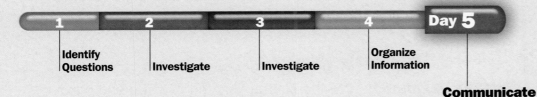

1	2	3	4	Day 5
Identify Questions	Investigate	Investigate	Organize Information	

Communicate

MORE READING FOR
Group Time

Use this Leveled Reader or other text at children's instructional level.

Advanced

Reviews
• Concept vocabulary
• Sequence

Group Time

DAY 1

1 Word Work

CONTRACTIONS Reteach p. 190n. Additional words to blend:

hasn't	he's	she'll	I'm	didn't

Then have children read and write the word pairs shown below and name the contraction they can form. Have them write the contractions and identify which letter or letters were left out to form the contraction.

there is	there's
was not	wasn't
we will	we'll
he will	he'll

SPELLING Reteach p. 190p. Model spelling *I'll* and *isn't*. You may wish to give children fewer words to learn.

2 Read Decodable Reader 7

BEFORE READING Review the contractions on p. 190q and have children blend these story words: *didn't, isn't, it'll, let's*. Be sure children understand meanings of words such as *it'll*.

Monitor Progress	Word and Story Reading
If... children have difficulty with any of these words,	**then...** reteach them by modeling. Have children practice the words, with feedback from you, until they can read them independently.
If... children have difficulty reading the story individually,	**then...** read a page aloud as children follow along. Then have the group reread the page. Continue reading in this way before children read individually.

3 Reread for Fluency

Use the Oral Reading Routine, p. 190q, and text at each child's independent reading level.

Decodable Reader 7

Jem Wasn't Happy

Written by Stephen Lewis
Illustrated by Ann Mitcham

Phonics Skill
Contractions n't, 'll, 'll, 'm
didn't   I'm   let's   it'll

MORE READING FOR

Group Time

Let's Play Baseball!

Use this Leveled Reader or other text at children's instructional level.

Below-Level

Reviews
- High-frequency words *certainly, either, great, laugh, second, worst, you're*
- Realism and fantasy

Check this database for additional titles.

Leveled Reader Database

ONLINE

sfsuccessnet.com

Advanced

DAY 1

1 Word Work

⊙ **Contractions _n't, 's, 'll, 'm_** If children know the words on first read, they may need no further practice. Practice items:

| couldn't | weren't | that's | haven't | there's |
| aren't | don't | they'll | we'll | won't |

Have children write other _n't, 's,_ and _'ll_ contractions. Have individuals choose several of the words to use in a sentence.

2 Read Advanced Selection 7

BEFORE READING Have children identify this oral vocabulary word: _compete_.

DURING READING Children may read silently. Provide guidance as needed.

AFTER READING Have children recall the most important idea in the selection. (The best Little League teams play in the Little League World Series.) Ask:
- In which kind of book would you most likely find this selection: one about famous baseball players, one about presidents who played Little League, a history of Little League, or a fiction book about a Little League player? Explain.

On the back of the selection page, have children write about a new idea for a World Series.

DI•10

3 Extend Concepts Through Inquiry

IDENTIFY QUESTIONS Have children choose either a baseball player to research or some aspect of the history of baseball, such as Negro leagues or women's leagues. During the week, they should learn more about their choices from reading, studying pictures, and talking with adults or older children. On Day 5, they will share what they learned. Guide children in brainstorming choices.
- Think about your choice. Why was your player famous? OR Why were Negro leagues formed? When and why did they dissolve? OR When did women start playing professional baseball? Are there women's leagues today?

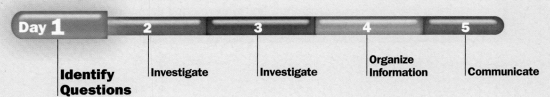

| Day 1 | 2 | 3 | 4 | 5 |
| Identify Questions | Investigate | Investigate | Organize Information | Communicate |

MORE READING FOR
Group Time

Use this Leveled Reader or other text at children's instructional level.

Advanced

Reviews
- Concept vocabulary
- Realism and fantasy

Group Time

Stuck

Written by Dan Archer
Illustrated by Jolie Foster

Phonics Skill
Contractions n't, 'll, 'll, 'm

194

Audio CD AudioText

DAY 2

Strategic Intervention

ROUTINE

1 Word Work

CONTRACTIONS Reteach p. 192c. Additional words to blend:

couldn't	haven't	hasn't	it's
she'll	wasn't	you'll	shouldn't

HIGH-FREQUENCY WORDS Reteach pp. 192–193. Have individuals practice reading the words from word cards.

2 Read Strategic Intervention Decodable Reader 7

BEFORE READING Before reading, review *certainly, either, great, laugh, second, worst,* and *you're* on the Word Wall. Read p. 2 with children and then have them predict what they think will happen next in the story.

AFTER READING Check comprehension by having children retell the story, including the characters, setting, and plot.

Have children locate contractions in the story. List words children name. Review the contraction spelling patterns. Have children sort the words they found below *can't* and *it's.*

can't	it's
hadn't	let's
wasn't	that's

3 Reread *Ronald Morgan Goes to Bat*

BEFORE READING Have children practice the words below—first as a group and then individually. Then use Guiding Comprehension, pp. 194–211, to monitor understanding.

deserve	chocolate	practice	watched
helmet	instead	raisins	whispered

Monitor Progress	Word and Story Reading
If... children have difficulty with any of these words,	**then...** reteach them by modeling. Have children practice the words, with feedback from you, until they can read them independently.
If... children have difficulty reading the story individually,	**then...** have them follow along in their books as they listen to the AudioText. You may also have them read pages of the selection aloud together, first with you and then without you, before reading individually.

Advanced

1 Read *Ronald Morgan Goes to Bat*

DURING READING Have children read silently to p. 204. Provide guidance as needed. Ask:
- Do you like Mr. Spano? Tell why or why not.
- What kind of person is Ronald? Give examples.

Have children read silently to p. 211. Provide guidance as needed. Ask:
- Why was Ronald an important member of the baseball team?
- Pretend the story continues. Do you think Ronald will become a good baseball player? Why or why not?

Realism and Fantasy Have children think about the story they just read. Discuss characteristics of realistic fiction.
- Can you picture a real boy like Ronald Morgan? Explain.
- Does the story seem like it could happen? Why or why not?

Prior Knowledge Children can scan the story, look at pictures, and write a short paragraph that includes what they already know about baseball or being on a team.

RESPONSE Have students pretend they are Ronald and write a journal entry telling about how he felt after practicing baseball with his father.

2 Extend Concepts Through Inquiry

INVESTIGATE Guide children in choosing material at their independent reading level to explore their topic. Some books that may be appropriate are *Negro Leagues: All-Black Baseball* by Laura Driscoll and *Promises to Keep: How Jackie Robinson Changed America* by Sharon Robinson. Continue to explain and model ways to research.

Help children decide how they will present their information. Children may use a graphic organizer, a written format, photographs, drawings, or models.

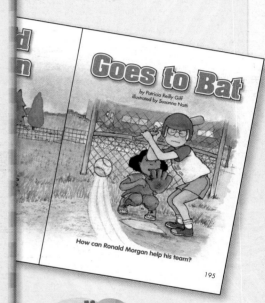

DAY 2

How can Ronald Morgan help his team?

195

Audio CD AudioText

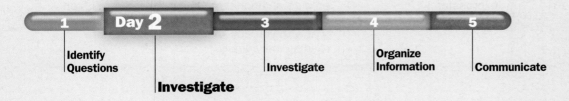

1	**Day 2**	3	4	5
Identify Questions	Investigate	Investigate	Organize Information	Communicate

Ronald Morgan Goes to Bat
Group Time

194

Audio CD AudioText

MORE READING FOR
Group Time

Use this Leveled Reader or other text at children's instructional level.

Below-Level

Reviews
- High-frequency words *certainly, either, great, laugh, second, worst, you're*
- Realism and fantasy

DAY 3

Strategic Intervention

ROUTINE

1 Word Work

REVIEW *r*-CONTROLLED *ar, or, ore* Review p. 212c, using these additional words. Have children sort the words into *ar, or, ore* lists.

adore	garden	organ	charm	orbit chore
artist	north	barber	before	darling stork

REVIEW SENTENCE READING Have individuals read these sentences to review decoding skills.

> Did Jordan place the large jar on the porch?
> My chore was to push the cart across the yard.
> A sharp thorn tore at the skin on my arm.
> When it is dark you can see stars and other orbs.

2 Comprehension

REALISM AND FANTASY/PRIOR KNOWLEDGE Reteach p. 192e. Have children respond to the Connect to Reading questions after completing step 3 Reread for Fluency.
- Now read the story again quietly. When you have finished, I'd like you to use clues in the pictures and story to tell if the story is realism or fantasy. Then ask yourself if this story reminds you of something you know or have read about.

3 Reread for Fluency

READ WITH EXPRESSION Teach p. 212f using text at children's independent level. Reading options include Student Edition selections, Decodable Readers, Strategic Intervention Decodable Readers, and Leveled Readers.

Monitor Progress	Fluency
If... children have difficulty reading with expression,	**then...** discuss with them the appropriate expression to be used with each passage and provide additional modeling. Have them listen to your model and then read aloud together, first with you and then without you, before reading individually.

Advanced

DAY 3

1 Read Self-Selected Reading

BEFORE READING Have children select a trade book or Leveled Reader to read independently. Guide children in selecting books of appropriate difficulty.

AFTER READING When they have finished, have each child select an interesting passage to read aloud to a partner.

2 Extend Concepts Through Inquiry

INVESTIGATE Give children time to investigate the baseball subject they are researching and to begin preparing their information. Help students with their chosen methods of presentation.

1	2	Day 3	4	5
Identify Questions	Investigate	**Investigate**	Organize Information	Communicate

Trade Books for Self-Selected Reading

CASEY AT THE BAT: A BALLAD OF THE REPUBLIC SUNG IN THE YEAR 1888 by Ernest Thayer and Christopher Bing, Handprint Books, 2000

MIGHTY JACKIE: THE STRIKE-OUT QUEEN, by Marissa Moss, Simon and Schuster, 2004

MORE READING FOR
Group Time

Use this Leveled Reader or other text at children's instructional level.

Advanced

Reviews
- Concept vocabulary
- Realism and fantasy

Group Time

DAY **4**

ROUTINE

1 Read "Spaceball"

BEFORE READING Have children practice the words below—first as a group and then individually. Then use Poetry, pp. 214–215.

mysterious   aliens   pitcher's   announcer

Monitor Progress	Word and Selection Reading
If... children have difficulty with any of these words,	**then...** have them practice in pairs reading word cards before reading the selection.
If... children have difficulty reading the selection individually,	**then...** have them follow along in their books as they listen to the AudioText. You may also have them read pages of the selection aloud together, first with you and then without you, before reading individually.

AudioText

2 Reread for Fluency

Preteach p. 215a, using text at children's independent reading level. Reading options include Student Edition selections, Decodable Readers, Strategic Intervention Decodable Readers, and Leveled Readers.

3 Build Concepts

Use the Oral Vocabulary Routine, p. DI•1–DI•2, DI•4, and the Amazing Words on p. DI•8.

MORE READING FOR
Group Time

Use this Leveled Reader or other text at children's instructional level.

Below-Level

Reviews
- High-frequency words *certainly, either, great, laugh, second, worst, you're*
- Realism and Fantasy

Advanced

ROUTINE

DAY 4

1 Read "Spaceball"

AFTER READING Ask:

- Compare *Ronald Morgan Goes to Bat* to "Spaceball". How are they alike? How are they different?
- The poet uses "end rhyme" in this poem. Which lines in each stanza use end rhyme?
- Is this poem realistic or fantasy? How do you know?

2 Vocabulary

Extend vocabulary with questions such as these:

- Can a game of baseball be *recreation* if teams *compete*? Why or why not?
- Did Ronald Morgan *mope* when he missed catching the ball in left field? Why or why not?
- Did Ronald Morgan *contribute* enough to the team to *deserve* to play? Why or why not?
- Would you say that a person might *tinker* in his or her garage for *recreation*? Explain.

Encourage children to use the words in their writing.

3 Extend Concepts Through **Inquiry**

ORGANIZE INFORMATION Give children time to continue reading about their baseball subject. Remind them that tomorrow they will share their information. By now they should have begun putting the information in a presentation format. Help those who need assistance.

AudioText

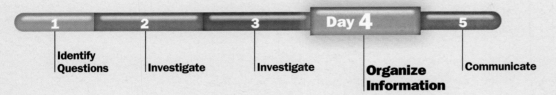

1	2	3	Day **4**	5
Identify Questions	Investigate	Investigate	Organize Information	Communicate

MORE READING FOR
Group Time

Use this Leveled Reader or other text at children's instructional level.

Advanced

Reviews
- Concept vocabulary
- Realism and fantasy

Group Time

Strategic Intervention

ROUTINE

1 Word Work

CONTRACTIONS Have children read aloud as you track the print. Call on individuals to blend the underlined words.

I'll see if **he's** the one **who's** at the door.
I'm sure this **isn't** the house **she's** renting.
I **can't** go to the party if I **haven't** done my chores.
There's the picture **she's** been painting.

HIGH-FREQUENCY WORDS Use pp. 192–193 to review *certainly, either, great, laugh, second, worst, you're.*

Monitor Progress	High-Frequency Words
If... children have difficulty with any of these words,	**then...** tell them the word and have them repeat it. Have children spell the word and tell what word they spelled. Have them practice in pairs with word cards.

2 Monitor Progress

SENTENCE READING SET A Use Set A on reproducible p. 216f to assess children's ability to read decodable and high-frequency words in sentences.

COMPREHENSION To assess comprehension, have each child read Strategic Intervention Decodable Reader 7 or other text at the child's independent level. Ask when and where the story takes place (setting), and have the child retell the story.

MORE READING FOR
Group Time

Use this Leveled Reader or other text at children's instructional level.

Below-Level

Reviews
- High-frequency words *certainly, either, great, laugh, second, worst, you're*
- Realism and Fantasy

Advanced

ROUTINE

1 Monitor Progress

SENTENCE READING SET C Use Set C on reproducible p. 216f to assess children's ability to read decodable and high-frequency words in sentences. If you have any questions about whether children have mastered this week's skills, have them read the Set B sentences.

COMPREHENSION Have each child read "Dora Can't Skate" on reproducible p. 216g. Ask for examples of realism in the story and have the child retell the passage. Use the Retelling Rubric on p. 212g to evaluate the child's retelling.

2 Extend Concepts Through Inquiry

COMMUNICATE Have partners share their reports on baseball.

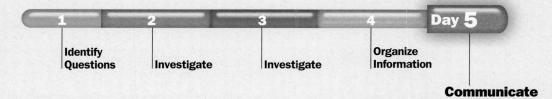

1	2	3	4	Day 5
Identify Questions	Investigate	Investigate	Organize Information	

Communicate

MORE READING FOR
Group Time

Use this Leveled Reader or other text at children's instructional level.

Advanced

Reviews
- Concept vocabulary
- Realism and fantasy

Group Time

Strategic Intervention

ROUTINE

1 Word Work

PHONEMIC AWARENESS Write the word pairs below one at a time. Model segmenting and blending each word in the pair; have children repeat after you. Then have them isolate the vowel sound in each word.

barn—burn   star—stir   porch—perch   for—fir

r-CONTROLLED *er, ir, ur* Reteach p. 218n. Additional words to blend:

purple   birch   purse   verb   whir

Have children spell *turn* with letter tiles. Monitor work and provide feedback.

- Change the *t* in *turn* to *f*, and change the *ur* to *er*. What is the new word?

f	e	r	n

- Change the *f* in *fern* to *h*. and change the *n* to *d*. What is the new word?

h	e	r	d

SPELLING Reteach p. 218p. Model spelling *serve* and *turtle*. You may wish to give children fewer words to learn.

2 Read Decodable Reader 8

BEFORE READING Review the *er, ir,* and *ur* words on p. 218q and have children blend these story words: *bird, Herb, butter, her, first, third, batter, stir, shirt, better, stirring, after, turned.* Be sure children understand the meanings of words such as *batter.*

Monitor Progress	Word and Story Reading
If... children have difficulty with any of these words,	**then...** reteach them by modeling. Have children practice the words, with feedback from you, until they can read them independently.
If... children have difficulty reading the story individually,	**then...** read a page aloud as children follow along. Then have the group reread the page. Continue reading in this way before children read individually.

3 Reread for Fluency

Use the Paired Reading Routine, p. 218q, and text at each child's independent reading level.

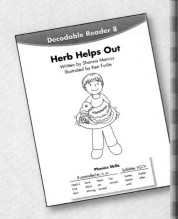

Decodable Reader 8

Herb Helps Out

Written by Shanna Marcus
Illustrated by Ken Furlie

Phonics Skills

MORE READING FOR
Group Time

Use this Leveled Reader or other text at children's instructional level.

Below-Level

Reviews
- High-frequency words *above, ago, enough, toward, word, whole*
- Sequence

Check this database for additional titles.

Leveled Reader Database
ONLINE
sfsuccessnet.com

Advanced

DAY 1

1 Word Work

🎯 **r-Controlled *er, ir, ur*; Syllable *-er*** Practice with longer words. If children know the words on first read, they may need no further practice. Practice items:

plural	stirrup	afterward	chirping	certainly
circular	emergency	hurdle	purchase	liberty
birch	thirsty	sturdy	bluebird	blurted

Have children circle the *r*-controlled *er, ir, ur*. Have individuals choose several words to use in a sentence.

2 Read Advanced Selection 8

BEFORE READING Have children identify these oral vocabulary words: *inhabit, conflict.*

DURING READING Children may read silently. Provide guidance as needed.

AFTER READING Have children think about what the author is trying to tell them about turtles. Ask:

• Why did the author write this selection? Did she succeed?

On the back of the selection page, have children write a riddle about an animal.

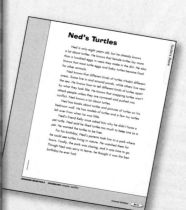

Ned's Turtles

DI•11

3 Extend Concepts Through Inquiry

IDENTIFY QUESTIONS Have children work in pairs to study the folk tale genre and find a short example. (Children might want to compare *Turtle's Race with Beaver* to Aesop's *The Tortoise and the Hare*.) During the week, they should learn more about their choices from reading, studying pictures, and talking with adults or older children. On Day 5 they will share what they learned. Guide children in selecting a folk tale for their example.

• Think about the folk tale genre. Is it fiction or nonfiction? What makes it different from other types of literature?

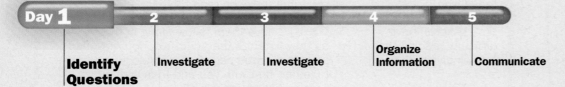

Day 1	2	3	4	5
Identify Questions	Investigate	Investigate	**Organize Information**	Communicate

MORE READING FOR
Group Time

Use this Leveled Reader or other text at children's instructional level.

SEA TURTLES AT RISK

Advanced

Reviews
• Concept vocabulary
• Sequence

Group Time

AudioText

Strategic Intervention

ROUTINE

1 Word Work

r-CONTROLLED *er, ir, ur* Reteach p. 220c. Additional words to blend:

term	girth	church	spurt
urge	flirt	shirk	perk

HIGH-FREQUENCY WORDS Reteach pp. 220–221. Have individuals practice reading the words form word cards.

2 Read Strategic Intervention Decodable Reader 8

BEFORE READING Before reading, review *above*, *ago*, *enough*, *toward*, *word*, and *whole* on the Word Wall. Then lead children on a picture walk through *Curt's Bike Trouble*.

AFTER READING Check comprehension by having children retell the story, including the characters, setting, and plot.

Have children locate *er, ir,* and *ur* words in the story. List words children name. Review the *er, ir,* and *ur* spelling patterns. Have children sort the words they found below *better, curb,* and *dirt*.

better	curb	dirt
corner	Curt	first
Fern	Curt's	Kirk
perked	hurt	
swerve	hurting	
	Nurse	
	turned	

3 Read *Turtle's Race with Beaver*

BEFORE READING Have children practice the words below—first as a group and then individually. Then use Guiding Comprehension, pp. 222–242, to monitor understanding.

beautiful	perfect	finishing	positions
settled	shallower	splendid	throughout

Monitor Progress	Word and Story Reading
If... children have difficulty with any of these words,	**then...** reteach them by modeling. Have children practice the words, with feedback from you, until they can read them independently.
If... children have difficulty reading the story individually,	**then...** have them follow along in their books as they listen to the AudioText. You may also have them read pages of the selection aloud together, first with you and then without you, before reading individually.

DAY 2

Strategic Intervention Decodable Reader 8

Curt's Bike Trouble

Written by Amanda Hopkins
Illustrated by Christopher Calvetti

Advanced

1 Read *Turtle's Race with Beaver*

DURING READING Have children read silently to p. 234. Provide guidance as needed. Ask:
- What did you learn about turtles and beavers from this story?
- Who do you think will win the race? Why do you think so?

Have children read silently to p. 242. Provide guidance as needed. Ask:
- Are you glad that Turtle won? Explain.

 sequence Have children think about the story they just read. Discuss the clue words used to indicate sequence in the story.
- What clue words are used on pp. 227 and 228?

summarize Children can write a short summary when they finish reading the story. Remind them to include Turtle's and Beaver's goals and how they tried to reach them.

RESPONSE Ask children to imagine a race between two other mismatched animals and write a paragraph describing the race.

2 Extend Concepts Through Inquiry

INVESTIGATE Guide children in choosing material at their independent reading level to explore their topic. Some books that may be appropriate are *Folk and Fairy Tales* edited by Martin Hallett and Barbara Karasek and *Swedish Folk Tales* by John Bauer and Holger Lundburgh.

Help children decide how they will present their information. Children may use a graphic organizer, a written format, drawings, or models.

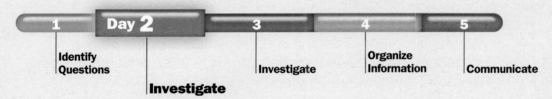

DAY **2**

Turtle's Race with Beaver

as told by Joseph Bruchac and James Bruchac
illustrated by Jose Aruego and Ariane Dewey

Why are Turtle and Beaver racing, and who will win?

223

Audio CD **AudioText**

Group Time

Audio CD   **AudioText**

DAY 3

Strategic Intervention

ROUTINE

1 Word Work

REVIEW **CONTRACTIONS** Review p. 243c, using these additional words. Have children list the word pairs and write a contraction that can be made from the two words.

did not	didn't		would not	wouldn't
he is	he's		it is	it's
they will	they'll		you will	you'll
I am	I'm		has not	hasn't

REVIEW **SENTENCE READING** Have individuals read these sentences to review decoding skills.

> I'm sure she didn't have the map.
> He's going to bring the cake, and you'll bring the forks.
> It's so dry because it hasn't rained in months.
> They'll pick me up so I'm on time for the play.

2 Comprehension

SEQUENCE/SUMMARIZE Reteach p. 220e. Have children respond to the Connect to Reading questions after completing step 3 Reread for Fluency.

- Now read the story again quietly. When you have finished, I'd like you use pictures and clue words to tell about the order of events and what this story is mostly about.

3 Reread for Fluency

EXPRESS CHARACTERIZATION Teach p. 243f using text at children's independent level. Reading options include Student Edition selections, Decodable Readers, Strategic Intervention Decodable Readers, and Leveled Readers.

Monitor Progress	Fluency
If... children have difficulty with any of these words,	**then...** discuss with them who is speaking each time they come across quotation marks, have them look at the pictures for clues, and provide additional modeling. Have them listen to your model and then read aloud together, first with you and then without you, before reading individually.

Advanced

DAY 3

1 Read Self-Selected Reading

BEFORE READING Have children select a trade book or Leveled Reader to read independently. Guide children in selecting books of appropriate difficulty.

AFTER READING When they have finished, have each child select an interesting passage to read aloud to a partner.

2 Extend Concepts Through Inquiry

INVESTIGATE Give children time to investigate the folk tale genre and to begin preparing their information. Help students with their chosen methods of presentation.

1	2	Day 3	4	5
Identify Questions	Investigate	Investigate	Organize Information	Communicate

Trade Books for Self-Selected Reading

TWO OF EVERYTHING: A CHINESE FOLKTALE by Lily Toy Hong, Albert Whitman & Company, 1993

THE STONE CUTTER by Gerald McDermott, Picture Puffin, 1975

MORE READING FOR
Group Time

Use this Leveled Reader or other text at children's instructional level.

Advanced

Reviews
• Concept vocabulary
• Sequence

Group Time

DAY 4

 AudioText

Strategic Intervention

ROUTINE

1 Read "The Secret Life of Ponds"

BEFORE READING Have children practice the words below—first as a group and then individually. Then use Science in Reading, pp. 246–249.

explored   awesome   definitely   possibilities

Monitor Progress	Word and Selection Reading
If... children have difficulty with any of these words,	**then...** have them practice in pairs reading word cards before reading the selection.
If... children have difficulty reading the story individually,	**then...** have them follow along in their books as they listen to the AudioText. You may also have them read pages of the selection aloud together, first with you and then without you, before reading individually.

2 Reread For Fluency

Preteach p. 249a, using text at children's independent reading level. Reading options include Student Edition selections, Decodable Readers, Strategic Intervention Decodable Readers, and Leveled Readers.

3 Build Concepts

Use the Oral Vocabulary Routine, pp. DI•1–DI•2, DI•5, and the Amazing Words on p. DI•8.

MORE READING FOR

Group Time

Use this Leveled Reader or other text at children's instructional level.

Below-Level

Reviews
- High-frequency words *above, ago, enough, toward, word, whole*
- Sequence

Advanced

1 **Read** "The Secret Life of Ponds"

AFTER READING Ask:
- Why do you think the animals mentioned on p. 247 need a pond? Give examples.
- Why do you think the artist drew so many different living things in the pond on p. 248?
- Look at p. 248. How many categories of living things can you find?

2 **Vocabulary**

Extend vocabulary with questions such as these:
- How did Turtle want to *resolve* the *conflict* with Beaver?
- If you bought a *serape* while you were on *vacation*, where might you have been?
- A fish *inhabits* a pond because it needs water to live in, but why did Turtle need a pond?
- Do you think you could *coax* a turtle up a *ramp*? Why or why not?

Encourage children to use the words in their writing.

3 **Extend Concepts Through** **Inquiry**

ORGANIZE INFORMATION Give children time to continue their genre study. Remind them that tomorrow they will share their information. By now they should have begun putting the information in a presentation format. Help those who need assistance.

1	2	3	Day 4	5
Identify Questions	Investigate	Investigate	Organize Information	Communicate

DAY 4

Audio CD   AudioText

MORE READING FOR
Group Time

SEA TURTLES AT RISK

Use this Leveled Reader or other text at children's instructional level.

Advanced

Reviews
- Concept vocabulary
- Sequence

Group Time

DAY 5

ROUTINE

1 Word Work

r-CONTROLLED *er, ir, ur* Have children read aloud as you track the print. Call on individuals to blend the underlined words.

> You have <u>dirt</u> on your <u>purple</u> <u>skirt</u>.
> I was the <u>third</u> <u>girl</u> who saw the <u>nurse</u> today.
> Look at the <u>bird</u> <u>perch</u> on the <u>urn</u>!
> The <u>clerk</u> in the red <u>shirt</u> is <u>her</u> <u>mother</u>.

HIGH-FREQUENCY WORDS Use pp. 220–221 to review *above, ago, enough, toward, whole, word.*

Monitor Progress	High-Frequency Words
If... children have difficulty with any of these words,	**then...** tell them the word and have them repeat it. Have children spell the word and tell what word they spelled. Have them practice in pairs with word cards.

2 Monitor Progress

SENTENCE READING SET A Use Set A on reproducible p. 250f to assess children's ability to read decodable and high-frequency words in sentences.

COMPREHENSION To assess comprehension, have each child read Strategic Intervention Decodable Reader 8 or other text at the child's independent level. Ask when and where the story takes place (setting), and have the child retell the story.

MORE READING FOR
Group Time

Use this Leveled Reader or other text at children's instructional level.

Below-Level

Reviews
- High-frequency words *above, ago, enough, toward, word, whole*
- Sequence

Advanced

DAY 5

1 Monitor Progress

SENTENCE READING SET C USE SET C on reproducible p. 250f to assess children's ability to read decodable and high-frequency words in sentences. If you have any questions about whether children have mastered this week's skills, have them read the Set B sentences.

COMPREHENSION Have each child read "The Purple Shirt" on reproducible p. 250g. Have the child retell the passage in sequence. Use the Retelling Rubric on p. 243g to evaluate the child's retelling.

2 Extend Concepts Through INquiry

COMMUNICATE Have partners share their reports on folk tales.

1	2	3	4	Day 5
Identify Questions	Investigate	Investigate	Organize Information	

Communicate

MORE READING FOR
Group Time

Use this Leveled Reader or other text at children's instructional level.

Advanced

Reviews
• Concept vocabulary
• Sequence

Group Time

Strategic Intervention

ROUTINE

1 Word Work

PLURALS -s, -es, -ies Reteach p. 252n. Additional words to blend:

branches	**chores**	**stories**	**vases**	**forests**

Have children form plurals by adding *-s*, *-es*, or *-ies* and sort the words into three columns. Then have children read each word and tell how the spelling changed when the endings were added. Monitor their work.

lunch	**beach**	**party**	**lamp**
puppy	**cup**	**wish**	**daddy**

SPELLING Reteach p. 252p. Model spelling *notes* and *switches*. You may wish to give children fewer words to learn.

2 Read Decodable Reader 9

BEFORE READING Review the plural words on p. 252q and have children blend these story words: *bases, classes, drives, Fletch's, notes, prize, tunes, crafts.* Be sure children understand meanings of words such as *tunes* and *crafts.*

Monitor Progress	Word and Story Reading
If... children have difficulty with any of these words,	**then...** reteach them by modeling. Have children practice the words, with feedback from you, until they can read them independently.
If... children have difficulty reading the story individually,	**then...** read a page aloud as children follow along. Then have the group reread the page. Continue reading in this way before children read individually.

3 Reread for Fluency

Use the Oral Reading Routine, p. 252q, and text at each child's independent reading level.

MORE READING FOR

Group Time

Use this Leveled Reader or other text at children's instructional level.

Below-Level

Reviews
• High-frequency words *bought, people, pleasant, probably, scared, sign, shall*
• Author's purpose

Check this database for additional titles.

Leveled Reader Database
ONLINE
sfsuccessnet.com

Advanced

1 Word Work

Plurals -s, -es, -ies Practice with longer words. If children know the words on first read, they may need no further practice. Practice items:

switches	peaches	torches	poppies	decisions
paddles	parakeets	indexes	hatches	countries
axes	groceries	melodies	tomatoes	watermelons

Have children circle the -s, -es, -ies endings. Have individuals choose several words to use in a sentence.

2 Read Advanced Selection 9

BEFORE READING Have children identify this oral vocabulary word: *solution*.

DURING READING Children may read silently. Provide guidance as needed.

AFTER READING Have children think about the author's purpose. (to tell how Capuchin monkeys are trained to help disabled people) Ask:
- Why would M.J. Willard think that Capuchin monkeys might be able to help disabled people?

On the back of the selection page, have children pretend they are a Capuchin monkey that has just come to live with a new human companion. Have them write what they would say if they could talk.

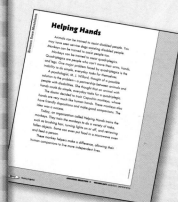

DI•12

3 Extend Concepts Through Inquiry

IDENTIFY QUESTIONS Have children work in pairs to study the life of Hans Christian Andersen. During the week, they should learn more from reading, studying pictures, and talking with adults or older children. On Day 5 they will share what they learned. Model how to research a person's life.
- Think about Hans Christian Andersen. What is he famous for? What was his life like? What made him decide to write tales?

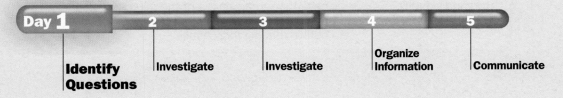

Day 1	2	3	4	5
Identify Questions	Investigate	Investigate	Organize Information	Communicate

MORE READING FOR
Group Time

Use this Leveled Reader or other text at children's instructional level.

Advanced

Reviews
- Concept vocabulary
- Author's purpose

Group Time

DAY 2

Audio CD · **AudioText**

1 Word Work

🔊 **PLURALS -s, -es, -ies** Reteach pp. 254c–254d. Additional words to blend:

families	desks	watches	glasses
globes	grapes	bushes	puppies

HIGH-FREQUENCY WORDS Reteach pp. 254–255. Have individuals practice reading the words from word cards.

2 Read Strategic Intervention Decodable Reader 9

BEFORE READING Before reading, review *bought, people, pleasant, probably, scared, sign,* and *shall* on the Word Wall. Lead children on a picture walk through *Stan* and ask them what each picture is about.

AFTER READING Check comprehension by having children retell the story, including the characters, setting, and plot.

Have children locate plural words in the story. List words children name. Review the *-s, -es,* and *-ies* spelling patterns. Have children sort the words they found below cards and dishes.

cards	dishes
lamps	lunches
notes	switches
things	

3 Read *The Bremen Town Musicians*

BEFORE READING Have children practice the words below—first as a group and then individually. Then use Guiding Comprehension, pp. 256–273, to monitor understanding.

donkey	heavy	knelt	farmyard
delicious	whispered	warmth	startled

Monitor Progress	Word and Story Reading
If... children have difficulty with any of these words,	**then...** reteach them by modeling. Have children practice the words, with feedback from you, until they can read them independently.
If... children have difficulty reading the story individually,	**then...** have them follow along in their books as they listen to the AudioText. You may also have them read pages of the selection aloud together, first with you and then without you, before reading individually.

Advanced

ROUTINE

1 Read *The Bremen Town Musicians*

DURING READING Have children read silently to p. 267. Provide guidance as needed. Ask:

- Why does the play need a narrator?

Have children read silently to p. 273. Provide guidance as needed. Ask:

- Could the animals have accomplished the same thing if they had not been together? Explain.

Author's Purpose Have children think about why the author might have written this play. Discuss the play's effect on the reader.

- Did you think of the play as primarily a lesson or entertainment? Explain.
- Did you find it easy to visualize, or make pictures in your mind, as you read the play? Explain.

Story Structure Children can work with a partner to complete a story structure chart. Draw a chart, or use Graphic Organizer 8. Ask children to analyze the author's use of setting, character, and plot.

RESPONSE Have children draw a statue of the four animals and write a brief description of what it represents.

Title
The Bremen Town Musicians

Characters
Donkey, Dog, Cat, Rooster, robbers

Settings
on the road to Bremen Town and in Bremen Town

Events
1. First: A donkey runs away.
2. Next: He meets a dog, cat, and rooster.
3. Then: The animals scare robbers from a house.
4. The animals become famous Bremen Town Musicians..

▲ **Graphic Organizer 8**

Audio CD **AudioText**

3 Extend Concepts Through Inquiry

INVESTIGATE Guide children in choosing material at their independent reading level. Some books that may be appropriate are *The Fairy Tale Life of Hans Christian Andersen* by Eva Moore and *A Fairy-Tale Life: A Story About Hans Christian Andersen Fables* by Joann Burch.

Help children decide how they will present their information. Children may use a graphic organizer, a written format, drawings, or models.

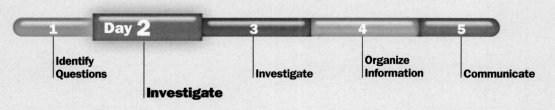

1	Day 2	3	4	5
Identify Questions	Investigate	Investigate	Organize Information	Communicate

Group Time

The Bremen Town Musicians

retold as a play by Carol Pugliano
illustrated by Jon Goodell

DAY 3

Audio CD **AudioText**

MORE READING FOR
Group Time

Use this Leveled Reader or other text at children's instructional level.

Below-Level

Reviews
• High-frequency words *bought, people, pleasant, probably, scared, sign, shall*
• Author's purpose

Strategic Intervention

ROUTINE

1 Word Work

REVIEW *r*-**CONTROLLED** *er, ir, ur* Review p. 274c, using these additional words. Have children sort the words into *er, ir,* and *ur* lists.

birds	chirp	nurse	girls	burst	circus
turkey	dirt	birch	person	first	verse

REVIEW **SENTENCE READING** Have individuals read these sentences to review decoding skills.

> **The birds hardly chirp at the nurse.**
> **The girls burst through the door to the circus.**
> **The turkey pecked the dirt by the birch tree.**
> **That person was the first to say the verse.**

2 Comprehension

AUTHOR'S PURPOSE/STORY STRUCTURE Reteach p. 254e. Have children respond to the Connect to Reading questions after completing step 3 Reread for Fluency.
• Now read the story again quietly. When you have finished, I'd like you to tell me why you think the author wrote the story, who the story is about, where and when it takes place, and what happens.

3 Reread for Fluency

READ WITH APPROPRIATE PHRASING Teach p. 274f using text at children's independent level. Reading options include Student Edition selections, Decodable Readers, Strategic Intervention Decodable Readers, and Leveled Readers.

Monitor Progress	Fluency
If... children have difficulty reading with appropriate phrasing,	**then...** discuss with them the appropriate phrasing to be used with each passage and provide additional modeling. Have them listen to your model and then read aloud together, first with you and then without you, before reading individually.

Advanced

ROUTINE

1 Read Self-Selected Reading

BEFORE READING Have children select a trade book or Leveled Reader to read independently. Guide children in selecting books of appropriate difficulty.

AFTER READING When they have finished, have each child select an interesting passage to read aloud to a partner.

2 Extend Concepts Through Inquiry

INVESTIGATE Give children time to investigate the author they are researching and to begin preparing their information. Help students with their chosen methods of presentation.

1	2	Day 3	4	5
Identify Questions	Investigate	Investigate	Organize Information	Communicate

DAY 3

Trade Books for Self-Selected Reading

CHESTER CRICKET'S PIGEON RIDE by George Selden, Farrar, Straus and Giroux, 2001

THE GIRL WHO LOVED WILD HORSES by Paul Goble, Aladdin, 1993

MORE READING FOR

Group Time

Use this Leveled Reader or other text at children's instructional level.

Advanced

Reviews
- Concept vocabulary
- Author's purpose

Group Time

DAY 4

Audio CD   **AudioText**

1 Read "Animals Helping Animals"

BEFORE READING Have children practice the words below—first as a group and then individually. Then use Science in Reading, pp. 276–279.

anemone   crocodile   badger   impalas

Monitor Progress	Word and Selection Reading
If... children have difficulty with any of these words,	**then...** have them practice in pairs reading word cards before reading the selection.
If... children have difficulty reading the story individually,	**then...** have them follow along in their books as they listen to the AudioText. You may also have them read pages of the selection aloud together, first with you and then without you, before reading individually.

2 Reread for Fluency

Preteach p. 279a, using text at children's independent reading level. Reading options include Student Edition selections, Decodable Readers, Strategic Intervention Decodable Readers, and Leveled Readers.

3 Build Concepts

Use the Oral Vocabulary Routine, p. DI•1–DI•2, DI•6, and the Amazing Words on p. DI•8.

MORE READING FOR
Group Time

Use this Leveled Reader or other text at children's instructional level.

Below-Level

Reviews
• High-frequency words *bought, people, pleasant, probably, scared, sign, shall*
• Author's purpose

Advanced

1 Read "Animals Helping Animals"

AFTER READING Ask:
- Does each animal get something in return for helping the other animal? Explain.
- Why do you think the sea anemone doesn't hurt the clown fish?
- If you wrote "People Helping People," what examples would you provide? Why?

2 Vocabulary

Extend vocabulary with questions such as these:
- Do you think the two pairs of animals on p. 279 have formed a *partnership* for *survival*? Explain.
- Did the *solution* to the Bremen Town Musicians' problems prove to be a good one? Why or why not?
- Would you describe Cat, on p. 262, as looking *miserable*? Why or why not?
- Do you think that the four Bremen Town animals were *struggling* for *survival*? Why or why not?

Encourage children to use the words in their writing.

Norman watched it all and laughed until tears came to his eyes. But soon he saw people becoming angry.

277

 AudioText

3 Extend Concepts Through Inquiry

ORGANIZE INFORMATION Give children time to continue reading about Hans Christian Andersen. Remind them that tomorrow they will share their information. By now they should have begun putting the information in a presentation format. Help those who need assistance.

1	2	3	Day 4	5
Identify Questions	Investigate	Investigate	Organize Information	Communicate

MORE READING FOR
Group Time

Use this Leveled Reader or other text at children's instructional level.

Advanced

Reviews
- Concept vocabulary
- Author's purpose

Group Time

DAY 5

Strategic Intervention

ROUTINE

1 Word Work

PLURALS *-s, -es, -ies* Have children read aloud as you track the print. Call on individuals to blend the underlined words.

I put the <u>pennies</u>, <u>nickels</u>, and <u>dimes</u> in my purse.
The <u>boys</u> and <u>girls</u> made <u>houses</u> out of <u>boxes</u>.
The <u>planes</u> landed in big <u>cities</u> and little <u>towns</u>.
We put the <u>branches</u> and <u>twigs</u> in <u>piles</u>.

HIGH-FREQUENCY WORDS Use pp. 254–255 to review *bought, people, pleasant, probably, scared, sign, shall.*

Monitor Progress	High-Frequency Words
If… children have difficulty with any of these words,	**then…** tell them the word and have them repeat it. Have children spell the word and tell what word they spelled. Have them practice in pairs with word cards.

2 Monitor Progress

SENTENCE READING SET A Use Set A on reproducible p. 280f to assess children's ability to read decodable and high-frequency words in sentences.

COMPREHENSION To assess comprehension, have each child read Strategic Intervention Decodable Reader 9 or other text at the child's independent level. Ask when and where the story takes place (setting) and have the child retell the story.

MORE READING FOR
Group Time

Use this Leveled Reader or other text at children's instructional level.

Below-Level

Reviews
- High-frequency words *bought, people, pleasant, probably, scared, sign, shall*
- Author's purpose

Advanced

DAY 5

① Monitor Progress

SENTENCE READING SET C Use Set C on reproducible p. 280f to assess children's ability to read decodable and high-frequency words in sentences. If you have any question about whether children have mastered this week's skills, have them read the Set B sentences.

COMPREHENSION Have each child read "Animal Wishes" on reproducible p. 280g. Ask what the author's purpose for writing the selection was. Then have the child retell the passage. Use the Retelling Rubric on p. 274g to evaluate the child's retelling.

② Extend Concepts Through **INquiry**

COMMUNICATE Have partners share their projects on Hans Christian Andersen.

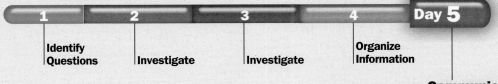

1	2	3	4	Day 5
Identify Questions	Investigate	Investigate	Organize Information	

Communicate

MORE READING FOR
Group Time

Use this Leveled Reader or other text at children's instructional level.

Advanced

Reviews
• Concept vocabulary
• Author's purpose

Group Time

DAY 1

ROUTINE

1 Word Work

PHONEMIC AWARENESS Write the word pairs below one at a time. Model segmenting and blending each word in the pair; have children repeat after you. Then have them isolate the vowel sound in each word.

brad—braid   **sad—say**   **pant—paint**   **bad—bay**

LONG *a: a, ai, ay* Reteach p. 282n. Additional words to blend:

lay   **train**   **today**   **may**   **nail**

Then have children spell rain with letter tiles. Monitor their work.

- Change the *in* in *rain* to *y*.
  What is the new word?

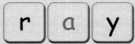

- Change the *r* in *ray* to *m*.
  What is the new word?

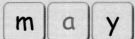

- Change the *y* in *may* to *in*.
  What is the new word?

SPELLING Reteach p. 282p. Model spelling *away* and *raise*. You may wish to give children fewer words to learn.

2 Read Decodable Reader 10

BEFORE READING Review the long a words on p. 282q and have children blend these story words: *main, getting, problem, scram, brain, swishes, that's, upset.* Be sure children understand meanings of words such as *raises*.

Monitor Progress	Word and Story Reading
If... children have difficulty with any of these words,	**then...** reteach them by modeling. Have children practice the words, with feedback from you, until they can read them independently.
If... children have difficulty reading the story individually,	**then...** read a page aloud as children follow along. Then have the group reread the page. Continue reading in this way before children read individually.

3 Reread for Fluency

Use the Paired Reading Routine, p. 282q, and text at each child's independent reading level.

Decodable Reader 10

Bert Does Not Like Bugs
Written by Julie Walsh
Illustrated by Carmen Billings

MORE READING FOR
Group Time

Use this Leveled Reader or other text at children's instructional level.

Below-Level

Reviews

Reviews
- High-frequency words *door, behind, brought, minute, promise, sorry, everybody*
- Draw conclusions

Check this database for additional titles.

Leveled Reader Database ONLINE

sfsuccessnet.com

Advanced

1 Word Work

LONG *a*: *a, ai, ay* Practice with longer words . If children know the words on first read, they may need no further practice. Practice items:

afraid	delay	faithful	patient	waist
crayon	stained	labor	equator	dismay
native	vacant	quail	explain	painter

Have children sort the words by long *a* spellings. Have individuals choose several words to use in a sentence.

2 Read Advanced Selection 10

BEFORE READING Have children identify these oral vocabulary words: *holiday, participate*.

DURING READING Children may read silently. Provide guidance as needed.

AFTER READING Have children think about the characters in the story. (Nicholas, his father, his mother) Ask:

- What conclusion can you make about Nicholas's father? How do you know?
- How do you think the rest of the day will go at Nicholas's house? What makes you think so?

On the back of the selection page, have children write a rhyme about turkeys or Thanksgiving.

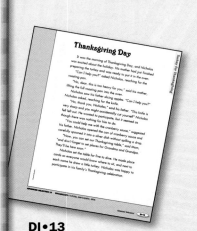

DI•13

3 Extend Concepts Through Inquiry

IDENTIFY QUESTIONS Have children work in pairs to study a holiday or celebration, such as New Year's Day, Mother's Day, Cinco de Mayo, Martin Luther King Day, Memorial Day. During the week, they should learn more about their choice from reading, studying pictures, and talking with adults or older children. On Day 5 they will share what they learned. Model how to research a holiday or celebration.

- Think about your choice. When does it happen? What is the reason for it?

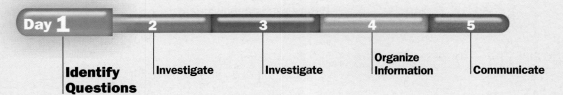

Day **1**	2	3	4	5
Identify Questions	Investigate	Investigate	Organize Information	Communicate

MORE READING FOR

Group Time

Use this Leveled Reader or other text at children's instructional level.

Advanced

Reviews
- Concept vocabulary
- Draw conclusions

Turkey for Thanksgiving   **DI•55**

Group Time

DAY 2

Strategic Intervention

1 Word Work

LONG *a: a, ai, ay* Reteach p. 284c. Additional words to blend:

waist	gray	grain	dismay
away	chain	say	jail

HIGH-FREQUENCY WORDS Reteach pp. 284–285. Have individuals practice reading the words form word cards.

2 Read Strategic Intervention Decodable Reader 10

BEFORE READING Before reading, review *door, behind, brought, minute, promise, sorry,* and *everybody* on the Word Wall. Point out quotation marks on p. 7 and explain that they show someone is talking.

AFTER READING Check comprehension by having children retell the story, including the characters, setting, and plot.

Have children locate long a words in the story. List words children name. Review the *ai* and *ay* spelling patterns. Have children sort the words they found below *day* and *rained*.

day	rained
play	wait
playing	
way	

3 Reread *A Turkey for Thanksgiving*

BEFORE READING Have children practice the words below—first as a group and then individually. Then use Guiding Comprehension, pp. 286–302, to monitor understanding.

straight	porcupine	pilgrims	sighed
wandered	dinnertime	bellowed	blundered

Monitor Progress	Word and Story Reading
If... children have difficulty with any of these words,	**then...** reteach them by modeling. Have children practice the words, with feedback from you, until they can read them independently.
If... children have difficulty reading the story individually,	**then...** have them follow along in their books as they listen to the AudioText. You may also have them read pages of the selection aloud together, first with you and then without you, before reading individually.

AudioText

Advanced

ROUTINE

1 Read *A Turkey for Thanksgiving*

DURING READING Have children read silently to p. 294. Provide guidance as needed. Ask:
- What in the story tells you that it is a fantasy?
- Why do you think the author tells the reader, in the first sentence on p. 293, how the earth smelled?

Have children read silently to p. 302. Provide guidance as needed. Ask:
- Why did Turkey run away from Mr. Moose?
- Were you surprised that Turkey was a guest instead of a meal? Why or why not?

Draw Conclusions Have children think about the story they just read. Discuss conclusions they can draw, or opinions they can form, from the story.
- How do you think Mr. and Mrs. Moose feel about each other? Explain.
- Do you think ice and snow are necessary to the setting of the story? Why or why not?

Visualize Children can draw pictures of something in the text that is not illustrated. Then have them discuss their pictures.

RESPONSE Ask children to design an attractive menu for the meal, listing the foods mentioned in the story.

AudioText

2 Extend Concepts Through Inquiry

INVESTIGATE Guide children in choosing material at their independent reading level to explore their topic. Some books that may be appropriate are *The Scholastic Big Book of Holidays Around the Year* by Susan Dillon and *Children Just Like Me: Celebrations!* by Anabel Kindersley, et al. Continue to explain and model ways to research.

Help children decide how they will present their information. Children may use a graphic organizer, a written format, photographs, drawings, or models.

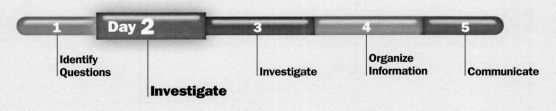

1 — Identify Questions
Day 2 — Investigate
3 — Investigate
4 — Organize Information
5 — Communicate

A Turkey for Thanksgiving

Group Time

DAY 3

A Turkey for Thanksgiving
by Eve Bunting
illustrated by Diane de Groat

AudioText

MORE READING FOR
Group Time

Use this Leveled Reader or other text at children's instructional level.

Below-Level

Reviews
• High-frequency words *door, behind, brought, minute, promise, sorry, everybody*
• Draw conclusions

Strategic Intervention

ROUTINE

1 Word Work

REVIEW PLURALS -s, -es, -ies Review p. 303c, using these additional words. Have children sort the words into -s, -es, and -ies lists.

buddies	bikes	homes	ladies	lunches	brushes
supplies	bins	boxes	toys	leashes	puppies

REVIEW SENTENCE READING Have individuals read these sentences to review decoding skills.

My buddies and I ride bikes to our homes.
The ladies will bring their lunches and drinks.
The art brushes and supplies go in the bins.
We will bring boxes of toys, food, and leashes for the puppies.

2 Comprehension

DRAW CONCLUSIONS/VISUALIZE Reteach p. 284e. Have children respond to the Connect to Reading questions after completing step 3 Reread for Fluency.
• Now read the story again quietly. When you have finished, I'd like you to picture what is happening and look for clues that will help you draw conclusions about the story you're reading.

3 Reread for Fluency

READ SILENTLY WITH FLUENCY Teach p. 303f using text at children's independent level. Reading options include Student Edition selections, Decodable Readers, Strategic Intervention Decodable Readers, and Leveled Readers.

Monitor Progress	Fluency
If... children have difficulty reading silently with fluency,	**then...** discuss with them where they are getting stuck, encourage them to sound out a word by syllables or word parts, and provide additional modeling. Have them listen to your model and then read aloud together, first with you and then without you, before reading individually.

Advanced

ROUTINE

DAY 3

1 Read Self-Selected Reading

BEFORE READING Have children select a trade book or Leveled Reader to read independently. Guide children in selecting books of appropriate difficulty.

AFTER READING When they have finished, have each child select a favorite passage to read aloud to a partner.

2 Extend Concepts Through Inquiry

INVESTIGATE Give children time to investigate the holiday or celebration they are researching and to begin preparing their information. Help students with their chosen methods of presentation.

1	2	Day 3	4	5
Identify Questions	Investigate		Organize Information	Communicate
		Investigate		

Trade Books for Self-Selected Reading

CELEBRATING CHINESE NEW YEAR by Diane Hoyt-Goldsmith, Holiday House, Inc., 1999

THANKS & GIVING: ALL YEAR LONG Marlo Thomas and Christopher Cerf (Editor), Simon & Schuster Children's Publishing, 2004

MORE READING FOR
Group Time

Use this Leveled Reader or other text at children's instructional level.

Advanced

Reviews
- Concept vocabulary
- Draw conclusions

Group Time

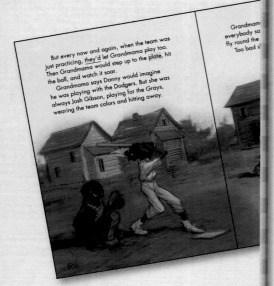

AudioText

MORE READING FOR
Group Time

Use this Leveled Reader or other text at children's instructional level.

Below-Level

Reviews
- High-frequency words *door, behind, brought, minute, promise, sorry, everybody*
- Draw conclusions

DAY 4

Strategic Intervention

ROUTINE

1 Read "Thanksgiving USA"

BEFORE READING Have children practice the words below—first as a group and then individually. Then use Social Studies in Reading, pp. 306–309.

hundred   sailed   Congress   chief   brought

Monitor Progress	Word and Selection Reading
If... children have difficulty with any of these words,	**then...** have them practice in pairs reading word cards before reading the selection.
If... children have difficulty reading the selection individually,	**then...** have them follow along in their books as they listen to the AudioText. You may also have them read pages of the selection aloud together, first with you and then without you, before reading individually.

2 Reread for Fluency

Preteach p. 309a, using text at children's independent reading level. Reading options include Student Edition selections, Decodable Readers, Strategic Intervention Decodable Readers, and Leveled Readers.

3 Build Concepts

Use the Oral Vocabulary Routine, p. DI•1–DI•2, DI•7, and the Amazing Words on p. DI•8.

Advanced

ROUTINE

1 Read "Thanksgiving USA"

AFTER READING Ask:
- Do you think it is important to know how to research topics on the Internet? Why or why not?
- Why do you think the choices Nadia found on the Web are called "links"?
- Do you think the Pilgrims would have celebrated a day of thanks in 1621 were it not for the Indians? Why or why not?

2 Vocabulary

Extend vocabulary with questions such as these:
- Do you think it's important to *decorate* for a *banquet*? Why or why not?
- Would you rather *dine* at home or at a restaurant? Explain.
- Would you like to *participate* in a celebration march? Why or why not?
- Which is your favorite *holiday*? Why?

Encourage children to use the words in their writing.

3 Extend Concepts Through **INquiry**

ORGANIZE INFORMATION Give children time to continue reading about their holiday or celebration. Remind them that tomorrow they will share their information. By now they should have begun putting the information in a presentation format. Help those who need assistance.

DAY 4

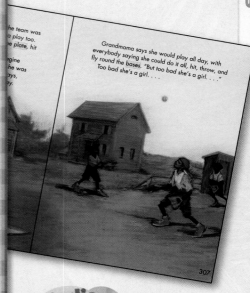

Grandmama says she would play all day, with everybody saying she could do it all, hit, throw, and fly round the bases. "But too bad she's a girl. . . ."

307

AudioText

1	2	3	Day 4	5
Identify Questions	Investigate	Investigate	Organize Information	Communicate

MORE READING FOR
Group Time

Use this Leveled Reader or other text at children's instructional level.

Advanced

Reviews
- Concept vocabulary
- Draw conclusions

Group Time

DAY 5

Strategic Intervention

ROUTINE

1 Word Work

🔊 **LONG *a: a, ai, ay*** Have children read aloud as you track the print. Call on individuals to blend the underlined words.

> <u>Today</u> I will take my <u>pail</u> to the <u>bay</u>.
> Are you going to <u>paint</u> or <u>stain</u> that <u>gray gate</u>?
> The <u>frail</u> <u>quail</u> <u>lay</u> by the pile of <u>hay</u>.
> I <u>may</u> not get the <u>mail</u> because of the <u>rain</u>.

HIGH-FREQUENCY WORDS Use pp. 284–285 to review *door, behind, brought, minute, promise, sorry, everybody*.

Monitor Progress	High-Frequency Words
If... children have difficulty with any of these words,	**then...** tell them the word and have them repeat it. Have children spell the word and tell what word they spelled. Have them practice in pairs with word cards.

2 Monitor Progress

SENTENCE READING SET A Use Set A on reproducible p. 310f to assess children's ability to read decodable and high-frequency words in sentences.

COMPREHENSION To assess comprehension, have each child read Strategic Intervention Decodable Reader 10 or other text at the child's independent level. Ask when and where the story takes place (setting), and have the child retell the story.

MORE READING FOR
Group Time

Use this Leveled Reader or other text at children's instructional level.

Below-Level

Reviews
• High-frequency words *door, behind, brought, minute, promise, sorry, everybody*
• Draw conclusions

Advanced

1 Monitor Progress

SENTENCE READING SET C Use Set C on reproducible p. 310f to assess children's ability to read decodable and high-frequency words in sentences. If you have any question about whether children have mastered this week's skills, have them read the Set B sentences.

COMPREHENSION Have each child read "The Day of the Mermaid" on reproducible p. 310g. Ask them to draw a conclusion about what David and Gail think of each other. Then have the child retell the passage. Use the Retelling Rubric on p. 303g to evaluate the child's retelling.

2 Extend Concepts Through INquiry

COMMUNICATE Have partners share their projects on holidays or celebrations.

1	2	3	4	Day 5
Identify Questions	Investigate	Investigate	Organize Information	

Communicate

MORE READING FOR

Group Time

Use this Leveled Reader or other text at children's instructional level.

Advanced

Reviews
• Concept vocabulary
• Draw conclusions

Tara and Tiree, Fearless Friends

r-Controlled *ar, or, ore*

1 TEACH

Emphasize the sounds /är/ as you say: It's not hard to see stars in the dark.

Emphasize the sounds /ôr/ as you say: Doris went to the store on a stormy morning.

Ask children which vowel sounds they heard repeated in each sentence.

Write *hard, stars,* and *dark* on the board. Tell children that *ar* stands for /är/. Underline the /är/ spelling pattern in each word.

Repeat the procedure for /ôr/ words in the second sentence. Tell children that *or* and *ore* can both stand for /ôr/.

2 PRACTICE AND ASSESS

Have children work in small groups. Provide each group with a piece of poster board. Tell children to divide the poster into three columns and write one of these words at the top of each column: *dark, corn,* and *shore.* Have them circle the letters in each word that stand for /är/or/ôr/.

Write the following words on index cards:

fork   score   target   more

before   bark   darken   order

corner   orbit   adore   market

Have a child choose one, read it aloud, and tell what letters stand for /ôr/ or /är/.

Children then find a word on their poster with the same spelling and write the selected word in the matching column.

Tara and Tiree, Fearless Friends

Sequence

1 TEACH

Explain that events in a story happen in a certain order. Remembering the events in order can help children remember the story. Often a story has clue words to help readers figure out the order of events. Write these clue words on the board, and review them with children: *first, second, next, then, last, finally.*

Prepare a chart showing the "Jack and Jill" nursery rhyme. With children, read the rhyme aloud. Help children assign clue words to each line to tell the order of events. Clue words *then* and *next* are interchangeable, as are *last* and *finally.*

Help children recognize that the story would have been different if the order of events had been different.

2 PRACTICE AND ASSESS

Write the nursery rhyme "Little Miss Muffet" on sentence strips.

Little Miss Muffet sat on a tuffet, eating her curds and whey.
Along came a spider,
And sat down beside her
And frightened Miss Muffet away.

Mix the order of the sentence strips. Invite children to place the strips in the correct order and give each a clue word. Then talk about how the story would have been different if the order of events had been different.

Have children recall other favorite nursery rhymes, such as "Hickory, Dickory, Dock!" and "Simple Simon," and have them assign clue words to each line.

Ronald Morgan Goes to Bat

Contractions *n't*, *'s*, *'ll*, *'m*

1 TEACH

Remind children that a contraction is a new word made by putting two words together and leaving out some letters. The apostrophe in a contraction stands for the letters that have been left out. Write these word pairs on the board:

I am	she is	you will
I'm	she's	you'll

Have children read each contraction and tell what letter or letters are replaced by the apostrophe. Write these sentences on chart paper, and have them read:

I wasn't sure if I should or shouldn't.
He didn't know if he could or he couldn't.
I didn't smile because I wasn't happy.

Have children circle each contraction and tell what two words are used to make the contraction.

2 PRACTICE AND ASSESS

Write the contractions below on the board. Invite children to write the two words that make up each contraction. Help them to identify letters replaced by apostrophes.

isn't (is not)	he'll (he will)
aren't (are not)	they'll (they will)
can't (can not)	we're (we are)

Give groups the contraction cards *'ll, n't, 's, 'm* and word cards *I, he, she, does* to build contractions. Tell them to make a list of the contractions they build. Invite groups to share their lists.

Ronald Morgan Goes to Bat

Realism and Fantasy

1 TEACH

Tell children that some stories are about make-believe characters and places. Things can happen in stories that could never really happen to real people. This kind of story is a *fantasy*.

Explain that other stories have characters and actions that might be real. This kind of story is called *realistic*.

Tell children you are going to describe some story characters. Ask them to tell whether the character could be real or in a fantasy:

an elf (fantasy)
a girl named Cassie (real)
a dragon that breathes fire (fantasy)
a rabbit that wears clothes and talks (fantasy)
a man who plays the piano (real)
a teacher (real)

2 PRACTICE AND ASSESS

Tell children you will tell them about some stories. They are to tell whether the story is a fantasy or could be real. Ask them to explain their answers.

A girl moves to a new school. (real)
Three bears go for a walk while their porridge cools. (fantasy)
A boy has trouble learning to fly a kite. (real)
A boy has trouble keeping his pet dinosaur a secret. (fantasy)
A frog wants to learn to fly. (fantasy)
An astronaut learns how to fly a space shuttle. (real)

Turtle's Race with Beaver

r-Controlled er, ir, ur

1 TEACH

Write the following sentence and have it read.

Her family went to the circus on Thursday.

Remind children that when the letter *r* follows a vowel, the *r* affects the sound of the vowel. Have them underline the words with the sounds /ėr/. Explain that the letters *er*, *ir*, and *ur* can stand for the same sounds, /ėr/. Circle those letters in the words *Her, circus, and Thursday.*

Write *enter, border,* and *farmer* and read the words aloud. Underline *er* at the end of each word. Tell children they can blend longer words with /ėr/ by dividing them into smaller parts. Explain that the words are usually divided between the two consonants. Have volunteers draw a line between the two syllables in each word and then blend them.

2 PRACTICE AND ASSESS

Write these sentences on the board:

A thirsty girl got dirt on her skirt.
A turtle turned in the surf.
He's certain to serve birthday cake.

Ask children to read the sentences and circle the letters that stand for /ėr/.

Prepare the following word cards:

hurry burger birth girl herd
curler first church germ dirty

Have children work in pairs or small groups. Give a pile of cards to each group. Tell them to read and sort the words by their vowel patterns: *er, ir, ur.*

Turtle's Race with Beaver

Sequence

1 TEACH

Remind children that events in a story happen in a certain order and that authors often use clue words to help readers figure out the order of events. Ask children to name clue words. Write the words on the board. (Possible responses: *first, second, next, then, last, finally*) Discuss with children how these words help them figure out the order in which things happen.

Ask volunteers to recall a favorite story and to name in sequence three things that happened in the story. Encourage children to use a clue word in each sentence. Discuss how the story would have been different if the order of events had been different.

2 PRACTICE AND ASSESS

Write the following sentences from *Turtle's Race with Beaver* on sentence strips.

Beaver challenged Turtle to a race.
Turtle agreed.
Beaver told other animals about the race.
Animals came to watch the race.
The race began.
Turtle tricked Beaver and bit the end of his tail.
Turtle won the race.

Mix the order of the sentence strips. Invite children to place the strips in the correct order and give each a beginning clue word. Then talk about how the story would have been different if the order of events had been different.

Plurals: -*s*, -*es*, -*ies*

1 TEACH

Say: The dogs bark at the big boxes.

Ask children how many dogs and boxes they pictured—one or more than one. How did they know? Write these words on the board:

dog	box	puppy
dogs	boxes	puppies

Circle the -*s* ending in *dogs* and the -*es* in *boxes*. Remind children that *s* or *es* can be added to a noun to show more that one. Explain that children can add *s* to most nouns to make the plural form, but words that end in ch, *sh, tch, ss, x,* or *zz* need the ending -*es*.

Explain that *puppies* means "more than one puppy." Circle the -*ies* in puppies. Tell children that to form the plural of nouns ending in *y*, change the *y* to *i* and add the -*es* ending.

2 PRACTICE AND ASSESS

Write the following words on cards and give one or two to each child.

Have each child read a word, identify the base word, and tell what ending was added: *s, es,* or changing the *y* to *i* and adding *es.*

Write *s, es,* and *ies* on the board, each at the top of a column. Write the words *baby, girl, peach, stamp, duckling, penny, star, fox, book,* and *story* on cards. Have children choose a card and read the word. Then have them say the plural form of the word and write it in the correct column.

Author's Purpose

1 TEACH

Write the following book titles on the board:

The Three Little Pigs
Recycling at Home
The Gingerbread Man
The First Astronauts

Read the titles aloud and ask children why they think the author wrote each story. Say: Sometimes authors write books to tell a good story. Sometimes they write to teach us facts about real things. Sometimes they want to convince us that something is important.

2 PRACTICE AND ASSESS

Show children the covers of fiction and nonfiction books that they have not read. With children, read the title of each book. Then display and discuss some of the pictures. Ask why children think the author wrote each book. As children answer, guide the discussion. Help them give reasons to support their answers.

Write "to tell a good story," "to persuade," and "to teach" as column heads on the board. Tell children to flip through *Working Together* and find stories that fit each category. Write the titles under the corresponding heading. Ask children to explain their thinking.

A Turkey for Thanksgiving

Long *a: a, ai, ay*

1 TEACH

Remind children that a long vowel sound says the name of the vowel. Write paint and way on the board and read them with children. Ask what vowel sound they hear in each word. Frame the letters *ai* in *paint* and *ay* in *way* and point out that *ai* and *ay* can stand for the long *a* sound.

Write *paper.* Remind children to blend longer words by dividing them into syllables. Tell them that when a syllable ends with a single vowel, like the *a* in *paper,* the vowel is usually long. Blend *paper.*

2 PRACTICE AND ASSESS

Write the sentences below on the board.

We paid to send the mail on the train.
I play every day in May.

Track the print with your finger as you read the sentences with children. Ask children to identify each word that has the long a sound and to underline them. Then invite volunteers to circle the letters in those words that stand for /ā/.

Pass out half sheets of gray and white paper to each child. Have children draw a large raindrop and write *rain* on the white paper and write *gray* on the gray paper.

Write the following words on the board and have them read.

bacon	paid	baby	sail	way
stay	today	tail	day	rain
play	fail	ray	pain	wait

Have children sort the words according to the spelling pattern for long *a*, writing *ay* words on the gray paper and *ai* words on the raindrop.

A Turkey for Thanksgiving

Draw Conclusions

1 TEACH

Explain that sometimes when you read a story, you can use what you know about real life and what the author tells you to figure out more about the characters and what is happening.

Say: If I were reading a story and one character in the story sees a rainbow, what does that tell me about the story? I know that a rainbow sometimes happens after it rains. I know that light from the sun causes a rainbow. Now I know that it rained and the sun is shining in the story. I am using information in the story plus what I know about real life to figure out more about the story.

2 PRACTICE AND ASSESS

Have children recall the story *The Bremen Town Musicians.* Encourage them to notice details in the text and in the pictures.

Ask these questions about the story:

Donkey is sad at the beginning of the story, but he also seems friendly, kind, and considerate. How do you know? (Possible response: When Donkey meets the dog he stops to talk to him and invites him to go with him to Bremen. I can tell this from what Donkey says and from how he looks in the pictures.)

How do the animals feel as they head for Bremen? How do you know? (Possible response: They feel happy because they are singing loudly and are marching proudly along their way. The pictures show smiles on their faces.

How do the robbers feel when they hear the animals singing? How do you know? (Possible response: The robbers feel scared because they run out of the house. They look scared too.)

Providing children with reading materials they can and want to read is an important step toward developing fluent readers. A running record allows you to determine each child's instructional and independent reading level. Information on how to take a running record is provided on pp. DI•71–DI•72.

Instructional Reading Level

Only approximately 1 in 10 words will be difficult when reading a selection from the Student Edition for children who are at grade level. (A typical second-grader reads approximately 90–100 words correct per minute.)

- Children reading at grade level should read regularly from the Student Edition and On-Level Leveled Readers, with teacher support as suggested in the Teacher's Editions.
- Children reading below grade level can read the Strategic Intervention Leveled Readers and the Decodable Readers. Instructional plans can be found in the Teacher's Edition and the Leveled Reader Teaching Guide.
- Children who are reading above grade level can use the Advanced Leveled Readers and the Advanced Selection in the Teacher's Edition. Instructional plans can be found in the Teacher's Edition and the Leveled Reader Teaching Guide.

Independent Reading Level

Children should read regularly in independent-level texts in which no more than approximately 1 in 20 words is difficult for the reader. Other factors that make a book easy to read include the child's interest in the topic, the amount of text on a page, how well illustrations support meaning, and the complexity and familiarity of the concepts. Suggested books for self-selected reading are provided with each lesson on pp. TR•22–TR•23 in this Teacher's Edition.

Guide children in learning how to self-select books at their independent reading level. As you talk about a book with children, discuss the challenging concepts in it, list new words children find in sampling the book, and ask children about their familiarity with the topic. A blackline master to help children evaluate books for independent reading is provided on p. DI•70.

Self-Selected/Independent Reading

While oral reading allows you to assess children's reading level and fluency, independent reading is of crucial importance to children's futures as readers and learners. Children need to develop their ability to read independently for increasing amounts of time.

- Schedule a regular time for sustained independent reading in your classroom. During the year, gradually increase the amount of time devoted to independent reading.
- More fluent readers may choose to read silently during independent reading time. Other children might read to a partner, to a stuffed animal, or to an adult volunteer.
- Help children track the amount of time they read independently and the number of pages they read in a given amount of time. Tracking will help motivate them to gradually increase their duration and speed. A blackline master for tracking independent reading is provided on p. DI•70.

Choosing a Book to Read by Yourself

These questions can help you pick a book to read.

_____ 1. Is this book about something that I like?

_____ 2. This book may be about a real person, about facts, or a made-up story. Do I like reading this kind of book?

_____ 3. Have I read other things by this author? Do I like the author?

If you say "yes" to question 1, 2, or 3, go on.

_____ 4. Were there fewer than 5 hard words on the first page?

_____ 5. Does the number of words on a page look about right to me?

If you say "yes" to questions 4 and 5, the book is right for you.

Silent Reading

Write the date, the title of the book, and the number of minutes you read.

Date	Title	Minutes

Taking a Running Record

A running record is an assessment of a child's oral reading accuracy and oral reading fluency. Reading accuracy is based on the number of words read correctly. Reading fluency is based on the reading rate (the number of words correct per minute) and the degree to which a child reads with a "natural flow."

How to Measure Reading Accuracy

1. Choose a grade-level text of about 80 to 120 words that is unfamiliar to the child.

2. Make a copy of the text for yourself. Make a copy for the child or have the child read aloud from a book.

3. Give the child the text and have the child read aloud. (You may wish to record the child's reading for later evaluation.)

4. On your copy of the text, mark any miscues or errors the child makes while reading. See the running record sample on page DI•72, which shows how to identify and mark miscues.

5. Count the total number of words in the text and the total number of errors made by the child. Note: If a child makes the same error more than once, such as mispronouncing the same word multiple times, count it as one error. Self-corrections do not count as actual errors. Use the following formula to calculate the percentage score, or accuracy rate:

$$\frac{\text{Total Number of Words} - \text{Total Number of Errors}}{\text{Total Number of Words}} \times 100 = \text{percentage score}$$

Interpreting the Results

- A child who reads **95–100%** of the words correctly is reading at an **independent level** and may need more challenging text.

- A child who reads **90–94%** of the words correctly is reading at an **instructional level** and will likely benefit from guided instruction.

- A child who reads **89%** or fewer of the words correctly is reading at a **frustrational level** and may benefit most from targeted instruction with lower-level texts and intervention.

How to Measure Reading Rate (WCPM)

1. Follow Steps 1–3 above.

2. Note the exact times when the child begins and finishes reading.

3. Use the following formula to calculate the number of words correct per minute (WCPM):

$$\frac{\text{Total Number of Words Read Correctly}}{\text{Total Number of Seconds}} \times 60 = \text{words correct per minute}$$

Interpreting the Results

An appropriate reading rate for a second-grader is 90–100 (WCPM).

Running Record Sample

Running Record Sample

Miscues

Just then a fly crawled near Fred.

and

Fred's long, sticky tongue shot out in a

/ti ne/

flash and caught the tiny insect.

H

"Delicious! I'm full now," he said

loudly. He had already eaten three other

insects and a worm in the past hour.

(SC)

Frankie overheard Fred and climbed

down a few branches. He moved quickly

and easily without falling.

"What are you doing, Fred?" he

asked in a friendly voice.

"I was just finishing up my lunch,"

there

Fred answered. "How is life up high

today, my friend?"

—From *Frog Friends*
On-Level Reader 2.4.3

Insertion
The student inserts words or parts of words that are not in the text.

Mispronunciation/Misreading
The student pronounces or reads a word incorrectly.

Hesitation
The student hesitates over a word, and the teacher provides the word. Wait several seconds before telling the student what the word is.

Self-Correction
The student reads a word incorrectly but then corrects the error. Do not count self-corrections as actual errors. However, noting self-corrections will help you identify words the student finds difficult.

Omission
The student omits words or word parts.

Substitution
The student substitutes words or parts of words for the words in the text.

Running Record Results ▶	**Reading Accuracy** ▶	**Reading Rate—WCPM**
Total Number of Words: **86**	$\dfrac{86-5}{86} = \dfrac{81}{86} = .9418 = 94\%$	$\dfrac{81}{64} \times 60 = 75.9 = 76$ words correct per minute
Number of Errors: **5**		
Reading Time: **64 seconds**	Accuracy Percentage Score: **94%**	Reading Rate: **76 WCPM**

Teacher Resources

Table of Contents

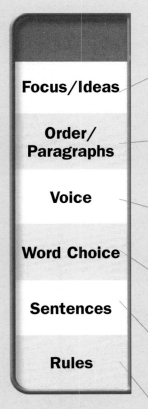

Writing Traits

- **Focus/Ideas** refers to the main purpose for writing and the details that make the subject clear and interesting. It includes development of ideas through support and elaboration.

- **Order/Paragraphs** refers to the overall structure of a piece of writing that guides readers. Within that structure, transitions show how ideas, sentences, and paragraphs are connected.

- **Voice** shows the writer's unique personality and establishes a connection between writer and reader. Voice, which contributes to style, should be suited to the audience and the purpose for writing.

- **Word Choice** is the use of precise, vivid words to communicate effectively and naturally. It helps create style through the use of specific nouns, lively verbs and adjectives, and accurate, well-placed modifiers.

- **Sentences** covers strong, well-built sentences that vary in length and type. Skillfully written sentences have pleasing rhythms and flow fluently.

- **Rules** refers to mechanical correctness and includes grammar, usage, spelling, punctuation, capitalization, and paragraphing.

Scoring Rubric — Narrative Writing

	6	5	4	3	2	1
Focus/Ideas	Excellent, focused narrative; well elaborated with quality details	Good, focused narrative; elaborated with telling details	Narrative focused; adequate elaboration	Generally focused narrative; some supporting details	Sometimes unfocused narrative; needs more supporting details	Rambling narrative; lacks development and detail
Organization/ Paragraphs	Strong beginning, middle, and end; appropriate order words	Coherent beginning, middle, and end; some order words	Beginning, middle, and end easily identifiable	Recognizable beginning, middle, and end; some order words	Little direction from beginning to end; few order words	Lacks beginning, middle, end; incorrect or no order words
Voice	Writer closely involved; engaging personality	Reveals personality	Pleasant but not compelling voice	Sincere voice but not fully engaged	Little writer involvement, personality	Careless writing with no feeling
Word Choice	Vivid, precise words that bring story to life	Clear words to bring story to life	Some specific word pictures	Language adequate but lacks color	Generally limited or redundant language	Vague, dull, or misused words
Sentences	Excellent variety of sentences; natural rhythm	Varied lengths, styles; generally smooth	Correct sentences with some variations in style	Correctly constructed sentences; some variety	May have simple, awkward, or wordy sentences; little variety	Choppy; many incomplete or run-on sentences
Rules	Excellent control; few or no errors	No serious errors to affect understanding	General mastery of conventions but some errors	Reasonable control; few distracting errors	Weak control; enough errors to affect understanding	Many errors that prevent understanding

Scoring Rubric — Narrative Writing

	5	4	3	2	1
Focus/Ideas	Excellent, focused narrative; well elaborated with quality details	Good, focused narrative; elaborated with telling details	Generally focused narrative; some supporting details	Sometimes unfocused narrative; needs more supporting details	Rambling narrative; lacks development and detail
Organization/ Paragraphs	Strong beginning, middle, and end; appropriate order words	Coherent beginning, middle, and end; some order words	Recognizable beginning, middle, and end; some order words	Little direction from beginning to end; few order words	Lacks beginning, middle, end; incorrect or no order words
Voice	Writer closely involved; engaging personality	Reveals personality	Sincere voice but not fully engaged	Little writer involvement, personality	Careless writing with no feeling
Word Choice	Vivid, precise words that bring story to life	Clear words to bring story to life	Language adequate but lacks color	Generally limited or redundant language	Vague, dull, or misused words
Sentences	Excellent variety of sentences; natural rhythm	Varied lengths, styles; generally smooth	Correctly constructed sentences; some variety	May have simple, awkward, or wordy sentences; little variety	Choppy; many incomplete or run-on sentences
Rules	Excellent control; few or no errors	No serious errors to affect understanding	Reasonable control; few distracting errors	Weak control; enough errors to affect understanding	Many errors that prevent understanding

Scoring Rubric — Narrative Writing

	3	2	1
Focus/Ideas	Excellent, focused narrative; well elaborated with quality details	Generally focused narrative; some supporting details	Rambling narrative; lacks development and detail
Organization/ Paragraphs	Strong beginning, middle, and end; appropriate order words	Recognizable beginning, middle, and end; some order words	Lacks beginning, middle, end; incorrect or no order words
Voice	Writer closely involved; engaging personality	Sincere voice but not fully engaged	Careless writing with no feeling
Word Choice	Vivid, precise words that bring story to life	Language adequate but lacks color	Vague, dull, or misused words
Sentences	Excellent variety of sentences; natural rhythm	Correctly constructed sentences; some variety	Choppy; many incomplete or run-on sentences
Rules	Excellent control; few or no errors	Reasonable control; few distracting errors	Many errors that prevent understanding

Scoring Rubric | Descriptive Writing

	6	5	4	3	2	1
Focus/Ideas	Excellent, focused description; well elaborated with quality details	Good, focused description; elaborated with telling details	Description focused; good elaboration	Generally focused description; some supporting details	Sometimes unfocused description; needs more supporting details	Rambling description; lacks development and detail
Organization/ Paragraphs	Compelling ideas enhanced by order, structure, and transitions	Appealing order, structure, and transitions	Structure identifiable and suitable; transitions used	Adequate order, structure, and some transitions to guide reader	Little direction from beginning to end; few transitions	Lacks direction and identifiable structure; no transitions
Voice	Writer closely involved; engaging personality	Reveals personality	Pleasant but not compelling voice	Sincere voice but not fully engaged	Little writer involvement, personality	Careless writing with no feeling
Word Choice	Vivid, precise words that create memorable pictures	Clear, interesting words to bring description to life	Some specific word pictures	Language adequate; appeals to senses	Generally limited or redundant language	Vague, dull, or misused words
Sentences	Excellent variety of sentences; natural rhythm	Varied lengths, styles; generally smooth	Correct sentences with variations in style	Correctly constructed sentences; some variety	May have simple, awkward, or wordy sentences; little variety	Choppy; many incomplete or run-on sentences
Rules	Excellent control; few or no errors	No serious errors to affect understanding	General mastery of conventions but some errors	Reasonable control; few distracting errors	Weak control; enough errors to affect understanding	Many errors that prevent understanding

Scoring Rubric | Descriptive Writing

	5	4	3	2	1
Focus/Ideas	Excellent, focused description; well elaborated with quality details	Good, focused description; elaborated with telling details	Generally focused description; some supporting details	Sometimes unfocused description; needs more supporting details	Rambling description; lacks development and detail
Organization/ Paragraphs	Compelling ideas enhanced by order, structure, and transitions	Appealing order, structure, and transitions	Adequate order, structure, and some transitions to guide reader	Little direction from beginning to end; few transitions	Lacks direction and identifiable structure; no transitions
Voice	Writer closely involved; engaging personality	Reveals personality	Sincere voice but not fully engaged	Little writer involvement, personality	Careless writing with no feeling
Word Choice	Vivid, precise words that create memorable pictures	Clear, interesting words to bring description to life	Language adequate; appeals to senses	Generally limited or redundant language	Vague, dull, or misused words
Sentences	Excellent variety of sentences; natural rhythm	Varied lengths, styles; generally smooth	Correctly constructed sentences; some variety	May have simple, awkward, or wordy sentences; little variety	Choppy; many incomplete or run-on sentences
Rules	Excellent control; few or no errors	No serious errors to affect understanding	Reasonable control; few distracting errors	Weak control; enough errors to affect understanding	Many errors that prevent understanding

Scoring Rubric | Descriptive Writing

	3	2	1
Focus/Ideas	Excellent, focused description; well elaborated with quality details	Generally focused description; some supporting details	Rambling description; lacks development and detail
Organization/ Paragraphs	Compelling ideas enhanced by order, structure, and transitions	Adequate order, structure, and some transitions to guide reader	Lacks direction and identifiable structure; no transitions
Voice	Writer closely involved; engaging personality	Sincere voice but not fully engaged	Careless writing with no feeling
Word Choice	Vivid, precise words that create memorable pictures	Language adequate; appeals to senses	Vague, dull, or misused words
Sentences	Excellent variety of sentences; natural rhythm	Correctly constructed sentences; some variety	Choppy; many incomplete or run-on sentences
Rules	Excellent control; few or no errors	Reasonable control; few distracting errors	Many errors that prevent understanding

Scoring Rubric — Persuasive Writing

	6	5	4	3	2	1
Focus/Ideas	Persuasive argument carefully built with quality details	Persuasive argument well supported with details	Persuasive argument focused; good elaboration	Persuasive argument with one or two convincing details	Persuasive piece sometimes unfocused; needs more support	Rambling persuasive argument; lacks development and detail
Organization/ Paragraphs	Information chosen and arranged for maximum effect	Evident progression of persuasive ideas	Progression and structure evident	Information arranged in a logical way with some lapses	Little structure or direction	No identifiable structure
Voice	Writer closely involved; persuasive but not overbearing	Maintains persuasive tone	Persuasive but not compelling voice	Sometimes uses persuasive voice	Little writer involvement, personality	Shows little conviction
Word Choice	Persuasive words carefully chosen for impact	Argument supported by persuasive language	Uses some persuasive words	Occasional persuasive language	Generally limited or redundant language	Vague, dull, or misused words; no persuasive words
Sentences	Excellent variety of sentences; natural rhythm	Varied lengths, styles; generally smooth	Correct sentences with variations in style	Carefully constructed sentences; some variety	Simple, awkward, or wordy sentences; little variety	Choppy; many incomplete or run-on sentences
Rules	Excellent control; few or no errors	No serious errors to affect understanding	General mastery of conventions but some errors	Reasonable control; few distracting errors	Weak control; enough errors to affect understanding	Many errors that prevent understanding

Scoring Rubric — Persuasive Writing

	5	4	3	2	1
Focus/Ideas	Persuasive argument carefully built with quality details	Persuasive argument well supported with details	Persuasive argument with one or two convincing details	Persuasive piece sometimes unfocused; needs more support	Rambling persuasive argument; lacks development and detail
Organization/ Paragraphs	Information chosen and arranged for maximum effect	Evident progression of persuasive ideas	Information arranged in a logical way with some lapses	Little structure or direction	No identifiable structure
Voice	Writer closely involved; persuasive but not overbearing	Maintains persuasive tone	Sometimes uses persuasive voice	Little writer involvement, personality	Shows little conviction
Word Choice	Persuasive words carefully chosen for impact	Argument supported by persuasive language	Occasional persuasive language	Generally limited or redundant language	Vague, dull, or misused words; no persuasive words
Sentences	Excellent variety of sentences; natural rhythm	Varied lengths, styles; generally smooth	Carefully constructed sentences; some variety	Simple, awkward, or wordy sentences; little variety	Choppy; many incomplete or run-on sentences
Rules	Excellent control; few or no errors	No serious errors to affect understanding	Reasonable control; few distracting errors	Weak control; enough errors to affect understanding	Many errors that prevent understanding

Scoring Rubric — Persuasive Writing

	3	2	1
Focus/Ideas	Persuasive argument carefully built with quality details	Persuasive argument with one or two convincing details	Rambling persuasive argument; lacks development and detail
Organization/ Paragraphs	Information chosen and arranged for maximum effect	Information arranged in a logical way with some lapses	No identifiable structure
Voice	Writer closely involved; persuasive but not overbearing	Sometimes uses persuasive voice	Shows little conviction
Word Choice	Persuasive words carefully chosen for impact	Occasional persuasive language	Vague, dull, or misused words; no persuasive words
Sentences	Excellent variety of sentences; natural rhythm	Carefully constructed sentences; some variety	Choppy; many incomplete or run-on sentences
Rules	Excellent control; few or no errors	Reasonable control; few distracting errors	Many errors that prevent understanding

Scoring Rubric | Expository Writing

	6	5	4	3	2	1
Focus/Ideas	Insightful, focused exposition; well elaborated with quality details	Informed, focused exposition; elaborated with telling details	Exposition focused, good elaboration	Generally focused exposition; some supporting details	Sometimes unfocused exposition needs more supporting details	Rambling exposition; lacks development and detail
Organization/ Paragraphs	Logical, consistent flow of ideas; good transitions	Logical sequencing of ideas; uses transitions	Ideas sequenced with some transitions	Sequenced ideas with some transitions	Little direction from beginning to end; few order words	Lacks structure and transitions
Voice	Writer closely involved; informative voice well suited to topic	Reveals personality; voice suited to topic	Pleasant but not compelling voice	Sincere voice suited to topic	Little writer involvement, personality	Careless writing with no feeling
Word Choice	Vivid, precise words to express ideas	Clear words to express ideas	Words correct and adequate	Language adequate but may lack precision	Generally limited or redundant language	Vague, dull, or misused words
Sentences	Strong topic sentence; fluent, varied structures	Good topic sentence; smooth sentence structure	Correct sentences that are sometimes fluent	Topic sentence correctly constructed; some sentence variety	Topic sentence unclear or missing; wordy, awkward sentences	No topic sentence; many incomplete or run-on sentences
Rules	Excellent control; few or no errors	No serious errors to affect understanding	General mastery of conventions but some errors	Reasonable control; few distracting errors	Weak control; enough errors to affect understanding	Many errors that prevent understanding

Scoring Rubric | Expository Writing

	5	4	3	2	1
Focus/Ideas	Insightful, focused exposition; well elaborated with quality details	Informed, focused exposition; elaborated with telling details	Generally focused exposition; some supporting details	Sometimes unfocused exposition needs more supporting details	Rambling exposition; lacks development and detail
Organization/ Paragraphs	Logical, consistent flow of ideas; good transitions	Logical sequencing of ideas; uses transitions	Sequenced ideas with some transitions	Little direction from beginning to end; few order words	Lacks structure and transitions
Voice	Writer closely involved; informative voice well suited to topic	Reveals personality; voice suited to topic	Language adequate but may lack precision	Little writer involvement, personality	Careless writing with no feeling
Word Choice	Vivid, precise words to express ideas	Clear words to express ideas	Topic sentence correctly constructed; some sentence variety	Generally limited or redundant language	Vague, dull, or misused words
Sentences	Strong topic sentence; fluent, varied structures	Good topic sentence; smooth sentence structure	Sincere voice suited to topic	Topic sentence unclear or missing; wordy, awkward sentences	No topic sentence; many incomplete or run-on sentences
Rules	Excellent control; few or no errors	No serious errors to affect understanding	Reasonable control; few distracting errors	Weak control; enough errors to affect understanding	Many errors that prevent understanding

Scoring Rubric | Expository Writing

	3	2	1
Focus/Ideas	Insightful, focused exposition; well elaborated with quality details	Generally focused exposition; some supporting details	Rambling exposition; lacks development and detail
Organization/ Paragraphs	Logical, consistent flow of ideas; good transitions	Sequenced ideas with some transitions	Lacks structure and transitions
Voice	Writer closely involved; informative voice well suited to topic	Sincere voice suited to topic	Careless writing with no feeling
Word Choice	Vivid, precise words to express ideas	Language adequate but may lack precision	Vague, dull, or misused words
Sentences	Strong topic sentence; fluent, varied structures	Topic sentence correctly constructed; some sentence variety	No topic sentence; many incomplete or run-on sentences
Rules	Excellent control; few or no errors	Reasonable control; few distracting errors	Many errors that prevent understanding

Iris and Walter

Short Vowels; Short e: ea

add	pack	peck	pink	knock	junk
ask	pan	red	quick	lock	just
back	pat	sled	rib	lots	luck
band	plan	speck	ring	pond	lump
bang	rang	step	rip	rock	mug
bank	sack	tell	sick	shock	must
black	sang	them	sing	slop	run
bland	sank	well	sink	sock	rust
brand	sat	went	six	sod	sung
camp	sad	when	slim	stock	truck
cap	slap	yell	sling	stop	trunk
cat	stack	big	slip	tock	tub
crack	tag	bring	still	top	tuck
drank	tank	cling	swing	bunk	tug
fast	track	crib	think	but	bread
grab	van	fill	thing	chunk	breath
grand	bed	fist	this	cup	dead
grass	bell	fit	tip	cut	dread
hand	bend	fix	will	drum	feather
hat	best	hill	win	duck	head
lack	check	his	wing	dunk	leather
hot	deck	hit	box	dust	meadow
land	desk	kid	clock	fun	read
last	dress	king	dock	gum	ready
man	end	lick	frog	hug	spread
map	get	list	got	hum	sweater
mask	less	mist	honk	hung	thread
mat	let	pick	jog	jump	weather

Spelling Words

chop
desk
drum
dust
job
list
mess
pack
rock
rib
sad
tag

High-Frequency/Tested Words

beautiful
country
friend*
front
someone
somewhere

Selection Words

amazing
ladder
meadow
roller-skate

Exploring Space with an Astronaut

Long Vowels CVCe; c/s/, g/j/, s/z/

age	pace	exercise	ride	lone	tube	
airplane	page	file	ripe	nose	tune	
ate	place	fine	shines	note	use	
bake	plane	hike	size	poke		
brave	plate	ice	slice	pose		
cage	race	inside	spice	rode		
cake	rage	kite	time	rose		
cape	rake	lice	twice	telescope		
date	safe	life	white	those		
drape	sage	like	wide	tone		
erase	shake	lime	wise	vote		
face	space	mice	bone	confuse		
game	spaceship	miles	broke	cube		
gape	stage	mime	chose	cute		
lace	take	mine	close	fuse		
lake	tame	nice	code	huge		
lane	wage	outside	dose	mule		
late	bite	pile	home	mute		
made	bride	price	hope	plume		
make	dice	quite	hose	rude		
mane	dime	rice	joke	rule		

Spelling Words

blaze
cube
fine
home
late
mice
nose
page
size
space
tune
vote

High-Frequency/Tested Words

everywhere
live*
machines
move
woman
work*
world

Selection Words

astronaut
experiment
gravity
shuttle
telescope

* = reviewed high-freque▸
word from grade 1

Henry and Mudge and the Starry Night

Consonant Blends

act	bride	croak	flock	land	pride	small	stars	stung
ant	bring	crows	flop	last	prop	smelly	state	tent
ask	brisk	crust	flute	long	raft	smile	step	trace
band	broke	drank	fly	lost	scrape	smack	stick	track
best	brush	dread	frame	mask	screech	snake	stink	tree
black	bust	dreams	frog	milk	scrub	snap	stone	tribe
blades	camp	drink	front	must	send	snuck	strand	trip
blame	clam	drool	glad	nest	skate	snuggle	strap	trunk
blank	clamp	drop	glide	next	skills	sound	stream	trust
blast	clank	drove	grace	past	skit	space	stress	tusk
blew	clap	dump	grand	pest	sky	splat	stretch	twice
blond	clean	dusk	grass	place	slat	split	strict	twigs
bluebird	close	dust	gray	plan	sleep	splint	stride	twin
branch	crackers	dwell	grind	plank	slept	spread	strike	trust
brand	craft	fast	groan	plant	slide	spring	string	went
brake	cramp	felt	hand	plate	slippery	spruce	stripe	west
brave	crate	flake	help	plug	slope	stage	strong	wind
bread	crept	flat	jump	plump	slow	stamp	stretch	
breeze	crest	flex	just	pond	slump	stand	stump	

Spelling Words

ask
brave
breeze
clip
hand
mask
nest
state
stop
strap
stream
twin

High-Frequency/Tested Words

bear
build
couldn't
father
love*
mother
straight

Selection Words

drooled
lanterns
shivered
snuggled

A Walk in the Desert

Base Words and Endings -s, -ed, -ing

-s				-ing	
amazes	pecks	dragged	peeled	amazing	playing
asks	pretends	dropped	petted	asking	racing
bakes	protects	filled	placed	bugging	riding
calls	races	gagged	raced	carving	rubbing
chips	rubs	gobbled	rested	confusing	running
cools	runs	grabbed	rubbed	dining	scaring
drags	seems	grinned	saved	dragging	shaking
eats	smiles	happened	smiled	hiding	sleeping
gets	uses	hiked	snapped	hiking	sliding
grows	wags	hopped	tagged	hopping	smiling
hikes	walks	hugged	traded	jumping	soaring
howls	wipes	jogged	wagged	lifting	sunning
jumps		jumped	walked	looking	trading
lies	-ed	lifted	watched	making	wagging
lives	added	looked	wiped	opening	walking
makes	amazed	nodded	yelled	patting	winning
	asked	patted			

Spelling Words

dropped
dropping
excited
exciting
hugged
hugging
lifted
lifting
smiled
smiling
talked
talking

High-Frequency/Tested Words

animals
early*
eyes*
full
water*
warm

Selection Words

cactus
climate
coyote
desert
harsh

The Strongest One

Consonant Diagraphs

arch	each	mash	shy	then	ditch	while	
bench	lunch	mush	splash	there	fetch	whim	
branches	much	shack	trash	they	hatch	whip	
bunch	pinch	shake	wash	thick	hutch	whirl	
chalk	such	shape	wish	thin	itch	whisk	
chase	teach	shell	bath	think	latch	whistle	
chat	watch	shin	everything	things	match	white	
check	which	shine	forth	third	patch		
chest	bash	ship	fourth	thirsty	pitch		
chick	blush	shirt	math	those	scratched		
chicken	brush	shone	mouth	thud	stitch		
chimp	bushes	shop	path	thumb	stretch		
chin	crush	shore	something	thump	watch		
chip	dash	shot	teeth	together	elsewhere		
chop	dish	show	than	batch	whale		
chose	fresh	shrimp	thank	catch	when		
church	fish	shrubs	that	clutch	where		
crouch	hush	shut	them	crutch	which		

Spelling Words

bunch
chase
itch
match
patch
shape
that
them
whale
what
when
wish

High-Frequency/Tested Words

gone
learn*
often
pieces
though
together*
very*

Selection Words

dangerous
gnaws
narrator
relatives

* = reviewed high-frequency
word from grade 1

Tara and Tiree, Fearless Friends

r-Controlled ar, or, ore; Syllables VCCV

ar	dark	shark	fork	**ore**	belly	packet
alarm	darling	smart	form	adore	bucket	panda
armies	far	star	fort	before	carpet	pepper
armor	farm	start	horse	bore	chicken	picnic
art	garden	target	morning	chore	corner	pocket
artist	hard	yard	north	more	correct	pompom
barber	harm		orbit	score	darling	problem
bark	harp	**or**	order	shore	distant	puppet
barn	jars	border	porch	sore	enlist	rabbits
car	lark	born	short	store	forget	ribbon
carp	mark	corn	sport	stories	gimmick	socket
carpet	market	corner	stork	therefore	insect	target
cart	parched	correct	storm		kitten	until
cartoon	part	forget	stormy	**VCCV**	mitten	winter
charm	party	forgot	thorn	basket	muffin	

Spelling Words

before
born
chore
corn
farm
hard
horse
more
part
porch
score
smart

Ronald Morgan Goes to Bat

Contractions

aren't	don't	how's	it's	there's	won't
can't	hadn't	I'll	let's	they'll	who's
couldn't	haven't	I'm	shouldn't	she'll	you'll
didn't	he's	isn't	she's	we'll	
doesn't	he'll	it'll	that's	wasn't	

Spelling Words

didn't
hadn't
hasn't
he's
I'll
I'm
isn't
it's
she's
wasn't
we'll
who'll

Turtle's Race with Beaver

r-Controlled er, ir, ur; Syllables VCCV

er	swerve	flirt	curl	turtle	corner	surface
clerk	term	shirk	curler	urge	curler	survive
fern	verse	shirt	disturb	urn	dirty	tender
germ		skirt	fur		disturb	thirty
her	**ir**	squirrel	furry	**VCCV**	enter	turkey
herd	birch	stir	hurry	after	gotten	under
herself	bird	third	hurt	almost	happens	until
certain	birdbath	thirsty	murmur	arrive	happy	winter
jerk	birth	thirty	nurse	batter	hurry	wonder
kernel	birthday	twirl	purple	better	kernel	
nerve	chirp		purse	border	murmur	
perch	circus	**ur**	return	bottom	perfect	
perfect	confirm	blurt	spurt	burger	plenty	
perk	dirt	burden	surf	butter	rabbit	
person	dirty	burger	surface	certain	sherbet	
pert	girl	burn	survive	challenge	sister	
serve	girth	burst	Thursday	chipmunk	splendid	
sherbet	firm	church	turkey	circus	squirrel	
stern	first	curb	turn	confirm	summer	

Spelling Words

birth
curb
curl
dirt
her
nurse
person
purse
serve
skirt
turn
turtle

The Bremen Town Musicians

Plurals -s, -es, -ies

-s

animals	drinks	monsters	towns	dishes	**-ies**
bags	ducklings	nails	toys	ditches	armies
bases	ducks	nickels	twigs	dresses	babies
baskets	experts	notes	tunes	foxes	berries
bikes	farms	orders	vases	glasses	buddies
bins	forests	papers	years	kisses	bunnies
books	friends	pencils		lashes	candies
boys	gerbils	piles	**-es**	leashes	cherries
cages	germs	places	ashes	lunches	cities
cards	girls	planes	batches	matches	daddies
centers	globes	plates	beaches	messes	families
cents	grapes	pockets	benches	mixes	flies
chores	hands	purses	boxes	patches	jellies
classmates	heels	races	branches	peaches	ladies
corners	holes	rocks	brushes	perches	lilies
crafts	homes	robbers	bunches	ranches	mommies
crops	hoses	roses	buses	scratches	nannies
cups	hours	spices	bushes	switches	parties
dancers	houses	stamps	churches	watches	pennies
desks	jobs	stands	classes	wishes	ponies
dimes	kittens	stars	circuses		puppies
dogs	lamps	stores	crashes		stories
	lots	things	crutches		supplies

Spelling Words

babies
baby
lunch
lunches
note
notes
stories
story
switch
switches
tune
tunes

High-Frequency/Tested Words

bought
people*
pleasant
probably
scared
shall
sign*

Selection Words

excitement
mill
monsters
musicians
robbers

A Turkey for Thanksgiving

Long a: a, ai, ay; Syllables VCV

a	claim	pain	**ay**	ray	famous
acorns	explain	paint	away	say	holiday
agent	fail	quail	bay	spray	lady
apron	faint	rail	day	stay	lazy
baby	frail	rain	dismay	stray	ever
famous	gain	raised	gray	sway	paper
lady	grain	sail	fray	today	visit
lazy	hail	snail	hay	stay	
paper	laid	stain	holiday	way	
table	maid	tail	lay		
	mail	train	may	**VCV**	
ai	main	waist	okay	acorn	
aim	nail	wait	pay	agent	
braid	paid		play	baby	
brain	pail		pray	began	

Spelling Words

away
brain
main
paint
play
raise
say
stay
tail
today
tray
wait

High-Frequency/Tested Words

behind*
brought
door*
everybody
minute
promise
sorry

Selection Words

hooves
lumbered
riverbank
Thanksgiving

* = reviewed high-frequency word from grade 1

Pearl and Wagner: Two Good Friends

Long e: e, ee, ea, y; Syllabels VCV

e
be
detail
equal
even
he
maybe
me
meter
recess
secret
she
we

ee
agree
bee
beet
breeze
creep
deep
feed
feel
feet
fifteen
green

greet
jeep
keep
meet
need
screech
seed
seek
seems
sleep
sleet
speech
steep
street
succeed
sweeping
sweet
teeth
three
tree
weed
week
wheel

ea
beach

beam
bean
beat
bleach
cheap
clean
cream
crease
dreamed
each
ease
easel
easy
eating
feast
heal
heap
leafy
leaping
leave
mean
meat
neat
pea
peach
peak

please
read
readers
seal
seat
squeak
stream
teach
teacher
team
tease
treat

y
any
anything
baby
bunny
city
cozy
dirty
everyone
everywhere
funny
happy
jolly

lady
lazy
leafy
lucky
only
party
pony
pretty
ready
really
shaky
silly
story
windy

VCV
city
detail
electric
even
meter
recess
remember
robins

Spelling Words
deep
easy
feel
leave
party
seat
sleep
team
teeth
wheel
windy

High-Frequency/Tested Words
guess
pretty
science*
shoe*
village
watch
won

Selection Words
electricity
robot
trash
wad

Dear Juno

Long o: o, oa, ow; Syllables VCV

o
almost
bold
cold
colt
donate
fold
gold
hello
hero
hold
host
locate
mold
moment
most
noticed
notion
ocean
old

open
over
photograph
post
postcard
rotate
scold
so
soda
sold
strolled
told
unfolded

oa
boast
boat
coach
coast
coat

croak
float
foamy
goal
goat
loaf
loan
moat
oath
oat
road
roam
roast
throat
toad
toast

ow
below
blow

blown
bowl
flow
flown
follow
glow
grow
grown
growth
know
mow
mower
own
owner
row
show
shown
slow
snow
throw

thrown
window
yellow

VCV
donate
favor
locate
moment
noticed
open
photograph
robot
soda
hero

Spelling Words
ago
bowl
float
goat
hold
most
open
show
slow
toad
toast
told

High-Frequency/Tested Words
answer*
company
faraway
parents
picture*
school*
wash

Selection Words
envelope
persimmons
photograph
smudged

* = reviewed high-frequen
word from grade 1

Anansi Goes Fishing

Compound Words

afternoon	carpool	grandpa	mailman	railroad	sunrise
airline	catfish	grandparents	maybe	raindrop	sunscreen
airplane	cowboy	grandson	myself	rainstorm	sunshine
airport	cupcake	grasshoppers	nearby	rainbow	suntan
anything	daylight	haircut	netmaker	riverbank	supermarket
babysit	daytime	halfway	network	riverboat	teacup
backpack	dishpan	haystack	nobody	rowboat	teammates
backyard	driveway	himself	nothing	sailboat	teardrop
baseball	drugstore	homemade	nowhere	sandpaper	thunderstorm
bathtub	everybody	homework	nutshell	schoolyard	treehouse
bedroom	everyone	inside	oatmeal	seashore	watermelon
bedtime	everything	landlord	outside	seaweed	weekend
beehive	everywhere	laptop	pancake	shortstop	whatever
birthday	faraway	ladybug	paycheck	snowflake	wherever
blackbird	fireplace	lipstick	peanuts	snowstorm	wildflower
brainstorm	flashlight	lookout	pinecone	someone	worksheet
breakfast	forever	lunchbox	pitchfork	something	yourself
buttermilk	goldfish	lunchtime	playmate	starfish	
cannot	granddad	mailbag	playoff	streetcar	
carefree	grandma	mailbox	popcorn	sunflowers	

Spelling Words

backyard
basketball
bathtub
bedtime
birthday
driveway
mailbox
raindrop
riverbank
someone
something
weekend

been
believe
caught
finally
today*
tomorrow
whatever

Selection Words

delicious
justice
lazy
weave

Rosa and Blanca

Long i: i, ie, igh, y

i	spider	lied	nightlight	fly
behind	wild	pie	right	hydrant
bind	tiger	tie	sigh	July
blind	tiny	tried	sight	myself
child	title		slight	nylon
cider		**igh**	thigh	shy
climb	**ie**	bright	tight	sky
find	cried	flight		sly
kind	cries	fright	**y**	try
lilac	die	high	by	why
mild	dried	knight	cry	
mind	flies	light	cycle	
pilot	fries	might	cyclone	
sign	lie	night	dry	

Spelling Words

blind
bright
child
cry
find
flight
fly
myself
right
sky
spider
wild

High-Frequency/ Tested Words

alone
buy
daughters
half
many*
their*
youngest

Selection Words

chiles
luckiest
tortillas

A Weed Is a Flower

Comparative Endings

bigger	heavier	sooner	brightest	highest	silliest
brighter	hotter	stranger	busiest	hottest	slowest
colder	higher	taller	closest	latest	smallest
fairer	lazier	thicker	coldest	laziest	smartest
fancier	littler	thinner	cutest	lightest	softest
faster	longer	tighter	fairest	littlest	sweetest
finer	nicer	tinier	fastest	longest	tallest
friendlier	prettier	uglier	finest	prettiest	thinnest
greener	redder	weaker	friendliest	nicest	tiniest
happier	sillier	wider	fullest	reddest	ugliest
harder	slower	biggest	happiest	ripest	weakest
harsher	softer	bravest	heaviest	saddest	widest

Spelling Words

busier
busiest
fatter
fattest
happier
happiest
hotter
hottest
smaller
smallest
sooner
soonest

High-Frequency/ Tested Words

clothes
hours
money
neighbor
only*
question
taught

Selection Words

agriculture
college
greenhouse
laboratory

* = reviewed high-frequency
word from grade 1

The Quilt Story

Syllables: Consonant +le

able	cradle	maple	rattle	stable	twinkle
ankle	cuddle	middle	riddle	staple	uncle
apple	dimple	mumble	rifle	startle	whistle
bottle	fable	nibble	ripple	struggle	wiggle
bubble	giggle	noble	sample	stumble	wobble
bugle	gobble	paddle	scribble	table	
bundle	handle	pickle	simple	tickle	
cable	jumble	puddle	snuggle	title	
candle	ladle	purple	sparkle	trouble	
cattle	little	puzzle	sprinkle	tumble	

Spelling Words

able
ankle
apple
bubble
bugle
bundle
cable
giggle
purple
sparkle
tickle
title

High-Frequency/Tested Words

blankets
pretended
quilt
stuffing
trunks
unpacked
wrapped

Selection Words

beautiful
country
friend
front
someone
somewhere

The Life Cycle of a Pumpkin

Vowels oo, u

oo	foot	nook	took	u	bushy
book	football	notebook	understood	bull	full
bookbag	footstep	overlook	wood	bulldog	fully
brook	good	root	wooden	bullet	pudding
cook	hood	shook	woodpile	bullfrog	pull
cookbook	hoof	soot	wool	bully	pulley
cookie	hook	stood		bush	push
crook	look	textbook		bushel	put

Spelling Words

brook
cook
full
hood
hook
July
pull
push
put
shook
stood
wood

High-Frequency/Tested Words

bumpy
fruit
harvest
root
smooth
soil
vine

Selection Words

everywhere
live
machines
move
woman
work
world

Frogs

Vowel Diphthongs ou, ow/ou/

ou	house	proud	ow	flower	towel
about	loud	round	allow	frown	towers
aloud	mouse	scout	bow	gown	town
amounts	mouth	shout	brown	growl	vow
around	ouch	sound	clown	how	vowel
bounce	ounce	south	cow	howl	
bound	our	sprout	cowboy	now	
cloud	out	stout	crowd	owl	
count	outside	trout	crown	plow	
crouch	pounce	voucher	down	powder	
found	pouch	without	downtown	powerful	
grouch	pound		drown	rowdy	
ground	pout		drowsy	shower	

Spelling Words

about
around
crown
downtown
flower
gown
ground
howl
mouse
pound
south

High-Frequency/Tested Words

crawls
insects
pond
powerful
shed
skin
wonderful

Selection Words

bear
build
couldn't
father
love
mother
straight

I Like Where I Am

Vowel Diphthongs *oi, oy/oi/*

oi			**oy**	
avoid	joint	point	annoy	joy
boil	joist	poise	boy	loyal
broil	hoist	poison	boyhood	oyster
choice	loiter	rejoice	cowboy	ploy
coil	moist	sirloin	coy	royal
coin	noise	soil	destroy	soy
foil	noisy	spoil	employ	toy
join	oily	toil	enjoy	voyage
	ointment	voice		

Spelling Words

broil
cowboy
destroy
enjoy
foil
joint
joy
loyal
moist
noise
royal
spoil

High-Frequency/Tested Words

block
chuckle
fair
giant
strong
tears
trouble

Selection Words

animals
early
eyes
full
water

Helen Keller and the Big Storm

Vowels *oo, ue, ew, ui*

oo			**ew**	**ue**	**ui**
bathroom	moo	spool	blew	blue	bruise
bloom	mood	spoon	brew	clue	cruise
boot	moon	stoop	chew	cue	fruit
broom	noon	too	crew	due	juice
classroom	pool	tool	drew	glue	nuisance
cool	proof	tooth	few	hue	recruit
food	raccoon	troop	flew	true	suit
goose	room	zoo	grew		
hoop	school	zoom	knew		
hoot	scoop		new		
loop	smooth		stew		
loose	snoop		threw		
	soon				

Spelling Words

blue
clue
cool
drew
flew
fruit
juice
new
spoon
suit
too
true

High-Frequency/Tested Words

angry
branches
clung
fingers
picnic
pressing
special

Selection Words

gone
learn
often
pieces
though
together
very

Firefighter!

Suffixes -ly, -ful, -er, -or

-ly		**-ful**	skillful	painter	creditor
boldly	lightly	boastful	thankful	player	director
bravely	loudly	careful	wonderful	rancher	editor
brightly	lovely	cheerful		reader	inventor
carefully	proudly	colorful	**-er**	singer	refrigerator
clearly	quickly	eventful	computer	storyteller	sailor
closely	quietly	graceful	dancer	teacher	supervisor
finally	slowly	harmful	driver	vacationer	visitor
firmly	smoothly	helpful	farmer	waiter	
fondly	softly	hopeful	fighter	writer	
gently	suddenly	joyful	firefighter		
gladly	sweetly	peaceful	gardener	**-or**	
hardly	tenderly	playful	helper	actor	
harshly	tightly	powerful	hiker	calculator	
kindly	weekly	restful	leader	conductor	

Spelling Words

cheerful
fighter
graceful
hardly
helper
quickly
sailor
slowly
teacher
visitor
weekly
yearly

High-Frequency/ Tested Words

building
burning
masks
quickly
roar
station
tightly

Selection Words

break
family
heard
listen
once
pull

One Dark Night

Prefixes un-, re-, pre-, dis-

un-	unlock	relight	**pre-**	**dis-**
unable	unmasks	remake	precooked	disagree
unclasp	unpack	repack	predate	disappear
undisturbed	unplug	repaint	preflight	disappointed
unglue	unroll	repave	preheat	disapprove
uneasy	unsafe	repeated	preorder	disconnect
uneven	unseen	replace	prepaid	discount
unfair	untie	replaced	preread	disinfect
unfinished	untrue	replay	preschool	disjoint
unfold		rerun	preteen	dislike
unfrozen	**re-**	resize	pretest	dislocate
unglue	react	rethink	pretreat	displace
unhappy	reclose	reuse	preview	displease
unhook	redrew	rewind	prewash	disprove
unkind	refilled	rewire		distrust
unlatch	refold	rework		
unload	reheated	rewrite		

Spelling Words

disagree
disappear
preheat
preschool
regroup
rerun
retie
rewind
unlock
unpack
unplug
unsafe

High-Frequency/ Tested Words

flashes
lightning
pounds
pours
rolling
storm
thunder

Selection Words

certainly
either
great
laugh
second
worst
you're

Bad Dog, Dodger!

Silent Consonants: kn, wr, gn, mb

kn	knot	wriggle	**gn**	**mb**
knee	know	wringing	design	climb
kneecap	knuckle	wrinkle	gnat	comb
kneel		wrist	gnaw	crumb
knew	**wr**	write	gnome	dumb
knickers	wrap	wrong	gnu	lamb
knife	wreath	wrote	resign	limb
knight	wreck		sign	numb
knit	wren			plumber
knob	wrench			thumb
knock	wrestle			tomb

Spelling Words

climb
comb
gnat
knee
knob
knock
lamb
sign
wrap
wren
write
wrong

High-Frequency/ Tested Words

chased
chewing
dripping
grabbed
practice
treat
wagged

Selection Words

above
ago
enough
toward
whole
word

Horace and Morris but mostly Dolores

ph, gh/f/

ph
alphabet
dolphin
elephant
gopher
graph
nephew
orphan

phantom
phase
pheasant
phone
phony
phooey
photo
phrase

sphere
telegraph
trophy

gh
autograph
cough
enough

laugh
rough
roughly
tough

Spelling Words

cliff
cough
enough
giraffe
graph
laugh
phone
photo
puff
rough
stuff
tough

High-Frequency/ Tested Words

adventure
climbed
clubhouse
exploring
greatest
truest
wondered

Selection Words

bought
people
pleasant
probably
scared
shall
sign

The Signmaker's Assistant

Vowels aw, au, augh, al

aw
awful
bawl
brawny
claw
crawl
draw
drawn
fawn
gnaw
hawk
jaw
law
lawn
paw

raw
saw
scrawl
shawl
squawk
straw
thaw
yawn

au
applaud
August
author
auto
because

cause
fault
haul
haunt
jaunt
launch
laundry
pause
sauce
sausage
vault

augh
caught
daughter

haughty
naughty
slaughter
taught

al
all
also
always
bald
ball
baseball
call
chalk
fall

false
malt
salt
small
talk
taller
walk
wall
walnut
waltz

Spelling Words

August
auto
because
caught
chalk
draw
fault
launch
talk
taught
thaw
walk

High-Frequency/ Tested Words

afternoon
blame
idea
important
signmaker
townspeople

Selection Words

behind
brought
door
everybody
minute
promise
sorry

Just Like Josh Gibson

Contractions

could've	she'd	we're	you'd
don't	should've	we've	you've
he'd	they'd	where'd	you're
I'd	they're	won't	
I've	they've	would've	

Spelling Words

can't
don't
he'd
I'd
I've
she'd
they'd
they're
we're
we've
won't
you're

bases
cheers
field
plate
sailed
threw

Selection Words

guess
pretty
science
shoe
village
watch
won

Red, White, and Blue: The Story of the American Flag

Base Words and Endings

added	cries	having	pinches	spotted
baking	crossed	heading	places	started
beginning	crying	helped	planning	stepped
belonged	danced	hiking	plans	stepping
bigger	dancing	hoped	pointed	steps
biggest	decided	hopes	pouncing	stopped
bombed	discovered	hoping	pounds	stopping
bounced	dropped	hopped	prepays	stops
bouncing	drops	hopping	prettiest	streets
bounces	drumming	hugged	propping	stripes
braver	ended	hurried	purred	talking
burned	erupted	jogging	replied	thanks
called	excited	joking	reapplied	thinking
carried	faster	judging	returns	thornier
carries	fastest	knows	richest	tied
carrying	fighting	landed	rides	tried
changes	fitted	loneliest	rolling	tries
chokes	flies	longest	rubbed	trying
cleaned	floated	luckier	rubbing	unhappier
cleaning	floating	luckiest	rushed	unluckiest
cleared	floats	making	sadder	used
clearer	flying	marched	sailed	visits
clearest	fried	minded	scampered	wanted
clearing	friendlier	moved	scared	watched
clears	funnier	named	sewing	waved
climbed	funniest	needed	shouted	waving
closed	glued	nicer	showed	wider
coming	going	nicest	singing	widest
continued	hammered	nodded	skipping	wishes
cooking	happened	opened	sleepiest	
crazier	happier	owned	smarter	
craziest	happiest	peeking	smiles	
cried	hardest	picked	spiciest	

Spelling Words

cried
crying
hiked
hiking
liked
liking
planned
planning
skipped
skipping
tried
trying

America
birthday
flag
freedom
nicknames
stars
stripes

Selection Words

answer
company
faraway
parents
picture
school
wash

A Birthday Basket for Tía

Syllables *tion, ture*

tion			**ture**	
action	fraction	section	adventure	lecturing
addition	location	station	capture	mixture
affection	lotion	suction	creature	moisture
caption	mention	tuitions	culture	nature
caution	motion	vacation	feature	picture
celebration	nation		fixture	puncture
creation	portion		fracture	sculpture
edition	position		furniture	vulture
fiction	potion		future	
	recreation			

Spelling Words

action
caution
feature
fixture
future
mixture
motion
nation
nature
picture
section
station

Selection Words

been
believe
caught
finally
today
tomorrow
whatever

Cowboys

Suffixes *-ness, -less*

-ness		sweetness	fearless	restless
awareness	illness	tenderness	flightless	shameless
cheerfulness	kindness	usefulness	friendless	shapeless
brightness	lateness	watchfulness	harmless	sleepless
darkness	laziness	weakness	heartless	speechless
emptiness	loneliness	weariness	helpless	spotless
fairness	loudness		hopeless	thankless
fitness	madness	**-less**	hopelessly	thoughtless
fondness	quickness	ageless	jobless	tireless
friendliness	redness	bottomless	joyless	toothless
fullness	rudeness	careless	meatless	useless
gentleness	sadness	cloudless	mindless	worthless
goodness	sickness	colorless	painless	
greatness	soreness	cordless	penniless	
happiness	stillness	countless	pointless	
	suddenness			

Spelling Words

careless
darkness
fearless
fitness
goodness
helpless
kindness
sadness
sickness
thankless
useless
weakness

Selection Words

alone
buy
daughters
half
many
their
youngest

Jingle Dancer

Prefixes *mis-, mid-*

misbehave	misguided	misprint	misunderstood	midsentence
misbehavior	misinform	misquote	midafternoon	midship
miscompute	misjudge	misread	midair	midsize
misconduct	mislabel	misreport	midcircle	midstream
miscopy	mislaid	misshape	midday	midtown
misdeed	mislead	misstep	midlife	midsummer
misdirect	misleading	misspoke	midline	midway
misfile	mismatch	mistreat	midnight	midweek
misfit	misplace	mistype	midpoint	midyear

Spelling Words

midair
midday
midway
midweek
midyear
misbehave
misdeed
mislead
mismatch
misplace
misprint
mistake

Selection Words

clothes
hours
money
neighbor
only
question
taught

Position for Writing

Left-handed and right-handed writers slant their papers differently from one another, but they sit and hold their pencils the same way.

Body Position

• Children should sit tall, with both feet flat on the floor and arms relaxed on a table or desk.

• Children should hold their papers with their non-writing hand.

Paper Slant

• Paper should be positioned at a slant that is approximately parallel to the writing arm.

• For left-handed children, the paper should slant from the right at the top to the left at the bottom.

• Right-handed children should slant the paper from the left at the top to the right at the bottom.

Pencil Grip

• Children should grasp the pencil lightly between the thumb and index finger, usually about an inch above the pencil point.

• For a child who grasps the pencil too close to the point, a simple remedy is to wrap a rubber band around the pencil about an inch above the point. Have the child hold the pencil above the rubber band.

Legibility

Legibility should be the goal of handwriting instruction. Children should be praised for writing legibly, even though their writing may deviate from a perfect model. Legibility is based on flexible but standard criteria for letter form, size, and slant, and for letter and word spacing.

Letter Form

• Standards for letter form enable each letter to be distinguished clearly from other letters.

• In the letter *a*, for example, the round part of the letter must be open, and the letter must be closed at the top. The letter *a* must not be confused with *u*, *d*, or *o*.

• The letters *t* and *f* must be crossed; the letters *i* and *j* dotted.

Letter Size

• Small letters sit on the bottom line and touch the middle line.

• Tall letters sit on the bottom line and touch the top line.

• Letters with descenders have tails that go down under the bottom line and touch the line below.

Letter Slant

• Letter slant should be consistent.

• All letters may slant to the right, to the left, or be straight up and down.

Letter and Word Spacing

• Letters in a word should be evenly spaced. They should not be written too close together or too far apart.

• There should be more space between words in a sentence than between letters in a word. This allows each word to stand out.

D'Nealian™ Alphabet

a b c d e f g h i

j k l m n o p q r s t

u v w x y z

A B C D E F G

H I J K L M N O

P Q R S T U V

W X Y Z . , ' ?

1 2 3 4 5 6

7 8 9 10

Manuscript Alphabet

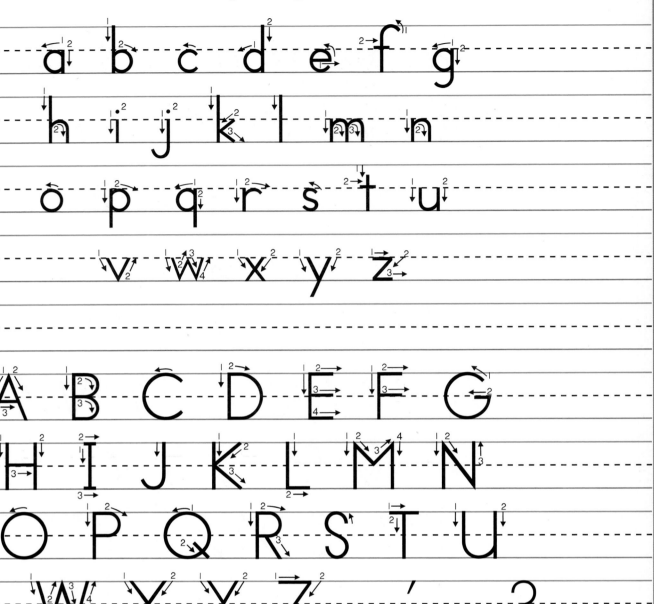

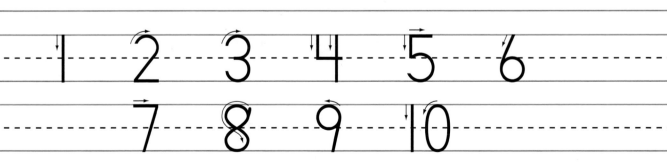

D'Nealian™ Cursive Alphabet

a b c d e f g

h i j k l m n

o p q r s t u

v w x y z

A B C D E F G

H I J K L M N

O P Q R S T U

V W X Y Z . , ' ?

1 2 3 4 5 6

7 8 9 10

Unit 2 *Working Together*

	Below-Level	On-Level	Advanced

Iris and Walter

To Read Aloud!
My Life with the Wave
by Catherine Cowan (Lothrop, Lee, and Shepard, 1997) In this beautifully illustrated book, a boy becomes friends with a wave.

Zelda and Ivy and the Boy Next Door

by Laura McGee Kvasnosky (Candlewick, 1999) Zelda and Ivy, the fox sisters, enjoy life together with their friend.

My Friend John

by Charlotte Zolotow (Doubleday, 2000) Simply and eloquently written, this book explores the gentle friendship between two boys.

The Bracelet

by Yoshiko Uchida (Philomel Books, 1993) A story about childhood friendship in a time of turmoil.

Exploring Space

To Read Aloud!
How Far is a Star?
by Sidney Rosen (Carolrhoda, 1992) Children will enjoy the question-and-answer approach this book uses to discuss the stars.

Zoom! Zoom! Zoom! I'm Off to the Moon!

by Dan Yaccarino (Scholastic, 1997) A young boy takes an exciting trip to the moon. Bright, clear illustrations and rhyming text are sure to please.

Follow the Moon

by Sarah Weeks (HarperCollins, 1995) A boy assists a baby sea turtle in following the moon to the ocean.

Moon

by Seymour Simon (Four Winds, 1984) The renowned nonfiction author introduces the moon, featuring photographs taken from space.

Henry and Mudge

To Read Aloud!
Scaredy Dog
by Jane Resh Thomas (Hyperion, 1997) With her love and kindness, Erin helps her adopted dog, Mac, overcome his fears.

Henry and Mudge and the Careful Cousin

by Cynthia Rylant (Simon and Schuster, 1994) Henry isn't quite sure how to be friends with his overly-cautious cousin when she visits.

Henry and Mudge Get the Cold Shivers

by Cynthia Rylant (Live Oak Media, 2001) When Mudge gets sick with a cold, Henry takes him to the vet and helps him feel better.

The Iguana Brothers

by Tony Johnston (Blue Sky, 1995) Dom and Tom, the iguana brothers, play, eat, and imagine together and eventually learn that they can be best friends.

A Walk in the Desert

To Read Aloud!
Welcome to the Greenhouse
by Jane Yolen (Putnam Publishing, 1993) This poem about the rainforest encompasses animals, colors, sounds, and all of the beauty inherent in this special endangered place.

The Adventures of Taxi Dog

by Debra and Sal Barracca (Putnam, 2000) Maxi accompanies a taxi driver on his route through hectic New York City.

Postcard Pest

by Patricia Reilly Giff (Yearling, 1994) In this Polk Street Kids Special, the class sends postcards all over the country and learns about stamp collections.

If You're Not From the Prairie

by David Bouchard (Atheneum Books, 1995) Beautiful Wyeth-esque illustrations accompany simple poetry about the sights, sounds, and feel of growing up on the prairie.

The Strongest One

To Read Aloud!
Two Bad Ants
by Chris Van Allsburg (Houghton Mifflin, 1988) When a troop of ants are sent to retrieve sugar crystals from a kitchen, two ants stay behind to feast and sleep in the sugar bowl.

We Love the Dirt

by Tony Johnston (Cartwheel, 1997) A farmer and the inhabitants of a farm each have a special affinity with the dirt.

Little Red Ant and the Big Crumb: A Mexican Fable

by Shirley Climo (Clarion, 1995) A tiny ant finds a crumb in a field and goes off to find other animals to help her carry it.

Exploding Ants: Amazing Facts about How Animals Adapt

by Joanne Settel (Atheneum Books, 1999) This book takes a humorous but factually accurate look at how various insects and animals defend themselves against the forces.

Unit 2 Reading Log

Name _____

Dates Read	Title and Author	What is it about?	How would you rate it?	Explain your rating.
From ____ to ____			Great 5 4 3 2 1 Awful	
From ____ to ____			Great 5 4 3 2 1 Awful	
From ____ to ____			Great 5 4 3 2 1 Awful	
From ____ to ____			Great 5 4 3 2 1 Awful	
From ____ to ____			Great 5 4 3 2 1 Awful	

Unit 2 Narrative Retelling Chart

Selection Title _____ Name _____ Date _____

Retelling Criteria/Teacher Prompt	Teacher-Aided Response	Student-Generated Response	Rubric Score (Circle one.)
Connections Does this story remind you of anything else?			4 3 2 1
Author's Purpose Why do you think the author wrote this story? What was the author trying to tell us?			4 3 2 1
Characters What can you tell me about ____ (use character's name)?			4 3 2 1
Setting Where and when did the story happen?			4 3 2 1
Plot What happened in the story?			4 3 2 1

Summative Retelling Score   4   3   2   1 _____

Comments _____

Unit 2 Expository Retelling Chart

Selection Title _____   **Name** _____   **Date** _____

Retelling Criteria/Teacher Prompt	Teacher-Aided Response	Student-Generated Response	Rubric Score (Circle one.)			
Connections Did this selection make you think about something else you have read? What did you learn about as you read this selection?			4	3	2	1
Author's Purpose Why do you think the author wrote this selection?			4	3	2	1
Topic What was the selection mostly about?			4	3	2	1
Important Ideas What is important for me to know about _____ (topic)?			4	3	2	1
Conclusions What did you learn from reading this selection?			4	3	2	1

Summative Retelling Score   4   3   2   1   _____

Comments _____

Reading

Concepts of Print and Print Awareness	Pre-K	K	1	2	3	4	5
Develop awareness that print represents spoken language and conveys and preserves meaning	•	•	•				
Recognize familiar books by their covers; hold book right side up	•	•					
Identify parts of a book and their functions (front cover, title page/title, back cover, page numbers)	•	•	•				
Understand the concepts of letter, word, sentence, paragraph, and story	•	•	•				
Track print (front to back of book, top to bottom of page, left to right on line, sweep back left for next line)	•	•	•				
Match spoken to printed words	•	•	•				
Know capital and lowercase letter names and match them	•	• T	•				
Know the order of the alphabet	•	•	•				
Recognize first name in print	•	•	•				
Recognize the uses of capitalization and punctuation		•	•				
Value print as a means of gaining information	•	•	•				

Phonological and Phonemic Awareness	Pre-K	K	1	2	3	4	5
Phonological Awareness							
Recognize and produce rhyming words	•	•	•				
Track and count each word in a spoken sentence and each syllable in a spoken word	•	•	•				
Segment and blend syllables in spoken words			•				
Segment and blend onset and rime in one-syllable words		•	•				
Recognize and produce words beginning with the same sound	•	•	•				
Identify beginning, middle, and/or ending sounds that are the same or different	•	•	•				
Understand that spoken words are made of sequences of sounds	•	•	•				
Phonemic Awareness							
Identify the position of sounds in words		•	•				
Identify and isolate initial, final, and medial sounds in spoken words	•	•	•				
Blend sounds orally to make words or syllables		•	•				
Segment a word or syllable into sounds; count phonemes in spoken words or syllables		•	•				
Manipulate sounds in words (add, delete, and/or substitute phonemes)	•	•	•				

Phonics and Decoding	Pre-K	K	1	2	3	4	5
Phonics							
Understand and apply the **alphabetic principle** that spoken words are composed of sounds that are represented by letters	•	•	•				
Know letter-sound relationships	•	• T	• T	• T			
Blend sounds of letters to decode		•	• T	• T	• T		
Consonants, consonant blends, and consonant digraphs		•	• T	• T	• T		
Short, long, and r-controlled vowels; vowel digraphs; diphthongs; common vowel patterns			• T	• T	• T		
Phonograms/word families		•	•	•	•		
Word Structure							
Decode words with common word parts		•	• T	• T	• T	•	•
Base words and inflected endings			• T	• T	•	•	•
Contractions and compound words			• T	• T	• T	•	•
Suffixes and prefixes			• T	• T	• T	•	•
Greek and Latin roots						•	•
Blend syllables to decode words			• T	• T	• T	•	•
Decoding Strategies							
Blending strategy: Apply knowledge of letter-sound relationships to decode unfamiliar words		•	•	•	•		
Apply knowledge of word structure to decode unfamiliar words		•	•	•	•	•	•
Use context and syntax along with letter-sound relationships and word structure to decode		•	•	•	•	•	•
Self-correct			•	•	•	•	•

Fluency	Pre-K	K	1	2	3	4	5
Read aloud fluently with accuracy, comprehension, appropriate pace/rate; with expression/intonation (prosody); with attention to punctuation and appropriate phrasing			• T	• T	• T	• T	• T
Practice fluency in a variety of ways, including choral reading, partner/paired reading, reader's theater, repeated oral reading, and tape-assisted reading		•	•	•	•	•	•

• instructional opportunity   **T** tested in standardized test f

	Pre-K	K	1	2	3	4	5	6
...k toward appropriate fluency goals by the end of each grade		• T	• T	• T	• T	• T	• T	• T
...d regularly in independent-level material		•	•	•	•	•	•	•
...d silently for increasing periods of time		•	•	•	•	•	•	•

Vocabulary (Oral and Written)

	Pre-K	K	1	2	3	4	5	6
...rd Recognition								
...ognize regular and irregular high-frequency words	•	•	• T	• T				
...ognize and understand selection vocabulary		•	•	• T	•	•	•	•
...erstand content-area vocabulary and specialized, technical, or topical words			•	•	•	•	•	•
...rd Learning Strategies								
...elop vocabulary through direct instruction, concrete experiences, reading, listening to text read aloud	•	•	•	•	•	•	•	•
...knowledge of word structure to figure out meanings of words			•	• T	• T	• T	• T	• T
...context clues for meanings of unfamiliar words, multiple-meaning words, homonyms, homographs			•	• T	• T	• T	• T	• T
...grade-appropriate reference sources to learn word meanings	•	•	•	•	• T	• T	• T	• T
...picture clues to help determine word meanings	•	•	•	•	•			
...new words in a variety of contexts	•	•	•	•	•	•	•	•
...mine word usage and effectiveness		•	•	•	•	•	•	•
...te and use graphic organizers to group, study, and retain vocabulary		•	•	•	•	•	•	•
...end Concepts and Word Knowledge								
...demic language	•	•	•	•	•	•	•	•
...sify and categorize	•	•	•	•	•	•	•	•
...nyms and synonyms			•	• T	• T	• T	• T	• T
...ographs, homonyms, and homophones				•	• T	• T	• T	• T
...iple-meaning words			•	•	• T	• T	• T	• T
...ted words and derivations					•	•	•	•
...ogies						•	•	
...notation/denotation						•	•	•
...rative language and idioms			•	•	•	•	•	•
...criptive words (location, size, color, shape, number, ideas, feelings)	•	•	•	•	•	•	•	•
...-utility words (shapes, colors, question words, position/directional words, and so on)	•	•	•	•				
...e and order words	•	•	•	•	•	•	•	•
...sition words						•	•	•
...d origins: Etymologies/word histories; words from other languages, regions, or cultures					•	•	•	•
...tened forms: abbreviations, acronyms, clipped words			•	•	•	•	• T	

...xt Comprehension

	Pre-K	K	1	2	3	4	5	6
...mprehension Strategies								
...iew the text and formulate questions	•	•	•	•	•	•	•	•
...and monitor purpose for reading and listening	•	•	•	•	•	•	•	•
...vate and use prior knowledge	•	•	•	•	•	•	•	•
...e predictions	•	•	•	•	•	•	•	•
...itor comprehension and use fix-up strategies to resolve difficulties in meaning: adjust reading rate, ...ad and read on, seek help from reference sources and/or other people, skim and scan, summarize, ...text features			•	•	•	•	•	•
...te and use graphic and semantic organizers		•	•	•	•	•	•	•
...wer questions (text explicit, text implicit, scriptal), including *who, what, when, where, why, what if, how*	•	•	•	•	•	•	•	•
...ok back in text for answers			•	•	•	•	•	•
...swer test-like questions			•	•	•	•	•	•
...erate clarifying questions, including *who, what, where, when, how, why,* and *what if*	•	•	•	•	•	•	•	•
...ognize text structure: story and informational (cause/effect, chronological, compare/contrast, ...cription, problem/solution, propostion/support)	•	•	•	•	•	•	•	•
...marize text		•	•	•	•	•	•	•
...ecall and retell stories	•	•	•	•	•	•	•	•
...entify and retell important/main ideas (nonfiction)	•	•	•	•	•	•	•	•
...entify and retell new information			•	•	•	•	•	•
...alize; use mental imagery		•	•	•	•	•	•	•
...strategies flexibly and in combination			•	•	•	•	•	•

Comprehension Skills

Skill	Pre-K	K	1	2	3	4	5
Author's purpose			• T	• T	• T	• T	• T
Author's viewpoint/bias/perspective					•	•	•
Categorize and classify	•	•	•	•			
Cause and effect		•	• T	• T	• T	• T	• T
Compare and contrast		•	• T	• T	• T	• T	• T
Details and facts		•	•	•	•	•	•
Draw conclusions		•	• T	• T	• T	• T	• T
Fact and opinion				• T	• T	• T	• T
Follow directions/steps in a process	•	•	•	•	•	•	•
Generalize					• T	• T	• T
Graphic sources		•	•	•	•	• T	• T
Main idea and supporting details		• T	• T	• T	• T	• T	• T
Paraphrase			•	•	•	•	•
Persuasive devices and propaganda				•	•	•	•
Realism/fantasy		•	• T	• T	• T	•	•
Sequence of events		• T	• T	• T	• T	• T	• T

Higher Order Thinking Skills

Skill	Pre-K	K	1	2	3	4	5
Analyze				•	•	•	•
Describe and connect the essential ideas, arguments, and perspectives of a text			•	•	•	•	•
Draw inferences, conclusions, or generalizations, support them with textual evidence and prior knowledge	•		•	•	•	•	•
Evaluate and critique ideas and text			•	•	•	•	•
Hypothesize						•	•
Make judgments about ideas and text			•	•	•	•	•
Organize and synthesize ideas and information			•			•	•

Literary Analysis, Response, & Appreciation

Genre and Its Characteristics

Skill	Pre-K	K	1	2	3	4	5
Recognize characteristics of a variety of genre	•	•	•	•	•	•	•
Distinguish fiction from nonfiction		•	•	•	•	•	•
Identify characteristics of literary texts, including drama, fantasy, traditional tales		•	•	•	•	•	•
Identify characteristics of nonfiction texts, including biography, interviews, newspaper articles		•	•	•	•	•	•
Identify characteristics of poetry and song, including nursery rhymes, limericks, blank verse	•	•	•	•	•	•	•

Literary Elements and Story Structure

Skill	Pre-K	K	1	2	3	4	5
Character	•	• T	• T	• T	• T	• T	• T
Recognize and describe traits, actions, feelings, and motives of characters		•	•	•	•	•	•
Analyze characters' relationships, changes, and points of view		•	•	•	•	•	•
Analyze characters' conflicts				•		•	•
Plot and plot structure	•	• T	• T	• T	• T	• T	• T
Beginning, middle, end	•	•	•	•	•		
Goal and outcome or problem and solution/resolution		•	•	•	•	•	•
Rising action, climax, and falling action/denouement; setbacks						•	•
Setting	•	• T	• T	• T	• T	• T	
Relate setting to problem/solution						•	•
Explain ways setting contributes to mood						•	•
Theme		•	• T	• T			
Use Literary Elements and Story Structure	•	•	•	•	•	•	•
Analyze and evaluate author's use of setting, plot, character				•	•	•	•
Identify similarities and differences of characters, events, and settings within or across selections/cultures	•	•	•	•	•	•	•

Literary Devices

Skill	Pre-K	K	1	2	3	4	5
Allusion							
Dialect						•	•
Dialogue and narration	•	•	•	•	•	•	•
Exaggeration/hyperbole					•	•	•
Figurative language: idiom, jargon, metaphor, simile, slang			•	•	•	•	•

• instructional opportunity   **T** tested in standardized test f

	Pre-K	K	1	2	3	4	5	6
hback						•	•	•
shadowing							•	•
nal and informal language				•	•	•	•	•
nor						•	•	•
gery and sensory words			•	•	•	•	•	•
d				•	•	•	•	•
sonification				•	•	•	•	•
t of view (first person, third person, omniscient)					•	•	•	•
s and word play				•	•	•	•	•
nd devices and poetic elements	•	•	•	•	•	•	•	•
literation, assonance, onomatopoeia	•	•	•	•	•	•	•	•
hyme, rhythm, repetition, and cadence	•	•	•	•	•	•	•	•
ord choice				•	•	•	•	•
bolism				•	•	•	•	•
e							•	•

thor's and Illustrator's Craft

	Pre-K	K	1	2	3	4	5	6
inguish the roles of author and illustrator		•	•	•				
ognize/analyze author's and illustrator's craft or style			•	•	•	•	•	•

erary Response

	Pre-K	K	1	2	3	4	5	6
llect, talk, and write about books	•	•	•	•	•	•	•	•
ect on reading and respond (through talk, movement, art, and so on)	•	•	•	•	•	•	•	•
k and answer questions about text	•	•	•	•	•	•	•	•
rite about what is read	•	•	•	•	•	•	•	•
se evidence from the text to support opinions, interpretations, or conclusions		•	•	•	•	•	•	•
upport ideas through reference to other texts and personal knowledge				•	•	•	•	•
cate materials on related topic, theme, or idea				•	•	•	•	•
enerate alternative endings to plots and identify the reason for, and the impact of, the alternatives	•	•		•	•	•	•	•
chesize and extend the literary experience through creative responses	•	•	•	•	•	•	•	•
e connections: text to self, text to text, text to world	•	•	•	•	•	•	•	•
uate and critique the quality of the literary experience				•	•	•	•	•
r observations, react, speculate in response to text				•	•	•	•	•

erary Appreciation/Motivation

	Pre-K	K	1	2	3	4	5	6
w an interest in books and reading; engage voluntarily in social interaction about books	•	•	•	•	•	•	•	•
ose text by drawing on personal interests, relying on knowledge of authors and genres, estimating text culty, and using recommendations of others	•	•	•	•	•	•	•	•
d a variety of grade-level appropriate narrative and expository texts		•	•	•	•	•	•	•
d from a wide variety of genres for a variety of purposes	•	•	•	•	•	•	•	•
d independently			•	•	•	•	•	•
blish familiarity with a topic			•	•	•	•	•	•

tural Awareness

	Pre-K	K	1	2	3	4	5	6
elop attitudes and abilities to interact with diverse groups and cultures	•	•	•	•	•	•	•	•
nect experiences and ideas with those from a variety of languages, cultures, customs, perspectives	•	•	•	•	•	•	•	•
erstand how attitudes and values in a culture or during a period in time affect the writing from that ure or time period						•	•	•
pare language and oral traditions (family stories) that reflect customs, regions, and cultures		•	•	•	•	•	•	•
ognize themes that cross cultures and bind them together in their common humanness						•	•	•

nguage Arts

iting	Pre-K	K	1	2	3	4	5	6
ncepts of Print for Writing								
elop gross and fine motor skills and hand/eye coordination	•	•	•					
t own name and other important words	•	•	•					
e using pictures, some letters, and transitional spelling to convey meaning	•	•	•					
ate messages or stories for others to write	•	•	•					

Skill	Pre-K	K	1	2	3	4	5	6
Create own written texts for others to read; write left to right on a line and top to bottom on a page	•	•	•					
Participate in shared and interactive writing	•	•	•					

Traits of Writing

Focus/Ideas

Skill	Pre-K	K	1	2	3	4	5	6
Maintain focus and sharpen ideas		•	•	•	•	•	•	
Use sensory details and concrete examples; elaborate		•	•	•	•	•	•	
Delete extraneous information			•	•	•	•	•	
Rearrange words and sentences to improve meaning and focus				•	•	•	•	
Use strategies, such as tone, style, consistent point of view, to achieve a sense of completeness						•	•	

Organization/Paragraphs

Skill	Pre-K	K	1	2	3	4	5	6
Use graphic organizers to group ideas		•	•	•	•	•	•	
Write coherent paragraphs that develop a central idea			•	•	•	•	•	
Use transitions to connect sentences and paragraphs			•	•	•	•	•	
Select an organizational structure based on purpose, audience, length						•	•	
Organize ideas in a logical progression, such as chronological order or by order of importance		•	•	•	•	•	•	
Write introductory, supporting, and concluding paragraphs					•	•	•	
Write a multi-paragraph paper				•	•	•	•	

Voice

Skill	Pre-K	K	1	2	3	4	5	6
Develop personal, identifiable voice and an individual tone/style			•	•	•	•	•	
Maintain consistent voice and point of view						•	•	
Use voice appropriate to audience, message, and purpose						•	•	

Word Choice

Skill	Pre-K	K	1	2	3	4	5	6
Use clear, precise, appropriate language		•	•	•	•	•	•	
Use figurative language and vivid words				•	•	•	•	
Select effective vocabulary using word walls, dictionary, or thesaurus		•	•	•	•	•	•	

Sentences

Skill	Pre-K	K	1	2	3	4	5	6
Combine, elaborate, and vary sentences		•	•	•	•	•	•	
Write topic sentence, supporting sentences with facts and details, and concluding sentence			•	•	•	•	•	
Use correct word order				•	•	•	•	
Use parallel structure in a sentence							•	

Conventions

Skill	Pre-K	K	1	2	3	4	5	6
Use correct spelling and grammar; capitalize and punctuate correctly		•	•	•	•	•	•	
Correct sentence fragments and run-ons					•	•	•	
Use correct paragraph indention				•	•	•	•	

The Writing Process

Skill	Pre-K	K	1	2	3	4	5	6
Prewrite using various strategies	•	•	•	•	•	•	•	
Develop first drafts of single- and multiple-paragraph compositions		•	•	•	•	•	•	
Revise drafts for varied purposes, including to clarify and to achieve purpose, sense of audience, precise word choice, vivid images, and elaboration	•	•	•	•	•	•	•	
Edit and proofread for correct spelling, grammar, usage, and mechanics		•	•	•	•	•	•	
Publish own work	•	•	•	•	•	•	•	

Types of Writing

Skill	Pre-K	K	1	2	3	4	5	6
Narrative writing (such as personal narratives, stories, biographies, autobiographies)	•	•	• T	• T	• T	• T	• T	•
Expository writing (such as essays, directions, explanations, news stories, research reports, summaries)		•	• T	• T	• T	• T	• T	
Descriptive writing (such as labels, captions, lists, plays, poems, response logs, songs)	•	•	• T	• T	• T	• T	• T	
Persuasive writing (such as ads, editorials, essays, letters to the editor, opinions, posters)		•	• T	• T	• T	• T	• T	

Writing Habits and Practices

Skill	Pre-K	K	1	2	3	4	5	6
Write on a daily basis	•	•	•	•	•	•	•	
Use writing as a tool for learning and self-discovery				•	•	•	•	
Write independently for extended periods of time			•	•	•	•	•	

ENGLISH LANGUAGE CONVENTIONS in WRITING and SPEAKING	Pre-K	K	1	2	3	4	5	

Grammar and Usage in Speaking and Writing

Sentences

Skill	Pre-K	K	1	2	3	4	5	6
Types (declarative, interrogative, exclamatory, imperative)	•	•	• T	• T	• T	• T	• T	
Structure (simple, compound, complex, compound-complex)	•	•	•	•	•	• T	• T	

• instructional opportunity   **T** tested in standardized test f...

	Pre-K	K	1	2	3	4	5	6
...rts (subjects/predicates: complete, simple, compound; phrases; clauses)				• T	•	• T	• T	• T
...agments and run-on sentences		•	•	•	•	•	•	•
...mbine sentences, elaborate			•	•	•	•	•	•
...s of speech: nouns, verbs and verb tenses, adjectives, adverbs, pronouns and antecedents, ...unctions, prepositions, interjections		•	• T	• T	• T	• T	• T	• T
...ge								
...bject-verb agreement		•	• T	•	•	• T	• T	• T
...onoun agreement/referents			• T	•	•	• T	• T	• T
...splaced modifiers						•	• T	• T
...sused words					•	•	•	• T
...gatives; avoid double negatives					•	•	•	•

Mechanics in Writing

	Pre-K	K	1	2	3	4	5	6
...talization (first word in sentence, proper nouns and adjectives, pronoun *I*, titles, and so on)	•	•	• T	• T	• T	• T	• T	• T
...ctuation (apostrophe, comma, period, question mark, exclamation mark, quotation marks, and so on)		•	• T	• T	• T	• T	• T	• T

Spelling

	Pre-K	K	1	2	3	4	5	6
...independently by using pre-phonetic knowledge, knowledge of letter names, sound-letter knowledge	•	•	•	•	•	•	•	•
...sound-letter knowledge to spell	•	•	•	•	•	•	•	•
...nsonants: single, double, blends, digraphs, silent letters, and unusual consonant spellings		•	•	•	•	•	•	•
...wels: short, long, *r*-controlled, digraphs, diphthongs, less common vowel patterns, schwa		•	•	•	•	•	•	•
...knowledge of word structure to spell		•	•	•	•	•	•	•
...se words and affixes (inflections, prefixes, suffixes), possessives, contractions and compound words		•	•	•	•	•	•	•
...eek and Latin roots, syllable patterns, multisyllabic words		•	•	•	•	•	•	•
...high-frequency, irregular words		•	•	•	•	•	•	•
...frequently misspelled words correctly, including homophones or homonyms		•	•	•	•	•	•	•
...meaning relationships to spell					•	•	•	•

Handwriting

	Pre-K	K	1	2	3	4	5	6
...increasing control of penmanship, including pencil grip, paper position, posture, stroke	•	•	•	•				
...e legibly, with control over letter size and form; letter slant; and letter, word, and sentence spacing		•	•	•	•	•	•	•
...e lowercase and capital letters	•	•	•	•				
...anuscript	•	•		•	•	•	•	•
...rsive				•	•	•	•	•
...e numerals	•	•	•					

Listening and Speaking

	Pre-K	K	1	2	3	4	5	6

Listening Skills and Strategies

	Pre-K	K	1	2	3	4	5	6
...en to a variety of presentations attentively and politely	•	•	•	•	•	•	•	•
...monitor comprehension while listening, using a variety of skills and strategies	•	•	•	•	•	•	•	•
...en for a purpose	•	•	•	•	•	•	•	•
...r enjoyment and appreciation	•	•	•	•	•	•	•	•
...expand vocabulary and concepts	•	•	•	•	•	•	•	•
...obtain information and ideas	•	•	•	•	•	•	•	•
...follow oral directions	•	•	•	•	•	•	•	•
...answer questions and solve problems	•	•	•	•	•	•	•	•
...participate in group discussions	•	•	•	•	•	•	•	•
...identify and analyze the musical elements of literary language	•	•	•	•	•	•	•	•
...gain knowledge of one's own culture, the culture of others, and the common elements of cultures	•		•	•	•	•	•	•
...ognize formal and informal language			•	•	•	•	•	•
...en critically to distinguish fact from opinion and to analyze and evaluate ideas, information, experiences		•		•	•	•	•	•
...uate a speaker's delivery				•	•	•	•	•
...pret a speaker's purpose, perspective, persuasive techniques, verbal and nonverbal messages, and ...of rhetorical devices						•	•	•

Speaking Skills and Strategies

	Pre-K	K	1	2	3	4	5	6
...ak clearly, accurately, and fluently, using appropriate delivery for a variety of audiences, and purposes	•	•	•	•	•	•	•	•
...proper intonation, volume, pitch, modulation, and phrasing		•	•	•	•	•	•	•
...ak with a command of standard English conventions	•	•		•	•	•	•	•
...appropriate language for formal and informal settings		•	•	•	•	•	•	•

	Pre-K	K	1	2	3	4	5
Speak for a purpose							
To ask and answer questions	•	•	•	•	•	•	•
To give directions and instructions	•	•	•	•	•	•	•
To retell, paraphrase, or explain information		•	•	•	•	•	•
To communicate needs and share ideas and experiences	•	•	•	•	•	•	•
To participate in conversations and discussions	•	•	•	•	•	•	•
To express an opinion	•	•	•	•	•	•	•
To deliver dramatic recitations, interpretations, or performances	•	•	•	•	•	•	•
To deliver presentations or oral reports (narrative, descriptive, persuasive, and informational)	•	•	•	•	•	•	•
Stay on topic	•	•	•	•	•	•	
Use appropriate verbal and nonverbal elements (such as facial expression, gestures, eye contact, posture)	•	•	•	•	•	•	•
Identify and/or demonstrate methods to manage or overcome communication anxiety						•	•

Viewing/Media	Pre-K	K	1	2	3	4	5
Interact with and respond to a variety of print and non-print media for a range of purposes	•	•	•	•	•	•	•
Compare and contrast print, visual, and electronic media					•	•	•
Analyze and evaluate media				•	•	•	•
Recognize purpose, bias, propaganda, and persuasive techniques in media messages				•	•	•	•

Research and Study Skills

Understand and Use Graphic Sources	Pre-K	K	1	2	3	4	5
Advertisement			•	•	•	•	•
Chart/table	•	•	•	•	•	•	•
Diagram/scale drawing			•	•	•	•	•
Graph (bar, circle, line, picture)		•	•	•	•	•	•
Illustration, photograph, caption, label	•	•	•	•	•	•	•
Map/globe	•	•	•	•	•	•	•
Order form/application						•	•
Poster/announcement	•	•	•	•	•	•	•
Schedule						•	•
Sign	•	•	•	•		•	
Time line				•	•	•	•

Understand and Use Reference Sources	Pre-K	K	1	2	3	4	5
Know and use parts of a book to locate information	•	•	•	•	•	•	•
Use alphabetical order			•	•	•	•	
Understand purpose, structure, and organization of reference sources (print, electronic, media, Internet)	•	•	•	•	•	•	•
Almanac						•	•
Atlas		•		•	•	•	•
Card catalog/library database				•	•	•	•
Dictionary/glossary		•	•	•	• T	• T	• T
Encyclopedia			•	•	•	•	•
Magazine/periodical				•	•	•	•
Newspaper and Newsletter			•	•	•	•	•
Readers' Guide to Periodical Literature						•	•
Technology (computer and non-computer electronic media)		•	•	•	•	•	•
Thesaurus				•	•	•	•

Study Skills and Strategies	Pre-K	K	1	2	3	4	5
Adjust reading rate			•	•	•	•	•
Clarify directions	•	•	•	•	•	•	•
Outline				•	•	•	•
Skim and scan			•	•	•	•	•
SQP3R						•	•
Summarize		•	•	•	•	•	•
Take notes, paraphrase, and synthesize			•	•	•	•	•
Use graphic and semantic organizers to organize information		•	•	•	•	•	•

• instructional opportunity   **T** tested in standardized test f

st-Taking Skills and Strategies	Pre-K	K	1	2	3	4	5	6
erstand the question, the vocabulary of tests, and key words			•	•	•	•	•	•
wer the question; use information from the text (stated or inferred)		•	•	•		•	•	TR33
e across texts			•	•	•	•	•	•
plete the sentence			•	•	•	•	•	•

chnology/New Literacies	Pre-K	K	1	2	3	4	5	6
n-Computer Electronic Media								
o tapes/CDs, video tapes/DVDs	•	•						
, television, and radio		•	•	•	•	•	•	•
mputer Programs and Services: Basic Operations and Concepts								
accurate computer terminology	•	•	•	•	•	•	•	•
ate, name, locate, open, save, delete, and organize files		•	•	•	•	•	•	•
input and output devices (such as mouse, keyboard, monitor, printer, touch screen)	•	•	•	•	•	•	•	•
basic keyboarding skills		•	•	•	•	•	•	•
ponsible Use of Technology Systems and Software								
k cooperatively and collaboratively with others; follow acceptable use policies	•	•	•	•	•	•	•	•
ognize hazards of Internet searches		•	•	•	•	•	•	•
pect intellectual property				•	•	•	•	•
ormation and Communication Technologies: Information Acquisition								
electronic web (non-linear) navigation, online resources, databases, keyword searches			•	•	•	•	•	•
visual and non-textual features of online resources	•	•	•	•	•	•	•	•
rnet inquiry			•	•	•	•	•	•
entify questions			•	•	•	•	•	•
cate, select, and collect information			•	•	•	•	•	•
nalyze information			•	•	•	•	•	•
Evaluate electronic information sources for accuracy, relevance, bias			•	•	•	•	•	•
Understand bias/subjectivity of electronic content (about this site, author search, date created)				•	•	•	•	•
nthesize information				•	•	•	•	•
ommunicate findings			•	•	•	•	•	•
fix-up strategies (such as clicking *Back, Forward.* or *Undo;* redoing a search; trimming the URL)			•	•	•	•	•	•
mmunication								
aborate, publish, present, and interact with others		•	•	•	•	•	•	•
online resources (e-mail, bulletin boards, newsgroups)			•	•	•	•	•	•
a variety of multimedia formats			•	•	•	•	•	•
blem Solving								
ect the appropriate software for the task	•	•	•	•	•	•	•	•
technology resources for solving problems and making informed decisions			•	•	•	•	•	•
ermine when technology is useful			•	•	•	•	•	•

e Research Process	Pre-K	K	1	2	3	4	5	6
ose and narrow the topic; frame and revise questions for inquiry		•	•	•	•	•	•	•
ose and evaluate appropriate reference sources		•	•	•	•	•	•	•
ate and collect information	•	•	•	•	•	•	•	•
e notes/record findings			•	•	•	•	•	•
bine and compare information			•	•	•	•	•	•
uate, interpret, and draw conclusions about key information		•	•	•	•	•	•	•
marize information		•	•	•	•	•	•	•
e an outline			•	•	•	•	•	•
anize content systematically		•	•	•	•	•	•	•
mmunicate information		•	•	•	•	•	•	•
rite and present a report			•	•	•	•	•	•
Include citations						•	•	•
Respect intellectual property/plagiarism						•	•	•
elect and organize visual aids		•	•	•	•	•	•	•

A

Achieving English proficiency. *See* **ELL (English language learners) suggestions.**

Accountability. *See* **Adequate yearly progress, Professional development.**

Activate prior knowledge. *See* **Prior knowledge.**

Adequate yearly progress (AYP), 2.1 10e–10f, 2.2 160e–160f, 2.3 314e–314f, 2.4 10e–10f, 2.5 152e–152f, 2.6 294e–294f

Advanced learners
build background, 2.1 12r, 42r, 68r, 96r, 128r, 2.2 162r, 190r, 218r, 252r, 282r, 2.3 316r, 344r, 372r, 402r, 426r, 2.4 12r, 42r, 66r, 96r, 124r, 2.5 154r, 180r, 208r, 234r, 264r, 2.6 296r, 322r, 350r, 376r, 408r
creative writing, 2.1 129d, 149a
fluency, 2.1 12q, 36f, 42q, 60f, 68q, 88f, 96q, 120f, 128q, 150f, 2.2 162q, 182f, 190q, 212f, 218q, 243f, 252q, 274f, 282q, 303f, 2.3 316q, 338f, 344q, 366f, 372q, 395f, 402q, 408f, 426q, 452f, 2.4 12q, 31f, 42q, 60f, 66q, 88f, 96q, 116f, 124q, 142f, 2.5 154q, 172f, 180q, 202f, 208q, 226q, 234q, 256f, 264q, 284f, 2.6 296q, 314f, 322q, 344f, 350q, 368f, 376q, 402f, 408q, 426f
group time, 2.1 12h–12i, 12p, 16a, 36e, 38d, 42h–42i, 42p, 46a, 60e, 62d, 66e, 68h–68i, 68p, 72a, 88e, 90d, 94d, 96h–96i, 96p, 100a, 122d, 126d, 128h–128i, 128p, 132a, 150e, 152d, 156d, 2.2 162h–168i, 162p, 166a, 182e, 184d, 188d, 190h–190i, 190p, 194a, 212e, 214d, 216d, 218h–218i, 218p, 222a, 243e, 246d, 250d, 252h–252i, 252p, 256a, 274e, 276d, 280d, 282h–282i, 282p, 286a, 303a, 306d, 310d, 311d, 2.3 316h–316i, 316p, 320a, 338e, 340d, 342d, 344h–344i, 344p, 348a, 366e, 368d, 370d, 372h–372i, 372p, 376a, 395e, 398d, 400d, 402h–402i, 402p, 406a, 418e, 420d, 424d, 426h–426i, 426p, 430a, 452e, 454d, 458d, 2.4 12h–12i, 12p, 34d, 39b, 40d, 42h–42i, 42p, 62d, 63b, 64d, 66h–66i, 66p, 90d, 93b, 94d, 96h–96i, 96p, 118d, 121b, 122d, 124h–124i, 124p, 144d, 147b, 148d, 2.5 154h–154i, 154p, 174d, 177b, 178d, 180h–180i, 180p, 204d, 205b, 206d, 208h–208i, 208p, 228d, 231b, 232d, 234h–234i, 234p, 258d, 261b, 262d, 264h–264i, 264p, 286d, 289b, 290d, 2.6 296h–296i, 296p, 316d, 319b, 320d, 322h–322i, 322p, 346d, 347b, 348d, 350h–350i, 350p, 370d, 373b, 374d, 376h–376i, 376p, 404d, 405b, 406d, 408h–408i, 408p, 428d, 431b, 432d
leveled readers, 2.1 LR7–LR9, LR16–LR18, LR25–LR27, LR34–LR36, LR43–LR45, 2.2 LR7–LR9, LR16–LR18, LR25–LR27, LR34–LR36, LR43–LR45, 2.3 LR7–LR9, LR16–LR18, LR25–LR27, LR34–LR36, LR43–LR45, 2.4 LR7–LR9, LR16–LR18, LR25–LR27, LR34–LR36, LR43–LR45, 2.5 LR7–LR9, LR16–LR18, LR25–LR27, LR34–LR36, LR43–LR45, 2.6 LR7–LR9, LR16–LR18, LR25–LR27, LR34–LR36, LR43–LR45
progress monitoring, 2.1 12n, 42n, 68n, 96n, 128n, 2.2 162n, 190n, 218n, 252n, 282n, 316n, 2.3 344n, 372n, 402n, 426n
phonics progress, 2.1 12n, 42n, 68n, 96n, 128n, 2.2 162n, 190n, 218n, 252n, 282n, 2.3 316n, 344n, 372n, 402n, 426n, 2.4 12n, 42n, 66n, 96n, 124n, 2.5 154n, 180n, 208n, 234n, 264n, 2.6 296n, 322n, 350n, 376n, 408n
resources, 2.1 12g, 42g, 68g, 96g, 128g,

2.2 162g, 190g, 218g, 252g, 282g, 2.3 316g, 344g, 372g, 402g, 426g, 2.4 12g, 42g, 66g, 96g, 124g, 2.5 154g, 180g, 208g, 234g, 264g, 2.6 296g, 322g, 350g, 376g, 408g
selections, 2.1 DI.8–DI.13, 2.2 DI.8–DI.13, 2.3 DI.8–DI.13, 2.4 DI.8–DI.13, 2.5 DI.8–DI.13, 2.6 DI.8–DI.13
vocabulary, 2.1 36e, 60e, 88e, 120e, 150e, 2.2 182e, 212e, 243e, 274e, 303e, 2.3 338e, 366e, 395e, 408e, 452e, 2.4 31e, 60e, 88e, 116e, 142e, 2.5 172e, 202e, 226e, 256e, 284e, 2.6 314e, 344e, 368e, 402e, 426e
writing, 2.1 13c, 35b, 39b, 43c, 59a, 65b, 69c, 87b, 93b, 97c, 119b, 125b, 129c, 149a, 155b, 2.2 163c, 181b, 187b, 191c, 211a, 215b, 219c, 242a, 249b, 253c, 273a, 279b, 283c, 302a, 309b, 2.3 317c, 337a, 341b, 345c, 365a, 369b, 373c, 394b, 399b, 403c, 417b, 423b, 427c, 451a, 457b, 2.4 13a, 43a, 67a, 97a, 125a, 2.5 155a, 181a, 209a, 235a, 265a, 2.6 297a, 323a, 351a, 377a, 409a

Affective domain. *See* **Habits and attitudes, Literary response and appreciation.**

Affixes. *See* **Word structure,** prefixes, suffixes.

Alphabetical order, 2.3 401a, 2.4 41a

Amazing Words. *See* **Oral vocabulary development.**

Analyzing. *See* **Reading across texts.** In addition, analytical thinking questions are raised throughout Guiding Comprehension and Reader Response.

Animal fantasy. *See* **Genres.**

Antonyms, 2.1 274a

Appreciating literature. *See* **Habits and attitudes, Literary response and appreciation.**

Art, interpreting. *See* **Literary craft,** illustrator's craft/style.

Ask questions. *See* **Prereading strategies,** ask questions, set purposes for reading; **Questions, asking.**

Assessment
classroom-based. *See* **Assessment,** progress monitoring. In addition, "If/then" assessment occurs throughout lessons and Guiding Comprehension.
fluency. *See* **Fluency,** reading.
formal, 2.1 37a, 40d, 61a, 66d, 89a, 94d, 121a, 126d, 151a, 156d, 2.2 183a, 188d, 213a, 216d, 245a, 250d, 275a, 280d, 305a, 310d, 2.3 339a, 342d, 367a, 370d, 397a, 400d, 419a, 424d, 453a, 458d, 2.4 33a, 40d, 61a, 64d, 89a, 94d, 117a, 122d, 143a, 148d, 2.5 173a, 178d, 203a, 206d, 227a, 232d, 257a, 262d, 285a, 290d, 2.6 315a, 320d, 345a, 348d, 369a, 374d, 403a, 406d, 427a, 432d
progress monitoring
comprehension, 2.1 40e, 66e, 94e, 126e, 156e, 2.2 188e, 216e, 250e, 280e, 310e, 2.3 242e, 370e, 400e, 424e, 2.4 40f, 64e, 94e, 122e, 148e, 178e, 206e, 232e, 262e, 290e, 2.6 320e, 348e, 374e, 406e, 432e
fluency, 2.1 36f, 40e–40f, 60f, 66e–66f, 88f, 94e–94f, 120f, 126g, 150f, 156e, 2.2 182f, 188e, 212f, 216e, 243f, 250e, 274f, 280e, 303f, 310e, 2.3 242e, 338f, 366f, 370e, 395f, 400e, 418f, 424e, 452f, 458e, 2.4 40f, 64e, 94e, 122e, 148e, 2.5 178e, 206e, 232e, 262e,

290e, 2.6 320e, 348e, 374e, 406e, 432e
phonics, 2.1 12o, 42o, 68o, 96o, 128o, 2.2 162o, 190o, 218o, 252o, 282o, 2.3 316o, 344o, 372o, 402o, 426o, 2.4 12o, 42o, 66o, 96o, 124o, 2.5 154o, 180o, 208o, 234o, 264o, 2.6 296o, 322o, 350o, 376o, 408o
retelling, 2.1 36g, 60g, 88g, 120g, 150g, 2.2 182g, 212g, 243g, 274g, 303g, 2.3 338g, 366g, 395g, 418g, 452g, 2.4 31g, 60g, 88g, 116g, 142g, 2.5 172g, 202g, 226g, 256g, 284g, 2.6 314g, 344g, 368g, 402g, 462g
regrouping and, 2.1 159l, 2.2 313l, 2.3 461l, 2.4 151l, 2.5 293l, 2.6 435l
scoring guide (rubric), 2.1 37a, 61a, 89a, 121a, 151a, TR2–TR5, 2.2 183a, 213a, 245a, 275a, 305a, TR2–TR5, 2.3 339a, 367a, 397a, 419a, 453a, TR2–TR5, 2.4 33a, 61a, 89a, 117a, 143a, TR2–TR5, 2.5 173a, 203a, 227a, 257a, 285a, TR2–TR5, 2.6 315a, 345a, 369a, 403a, 427a, TR2–TR5
spelling, 2.1 40d, 66d, 94d, 126d, 156d, 2.2 188d, 216d, 250d, 280d, 310d, 2.3 342d, 370d, 400d, 424d, 458d, 2.4 40d, 64d, 94d, 122d, 148d, 2.5 178d, 206d, 232d, 262d, 290d, 2.6 320d, 348d, 374d, 406d, 432d

Attitudes, personal. *See* **Habits and attitudes.**

Authors (of reading selections)
Abercrombie, Barbara, 2.5 212–225
Aliki, 2.3 430–451
Arnold, Caroline, 2.1 100–119
Arnold, Tedd, 2.5 268–283
Bagert, Brod, 2.2 214–215
Bauer, Marion Dane, 2.4 144–147
Blair, Eric, 2.3 420–423
Bruchac, James, 2.2 222–242
Bruchac, Joseph, 2.1 132–149, 2.2 222–242
Bunting, Eve, 2.2 286–302
Carpenter, Connie, 2.5 174–177
Clements, Andrew, 2.2 166–181
Cody, Tod, 2.6 404–405
Cohan, George M., 2.6 346–347
Coombs, L.B., 2.5 228–231
Esterer, Arnulf K., 2.3 368–369
Esterer, Louise A., 2.3 368–369
Fridell, Ron, 2.4 46–59
Gibbons, Gail, 2.4 70–87
Giff, Patricia Reilly, 2.2 194–211
Gifford, Clive, 2.3 340–341
Glaser, Isabel Joshlin, 2.5 204
Guest, Elissa Haden, 2.1 16–35
Harper, Jessica, 2.4 100–115
Hayes, Joe, 2.3 406–417
Herman, John, 2.6 326–343
Howe, James, 2.5 238–255
Hoyt-Goldsmith, Diane, 2.6 428–431
Hutchins, Hazel, 2.5 184–201
Jacobs, John, 2.1 152–155
Johnson, Angela, 2.6 300–313
Johnston, Tony, 2.4 16–30
Katz, Bobbi, 2.1 38–39
Kimmel, Eric A., 2.3 376–394
Koss, Amy Goldman, 2.3 398–399, 2.4 62–63
Lakin, Patricia, 2.4 128–141
McCombs, Lorraine, 2.1 90–93
McMullan, Kate, 2.3 320–337
Merriam, Eve, 2.5 205
Mora, Pat, 2.6 354–367
Moran, Rena, 2.2 184–187
Murphy, Patricia J., 2.1 46–59
Pak, Soyung, 2.3 348–365

concepts, Spelling, all Writing categories.

Language, oral. *See* **Oral language and concepts,** oral language activities.

Large group discussion. *See* **Oral language and concepts,** oral language activities.

Learning centers. *See* **Literacy Centers.**

Less-able readers. *See* **Intervention.**

Leveled readers, 2.1 LR1–LR48, 2.2 LR1–LR48, 2.3 LR1–LR48, 2.4 LR1–LR48, 2.5 LR1–LR48, 2.6 LR1–LR48

Levels of thinking. *See* **Critical thinking.**

Limited English proficient children. *See* **ELL (English language learners) suggestions.**

Listening. *See* **Oral language and concepts.**

Literacy Centers
  listening, 2.1 12j, 42j, 68j, 96j, 128j, 2.2 162j, 190j, 218j, 252j, 282j, 2.3 316j, 344j, 372j, 402j, 426j, 2.4 12j, 42j, 66j, 96j, 124j, 2.5 154j, 180j, 208j, 234j, 264j, 2.6 296j, 322j, 350j, 376j, 408j
  reading/library, 2.1 12j, 42j, 68j, 96j, 128j, 2.2 162j, 190j, 218j, 252j, 282j, 2.3 316j, 344j, 372j, 402j, 426j, 2.4 12j, 42j, 66j, 96j, 124j, 2.5 154j, 180j, 208j, 234j, 264j, 2.6 296j, 322j, 350j, 376j, 408j
  science, 2.1 42k, 68k, 96k, 2.2 218k, 252k, 2.3 316k, 372k, 426k, 2.4 42k
  social studies, 12k, 128k, 2.2 162k, 190k, 282k, 2.3 344k, 402k, 2.4 12k, 96k, 124k, 2.5 154k, 208k, 234k, 2.6 296k, 322j, 322k, 350k, 376j, 408k,
  technology, 2.1 12k, 42k, 68k, 96k, 128k, 2.2 162k, 190k, 218k, 252k, 282k, 2.3 316k, 344k, 372k, 402k, 426k, 2.4 12k, 42k, 66k, 96k, 124k, 2.5 154k, 180k, 208k, 234k, 264k, 2.6 296k, 322k, 350k, 376k, 408k
  word work, 2.1 12j, 42j, 68j, 96j, 128j, 2.2 162j, 190j, 218j, 252j, 282j, 2.3 316j, 344j, 372j, 402j, 426j, 2.4 12j, 42j, 66j, 96j, 124j, 2.5 154j, 180j, 208j, 234j, 264j, 2.6 296j, 322j, 350j, 376j, 408j
  writing, 2.1 12k, 42k, 68k, 96k, 128k, 2.2 162k, 190k, 218k, 252k, 282k, 2.3 316k, 344k, 372k, 402k, 426k, 2.4 12k, 42k, 66k, 96k, 124k, 2.5 154k, 180k, 208k, 234k, 264k, 2.6 296k, 322k, 350k, 376k, 408k

Literal comprehension. Literal comprehension questions appear throughout Guiding Comprehension in each lesson.

Literary craft
  author's craft/style/language, 2.6 302–303
  illustrator's craft/style, 2.4 28–29

Literary devices
  dialogue, 2.5 272–273
  exaggeration, 2.6 302–303
  figurative language, 2.2 228–229
  formal/informal language, 2.3 326–327
  idiom, 2.1 196–197, 2.2 196–197
  imagery and sensory words, 2.4 140–141, 2.6 418–419
  narration, 2.3 382–383
  personification, 2.2 228–229, 292–293
  pun, 2.5 240–241
  repetition, 2.4 102–103
  simile, 2.1 36e, 2.2 303e, 2.5 188–189
  word choice, 2.3 432–433
  See also **Figurative language, Sound devices**

and poetic elements.

Literary genres. *See* **Genres.**

Literary response and appreciation
  appreciation of author's craft/style, 2.6 302–303
  appreciation of illustrator's craft/style, 2.4 28–29
  enjoyment of literature, 2.1 36g, 60g, 88g, 120g, 150g, 2.2 182g, 212g, 243g, 274g, 303g, 2.3 338g, 366g, 395g, 418g, 452g, 2.4 31g, 60g, 88g, 116g, 142g, 2.5 172g, 202g, 226g, 256g, 284g, 2.6 314g, 344g, 368g, 402g, 462g
  See also **Habits and attitudes.**

Literature selections
  "Anansi Goes Fishing," Eric A. Kimmel, 2.3 376–394
  "Animals Helping Animals," Jacquelyn Siki, 2.2 276–279
  "Anteaters," John Jacobs, 2.1 152–155
  "Bad Dog, Dodger!," Barbara Abercrombie, 2.5 212–225
  "Birthday Basket for Tiá, A," Pat Mora, 2.6 354–367
  "Bremen Town Musicians, The," Carol Pugliano-Martin, 2.2 256–273
  "Celebrating the Buffalo Days," Diane Hoyt-Goldsmith, 2.6 428–431
  "Cowboy Gear," Tod Cody, 2.6 404–405
  "Cowboys," Lucille Recht Penner, 2.6 380–401
  "Crow and the Pitcher, The," Eric Blair, 2.3 420–423
  "Dear Juno," Soyung Pak, 2.3 348–365
  "Exploring Space with an Astronaut," Patricia J. Murphy, 2.1 46–59
  "Family Traditions: Birthdays," Internet article, 2.6 370–373
  "Fire Fighter!," Angela Royston, 2.5 158–171
  "Fire Fighting Teamwork," Connie Carpenter, 2.5 174–177
  "Frogs," Gail Gibbons, 2.4 70–87
  "From Egg to Egg," Michael Elsohn Ross, 2.4 90–93
  "Good Kicking," Rich Richardson, 2.5 258–261
  "Helen Keller and the Big Storm," Patricia Lakin, 2.4 128–141
  "Helping Hand," Internet article, 2.5 286–289
  "Henry and Mudge and the Starry Night," Cynthia Rylant, 2.1 72–87
  "Horace and Morris but Mostly Dolores," James Howe, 2.5 238–255
  "How Baseball Began," Tammy Terry, 2.6 316–319
  "How to Train Your Puppy," L.B. Coombs, 2.5 228–231
  "I Like Where I Am," Jessica Harper, 2.4 100–115
  "Iris and Walter," Elissa Haden Guest, 2.1 16–35
  "Jingle Dancer," Cynthia Leitich Smith, 2.6 412–425
  "Just Like Josh Gibson," Angela Johnson, 2.6 300–313
  "Life Cycle of a Pumpkin," Ron Fridell and Patricia Walsh, 2.4 46–59
  "Making Memories Changing with the Times," Myka-Lynne Sokoloff, 2.4 34–39
  "New Home, A," Internet article, 2.4 118–121
  "One Dark Night," Hazel Hutchins, 2.5 184–201
  "Pearl and Wagner: Two Good Friends," Kate McMullan, 2.3 320–337
  "Quilt Story, The" Tony Johnston, 2.4 16–30
  "Red, White and Blue: The Story of The

American Flag," John Herman, 2.6 326–343
  "Rescue Dogs," Rena Moran, 2.2 184–187
  "Robots at Home," Clive Gifford, 2.3 340–341
  "Ronald Morgan Goes to Bat," Patricia Reilly Giff, 2.2 194–211
  "Rosa and Blanca," Joe Hayes, 2.3 406–417
  "Saying It Without Words: Signs and Symbols," Arnulf K. Esterer and Louise A. Esterer, 2.3 368–369
  "Secret Life of Ponds, The," Elizabeth Schleicher, 2.2 246–249
  "Signmaker's Assistant, The," Ted Arnold, 2.5 268–283
  "Star Pictures in the Sky," Lorraine McCombs, 2.1 90–93
  "Strongest One, The," Joseph Bruchac, 2.1 132–149
  "Tara and Tiree, Fearless Friends," Andrew Clements, 2.2 166–181
  "Thanksgiving USA," Internet article, 2.2 306–309
  "Trip to Space Camp, A," Ann Weil, 2.1 62–65
  "Turkey for Thanksgiving, A," Eve Bunting, 2.2 286–302
  "Turtle's Race with Beaver," Joseph Bruchac and James Bruchac, 2.2 222–242
  "Types of Forests," Internet article, 2.1 122–125
  "Walk in the Desert, A," Caroline Arnold, 2.1 100–119
  "Weed Is a Flower: The Life of George Washington Carver, A," Aliki, 2.3 430–451
  "What's Made from Corn?," Internet article, 2.3 454–457
  "Wind," Marion Dane Bauer, 2.4 144–147
  See also **Genre, Phonics stories, Poetry selections.**

Logs. *See* **Journal writing; Writing, forms/products.**

M

Main idea and details, 2.1 32–33, 43a–43b, 44e, 54–55, 61b, 97a–97b, 97d, 98e, 102–103, 121b, DI.24, DI.26, DI.28, DI.30, DI.32, DI.44, DI.46, DI.48, DI.50, DI.52, 2.4 132–133, 2.5 155b, 160–161, 173b, DI.64, 2.6 338–339

Making connections. *See* **Connections, making.**

Map/globe. *See* **Graphic sources,** map/globe.

Mapping selections. *See* **Graphic and semantic organizers.**

Mass media. *See* **Viewing.**

Mechanics (of English grammar and writing)
  capitalization, 2.2 254a
    letter format, 2.4 115a
    nouns, proper, 2.2 191d, 211b, 213b, 215c, 216–217, 2.4 141b
    sentence, 2.1 35b, 35c, 37b, 39c, 59a, 97d, 119c, 2.2 181b, 302a, 2.4 141b
    titles, 2.1 35b
  punctuation
    apostrophe, 2.2 191d, 2.5 265b, 283b, 289c, 2.6 296m, 344c
    colon, 2.4 34e
    comma, 2.4 115a, 2.6 351b
    end marks,
      period, 2.1 13d, 35b, 35c, 37b, 39c, 43d, 59a, 97d, 125c, 126, 2.2 181b, 254a, 302a, 2.4 141b

DI.65, **2.6** DI.68

suffixes, **2.5** 154n–154o, 154q, 155b, 156o, 172e, 174d, 178c, 202c, DI.64, **2.6** 426c, DI.67

syllable patterns
final syllable -le, **2.4** 12n–12o, 12q, 13b, 14c–14d, 31c, 31d, 34c, 40c, 60c, DI.64, **2.5** 286c
final syllable -tion, -ture, **2.6** 368d, 402c, DI.66
See also **Spelling,** word structure.

Word study. See **Context clues, Dictionary/ glossary, Vocabulary strategies, Word structure.**

Word Wall, **2.1** 12q, 14d, 42q, 44d, 68q, 70d, 96q, 98d, 128q, 130d, **2.2** 162q, 164d, 182d, 190q, 192d, 218q, 220d, 252q, 254d, 282q, 284d, **2.3** 316q, 318d, 344q, 346d, 372q, 374d, 402q, 404d, 426q, 428d, **2.4** 14d, 44d, 68d, 98d, 126d, **2.5** 156d, 182d, 210d, 236d, 266d, **2.6** 298d, 324d, 352d, 378d, 410d

Work stations. See **Literacy Centers.**

Working with words. See **Context clues for meaning, Dictionary/glossary, Vocabulary building, Vocabulary strategies.**

Writer's craft. See **Literary craft,** author's craft/ style/language.

Writing across the curriculum, **2.1** 39b, 65b, 93b, 125b, 155b, **2.2** 187b, 215b, 249b, 279b, 309b, **2.3** 341b, 369b, 399b, 423b, 457b, **2.4** 39b, 63b, 93b, 121b, 147b, **2.5** 177b, 205b, 231b, 261b, 289b, **2.6** 319b, 347b, 373b, 405b, 431b

Writing and grammar, **2.1** 37b, 40–41, 61b, 66–67, 89b, 94–95, 121b, 126–127, 151b, 156–157, **2.2** 183b, 188–189, 213b, 216–217, 245b, 250–251, 275b, 280–281, 305b, 310–311, **2.3** 339b, 342–343, 367b, 370–371, 397b, 400–401, 419b, 424–425, 453b, 458–459, **2.4** 33b, 40–41, 61b, 64–65, 89b, 94–95, 117b, 122–123, 143b, 148–149, **2.5** 173b, 178–179, 203b, 206–207, 227b, 232–233, 257b, 262–262, 285b, 290–291, **2.6** 315b, 320–321, 345b, 348–348, 369b, 374–374, 403b, 406–406, 427b, 432–433

signal words, **2.4** 30a

Writing and spelling, **2.1** 14d, 44d, 70d, 98d, 130d, **2.2** 164d, 192d, 220d, 254d, 284d, **2.3** 318d, 346d, 374d, 404d, 428d, **2.4** 34d, 62d, 90d, 118d, 144d, **2.5** 174d, 204d, 228d, 258d, 286d, **2.6** 316d, 346d, 370d, 404d, 428d

Writing forms/products
advertisement, **2.1** 119b, **2.3** 403c, **2.4** 87b
advice, **2.3** 373c, **2.5** 235a
biography, **2.3** 427c
caption, **2.1** 93b
chart, **2.1** 39b, 65b, **2.2** 215b
comparison/contrast, **2.4** 39b, 67a, **2.6** 347b
dialogue, **2.3** 394b
directions, **2.2** 163c, **2.3** 451a, **2.4** 30a, **2.5** 225b
explanation, **2.4** 89a
flow chart, **2.3** 341b
invitation, **2.2** 283c
journal, **2.1** 16a, 46a, 72a, 100a, 132a, **2.2** 166a, 194a, 222a, 256a, 286a, **2.3** 320a, 348a, 376a, 406a, 430a, **2.4** 39b
labels, **2.3** 341b, **2.6** 405b
letter, **2.1** 87b, **2.3** 365a, **2.4** 115a, **2.5** 235a, 283a, **2.6** 313b
list, **2.1** 43c, **2.2** 187b, 191c, 302a, 309b, **2.3** 345c, **2.5** 177b

map, **2.6** 431b
news story, **2.4** 125a
note, **2.3** 417b
notes, **2.2** 181b, **2.4** 59b
opinion, **2.4** 141b
outline, **2.2** 211a
paragraph, **2.1** 35b, **2.2** 242a, **2.3** 337a
plan, **2.1** 13c, **2.2** 219c, **2.3** 317c
poem, **2.4** 97a
poster, **2.2** 253c, **2.3** 427c, **2.5** 171b
presentation, **2.3** 461b
problem/solution, **2.1** 37a, **2.5** 255b
questions and/or answers, **2.1** 59a, **2.2** 273a
report, **2.1** 97c, **2.5** 155a
response to literature, **2.1** 37a, 61a, 89a, 121a, 151a, **2.2** 183a, 213a, 245a, 275a, 305a, **2.3** 339a, 367a, 397a, 419a, 453a, **2.4** 33a, 61a, 89a, 117a, 143a, **2.5** 173a, 203a, 227a, 257a, 285a, **2.6** 315a, 345a, 369a, 403a, 427a
review, **2.4** 43a
riddle, **2.4** 13a
rules, **2.5** 209a
sentence, **2.1** 13c, 37b
sign, **2.5** 265a, 289b
song, **2.4** 67a
story, **2.1** 69c, **2.2** 279b, **2.3** 461b, **2.5** 201b, **2.6** 373b
Venn diagram, **2.6** 347b
web, **2.1** 125b

Writing modes
descriptive, **2.2** 183a, 187b, 309b, **2.3** 345c, **2.4** 13a, 33a, 39a, 43a, 87b, 125a
expository, **2.1** 13c, 37a, 97c, 125b, 341b, **2.2** 163c, 211a, 215b, 242a, 273a, 283c, 302a, **2.3** 317c, 345c, 373c, 427c, **2.4** 59b, 61a, 141b, 143a, **2.5** 155a, 177b, 209a, 225b, 255b, 283a, **2.6** 347b, 405b, 431b
expressive, **2.4** 97a, 115a
interactive writing, **2.1** 35b, 59a, 87b, 119b, 149b, **2.2** 181b, 211a, 242a, 273a, 302a, **2.3** 337a, 365a, 394b, 417b, 451a, **2.4** 30a, 59b, 87b, 115a, 141b, **2.5** 171b, 201b, 225b, 255b, 283a, **2.6** 313b, 343b, 367b, 401b, 425b
narrative, **2.1** 35b, **2.2** 181b, 279b, **2.5** 201b, **2.6** 373b
persuasive, **2.1** 119b, **2.2** 253c, **2.3** 403c, **2.5** 171b, 265a
shared writing, **2.1** 13c, 43c, 69c, 97c, 129c, **2.2** 163c, 191c, 219c, 253c, 283c, **2.3** 317c, 345c, 373c, 403c, 427c, **2.4** 13a, 43a, 67a, 97a, 125a, **2.5** 155a, 181a, 209a, 235a, 265a, **2.6** 297a, 323a, 351a, 377a, 409a

Writing process, **2.1** 159a–159h, **2.2** 313a–313h, **2.3** 461a–461h, **2.4** 151a–151h, **2.5** 293a–293h, **2.6** 435a–435h
assessing. See **Assessment,** scoring guide (rubric).

Writing purpose
clarify information, **2.1** 59a, 119b, **2.2** 244b, 273a, **2.4** 87b, 141b
express ideas, **2.1** 13c, **2.2** 187b, 191c, **2.3** 403c, 427c, **2.4** 115a, **2.5** 283a
respond to ideas, **2.1** 37a, 61a, 89a, 121a, 151a, **2.2** 183a, 213a, 245a, 275a, 305a, **2.3** 339a, 367a, 397a, 419a, 453a, **2.4** 59b, 61a
share experiences, **2.1** 69c, **2.2** 219c, 242a, 302a, 309b, **2.3** 337a, 365a, 373c, 451a, **2.4** 39b, 43a, 67a, 97a, 125a, 141b, **2.5** 177b
share ideas/information, **2.1** 35b, 39b, 43c, 97c, 125b, **2.2** 163c, 187b, 211a, 215b, 219c, 242a,

249b, 253c, 283c, 302a, **2.3** 317c, 337a, 341b, 451a, 345c, 323c, 427c, 461b, **2.4** 30a, 33a, 61a, 87b, 125a, 141b, 143a, **2.5** 155a, 171b, 209a, 225b, 255b, 265a, **2.6** 347b, 405b, 431b
share rhymes and stories, **2.2** 181b, **2.3** 394b, 417b, **2.4** 13a, 27a, **2.5** 201b, **2.6** 373b
specific audience, **2.1** 119b, **2.4** 115a, **2.6** 313b

Writing, six-trait. See **Six-trait writing.**

Writing strategies. See **Assessment,** scoring guide (rubric); **Writing process.**

Teacher's Edition

Text

KWL Strategy: The KWL Interactive Reading Strategy was developed and is used by permission of Donna Ogle, National-Louis University, Evanston, Illinois, co-author of *Reading Today and Tomorrow*, Holt, Rinehart & Winston Publishers, 1988. (See also *The Reading Teacher*, February 1986, pp. 564–570.)

Artists

Scott Gustafson: cover, page i

Luciana Navarro Alves: page 191B

Kenneth Spengler: page 253B

Photographs

Every effort has been made to secure permission and provide appropriate credit for photographic material. The publisher deeply regrets any omission and pledges to correct errors called to its attention in subsequent editions.

Unless otherwise acknowledged, all photographs are the property of Scott Foresman, a division of Pearson Education.

Photo locators denoted as follows: Top (T), Center (C), Bottom (B), Left (L), Right (R), Background (Bkgd).

Page 252J: Corbis

Page 283B (BR:) Digital Vision, (CR) Getty Images